T0184266

Lecture Notes of the Institute for Computer Sciences, Social Informatics and Telecommunications Engineering 326

More information about this series at http://www.springer.com/series/8197

Yu-Dong Zhang · Shui-Hua Wang ·
Shuai Liu (Eds.)

Multimedia Technology and Enhanced Learning

Second EAI International Conference, ICMTEL 2020
Leicester, UK, April 10–11, 2020
Proceedings, Part I

 Springer

Editors
Yu-Dong Zhang 🆔
School of Informatics
University of Leicester
Leicestershire, UK

Shui-Hua Wang 🆔
University of Leicester
Leicestershire, UK

Shuai Liu 🆔
Human Normal University
Changsha, China

ISSN 1867-8211 ISSN 1867-822X (electronic)
Lecture Notes of the Institute for Computer Sciences, Social Informatics
and Telecommunications Engineering
ISBN 978-3-030-51099-2 ISBN 978-3-030-51100-5 (eBook)
https://doi.org/10.1007/978-3-030-51100-5

This Springer imprint is published by the registered company Springer Nature Switzerland AG
The registered company address is: Gewerbestrasse 11, 6330 Cham, Switzerland

Preface

We are delighted to introduce the proceedings of the second European Alliance for Innovation (EAI) International Conference on Multimedia Technology and Enhanced Learning (ICMTEL). This conference has brought together researchers, developers, engineers, scientists, and practitioners from around the world. Participants shared their knowledge in leveraging and developing multimedia technology with machine learning, especially enhanced learning. The theme of ICMTEL 2020 was "Deep learning driven multimedia technology in academy, industry and society."

The proceeding of ICMTEL 2020 consists of 83 full papers, all presented in YouTube Live due to the impact of coronavirus. Aside from the high-quality academic and technical paper presentations, the technical program also featured three keynote speeches and five workshops. The three keynote speeches were presented by Prof. Lu Liu, Head of School of Informatics from University of Leicester, UK; Dr. Shui-hua Wang, Research Fellow at University of Loughborough, UK, and Prof. Shuai Liu, Head of School of Artificial Intelligence from Hunan Normal University, China. The five workshops organized were (i) International Workshop on Data fusion filter and Machine Learning for Statistical Signal Processing (DFMLSSP 2020); (ii) International Workshop on Intelligent Technology and Design for Special Education/Rehabilitation (ITD 2020); (iii) International Workshop on Intelligent Technology and Design for Special Education/Rehabilitation (ITD 2020); (iv) International Workshop on Weather Radar and Antenna Design (WRAD 2020); and (iv) International Workshop on Digital Image Processing, Analysis and Application Based on Machine Learning (DIPAA 2020).

Support from the steering chair Prof. Imrich Chlamtac was essential for the success of the conference. We sincerely appreciate his constant support and guidance. It was also a great pleasure to work with such an excellent Organizing Committee, and we are grateful for their hard work in organizing and supporting the conference. In particular, the Technical Program Committee (TPC), led by our TPC chair: Prof. Zhengchao Dong, and TPC co-chairs: Prof. Vishnu Varthanan Govindaraj, Prof. Raymond F. Muzic, Jr., Prof. Gautam Srivastava, Dr. Preetha Phillips, Prof. Amin Taheri-Garavand, Prof. Vikrant Bhateja, Prof. Seifedine Kadry, Prof. Yuriy S. Shmaliy, Prof. Mohammad R. Khosravi, Dr. Muhammad Attique Khan, Dr. Suresh Chandra Satapathy, Dr. Deepak Ranjan Nayak, Dr. Mohammad Momeny, Prof. Juan Manuel Górriz, Dr. Yeliz Karaca, Dr. Miguel Martínez García, and other co-chairs who contributed to the peer-review process of technical papers. We are also grateful to our conference manager, Lukas Skolek, for his support and all the authors who submitted their papers to the ICMTEL 2020 conference and workshops.

We strongly believe that the ICMTEL 2020 conference provided a beneficial forum for all researchers, developers, engineers, scientists, and practitioners to discuss scientific and technological aspects that are relevant to multimedia technology, machine learning, and artificial intelligence. We also expect that the future ICMTEL conferences will be more successful than the contributions presented in this volume.

May 2020   Yu-Dong Zhang
                                                              Shuai Liu

Organization

Steering Committee

Imrich Chlamtac	University of Trento, Italy
Yu-Dong Zhang	University of Leicester, UK

Organizing Committee

General Chair

Yu-Dong Zhang   University of Leicester, UK

General Co-chairs

Shui-Hua Wang	Loughborough University, UK
Shuai Liu	Inner Mongolia University, China
Juan Manuel Górriz	University of Granada, Spain

TPC Chair

Zhengchao Dong   Columbia University, USA

TPC Co-chairs

Xinhua Mao	Nanjing University of Aeronautics and Astronautics, China
Mingwei Shen	Hohai University, China
Vishnu Varthanan Govindaraj	Kalasalingam Academy of Research and Education, India
Guodong Han	The 54th Research Institute of CETC, China
Pengjiang Qian	Jiangnan University, China
Raymond F. Muzic, Jr.	Case Western Reserve University, USA
Gautam Srivastava	Brandon University, Canada
Preetha Phillips	West Virginia School of Osteopathic Medicine, USA
Amin Taheri-Garavand	Lorestan University, Iran
Vikrant Bhateja	SRMGPC, India
Xianwei Jiang	Nanjing Normal University of Special Education, China
Nianyin Zeng	Xiamen University, China
Seifedine Kadry	Beirut Arab University, Lebanon
Yuriy S. Shmaliy	Universidad de Guanajuato, Mexico
Yuan Xu	University of Jinan, China
Kaijian Xia	The Affiliated Changshu Hospital of Soochow University, China

Mohammad R. Khosravi	Shiraz University of Technology, Iran
Zhihai Lu	Nanjing Normal University, China
Muhammad Attique Khan	HITEC University, Pakistan
Suresh Chandra Satapathy	KIIT Deemed to University, India
Deepak Ranjan Nayak	Sardar Vallabhbhai National Institute of Technology, India
Zhi-Hai Lu	Nanjing Normal University, China
Chenxi Huang	Xiamen University, China
Jin Hong Tan	National University of Singapore, Singapore
Honghao Gao	Shanghai University, China
Mohammad Momeny	Yazd University, Iran
Yeliz Karaca	University of Massachusetts Medical School, USA
Miguel Martínez García	Loughborough University, UK

Local Chair

| Xiang Yu | University of Leicester, UK |

Workshop Chair

| Xinhua Mao | Nanjing University of Aeronautics and Astronautics, China |

Publicity and Social Media Chairs

Cheng Kang	University of Leicester, UK
Qinghua Zhou	University of Leicester, UK
Rossi Kamal	Shanto-Marium University of Creative Technology, Bangladesh

Publications Chair

| Yizhang Jiang | Jiangnan University, China |

Web Chair

| Lijia Deng | University of Leicester, UK |

Technical Program Committee

Abdon Atangana	University of the Free State, South Africa
Aijun Liu	Arizona State University, USA
Amin Taheri-Garavand	Lorestan University, Iran
Arifur Nayeem	Saidpur Government Technical School and College, Bangladesh
Arun Kumar Sangaiah	Vellore Institute of Technology, India
Atiena Pereira	University of Campinas, Brazil
Carlo Cattani	University of Tuscia, Italy
Chenxi Huang	Tongji University, China

Chunlei Shan	Shanghai University of Traditional Chinese Medicine (SHUTCM), China
Chunxia Xiao	Wuhan University, China
Dan Sui	California State Polytechnic University, USA
Dang Thanh	Hue College of Industry, Vietnam
David Guttery	University of Leicester, UK
Debesh Jha	Chosun University, South Korea
Dimas Lima	Federal University of Santa Catarina, Brazil
Elijah Nguyen	Flinders University, Australia
Elizabeth Lee	Chattanooga State Community College, USA
Fidel Evans	University of Florida, USA
Foxen Cod	Middlesex University, UK
Frank Vanhoenshoven	University of Hasselt, Belgium
Gautam Srivastava	Brandon University, Canada
Ge Liu	Tennessee State University, USA
Gonzalo Napoles Ruiz	University of Hasselt, Belgium
Guangzhou Yu	Guangdong Ocean University, China
Guodong Han	The 54th Research Institute of CETC, China
Hari Mohan Pandey	Edge Hill University, UK
Heng Li	Henan Finance University, China
Hong Cheng	First Affiliated Hospital of Nanjing Medical University, China
Honghao Gao	Shanghai University, China
Jianfeng Cui	Xiamen University of Technology, China
Jitendra Pandey	Middle East College, Oman,
John Liu	Michigan State University, USA
Juan Manuel Górriz	University of Granada, Spain
Koji Nakamura	Kyushu Institute of Technology, Japan
Lei Ma	Beijing Polytechnic University, China
Leonid Snetkov	ITMO University, Russia
Liam O'Donnell	University of Limerick, Ireland
Liangxiu Han	Manchester Metropolitan University, UK
Linkai Niu	Taiyuan University of Technology, China
Logan Graham	Ryerson University, Canada
Mackenzie Brown	Edith Cowan University, Australia
Miguel Martínez García	Loughborough University, UK
Ming Pei	West Virginia University, USA
Mingwei Shen	Hohai University, China
Mohamed Elhoseny	Mansoura University, Egypt
Mohammad Momeny	Yazd University, Iran
Muhammad Bilal	Hankuk University of Foreign Studies, South Korea
Matben Suchkov	Kazan Federal University, Russia
Neeraj Kumar	Thapar University, India
Nianyin Zeng	Xiamen University, China
Peng Chen	Columbia University, USA
Pengjiqiang Qian	Jiangnan University, China

Praveen Agarwal	Anand International College of Engineering, India
Preetha Phillips	West Virginia School of Osteopathic Medicine, USA
Qingmei Lu	Bioengieering, University of Louisville, USA
Ravipudi Venkata Rao	Sardar Vallabhbhai National Institute of Technology, India
Rayan S Cloutier	Carleton University, Canada
Raymond F. Muzic, Jr.	Case Western Reserve University, USA
Rik Crutzen	Maastricht University, The Netherlands
Rodney Payne	Clemson University, USA
Seifedine Kadry	Beirut Arab University, Lebanon
Shipeng Xie	Nanjing University of Posts and Telecommunications, China
Shuai Yang	Changchun University of Technology, China
Shui-Hua Wang	Loughborough University, UK
Sunil Kumar	National Institute of Technology, India
Tanveer Hussain	Sejong University, South Korea
Tianming Zhan	Nanjing Audit University, China
Vikrant Bhateja	SRMGPC, India
Vishnu Varthanan Govindaraj	Kalasalingam Academy of Research and Education, India
Wagner Quinn	University College Cork, Ireland
Weibo Liu	Brunel University London, UK
Weiguo Zhu	Huaiyin Institute of Technology, China
Weiling Bai	Inner Mongolia University, China
Wenbo Fu	Datong University, China
Xianwei Jiang	Nanjing Normal University of Special Education, China
Xinhua Mao	Nanjing University of Aeronautics and Astronautics, China
Xuanyue Tong	Nanyang Institute of Technology, Singapore
Yang Wang	School of Electronics and Information Engineering, China
Yeliz Karaca	University of Massachusetts Medical School, USA
Yi-Ding Lv	Nanjing Medical University, China
Yin Zhang	University of Economics and Law, China
Ying Shao	Harvard University, USA
Yongjun Qin	Guilin Normal College, China
Yuan Xu	University of Jinan, China
Yuankai Huo	Vanderbilt University, USA
Yuriy S. Shmaliy	Universidad de Guanajuato, Mexico
Zehong Cao	University of Tasmania, Australia
Zheng Zhang	University of Southern California, USA
Zhimin Chen	Shanghai Dianji University, China
Zhou Zhang	Stevens Institute of Technology, USA
Zhuo Tao	Nanyang Technological University, Singapore
Zhuqing Jiao	Changzhou University, China

Contents – Part I

Contents – Part II

Multimedia Technology and Enhanced Learning

Digital Image Processing, Analysis and Application Based on Machine Learning

Data Fusion Filter and Machine Learning for Statistical Signal Processing

Intelligent Technology and Design for Special Education/ Rehabilitation

Transfer Learning Methods Used in Medical Imaging and Health Informatics

Weather Radar and Antenna Design

Multimedia Technology and Enhanced Learning

Identification of Tea Leaf Based on Histogram Equalization, Gray-Level Co-Occurrence Matrix and Support Vector Machine Algorithm

Yihao Chen[✉]

Department of Informatics, University of Leicester, Leicester LE1 7RH, UK
yc306@le.ac.uk

Abstract. To identify tea categories more automatically and efficiently, we proposed an improved tea identification system based on Histogram Equalization (HE), Gray-Level Co-Occurrence Matrix (GLCM) and Support Vector Machine (SVM) algorithm. In our previous project, 25 images per class might be not enough to classify, and a small size of dataset will cause overfitting. Therefore, we collected 10 kinds of typical processed Chinese tea, photographed 300 images each category by Canon EOS 80D camera, and regarded them as a first-hand dataset. The dataset was randomly divided into training set and testing set, which both contain 1500 images. And we applied data augmentation methods to augment the training set to a 9000-image training set. All the images were resized to 256 * 256 pixels as the input of feature extraction process. We enhanced the image features through Histogram Equalization (HE) and extracted features from each image which were trained through Gray-Level Co-Occurrence Matrix (GLCM). The results show that the average accuracy reached 94.64%. The proposed method is effective for tea identification process.

Keywords: Tea leaves identification · Data augmentation · Histogram Equalization (HE) · Gray-Level Co-Occurrence Matrix (GLCM) · Cross-Validation (CV) · Support Vector Machine (SVM)

1 Introduction

Tea is a popular drink all over the world. There are a variety of functions and effects, such as promoting the absorption of iron in the body, helping to regulate cholesterol levels in the body, promoting metabolism, and even inhibiting the occurrence of cancer [1]. The record of the United Nations Food and Agriculture Organization and Wang' s researches on Chinese tea culture illustrate [2] that in China alone people grow, ferment and bake black tea, green tea, oolong tea, scented tea and other varieties of tea. The production process of tea is extremely complicated. Different production processes, time periods and fermentation levels will affect the properties of tea products. Moreover, there are many varieties of tea leaves, and even the tea products made with the same leaf through different processes have different characteristics, colors and fragrances [3].

© ICST Institute for Computer Sciences, Social Informatics and Telecommunications Engineering 2020
Published by Springer Nature Switzerland AG 2020. All Rights Reserved
Y.-D. Zhang et al. (Eds.): ICMTEL 2020, LNICST 326, pp. 3–16, 2020.
https://doi.org/10.1007/978-3-030-51100-5_1

Over the years, the computer processing and analysis of data more and more accurate and efficient, related algorithms are also improving. In the field of machine learning and artificial intelligence, image processing is one of the most studied topics, such as medical image analysis, biological image classification, etc. These advances are attributed to the formation of image analysis algorithm, the improvement of classifier and the development of convolutional neural network. The work of tea classification has been improved a lot, but they are based on different standards, original data types and algorithms, and the results are quite different. Since the appearance of processed tea leaves is quite different from that of fresh tea leaves, it can be further explored to use tea products as the research object. If the algorithm and results of this project can be applied to industrial production process or application development of mobile terminals, then this project might have a very good prospect.

Previously, Wu, Chen (2009) [4] proposed a tea identification method using discrete cosine transform (DCT) and least squares-support vector machine (LS-SVM) based on multi-spectral digital image texture features. They used a multispectral digital imager to take images of different bands of tea leaves and combine them into a new image of one object. They trained the dataset with 80 filters and classified it with a classifier. Although the accuracy of this method can reach a considerable 100% due to the maturity of the filter and classifier design, it has the disadvantage that is requiring the use of additional scanning imagers. It means that the acquisition of data sets will cost too much.

Similarly, Zhang and HE (2014) [5] designed a system for identifying green tea brands based on hyperspectral imaging techniques and the Gray-level Co-occurrence Matrix (GLCM) and LS-SVM classifier. In this system, the dataset and the algorithm are perfect, and the results are accurate. However, the collection of the data set still needs to be finished by peripheral devices. Zhao, Chen (2006) [6] used near-infrared spectroscopy to identify green tea, Oolong tea and black tea quickly. By collecting the different spectral features of each tea in the near-infrared spectroscopy, they used these features as input to the support vector machine (SVM) classifier. Their study was more than 90% accurate.

All the above methods have achieved good recognition results, but they needed to collect data with additional equipment, which leads to the acquisition of data sets that require material and time. Therefore, we tried to use the image recognition technology to identify the common tea product image. The advantage of this approach is that it is simpler, more efficient and less costly without expensive equipment and cumbersome processes. For example, Borah, Hines (2007) [7] proposed an algorithm for image texture analysis based on wavelet transform. The technique directly processes the feature information of a group of images and then analyzes it. Yang (2015) [8] created a system to identify green teas, Oolong teas and black teas based on wavelet packet entropy and fuzzy support vector machine. It was an efficient method and the accuracy was over 97%. Tang (2018) [9] experimented that tested Convolutional neural network provides us with an inspiration. In our previous study [10], we used the Gray-Level Co-Occurrence Matrix (GLCM) model and k-nearest neighbors algorithm to extract features from images which were taken by ourselves. Moreover, we got a good result that showed the accuracy was over 86%. However, one of the disadvantages is that this project is not automatic enough because we just called in the classification function in MATLAB software to test the initial performance of GLCM on this set of images.

In the previous study, since GLCM with fewer parameters and less operation can effectively extract features from images, we continued to use this model in this study. GLCM is a commonly used image processing technology, which can reflect the joint distribution between two pixel points with different spatial position relations [11]. In the feature extraction step, MATLAB was used to run GLCM algorithm to extract feature dataset, and the input images were digitized to obtain the feature matrix. Each of the characteristic values in these matrixes was a sorted input. After the training and testing of the classifier and the verification of the multi-fold cross-validation process, the accuracy of the test data set can be finally calculated. In this process, using GLCM algorithm to extract features was a key step.

The aim of this study is to design a tea identification system based on traditional computer vision methods using our own dataset and to test the classification performance of a combination of Histogram Equalization (HE), Gray-Level Co-Occurrence Matrix (GLCM) and Support Vector Machine (SVM).

In order to test the classification performance of our model, this study used the pictures of ten kinds of tea, which were, respectively, Anji White tea, Chrysanthemum Tea, Huangshanhoukui Green Tea, Jasmine Tea, Longjing Green Tea, Tawthron Black Tea, Tieguanyin, Xiangxin Black Tea, Yixing black tea and Zhengshanxiaozhong Black Tea, as the original data. For instance, there are three green teas which have similar features, such as leaf shape and color. However, there is a slight whitening change during the growth of white tea, and this feature still exists in the processed tea.

2   Methodology

2.1   Data Acquisition

In our previous study, the high-resolution tea pictures we photographed and collected by ourselves stored enough useful information, such as leaf texture feature, pixel value. Thus, we continued to use the similar set of pictures as the data set in this study. The categories of these teas are, respectively, Anji White tea, Chrysanthemum Tea, Huangshanhoukui Green Tea, Jasmine Tea, Longjing Green Tea, Tawthron Black Tea, Tieguanyin, Xiangxin Black Tea, Yixing black tea and Zhengshanxiaozhong Black Tea (10 categories tea). The tea leaves were photographed in two different shades of light, with half in the sun light and the other half in a warm LED light of 8 W. It was obvious to find that the tea images in these two environments were different, which are shown in Fig. 1. To reduce the influence of the reflected light of the background, we placed all the tea leaves on dark background. Finally, 300 high-quality images were selected for each category of tea, and the images from different environments were selected randomly.

The images we selected were approximately 4 MB in size and had a pixel value of about 4000 * 4000. These images contain enough tea information, such as color, leaf shape, texture, quantity, etc. Generally, image recognition only needs a small size to

(a) Anji white tea in the warm LED light.   (b) Anji white tea in the sun light.

Fig. 1. The positions of Anji white tea

remain the program efficiency, so we resized these images to 256 * 256 pixels in batch through MATLAB software.

2.2 Data Augmentation

In our last experiment, Although the program can be run in the previous experiment, the average accuracy is about 65% [10]. The insufficiently sized dataset may be a main reason for the low accuracy. Besides, overfitting might be caused by a small number of samples [12]. The raw data sets are divided into two parts randomly, which are used as training sets and test sets respectively. 1500 samples are in the training set, and rest of them are tested as the testing set. We used data augmentation technology to rotate, mirror, crop and other operations on the acquired images [13].

Since our data set was small before, we applied this technique to increase the training data set and make the data set diverse. Since the larger dataset can be show a better performance of classification, we augmented the training set from 1500 images to 9000 images. Some samples are shown in Fig. 2: (i) is the raw image, (ii) is mirrored, (iii) is added zero-mean, Gaussian white noise with variance of 0.01, (iv) is enhanced contrast in a new range of intensity which is from 0.1 to 0.9, and (v), (vi) and (vii) are rotated 5°, 10°, 15° clockwise, respectively. These images were stored uniformly in a folder.

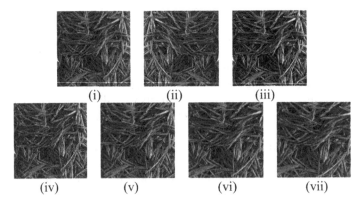

Fig. 2. Proposed samples of Anji White Tea

2.3   Feature Extraction

To reduce the influence of different intensities of light and unify the overall grayscale of the images, we introduced the method of HE. It can enhance the local contrast without affecting the overall contrast to present details of images. The process of HE is as following: (1) The frequency of occurrence of each gray level of the histogram is counted and normalized to [0,1]. The probability of a pixel with a grayscale of i is

$$p_x(i) = \frac{n_i}{n}, i \in 0, 1\ldots, L-1, \tag{1}$$

where n represents the number of times a certain grayscale occurs, L represents gray level.

(2) Accumulate normalization histogram:

$$cdf_x(i) = \sum_{j=0}^{i} p_x(j). \tag{2}$$

To summarize, the gray value is:

$$h(v) = round\left(\frac{cdf(v) - cdf_{min}}{(M \times N) - cdf_{min}} \times (L-1)\right), \tag{3}$$

where $round()$ represents the returning the integral value that is nearest to the argument. M and N represent the number of pixels in length and width of the image.

GLCM represents the correlation between different gray pixels in the image. Texture feature extraction [14] is divided into four parts: extraction of gray image, gray level quantization, calculation of eigenvalue, and generation of texture feature maps [14]. Compared with wavelet transform, GLCM can better describe spatial relations. By extracting the original three-channel image and then processing the gray level, we can obtain the required gray level image. This was useful for determining the grayscale value of each pixel in the image [15].

Suppose that f(x, y) presents a two-dimensional image, the size of which is M × N. Then, relative frequencies in this image P(i, j) will satisfy the following condition:

$$P(i,j) = \#\{(x_1, y_1), (x_2, y_2) \in M \times N | f(x_1, y_1) = i, f(x_2, y_2) = j\}, \tag{4}$$

where #(x) presents the number of elements in the set.

The adjacent relations between the gray values of different pixels, the features, can be extracted, and then stored in one matrix [16–19]. The gray-level co-occurrence matrix can be obtained through this step. Through this process, we can represent larger color or gray images by images with smaller pixel features. If the gray value of pixels in the image are similar, the features in the matrix will be concentrated on the main diagonal. As shown in Fig. 3, a window which is set as 1 × 2 moves from the first two blocks to the end in horizontal direction, and the value of the step distance is 1.

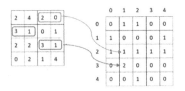

Fig. 3. A sample of GLCM

Many statistics can be used to describe texture features in GLCM, among which the more typical ones are contrast, correlation, energy and homogeneity. Contrast directly describes the brightness difference between pixels in an image. Mathematically,

$$CON = \sum_i^k \sum_j^k |i - j|^2 \cdot G(i,j),\tag{5}$$

where $G(i,j)$ represents the relative frequencies, k represents the maximum number of pixels.

Correlation indicates the similarity of features in horizontal and vertical directions. It can be calculated as,

$$COR = \sum_{i=1}^k \sum_{j=1}^k \frac{(i \cdot j) \cdot G(i,j) - U_i U_j}{S_i S_j} \cdot (S_i S_j \neq 0),\tag{6}$$

where

$$U_i = \sum_{i-1}^k \sum_{j=1}^k i \cdot G(i,j),\tag{7}$$

$$U_j = \sum_{i=1}^k \sum_{j=1}^k j \cdot G(i,j),\tag{8}$$

$$S_i^2 = \sum_{i=1}^k \sum_{j=1}^k G(i,j)(i - U_i)^2,\tag{9}$$

$$S_j^2 = \sum_{i=1}^k \sum_{j=1}^k G(i,j)(j - U_j)^2.\tag{10}$$

The ASM (Angular second moment) energy reflects the stability of the grayscale change of the image texture. The higher the energy value is the more uniform the texture will be. Homogeneity describes the local stability of the image. Mathematically,

$$ASM = \sum_i^k \sum_j^k (G(i,j))^2\tag{11}$$

$$HOM = \sum_i^k \sum_j^k \frac{G(i,j)}{1 + |i - j|}\tag{12}$$

In this project, we scanned the images in $0°$, $45°$, $90°$, $135°$ respectively, so the feature map is a 4-channel matrix. It represents the preprocessed 256 * 256-pixels image as an 8 * 8 * 4-pixels image, and it is also an 8 * 8 * 4-matrix. Each number in the matrix represents the overall features and local features of the image. The four features mentioned above were also utilized. Different images of one same tea have similar texture characteristics, color and structure. Therefore, the feature matrix will have similar overall structure and specific feature values. In the future, we shall test other feature extraction methods, such as convolutional neural network [20–24].

2.4   Classification

Support vector machine (SVM) [25] is a popular learning model and classifier recently. The standard support vector machine mainly solves the binary classification problem, but after the algorithm improvement, the multi-classification problem can also be solved by it. We do not use deep learning methods [26–31] or transfer learning methods [32–35] since our dataset is small.

The algorithm and steps of standard SVM can be used to construct multiple classification boundaries, so as to realize one-against-all multi-classification [36]. Although support vector machine cannot solve outliers and noise, the classic SVM is worth using because it can show a good performance in the small sample classifying experiments. In Wu, Chen (2009) [4]'s study, Least Squares-Support Vector Machine was applied well. In Yang (2015) [8]'s research, they used fuzzy support vector machines and got good results.

We suppose that there are a set of inputs called $X = \{X_1, X_2, \ldots, X_N\}$ and a goal called $Y = \{y_1, y_2, \ldots, y_N\}$. Each item of data contains the feature space $X_i = \{x_1, x_2, \ldots, x_N\}$ and the binary goal $y = \{-1, 1\}$. We suppose to regard the input feature space as a hyperplane of the decision boundary, and the goal set can be divided into positive and negative categories. The hyperplane can be represented as

$$\omega^T X + b = 0. \tag{13}$$

The point to the plane distance D can be represented as

$$D = y_i(\omega^T X_i + b), \tag{14}$$

where ω represents normal vector and b represents intercept to the hyperplane.

In fact, the decision boundaries used to separate the samples were created. As shown in Fig. 4, the positive class (Class B) corresponding to the boundary $y_i = +1$ is $\omega^T X_i + b \geq +1$. The negative class (Class A) corresponding to the boundary $y_i = -1$ is $\omega^T X_i + b \leq -1$. We can deduce this method into multiple classification problems. Two interval boundaries are calculated for every two samples in the M groups of input samples, so that we can get [M * (M − 1)]/2 boundaries totally. SVM has a good performance in both binary and multi-classification problems.

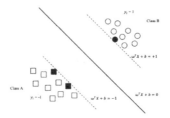

Fig. 4. SVM model

The original Support vector machine (SVM) is designed for the binary classification projects. However, in our study we have 10 classes. One solution to multi-classification is to regards one class as the positive set and the rest of the classes are negative set and every class should be looped to train the model, which is one-versus-rest (OVR).

3 Experiments and Results

This system was developed via the Grayscale Processing Toolbox in MATLAB R2018b. The programs were run on the HP laptop with 2.30 GHz i5–8300H CPU, 8 GB RAM, and Windows 10 operating system.

3.1 Data Acquisition

A set of raw images have been photographed by us via a digital camera with a 35-mm lens, which have 300 images in each class\category. Some samples are shown in Fig. 5. We randomly divided each category of images into two equal groups as testing set and training set, respectively.

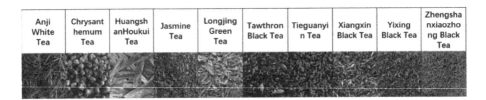

Anji White Tea	Chrysanthemum Tea	Huangshan Houkui Tea	Jasmine Tea	Longjing Green Tea	Tawthron Black Tea	Tieguanyin Tea	Xiangxin Black Tea	Yixing Black Tea	Zhengshanxiaozhong Black Tea

Fig. 5. Some samples of tea leaf images

3.2 Data Augmentation

Firstly, we used MATLAB to resize the images because it was not necessary to scan a large image that is at 4000 * 4000-pixels. All images were processed into 256 * 256-pixels square images. The purpose of this preprocessing operation is to compress the image while retaining the information of the image itself to improve the efficiency.

We rotated the training images clockwise by following angles: 5°, 10°, 15°, mirrored each class of images separately, changed the contrast, added gaussian noise which are shown in Fig. 2. In order to utilize this dataset in our future work, we reserved this dataset and named it CTset, which shows in Table 1.

Table 1. Statistic of CTset

Training set	9000
Testing set	1500
Total number	10500

3.3 Histogram Equalization

Before extracting features, we first grayscaled the image. But the overall contrast of the image will be affected by many factors, such as lighting angle, light intensity, etc., so that the feature details in the grayscale image will not be clearly displayed. Therefore, HE was utilized to preprocess the grayscaled images. The output images contain 64-bins default. A sample of difference between one raw image and a processed image and their histograms are as showing in Fig. 6. (a) is an original grayscaled image. (b) is an image after histogram equalization. (c) and (d) are the histograms of (a) and (b) respectively.

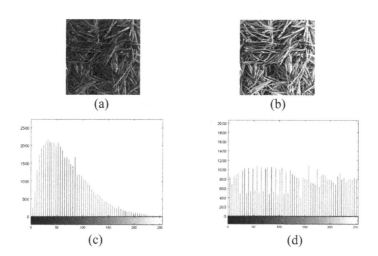

Fig. 6. A sample of histogram equalization

3.4 Feature Extraction

There is a grayscale processing toolbox which already contains the developed program command GLCM = graycomatrix (I) in MATLAB software, which can directly input and scan the input image. Based on our previous experimental results, we set the size of the output to 8 * 8 * 4. Regarding the obtained GLCM, most eigenvalues are distributed along the main diagonal of the matrix. One of the grayscale matrices in one channel is shown in Table 2.

Table 2. An 8 * 8 example of Anji white tea's GLCM in one channel

8591	2996	256	9	0	0	0	0
3027	11094	323	382	8	0	0	0
232	3550	7393	1968	1960	117	0	0
9	340	1973	2947	2953	465	3	0
4	341	1956	1490	2952	346	57	28
0	0	34	739	1028	597	208	5
0	0	25	12	194	130	98	40
0	0	0	7	5	8	18	11

Then, we combined all the training set matrixes and testing set matrixes of into one training matrix and one testing set respectively, the size of which are 9000 * 256 and 1500 * 256. They contain gray-level co-occurrence matrix features of the raw grayscaled matrix in which each row represents one image. We named them as A_TR and A_TE. We also extracted the contrast, correlation, energy values, and homogeneity of the matrix from the stats = graycoprops(A) command and stored them in 9000 * 16 and 1500 * 16 matrixes named B_TR and B_TE.

We artificially labeled each category of tea leaf from 1 to 10. The label matrix is called matrix C_TR and C_TE. The matrix A_TR and C_TR needed to be combined into an augmented matrix D_TR. And we combined B_TR and C_TR into E_TR to test the GLCM feature maps (same operation needs to apply in the testing set, D_TE and E_TE). The size of the D_TR and E_TR are 9000 * 257 and 9000 * 17. Through the above operations, we have used a matrix to represent all the data, where each element was the characteristic parameter of each image and each row represented the overall feature of each image.

Table 3. The classification accuracy with and without HE

Model	Average accuracy
GLCM+SVM	93.07%
HE+GLCM+SVM	**94.64%**

(Bold means the best.)

3.5   Classification

In order to reflect the advantages of the Histogram Equalization, we compared the classification results of our HE+GLCM+SVM model and GLCM+SVM model, which shows in Table 3. We ran the experiments for 10 times and obtained an average accuracy to avoid contingency. Table 3 shows that the proposed models achieves good results. The Histogram Equalization method benefits to our classification problem by increasing the average accuracy (about 1.57%).

Table 4. The comparison of GLCM features (Bold means the best.)

Classifier	Average accuracy
Contrast	**73.61%**
Correlation	65.93%
Energy	69.08%
Homogeneity	65.47%

We proposed to test the four main GLCM features separately to discover the most motivating feature for this problem, which are contrast, correlation, energy and homogeneity. The results are shown in Table 4. The contrast achieves the highest average classification accuracy in this study.

Table 5. The classification accuracy of common classifiers

Classifier	Average accuracy
KNN	94.38%
NBS	83.58%
DT	92.62%
RF	92.81%
HE+GLCM+SVM (Ours)	**94.64%**

(Bold means the best.)

We compared the results of this study with our previous experiments which is based on GLCM and K-Nearest Neighbor (KNN) [10], Naive Bayes Classifier [37], Decision Tree [38], and Random Forest [39]. The results on the testing set are listed in Table 5, each of which are tested in 10 times.

To summarize, the proposed HE+GLCM+SVM model demonstrates the best performance of classification, and the average accuracy reaches 94.64%. This model focuses more on the texture features through GLCM method and benefits from HE method by enhancing the feature details.

4   Conclusion

The aim of this project is to develop an automatic tea identification/classification system with a high accuracy. Compared with our previous work and some classic classifies, we have augmented the dataset and improved the model. It is conceivable that larger data sets can be tested to obtain better results and avoid overfitting. The system was created based on Histogram Equalization (HE), Gray-Level Co-Occurrence Matrix (GLCM) and support vector machine (SVM) to cope with the ten-class problem. The results showed that this model can successfully identify and classify different tea varieties, and the average accuracy reaches 94.64%.

In the future, we will collect more kinds of tea images or build a larger dataset, test other classifiers, and design a model based on Convolutional neural network (CNN) and other machine learning methods. Besides, our system has been proved to be successful only on our dataset, and it is not certain whether it is suitable for the common classification dataset. We shall collect more samples and classes of tea images and build a higher performance system.

References

1. Conney, A., et al.: Inhibitory effect of green and black tea on tumor growth. Proc. Soc. Exp. Biol. Med. **220**(4), 229–233 (1999)
2. Wang, L.: Tea and Chinese Culture. Long River Press (2005)
3. Zhang, L., et al.: Effect of drying methods on the aromatic character of Pu-erh Tea. **1**, 71–75 (2007)
4. Wu, D., et al.: Application of multispectral image texture to discriminating tea categories based on DCT and LS-SVM. Spectroscopy Spectral Anal. **29**(5), 1382–1385 (2009)
5. Zhang, H.-L., et al.: Identification of green tea brand based on hyperspectra imaging technology. Spectroscopy Spectral Anal. **34**(5), 1373–1377 (2014)
6. Zhao, J., et al.: Qualitative identification of tea categories by near infrared spectroscopy and support vector machine. J. Pharmaceutical Biomed. Anal. **41**(4), 1198–1204 (2006)
7. Borah, S., et al.: Wavelet transform based image texture analysis for size estimation applied to the sorting of tea granules. J. Food Eng. **79**(2), 629–639 (2007)
8. Yang, J.: Identification of green, Oolong and black teas in China via wavelet packet entropy and fuzzy support vector machine. Entropy **17**(10), 6663–6682 (2015)
9. Zhang, Y.-D., Muhammad, K., Tang, C.: Twelve-layer deep convolutional neural network with stochastic pooling for tea category classification on GPU platform. Multimedia Tools Appl. **77**(17), 22821–22839 (2018). https://doi.org/10.1007/s11042-018-5765-3
10. Chen, Y., et al.: Tea leaves identification based on gray-level co-occurrence matrix and K-nearest neighbors algorithm. In: AIP Conference Proceedings, p. 020084. AIP Publishing LLC (2019)
11. Benčo, M., et al.: Novel method for color textures features extraction based on GLCM. Radioengineering **16**(4), 65 (2007)
12. Tetko, I.V., et al.: Neural network studies. 1. Comparison of overfitting and overtraining. **35**(5), 826–833 (1995)
13. Tanner, M.A., et al.: The calculation of posterior distributions by data augmentation. J. Am. Stat. Assoc. **82**(398), 528–540 (1987)
14. Pagani, L., et al.: Towards a new definition of areal surface texture parameters on freeform surface: Re-entrant features and functional parameters. Measurement **141**, 442–459 (2019)
15. Nanni, L., et al.: Texture descriptors for representing feature vectors. Expert Syst. Appl. **122**, 163–172 (2019)
16. Bradley, P.S.: A support-based reconstruction for SENSE MRI. Sensors **13**(4), 4029–4040 (2013)

17. Wu, L.N.: Segment-based coding of color images. Sci. China Ser. F-Inf. Sci. **52**(6), 914–925 (2009)
18. Wu, L.N.: Pattern recognition via PCNN and tsallis entropy. Sensors **8**(11), 7518–7529 (2008)
19. Wu, L.N.: Improved image filter based on SPCNN. Sci. China Ser. F-Inf. Sci. **51**(12), 2115–2125 (2008)
20. Zhang, Y.-D., Jiang, Y., Zhu, W., Lu, S., Zhao, G.: Exploring a smart pathological brain detection method on pseudo Zernike moment. Multimedia Tools Appl. **77**(17), 22589–22604 (2017). https://doi.org/10.1007/s11042-017-4703-0
21. Cheng, H.: Multiple sclerosis identification based on fractional Fourier entropy and a modified Jaya algorithm. Entropy **20**(4) (2018). Article ID. 254
22. Zhang, Y.-D., Sun, J.: Preliminary study on angiosperm genus classification by weight decay and combination of most abundant color index with fractional Fourier entropy. Multimedia Tools Appl. **77**(17), 22671–22688 (2017). https://doi.org/10.1007/s11042-017-5146-3
23. Lu, S.: Pathological brain detection based on alexnet and transfer learning. J. Comput. Sci. **30**, 41–47 (2019)
24. Yang, J.: Preclinical diagnosis of magnetic resonance (MR) brain images via discrete wavelet packet transform with Tsallis entropy and generalized eigenvalue proximal support vector machine (GEPSVM). Entropy **17**(4), 1795–1813 (2015)
25. Parhizkar, E., et al.: Partial least squares- least squares- support vector machine modeling of ATR-IR as a spectrophotometric method for detection and determination of iron in pharmaceutical formulations. Iranian J. Pharmaceutical Res. **18**(1), 72–79 (2019)
26. Zhang, Y.-D., Dong, Z., Chen, X., Jia, W., Du, S., Muhammad, K., Wang, S.-H.: Image based fruit category classification by 13-layer deep convolutional neural network and data augmentation. Multimedia Tools Appl. **78**(3), 3613–3632 (2017). https://doi.org/10.1007/s11042-017-5243-3
27. Li, Z.: Teeth category classification via seven-layer deep convolutional neural network with max pooling and global average pooling. Int. J. Imaging Syst. Technol. **29**(4), 577–583 (2019)
28. Tang, C.: Cerebral micro-bleeding detection based on densely connected neural network. Front. Neurosci. **13** (2019). Article ID. 422
29. Jia, W., Muhammad, K., Wang, S.-H., Zhang, Y.-D.: Five-category classification of pathological brain images based on deep stacked sparse autoencoder. Multimedia Tools Appl. **78**(4), 4045–4064 (2017). https://doi.org/10.1007/s11042-017-5174-z
30. Chen, Y.: Cerebral micro-bleeding identification based on a nine-layer convolutional neural network with stochastic pooling. Concurrency Comput.: Practice Exp. **31**(1), e5130 (2020)
31. Wang, S.-H., Muhammad, K., Hong, J., Sangaiah, A.K., Zhang, Y.-D.: Alcoholism identification via convolutional neural network based on parametric ReLU, dropout, and batch normalization. Neural Comput. Appl. **32**(3), 665–680 (2018). https://doi.org/10.1007/s00521-018-3924-0
32. Xie, S.: Alcoholism identification based on an AlexNet transfer learning model. Front. Psychiatry **10** (2019). Article ID. 205
33. Hong, J., Cheng, H., Zhang, Y.-D., Liu, J.: Detecting cerebral microbleeds with transfer learning. Mach. Vis. Appl. **30**(3), 1123–1133 (2019). https://doi.org/10.1007/s00138-019-01029-5
34. Jiang, X., et al.: Classification of Alzheimer's disease via eight-layer convolutional neural network with batch normalization and dropout techniques. J. Med. Imaging Health Inform. **10**(5), 1040–1048 (2020)

35. Govindaraj, V.V.: High performance multiple sclerosis classification by data augmentation and AlexNet transfer learning model. J. Med. Imaging Health Inform. **9**(9), 2012–2021 (2019)
36. Hsu, C.-W., et al.: *A comparison of methods for multiclass support vector machines.* IEEE Trans. Neural Netw. **13**(2), 415–425 (2002)
37. Rish, I.: An empirical study of the naive Bayes classifier. In: IJCAI 2001 Workshop on Empirical Methods in Artificial Intelligence, pp. 41–46. IBM New York (2001)
38. Safavian, S.R., et al.: A survey of decision tree classifier methodology. IEEE Trans. Syst. Man Cybern. **21**(3), 660–674 (1991)
39. Liaw, A., et al.: Classification and regression by randomForest. **2**(3), 18–22 2002

Research on Durability Test for Composite Pipe Fitting Materials of Automobile

Ang Li[1(✉)] and Juan Du[2]

[1] Basic Education School, Zhuhai College of Jilin University, Zhuhai 122000, China
wangyan201711@163.com
[2] School of Computer Science, Wuhan University, Wuhan 430072, China

Abstract. The automobile industry is one of the most promising industries in China. The increase of the number of vehicles is accompanied by the increase of traffic accidents. Therefore, the application of composite pipe materials has a broad prospect and become the basis of the automobile industry. In this paper, the durability of the composite material is tested, and it is used in the manufacture of stainless steel pipe fittings of automobile, which can produce low-cost, high-performance and ideal automobile parts. The application of the composite material in automobile field can effectively improve the production efficiency and use efficiency.

Keywords: Automobile industry · Composite pipe fitting materials · Durability · Research

1 Introduction

It has been proved that the car was invented in 1976, although it is quite controversial. Since 1885, the invention of diesel engine, through the unremitting efforts of engineers and designers, can be said that the automobile industry has become the largest automobile industry in the world. The most complex industry.. the sustainable development of the industry needs to consider the factors of price, performance, safety, market demand, etc. from the distribution diagram of automobiles, it can be seen that the automobiles owned by every 1000 people are not only the needs of human production and life at present, but also the demand for automobiles in the future will increase greatly. With the rapid decline of automobile price and the increase of per capita income, the development of automobile industry is faster and faster. In these areas, the ecological environment is relatively different in China's national economic level and per capita income level. People's consumption of automobiles has gradually shifted from developed areas such as Beijing, Shanghai and Guangzhou to sub developed areas [1]. At present, there are fewer car owners in many coastal areas than in Beijing, but the per capita income of these areas does not affect the future development of the automobile industry. The population of these areas is far higher than that of Beijing, nearly 300 million, which is equivalent to that of developed areas.

Nowadays, the automobile industry is getting better and better, and people's consumption concept is also changing. China's automobile market has entered the new

Y.-D. Zhang et al. (Eds.): ICMTEL 2020, LNICST 326, pp. 17–27, 2020.
https://doi.org/10.1007/978-3-030-51100-5_2

normal of "micro growth", and it is in urgent need of macro-control economy. The saturation of the primary and secondary markets and the change of consumer mentality have led to the golden age of double-digit growth in automobile sales. The most important thing is that the existing automotive energy absorption pipe is metal energy absorption box. Ordinary metal materials are usually very heavy, mainly rely on plastic deformation metal materials to manufacture and absorb energy, but their energy absorption rate is low, which can not meet the development trend of lightweight and safety of automobile. We must spend the most time to apply the capable materials to lay the foundation for the production of automobiles. Therefore, the price of composite pipe fitting materials is getting higher and higher, which has attracted attention in this field.

2 Research on Durability Test for Composite Pipe Fitting Materials of Automobile

The definition of composite pipe fittings is to establish an isotropic material model through the constitutive model of metal materials (elastoplastic material) and its failure theory. The composite pipe is developed and produced by few manufacturers, and it is widely used abroad [2]. The technical parameters of the composite pipe material are shown in Table 1.

Table 1. Technical parameters of the composite pipe material

Parameter	Fitting
Torus bending strength	≥ 180
Circular bending modulus of elasticity	≥ 13
Axial bending strength	≥ 180
Axial bending modulus of elasticity	≥ 10
Cyclic tensile strength	≥ 130
Elastic modulus of cyclic tensile	≥ 13
Axial tensile strength	≥ 130
Axial tensile elastic modulus	≥ 13
Fracture ELongation	≥ 0.25

The durability of the composite pipe material is reflected in the following points:

(1) Excellent corrosion resistance and long service life
    The pipe fitting material has good corrosion resistance of many chemical fluids such as acid, alkali and salt. It can transport drinking water, rainwater, sewage and many chemical fluids. The designed service life is 50 years.

(2) Excellent characteristics

The composite pipe material has a smooth inner wall and a roughness coefficient of 0.0084. Automotive materials often suffer from the localized corrosion and become rougher, while composite pipe materials always maintain a smooth surface [3].

(3) Health and safety, no pollution

The composite pipe material used in the car is made of food grade materials and is hygienic and safe. The inner surface of the composite pipe fitting material is smooth, no scaling and no corrosion, and no secondary pollution to the water quality [4]. Metal or PCCP pipes will produce rust water over time, polluting water quality.

(4) Good heat and frost resistance

The temperature of the composite pipe material is generally between −40 °C and 70 °C; the composite pipe material made of special resin can be used up to 120 °C; the composite pipe material has a small thermal expansion coefficient, and the thermal expansion coefficient of PE pipe is about 8 times of the composite pipe fitting materials [5, 6].

(5) Good electrical and thermal insulation

The composite pipe material is non-conductor, the pipe has good insulation and the heat transfer coefficient is small, so the heat preservation of the pipe is good with few heat loss [7, 8].

Different types of composite pipe materials have different properties and indicators, as shown in Table 2.

Table 2. List of indicators and specifications

Pipediameter (mm)	Wall thickness (mm)	Weight (kg/m)
68	9	11.75
70	10.5	13.48
73	9	12.12
76	7	13.25

At the same time, the composite pipe material and the metal pipe material are also very different in performance, as shown in Table 3.

Table 3. Performance comparison between composite pipe fittings and metal pipe fittings

Comparison program	Metal pipe fitting material	Composite pipe fitting material
Designability	Isotropy	Anisotropy
Intensity	Low	High
Corrosivity	Poor corrosion resistance	No sign of corrosion
Flexible life	300–500	>10000
Wall signal line	Unachievable	Achievable

The composite pipe fittings with different lengths have different bearing capacities. The shorter composite pipes are reduced in thickness while increasing the thickness at both ends, which not only facilitates the connection with other composite pipes, but also satisfies the requirements of bearing, has certain operability and saves the cost of fittings.

It is assumed that the bearing capacity of the composite pipe fittings is P, the elastic modulus is E, the longitudinal moment of inertia is u, the length is L, and the thickness is D. Then:

$$P = \frac{2E}{1 - u} \left(\frac{D}{L} \right) \tag{1}$$

When the thickness of the composite pipe is constant, the effect of the length on the bearing capacity is shown in Fig. 1.

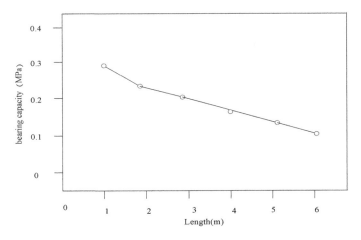

Fig. 1. Effect of the length on the bearing capacity of composite pipe fitting

It can be seen from the figure that as the length of the composite pipe is increased, the bearing capacity is gradually reduced and slowly decayed.

When the length of the composite pipe is constant, the effect of thickness on the bearing capacity is shown in Fig. 2.

It can be seen from the figure that as the thickness of the composite pipe is increased, the bearing capacity is gradually increased to become a slowly rising state [9, 10].

Therefore, the method of reducing the length of the pipe and increasing the thickness at the joint can ensure the bearing capacity and is also convenient to use.

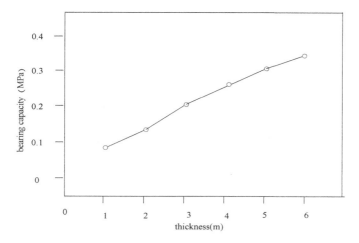

Fig. 2. Effect of thickness on the bearing capacity of composite pipe fitting

The composite pipe material is characterized by light weight, smooth inner wall, low resistance and good corrosion resistance [11, 12]. The composite pipe adopts the international advanced composite material [13, 14]. The composite pipe has better thermal insulation performance, the inner and outer walls are not easy to corrode, the inner wall is smooth, and the resistance to the fluid is small; and because it can be bent at will, the installation and construction are convenient [15]. As an auto parts, composite pipe fittings have sufficient strength. This unique process has high production efficiency, easy process control and high composite quality.

3   Test Analysis

Computer simulation technology is widely used in various aspects of national defense, industry and other human production and life. The ultrasonic detection based on computer simulation technology is a commonly used technique for pipe fitting detection. It is the nature of the acoustics transmitted by ultrasonic waves, and the properties or characteristics of the pipe itself are tested to judge the durability of the pipe. The system chart of the ultrasonic detector is shown in Fig. 3 (Fig. 4).

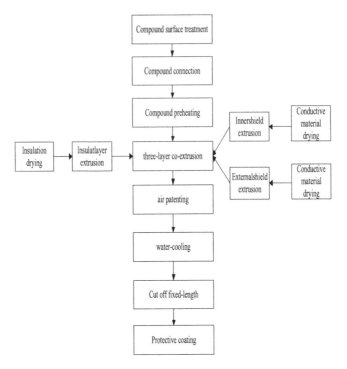

Fig. 3. Production process of composite pipe material

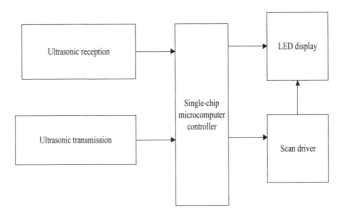

Fig. 4. System chart of the ultrasonic detector

Ultrasonic testing program:

```
Begin                    //Set baud rate

pinMode(ting,OUTPUT);    //Connect the pins of SR04

pinMode(echo,INPUT);     //Set input status

Serial.println("ultrasonic sensor");

digitalWrite(ting,LOW);  //Generate a 10US high pulse to trigger Trigpin

delayMicroseconds(2);

delayMicroseconds(10);

digitalWrite(ting,LOW);

const int ting=2;        //Set SR04 to connect to Arduino

const int echo=3;        //Set SR04 to connect to Arduino

float distance;          //Define a floating point variable

void setup()

sbit Tr = P2^0;          //Ultrasonic trigger

sbit Ec = P2^1;          //Ultrasonic output

sbit key = P2^4;         //click the button

sbit encC = P2^5;        //38 decoder

sbit encB = P2^6;

sbit encA = P2^7;            //P0 port digital tube

                            //Defining variables

float L = 0;             //Distance length（mm）

unsigned char code LED[] = {0x3F, 0x06, 0x5B, 0x4F, 0x66, 0x6D, 0x7D, 0x07,
0x7F, 0x6F};//Function declaration

Serial.print(distance);

Serial.print("cm");
```

```
serial.println();

while(!Ec);                //Wait high level

TR0 = 1;                   //Open timer

while(Ec);                 //Wait low level

TR0 = 0;                   //Turn off the timer

void ultInit();            //Ultrasonic initialization

void ultStart();           //Ultrasonic trigger

void count();              //Calculate the distance

void show();               //Display distance on the screen

void delay();              //Delay function

P0 = LED[(int)L%10];

encC = 0; encB = 1; encA = 1;

P0 = LED[(int)L/10%10];

encC = 0; encB = 1; encA = 0;

P0 = LED[(int)L/100%10];

encC = 0; encB = 0; encA = 1;

P0 = LED[(int)L/1000%10];

encC = 0; encB = 0; encA = 0;

Serial.print(distance);

Serial.print("cm");

serial.println();

distance=outcomeH;         //The upper 8 bits of the measurement result
```

```
distance<<=8;        //The upper 8 bits put in the 16-bit

distance=distance|outcomeL;        //Combine with the lower 8 bits to become

16-bit result data

distance*=12;        //Because the timer defaults to 12 division

    distance/=58;

    Serial.print(distance);

    Serial.print("cm");

    serial.println();

    void exter()

    interrupt 0                // External interrupt is 0

outcomeH =TH0;    //Take the value of the timer out

outcomeL =TL0;    //Take the value of the timer out

    End
```

It's assumed that the composite pipe length is L, R is the mid-surface radius, and U is the pressure resistance.

$$\varepsilon 1 = \frac{X}{L} - \frac{Y}{L} \tag{2}$$

$$\varepsilon 2 = \frac{r}{L} \tag{3}$$

$$U = \int \int \int \left[\varepsilon 1 + \varepsilon 2 + 2t\varepsilon 1\varepsilon 2 + \frac{1-t}{2} r \right] dt \tag{4}$$

The test was carried out by the above formula, and the result is shown in Fig. 5.

It can be seen from the figure that in the same time, the compressive capacity of the composite pipe material used by the automobile is much higher than that of the conventional material, and the higher the pressure resistance, the higher the durability.

The pipe produced under the condition of energy saving, non-toxic and non-polluting equipment is a new environmentally friendly product. There are no special requirements for water, electricity, gas and raw materials used in production, which is easy to solve in China. In the production process, no water is needed, which reduces the consumption and pollution of water; the product has the characteristics of good durability, corrosion resistance, convenient connection and firmness, which prolongs

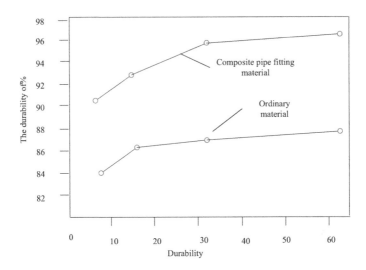

Fig. 5. Durability of two materials for automobiles

the service life of the structure and broadens the adaptability of structure to the environment, thus saving material consumption, manpower and material resources, reducing resource consumption. After the waste is crushed and processed, it can be recycled as raw materials without polluting or burdening the environment. Therefore, in this project, the (3R principle) eco-industrial characteristics such as "reduce" of resources, "reuse" of waste and "recycle" of pollutant discharge are fully reflected in this project. In the production process, no waste water (no water in the production process) and waste, a large amount of water is needed in the process of producing ordinary pipes, and clean production and environmentally friendly production are realized.

Compared with metal pipe fittings, composite pipe fittings have great advantages in terms of corrosion resistance and bending degree. Therefore, we should wait for the application of composite pipe fittings in the automotive industry. There are still many problems in the research of composite pipe fitting materials in the automotive industry. Although progress has been made, the latter research and testing will be strengthened. It is recommended that manufacturers can learn from foreign research results and technical means of composite pipe fitting materials, learn from each other's strengths, and promote the rapid development of China's automobile industry.

4 Conclusions

In order to reduce the occurrence of accidents, the conclusion of this study is: on the one hand, the government must establish strict automobile safety performance standards; on the other hand, automobile manufacturers should take measures to pay attention to the quality of products, especially in terms of crashworthiness and durability, composite pipe materials can improve the durability of automobiles, while reducing the weight of automobiles. In general, China's automobile industry still has a lot of room for development, and composite pipe will play a great role in the specific application field of the automobile industry in the future.

Fund Project. Project of Higher Education 2017002 of Guangdong Province.

References

1. Endo, M., Takeuchi, K., Kobori, K., et al.: Pyrolytic carbon nanotubes from vapor-grown carbon fibers. Carbon **33**(12), 56–58 (2017)
2. Jindal, P., Jindal, V.K.: Strains in axial and lateral directions in carbon nanotubes. **11**(2), 127–134 (2017)
3. Punetha, V.D., Rana, S., Yoo, H.J., et al.: Functionalization of carbon nanomaterials for advanced polymer nanocomposites. A Comparison Study between CNT and Graphene. **19**(2), 37–38 (2017)
4. Gilbert: Ultrasonic detection based on computer simulation technology. **31**(10), 23–24 (2017)
5. Lei, S.X., Cheng, X.U.: Electrical Property of MWNTs/PS-PVC Composites. Fuhe Cailiao Xue bao Materiae Compositae Sinica **23**(1), 52–56 (2017)
6. Saha, S., Bandyopadhyay, S.: MRI brain image segmentation by fuzzy symmetry based genetic clustering technique. IEEE Congress Evoi. Comput. **23**(1), 52–56 (2017)
7. Chuang, K.S., Tzang, H.L., Chen, T.-J.: Fuzzy c-means clustering with spatial information for image segmentation. Comput. Med. Imaging Graph **3**(10), 123–124 (2017)
8. Zhang, D.-Q., Chen, S.-C.: A novel kemelized fuzzy c-means algorithm with application in medical image sementation. Artif. Intell. Med. **19**(2), 37–38 (2017)
9. Bricq, S., Collet, C.H., Armspach, J.P.: Unifying framework for multimodal brain MRI segmentation based on hidden Markov chains. Med. Image **23**(12), 22–25 (2017)
10. Chabat, F., Yang, G.-Z., Hansell, D.-M.: Obstructive lung diseases: texture classification for differentiation at CT. Radiology **5**(34), 57–58 (2017)
11. Wang, J., Shao, J., Long, M., et al.: Multifactor mechanical aging properties and electrical performance research on composite material tower and samples: aging properties and electrical performance of composite tower and samples. **13**(2), 26–31 (2018)
12. Luo, X., Meng, X.: Research on bond durability among different core materials and zirconia ceramic cemented by self-adhesive resin cements. **35**(1), 89–92 (2017)
13. Yao, Y., Jin, H., Chen, X., et al.: Research on numerical simulation method of stress distribution for composite multiple bolted joints. J. Wuhan Univ. Technol. (Transp. Sci. Eng.) **41**(1), 161–164 (2017)
14. Leigh, S.S.: A review of impact testing on marine composite materials: part III - damage tolerance and durability. Compos. Struct. **118**(1), 512–518 (2018)
15. Tan, J., Ma, X., Qin, Z.: Study on axial compression performance of 2D braided composites tubes. Fiber Reinforced Plastics/Compos. **12**, 57–59 (2017)

Method for Extracting Information
of Database of Smart Phone Terminal
in Lock Screen Mode

Juan Du[(⊠)] and Rong Xie

School of Computer Science, Wuhan University, Wuhan 430072, China
dujuan1234l@163.com

Abstract. In order to improve the database management and scheduling ability of smartphone terminal, it is necessary to optimize the information extraction of smartphone terminal database in lock screen mode. through the dynamic mining of smartphone terminal database data, the optimal processing of smart phone terminal database data information is realized, and this paper proposes an algorithm to extract the resource information of the smartphone terminal database under the lock screen mode based on the Internet. Using distributed wireless sensor to form the Internet model of smart phone database collection, and the optimal deployment design of data acquisition Internet of things node is carried out. The spectrum analysis method is used to detect the abnormal resource information of smart phone terminal database in lock screen mode, and the detection results are fuzzy clustering to realize the extraction of smart phone terminal database resource information in locked screen mode under the environment of Internet of things. The simulation results show that the algorithm has high accuracy, good recall, strong anti-interference ability and good adaptive ability to collect the resource information of smart phone terminal database in lock screen mode.

Keywords: Lock screen mode · Smartphone · Terminal database · Resource information · Extraction

1 Introduction

The smart phone terminal database resource information collection system in the lock screen mode continuously provides the security information service for the smart phone transmission, including automatic crash alarm, road aid, remote unlock service, hands-free telephone, and road navigation, etc. [1, 2].

In the design of smart phone terminal database resource information collection algorithm and system design in the locked screen mode, The key is to establish the communication network system of relevant workshop. Based on the Internet of Things, the smart phone terminal database information networking between vehicles and roads is constructed [3]. At present, in the locked screen mode, the resource information acquisition method of smartphone terminal database is mainly used for domain feature

Y.-D. Zhang et al. (Eds.): ICMTEL 2020, LNICST 326, pp. 28–40, 2020.
https://doi.org/10.1007/978-3-030-51100-5_3

analysis method, etc. In addition, the feature sampling of smartphone terminal database resource information in the locked screen mode is carried out. In reference [4], a resource information extraction method for smart phone terminal database in QoS constrained lock screen mode is proposed, which merges the sampled data sparsely, and carries on the classification and repair after dynamic data acquisition combined with autocorrelation feature matching method, in order to make data collection more accurate but this method is easy to be interfered by dynamic disturbance features, which leads to the poor accuracy of acquisition, which reduces the extraction effect. In reference [5], a dynamic data acquisition algorithm for smart phone terminal database Internet of things network in the physical layer network coding method is proposed in the cloud computing environment is used for quantitative coding of data, the data of encoded data are processed blindly by CPM, and the ability of collecting and balancing the resource information of smartphone terminal database in locked screen mode is improved. However, the computational overhead of the algorithm is too large and the real-time performance of data acquisition is not good [6].

In order to solve the above problems, this paper proposes a resource information extraction algorithm for smart phone terminal database based on Internet of things lock screen mode. The adaptive weighting algorithm is used to fuse the resource information of smart phone terminal database in lock screen mode, and the spectral characteristic quantity of smart phone terminal database resource information in lock screen mode is extracted. The spectrum analysis method is used to detect the abnormal resource information of smart phone terminal database in lock screen mode, and the detection results to realize the extraction of smart phone terminal database resource information in locked screen mode in a network environment. Finally, the method of simulation experiment is used to verify its application performance in improving intelligence and accuracy of smart phone terminal database information in lock screen mode [7].

2 Internet of Things Node Distribution and Data Pre-processing of the Database Resource Information of the Smart Phone Terminal

2.1 Optimal Deployment of Internet of Things Node for Resource Information Collection of Smart Phone Terminal Database in Lock Screen Mode

In order to collect the resource information of smart phone terminal database accurately in lock screen mode, the method is used to design the node distribution of Internet of things, in the lock screen mode, the statistical feature analysis method is used to extract the resource information of the smartphone terminal database and the node distribution model of Internet of things of smart phone terminal database information distribution in lock screen mode is constructed [8]. The omni-directional node tree model of FP-tree microcell is used to construct the distributed node model of smart phone terminal database resource information distribution Internet of things in lock screen mode, as shown in Fig. 1.

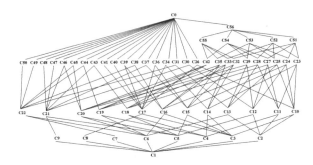

Fig. 1. Node communication graph model of database resource information distribution network of smart phone terminal

In the node communication graph of the database resource information distribution of the smart phone terminal database in the lock screen mode shown in Fig. 1, the sink node of the network of the intelligent mobile phone terminal database resource information collection object networking network in the lock screen mode is represented by four-tuple $\{S_1, S_2, \cdots, S_L\}$, obtaining the interrupt node of the database resource information distribution network of the smart phone terminal database in the lock screen mode as $node_j$, and performing the sparse characteristic reconstruction by the transmission information fusion method in the neighbor information table, constructing a state transition matrix of a network transmission channel of a database resource information distribution object of a smart phone terminal in a lock screen mode, which comprises the following steps of:

$$x(k+1) = A(k)x(k) + \Gamma(k)w(k) \tag{1}$$

$$z_i(k) = H_i(k)x(k) + u_i(k), \quad i = 1, 2, \cdots, N \tag{2}$$

The method comprises the following steps of: carrying out self-correlation characteristic sampling on transmission data in a database resource information distribution network channel of a smart phone terminal database in a lock screen mode, the loop iteration and loop iteration process in the database resource information acquisition process of the smart phone terminal in the lock screen mode are carried out by adopting a fuzzy directional clustering method, as shown in Fig. 2.

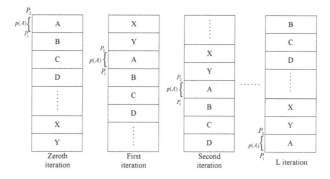

Fig. 2. Cyclic iterative process of resource information collection in smartphone terminal database in lock screen mode

According to the iterative process of data acquisition given in Fig. 2, set $x(t)$, $t = 0, 1, \cdots, n - 1$, is made as a training sequence, and the initialization pointer count G in the process of collecting resource information of smartphone terminal database in lock screen mode is counted. The number of data scale samples of smartphone terminal database in the input Internet of things is N, in which the training vector mode is based on the analysis. Using distributed wireless sensor to build data collection model of smartphone, and the optimal deployment design of data acquisition node is carried out [9–11].

2.2   Information Fusion Processing of Smartphone Terminal Database Resources in Lock Screen Mode

On the basis of designing and optimizing the deployment of Internet of things nodes collected by smart phone terminal database information in lock screen mode, the fusion processing of smart phone terminal database resource information in lock screen mode is carried out, and the distance between the distributed search result of smartphone terminal database data Internet of things $x(t)$ and the connection weight vector ω_j of smart phone terminal database resource information clustering center in all lock screen mode is calculated. Represented as Euclidean distance

$$d_j = \sum_{i=0}^{k-1} (x_i(t) - \omega_{ij}(t))^2, j = 0, 1, \cdots, N - 1 \tag{3}$$

In the node connection diagram of smart phone terminal database resource information distribution Internet of things in lock screen mode, the sampling amplitude of the node transmission data of smart phone terminal database resource information distribution Internet of things in lock screen mode is obtained:

$$\alpha_{desira}^i = \alpha_1 \cdot \frac{Density_i}{\sum_i Density_i} + \alpha_2 \frac{AP_i}{AP_{init}} \tag{4}$$

Wherein the weighting coefficient of the data self-adaptive fusion of the smart phone terminal database data is met:

$$\begin{cases} \alpha_1 + \alpha_2 = 1, \alpha_1, \alpha_2 \in [0, 1] \\ \alpha_2 = \dfrac{\max\limits_i (AP_i) - \min\limits_i (AP_i)}{AP_{init}} \end{cases} \tag{5}$$

Under different transmission medium attenuation modes, the information fusion support vector set of smart phone terminal database resource information under lock screen mode is as follows: under the mode of Internet of things breakpoint locking screen, the information fusion support vector set of smart phone terminal database resource information is as follows:

$$\begin{aligned} x_{id}(t+1) &= wx_{id}(t) + c_1 r_1 [r_3^{t_o > T_o} p_{id} - x_{id}(t)] \\ &\quad + c_2 r_2 [r_4^{t_g > T_g} p_{gd} - x_{id}(t)] \end{aligned} \tag{6}$$

Thereby realizing the data sampling of the nodes connected with the database resource information distribution network of the smart phone terminal in the lock screen mode, under the routing mechanism, and obtaining the confidence probability of the data acquisition accuracy distribution as follows:

$$K_{wpg}(x, y, w_i) = \begin{cases} 1 & d(\omega_i, k) \leq r - r_u \\ u(\frac{-\alpha_1 \theta \beta_1}{\theta_2 \beta_2}) + \alpha_2 & r - r_u < d(\omega_i, k) < r + r_u \\ 0 & \text{else} \end{cases} \tag{7}$$

In the above formula, $r_u (0 < r_u < r)$ represents the adaptive weighting operator of static routing sub-node, and $\alpha_1, a_2, \beta_1, \beta_2$ respectively corresponds tounclear logic control detection coefficient of Internet of Things routing in smart phone terminal database [12]. After n jump, the probability of accurate transmission between the middle layer and the layer of the link layer of the Internet of Things collected by the database resource information of the smartphone terminal in the lock screen mode is:

$$P_{graph} = \left\{ 1 - \left[1 - (1 - P_e)^2 (1 - P_d) \right]^m \right\}^n \tag{8}$$

The detection method is used to design the routing of smart phone terminal database resource information in lock screen mode. The optimal distribution probability of smart phone terminal database resource information fusion in n-hop lock screen mode is obtained by P_{AOMDV}:

$$P_{\text{AOMDV}} = (1 - P_d)^2 \left\{ 1 - \left[1 - (1 - P_e)^n (1 - P_d)^{n-1} \right]^m \right\} \tag{9}$$

In that lock screen mode, the information flow of the database resource information of the smart phone terminal in the lock screen mode is partitioned by a sparse fusion method, so that the data information fusion process of the database of the smart phone terminal is realized, and the anti-interference capability of the output acquisition is improved.

3   Optimal Implementation of Resource Information Extraction Algorithm

3.1   Extraction of Spectral Feature Quantity from Database Information of Smart Phone Terminal in Lock Screen Mode

The feature decomposition method is used to reconstruct the neighbor cluster head of the Sink node of the linearly, and the output feature quantity is expressed as $R_i(k) = E[\tilde{v}_i(k)\tilde{v}_i^T(k)]$. In combination with the following repair methods suitable for routing, the forwarding protocol of the digital fusion link layer for the resource information collection of the smart phone terminal database in the lock screen mode is obtained as follows:

$$CT_{ID_j} = \{C_1', C_2', C_3', C_4', C_5'\}$$
$$= \{(C_1 rk_{1ij})^{rk_{3ij}}, (C_2 rk_{2ij})^{rk_{3ij}}, C_3 k', C_4 k', C_5 rk_{6ij}\} \tag{10}$$

In the above formula, C_1, C_2, C_3 represent the distributed frequency band of resource information extraction, according to the correlation degree of the data fusion center, carries on the autocorrelation matching, obtains the data sampling frequency band interval:

$$c = z \cdot \left|\frac{x_0}{2}\right| = (q_p(z)p + r_p(z)) \cdot \left|\frac{x_0}{2}\right|$$
$$= q_p(z)p \cdot \left\lfloor\frac{x_0}{2}\right\rfloor + r_p(z) \cdot \left\lfloor\frac{x_0}{2}\right\rfloor \tag{11}$$

According to the sampling time interval and beam distribution interval of smart phone terminal database resource information in lock screen mode, the adaptive fusion and optimal channel allocation of resource information extraction are carried out. On this basis, the spectral features of smart phone terminal database resource information in locked screen mode are extracted, and the results of frequency feature extraction of transmission data are explained, database information distribution in locked screen mode are described as follows:

$$S_b = \sum_{i=1}^{e} p(\omega_i)(u_i - u)(u_i - u)^T \tag{12}$$

$$S_\omega = \sum_{i=1}^{e} p(\omega_i)E\left[\frac{(u_i - u)(u_i - u)^T}{\omega_i}\right] \tag{13}$$

$$S_i = S_b + S_\omega \tag{14}$$

And carrying out normalization processing on the information flow reorganization model $X(t)$ of the database resource information of the smart phone terminal in the lock screen mode, and improving the accuracy of the feature extraction.

3.2 Collection and Output of Resource Information of Smart Phone Terminal Database in Lock Screen Mode

By adopting the spectrum analysis method, the abnormal detection of the database resource information of the smart phone terminal database in the lock screen mode is carried out, and the sparse random sampling mode function of the database resource information of the smart phone terminal in the lock screen mode is met:

$$X'(t) = X(t)/\|X(t)\| \tag{15}$$

The anti-interference processing is carried out by the data filtering method, and $\tau + 1$ samples are randomly sampled in the node of the resource information extraction to obtain the data transmission key of the database of the smart phone terminal.

$$pk = \langle x_0, x_1, \ldots, x_\tau \rangle \tag{16}$$

The distribution model of smartphone data transmission that terminal database information distribution Internet of things in lock screen mode is constructed, and the output number acquisition sequence $x_0, x_1, \ldots, x_\tau$, is obviously:

$$parity(r_p(z)) = Decrypt(sk, c) \tag{17}$$

$$parity(q_p(z)) = parity(r_p(z)) \oplus parity(z) \tag{18}$$

The fuzzy clustering is carried out on the detection result, the data clustering is carried out by adopting the fuzzy clustering method, and the acquisition result of the database resource information of the smart phone terminal database under the output lock screen mode is as follows:

$$
\begin{aligned}
\frac{C_3 e(sk_{i2}, C_2^{x_i^{-1}})}{e(C_1^{x_i^{-1}}, sk_{i1})} &= me(g_1, g_2)^r e(g_1, g^{u_i(H_1(ID_i, upk_i) - H_1(g, g_1, g_2, g_3, h))})^r \\
&\quad \cdot \frac{e[g^{u_i}, (g_1^{H_1(g, g_1, g_2, g_3, h)} h)^r]}{e[g_2^a(g_1^{H_1(ID_i, upk_i)} h)^{u_i}, g^r]} \\
&= me(g_1, g_2)^r e(g_1, g^{u_i(H_1(ID_i, upk_i) - H_1(g, g_1, g_2, g_3, h))})^r \\
&\quad \cdot \frac{e[g^r, (g_1^{H_1(g, g_1, g_2, g_3, h)} h)^{u_i}]}{e(g_2^a, g^r) e[(g_1^{H_1(ID_i, upk_i)} h)^{u_i}, g^r]} \\
&= m
\end{aligned}
\tag{19}
$$

The autoregression linear equilibrium method is used to decompose the resource information of smart phone terminal database in locked screen mode linearly in the link layer.

$$\frac{n}{8} = r_1 = 2r_2 = 2^2 r_3 = \ldots = 2^{i-1} r_i = \ldots \tag{20}$$

The construction test statistics are as follows:

$$Q = \frac{V_n - 2n\pi(1 - \pi)}{2\sqrt{n\pi}(1 - \pi)} \tag{21}$$

According to the test statistics, the sampling decision is carried out to improve the accuracy of extracting resource information from smartphone terminal database in lock screen mode [13], the specific process is as follows (Fig. 3):

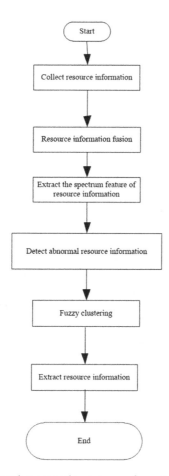

Fig. 3. Resource information extraction process of smartphone terminal database

4 Simulation Experiment and Performance Analysis

In order to verify the application performance of this method in the realization of smart phone terminal database resource information collection in lock screen mode, the simulation experiment is carried out. This experiment is carried out in Matlab environment. The experimental results are as follows: IntelCore4-530 1G memory, operating system Windows 7, distributed Internet of things transmission link capacity of smart phone terminal database resource information collection in lock screen mode is 120 Mbps. The time delay of resource information extraction is 18 ms, the initial data length is 1024. The frequency is $f_1 = 1.25$ Hz, of smartphone terminal database resource information in lock screen mode is terminated by using frequency GHz, lock screen mode. The energy attenuation coefficient of resource information distribution Internet of things node is $\lambda = 0.56$, the distribution grid unit from resource information is 200×200, and the packet size is 1200 Bps. The inertia weight of data filtering is 1.25. The channel attenuation intensity of smartphone terminal database resource information transmission link layer in lock screen mode is 295 pJ/(bit ·m4). The transmission frequency is 10 kHz, 16 kHz, 26 kHz and 32 kHz. According to the above simulation environment and parameter setting, the simulation experiment of smart phone terminal database resource information collection in lock screen mode is carried out. The output time domain waveform diagram of smart phone terminal database information collected by each frequency point in lock screen mode is shown in Fig. 4.

The results of Fig. 4 show that the data of smartphone terminal database with different frequency points can be accurately extracted by using this method to collect the resource information of smartphone terminal database in lock screen mode. The change of signal amplitude has significant positive correlation with the increase of distance, which indicates that the dynamic acquisition and tracking performance of smartphone terminal database number is better. In order to compare the performance, the signal-to-noise ratio (SNR) of 10000 Monte Carlo experiments is set to −20–20 dB, and the curve of accurate data acquisition is shown in Fig. 5.

Analysis of Fig. 5 shows that the accuracy rate of the method in this paper reaches the highest when the number of iterations is 80, the accuracy rate of the method in literature [5] is the highest when the number of iterations is 100, and the accuracy rate of the method in literature [4] is only 96%. It shows that the method of this paper has high accuracy of resource information extraction, good data recall performance, strong anti-interference ability of smart phone terminal, strong database information extraction process, and good adaptive ability.

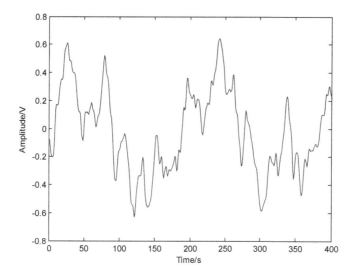

(a) 10kHz/16kHz frequency

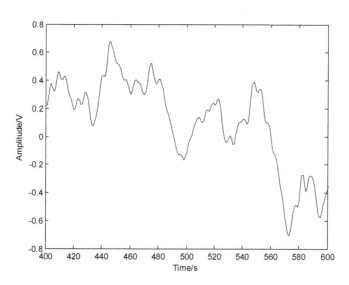

(b)26KHz/32KHz frequency

Fig. 4. Output time domain waveform of smartphone terminal database information acquisition in lock screen mode

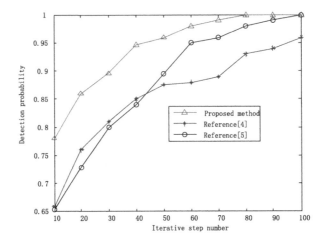

Fig. 5. Comparison of the accuracy of the information extraction of the database of the smart phone terminal

In order to verify this method, the data collection accuracy of the smartphone terminal database of the method in this paper, the method in literature [4] and the method in literature [5] are compared and analyzed, and the comparison results are shown in Fig. 6.

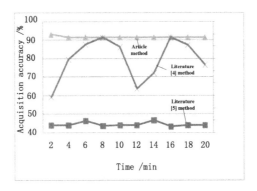

Fig. 6. Comparison results of information collection accuracy of smartphone terminal database

According to Fig. 6, the collection precision of the smartphone terminal database information of the method in this paper presents a stable state with the growth of time, and the collection precision can reach 92%, while the collection precision of the smartphone terminal database information of the methods in literature [4] and literature [5] is only 77% and 46% when the time is 20 min. The method in this paper is more accurate than the literature method, which shows that this method can extract the information of smartphone terminal database accurately.

5   Conclusions

Due to the low precision of extracting resource information from smartphone database in the traditional lock screen mode, an algorithm of extracting resource information from smartphone terminal database based on the Internet of things is proposed. Carrying out fusion processing of the database resource information of the smart phone terminal database under the lock screen mode by adopting an adaptive weighting algorithm, and extracting the spectral characteristic quantity of the database resource information of the smart phone terminal database in the lock screen mode, By adopting the spectrum analysis method, the abnormal detection of the database resource information of the smart phone terminal in the lock screen mode is carried out, and the detection result is subjected to fuzzy clustering, and the information extraction of the database resources of the smart phone terminal in the lock screen mode under the Internet of Things environment is realized. The experimental results show that under the lock screen mode of this method, the accuracy of resource information extraction of smartphone terminal database is better, the anti-interference is strong, and the intelligent mobile phone terminal database information dynamic management has good application value in the dynamic management of the database information of the smart phone terminal. Because the problem of extraction time is not considered when extracting the resource information of smart phone terminal database in lock screen mode, in the future research, we will compare the extraction time of the resource information of smart phone terminal database to further verify the reliability of this method.

References

1. Rui, L., Li, Q.: Short-term traffic flow prediction algorithm based on combined model. JEIT **38**(5), 1227–1233 (2016)
2. Ioannou, E., Garofalakis, M.: Holistic query evaluation over information extraction pipelines. Proc. Vldb Endow. **11**(2), 217–229 (2017)
3. Krebs, J., Corovic, H., Dietrich, G., et al.: Semi-automatic terminology generation for information extraction from german chest X-ray reports. **243**, 80 (2017)
4. Figueiredo, L.N.L., de Assis, G.T., Ferreira, A.A.: DERIN: a data extraction method based on rendering information and n-gram. Inf. Process. Manag. **53**(5), 1120–1138 (2017)
5. Xing, S., Liu, F., Zhao, X.: Parallel high utility pattern mining algorithm based on cluster partition. J. Comput. Appl. **36**(8), 2202–2206 (2016)
6. Chuanyu, L.V.: Construction of chemical information database based on optical structure recognition technique. **50**(2), 352–357 (2018)
7. Tahsin, T., Weissenbacher, D., Rivera, R., et al.: A high-precision rule-based extraction system for expanding geospatial metadata in GenBank records. **23**(5), 934 (2017)
8. Liu, X., Tao, X., Duan, Y., et al.: Visual information assisted UAV positioning using priori remote-sensing information (6), 1–20 (2017)
9. Gallacher, C., Thomas, R., Lord, R., et al.: Comprehensive database of manufactured gas plant tars - part c heterocyclic and hydroxylated PAHs. Rapid Commun. Mass Spectrometry **31**(15), 1250 (2017)

10. Ni, X., Gole, A.M., Zhao, C., et al.: An improved measure of ac system strength for performance analysis of multi-infeed HVdc systems including VSC and LCC converters. IEEE Trans. Power Deliv. **33**(1), 169–178 (2018)
11. Amirat, Y., Münch, A.: On the controllability of an advection-diffusion equation with respect to the diffusion parameter: asymptotic analysis and numerical simulations. Acta Mathematicae Applicatae Sinica English Serie **35**(1), 54–110 (2019)
12. Wang, W., Wang, Y.: The well-posedness of solution to semilinear pseudo-parabolic equation. Acta Mathematicae Applicatae Sinica English Serie **35**(2), 386–400 (2019)
13. Yang, J., Wei, C.: Testing serial correlation in partially linear additive models. Acta Mathematicae Applicatae Sinica English Serie **35**(2), 401–411 (2019)

Quality Detection Method of Phase Change Energy Storage and Thermal Insulation Building Materials Based on Neural Network

Shan-qin Sun[(⊠)]

Hunan Institute of Microbiology (Testing Center), Changsha 410001, China
lining144165855@163.com

Abstract. In order to improve the quality detection ability of thermal insulation building material, a phase change energy storage thermal insulation building material quality detection method based on neural network is put forward. The double broken line model is used to detect and evaluate the quality of phase change energy storage thermal insulation building material. Combined with the material stress characteristics and dissipation characteristics, the seismic evaluation of phase change energy storage thermal insulation building material is carried out, and the self-recovery energy dissipation support model of phase change energy storage thermal insulation building material is established. Under the constraint of quality parameter constraint model and neural network control model, the quality of phase change energy storage thermal insulation building materials is evaluated quantitatively by using network adaptive control method, and the stress distribution characteristic parameters of phase change energy storage thermal insulation building materials are calculated respectively to realize the quality detection of phase change energy storage thermal insulation building materials. The simulation results show that the accuracy of phase change energy storage and thermal insulation building material quality detection is high, the accuracy of parameter evaluation is good, and the quality detection ability is very good.

Keywords: Neural network · Phase change energy storage · Thermal insulation building materials · Quality inspection

1 Introduction

With the rapid development of China's economy, the pace of urbanization in China is moving forward. Various industries in the city have sprung up after a spring rain, and the urban construction industry is developing particularly rapidly. The development of urban construction infrastructure related industries has become more attractive, and the quality of the overall construction project is the most important [1]. The decisive factors affecting the quality of the whole building project are thermal insulation building materials and building infrastructure, which are the foundation to ensure the quality of the whole building construction project. Therefore, the quality of thermal insulation building materials should be strictly tested in the construction process to prevent the application of unqualified thermal insulation building materials to

Y.-D. Zhang et al. (Eds.): ICMTEL 2020, LNICST 326, pp. 41–53, 2020.
https://doi.org/10.1007/978-3-030-51100-5_4

infrastructure construction, which requires strict inspection and analysis of thermal insulation building materials by scientific and technical means [2]. In the construction process of housing construction project, how to optimize the selection is the key, and the housing construction project is based on the related material quality inspection, which will have a direct impact on the whole process. Therefore, in order to ensure the smooth and orderly construction process and all the processes meet the requirements, we must do a good job of material quality inspection and analysis, and actively optimize the detection and improve the feasibility.

With the wide application of phase change energy storage thermal insulation building materials in buildings, the strength and stability of phase change energy storage thermal insulation building materials have attracted people's attention. In reference [3], a nondestructive testing method of steel structure based on BIM and surface image analysis is proposed. The wavelet decomposition method is used to denoise the detection image of steel structure of building. The clarity of the detection image is enhanced through expansion and corrosion treatment. Infrared image technology is used to extract the defect edge in turn through rotation tracking method according to the change rate of the detection image recovery at the defect edge. Based on B Im's steel structure detection model for green construction in seismic area, fully control the material, nondestructive testing and management process of green construction steel structure in seismic area, control the whole life cycle of building steel structure, and complete the nondestructive testing of building steel structure. Literature [4] on the basis of expounding the connotation of the quality inspection of the main structure of the construction project, analyzes its specific inspection process and methods, and points out the specific application of the quality inspection technology of the main structure. But the accuracy of building materials quality inspection of the above two methods is low.

In view of the above problems, this paper proposes a method of phase change energy storage and thermal insulation building material quality detection based on neural network. Firstly, the finite element simulation analysis model of phase change energy storage and thermal insulation building materials is established, and then the neural network adaptive control method is used to quantitatively evaluate the quality of phase change energy storage thermal insulation building materials to realize the quality detection of phase change energy storage thermal insulation building materials. Finally, the simulation experiment is carried out, and the effective conclusion is obtained.

2   The Significance and Method of Quality Inspection of Heat-Insulating Building Material

2.1   Significance of Quality Inspection of Thermal Insulation Building Materials

In the process of testing the materials used in the building, it is particularly important to ensure the accuracy of the test results. It is necessary not only to test the quality of the construction materials used in the construction of the building project, but also to understand its performance, so as to ensure the completion of high quality in the construction process of the building project. In order to ensure that the methods and methods of testing are scientific and effective, it is necessary to carry out the inspection of the related materials used in houses and buildings in combination with the specifications in this area and follow the standards in order to ensure that the methods and methods of testing are scientific and effective. Thus it can be seen that no matter what type of housing construction project, in the whole process of construction, it is necessary to carefully detect the materials involved in the relevant housing construction, which is not only conducive to fully ensuring the construction quality of the housing construction project, but also effectively ensures that the safety of the construction personnel is not threatened [5–7].

2.2 Purpose and Method of Quality Inspection of Thermal Insulation Building Materials

(1) Material quality inspection project.

Thermal insulation building materials have great influence on the quality of building engineering, so we must pay great attention to it. In the process of quality inspection, appropriate schemes and measures should be taken. For material quality inspection and test, the corresponding testing methods and means should be adopted according to the specific texture of the material. From the current actual situation, the thermal insulation construction materials in the housing construction industry can be described as a variety of materials, such as stone, cement and so on, these belong to structural materials, such as paint, tiles and so on, these belong to decorative materials [8]. In the specific construction process, will involve all aspects of construction materials, functions and types are relatively complete. These materials are basically provided by suppliers, the quality and compliance of these materials can not be guaranteed, so all incoming materials must be checked, and the quality inspection objectives should be used as the basis of testing in accordance with the unified national regulations, so as to ensure that all material tests can meet the eligibility standards. For example, taking cement as an example, it is necessary to test its stability and strength, and to carry out omni-directional testing for different types and functions of thermal insulation building materials, so as to promote the detection and test of thermal insulation building materials to reach the standard [9].

(2) Sampling test.

In the process of sampling, more typical samples should be taken. Usually, the specified quantity of samples should be taken arbitrarily at different positions of a batch of materials, not only to ensure the correct sampling quantity, but also to extract according to the requirements. The sampling quantity is closely related to the accuracy of the test results. Too little sampling quantity, or if the sampling method and position are wrong, will increase the test error, and even obtain the opposite results. However, in practice, sampling atypical cases often occur.

(3) Control the humidity and temperature of the detection environment.

Because the temperature and humidity of the environment will seriously affect some thermal insulation building materials, it is necessary to strictly follow the relevant environmental standards to adjust and control the humidity and temperature when testing the quality of thermal insulation building materials. For example, in the process of concrete mixing test in summer, the temperature of water should not be higher than 20 °C, and the cold water of deep well should be the best.

(4) Scientific processing of data.
In the course of the test, due to the influence and distress of many factors, the test results are not satisfactory. For the same group of specimens, their test results are likely to appear greater discreteness. In order to minimize this error, it is necessary to give appropriate data processing to the test results. It should also be noted that there is a big gap between the test results and the expected results, and the results are very different. For the test results, the experimenters need to be carefully analyzed, and the causes of its formation are analyzed, and the results of the relatively wide disparity need to be tested repeatedly until the reasons are found out, so as to ensure the availability of the test results [10].

3   Finite Element Simulation of Phase Change Energy Storage and Thermal Insulation Building Materials

3.1   Finite Element Simulation Analysis of Phase Change Energy Storage and Thermal Insulation Building Materials

In order to realize the quality detection of phase change energy storage and thermal insulation building materials, the support finite element simulation analysis model of phase change energy storage thermal insulation building materials is established. The double broken line model is used to detect the quality of phase change energy storage thermal insulation building materials, and the finite element simulation and support double structure simulation methods are used to detect the support finite element characteristics of phase change energy storage thermal insulation building materials [11]. The finite element analysis model of phase change energy storage thermal insulation building material is established, and the neural network model is used to detect the quality of phase change energy storage thermal insulation building material. The neural network model is shown in Fig. 1.

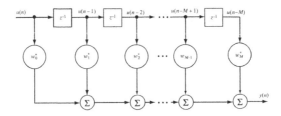

Fig. 1. Neural network model

The joint distribution model of main physical parameters for automatic quality detection of phase change energy storage thermal insulation building materials is established. The steady state characteristic equation of phase change energy storage thermal insulation building materials under sinusoidal excitation is obtained as follows:

$$
\begin{aligned}
T = &\tfrac{1}{2}M_{RL}\dot{X}_{RL}^2 + \tfrac{1}{2}M_{RR}\dot{X}_{RR}^2 + \tfrac{1}{2}J_{RL}\dot{\theta}_{RL}^2 + \tfrac{1}{2}J_{RR}\dot{\theta}_{RR}^2 \\
&+ \tfrac{1}{2}M_p\left[\left(\dot{\theta}_p L\cos\theta_p + \dot{X}_{RM}\right)^2 + \left(-\dot{\theta}_p L\cos\theta_p\right)^2\right] + \tfrac{1}{2}J_{P\theta}\dot{\theta}_P^2 \\
&+ \tfrac{1}{2}J_{P\delta}\dot{\delta}^2
\end{aligned}
\tag{1}
$$

$$
V = M_P g L\cos_{\theta_P}
\tag{2}
$$

When it is restored to the origin, NSYS finite element simulation is used to match the model features of phase change energy storage and thermal insulation building material quality detection, a nonlinear differential equation is used to detect the quality of phase change energy storage thermal insulation building material [12], double Bouc-Wen model is used to analyze the seismic strengthening strength of phase change energy storage thermal insulation building material, and the method of series detection of internal pipe and guide shaft is adopted. The seismic prestress distribution of phase change energy storage and thermal insulation building materials is carried out to meet the requirements of:

$$
\begin{aligned}
0 \le \ &-2\sum_{i=1}^{n} t_{i1}f_i(y_i(t))[f_i(y_i(t)) - \rho_i y_i(t)] \\
&-2\sum_{i=1}^{n} t_{i2}f_i(y_i(t-\delta(t)))[f_i(y_i(t-\delta(t))) - \rho_i y_i(t-\delta(t))] \\
=\ &-2f^T(y(t))T_1 f(y(t)) - 2f^T(y(t-\delta(t)))T_2 f(y(t-\delta(t))) \\
&+2y^T(t)\Sigma T_1 f(y(t)) + 2y^T(t-\delta(t))\Sigma T_2 f(y(t-\delta(t))).
\end{aligned}
\tag{3}
$$

Under the constraint condition of self-reset damping energy dissipation braces, the characteristic expression of building structure quality detection is obtained as follows:

$$
\begin{cases}
e = z_1 - y \\
\dot{z}_1 = z_2 - \beta_1 e \\
\dot{z}_2 = z_3 - \beta_2 fal(e, 0.5, \delta) \\
\dot{z}_3 = -\beta_3 fal(1, 0.25, \delta) + bu
\end{cases}
\tag{4}
$$

In that formula, z_1, z_2 is the characteristic quantity of the damping energy dissipation support distribution, and y is the characteristic quantity of the load separation, and the test method of the vibration characteristic of the seismic wave output is adopted to carry out the support finite element simulation of the phase-change energy-storage heat-insulation building material, and the state transition equation of the seismic wave is obtained as follows:

$$
\frac{\partial}{\partial t}(\rho u_i) + \frac{\partial}{\partial x_j}(\rho u_i u_j) = -\frac{\partial p}{\partial x_i} + \frac{\partial \tau_{ij}}{\partial x_j} + \rho g_i + F_i
\tag{5}
$$

Wherein

$$\tau_{ij} = [\mu(\frac{\partial u_i}{\partial x_j} + \frac{\partial u_j}{\partial x_i})] - \frac{2}{3}\mu\frac{\partial u_i}{\partial x_i}\delta_{ij} \tag{6}$$

Combined with the double broken line model for quality detection to improve the output stability of phase change energy storage and insulation building materials [13].

3.2 Quality Evaluation of Phase Change Energy Storage and Thermal Insulation Building Materials

According to the stress characteristics and dissipation characteristics of phase change energy storage thermal insulation building materials, the seismic evaluation of phase change energy storage thermal insulation building materials is carried out, and the self-recovery energy dissipation bracing model of phase change energy storage thermal insulation building materials is established [14]. The fusion model of stress characteristic parameters for phase change energy storage thermal insulation building materials quality detection is expressed as follows:

$$
\begin{aligned}
\max \quad & \Theta_{Q_i} = \frac{a_{Q_i}}{a_{Q_i} + c_{Q_i}} \\
\max \quad & \Theta_{E_i} = \frac{a_{E_i}}{a_{E_i} + c_{E_i}} \\
\max \quad & \Theta_{C_i} = \frac{a_{C_i}}{a_{C_i} + c_{C_i}} \\
S.t. \quad & Q_i \geq Q_{th} \\
& E_i \geq E_{th} \\
& C_i \leq C_{th} \\
& Q_{jk} \geq 0, E_{jk} \geq 0, C_{jk} \geq 0 \\
& \sum_{j=1}^{Nj} x_{jk} = 1, \forall i, 1 \leq k \leq M, 1 \leq j \leq N_j
\end{aligned}
\tag{7}
$$

In the above formula, Θ is referred to as the detection statistic under the action of damping energy dissipation support, and the characteristic transfer control is carried out according to the description support hysteresis characteristic, and the viscous coefficient of the damping support material is $\{F_i, F_U\}$, and the degree of association is as follows:

$$\mu_{B_i} = a_{B_i} + b_{B_i}\Delta + c_{B_i}\Phi \tag{8}$$

Wherein, $a_{B_i} = \frac{B_i}{B_U + B_v}$, $b_{B_i} = \frac{(B_U - B_i)(B_i - B_v)}{(B_U + B_v)B_i}$, $c_{B_i} = \frac{B_U B_v}{(B_U + B_v)B_i}$, in the assembly integral model structure, in the early elastic stage and plastic stage, the yield strength of the building structure is S, and the seismic structure frequency S is tested under the condition of fine oblique cracks formed at the angle of the connecting beam. The quality distribution of phase change energy storage and thermal insulation building materials under earthquake action is as follows:

$$s(x) = [N(x), M(x)]^{\mathrm{T}} \tag{9}$$

In the above formula, the $N(x)$ represents the tensile strength, $M(x)$ is the yield response characteristic distribution of the tensile stress, and the peak of the acceleration wave acceleration is input to obtain the power increment:

$$f_t = \frac{\Delta V_t}{V_{t1}} = \frac{V_{t1} - V_{u1}}{V_{t1}} \tag{10}$$

Under the condition that the decrease of the first third order frequency is the same, the elastic-plastic displacement of the building structure is as follows:

$$d_i = d_{ei} + d_{pti} \tag{11}$$

With the peak acceleration of the input tension wave, the characteristic components of the tensile stability detection are obtained as follows:

$$D_e = \sum_i d_{ei} \tag{12}$$

Based on the analysis, the parameter evaluation of phase change energy storage and thermal insulation building material quality inspection is realized [15].

4 Quality Inspection and Optimization of Phase Change Energy Storage and Thermal Insulation Building Materials

4.1 Self-recovery Energy Dissipation Bracing Model for Phase Change Energy Storage and Thermal Insulation Building Materials

Under the constraint of quality parameter index constraint model and neural network control model, the neural network adaptive control method is used to quantitatively evaluate the quality of phase change energy storage and thermal insulation building materials. The internal force distribution of tension resistance is expressed as follows:

$$e(x) = \sum_i d_{ei} D_s B(x).d_e \tag{13}$$

In the formula, $B(x)$ represents the joint characteristic distribution of the self-recovery energy dissipation braces of the phase change energy storage and thermal insulation building materials, and the maximum floor shear force of the integral structure is as follows:

$$B = \begin{bmatrix} -1 & 0 & 0 & -1 & 0 & 0 \\ 0 & 6\xi/L & 3\xi - 1 & 0 & 6\xi/L & 3\xi - 1 \end{bmatrix} \tag{14}$$

Wherein, $\xi \in [-1, 1]$, denotes the order of tension wave, under the constraint of statistical characteristic quantity, the tension action is nonlinear distribution, and the dynamic control equation of steel structure is as follows:

$$\begin{bmatrix} m_b & \\ & m_s \end{bmatrix} \begin{Bmatrix} \ddot{x}_b \\ \ddot{x}_s \end{Bmatrix} + \begin{bmatrix} c_b & -c_b \\ -c_b & c_b + c_s \end{bmatrix} \begin{Bmatrix} \dot{x}_b \\ \dot{x}_s \end{Bmatrix}$$
$$+ \begin{bmatrix} k_b & -k_b \\ -k_b & k_b + k_s \end{bmatrix} \begin{Bmatrix} x_b \\ x_b \end{Bmatrix} + \begin{bmatrix} m_b & \\ & m_s \end{bmatrix} \begin{Bmatrix} u_b \\ u_s \end{Bmatrix} = 0 \tag{15}$$

In the above formula, u_b represents the maximum overturning moment and c_s represents the increment of elastic internal force of the section. In the elastic stage, the load of the assembly integral structure is as follows:

$$d_i = \begin{bmatrix} k_b & -k_b \\ -k_b & k_b + k_s \end{bmatrix} \begin{Bmatrix} x_b \\ x_b \end{Bmatrix} + \begin{bmatrix} m_b & \\ & m_s \end{bmatrix} \begin{Bmatrix} u_b \\ u_s \end{Bmatrix} d_{ei} \tag{16}$$

The yield response of phase change energy storage thermal insulation building material is set in advance. The output stress load increases gradually with the order of input tension wave, and the output is as follows:

$$x'_{ij} = x_i - \rho + j\frac{2\rho}{n} \tag{17}$$

In the formula, ρ represents the self-recovery energy dissipation supporting force of the phase-change energy-storage heat-insulating building material under the action of the pulling force, x_i is the maximum interlayer displacement of the assembled integral structure, The quantitative evaluation of the quality of the phase-change energy-storage building material is carried out by using the neural network adaptive control method.

4.2   Quality Inspection of Phase Change Energy Storage and Thermal Insulation Building Materials

The stress distribution characteristic parameters of the thermal insulation material are respectively calculated, the quality detection of the phase-change energy-storage heat-insulation building material is realized, and the model strain increment of the building structure under the iteration conditions of the $n + 1$, n-step is as follows:

$$d(t) = \begin{cases} \arctan\left(\frac{X'_2(t)}{X'_1(t)}\right), & X'_1(t) > 0 \\ \arctan\left(\frac{X'_2(t)}{X'_1(t)}\right) + \pi, & X'_1(t) < 0, \ t = 1, 2, \ldots, T \\ \pi/2, & X'_1(t) = 0 X'_1(t) = 0 \end{cases} \tag{18}$$

Under the effect of concentrated load, the mass state quantity of the phase-change energy-storage building material is $x_0(x_0 = [\varphi_0, \dot{\varphi}_0, \theta_0]^T)$, and the overturning moment of the bottom layer under the action of the tension wave is as follows:

$$\begin{cases} mV\Delta\dot{\theta} = \left(c_y^{\alpha}qS_M + P\right)\Delta\alpha + mg\ \sin\theta\Delta\theta + P\Delta\delta_{\varphi} \\ \qquad + m_R l_R \Delta\ddot{\delta}_{\varphi} + F_{gr} \\ J_{Z1}\Delta\ddot{\varphi} = -c_y^{\alpha}qS_M\left(x_g - x_T\right)\Delta\alpha - qS_M m_{dz} l_k^2 \Delta\dot{\varphi}/V \\ \qquad - P(x_R - x_T)\Delta\delta_{\varphi} - m_R \dot{W}_{x1} l_R \Delta\delta_{\varphi} \\ \qquad - m_R l_R \Delta\ddot{\delta}_{\varphi}(x_R - x_T) - J_R \Delta\ddot{\delta}_{\varphi} + M_{gr} \end{cases} \tag{19}$$

Due to the different response values under the action of tensile wave, according to the interstory displacement of building structure, the tensile stress equation of building is obtained as follows:

$$(\frac{1}{2}(u_A^+ - u_A^-) - \frac{1}{2}F_{A_1}, \frac{1}{2}(u_A^+ - u_A^-) - \frac{1}{2}(F_B + F_{A_2})) \tag{20}$$

The stress distribution characteristic parameters of thermal insulation materials are calculated respectively, and the quality detection of phase change energy storage thermal insulation building materials is realized. The expression of yield response characteristic quantity of rectangular plate is defined as follows:

$$C_{ijkl} = 2\frac{1}{V}W^*\overline{\varepsilon_{ij}}\frac{1}{\varepsilon_{ij}^2}\ i=j, k=l, i=k \tag{21}$$

$$C_{ijkl} = \frac{1}{2V}W^*\overline{\varepsilon_{ij}}\frac{1}{\varepsilon_{ij}^2}\ i\neq j, k\neq l, i=k, j=l \tag{22}$$

$$C_{ijkl} = \frac{1}{4V}\frac{(W^*\overline{\varepsilon_{ij}\,\varepsilon_{kl}}) - W^*\overline{\varepsilon_{ij}} - W^*\overline{\varepsilon_{kl}}}{\overline{\varepsilon_{ij}}\,\overline{\varepsilon_{kl}}}\ i\neq j, k\neq l \tag{23}$$

$$C_{ijkl} = \frac{1}{2V}\frac{(W^*\overline{\varepsilon_{ij}\,\varepsilon_{kl}}) - W^*\overline{\varepsilon_{ij}} - W^*\overline{\varepsilon_{kl}}}{\overline{\varepsilon_{ij}}\,\overline{\varepsilon_{kl}}}\ i=j, k\neq l \tag{24}$$

The quality detection and optimization design of the phase-change energy storage and heat-insulating building material is realized.

5 Experimental Test Analysis

In order to test the application performance of this method in the quality detection of phase change energy storage and thermal insulation building materials, the experimental analysis is carried out. It is assumed that the strength of the input tensile wave is 250 MPa, the curve shape parameter is 1.24, the elastic modulus of phase change energy storage thermal insulation building material $Es = 23.45 \times 10^6$ psi, Mor is 0.43, the valley deflection is 2.45, and the structural parameters are set in Table 1.

Table 1. Parameter description of phase change energy storage and thermal insulation building materials

Finite element point	Coordinate x (m)	Coordinate y (m)	Coordinate z (m)	Stress (N)
1	4.45	5.54	7.56	14.56
2	3.64	9.43	9.78	37.32
3	8.33	8.42	5.73	53.34
4	0.23	6.68	8.34	54.56
5	7.45	8.86	1.56	14.53
6	9.67	6.65	9.78	23.46
7	9.45	3.64	2.65	43.64
8	7.43	2.78	2.63	54.32
9	4.43	3.85	8.45	64.73
10	5.56	5.54	7.52	76.45
11	2.32	7.56	1.32	41.43
12	6.36	3.63	0.45	32.11
13	3.65	8.53	8.34	42.72

According to the above parameters, the quality of phase change energy storage and thermal insulation building materials is tested, and the finite element model is shown in Fig. 2.

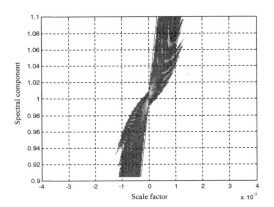

Fig. 2. Finite element model for the detection

According to the detection model of Fig. 2, the quality of phase change energy storage and thermal insulation building materials is tested, and the test results are shown in Fig. 3.

The analysis of Fig. 3 shows that the method can effectively realize the accuracy of phase change energy storage thermal insulation building material quality detection, the accuracy of parameter evaluation is good, and has good quality detection ability. It has good application value in phase change energy storage thermal insulation building material tension resistance and disaster prevention.

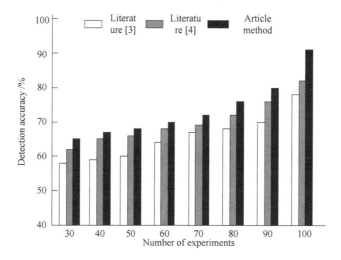

Fig. 3. Quality test results of phase change energy storage and thermal insulation building materials

In order to further verify the effectiveness of the method in this paper, the error of phase change energy storage and thermal insulation building material quality test results of the method in this paper, the method in literature [3] and the method in literature [4] are compared and analyzed, and the comparison results are shown in Fig. 4.

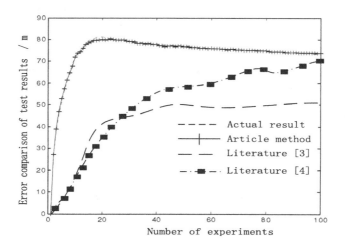

Fig. 4. Error comparison of test results

According to Fig. 4, the fitting degree between the quality test results of phase change energy storage and thermal insulation building materials in this method and the actual test results is 100%, while the quality test results of phase change energy storage and thermal insulation building materials in literature [3] and literature [4] are quite different from the actual test results, indicating that this method has a high quality test effect of phase change energy storage and thermal insulation building materials.

6 Conclusions

In conclusion, the quality detection technology of the heat-insulating building material can be reasonably applied, and the quality of the materials applied to the construction of the building construction can be ensured to be in accordance with the engineering requirements, and the construction work can be successfully completed, so that the construction progress and the quality of the building are guaranteed, It is of great significance to reduce the construction effect of the project. In the background of the continuous construction of the modern building construction, the types of the building construction materials are increased, and the quality detection technology of the engineering materials also has higher requirements, which requires the relevant construction personnel to have a deep understanding of the importance of the quality of the material quality detection, In addition, the quality inspection of the material is carried out in combination with the engineering demand, which lays a theoretical foundation for promoting the overall development of the building construction enterprises in China.

In order to improve that strength of the phase-change energy-storage heat-insulation building material by analyzing the quality of the phase-change energy-storage heat-insulation building material, the strength of the phase-change energy-storage heat-insulation building material is improved, and the quality detection method of the phase-change energy-storage heat-insulation building material based on the neural network is proposed the invention discloses a support finite element simulation analysis model for building a phase-change energy-storage heat-insulation building material, the quantitative evaluation of the quality of the phase-change energy-storage and heat-insulating building material is carried out by adopting a neural network adaptive control method, the stress distribution characteristic parameters of the thermal insulation material are calculated respectively, and the quality detection of the phase-change energy-storage heat-insulation building material is the method has the advantages of high accuracy of quality detection of the phase-change energy-storage heat-insulation building material by adopting the method, good accuracy of parameter evaluation, good quality detection capability and good engineering application value. Because this paper does not consider the detection time when studying the quality detection method of phase change energy storage and thermal insulation building materials based on neural network, in the future research, the detection time is taken as the experimental index to further verify the effectiveness of this method.

References

1. Iglesias, C., Martínez, J., Taboada, J.: Automated vision system for quality inspection of slate slabs. Comput. Ind. **99**, 119–129 (2018)
2. Zhang, J., Song, C., Wei, B.: Research and practice on quality inspection of underground space surveying. J. Geomatics **42**(4), 105–107 (2017)
3. Ma, Z., Wang, X., Wang, Z.: Nondestructive testing method for steel structure combined with BIM and surface image analysis. J. Seismic Eng. **4**, 1079–1085 (2019)
4. Li, X.: Study on the inspection method of the main structure quality of building engineering. Build. Mater. Decoration **51**, 46–47 (2018)
5. Wenjun, L., Tianyi, W., Zhou, Yu., et al.: Terahertz non-destructive inspection of air defect within adhesive layers of multi-layer bonded structure. Acta Optica Sinica **37**(1), 0111002 (2017)
6. Colonna, S., Imperatore, S., Zucconi, M., et al.: Post-seismic damage assessment of a historical masonry building: the case study of a school in Teramo. Key Eng. Mater. **747**, 620–627 (2017)
7. Bai, X., Sun, H., Wang, H.: M&A: behaviors and market power: an analysis based on Chinese a-share enterprises. Contemp. Econ. Sci. **03**, 106–113 (2016)
8. Garkina, I., Danilov, A.: Tasks of building materials from the viewpoint of control theory. Key Eng. Mater. **737**, 578–582 (2017)
9. Rusu, C., Mendez-Rial, R., Gonzalez-Prelcic, N., et al.: Low complexity hybrid precoding strategies for millimeter wave communication systems. IEEE Trans. Wireless Commun. **15**(12), 8380–8393 (2016)
10. Xing, S., Liu, F., Zhao, X.: Parallel high utility pattern mining algorithm based on cluster partition. J. Comput. Appl. **36**(8), 2202–2206 (2016)
11. Yahyaoui, H., Al-mutairi, A.: A feature-based trust sequence classification algorithm. Inf. Sci. **328**, 455–484 (2016)
12. Polatidis, N., Georgiadis, C.K.: A multi-level collaborative filtering method that improves recommendations. Expert Syst. Appl. **48**, 100–110 (2016)
13. Huang, T., Ma, L., Hu, X., Huang, S., et al.: Practical hybrid precoding algorithm for millimeter wave massive MIMO. JEIT **39**(8), 1788–1795 (2017)
14. Patel, H.: Accelerated PSO swarm search feature selection with SVM for data stream mining big data. Int. J. Res. Eng. **3**(9), 15761–15765 (2016)
15. Polatidis, N., Georgiadis, C.K.: A multi-level collaborative filtering method that improves recommendations. Expert Syst. Appl. **48**, 100–110 (2016)

Automatic Monitoring System of Vehicle Pollutant Emission Based on Fusion Algorithm

Shan-qin Sun[✉]

Hunan Institute of Microbiology (Testing Center), Changsha 410001, China
lining144165855@163.com

Abstract. To improve that automatic monitoring capability of the vehicle's pollutant discharge, a design method of the auto-monitor system for the emission of vehicle pollutant is proposed based on the fusion algorithm. The system design includes a large data analysis model design and system software for automatic monitoring of vehicle pollutant discharge. In that method, a quantitative statistical analysis method is adopt to carry out cloud computing fusion processing of automatic monitoring of pollutant discharge of a motor vehicle, and the invention relates to an information fusion and recombination model for automatically monitoring large data of pollutant discharge of a motor vehicle, the method of automatic monitoring of vehicle pollutant discharge based on the fusion algorithm is improved by the effective feature of the automatic monitoring of the pollutant discharge of the motor vehicle. In the development of B/S and embedded PCI bus, the software development and design of the automatic monitoring system for pollutant discharge of motor vehicle are carried out, and the hardware structure and software development of the automatic monitoring system for pollutant discharge of motor vehicle are carried out. The results of the test show that the automatic monitoring system for motor vehicle pollutant discharge is good in stability and strong in the sampling and statistical analysis of the physical information.

Keywords: Fusion algorithm · Motor vehicle · Pollutant · Discharge · Automatic monitoring system

1 Introduction

With the improvement of the people's living standard and the rapid development of the transportation and transportation industry in our country, the number of cars has risen sharply, and the transportation line is also getting busy [1]. In the course of carrying out the transportation, the automobile can discharge a large amount of tail gas, which has a great burden on the air and the environment pollution.

Under the information management platform, a database management platform of a motor vehicle pollutant discharge automatic monitoring system is designed, a database management platform of a motor vehicle pollutant discharge automatic monitoring system is constructed, a large data analysis method is adopted, the development and design of the automatic monitoring system for pollutant discharge of the motor vehicle, the combination of the combination networking technology and the embedded

Y.-D. Zhang et al. (Eds.): ICMTEL 2020, LNICST 326, pp. 54–65, 2020.
https://doi.org/10.1007/978-3-030-51100-5_5

technology are carried out, and the algorithm design and software development of the vehicle pollutant discharge automatic monitoring system are carried out. The man-machine interaction and information management platform of the automatic monitoring system for the pollutant discharge of the motor vehicle is established, the bus scheduling of the vehicle pollutant discharge automatic monitoring system is carried out by adopting the embedded ARM addressing technology, the database development design of the system and the development of the control platform are carried out, the research on the design method of the auto-monitoring system for pollutant discharge of motor-driven vehicles is of great concern to people. Literature [3] analyzed the law of vehicle pollution emission changing with traffic parameters by monitoring the low altitude vehicle emission data, and proposed the vehicle pollution emission factor model for different vehicle types. The model is calibrated and tested, and the results can effectively reflect the real emissions of road vehicles. Literature [4] obtained the environmental basic data of freight hub through the real-time monitoring of vehicle pollutant emission in freight station, The emission characteristics of three functional areas in the station, i.e. cargo handling area, internal road intersection and entrance and exit, are studied. It is found that the concentration of NOx and particulate pollutants is positively correlated with the vehicle flow; the proportion of large and medium-sized trucks in the vehicle flow has a significant impact on the emission of NOx and particulate matters; the increase of pollutant emission during forklift operation is the most serious pollution in the loading and unloading area of the station Important reasons. However, the automatic monitoring accuracy of vehicle pollutant emission in the above two methods is low.

In view of the above problems, this paper proposes a design method of vehicle emission automatic monitoring system based on fusion algorithm. The system design includes the design and system software of the large data analysis model for the automatic monitoring of the pollutant discharge of the motor vehicle, firstly the algorithm design of the vehicle pollutant discharge automatic monitoring system is carried out, and then the software development design of the automatic monitoring system for the pollutant discharge of the motor vehicle is carried out, Finally, the simulation test is carried out to show the superiority of the method in the improvement of the automatic monitoring and information management capability of the vehicle's pollutant discharge.

2   Composition of Motor Vehicle Pollutants and Its Impact on Environmental Pollution

With the increase of the motor vehicle and the congestion of the transportation line, the pollutant discharge of the motor vehicle is increased day by day, and the pollutant of the motor vehicle can cause a fatal harm to the environment, and the CO, NOx, SOx and unburned hydrocarbon HC discharged by the automobile can seriously damage the ozone layer and generate acid rain, the greenhouse effect and the haze, etc., in which toxic substances such as hydrocarbons, nitrogen oxides, lead compounds, benzene, and the like in motor vehicle pollutants can cause harm to the human body and the animals and plants, therefore, it is necessary to increase the prevention and treatment of motor vehicle pollutants and reduce the emission of tail gas. The main pollutants discharged by the automobile are carbon monoxide (CO), hydrocarbon (HC) and the like, and the combustion of the gasoline in the engine cylinder does not fully produce other nitrogen oxides such as NO2, and the nitrous acid and the nitric acid are generated in the air and the oxides, After being inhaled by a human body, a great harm to the lung can be generated, the exhaust pollution of the motor vehicle is also great to the environment and the health of people, the pollutants of the motor vehicle are mainly composed of the pollutants such as CO, NOx, Sox and the like, and the content of the CO and the sulfide in the tail gas accounts for the main part through the chemical analysis. In addition, CO2 is an important component of that vehicle's pollutant, and with the increase of CO2, the greenhouse effect is caused, according to the analysis, 30% of the CO2 in the air content is about from the vehicle exhaust, wherein the CO2 and the CO are harmful substances discharged from the combustion chamber for insufficient fuel combustion of the motor vehicle, In addition, the particulate matter discharged from the tail gas of the motor vehicle forms a solid carbide, as well as a hydrocarbon, a sulfide, and ash containing a metal component, and the like. The inhalation of these harmful substances in the human body makes it difficult for the person to breathe, the red and the throat of the eye, and the brain is faint. NOx is an exhaust gas that has a pungent smell in the vehicle's pollutants, and can form nitrous acid and nitric acid after entering the alveoli, and has great harm to the ecological environment and the plant and plant. In a comprehensive analysis, the harmful substances in the composition of motor vehicle pollutants are more harmful to the human body and the environment, and the pollution of motor vehicle pollutants to the environment is mainly manifested in the following aspects:

The main results are as follows:

(1) The excessive emission of motor vehicle pollutants will cause Greenhouse Effect and make the global climate warm. The sharp increase of CO_2 is the main cause of Greenhouse Effect, the global temperature will be listed, the north and south polar ice will melt, the sea level will rise, and the damage to the ecological environment will be enormous, while the main production of CO2 comes from motor vehicle pollutants, which intensifies with the increase of the number of cars. It is necessary to strict automobile emission standards, adopt end-of-life renewal, improve engine technology and reduce exhaust pollution.

(2) Harmful substances in motor vehicle pollutants will destroy the ecological balance. A large number of hydrocarbons, sulfides and metal components in motor vehicle pollutants have a great influence on animals and plants. When diesel engine fuel combustion is incomplete, hydrocarbons (HC) and sulfides will be produced, which will affect plant photosynthesis, cause vegetation damage, animals and humans inhaled such harmful substances, and will cause congenital defect diseases.

(3) Excessive emission of motor vehicle pollutants will cause great harm to human health. After absorbing human body, CO in motor vehicle pollutants binds to hemoglobin of human body, which causes toxic symptoms such as headache, dizziness, vomiting and so on. Respiratory failure and lung tissue diseases will be produced by inhaling NOx and HC in respiratory tract. NO2 and other nitrogen oxides in motor vehicle pollutants have severe stimulating effects on lung tissue. To sum up, motor vehicle pollutants are of great harm to the environment and ecology, and seriously

pollute the environment. It is necessary to take corresponding measures to reduce the emissions of motor vehicle pollutants, improve engine technology, reduce traffic congestion, improve fuel combustion efficiency, make fuel combustion sufficient, reduce CO and CO2 emissions in exhaust gas, and effectively reduce traffic congestion. In order to reduce the emission of motor vehicle pollutants and reduce the impact of motor vehicle pollutants on environmental pollution [5].

3 Big Data Analysis and Feature Extraction of Auto-Monitoring Vehicle Pollutant Emissions

3.1 Big Data Analysis of the Auto-Monitoring of the Emission of Motor Vehicles

Based on the above analysis of the composition of vehicle pollutants and its impact on environmental pollution, the big data of vehicle pollutant emissions are analyzed and feature extraction is carried out. Firstly, a big data information collection model for automatic monitoring of vehicle pollutant emission is established, and the method of combining fuzzy correlation feature detection and big data collection is used for detection and big data collection, the real-time data acquisition and the level analysis of the automatic monitoring of the pollutant discharge of the motor vehicle are carried out, a directed graph $G_1 = \left(M_1^\alpha, M_1^\beta, Y_1 \right)$ and $G_2 = \left(M_2^\alpha, M_2^\beta, Y_2 \right)$ are adopted as the candidate set of the automatic monitoring data liniment for the pollutant discharge of the motor vehicle, in that invention, $A = \{a_1, a_2, \ldots, a_n\}$ is a real-time health information distribution feature set for automatically monitoring the pollutant discharge of a motor vehicle, a statistical analysis method is adopted to establish a large-data information acquisition model for automatic monitoring of pollutant discharge of a motor vehicle, and in a cloud computing environment, a fusion scheduling model of automatic monitoring data for pollutant discharge of a motor vehicle is established through the automatic monitoring data distributed structure recombination of the pollutant discharge of the motor vehicle, and the physical health service description is carried out, In that cloud computing environment, the automatic monitoring data for pollutant discharge of the motor vehicle is sample to obtain the information acquisition and fusion model of the automatic monitoring data of the pollutant discharge of the motor vehicle [6].

The finite feature distribution set of automatic monitoring data of motor vehicle pollutant emissions is represented by quaternion $O = (C, I, P, Hc, R, A^0)$. C is the utility threshold item set of sampling time series of automatic monitoring data of motor vehicle pollutant emissions, I is the statistical feature distribution set of massive automatic monitoring data of motor vehicle pollutant emissions, and the efficient use itemsets of automatic monitoring of motor vehicle pollutant emissions are as follows:

$$x(t) = \sum_{i=0}^{p} a(\theta_i) s_i(t) + n(t) \tag{1}$$

wherein, p is the number of the minimum utility threshold of the automatic monitoring data of motor vehicle pollutant emissions, $s_i(t)$ is the statistical characteristic item of the automatic monitoring data of motor vehicle pollutant emissions, $a(\theta_i)$ is the fuzzy clustering measure of the automatic monitoring data of motor vehicle pollutant emissions, and H is the automatic monitoring data set of motor vehicle pollutant emissions. At this time, the data updating rules of automatic monitoring of motor vehicle pollutant emissions meet.

$$R_s^{(0)} = \sum_{n=0}^{k} \left\langle R_s^{(n)}, d_{\gamma n} \right\rangle d_{\gamma n} + R_s^{(k+1)} \tag{2}$$

According to the above analysis, the big data sampling analysis model of automatic monitoring of motor vehicle pollutant emissions is constructed, the cloud computing fusion of automatic monitoring of motor vehicle pollutant emissions is carried out by using quantitative statistical analysis method, the grid distribution structure model of automatic monitoring of motor vehicle pollutant emissions is constructed, and the system design and information distributed reorganization of automatic monitoring of motor vehicle pollutant emissions are carried out on the platform of cloud computing. Improve big data's management and information fusion ability for automatic monitoring of motor vehicle pollutant emissions [7].

3.2 Large-Data Feature Extraction for Automatic Monitoring of Pollutant Discharge of Motor Vehicles

The quantitative statistical analysis method is used to carry out the cloud computing fusion processing of automatic monitoring of motor vehicle pollutant emissions, and the method of block feature criticism and template data analysis is used to carry out big data information fusion and cluster analysis of automatic monitoring of motor vehicle pollutant emissions. Combined with adaptive learning algorithm, the optimization learning in the process of automatic monitoring of motor vehicle pollutant emissions is realized, and the automatic monitoring ability of motor vehicle pollutant emissions is improved [8]. The difference value of motor vehicle pollutant emission automatic monitoring project score is analyzed, and the correlation feature extraction model of big data, which is constructed for automatic monitoring of motor vehicle pollutant emission, is expressed as follows:

$$\begin{cases} x = (x_1, x_2, \ldots, x_n) \\ y = F(x) = (f_1(x), f_1(x), \ldots, f_m(x))^T \end{cases} \tag{3}$$

By adopting the self-adaptive learning algorithm, the optimized characteristic matching of the automatic monitoring of the pollutant discharge of the motor vehicle is carried out [9], and the characteristic matching set of the automatic monitoring of the pollutant discharge of the motor vehicle is obtained as follows:

$$RTT_s = (1 - \alpha) \times RTT_s + \alpha \times RTT \tag{4}$$

According to the difference control, the spatial ambiguity cluster analysis model of automatic monitoring of vehicle pollutant emissions is established by adding the difference factor. The optimal value of ambiguity function $\overline{Q}$ of automatic monitoring of motor vehicle pollutant emissions is as follows:

$$Opti = \sum_{k=1}^{m} \alpha_i^{-1} \alpha_k t_{i,k} \alpha_k^{-1} \alpha_j t_{k,j} = \sum_{k=1}^{m} t_{i,k} t_{k,j} = \begin{cases} 1 & i = j \\ 0 & i \neq j \end{cases} \tag{5}$$

By using the method of feature alignment, combined with the sampling time delay, the global effective quantitative feature distribution set of automatic monitoring data of motor vehicle pollutant emissions is extracted [10–12], and the limited data set of automatic monitoring data of motor vehicle pollutant emissions is obtained as:

$$X = \{x_1, x_2, \cdots, x_n\} \subset R^s \tag{6}$$

Wherein, the automatic monitoring data set of motor vehicle pollutant emissions contains n samples, for sample x_i, $i = 1, 2, \cdots, n$. The quantitative relationship between the process of automatic monitoring of motor vehicle pollutant emissions is obtained by using the method of identifying related parameters.

$$h(t) = \sum_i a_i(t) e^{j\theta_i(t)} \delta(t - iT_s) \tag{7}$$

The association rules of automatic monitoring data of motor vehicle pollutant emissions are excavated. By using the method of autoregression analysis, the fuzzy index set of the process of automatic monitoring of motor vehicle pollutant emissions is obtained as follows:

$$\Lambda_0 = \left\{ \beta \in \Gamma : |\langle f, d_{\gamma_0} \rangle| \geq a. \sup_{\gamma \in \Gamma} |\langle f, d_\gamma \rangle| \right\} \tag{8}$$

By the analysis, a fuzzy information clustering and fusion method is adopted for automatically monitoring the relevance feature extraction of the large data of vehicle pollutant discharge, and the effective characteristic quantity of the automatic monitoring of the pollutant discharge of the motor vehicle is excavated, to improve the adaptability of the automatic monitoring of the pollutant discharge of the motor vehicle [13].

4 Automatic Monitoring of Pollutant Discharge of Motor Vehicle

Based on the analysis and feature extraction of big data of vehicle pollutant emission, the vehicle pollutant emission is monitored automatically. In that method, a block characteristic criticism and a template data analysis method are adopted to automatically monitor large data information fusion and cluster analysis of vehicle pollutant discharge, and the optimized monitoring index is (RT_1, RT_2), and the degree of fuzzy clustering is RW, a fuzzy information clustering and fusion method is adopted to sample the automatic monitoring data of vehicle pollutant discharge, and the fuzzy degree function is obtained as follows:

$$F_j = \sum_{k=1}^{n} X_{kj}, \; Q_j = \sum_{k=1}^{n} \left(X_{kj}\right)^2 \tag{9}$$

The method comprises the following steps of: acquiring a sample set length of a vehicle pollutant discharge automatic monitoring data flow time sequence of $\{x(t_0 + i\Delta t)\}$, $i = 0, 1, \ldots, N - 1$ and motor vehicle pollutant discharge automatic monitoring data by adopting a fuzzy association degree mining method, wherein the sample set length is K. The fuzzy convergence control function for automatic monitoring of pollutant discharge of motor vehicle is as follows:

$$
\begin{aligned}
M_v = w_1 \sum_{i=1}^{m \times n} (H_i - S_i) + M_h w_2 \sum_{i=1}^{m \times n} (S_i - V_i) \\
+ w_3 \sum_{i=1}^{m \times n} (V_i - H_i)
\end{aligned} \tag{10}
$$

Carrying out the correlation analysis of the automatic monitoring of the pollutant discharge of the motor vehicle, obtaining the load of the automatic monitoring data of the pollutant discharge of the motor vehicle as the M_h, the high-order statistical characteristic distribution function is V, and the large data fusion scheduling of the automatic monitoring of the pollutant discharge of the motor vehicle is carried out, the statistical feature quantity of the obtained data fusion is as follows:

$$s(t) = s_c(t) e^{j2\pi f_0 t} = \frac{1}{\sqrt{T}} rect(\frac{t}{T}) e^{j2\pi(f_0 t + Kt^2)/2} \tag{11}$$

The invention discloses a cloud computing quantitative characteristic decomposition function of automatic monitoring of pollutant discharge of a motor vehicle, which comprises the following steps of:

$$f(k) = \begin{cases} f(k-1) - \frac{1}{n}, 1 \leq k < n \\ 1, k = n \end{cases} \tag{12}$$

wherein, k represents the clustering center of distributed automatic monitoring of vehicle pollutant emissions, and the optimized monitoring output function model is as follows:

$$\left.\begin{aligned}
&\min_{\alpha} \frac{1}{2}\sum_{i=1}^{l}\sum_{j=1}^{l} y_i y_j \alpha_i \alpha_j K(x_i, x_j) - \sum_{j=1}^{l} \alpha_j \\
&s.t. \quad \sum_{j=1}^{l} y_j \alpha_j = 0 \\
&\qquad 0 \le \alpha_j \le u(x_j)C, \qquad j = 1, 2, \ldots, l
\end{aligned}\right\} \tag{13}$$

According to the above analysis, a fuzzy information clustering and fusion method is adopted to automatically monitor large data fusion of vehicle pollutant discharge, and a binary structure combination method is adopted to carry out hierarchical clustering, and the self-adaptability of the automatic monitoring of the pollutant discharge of the motor vehicle is improved according to the clustering result [14].

5   System Software Development and Design

By adopting the RFID technology and the multi-mode VIX bus technology to carry out the automatic monitoring information sampling of the pollutant discharge of the motor vehicle, a large data characteristic analysis is carried out on the collected automatic monitoring data of the pollutant discharge of the motor vehicle, and a communication module is established [15], the bus transmission control and the remote communication design of the vehicle pollutant discharge automatic monitoring system are carried out, and the bus transmission and the optimization control of the vehicle pollutant discharge automatic monitoring system are completed by the ARM chip controller, and the overall design framework of the system is shown in Fig. 1.

In that B/S and the SOA framework system, the cross-compile control of the automatic monitoring system of the emission of the motor vehicle is carried out, and the information cross-compilation of the automatic monitoring system for the emission of the vehicle pollutant is carried out by executing the "Make menuconfig" program, the bus development of the automatic monitoring system of vehicle pollutant discharge is carried out on the embedded Linux kernel platform.

6   Experimental Test Analysis

In order to test the application performance of this method in the automatic monitoring of motor vehicle pollutant emissions, the simulation experiment is carried out with Matlab and C tools. The kernel of the automatic monitoring system for motor vehicle pollutant emissions is started based on B/S mode and SOA architecture technology, and the software integration design of the automatic monitoring system for motor vehicle pollutant emissions is carried out under the environment of Linux2.6.32 kernel.

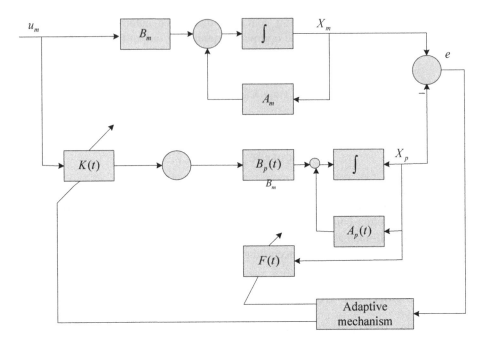

Fig. 1. Overall framework of automatic monitoring system for motor vehicle pollutant emissions

The output response of automatic monitoring of vehicle pollutant emissions is carried out by the test system, and the results are shown in Fig. 2.

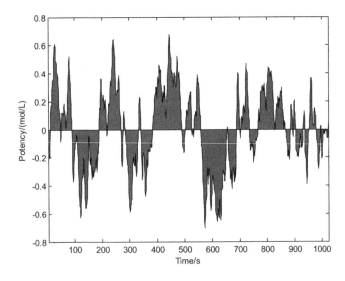

Fig. 2. Output response of automatic monitoring of vehicle pollutant emissions

According to the analysis Fig. 2, the method carries out the automatic monitoring output response of the pollutant discharge of the motor vehicle, and the accuracy of the automatic monitoring of the pollutant discharge of the motor vehicle is tested according to different methods, the comparison result is shown in Table 1.

Table 1. Comparison of accuracy of automatic monitoring of vehicle pollutant emission

Iterations	Proposed method	Reference [3]	Reference [4]
100	0.925	0.854	0.845
200	0.956	0.865	0.875
300	0.987	0.912	0.943
400	0.999	0.935	0.976

According to Table 1, the automatic monitoring accuracy of vehicle pollutant emission in this paper can reach 99.9%, which is higher than that of the literature method.

In order to further verify the effectiveness of the method in this paper, the error of vehicle pollutant emission automatic monitoring results of the method in this paper, the method in literature [3] and the method in literature [4] are compared and analyzed, and the comparison results are shown in Fig. 3.

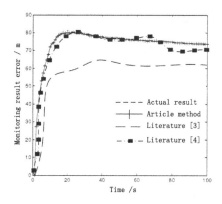

Fig. 3. Error comparison of monitoring results

According to Fig. 3, the fitting degree between the auto monitoring results of vehicle pollutant emission in this method and the auto monitoring results of vehicle pollutant emission in actual test is 100%, while the auto monitoring results of vehicle pollutant emission in literature [3] and literature [4] are quite different from the auto monitoring results of vehicle pollutant emission in actual test, which shows that this method has high vehicle pollution Automatic monitoring effect of material emission.

7   Conclusions

Because of the low precision of the traditional auto monitoring system, a design method of auto monitoring system based on fusion algorithm is proposed. In this paper, the database management platform of the automatic monitoring system for pollutant discharge of motor vehicle is constructed, and the development and design of the automatic monitoring system for pollutant discharge of motor vehicle are carried out by using the method of big data analysis. The invention relates to a large-data sampling analysis model for automatically monitoring the pollutant discharge of a motor vehicle, in that method, a block characteristic criticism and a template data analysis method are adopted to automatically monitor large-data information fusion and cluster analysis of vehicle pollutant discharge, By means of the fuzzy information clustering and the fusion method, the correlation feature extraction of the vehicle's pollutant discharge is automatically monitored, the effective feature quantity of the automatic monitoring of the pollutant discharge of the motor vehicle is excavated, and the improvement of the automatic monitoring algorithm for the pollutant discharge of the motor vehicle based on the fusion algorithm is realized. By adopting the RFID technology and the multi-mode VIX bus technology to carry out automatic monitoring information sampling of the pollutant discharge of the motor vehicle, a large data characteristic analysis is carried out on the collected automatic monitoring data of the pollutant discharge amount of the motor vehicle, and a communication module and a cloud computing platform are established, to realize the optimal design of the automatic monitoring system for the pollutant discharge of the motor vehicle. In this paper, the output stability of vehicle pollutant discharge automatic monitoring system is good and the automatic monitoring accuracy of vehicle pollutant emission is high. Since the change of traffic parameters is not considered in the research process, in the future research, the law of vehicle pollution emission with the change of traffic parameters will be analyzed by monitoring the emission data of low altitude vehicles on the road, and the model of vehicle pollution emission factor will be constructed for different vehicle types, and the model will be calibrated and tested.

References

1. Shan, Y., Wang, J.: Robust object tracking method of adaptive scale and direction. Comput. Eng. Appl. **54**(21), 208–216 (2018)
2. Razavian, A.S., Sullivan, J., Carlsson, S.: Visual instance retrieval with deep convolutional networks. ITE Trans. Media Technol. Appl. **4**(3), 251–258 (2016)
3. Xiao, Z.: Temporal and spatial prediction and distribution of urban motor vehicle pollution emission. J. Shanghai Maritime Univ. **38**(4), 79–83 (2017)
4. Chen, Y., Qin, W., Li, X., et al.: Monitoring and pollution characteristics of motor vehicle contamination at freight station. J. Chongqing Jiaotong Univ. (Nat. Sci. Edn.) **37**(9), 60–65 (2018)
5. Al-Rawas, G., Abdul-Wahab, S., Charabi, Y., Al-Wardy, M., Fadlallah, S.: Modelling the trends of vehicle-emitted pollutants in Salalah, Sultanate of Oman, over a 10-year period. Stoch. Environ. Res. Risk Assess. **32**(5), 1355–1373 (2017). https://doi.org/10.1007/s00477-017-1464-2

6. Quintana, P.J.E., Khalighi, M., Quiñones, J.E.C., et al.: Traffic pollutants measured inside vehicles waiting in line at a major US-Mexico Port of Entry. Sci. Total Environ. **622–623**, 236–243 (2017)
7. Kosek, K., Kozak, K., Kozioł, K., et al.: The interaction between bacterial abundance and selected pollutants concentration levels in an arctic catchment (southwest Spitsbergen, Svalbard). Sci. Total Environ. **622–623**, 913–923 (2017)
8. Chen, C., Wen, T., Junlin, A.N., et al.: Characteristic of air pollutants in Tianjin before, during and after the Beijing Military Parade in 2015. Chin. J. Environ. Eng. **11**(10), 5446–5456 (2017)
9. Ding, Y., Li, N.: Image quality assessment based on non-local high dimensional feature analysis. J. Electron. Inf. **38**(9), 2365–2370 (2016)
10. Nayeb Yazdi, M., Arhami, M., Delavarrafiee, M., Ketabchy, M.: Developing air exchange rate models by evaluating vehicle in-cabin air pollutant exposures in a highway and tunnel setting: case study of Tehran, Iran. Environ. Sci. Pollut. Res. **26**(1), 501–513 (2018). https://doi.org/10.1007/s11356-018-3611-9
11. Shang, F., Guo, H., Li, G., Zhang, L.: Novel image segmentation method with noise based on one-class SVM. J. Comput. Appl. **39**(3), 874–881 (2019)
12. Anh, H.Q., et al.: Comprehensive analysis of 942 organic micro-pollutants in settled dusts from northern Vietnam: pollution status and implications for human exposure. J. Mater. Cycles Waste Manag. **21**(1), 57–66 (2018). https://doi.org/10.1007/s10163-018-0745-2
13. Zhao, Y., Yuan, Q., Meng, X.: Multi-pose face recognition algorithm based on sparse coding and machine learning. J. Jilin Univ. (Sci. Edn.) **56**(02), 340–346 (2018)
14. Hu, H., Zheng, M., Wang, H.: Optimization of MVB periodic scheduling table based on genetic algorithm. J. Jilin Univ. Sci. Edn. **57**(03), 613–618 (2019)
15. Cai, J., Chen, Y., Zhang, M., et al.: Pollutant emission analysis-oriented application of multi-source heterogeneous data on capital-entering nonlocal trucks. Beijing Gongye Daxue Xuebao **43**(3), 428–433 (2017)

Research on Multi-source Heterogeneous Sensor Information Fusion Method Under Internet of Things Technology

Feng Jin[1(✉)] and Li-li Xu[2]

[1] Information and Communication College,
National University of Defense Technology, Changsha, China
jingfeng250052@sohu.com
[2] 95795 Troop of Guilin City in Guangxi, Xi'an, China

Abstract. Multi-heterogeneous sensor information fusion under traditional technology conditions was slow, inaccurate, incomplete, and inconsistent, which led to errors in data analysis and affect evaluation results. To this end, IoT technology was used to study the multi-source heterogeneous sensor information fusion method. Four methods of data acquisition, data abstraction and access, feature fusion algorithm design of high attribute dimension data, and feature level information fusion method were used to creatively change the traditional operation method. The experiment proved that the IoT data information presented new characteristics under the universal characteristics of the Internet of Things, and used the high-level knowledge evolution mechanism of the information resource development chain to study the state evolution of the Internet of Things information in its life cycle. The mechanism was to customize the guiding strategy for the integration of high-quality information in the Internet of Things.

Keywords: Information fusion · Internet of Things · Multiple heterogeneous sensors · Noumenon

1 Introduction

The concept of the Internet of Things originated from the Auto-ID Labs, which was founded by the Massachusetts Institute of Technology (MIT) in 1999. The center hopes to pass all the items through the RF by building a network radio frequency identification (RFID) system. Identification and other sensing devices are connected to the Internet to complete the intelligent identification and management of items [1]. The initial Internet of Things was developed and developed with the background of the logistics industry as its target. Based on radio frequency identification technology, it realized the intelligent management of the logistics system [2]. With the rapid development of science and technology, the connotation of the Internet of Things has been further deepened. In 2005, at the World Summit on the Information Society (WSIS) in

© ICST Institute for Computer Sciences, Social Informatics and Telecommunications Engineering 2020
Published by Springer Nature Switzerland AG 2020. All Rights Reserved
Y.-D. Zhang et al. (Eds.): ICMTEL 2020, LNICST 326, pp. 66–74, 2020.
https://doi.org/10.1007/978-3-030-51100-5_6

Tunis, the International Telecommunication Union (ITU: International Telecommunication Union) released the ITU Internet reports 2005 the Internet of things, which officially defined the concept of "Internet of Things" and elaborated on it. The characteristics of networking, related technologies, possible challenges and future global market opportunities [3]. At present, related technologies and applications of the Internet of Things include: intelligent industry, smart agriculture, intelligent logistics, intelligent transportation, smart grid, environmental protection, security protection, smart medical care and smart home. Even IBM and Google have launched a larger IoT program: IBM's Smarter Planet program and Google's Internet of Planet program, exploring large-scale application of the Internet of Things through cross-regional and cross-industry joint research [4].

With the development of Internet of things technology, information fusion technology of Internet of things has made some achievements. Information fusion technology refers to the process of collecting, analyzing, refining and processing a large amount of information data obtained by sensors according to certain rules and conditions in a certain sequence by using computer information technology. Through the information fusion technology, obtain the required accurate information data. It can be said that information fusion is the process of refining and integrating a large number of different information to obtain more refined and accurate data through information fusion, providing information data support for certain decision-making needs or data requirements. The main function of information fusion is to refine the information and improve the availability of information. With the continuous development of the information fusion technology, information fusion and widening applications from military to civilian in the field of application of the Internet of things technology rapid development today, but also plays an important role in information fusion technology, under the circumstances of Internet of things technology multiple heterogeneous sensor fusion method is studied.

2 IoT Multi-source Heterogeneous Sensor Information Fusion Method

2.1 Raw Data Collection

Using the IRIS series of nodes, we deployed a sensor network that monitors the indoor environment of the lab in three lab rooms, as shown in Fig. 1. The sensor node has a temperature sensor, an air humidity sensor, an illumination sensor, an atmospheric pressure sensor, etc. [5]. The data store uses experimental observations collected by SQL Server 2008 storage.

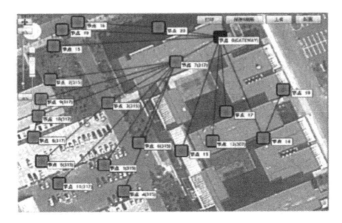

Fig. 1. Device deployment extreme network topology

2.2 Data Abstraction and Access

The D2RQ platform is an open source system that can establish a virtual mapping between read-only RDF data and a relational database, thereby enabling query and access to data existing in a relational database using RDF data access methods [6]. Based on a customized description model of the target object, we use the D2RQ mapping language to map the data in the relational database with the RDF type data. We first construct an observation-based ontology description model based on the semantic sensor network description model (W3C SSN Ontology) (as shown in Fig. 2). Table 1 shows the associated attributes used by the ontology description model and their descriptions, and then applies the D2RQ mapping language to convert the collected monitoring data stored in the relational database SQL Server 2008 into RDF data form for the next realization of the foundation for annotation and abstraction of monitoring data.

Table 1. Association properties between system models

Property name	Explanation
ssn:observationResult	Points to the time when the observation result
ssn:observedBy	Points to a sensor which produced the observation
ssn:observedBy	Points to the specific quality of the feature
eos:hasParent	Points to the parent nodes
eos:hasBoard	Points to the sensor board ID
ssn:hasValue	Points to the actual value of the observation data
eos:roomBelong	Points to the room ID which the nodes belong to
eos:unit	Points to the measuring unit of the observation

As can be seen from the table, SPARQL is a query and acquisition protocol developed for RDF data. It is the W3C recommendation for RDF data query on the Internet [7]. We can use the SPARQL tool to query and integrate multi-source associated data information represented by resources, thus enabling further fusion of multi-source heterogeneous data.

2.3 Feature Fusion Algorithm Design for High Attribute Dimensional Data

In order to improve the efficiency of high-dimensional IoT data feature fusion calculation, we present an efficient algorithm [8].

Suppose the data fusion model is K, and the data fusion model has its standard template feature vector, expressed as $Z_1, Z_2, Z_3, Z_4, Z_5...Z_m$, therefore, the length between the unknown data fusion model vector X and the standard vector Z_i of the W_i model is:

$$D_i(X) = d(X, Z_i) = |X - Z_i| = \sqrt{X - Z_i^n}(X - Z_i) \tag{1}$$

Where $i = 2, 4, 6, ...K$.

This algorithm is based on the idea of partitioning, cutting high attribute dimensional data into data of relatively low attribute dimensions. Firstly, the data of these relatively low attribute dimensions are processed, and then the necessary feature attributes of the original high attribute dimensional data are calculated by using these processing results to ensure that the obtained result is the same as the direct calculation of the high attribute dimensional data directly [9].

$$\mu_A(X)e^{-D(x)} \tag{2}$$

Where

$$\mu_{A1}(X), \mu_{A2}(X), \mu_{A3}(X), \mu_{A4}(X) \tag{3}$$

Based on this formula, the trust function is:
When $\mu_A(X) = \alpha$, then X belongs to the original data.
When $\mu_A(X) = \beta$, then X belongs to third-party data.
When $\mu_A(X) = \delta$, then X belongs to the basic data (Table 2).

Table 2. Differences in different sensor types (measurement unit: V/g)

	a	b	c	d	e	f
U	3	0.23	5.61	6.72	14.12	7.45
B	2	0.41	*	6.21	11.21	7.82
D	3.64	0.72	6.26	5.27	*	7.31
S	0.974	2	5.85	2	2	8
A	4	6.6	0.64	7	1	*

Our algorithm is divided into four steps: data preprocessing and modeling, high-dimensional data partitioning, nuclear attribute set calculation at all levels, and feature selection calculation. The data preprocessing mainly ensures that the data information collected by the sensor is comparable within the same kind of attributes through methods such as quantization mapping and continuous data discretization method, so that the data can reflect the corresponding distinguishing ability.

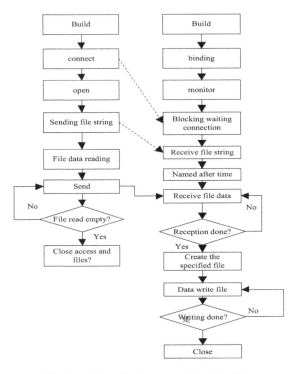

Fig. 2. Schematic diagram of the algorithm

In order to improve the efficiency of high-dimensional dimension IoT data feature fusion calculation, the algorithm is based on the idea of partitioning, and the data is cut into data of relatively low attribute dimensions according to the division of high-dimensional attributes. First, the data of these relatively low attribute dimensions are processed, and then the necessary feature attributes of the original high attribute dimensional data are calculated by using these processing results to ensure that the obtained result is the same as that obtained by direct calculation [10].

2.4   Implement Feature Level Information Fusion

The key issue of feature-level information fusion is how to effectively correlate the information describing the unified entity, and form an IoT view through data association. The data association problem first arises from the uncertainty of multi-information source transmission information and the uncertainty of multi-objective decision-making environment under the network. The actual information collection system always has measurement and description errors inevitably, and lacks prior knowledge of the monitored environmental entities. In the real-time multi-target monitoring process, the measurement or description acquired by the same target on multiple sources must have some similar characteristics due to the same physical source. Such as from the same source, the description object name is the same, the time or location is the same. At the same time, the characteristics of these descriptions and measurements must not be exactly the same due to the angle of concern or the insta-bility of the information collector's own performance. The purpose of data association is to use the similar features of the description to determine whether the measurements or descriptions whose characteristics are not identical are derived from the same target, thereby performing data association, constructing a complete description of the same target, and forming an Internet of Things state. The dynamic view below is shown in Fig. 3.

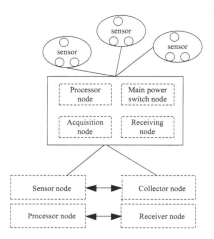

Fig. 3. Dynamic view of the Internet of Things

3 Experimental Results and Analysis

In order to ensure the effectiveness of the research on multi-source heterogeneous sensor information fusion method under the Internet of Things technology, the experimental demonstration was carried out. Two different types of target sensors were selected for the multi-source heterogeneous sensor information fusion method under the Internet of Things technology. In the experiment, the two types of sensors were placed under the same conditions to observe the experimental objectives of different methods and record the data at any time. Among them, the multi-source heterogeneous sensor information fusion effect of different methods is shown in Fig. 4.

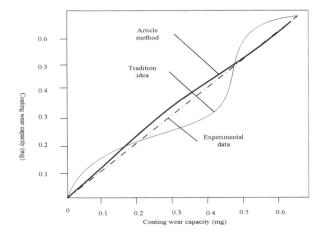

Fig. 4. Comparison of experimental results

In Fig. 4, the traditional idea refers to the multi-source heterogeneous sensor information fusion method based on statistics. Experimental data refers to the experimental data which is closest to the actual value after the fusion of the two kinds of sensor information, through multiple comparisons, screening and improvement. Analysis of the above figure shows that the information fusion results of traditional ideas far deviate from the experimental data, and the information fusion results of this method are close to the experimental data, so it can be shown that the information fusion precision of this method is high, and the actual application effect is better.

On the basis of the above experiments, the time of information fusion is compared, and the experimental results are shown in Fig. 5.

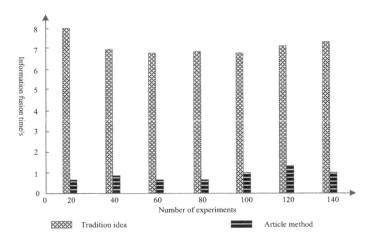

Fig. 5. Time comparison of information fusion

The shorter the time of information fusion, the higher the efficiency of information fusion, which can realize multi-source heterogeneous sensor information fusion in a short time. According to Fig. 5, the information fusion time of traditional ideas varies between 6.8 s and 8.0 s, while the information fusion time of the method in this paper is. With the change between 07 s–1.2 s, the information fusion time is far lower than the traditional thought, which indicates that this method can realize the information fusion of multi-source and heterogeneous sensors in a relatively short time, and the information fusion efficiency is high. The method has low information fusion time because this method adopts data acquisition, data extraction and access, high attribute dimensional data fusion algorithm design, characteristics of four kinds of methods, such as information fusion, creatively changed the traditional operation method, improve the effect of information fusion at the same time improve the efficiency of information fusion.

4   Conclusion

This paper mainly studies the multi-source heterogeneous sensor information fusion method under the Internet of Things technology, which can effectively obtain information resources from multi-source heterogeneous sensors by using Internet of Things technology. The identification and fusion of information resources to help us obtain more meaningful multi-source heterogeneous sensor information provides a valuable means for us to develop a fusion method for multi-source heterogeneous sensor information resources.

Through the elaboration and research and analysis of this paper, we can know that the research on multi-source heterogeneous sensor information fusion method under IoT technology has obvious and far-reaching significance. Even though the multi-source heterogeneous sensor information fusion method under the Internet of Things technology has made some obvious progress in recent years, there are still many research gaps waiting for us to explore. In this regard, we must be brave in innovation, aggressive, and strive to acquire and study the multi-source heterogeneous sensor information fusion method under the Internet of Things technology. Thereby obtaining effective resource information, and thus better serving the multi-source heterogeneous sensor information fusion business under the Internet of Things technology in China.

References

1. Saghafian, S., Tomlin, B., Biller, S.: The internet of things and information fusion: who talks to who? Soc. Sci. Electron. Publ. **6**(1), 39–51 (2018)
2. Blasch, E., Kadar, I., Grewe, L.L., et al.: Panel summary of cyber-physical systems (CPS) and Internet of Things (IoT) opportunities with information fusion. Sig. Process., Sens./Inf. Fus. Target Recogn. XXVI **111**(9), 2–12 (2017)
3. Bo, S., Rho, S., Zhou, X., et al.: A delay-aware schedule method for distributed information fusion with elastic and inelastic traffic. Inf. Fus. **36**(2), 68–79 (2017)

4. Guo, K., Tang, Y., Zhang, P.: CSF: crowd sourcing semantic fusion for heterogeneous media big data in the internet of things. Inf. Fus. **37**(2), 77–85 (2017)
5. Xie, N.F., Cao, C.G., Guo, H.Y.: A knowledge fusion model for web information. In: Proceedings of IEEE/WIC/ACM International Conference on Web Intelligence, vol. 12, no. 5, pp. 67–72, Compiegne Cedex (2018)
6. Ruta, M., Scioscia, F., Gramegna, F., et al.: A knowledge fusion approach for context awareness in vehicular networks. IEEE Internet Things J. **5**(4), 2407–2419 (2018)
7. Iacca, G., Iacca, G., Tejada, A., et al.: Spatial anomaly detection in sensor networks using neighborhood information. Inf. Fus. **33**, 41–56 (2017)
8. Li, G., Zhang, L., Sun, Y., Kong, J.: Towards the sEMG hand: internet of things sensors and haptic feedback application. Multimedia Tools Appl. **78**(21), 29765–29782 (2018). https://doi.org/10.1007/s11042-018-6293-x
9. Liu, S., Fu, W., Zhao, W.: A novel fusion method by static and moving facial capture. Math. Probl. Eng. (2013). https://doi.org/10.1155/2013/503924
10. Wenzhao, W., Peihao, Z., Xinzhong, T., et al.: Multiple access protocol based on TDMA and FDMA fusion in internet of things. J. Comput. Theor. Nanosci. **14**(11), 5155–5159 (2017)

Analysis of Guangdong-Hong Kong-Macao Greater Bay Area's Economic Growth Trend Based on Big Data Mining

Chao-ping Ma[1(✉)] and Xiao-yun Lin[2]

[1] Department of Economics and Trade, Guangzhou College of Technology
and Business, Guangzhou 510850, China
`machaoping369@163.com`
[2] Library, Guangzhou College of Technology and Business,
Guangzhou 510850, China

Abstract. For the sake of improving the optimal management and dispatching ability of Guangdong-Hong Kong-Macao Greater Bay Area's economy, it is essential to optimize and predict the growth trend of the Greater Bay Area's economy, put forward the optimization prediction method of the Greater Bay Area economic growth trend based on 3500 mining, and construct the economic growth model of statistical sequence distribution. Big data mining method is chosen to model the big data statistical information of the area's economic growth, extract the characteristic quantity of the association rules of the big data economic growth trend, use the fuzzy fusion clustering method to carry on the automatic clustering processing to the economic growth trend, and establish the optimal iterative model of the prediction of the economic growth trend. Combined with adaptive optimization algorithm, the Greater Bay Area's economic growth trend is optimized and predicted. The simulation outputs show that the method has good adaptability to predict economic growth trend of the area we talked about, and has high accuracy in predicting growth trend, which improves the adaptive scheduling and management ability of the economy in the bay area.

Keywords: Guangdong-Hong Kong-Macao Greater Bay Area · Economic growth · Big data mining · Trend analysis

1 Introduction

It is of great significance to study the economic growth trend of the bay area of Guangdong, Hong Kong and Macao [1, 2]. The prediction algorithm of the economic growth trend and the prediction algorithm based on the Markov model are proposed. However, the fuzzy degree of the method is large, and the adaptability of the prediction process is not good enough. To consider the above problems, based on big data mining, this paper suggests a prediction method to the economic growth trend of bay area, and constructs a statistical sequence distribution model for the growth trend of bay area economic [3, 4]. Using big data mining method, this paper builds a big data statistical information model for the economic growth trend of the Greater Bay Area, extracts the characteristics of the relevant laws of the economic growth trend and uses the fuzzy big

Y.-D. Zhang et al. (Eds.): ICMTEL 2020, LNICST 326, pp. 75–84, 2020.
https://doi.org/10.1007/978-3-030-51100-5_7

data fusion clustering method to automatically cluster the economic growth, and establishes the big bay optimal iteration model for the prediction of the economic growth trend, and the economic trending of the bay area is predicted. Combined with the adaptive optimization algorithm, the optimization of Guangdong and Macao region is implemented. Finally, the performance of improving the prediction ability of economic growth trend of Guangdong, Hong Kong and Macao region is verified by simulation experiment.

2   Analysis on the Trending of Regional Economy in the Area of Hong Kong and Macao

This paper sets up an information management model of the economy of the Hong Kong, Macao and Guangdong area, and the economic growth trend of that region is optimized, and the automatic dispatching and information management capability of the economy in the Hong Kong and Macao is improved. On the basis of the optimization and prediction of the economic trend in the big bay area, the paper analyses and analyzes the big data of the economy in the district. It is greatly significant to study the trend of the bay area's economic growth. The distribution is shown in Fig. 1.

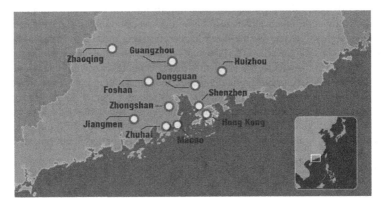

Fig. 1. Guangdong-Hong Kong-Macao Greater Bay Area's distribution

2.1   Shortcomings of Guangdong-Macao-Hong Kong Greater Bay Area's Regional Economy

The Greater Bay Area of Guangdong, Macao and Hong Kong gave full play to the geographical advantages of coastal areas and made great progress in the early stage of reform and openness. At the same time, it also led to the improvement of the economy in the surrounding areas to varying degrees. However, due to the limitations of innate regional conditions, the development of the bay district also has many deficiencies, mainly manifested in: first, the industrial structure of different areas is increasingly convergent. Repeat the low level of construction and other problems, resulting in waste of resources, resulting in low economic benefits. The second is the regional poverty [5]. Although the economy of that region is relatively developed, there are still some areas where the economy is backward and the infrastructure construction is seriously lagging behind, which leads to the poverty of the whole region, the imperfect industrial structure, and the lack of motivation for development. Third, the gap between different regions is further widened, which leads to different geographical regions driven by interests to form different forms of local protection barriers, which increases the difficulty of forming the overall market of economic development.

2.2 The Influences of the Economic Development in the Region of Hong Kong and Macao

By analyzing the bay region's economic development, we can conclude that the main influences of the regional economic development are as follows: first, the coordination mechanism between different geographical regions still has great disadvantages, including the ecological compensation mechanism and the resource development mechanism, in which the ecological mechanism is not perfect, and the compensation theory is not systematic, coupled with the lack of unity of the standards of ecological compensation. As a result, there are great differences in many aspects of compensation, so that the consensus of compensation cannot be formed, the mechanism of resource development is not perfect, the overall value of resource products is low, there is great uncertainty in price, and the abundance of resources cannot be transformed into the driving force of economic development. Second, there is a lack of overall planning in the management policies of different regions, and there is no pertinence in formulating the economic policies of the region. Even when the specific regional planning is issued, there is a lack of clear development direction and development goals, which affects the regional economic development [6].

3 Construction and Feature Analysis of Statistical Big Data Model

3.1 Statistical Big Data Modeling of the Economic Growth in the Bay Area of Guangdong, Hong Kong and Macao

To predict the trending of regional economic growth, the statistical sequence analysis and adaptive big data mining are used to design the prediction algorithm. Firstly, it is critical to construct the statistical sequence analysis model, and to use the interactive information scheduling model to sample the growth trend [6]. The specific process is shown in Fig. 2.

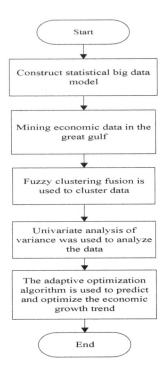

Fig. 2. The regional economic trending analysis flow chat based on big data mining

According to the results of information collection, the automatic prediction is carried out, and the statistical sequence distribution model is constructed [7]. The big data mining is used to predict the big data economic growth trend adaptively. Combined with the parameter aggregation analysis way, the nonlinear statistical analysis model nd is described by statistical time series.

$$x_n = x(t_0 + n\Delta t) = h[z(t_0 + n\Delta t)] + \omega_n \tag{1}$$

In the formula, $h(.)$ is the scalar distribution sequence according to the previous statistical results, which is a multivariate quantitative value function, and ω_n is the measurement error of Guangdong-Hong Kong-Macao Greater Bay Area's economic growth trend prediction. It is assumed that the time series monitored by a given amount is expressed as follows:

$$U = \{U_1, U_2, \cdots, U_N\} \tag{2}$$

In which, U_i is a random variable whose dimension is d-dimension, a regression analysis model of prediction in the region is constructed by using a statistical analysis method, The statistical data of the economic growth trend in the large-bay area of Guangdong-Hong Kong-Macao Greater Bay Area has formed a fuzzy rough set in the three-dimensional space [8].

The above formula represents the randomly sampled scalar sequence. Combined with the fuzzy information fusion method, the sampling results of statistical sequence are obtained as follows:

$$X = K[s_1, s_2, \cdots s_K]_\mathbf{n} = K(x_n, x_{n-\tau}, \cdots, x_{n-(m-1)\tau}) \tag{3}$$

Wherein, $K = N - (m-1)\tau$ represents the subspace clustering dimension of statistical sequence, which is a time delay. According to the above information flow model, it provides an accurate data analysis basis optimization prediction [9].

3.2   Statistical Characteristic Analysis

The statistical sequence distribution model of the economic growth trend is built, the large data statistical modeling is carried out by adopting a large data mining method, the economic growth trend prediction model is established, the discrete characteristic component of the economic demand information is $s_i = (x_i, x_{i+\tau}, \cdots, x_{i+(m-1)\tau})^T$, the above formula is a group of short-time discrete information distribution set, and in the embedded space of the economic growth trend prediction [10], the distribution function of the state-set distribution function is shown as follows:

$$\frac{dz(t)}{dt} = F(z) \tag{4}$$

Combined with the above formula, the effective probability density is higher by selecting the appropriate m and τ. At this time, the statistical regression analysis probability density characteristics are expressed as follows:

$$R_1 = \{X_1, X_2, X_3, \cdots, X_d\}^T \tag{5}$$

By using the continuous descriptive statistical analysis method, multiple comparative analysis was carried out to obtain the correlation function:

$$R_1^T R_1 = \{X_1, X_2, \cdots, X_m\}\{X_1, X_2, \cdots, X_m\}^T \tag{6}$$

Set up a meter to calculate the best characteristic decomposition value. The characteristic decomposition expression of the prediction is as follows:

$$R_1^T R_1 = V_1 \sum {}_1 V_1^T \tag{7}$$

The fuzzy analogy of the economic forecast is expressed as follows:

$$R_2^T R_2 = V_2 \sum {}_2 V_2^T \tag{8}$$

$$R_2 = \{X_{d+1}, X_{d+2}, \cdots X_{d+m}\}^T \tag{9}$$

$$R_2^T R_2 = \{X_{d+1}, X_{d+2}, \cdots X_{d+m}\}\{X_{d+1}, X_{d+2}, \cdots X_{d+m}\}^T \tag{10}$$

In the formula, the wide area characteristic components of the prediction are expressed as follows:

$$V = [V_1, V_2, \cdots, V_m] \in R^{m \times m} \tag{11}$$

On the basis the analysis of variance of univariate, according to the evolution characteristics of load value X_m and X_k, the predicted load is X_{m+1} and X_{k+1}.

4 Optimization of Guangdong-Hong Kong-Macao Greater Bay Area's Economic Growth Trend Prediction Algorithm

4.1 Extracting the Features from Relevance Rules

The mean of big data mining is used to model the economic development by big data statistical big data, and the association rules' characteristic quantity is extracted [11]. The association characteristics of the growth trend at the level of salience are represented as:

$$W_x(t, v) = \int_{-\infty}^{+\infty} X(v + \xi/2)X^*(v - \xi/2)e^{j2\pi\xi t}d\xi \tag{12}$$

Taking the quantitative average value of the persistent statistical value, the following are obtained:

$$E_x = \int_{-\infty}^{+\infty} \int_{-\infty}^{+\infty} W_x(t, v)dtdv \tag{13}$$

Wherein, $W_x(t, v)$ represents the decisive factor of the economic demand forecast:

$$\begin{cases} \int_{-\infty}^{+\infty} W_x(t, v)dt = |X(v)|^2 \\ \int_{-\infty}^{+\infty} W_x(t, v)dv = |x(t)|^2 \end{cases} \tag{14}$$

On the basis of a comprehensive analysis, the correlation rule feature extraction is carried out, and the automatic prediction of the economic growth trend is carried out according to the feature extraction results [12].

4.2 Fuzzy Clustering and Adaptive Prediction

On the basis of extracting the characteristics of association rules, the fuzzy data fusion clustering method is set to automatically cluster the regional economic growth [13, 14], and the univariate variance analysis is made use of analyzing the orthogonal eigenvector solution [15, 16]. It is assumed that the single component of the growth trend is unknown, and the results are as follows:

$$VV^T = I_M \tag{15}$$

$$\sum = diag(\sigma_1, \sigma_2, \cdots, \sigma_m) \in R^{m \times m} \tag{16}$$

Under the constraint of surplus probability, the order of eigenvalues is as follows:

$$\sigma_1 > \sigma_2 > \sigma_3 > \cdots > \sigma_{s+1} > \sigma_m \tag{17}$$

Under the evolutionary game, the new characteristic sequence of trending forecast is:

$$X_{m+1}(m) = X_{k+1}(m) \\ \pm \sqrt{(d_m(0)e^{\lambda_1} +)^2 - \sum_{i=1}^{m-1} [X_{m+1}(i) - X_{k+1}(i)]^2} \tag{18}$$

A new group of time series y_k, which replaces regional economic growth trend, is produced, and the forecast results are as follows:

$$D_k = D_{k-1} - N_{k-1}^2 / D_{k-1} \tag{19}$$

$$\phi_{kk} = N_k / D_k \tag{20}$$

$$\phi_{kj} = \phi_{k-1,j} - \phi_{kk} \cdot \phi_{k-1,k-j} \tag{21}$$

An initial value $N(0, 1)$, is generated in the Gaussian distribution $N(0, 1)$ to realize the improved design of prediction algorithm [17, 18].

5 Analysis of Experiment Results

In the sake of testing the application performance in the prediction of the economic growth, the experimental analysis is carried out, and the trending prediction simulation is carried out with SPSS statistical analysis software and Matlab simulation software. The descriptive statistical analysis is used to compare and analyze the linear proportion. The analysis results are shown in Table 1.

Table 1. Results of the multiple comparative analysis based on the annual

Year	2009–2012	2013–2016	2017–2019
2009–2012	1	–	–
2013–2016	0.043	1	–
2017–2019	0.056**	0.018*	1

Note: * indicates significant at 0.05 level.

According to the results of the above comparative analysis, it is found that the annual surplus has a significant impact on the economic, but it is not a decisive factor. On this basis, the descriptive statistical analysis is carried out, and the results are shown in Table 2.

Table 2. Results of continuous descriptive statistics

Year	Sample number	Standard deviation	Max value	Min value	Average value
2014	478	0.343	467.89	12.86	42.32
2015	346	0.256	547.86	24.56	44.56
2016	578	0.578	326.45	27.54	76.76
2017	865	0.437	655.68	45.65	76.78
2018	546	0.785	544.67	35.32	65.98
2019	489	0.893	543.45	43.45	56.75

According to the above descriptive statistical analysis results, the statistical analysis value is shown in Fig. 3.

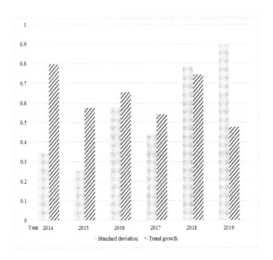

Fig. 3. Statistical Analysis Results of the prediction of the Economic Growth Trend in the district.

According to the statistical analysis results of Fig. 3, the prediction is realized, and the prediction accuracy is tested. The comparative results are shown in Fig. 3. The analysis of Fig. 4 shows that the prediction of the Greater Bay Area economy by using this method is more accurate.

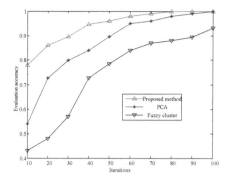

Fig. 4. Comparison of prediction accuracy

6 Conclusions

Based on the optimization and prediction of the economic growth trend of Guangdong-Hong Kong-Macao Greater Bay Area, the automatic dispatching and information management ability of the economy in Guangdong and Macao is improved. In this paper, the economic growth trend optimization and prediction with big data mining is put forward. Through the phase space reconstruction, the correlation statistical sequence distribution of the economic growth trend prediction of the Greater Bay Area is obtained, and the large-data statistical large-data modeling of the economic growth trend of the big bay region is carried out by adopting a large data mining method. With the fuzzy large-data fusion clustering way, the trending is automatically clustered, and the orthogonal feature vector solution analysis of the economic growth trend is carried out by using the variance analysis method of the single variable. And by using fusion clustering, the trend of economic in the large-bay area of the three districts is automatically cluster-treated by means of the fuzzy large-data fusion clustering method, and the optimization and prediction of the economic growth trend of the region of Hong Kong and Macao are realized by using the self-adaptive optimization algorithm. The outcomes show that the adaptive scheduling and management ability of the economic growth trend of the bay region of Guangdong, Hong Kong and Macao is better, the prediction accuracy is higher, and the self-adaptive scheduling and management ability of the large-bay district is improved.

Acknowledgements. Supported by Guangdong Provincial Philosophy and Social Sciences "13th Five-Year Plan" 2018 Project: "Guangdong-Hong Kong-Macao Greater Bay Area 'One Country, Two Systems, Three Levels and Four Cores' Fusion Development Study" (Approval No.: GD18XYJ22).

References

1. Aslanidis, N., Christiansen, C.: Smooth transition patterns in the realized stock-bond correlation. J. Empir. Finance **19**(4), 454–464 (2012)
2. Parvin, H., Mirnabibaboli, M., Alinejad-Rokny, H.: Proposing a classifier ensemble framework based on classifier selection and decision tree. Eng. Appl. Artif. Intell. **37**, 34–42 (2015)
3. Hwang, Y., Yu, T.Y., Lakshmanan, V., et al.: Neuro-fuzzy gust front detection algorithm with S-band polarimetric radar. IEEE Trans. Geosci. Remote Sens. **55**(3), 1618–1628 (2017)
4. Bin, M.A., Xianzhong, X.I.E.: PSHO-HF-PM: an efficient proactive spectrum handover mechanism in cognitive radio networks. Wireless Pers. Commun. **79**(3), 1–23 (2014)
5. Chaowen, C.: Discussions on the reform of Tanching practice for computer science majors. J. Nanning Teach. Coll. **22**(3), 75–77 (2005)
6. Tao, W.U.: Research on the infiltration of tea painting art in art education in colleges and universities. Tea Fujian **24**(4), 45–47 (2018)
7. Maheshwari, P., Singh, A.K.: A survey on spectrum handoff techniques in cognitive radio networks. In: 2014 International Conference on Contemporary Computing and Informatics (IC3I), pp. 996–1001. IEEE (2014)
8. Ding, X.M., Fuh, J.Y., Lee, K.S.: Interference detection for 3-axis mold machining. Comput. Aided Des. **33**(8), 561–569 (2001)
9. Lasemi, A., Xue, D., Gu, P.: Recent development in CNC machining of freeform surfaces: a state-of-the-art review. Comput. Aided Des. **42**(7), 641–654 (2010)
10. Wu, Y.X., Wen, X.: Short-term stock price forecast based on ARIMA model. Stat. Decis. **(23)**, 83–86 (2016)
11. Li, X., Peng, L., Hu, Y., Shao, J., et al.: Deep learning architecture for air quality predictions. Environ. Sci. Pollut. Res. **23**(22), 22408–22417 (2016)
12. Zaho, X., Wu, Y., Huang, H.Y., et al.: New generation of migrant workers housing purchasing power and the housing sales to inventory constraints relationship model – taking Zengcheng area as an example. Manag. Eng. **22**(1), 8–13 (2017)
13. Wang, Q., Bai, X., Feng, N.: The systemic risk measurement and influencing factors of commercial banks—an analysis based on CCA-POT-Copula Method **02**, 1–9 (2016)
14. Yao, L., Yao, W.X.: Research on the policy effect of incremental expansion of margin and securities lending: based on the multi period DID model and Hausman's test. Int. Financ. Res. **349**(5), 85–96 (2016)
15. Ning, C., You, F.: Data-driven adaptive nested robust optimization: general modeling framework and efficient computational algorithm for decision making under uncertainty. AIChE J. **63**(9), 3790–3817 (2017)
16. Feng, W., Heng, Z., Kangshun, L., et al.: A hybrid particle swarm optimization algorithm using adaptive learning strategy. Inf. Sci. **36**(4), 162–177 (2018)
17. Laizhong, C., Genghui, L., Xizhao, W., et al.: A ranking-based adaptive artificial bee colony algorithm for global numerical optimization. Inf. Sci. **417**(10), 169–185 (2017)
18. Konstantinos, A.T., George, N.: Optimization of a fully adaptive quality and maintenance model in the presence of multiple location and scale quality shifts. Appl. Math. Model. **54**(6), 64–81 (2017)

Analysis on the Development Path of Urban Agglomeration in Gulf Region of Guangdong, Hong Kong, Macao Under the Background of Big Data

Chao-ping Ma[1(✉)] and Xiao-yun Lin[2]

[1] Department of Economics and Trade,
Guangzhou College of Technology and Business, Guangzhou 510850, China
machaoping369@163.com
[2] Library, Guangzhou College of Technology and Business,
Guangzhou 510850, China

Abstract. China realize the sustainable development of socialism, and promote the integration and development of Guangdong, Hong Kong, Macao and the Gulf region. This paper analyzes the development path of the urban agglomeration in Da Wan District of Guangdong, Hong Kong and Macao under the backdrop of big data. A statistical sequence distribution model of the GDP index of the city group development in the Big Gulf Region of These city is constructed, the big data statistical information model of the GDP index of the city group development in the Big Gulf Region of These city is built by using a big data mining method, the association rule characteristic quantity of the GDP index of the city group development in the Big Gulf Region of These city is extracted, the big data of the GDP index of the city group development in the Big Gulf Region of These city under the big An optimization iteration model for the prediction of the GDP index for the development of the large bay area urban agglomeration in These city is established. Under the backdrop of big data, the development path analysis and adaptive adjustment of the large bay area urban agglomeration in These city are carried out to realize the analysis and optimization of the development path of the large bay area urban agglomeration The simulation results show that the prediction accuracy of the GDP index of These city and the gulf city assembly development is high, and the adaptability and convergence of the GDP index prediction of These city and the gulf city assembly development are improved.

Keywords: Big data backdrop · Big Gulf Region · Urban agglomeration · Development path · GDP

1 Introduction

In the Hong Kong Bay and Macao Bay, and including Hong Kong, Macao and Guangdong, it shows a state of strong economic vitality and is also in the leading position in the overall development of the country. General secretary Xi Jinping has also pointed out that "promoting the construction of Guangdong, Hong Kong, Macao and the

Y.-D. Zhang et al. (Eds.): ICMTEL 2020, LNICST 326, pp. 85–98, 2020.
https://doi.org/10.1007/978-3-030-51100-5_8

great bay area" is a major national development strategy and the only way to achieve sustainable socialist development [1]. These areas are located along the coast and have a sound system of port groups, it is an important one in the "one belt, one road initiative". It is an important shipping route between the Pacific Ocean and the Indian Ocean, with a developed shipping industry and marine economy. According to the statistics of the World Shipping Union, in 2016, three of the world's top 10 container ports will come from Guangdong, Hong Kong, Macao and the Bay Area (Shenzhen, Hong Kong and Guangzhou), with a total container throughput of 61.49 million containers, which is about Four point five times the total of the world's three Bay Areas. Among them, Shenzhen and Hong Kong are mainly oriented to overseas trade while Guangzhou is mainly oriented to domestic trade, thus making the task divide clear in the ports in the Bay Area and forming a complete shipping industry chain. The Bay Area of These three cities can be divided into three major combinations: Guangzhou-Foshan-Zhao Economic Circle with Guangzhou as its core in the north, Shenzhen-Dongguan-Hui Economic Circle with Shenzhen as its core in the east, and Zhuhai-Hong Kong-Macao Economic Circle with Hong Kong as its core in the south. No matter which coastal city has its own focus on its pillar industries. For example,Guangzhou's main industries are advanced manufacturing industry, high-tech industry and modern service industry, Shenzhen is dominated by high-tech industries, Hong Kong is dominated by financial and technological service industries, Zhuhai is mainly developing strategic emerging industrial industries, power energy industries and household electrical appliances, while Jiangmen is characterized by modern agriculture [2].

With the continuous progress of the construction of the Big gulf city assembly. In this paper, the third city, especially the megalopolis in the Great Bay area, is mentioned, and the management of them is becoming more and more refined. The development of coastal cities is reflected in GDP indicators, so the information management and scheduling of GDP indicators is particularly important for other sectors under the backdrop of big data, to establish an information management model for the GDP index for a study on the development of urban agglomerations in the Gulf region mentioned in this paper under the backdrop of big data, and to predict the GDP index for Under the backdrop of big data, the characteristics of the GDP index for the development of the Big gulf city assembly in these three cities are analyzed and self-adaptive prediction is carried out to improve the autonomy of the GDP index for the development of the Big gulf city assembly in these three cities under the backdrop of big data, the optimal scheduling model for the Big gulf city assembly in these three citiese is studied, the informatization management model for the Big Gulf Region Hong Kong Guangdong macao city group is established, and the prediction ability of the GDP index for This paper makes an analysis of the GDP index of the urban agglomeration in the Big Gulf Region of Guangdong, Hong Kong, Macao under the backdrop of Internet Age and analyzes the deviation of the GDP index of the urban agglomeration in the Big Gulf Region of Guangdong, Hong Kong, Macao under the backdrop of big data. This paper puts forward an analysis model of the development path of the urban agglomeration in the Big Gulf Region of Guangdong, Hong Kong, Macao under the backdrop of big data. The statistical sequence distribution model of the develop the economy growth index of the Big Gulf Region Hong Kong Guangdong macao city group, Macao is established, and the optimization iteration model of the develop the economy growth index prediction of the Big Gulf Region Hong Kong Guangdong macao city group is established [3–5]. The prediction of the develop the economy growth index of the Big Gulf Region Hong Kong Guangdong macao city group is realized by combining the adaptive optimization model, and the development path analysis and adaptive adjustment of the Big Gulf Region Hong Kong Guangdong macao city group are carried out in this context, Through the simulation test, it is proved that this method has the superiority in improving the system analysis ability development path of the urban agglomeration in the Da Wan District of Guangdong, Hong Kong, Macao [6].

2   Statistical Information Model Construction and Feature Analysis

2.1   Statistical Information Modeling of GDP Index for Urban Agglomeration Development in Big Gulf Region of Guangdong, Hong Kong, Macao

In order to realize the prediction of the GDP index of the city group development in the Big Gulf Region of Guangdong, Hong Kong, Macao, linear regression analysis and test statistical analysis methods are adopted to analyze the characteristics of the GDP index of the city group development in the Big Gulf Region of Guangdong, Hong Kong, Macao. combined with data tracking analysis method, the prediction pattern design of the GDP index of the city group development in the Big Gulf Region of these three cities is carried. Firstly, the statistical sequence analysis model of the GDP index of the city group development in the Big Gulf Region. An interactive information scheduling model is used to analyze the statistical characteristics of the GDP index of the urban agglomeration development in the Big Gulf Region of Guangdong, Hong Kong, Macao. according to the distributed scheduling results of the GDP index information of the urban agglomeration development in the Big Gulf Region of these three citiese, the characteristic detection and optimal scheduling of the GDP index of the urban agglomeration development in the Big Gulf Region of these three citiese are carried out under the backdrop of big data, and a statistical sequence distribution model of the GDP index of the urban agglomeration development in the Big Gulf Region of Guangdong Using data tracking analysis method to carry out the adaptive prediction of the GDP index of these three citiese Big gulf city assembly development, using fuzzy correlation characteristic clustering analysis method to carry out statistical analysis and adaptive clustering, the non-linear statistical analysis model of the GDP index of these three citiese Big gulf city assembly development is described as follows:

$$x_n = x(t_0 + n\Delta t) = h[z(t_0 + n\Delta t)] + \omega_n \tag{1}$$

In the formula, $h(.)$ is the information association characteristic detection method, carries on These Gulf city complexes develop the economy growth index characteristic scalar distribution sequence, obtains a big data backdrop Guangdong-Hong Kong-Macao Greater Bay Area urban agglomeration develop the economy growth index multivariate quantity value function, ω_n is the measurement error to These Gulf city complexes develop the economy growth index forecast. Suppose that the time series of These Gulf city complexes develop the economy growth index is expressed as:

$$U = \{U_1, U_2, \cdots, U_N\} \tag{2}$$

Wherein, U_i is a random variable with dimension d. A regression analysis model for predicting the GDP index of Guangdong, Hong Kong, Macao and the gulf city assembly development is established by using descriptive statistical analysis method. In the d-dimensional phase space, M is the characteristic distribution function of association rules of DF dimension and a fuzzy function on h. The statistical data of the GDP index of these three citiese and the gulf city assembly development form a fuzzy rough set in the dimensional phase space. Using multiple linear regression analysis method, the probability density function of distributed prediction of the GDP index of these three citiese and the gulf city assembly development is obtained as follows:

$$p(U|\Theta) = \sum_{k=1}^{K} \alpha_k G(U|u_k, \sum{}_k) \tag{3}$$

$$\Theta = \left[\alpha, u, \sum{}\right] \tag{4}$$

Wherein, $\alpha_k \geq 0$, $\sum_{k=1}^{K} \alpha_k = 1$, and:

$$\begin{aligned}
G(U|\mu_k, \sum{}_k) &= (2\pi)^{-d/2} \left|\sum{}_k\right|^{-1/2} \\
&\times \exp\left[-\frac{1}{2}(U - u_k)^T \sum{}_k^{-1} (U - u_k)\right]
\end{aligned} \tag{5}$$

Among them, $G(U|\mu_k, \sum_k)$ is the sample regression analysis value of the develop the economy growth index of these three citiese Big gulf city assembly under the backdrop of big data, $p(U|\Theta)$ it is the weighted value of the random probability density function, and by adopting the characteristic space clustering analysis method [7–9], it is obtained that the correlation statistical sequence distribution of the develop the economy growth index prediction of these three citiese Big gulf city assembly meets the following requirements:

$$\begin{aligned}
CW_{min}^{l_M} &= CW_{min}^{l_{M-1}} \times (1 + \overline{D}_{l_{M-1}})^{\chi} \\
&= CW_{min}^{0} \times (1 + \overline{D}_{l_0})^{\chi} \times (1 + \overline{D}_{l_1})^{\chi} \times \cdots \times (1 + \overline{D}_{l_{M-1}})^{\chi} \\
&= CW_{min}^{0} \times [(1 + \overline{D}_{l_0}) \times (1 + \overline{D}_{l_1}) \times \cdots \times (1 + \overline{D}_{l_{M-1}})]^{\chi}
\end{aligned} \tag{6}$$

Wherein

$$[(1+\overline{D}_{l_0}) \times (1+\overline{D}_{l_1}) \times \ldots \times (1+\overline{D}_{l_{M-1}})]$$
$$\leq ((1+\overline{D}_{l_0}+1+\overline{D}_{l_1}+\cdots+1+\overline{D}_{l_{m-1}})/M)^M \qquad (7)$$
$$= (1+\overline{D})^M$$

The above formula represents the scalar sequence of the GDP index of these three citiese and Big gulf city assembly based on fuzzy information sampling. Combining with the fuzzy information fusion method, the statistical sequence sampling results of the GDP index of these three citiese and Big gulf city assembly are as follows:

$$X = K[s_1, s_2, \cdots s_K]_{\mathbf{n}} = K(x_n, x_{n-\tau}, \cdots, x_{n-(m-1)\tau}) \qquad (8)$$

Wherein, $K = N - (m - 1)\tau$ represents the subspace clustering dimension of the GDP index of the Big Gulf Region these three citiese's city group Big Gulf Region, and SD is the time delay. From the above, a big data analysis model for forecasting the GDP index of the Big Gulf Region these three citiese's city group Big Gulf Region is established, and the development path analysis of the Big Gulf Region these three citiese's city group under the big data backdrop is carried out in combination with the analysis results of the big data characteristics [10].

2.2   Analysis on Characteristics of GDP Index for Urban Agglomeration Development

The trust perception method is used to model the big data statistical information of the develop the economy growth index of the Big Gulf Region these three citiese's city group. The association rule characteristic quantity of the develop the economy growth index of the Big Gulf Region these three citiese's city group is extracted [11]. The association characteristic of the develop the economy growth index of the Big Gulf Region these three citiese's city group Big Gulf Region on the significance level is expressed as follows:

$$W_x(t, v) = \int_{-\infty}^{+\infty} X(v + \xi/2)X^*(v - \xi/2)e^{j2\pi\xi t}d\xi \qquad (9)$$

In the above formula, ξ is the fuzzy attenuation coefficient of the develop the economy growth index of the Big Gulf Region these three citiese's city group Big Gulf Region under the backdrop of big data, X is the statistical characteristic value of the develop the economy growth index of the Big Gulf Region these three citiese's city group Big Gulf Region, indicating that taking complex conjugate, the quantitative average value of the develop the economy growth index of the Big Gulf Region these three citiese's city group Big Gulf Region is analyzed, and the following results are obtained:

$$E_x = \int_{-\infty}^{+\infty} \int_{-\infty}^{+\infty} W_x(t, v)dtdv \qquad (10)$$

Wherein, $W_x(t, v)$ indicates the decisive factor for the development of GDP index in the Big gulf city assembly of Guangdong, Hong Kong, Macao Big Gulf Region under the backdrop of big data. fuzzy clustering is carried out on the constraint characteristics of GDP index in the Big gulf city assembly of Guangdong, Hong Kong, Macao Big Gulf Region under the backdrop of big data, and the significant difference value is satisfied:

$$
\begin{cases}
\int_{-\infty}^{+\infty} W_x(t, v)dt = |X(v)|^2 \\
\int_{-\infty}^{+\infty} W_x(t, v)dv = |x(t)|^2
\end{cases}
\tag{11}
$$

In the above formula, $|X(v)|$ indicates the association rule item for the prediction of the GDP index of the city group development in the Big Gulf Region of Guangdong, Hong Kong, Macao Big Gulf Region. through statistical analysis results, the scalar sequence of the GDP index of the city group development in the Big Gulf Region of Guangdong, Hong Kong, Macao Big Gulf Region is obtained. $\{x(t_0 + i\Delta t)\}$, $i = 0, 1, \cdots, N - 1$, the relative characteristic distribution set of the GDP index of the city group development in the Big Gulf Region of Guangdong, Hong Kong, Macao Big Gulf Region is:

$$
X = [s_1, s_2, \cdots s_K]_\mathbf{n} = (x_n, x_{n-\tau}, \cdots, x_{n-(m-1)\tau})
\tag{12}
$$

Wherein, $K = N - (m - 1)\tau$ is the orthogonal feature vector for the prediction of GDP index of the city group in the Big Gulf Region of Guangdong, Hong Kong, Macao Big Gulf Region. τ is the time delay for sampling the statistical information of GDP index of the city group in the Big Gulf Region of Guangdong, Hong Kong, Macao Big Gulf Region. m is the fuzzy clustering dimension and $s_i = (x_i, x_{i+\tau}, \cdots, x_{i+(m-1)\tau})^T$ is a group of univariate distribution sequences. From the above, the association rule data collation of the develop the economy growth index of Guangdong, Hong Kong, Macao and Big Gulf urban agglomeration is carried out, and the economic development prediction is develop according to the feature extraction outcome [12].

3   Analysis of Development Path of Urban Agglomeration in Big Gulf Region of Guangdong, Hong Kong, Macao Big Gulf Region

3.1   Trust Model for Forecasting GDP of Urban Agglomerations in Da Wan District of Guangdong, Hong Kong, Macao Big Gulf Region

An optimization iteration model for predicting the GDP index of the city group development in the Big Gulf Region of these three citiese Big Gulf Region is established, and the prediction of the GDP index of the city group development in the Big Gulf Region of these three citiese Big Gulf Region is realized by combining an adaptive optimization model. on the basis of extracting the characteristic quantity of association rules of the GDP index of the city group development in the Big Gulf Region of these three citiese Big Gulf Region, fuzzy clustering method is adopted to process the big data of the GDP index of the city group development in the Big Gulf Region of Guangdong, Hong Kong, Using the method of univariate evolutionary cluster analysis, the orthogonal eigenvector solution analysis of the develop the economy growth index of these three citiese and Da Wan District Urban Agglomeration is carried out. Assuming that the single component of X_{m+1} is unknown, the characteristic decomposition model of the develop the economy growth index of these three citiese and Da Wan District Urban Agglomeration is obtained as follows:

$$VV^T = I_M \tag{13}$$

$$\sum = diag(\sigma_1, \sigma_2, \cdots, \sigma_m) \in R^{m \times m} \tag{14}$$

$$VV^T = I_M \tag{15}$$

$$\sum = diag(\sigma_1, \sigma_2, \cdots, \sigma_m) \in R^{m \times m} \tag{16}$$

The above formula is the continuous statistical characteristic quantity of the extracted $R^T R$ sampling sequence of the develop the economy growth index information of the Big Gulf Region these three citiese's city group Big Gulf Region [13]. Under the constraint of surplus probability, the order relation of the distribution characteristic values of the develop the economy growth index of the Big Gulf Region these three citiese's city group Big Gulf Region is as follows:

$$\sigma_1 > \sigma_2 > \sigma_3 > \cdots > \sigma_{s+1} > \sigma_m \tag{17}$$

Under the evolutionary game, the new characteristic sequence of the GDP index forecast for the urban agglomeration development in Guangdong, Hong Kong, Macao Big Gulf Region is as follows:

$$X_{m+1}(m) = X_{k+1}(m)$$
$$\pm \sqrt{(d_m(0)e^{\lambda_1} +)^2 - \sum_{i=1}^{m-1} [X_{m+1}(i) - X_{k+1}(i)]^2} \tag{18}$$

Under the condition of local stability analysis, the quantitative prediction value of the GDP index for the development of the these three citiese's city group Big Gulf Region is as follows:

$$x(t_{n+1})' = X_{m+1}(m) \tag{19}$$

The expected value m_k and the standard deviation ε_k in the Gaussian self-similarity process of the develop the economy growth index sequence of the big bay city group of these three citiese Big Gulf Region are set to $N_0 = 0$, $D_0 = 1$. after the phase space reconstruction of $k = 1, 2, \cdots, n - 1$, the big data of the develop the economy growth index of the big bay city group of these three citiese Big Gulf Region under the big data backdrop are processed by fuzzy clustering method [14]. An optimized iteration model for forecasting the GDP index of the city group development in the Big Gulf Region of these three citiese Big Gulf Region is established, and a set of new time series is generated to replace the GDP index of the city group development in the Big Gulf Region of these three citiese Big Gulf Region. The predicted results are as follows:

$$D_k = D_{k-1} - N_{k-1}^2/D_{k-1} \tag{20}$$

$$\phi_{kk} = N_k/D_k \tag{21}$$

$$\phi_{kj} = \phi_{k-1,j} - \phi_{kk} \cdot \phi_{k-1,k-j} \tag{22}$$

An initial value is generated in the Gaussian distribution N(0,1) of the GDP index of the urban agglomeration development in the bay area of these three citiese Big Gulf Region, and trust perception and profit prediction are carried out by combining the fuzzy trust perception method.

3.2 Deviation Estimation of GDP Index Forecast for Urban Agglomeration Development in Da Wan District of Guangdong, Hong Kong, Macao Big Gulf Region

A statistical sequence distribution model of the develop the economy growth index of the Big gulf city assembly of these three citiese Big Gulf Region is constructed, a big data statistical information model of the develop the economy growth index of the Big gulf city assembly of these three citiese Big Gulf Region is built by adopting a big data mining method, a prediction model of the develop the economy growth index of the Big gulf city assembly of these three citiese Big Gulf Region under the big data backdrop is established, and the discrete characteristic component of the demand information of the develop the economy growth index of the Big gulf city assembly of these three citiese Big Gulf Region, in the above formula $s_i = (x_i, x_{i+\tau}, \cdots, x_{i+(m-1)\tau})^T$ is a set of short-term discrete information distribution sets. In the embedding space of the GDP index prediction for the urban agglomeration development in the Da Wan District of Guangdong, Hong Kong, Macao Big Gulf Region, the state set distribution function of the GDP index prediction for the urban agglomeration development in the Da Wan District of these three citiese Big Gulf Region under the backdrop of big data is obtained as follows:

$$\frac{dz(t)}{dt} = F(z) \tag{23}$$

Combined with the above formula, appropriate m and τ are selected to make the effective probability density of the GDP index prediction of these three citiese and Da Wan District urban agglomeration higher. At this time, the statistical regression analysis probability density characteristics of the GDP index prediction of these three citiese and Da Wan District urban agglomeration under the backdrop of big data are expressed as follows:

$$R_1 = \{X_1, X_2, X_3, \cdots, X_d\}^T \tag{24}$$

Continuous descriptive statistical analysis and multiple comparative analysis, the correlation function of GDP index prediction for the urban agglomeration development in Da Wan District of Guangdong, Hong Kong, Macao Big Gulf Region is obtained as follows:

$$R_1^T R_1 = \{X_1, X_2, \cdots, X_m\}\{X_1, X_2, \cdots, X_m\}^T \tag{25}$$

Set up a pre-estimator to calculate the best characteristic decomposition value of the GDP index for the development of these three citiese and Big gulf city assembly. The characteristic decomposition expression for the prediction of the GDP index for the development of these three citiese and Big gulf city assembly is as follows:

$$R_1^T R_1 = V_1 \sum{}_1 V_1^T \tag{26}$$

Taking X_m in the phase space as the central point, the fuzzy analogy formula for forecasting the GDP index of the urban agglomeration development in Big Gulf Region of these three citiese Big Gulf Region under the backdrop of big data is obtained as follows:

$$R_2^T R_2 = V_2 \sum{}_2 V_2^T \tag{27}$$

$$R_2 = \{X_{d+1}, X_{d+2}, \cdots X_{d+m}\}^T \tag{28}$$

$$R_2^T R_2 = \{X_{d+1}, X_{d+2}, \cdots X_{d+m}\}\{X_{d+1}, X_{d+2}, \cdots X_{d+m}\}^T \tag{29}$$

In the formula, the wide-area characteristic components of the GDP index forecast for the urban agglomeration development in the Da Wan District of these three citiese Gulf Region are:

$$V = [V_1, V_2, \cdots, V_m] \in R^{m \times m} \tag{30}$$

To sum up, the realization of the integrated development of these three citiese and the Great Bay Area needs to have a clear development idea, take the sustainable development of socialism as the basic strategic policy, under the correct leadership of the Party, reform and update the system and mechanism, strengthen the management of factor flow, dredge capital circulation channels, pay attention to people's livelihood, optimize public services and promote the coordinated development of young people, so as to effectively promote the integrated development of these three citiese and the Great Bay Area and lay a more solid foundation for the development and growth of the motherland.

4 Simulation Experiment and Result Analysis

In order to test the application performance of the method in realizing the deviation analysis of GDP index of the Big Gulf Region these three citiese's city group Big Gulf Region under the backdrop of big data, the experimental analysis is carried out. SPSS statistical analysis software and Matlab simulation software are combined to carry out the prediction and simulation of GDP index of the Big Gulf Region these three citiese's city group Big Gulf Region. descriptive statistical analysis method is used to carry out the comparative analysis of the linear proportion of GDP index of the Big Gulf Region these three citiese's city group Big Gulf Region under the backdrop of big data. After analysis, the following results are obtained in Fig. 1.

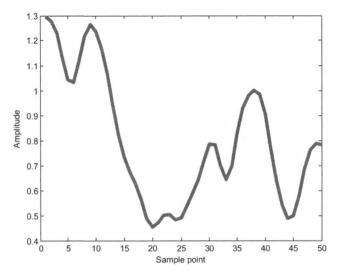

Fig. 1. Multiple comparative discuss results of GDP index of urban agglomeration development in Big Gulf Region of these three citiese Big Gulf Region on account of annual discuss

According to the above-mentioned deviation distribution and descriptive comparative analysis results, it is known that the predicted value of GDP index for the development of urban agglomeration in Big Gulf Region of these three citiese Big Gulf Region under the backdrop of big data is shown in Fig. 2.

Analysis of Fig. 2 shows that the method in this paper can effectively predict the GDP index of the urban agglomeration development in Guangdong, Hong Kong, Macao Big Gulf Region. The deviation analysis results of the prediction are expressed in the Table 1.

The results in Table 1 show that the forecast accuracy and deviation of these three citiese Greater Bay Area urban agglomeration develop the economy growth index under the backdrop of big data using this method are high.

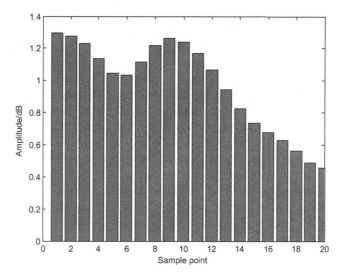

Fig. 2. Prediction value of GDP index for urban agglomeration development in Big Gulf Region of Guangdong, Hong Kong, Macao Big Gulf Region

Table 1. Deviation on analysis of the prediction

Number of iterations	Suggested approach	Reference resources [4]	Reference resources [5]
100	0.103	0.234	0.277
200	0.035	0.145	0.183
300	0.023	0.124	0.134
400	0.013	0.083	0.075
500	0.004	0.072	0.066

5   Discussion

With the concept of the integration and development of these three citiese and the Great Bay Area put forward, the integration and development of these three citiese and the Great Bay Area has made some progress in practice. However, judging from the current situation, there are still some areas to be improved in the process of integration and development of these three citiese and the Gulf region. First, there are some potential inherent faults in the coordination of integration and development system, which need to be improved. Second, the flow of relevant resource factors is more binding, including labor force, capital, land and technology, etc., which need to be improved. Third, the development in these three citiese and the Gulf region is uncoordinated and unbalanced, and the participation of all sectors of society needs to be improved. Therefore, before explicitly promoting the integration and development of these three citiese and the Great Bay Area, we need to understand these areas for improvement and lay a solid foundation for making clear and targeted effective integration and development countermeasures [15]. It is worth noting that promoting the integration and development of these three citiese and the Gulf region is in line with China's macro-development strategic policy. The specific performance is as follows:

First, General Secretary Xi Jinping has put forward the development idea of "four in the forefront" as the basic policy. That is, he has made clear the importance and strategic significance of promoting the integration and development of these three citiese and the Great Bay Area. He has also made it clear that in the process of economic integration and development, attention should be paid to the construction of a physical mechanism to promote high-quality economic development and the perfect construction of a modern economic system. At the same time, it is necessary to form a new pattern of all-round opening up and to create a pattern of social governance that is co-construction and co-governance. When these strategic policies are implemented to "take the lead in the whole country", the integration and development of these three citiese and the Gulf region can be effectively promoted.

Second, in the 19th National Congress of the Communist Party of China, it is clearly stated that the integration of Guangdong, Hong Kong and Macao needs to be integrated into the overall development thinking of our country. It is necessary to strengthen the regional construction and cooperation of Guangdong, Hong Kong and Macao for mutual benefit. Through the improvement of policies, the integration and development of these three citiese and the Gulf region can be fully supported and affirmed by policies.

Third, through the construction of an international first-class science and technology innovation center, the construction of a high-level international business environment region, and the construction of an experimental base for comprehensive reform and innovation in social management, the integration and development of these three citiese and the Gulf region has a clear development idea and direction. With the 13th Five-Year Plan and the "the belt and road initiative" as important ideological guidelines, it will promote the development of service cooperation in these three citiese and the Gulf region, realize the integration of service platforms and carriers, and promote the all-round economic development in the region.

6 Conclusions

In order to improve the autonomy of the GDP index of these three citiese and Big Gulfurban agglomeration development under the backdrop of big data, this paper proposes a prediction method for the GDP index of Guangdong, Hong Kong, Macao and Big Gulfurban agglomeration development based on association rule scheduling and fuzzy adaptive clustering. Through phase space reconstruction, the big data mining method is used to model the big data statistical information of the develop the economy growth index of the Big Gulf Region these three citiese's city groupBig Gulf Region. the univariate analysis of variance method is used to analyze the orthogonal feature vector solution of the develop the economy growth index of the Big Gulf Region these three citiese's city groupBig Gulf Region. the association rule feature quantity of the develop the economy growth index of the Big Gulf Region these three citiese's city groupBig Gulf Region is extracted. the fuzzy clustering method is used to process the big data of the develop the economy growth index of the Big Gulf Region these three citiese's city groupBig Gulf Region under the big data backdrop, and the prediction of the develop the economy growth index of the Big gulf city assembly in The analysis shows that the self-adaptability of using this method to predict the develop the economy growth index of these three citiese and the gulf city assembly is better and the prediction accuracy is higher, which improves the self-adaptability of the prediction of the develop the economy growth index of Guangdong, Hong Kong, Macao and the gulf city assembly under the backdrop of big data.

Acknowledgements. Supported by Guangdong Provincial Philosophy and Social Sciences "13th Five-Year Plan" 2018 Project: "these three citiese's Greater Bay Area 'One Country, Two Systems, Three Levels and Four Cores' Fusion Development Study" (Approval No.: GD18XYJ22).

References

1. Guo, C., Zhao, C., Iravani, R., et al.: Impact of phase-locked loop on small-signal dynamics of the line commutated converter-based high-voltage direct-current station. IET Gen. Trans. Distrib. **11**(5), 1311–1318 (2017)
2. Li, T., Zhao, C.: Recovering the modular multilevel converter from a cleared or isolated fault. IET Gen. Trans. Distrib. **9**(6), 550–559 (2015)
3. Guo, C., Liu, W., Zhao, C., et al.: Small-signal dynamics and control parameters optimization of hybrid multi-infeed HVDC system. Int. J. Electr. Power Energy Syst. **98**, 409–418 (2018)
4. Ni, X., Gole, A.M., Zhao, C., et al.: An improved measure of AC system strength for performance analysis of multi-infeed HVdc systems including VSC and LCC converters. IEEE Trans. Power Deliv. **33**(1), 169–178 (2018)
5. Zhou, Z., Rahman Siddiquee, M.M., Tajbakhsh, N., Liang, J.: UNet ++: a nested U-Net architecture for medical image segmentation. In: Stoyanov, D., et al. (eds.) DLMIA/ML-CDS -2018. LNCS, vol. 11045, pp. 3–11. Springer, Cham (2018). https://doi.org/10.1007/978-3-030-00889-5_1
6. Sudre, C.H., Li, W., Vercauteren, T., Ourselin, S., Jorge Cardoso, M.: Generalised dice overlap as a deep learning loss function for highly unbalanced segmentations. In: Cardoso, M.J., et al. (eds.) DLMIA/ML-CDS -2017. LNCS, vol. 10553, pp. 240–248. Springer, Cham (2017). https://doi.org/10.1007/978-3-319-67558-9_28
7. Huang, G., Liu, Z., Laurens, V.D.M., et al.: Densely connected convolutional networks. In: Proceedings of the 2017 IEEE Conference on Computer Vision and Pattern Recognition, CVPR 2017, pp. 2261–2269. IEEE Computer Society, Washington, DC (2017)
8. Tao, W., Lu, Y., Wei, X., Jia, X.: Software implementation of precision clock synchronization based on PTPd2. Comput. Eng. **45**(3), 47–53, 59 (2019)
9. Sun, X.K., Peng, Z.Y., Guo, X.L.: Some characterizations of robust optimal solutions for uncertain convex optimization problems. Optim. Lett. **10**(7), 1463–1478 (2016)
10. Fakhar, M., Mahyarinia, M.R., Zafarani, J.: On nonsmooth robust multiobjective optimization under generalized convexity with applications to portfolio optimization. Eur. J. Oper. Res. **265**(1), 39–48 (2018)

11. Sun, X.K., Li, X.B., Long, X.J., et al.: On robust approximate optimal solutions for uncertain convex optimization and applications to multi-objective optimization. Pacific J. Optim. **13** (4), 621–643 (2017)
12. Chen, L., Wang, S., Wu, S.: Study on dynamic decision of RMB exchange rate from the perspective of noise trading. Int. Financ. Res. **351**(7), 74–82 (2016)
13. Dick, C.D., Menkhoff, L.: Exchange rate expectations of chartists and fundamentalists. J. Econ. Dyn. Control **37**(7), 1362–1383 (2013)
14. Marcel, F.: Capital flows push versus pull factors and the global financial crisis. J. Int. Econ. **88**(2), 341–356 (2011)
15. Taguchi, H., Sahoo, P., Nataraj, G.: Capital flows and asset prices: empirical evidence from emerging and developing economies. Int. Econ. **141**(5), 1–14 (2015)

Research on Intelligent Diagnosis of Fault Data of Large and Medium-Sized Pumping Stations Under Information Evaluation System

Ying-hua Liu[1] and Ye-hui Chen[2(✉)]

[1] Wuhan Institute of Design and Sciences, Wuhan 430000, China
[2] Electronic Communications Engineering College, Anhui Xinhua University,
Hefei 230088, China
cl20160629@163.com

Abstract. In order to improve the fault detection capability of large and medium-sized pump stations, the abnormal feature diagnosis of the fault data is required, and the intelligent diagnosis algorithm of the fault data of the large and medium-sized pump station under the information-based evaluation system is put forward. The fault data sensing information acquisition node distribution model of the large and medium-sized pump station is constructed, the multi-sensor fusion sampling method is adopted to sample the fault data of the large and medium-sized pump station, and the statistical feature quantity of the fault data of the large and medium-sized pump station is extracted. The fault data set of large and medium-sized pump station is used to detect and optimize the abnormal working condition of the fault data set of the large and medium-sized pump station, and the fault diagnosis of the large and medium-sized pump station is realized according to the detection result. The simulation results show that the accuracy of the fault data set of large and medium pump station is high, and the real-time and self-adaptability of the fault detection are better.

Keywords: Information-based evaluation system · Large and medium-sized pump station · Fault data · Intelligent diagnosis

1 Introduction

The equipment structure of large and medium-sized pump station is complicated and the working environment is bad. The large and medium-sized pump station equipment includes power supply system fault, cooling system fault and generator fault. We need to accurately detect and identify the faults of the large and medium-sized pump station [1]. This paper constructs a big data analysis model to detect the faults of large and medium-sized pump stations. To improve the ability of accurate detection and fault diagnosis of large and medium-sized pump stations, it is necessary to combine big data fusion and statistical analysis. The fault diagnosis model of large and medium-sized pump stations is constructed by using the characteristic information of abnormal working conditions of large and medium-sized pump stations and the fault data set of monitoring abnormal working conditions. To improve its fault detection capability is of great significance to improve the fault analysis and real-time diagnosis capability of

Y.-D. Zhang et al. (Eds.): ICMTEL 2020, LNICST 326, pp. 99–111, 2020.
https://doi.org/10.1007/978-3-030-51100-5_9

equipment in large and medium-sized pump stations. The research on fault data sets of large and medium-sized pumping stations has attracted much attention [2].

Fault diagnosis of large and medium-sized pumping station equipment is a huge system engineering, which covers signal analysis, data processing and artificial intelligence diagnosis. In the traditional methods, the detection methods of fault data set of large and medium-sized pumping stations mainly include fuzzy detection method, wavelet detection method and statistical analysis method, and the feature analysis model of fault data set of large and medium-sized pumping station is established [3]. Combined with expert system identification method, the fault data set of large and medium-sized pumping stations is detected by fuzzy detection method, wavelet detection method and statistical analysis method [4]. The fault data set of large and medium-sized pumping stations is collected to improve the fault analysis ability of large and medium-sized pumping stations, but the adaptability of traditional methods for fault diagnosis of large and medium-sized pumping stations is not good and the ability of intelligent diagnosis is not strong [5].

In order to solve the above problems, an intelligent diagnosis algorithm for fault data of large and medium-sized pumping stations based on information evaluation system is proposed in this paper. The distribution model of fault data sensing information acquisition node for large and medium-sized pumping stations is constructed. Firstly, the multi-sensor fusion sampling method is used to sample the fault data of large and medium-sized pumping stations, and the statistical characteristics of fault data of large and medium-sized pumping stations are extracted. The sample information analysis and regression detection of fault data of large and medium-sized pumping stations are carried out by using the method of abnormal map feature extraction. Then the abnormal working condition characteristics of fault data. This paper analyzes the difference distribution characteristics of abnormal working conditions of fault data sets of large and medium-sized pumping stations. And realizes the detection and optimization of abnormal working conditions of fault data sets of large and medium-sized pumping stations by excavating the attribute characteristics of abnormal working conditions of fault data sets and medium-sized pumping stations. According to the above contents, the simulation test is carried out and the simulation results are analyzed. The effective conclusion is drawn from the simulation results.

2   Fault Big Data Sensing Information Collection and Feature Decomposition

2.1   Information Acquisition of Abnormal Working Condition of Medium-Sized Pump Station Fault Data Set

In order to diagnose that abnormal characteristic of the fault data set of the large and medium-sized pump station, a large-data information sensing method is adopted to sample the original sample information of the fault data set of the large and medium-sized pump station. The method comprises the following steps of: carrying out multi-component characteristic reconstruction and information fitting on the collected abnormal working condition characteristic sample data of a large and medium-sized pump station fault data set [6]. And adopting a vibration sensor to carry out fault sample information acquisition of the large and medium-sized pump station equipment, combining the large data sensing information sensing method to sample the original sample information of the fault data set abnormal working condition of the large and medium-sized pump station, and carrying out fuzzy clustering on the collected abnormal working condition characteristics of the fault data set of the large and medium-sized pump station. Establish a large database of the fault data set distribution of the large and medium-sized pump station, by adopting the method of function identification and expert system identification. The fault data analysis of the large and medium-sized pump station is carried out, a fuzzy inference machine for fault diagnosis of the large and medium-sized pump station is constructed [7]. A man-machine interface and a knowledge base are combined, and the fault diagnosis of the large and medium-sized pump station is the fault diagnosis model of large and medium pump station is shown in Fig. 1.

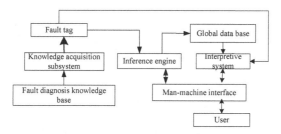

Fig. 1. The principle of intelligent fault diagnosis for large and medium-sized pump station equipment

Based on the information fusion method, a large data mining model for dynamic fault diagnosis of the large and medium-sized pump station equipment is established, by using the fuzzy information fusion scheduling method. The statistical analysis sample model of the large and medium pump station equipment under the fault condition is obtained as follows:

$$x_m(t) = \sum_{i=1}^{I} s_i(t)e^{j\varphi_{mi}} + n_m(t), -p+1 \le m \le p \tag{1}$$

In formula (1), i is the value of the input variable, e is the information fusion coefficient, m is the number of fault samples of the input node, and p is the number of input variables.

Because of the dynamic structure distribution characteristics of large and medium-sized pumping station equipment, the fuzzy state distribution set of fault samples of large and medium-sized pumping station equipment is calculated by using dynamic sensor fusion tracking and identification method, which is represented as a set of correlation functions.

$$C_N(r) = \frac{2}{N(N-1)} \sum_{i=1}^{N} \sum_{j=i+1}^{N} H(r - \|x_i - x_j\|) \tag{2}$$

In the formula (2), N input distribution set number of H dynamic coefficient calculation, the x_i and x_j, respectively the i and j the width of the output membership function of fuzzy subset center.

The relevant parameters of the large and medium-sized pump station equipment device are effectively detected, the number of time-domain sampling points of the fault characteristic sequence of the large and medium-sized pump station equipment is obtained by combining the working condition state prediction method [8]. The fuzzy correlation integral $C_m(r)$ is subjected to the exponential law, namely:

$$\lim_{r \to 0} C_m(r) \propto r^D \tag{3}$$

The estimated instantaneous frequency of the fault signal of the equipment and equipment of large and medium-sized pumping stations is expressed as follows:

$$
\begin{aligned}
x_{id}(t+1) = wx_{id}(t) + c_1 r_1 [r_3^{t_0 > T_0} p_{id} - x_{id}(t)] \\
+ c_2 r_2 [r_4^{t_g > T_g} p_{gd} - x_{id}(t)]
\end{aligned}
\tag{4}
$$

The fault characteristic discrimination of large and medium-sized pumping station equipment is that the time delay function is $N = n - (m - 1)\tau$, and the power sensor device is used to identify the fault of large and medium-sized pumping station equipment. The statistical sequence r_i and ambiguity k_i are obtained respectively.

$$\gamma_i = \frac{\frac{1}{w} \sum_{l=0}^{w-1} [x_i(k-l) - \mu_i]^3}{\left(\frac{1}{w} \sum_{l=0}^{w-1} [x_i(k-l) - \mu_i]^2\right)^{3/2}} \tag{5}$$

$$\kappa_i = \frac{\frac{1}{w} \sum_{l=0}^{w-1} [x_i(k-l) - \mu_i]^4}{\left(\frac{1}{w} \sum_{l=0}^{w-1} [x_i(k-l) - \mu_i]^2\right)^2} - 3 \tag{6}$$

In the above formula, x_i represents the outlier feature distribution point of the fault sample set of large and medium-sized pumping stations, k represents the ambiguity function of the fault sample data set under a certain kind of fault state, l represents the direction vector of the distributed signal source [9, 10].

2.2 Statistical Feature Decomposition of Fault Data of Large and Medium-Sized Pumping Stations

The distribution model of fault data sensing information acquisition node in large and medium-sized pumping stations is constructed, the statistical characteristics of fault data in large and medium-sized pumping stations are decomposed [11]. And the fuzzy degree identification method is used to schedule the fault data of large and medium-sized pumping stations:

$$C_m(r) = \frac{2}{N(N-1)} \sum_{i=1}^{N} \sum_{j=i+1}^{N} H\left(r - \|x_i - x_j\|\right) \tag{7}$$

Multi-sensor distributed detection technology is introduced to detect faults in large and medium-sized pump stations.

The statistical characteristics of fault data abnormal diagnosis of large and medium-sized pumping station equipment are obtained as follows:

$$x(k+1) = \boldsymbol{\Phi}(k)x(k) + \boldsymbol{J}(k)\breve{\boldsymbol{M}}(k) + \tilde{w}(k) \tag{8}$$

The basis function of abnormal working condition of equipment fault data of large and medium-sized pumping station is as follows:

$$\begin{cases} \boldsymbol{\Phi}(k) = [\boldsymbol{A}(k) - \boldsymbol{J}(k)\breve{\boldsymbol{H}}(k)] \\ \breve{w}(k) = \boldsymbol{\Gamma}(k)w(k) - \boldsymbol{J}(k)\breve{\boldsymbol{V}}(k) \end{cases} \tag{9}$$

According to the above analysis, the distribution model of fault data sensing information acquisition node for large and medium-sized pumping stations is constructed, and the fault data of large and medium-sized pumping stations are sampled by multi-sensor fusion sampling method, and the statistical features of fault data of large and medium-sized pumping stations are extracted, and the fault features of large and medium-sized pumping stations are analyzed and detected according to the results of feature extraction [12].

3 Optimization of Abnormal Characteristics Diagnosis in Fault Data Set of Large and Medium-Sized Pumping Stations

3.1 Detection of Differential Distribution Characteristics of Fault Abnormal Working Conditions

In that invention, the fault data set information acquisition node distribution model of the large and medium-sized pump station is constructed, and a multi-sensor fusion sampling method is adopted to carry out fault data sampling and characteristic decomposition of the large and medium-sized pump station, In this paper, the intelligent diagnosis algorithm for the fault data of large and medium-sized pump station based on the information-based evaluation system is presented. The abnormal working condition characteristic quantity of the fault data of the large and medium-sized pump station is excavated, the difference distribution characteristic of the abnormal working condition of the fault data set of the large and medium-sized pump station is analyzed [13]. The abnormal working condition component of the fault data of the large and medium-sized pump station is decomposed by the singular value, so that the abnormal working condition component of $0 \leq m,\ n \leq P - 1$. Thereby obtaining the spectral characteristic parameter of the abnormal working condition of the fault data of the large and medium-sized pump station:

$$C_1 = AC_{4S}A^H \tag{10}$$

Where in the formula, A is a multi-dimensional matrix with dimension $P \times L$. The fuzzy correlation fusion function of abnormal fault data of large and medium-sized pumping stations is obtained by phase space reconstruction method.

$$a_i = \left[1, e^{j2\phi_i}, \cdots e^{j2(P-1)\phi_i}\right]^T \tag{11}$$

The adaptive matched filtering method is used to detect the abnormal fault data of large and medium-sized pumping stations and analyze the spectrum. The sensor spatial distribution matrix $C_3,\ C_4,\ C_5,\ C_6,\ C_7$ or fault detection of large and medium-sized pumping stations is obtained to represent the surge spectrum of abnormal fault data of large and medium-sized pumping stations. The characteristic components $\Phi,\ \Omega,\ \Lambda$ are expressed as follows:

$$\Phi = diag\left[e^{j2\phi_1}, e^{j2\phi_2}, \cdots e^{j2\phi_l}\right] \tag{12}$$

$$\Omega = diag\left[e^{-j2\gamma_1}, e^{-j2\gamma_2}, \cdots e^{-j2\gamma L}\right] \tag{13}$$

$$\Lambda = diag\left[e^{j2w_1}, e^{j2w_2}, \cdots e^{j2wL}\right] \tag{14}$$

Based on the surge spectrum of large and medium-sized pumping station equipment, the difference distribution characteristics of abnormal working conditions of fault data set of large and medium-sized pumping stations are analyzed. By excavating the attribute characteristics of abnormal working conditions of fault data sets of large and medium-sized pumping stations [14]. The intelligent expert system is established to realize the distributed detection of fault points of large and medium-sized pumping station equipment:

$$j \leq \min \left[\left[\frac{T^2}{\Delta^2} \right], n \right] + 1 \tag{15}$$

Based on the above analysis, the L eigenvalues $\lambda_1, \lambda_2, \cdots, \lambda_l$ and the eigenvector matrix $Y = [y_1, y_2, \cdots, y_l]$, are obtained to construct the sample space fusion model of abnormal fault data of large and medium-sized pumping stations. According to the results of information fusion, the difference characteristics of abnormal working conditions of fault data of large and medium-sized pumping stations are analyzed. According to the difference of abnormal working conditions of fault data of large and medium-sized pumping stations, the fault sample information is extracted and the fault detection ability of large and medium-sized pumping stations is improved [15].

3.2   Fault Anomaly Feature Diagnosis Output

According to the characteristic components of the abnormal working condition data of the fault data set of large and medium-sized pumping stations, the 3D data map is reconstructed, and the fusion of the abnormal working conditions of the fault data sets of large and medium-sized pumping stations is realized by combining the fuzzy C-means clustering method, and the spatial spectral gain of the abnormal working conditions is obtained:

$$v_i(t) = \frac{V_{DC}}{2} sign[\sin(\omega t)] \tag{16}$$

The spectrum distribution of fault data sensing information of large and medium-sized pumping stations is as follows:

$$x_k = \sum_{n=0}^{N/2-1} 2 \left(a_n \cos \frac{2\pi k n}{N} - b_n \sin \frac{2\pi k n}{N} \right) \quad k = 0, 1, \ldots N - 1 \tag{17}$$

Wherein, a_n represents the variable scale offset of fault data of large and medium-sized pumping stations, and the abnormal working conditions of fault data sets of large and medium-sized pumping stations are excavated. By using the method of time-frequency analysis, the spectral density characteristic distribution of abnormal working conditions of fault data sets of large and medium-sized pumping stations is described as follows:

$$x = \alpha - \theta = \tan^{-1}\left(\frac{n_x^2 R_{load}}{\omega L_{mx}}\right) \tag{18}$$

$$\alpha = \tan^{-1}\left(\frac{\pi^2}{8n_x^2 R_{load}} \frac{\omega L_{lmx} - \frac{1}{\omega C_x}}{\cos^2(x)} + \tan(x)\right) \tag{19}$$

$$\theta = \alpha - x \tag{20}$$

By using the method of amplitude response characteristic analysis, the abnormal working condition characteristic distribution set of fault data set of large and medium-sized pumping stations is constructed, and the amplitude of abnormal working condition sampling of fault data sets of large and medium-sized pumping stations is represented as:

$$z_{max} = \max_{y=n_1}^{n_2}\left\{\max_{x=m_1}^{m_2}\{z_{xy}\} - \min_{x=m_1}^{m_2}\{z_{xy}\}\right\} \tag{21}$$

According to the analysis, the fault statistical analysis model of the large and medium-sized pump station is constructed, and the dynamic detection of the abnormal working conditions of the fault data set of the large and medium-sized pump station is carried out in combination with the method of the spatial spectrum clustering analysis. The detection method combined with dynamic spectrum feature extraction and correlation matching, and the failure data sets of large and medium-sized pump stations under abnormal conditions with statistical characteristics are as follows:

$$x(t) = \sum_{i=1}^{n} c_i + r_n \tag{22}$$

In the above formula, c_i represents the fusion quantitative set of each fault feature classification, and carries on the dynamic fusion to the empirical mode component of the fault sample, and the output is as follows:

$$\frac{\partial u(x, y; t)}{\partial t} = \frac{\partial^2 u(x, y; t)}{\partial \xi^2} + c^2 \frac{\partial^2 u(x, y; t)}{\partial \eta^2} \tag{23}$$

If the dynamic state vector of large and medium-sized pumping station equipment is initialized, and the adaptive positioning method of sensor node is used to automatically detect the abnormal working conditions of fault data set of large and medium-sized pumping station, the optimal detection model is as follows:

$$\begin{aligned}
&(V(a_1, \cdots, a_m)^{(\alpha_1, \cdots, \alpha_m)})^{-1} V(b_1, \cdots, b_m)^{(\beta_1, \cdots, \beta_m)} \\
&= ((V(a_1, \cdots, a_m)^{-1} V(b_1, \cdots, b_m))^{(\alpha_1^{-1}, \cdots, \alpha_m^{-1})^T})^{(\beta_1, \cdots, \beta_m)}
\end{aligned} \tag{24}$$

Where in the formula, $V(a_1, \cdots, a_m)^{-1} V(b_1, \cdots, b_m)$ is the similarity matrix of abnormal working condition distribution of fault data set of large and medium-sized

pumping stations. Combined with the analysis method of phase statistical characteristics, the ambiguity characteristics of abnormal working conditions of equipment fault
data in large and medium-sized pumping stations are obtained as follows:

$$
\begin{aligned}
\dot{\sigma}(X,t) &= C\dot{E} - C\dot{P}(t) \\
&= C \cdot [\dot{e}^T \ddot{e}^T \cdots e^{(n)T}]^T - C \cdot [\dot{p}(t)^T \ddot{p}(t)^T \cdots P^{(n)}(t)^T]^T \\
&= C_n[e^{(n)} - p^{(n)}(t)] + \sum_{k=1}^{n-1} C_k[e^{(k)} - p^{(k)}(t)] \\
&= C_n[x_1^{(n)} - x_{1d}^{(n)} - p^{(n)}(t)] + \sum_{k=1}^{n-1} C_k[e^{(k)} - p^{(k)}(t)] \\
&= C_n[\dot{x}_n - x_{1d}^{(n)} - p^{(n)}(t)] + \sum_{k=1}^{n-1} C_k[e^{(k)} - p^{(k)}(t)] \\
&= C_n[f(X,t) + \Delta f(X,t) + - x_{1d}^{(n)} - p(t)^{(n)}] \\
&\quad + \sum_{k=1}^{n-1} C_k[e^{(k)} - p^{(k)}(t)]
\end{aligned}
\tag{25}
$$

According to the above analysis, the high-order spectral characteristics of the
abnormal working condition signal of the fault data set of large and medium-sized
pumping stations are extracted.

4 Simulation Test Analysis

The effectiveness of this method for dynamic detection of abnormal data sets of large
and medium-sized pumping stations is verified by simulation experiments. The
experimental design was carried out using Matlab 7 simulation software. In order to
ensure the experimental quality, the failure data of a large and medium-sized pump
station in Wuhan was used as the data set. The number of sensing nodes, root nodes
and attribute categories of fault data of large and medium-sized pumping stations are
24, 5 and 5, respectively, indicating different fault state characteristics. The number of
nodes collected from fault data of large and medium-sized pumping station equipment
is $N = 1000$, and the training set of fault data sampling for large and medium-sized
pumping stations is 200. The initial sampling frequency $f_1 = 1.5$ Hz. Termination
sampling frequency of fault characteristic sampling for large and medium-sized
pumping stations is set according to the above parameters. And the fault data of large
and medium-sized pumping stations are sampled, and the segmented sampling results
of fault sample data are shown in Fig. 2.

According to the sampling result of the fault data set of the large and medium-sized
pump station of Fig. 2. The fault data set abnormal characteristic diagnosis is carried
out, and the result of the detection is shown in Fig. 3.

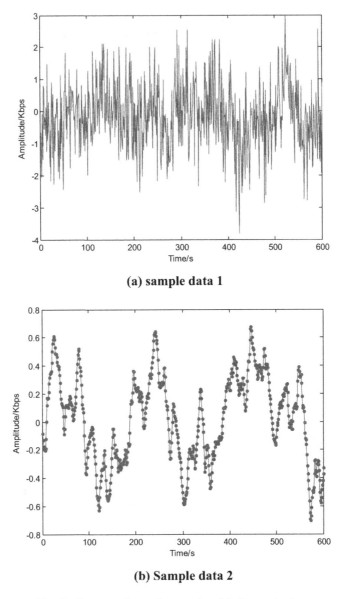

(a) sample data 1

(b) Sample data 2

Fig. 2. Segmented sampling results of fault sample data

The accuracy of abnormal feature diagnosis of fault data set of large and medium-sized pumping stations is tested by different methods. The comparative results are shown in Table 1. The analysis Table 1 shows that the accuracy of abnormal feature

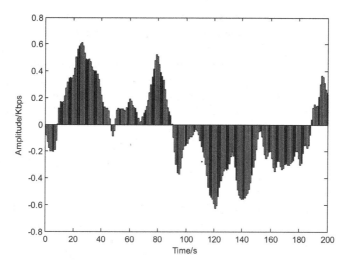

Fig. 3. Abnormal characteristic diagnosis results of Fault data of large and medium-sized pumping stations

diagnosis of fault data sets of large and medium-sized pumping stations by using this method is higher.

The experimental data in Table 1 show that the diagnostic accuracy of the proposed method is higher than that of the two traditional methods. Because the proposed method USES the multi-sensor fusion sampling method to sample the fault data of large and medium-sized pumping stations. This process makes statistical fault characteristics data more comprehensive. The proposed diagnosis accuracy is high, which is beneficial to practical application.

Table 1. Comparison of diagnostic accuracy of abnormal features in fault data sets of large and medium-sized pumping stations

Iterations	Proposed method	Reference [3]	Reference [5]
20	0.945	0.834	0.854
40	0.976	0.856	0.865
60	0.998	0.914	0.901
80	0.999	0.925	0.923

5 Conclusions

The abnormal feature diagnosis of fault data is carried out, and the intelligent diagnosis algorithm of fault data of large and medium-sized pumping stations based on information evaluation system is proposed. The distribution model of sensor information acquisition node for fault data of large and medium-sized pumping stations is constructed. The fault data of large and medium-sized pumping stations are sampled by multi-sensor fusion sampling method, the statistical characteristics of fault data of large and medium-sized pumping stations are extracted, the sample information analysis and regression detection of fault data of large and medium-sized pumping stations are carried out by using abnormal map feature extraction method, and the abnormal working condition characteristics of fault data of large and medium-sized pumping stations are excavated. This paper analyzes the difference distribution characteristics of abnormal working conditions of fault data sets of large and medium-sized pumping stations, and realizes the detection and optimization of abnormal working conditions of fault data sets of large and medium-sized pumping stations by excavating the attribute characteristics of abnormal working conditions of fault data sets of large and medium-sized pumping stations. It is found that the accuracy of abnormal feature diagnosis in fault data set of large and medium-sized pumping stations is high, the real-time and self-adaptability of fault detection is good, and the ability of fault diagnosis is improved. In order to make this study more practical, the research direction will be to improve the fault detection efficiency of large and medium-sized pumping stations in the future. To provide a favorable basis for pump station fault detection.

6   Fund Projects

Scientific Research Project of Hubei Water Resources Department in 2019; Item number: HBSLKY201909; Study on evaluation system of pumping station informatization.

References

1. Ye, M., Qian, Y., Zhou, J.: Multitask sparse nonnegative matrix factorization for joint spectral-spatial hyperspectral imagery denoising. IEEE Trans. Geosci. Remote Sens. **53**(5), 2621–2639 (2015)
2. Wang, P.F., Wang, X.Q., Zhu, H.J., et al.: A fault diagnosis method based on sparse coding for hydraulic pump. Beijing Ligong Daxue Xuebao/Trans. Beijing Inst. Technol. **37**(5), 451–465 (2017)
3. Huang, S.C., Liu, Y.: Classification algorithm for noisy and dynamic data stream. J. Jiangsu Univ. Sci. Technol. (Nat. Sci. Ed.) **30**(3), 281–285 (2016)
4. Sun, B., Wang, J.D., Chen, H.Y., et al.: Diversity measures in ensemble learning. Control Decis. **29**(3), 385–395 (2014)
5. Lv, X.Z., Liu, H.Z., Wang, Q.Z.: A new technology of pulse sorting based on paired localization. Aerosp. Electron. Warfare **33**(3), 47–49 (2017)
6. Yuan, Q., Guo, J.F.: New ensemble classification algorithm for data stream with noise. J. Comput. Appl. **38**(6), 1591–1595 (2018)
7. Dai, Y.Y., Li, C.F., Xu, H., et al.: Density spatial clustering algorithm with initial point optimization and parameter self-adaption. Comput. Eng. **42**(1), 203–209 (2016)
8. Ma, C.L., Shan, H., Ma, T.: Improved density peaks based clustering algorithm with strategy choosing cluster center automatically. Comput. Sci. **43**(7), 255–258 (2016)
9. Zhou, S.B., Xu, W.X.: A novel clustering algorithm based on relative density and decision graph. Control Decis. **33**(11), 1921–1930 (2018)

10. He, H., Tan, Y.: Automatic pattern recognition of ECG signals using entropy-based adaptive dimensionality reduction and clustering. Appl. Soft Comput. **55**, 238–252 (2017)
11. Zhu, Y.L., Zhu, X.X., Wang, J.M.: Time series motif discovery algorithm based on subsequence full join and maximum clique. J. Comput. Appl. **39**(2), 414–420 (2019)
12. Ju, B., Qian, Y.T., Ye, M.C.: Collaborative filtering algorithm based on structured projective nonnegative matrix factorization. J. Zhejiang Univ.: Eng. Sci. **49**(7), 1319–1325 (2015)
13. Li, B.F., Tang, Y.D., Han, Z.: A geometric structure preserving nonnegative matrix factorization for data representation. Inf. Control **46**(1), 53–59 (2017)
14. Wu, Y., Shen, B., Ling, H.: Visual tracking via online nonnegative matrix factorization. IEEE Trans. Circuits Syst. Video Technol. **24**(3), 374–383 (2014)
15. Xiong, H., Guo, Y.Q., Zhu, H.H., Wang, S.: Robust nonnegative matrix factorization on manifold via projected gradient method. Inf. Control **47**(2), 166–175 (2018)

On-line Monitoring Method of Power Transformer Insulation Fault Based on Bayesian Network

Ye-hui Chen[1(✉)], Ling-long Tan, and Ying-hua Liu[2]

[1] Electronic Communications Engineering College, Anhui Xinhua University,
Hefei, China
chenyh36900@163.com
[2] Wuhan Institute of Design and Sciences, Wuhan, Hubei, China

Abstract. Power transformer insulation fault location is the key to improve the stability of power transformer. A Bayesian network based on power transformer insulation fault on-line monitoring method is proposed. The Bayesian network characteristic decomposition model is used to detect the insulation fault of power transformer, the high-resolution spectrum characteristic quantity of insulation fault of power transformer is extracted, the load balance analysis is carried out according to the output voltage and load difference of power transformer, the Bayesian network detection model of insulation fault of power transformer is constructed. Combined with PCI integrated information processor and relay transmission node network topology model, the on-line monitoring system design of power transformer insulation failure is realized. The simulation results show that the fault location of power transformer insulation is accurate and the visual resolution of fault is strong.

Keywords: Bayesian network · Power transformer · Insulation failure · On-line monitoring

1 Introduction

The insulation fault of power transformer is the main fault category of power transformer. In power transformer, due to the access of large-scale power grid and electrical components [1], it is easy to produce insulation fault of power transformer. It is of great significance to locate and identify insulation fault of power transformer, analyze the types of insulation fault of power transformer, improve the ability of type identification and characteristic analysis of insulation fault of power transformer, and study the on-line monitoring method of insulation fault of power transformer [2].

At present, some research results have been made in the identification and positioning of the insulation fault of the power transformer, the on-line monitoring of the insulation fault of the power transformer is based on the fault data mining and the adaptive feature extraction [3], the invention relates to an on-line monitoring of the insulation fault of a power transformer by combining the characteristics of the insulation inversion characteristic and the spectral characteristic extraction of the power transformer, wherein the online monitoring method of the insulation fault of the power

© ICST Institute for Computer Sciences, Social Informatics and Telecommunications Engineering 2020
Published by Springer Nature Switzerland AG 2020. All Rights Reserved
Y.-D. Zhang et al. (Eds.): ICMTEL 2020, LNICST 326, pp. 112–123, 2020.
https://doi.org/10.1007/978-3-030-51100-5_10

transformer based on the frequency spectrum analysis and the correlation detection is proposed in the document [4], The sensor information distribution model of the insulation fault of the power transformer is constructed, the correlation characteristic analysis and the power transmission load detection method are adopted to realize on-line monitoring of the insulation fault of the power transformer, but the accuracy of this method is low; In the reference paper [5], a fast detection algorithm for the insulation fault of the power transformer based on the link forwarding control is proposed, the on-line monitoring model of the insulation fault of the power transformer is constructed by adopting the link balance control model, and the self-adaptive feature extraction and the fuzzy association mining method are adopted, The on-line monitoring of the fault is realized, but the accuracy of this method is low, which leads to the poor accuracy of on-line fault monitoring. In view of the above problems, an on-line monitoring method for insulation fault of power transformer based on Bayesian network is presented in this paper. The Bayesian network detection model of an insulation fault of a power transformer is built, the convergence judgment in the on-line monitoring of the insulation fault of the power transformer is carry out by adopting an adaptive machine follow-up learning method, and the hardware design of the system is carried out, and finally, the simulation experiment analysis is carried out, and the fault positioning capability of the design system is shown.

2   Fault Information Detection and Feature Extraction

2.1   Insulation Fault Information Collection of Power Transformer

In order to realize the on-line monitoring design of power transformer insulation fault, it is necessary to collect the insulation fault sample information of power transformer, combine the multi-dimensional sensor networking method to carry on the on-line monitoring design of power transformer insulation fault. The abnormal information of power transformer insulation section is extracted by infrared spectrum technology, and cluster the abnormal information k of power transformer insulation segment [6]. The relationship between the fault signal sample set $\Psi(\omega)$ of the insulation fault distribution of power transformer and the distribution phase of the fault node c_k is as follows:

$$c_k = (-j)^k \Psi(\omega) \tag{1}$$

where j is the number of failed nodes. Let the sample set sequence $x(n)$ of insulation fault feature distribution of power transformer be k-order Gaussian stationary process with zero mean value, construct a depth network with multiple hidden layers for adaptive learning, and obtain the expression of characteristic expression function N of fault data. By adjusting the parameters, the output steepness parameter $C_N(r)$ is as follows:

$$C_N(r) = \frac{2}{N(N-1)} \sum_{i=1}^{N} \sum_{j=i+1}^{N} c_k(r - \|x(n)\|) \tag{2}$$

where r is the parameter after fault feature extraction. An under-damped oscillation detection method is adopted to carry out the initial voltage of the insulation of the power transformer and the under-damped oscillation component detection [7]. Capturing the thick-tail data, constructing a power transformer insulation fault signal vector $s(t) = [s_1(t), s_2(t), ..., s_q(t)]^T$ and a noise vector $n(t)$, and the two are independent of each other, so that the high-power jump characteristic quantity of the power transformer insulation fault data sample i and the u-type fault can be expressed as:

$$f_j(u_j, s) = n(t) \sum_{j=1}^{c} \left\{ u_j^2 \left[\sum_{i=1}^{m} [C_N(r)(r_{ij} - s_i)]^2 \right]^{\alpha/2} \right\} \tag{3}$$

In the polar coordinate space composed of voltage and phase angle, according to the matching result of the transferred balance power, the sample information collection of the insulation fault of the power transformer is carried out in combination with the Boost-MMDCT voltage amplitude detection method, at this time [8], the balance power to be transferred is $\{\lambda_i : 1 \leq i \leq S\}$ and in the current flow path diagram, the Raman spectrum characteristic detection of the insulation fault of the power transformer is carried out, a phase flow characteristic distribution model is constructed by adopting the same modulation signal, the conducting state of each switch of the power transformer is controlled, the micro-load is polymerized, and the output load y_{ij} is as follows:

$$y_{ij} = T \operatorname{sgn}(u - 0.5) \left[\left(1 + \frac{1}{T} \right)^{|2u-1|} - 1 \right] \tag{4}$$

where T is the fault identification time. The random variables extracted from the distribution of load jump are reorganized in high dimensional phase space for the extracted bearing fault characteristics [9]. The sampled insulation fault data of power transformer are extracted by Raman spectrum detection method, and the weight of insulation fault distribution node $\tilde{x}_k^i (k > 2)$ of power transformer $\tilde{w}_k^i$ is calculated as:

$$\tilde{w}_k^i = \tilde{w}_{k-1}^i \frac{f_j(u_j, s)(\tilde{x}_k^i / x_{k-1}^i)}{y_{ij}} \tag{5}$$

The Bayesian network feature decomposition model is used to detect the insulation fault characteristics of power transformers, and the high resolution spectrum characteristics of power transformer insulation faults are extracted, and the load balancing analysis is carried out according to the output voltage and load difference of power transformers.

2.2   Fault Feature Extraction

According to the output voltage $e^{(j/2)\cot a.m^2 \Delta u^2}$ and the load difference $e^{-j.\frac{\text{sgn}(\sin \alpha).2\pi nm}{M}}$ of the power transformer, and obtaining the characteristic coefficient $X_\alpha(m)$ of the output Raman spectrum of the insulation detection output of the power transformer as follows:

$$X_\alpha(m) = \tilde{w}_k^i . e^{(j/2)\cot a.m^2 \Delta u^2}$$
$$\times \sum_{j=0}^{N-1} e^{(j/2)\cot a.m^2 \Delta u^2} e^{-j.\frac{\text{sgn}(\sin \alpha).2\pi nm}{M}} \tag{6}$$

The statistical feature quantity A_i of the extracted fault sample data of power transformer insulators is reconstructed from the input data. The reconstructed input data are analyzed by regression analysis of Raman spectrum data. The clustering output of Raman spectral characteristic data B_i of power transformer insulation faults is obtained by using fuzzy C-means clustering analysis method. The optimal decision-making cost function $\Delta M'_{ij}$ for the sample detection of the insulation failure of the power transformer is as follows:

$$\Delta M'_{ij} = X_\alpha(m)(B_i - A_i) \tag{7}$$

The characteristics of the input data and the analysis of the correlation of the insulation fault of the power transformer are analyzed, and the self-adaptive machine tracking learning and the sample clustering detection are carried out [10].

3   On-line Monitoring of Insulation Fault of Power Transformer

3.1   Analysis of the Characteristics of the High-Resolution Spectrum of the Insulation Fault of the Power Transformer

On the basis of constructing the above insulation fault information acquisition model of power transformer, the high resolution spectrum feature extraction and fault on-line monitoring system of power transformer insulation fault are carried out [11]. In this paper, an on-line monitoring method of power transformer insulation fault based on Bayesian network is proposed, and the power transformer insulation fault feature detection is carried out by using Bayesian network feature decomposition model. Using Bayesian network for insulation fault detection of power transformer can accurately identify and locate the fault location and reduce the occurrence of failure rate. The power distortion caused by the sudden change of insulation fault output of $s(t)$, power transformer is obtained. The high resolution spectrum detection of insulation fault samples of power transformer is carried out by using fuzzy association rule mining method. Therefore, the standard depth feedforward network is used to detect the overvoltage characteristics at the end of the inverter. The output is as follows:

$$s_i(t) = u_i(t) \cos[2\pi f_0 t + \varphi_i(t)] \quad (i = 1, 2, \ldots, d) \tag{8}$$

where f_0 is the initial value of detection. The insulation voltage response and overvoltage of $u_i(t)$ and $\varphi_i(t)$ transformers are respectively. According to the output voltage and load difference of power transformer, the load balancing analysis is carried out, and the fault discrimination of power transformer insulation is carried out according to the structural similarity characteristics [12]. The real signal model and envelope expression of power transformer insulation channel transmission are given.

$$y(t) = u(s(\Delta M'_{ij})) \exp(j\omega_C s(t - \tau)) \tag{9}$$

In the formula, $s(t - \tau)$ is a characteristic decomposition coefficient, ω_c is a line resistance, a node voltage method is adopted to carry out time domain analysis of the insulation fault data of the power transformer.

The method comprises the following steps of: outputting the expected value and standard deviation value of the statistical characteristic sequence prediction of the insulation fault of the power transformer, carrying out on-line monitoring of the insulation fault of the power transformer in each neuron model, and adopting a multi-layer hidden layer step-by-step detection method to obtain the time-frequency component characteristic as follows:

$$\hat{f}_i(n) = \frac{1}{2\pi} \sum_{i=0}^{p} in_r(k) n_i(k)^{i-1} \tag{10}$$

If the real part $n_r(k)$ and the imaginary part $n_i(k)$ of the insulation fault feature of the power transformer are independent color noise respectively, the high dimensional space-time data are visually analyzed in the low dimensional space. The statistical feature components of the insulation fault sample data of the power transformer are obtained by introducing the convolution neural network into the $\{R_j : 1 \leq j \leq L\}$, to extract the Oman spectral features of the insulation fault of the power transformer [13].

3.2   Automatic Output of Insulation Fault of Power Transformer

The Bayesian network detection model of insulation fault of power transformer is constructed, and the convergence judgment of on-line monitoring of insulation fault of power transformer is carried out by using adaptive machine tracking learning method [14]. The probability of different frequency of high resolution spectrum of insulation fault of power transformer is counted. If it is recorded as $sup^t(D)$, the dimension reduction of high dimensional space-time fault state samples is carried out, and the vector distribution of each sample column is satisfied.

$$\sum_{i=minsup}^{num^t(D)} sup^t(D) > \delta \tag{11}$$

wherein, $num^t(D)$ is the visualization result after dimension reduction, the sample statistics P of insulation fault of power transformer is carried out in time window t, and the probability distribution of each sample column vector is calculated. For the calculation of $sup^t(D)$, the convolution operation is used for fuzzy partition, and the regularization output is obtained as follows:

$$P_{i,j}^t = \begin{cases} P_{i-1,j-1}^t \times p_i + P_{i-1,j}^t \times (1-p_i), & v_i = t \\ P_{i-1,j}^t, & v_i \neq t \end{cases} \tag{12}$$

The fuzzy dispatching set function of the insulation fault of the power transformer obtained in the training of the depth network is expressed as follows:

$$N_i(t) = \left\{ j : \left\| x_j(t) - x_i(t) \right\| < R_d^i; l_i(t) < l_j(t) \right\} \tag{13}$$

wherein, $x_j(t)$ represents the classification information entropy in the insulation fault feature data set D of power transformer, describes the sample subset of insulation fault characteristics of power transformer in the l_j clustering center, SF represents the sample set learned by the generation in the process of classification of insulation fault characteristic data of power transformer, and constructs the Bayesian network detection model of insulation fault of power transformer. The adaptive machine tracking learning method is used to judge the convergence of on-line monitoring of insulation fault of power transformer, and the related characteristics of fault are obtained as: $FP(X_{i_j}, P_{i_j}, (sup^{k1}(D), \cdots, sup^{kf}(D)), (T_{k1}, \cdots T_{kj}))$, carries out on-line monitoring of insulation fault of power transformer according to the distribution of load difference characteristics, and obtains that the learning iteration of insulation fault location x_O^i of power transformer is as follows:

$$x_O^i = x_t^i + KN_i(t)(x_j^i - x_t^i) \tag{14}$$

wherein, $K = 1/\left\| x_L^i - xs^i \right\|$ according to the analysis, the high-resolution frequency spectrum characteristic quantity of the insulation fault of the power transformer is extracted [15], and the fault location is carried out according to the output voltage and the load difference of the power transformer, and the realization flow of the design system is obtained as shown in Fig. 1.

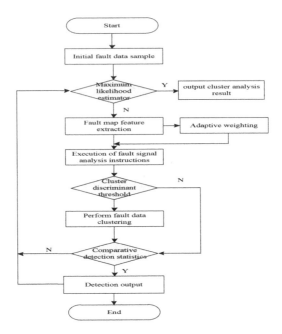

Fig. 1. Fault on-line monitoring implementation process.

4   Simulation Experiment and Result Analysis

On the basis of constructing the insulation fault location algorithm of power transformer based on Bayesian network, the positioning system design and simulation experiment are carried out. The experimental environment is: Using MATLAB simulation tool, Microsoft Windows XP operating system, Intel (R) Celeron (R) 2.6 GHz processor, 24 GB memory. Combined with PCI integrated information processor and relay transmission node network topology model, the on-line monitoring system of power transformer insulation fault is designed. Figure 2 is an on-line monitoring system for transformer insulation fault.

Fig. 2. On line monitoring system of transformer insulation fault

According to the above experimental environment, a total of 5000 fault samples, 2000 training samples and 3000 test samples were collected by the on-line monitoring system of power transformer insulation fault. The equivalent circuit model of on-line monitoring of power transformer insulation fault is shown in Fig. 3.

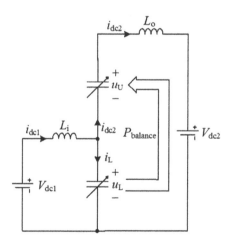

Fig. 3. Equivalent circuit model

In the equivalent circuit model shown in Fig. 3, the variable ratio of DC transformer is set to 0.23, the transmission power of converter is 2300 kW, and the average input voltage of upper and lower bridge arm is 200. The topological structure of fault location system is obtained as shown in Fig. 4.

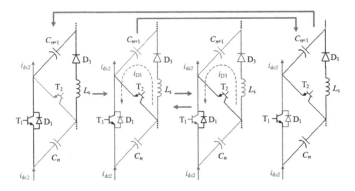

Fig. 4. Topology structure of the fault location system

According to the above system design, the fault location efficiency is tested, and the simulation results of fault location detection are shown in Fig. 5.

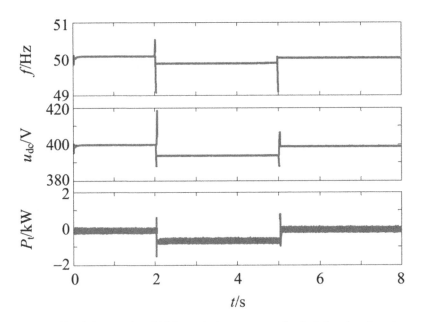

Fig. 5. Simulation results of high resolution spectrum for fault location detection

The analysis of Fig. 5 shows that the insulation fault location detection of power transformer can be effectively realized by using this method, and the accuracy of detection is high, and the peak value of high resolution spectrum is the fault location.

In order to further verify the effectiveness of the method in this paper, the accuracy of insulation fault location of power transformer in this method, literature [4] method and literature [5] method are compared and analyzed, and the comparison results are shown in Fig. 6.

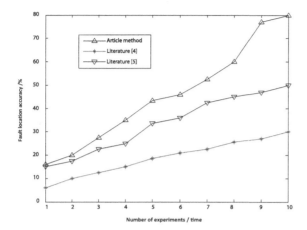

Fig. 6. Comparison results of fault location accuracy

According to Fig. 6, with the increase of the number of experiments, the insulation fault location accuracy of the power transformer in this method can reach up to 80%, while the insulation fault location accuracy of the power transformer in literature [4] and literature [5] is only 30% and 50%. The insulation fault location accuracy of the power transformer in this method is higher than that in literature [4] and literature [5], indicating that this method can accurately monitor the insulation fault of power transformer on line.

5   Conclusions

In this paper, an on-line monitoring method of insulation fault of power transformer based on Bayesian network is proposed. Based on the feature analysis of transformer insulation fault in power system, combined with large-scale fault feature data mining and clustering analysis method, the insulation fault discrimination of power transformer is realized, and the classification and identification ability of power transformer insulation fault is improved. The underdamped oscillation detection method is used to detect the initial voltage and underdamped oscillation component of power transformer insulation, the information is reconstructed from the input data, the Bayesian network detection model of power transformer insulation fault is constructed, and the convergence judgment in on-line monitoring of power transformer insulation fault is carried out by using adaptive machine tracking learning method. On-line monitoring of insulation fault of power transformer is carried out according to the distribution of load difference characteristics. It is found that the accuracy and automaticity of this method for insulation fault location of power transformer are high. And has a high power transformer insulation fault on-line monitoring effect. The research on the insulation fault diagnosis of power transformer has attracted much attention of researchers. In the future, the insulation state evaluation system of power transformer will be established, and the classification will be carried out to improve the on-line monitoring of the insulation fault of power transformer, further improve the intelligent diagnosis technology of transformer fault, and provide a new method for the condition based maintenance of transformer.

6   Fund Projects

The Key Research Project of High Education Natural Science of Anhui Province (NO. KJ2016A618).

The Key Research Project of High Education Natural Science of Anhui Xinhua University (NO. KJ2017zr001).

References

1. Ma, M., Wang, J., Wang, Z., Li, P., Xiong, L.: Transient stability analysis of the global phase portraits in multi-machine system. Proc. CSEE **39**(15), 4385–4394 (2019)
2. Wei, S., Yang, M., Han, X., et al.: Online identification for transient angle stability based on MLE index of phase trajectory. Autom. Electr. Power Syst. **41**(16), 71–79 (2017)
3. Zhou, Y., Wu, J., Yu, Z., et al.: Power system transient stability assessment based on cluster features of rotor angle trajectories. Power Syst. Technol. **40**(5), 1482–1487 (2016)
4. Martínez, Y.P., Vidal, C.: Classification of global phase portraits and bifurcation diagrams of Hamiltonian systems with rational potential. J. Differ. Equ. **261**(11), 5923–5948 (2016)
5. Wang, T., Chiang, H.D.: On the number of unstable equilibrium points on spatially-periodic stability boundary. IEEE Trans. Autom. Control **61**(9), 2553–2558 (2016)
6. Meng, H., Xu, H., Song, X.: Transformer fault diagnosis based on attribute reduction of rough set and SVM. Nanjing Hangkong Hangtian Daxue Xuebao/J. Nanjing Univ. Aeronaut. Astronaut. **49**(4), 504–510 (2017)
7. Arani, M.F.M., Mohamed, Y.A.R.I.: Analysis and performance enhancement of vector-controlled VSC in HVDC links connected to very weak grids. IEEE Trans. Power Syst. **32**(1), 684–693 (2017)
8. Zhang, H., Chen, W.: Tungsten oxide (WO3) micro balls composed of curly nanosheets for transformer fault gas diagnosis. J. Nanoelectron. Optoelectron. **12**(12), 1305–1308 (2017)
9. Guo, C., Liu, W., Zhao, C., Ni, X.: Small-signal dynamics and control parameters optimization of hybrid multi-infeed HVDC system. Int. J. Electr. Power Energy Syst. **98**, 409–418 (2018)
10. Ni, X., Gole, A.M., Zhao, C., Guo, C., et al.: An improved measure of AC system strength for performance analysis of multi-infeed HVDC systems including VSC and LCC converters. IEEE Trans. Power Delivery **33**(1), 169–178 (2018)
11. Sreewirote, B., Ngaopitakkul, A.: Analysis on behaviour of wavelet coefficient during fault occurrence in transformer. IOP Conf. Ser. Earth Environ. Sci. **127**(1), 012008 (2018)
12. Lim, K., Bastawrous, H.A., Duong, V.H., et al.: Fading Kalman filter-based real-time state of charge estimation in LiFePO4, battery-powered electric vehicles. Appl. Energy **169**, 40–48 (2016)

13. Di, B., Zhou, R., Dong, Z.N.: Cooperative localization and tracking of multiple targets with the communication-aware unmanned aerial vehicle system. Control Dec. **31**(04), 616–622 (2016)
14. Mejia-Barron, A., Valtierra-Rodriguez, M., Granados-Lieberman, D., et al.: Experimental data-based transient-stationary current model for inter-turn fault diagnostics in a transformer. Electr. Power Syst. Res. **152**, 306–315 (2017)
15. Majchrzak, V., Parent, G., Brudny, J.-F.: Influence of the electrical circuit configurations of a DVR coupling transformer with a magnetic bypass. COMPEL Int. J. Comput. Math. Electr. Electron. Eng. **36**(3), 804–810 (2017)

Mining and Analyzing Behavior Patterns of Smart Home Users Based on Cloud Computing

Xing-hua Lu[(✉)], Chang-shen Mo, Xiao-qi Wang, and Qing-qing Ma

Huali College Guangdong University of Technology, Guangzhou 511325, China
luxinghua5454565@163.com

Abstract. Aiming at the problem of poor robustness of traditional user behavior pattern mining analysis method, a cloud computing-based intelligent home user behavior pattern mining analysis method is designed. Intelligent household IoT from using cloud computing method and data mining the user behavior patterns, establish a two-layer neural network level of data is divided into 2 kinds, the user behavior mode by setting the input weight vector calculation after classifying data correlation between user behavior model, using Apriori algorithm, input minimum support and minimum confidence, on the basis of analyzing the correlation between data, and establish the user behavior mode decision tree, on the basis of complete analysis of cloud computing smart home user behavior patterns mining method design. Through the comparison experiment with the traditional method, it is concluded that the designed mining analysis method based on cloud computing has higher robustness, the proposed cloud computing-based intelligent home user behavior pattern mining method has good application space.

Keywords: Cloud computing · Smart home · User behavior pattern

1 Introduction

Smart home is a residential platform, using integrated wiring technology, network communication technology, security technology, automatic control technology, audio and video technology to integrate home life related facilities, and build an efficient management system for residential facilities and family schedules. Unlike traditional home systems, smart home systems based on IoT technology are systems that use communication networks to connect critical appliances and services and allow remote control, monitoring or access. According to the three-layer architecture of the Internet of Things, the first layer of the Internet of Things is a perceptual extension system, which is mainly responsible for collecting information and control equipment. The second layer is a heterogeneous converged ubiquitous communication network, which is mainly responsible for the interconnection and storage of heterogeneous networks. Processing; the third layer is the application and service layer, mainly responsible for data monitoring, data analysis, etc.

Published by Springer Nature Switzerland AG 2020. All Rights Reserved
Y.-D. Zhang et al. (Eds.): ICMTEL 2020, LNICST 326, pp. 124–135, 2020.
https://doi.org/10.1007/978-3-030-51100-5_11

Literature [3] based on the Internet of Things and cloud computing, research on smart home security access control technology, through analysis of existing home appliance control systems, propose improvements in remote control and information security, and apply the improved solution to home appliance control systems This system enables access based on webpage and Android smartphone control mode, and can wirelessly remotely control household appliances such as color TVs, air conditioners, and fans. Through the communication interface provided by the system, the scene mode control with security alarms and environmental monitoring in the home is realized. However, the robustness of this method is poor.

The method of reference [3] divides the behavior pattern of mobile users into three grades according to the degree of interest, namely, low interest, ZTE interest and pleasure, retaining the behavior pattern with high interest, eliminating the behavior pattern with low interest, and then mining the association rule of behavior pattern with higher interest degree by using data mining method. Use these rules to make certain recommended services to users in order to provide better service for mobile users. Although the method can classify user behavior patterns according to grade, it is not suitable for smart home users.

Through the mining and analysis of user behavior patterns, the home system can better understand the user's living habits, and design the electrical switch time and the electrical start-up amount according to the user's habits, so as to simplify the user's life, environmental protection and low power consumption. Cloud computing is a kind of distributed computing. It refers to the decomposition of huge data calculation processing programs into countless small programs through the network "cloud". Then, through the system composed of multiple servers, processing and analyzing these small programs to obtain the results. And return to the user. The related performance of cloud computing can meet the mining and analysis of intelligent user behavior patterns. Based on the above analysis, this paper studies the cloud computing-based smart home user behavior pattern mining analysis method, the following is the research content.

2   Cloud Computing-Based Smart Home User Behavior Pattern Mining Analysis Method

2.1   Cloud Computing Mining User Behavior Pattern Data

In the cloud computing environment, the user behavior pattern is mined. User functions are mined using Map and Reduce functions of the MapReduce parallel programming model. The main idea of MapReduce processing data is to divide a relatively large data set into smaller data sets, hand a small data set to each node in the cluster for calculation, and then aggregate the key-value pairs with the same key value. Then, it is handed over to different nodes for calculation and the final result is obtained [3]. The MapReduce mining data process diagram is shown below.

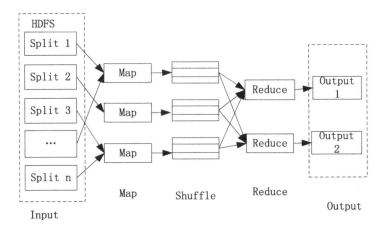

Fig. 1. Data mining process diagram

In the mining of smart home user behavior pattern data, each node calculates data from the smart home Internet of Things according to the data clustering principle. The calculation formula of each node, that is, the smart home user behavior pattern similarity matrix is as follows.

$$Q_{mn} = \begin{bmatrix} q_{11} & q_{12} & \cdots & q_{1n} \\ q_{21} & q_{22} & \cdots & q_{2n} \\ \vdots & \vdots & \ddots & \vdots \\ q_{m1} & q_{m2} & \cdots & q_{mn} \end{bmatrix} \tag{1}$$

In the formula (1), q_{mn} represents the similarity between the smart home user behavior pattern data m and the smart home user behavior pattern data template n. The similarity matrix between the data of the two smart home user behavior patterns is as shown in the following figure [4].

$$R_{mn} = \begin{bmatrix} r_{11} & r_{12} & \cdots & r_{1n} \\ & r_{22} & \cdots & r_{2n} \\ & & \ddots & \vdots \\ & & & r_{mn} \end{bmatrix} \tag{2}$$

In formula (2), R_{mn} represents the similarity between the two smart home user behavior pattern data of mode data m and mode data n.

According to the process diagram shown in Fig. 1, the user behavior pattern data in the smart home is extracted from the Internet of Things. Store the mined user behavior pattern data in HDFS. HDFS is able to split large file data into many small blocks of data. Modify the size of the block as needed. The default size is 64 MB. HDFS follows the three-way replication system, ensuring that files residing in HDFS remain unchanged in three different node assignments, as shown in the following figure [5] (Fig. 2).

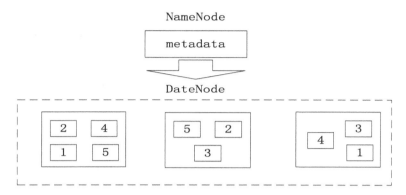

Fig. 2. HDFS block multi-copy storage

Storing with multiple copies allows you to read data from any node that has a block of data, thereby increasing the speed at which data is read. At the same time, it is also beneficial to compare between different copies to ensure the accuracy of the data. When a DataNode is down or the data disappears, it can be retrieved from other copies. When HDFS stores new files, it calculates its own checksum for the new file and keeps the checksum in its own namespace to hide the file independently. The checksum is sent to the client together with the data. After receiving the data, the client performs local check. If the locally calculated checksum is different from the checksum in the data, the data is sent incorrectly and needs to be retrieved from other nodes. This data. After mining the smart home user behavior pattern data using cloud computing, the user behavior patterns are classified for subsequent analysis and processing.

2.2   User Behavior Pattern Classification

In a smart home system, there are many variations in user behavior. In view of the classification of smart home users, they can be divided into entertainment, security, health and other categories. Considering the security of smart homes, this section divides all the user behavior patterns of cloud data storage into two types, which can be directly executed. And cannot be executed directly. The smart home user behavior mode that can be directly executed means that the user behavior action can be controlled by the smart home gateway and directly executed by the smart home terminal, without first confirming whether the event is executed by the user. The smart home behavior mode that cannot be directly executed means that this type of user action may affect the daily life of the user after execution, and may even affect the user's life safety. Such behavior requires the cloud to first alert the user through the smart home gateway after matching the user behavior. After the user selects, the smart home system will perform related events.

Set the primary input data set containing n data to $X = (x_1, x_2, \cdots, x_n)$, where $x_1, x_2, \cdots, x_{20}$ is used for primary mode identification and $x_{21}, x_{22}, \cdots, x_n$ is used for secondary mode classification. In these n items, if an item matches, the item is set to 1, and vice versa. With the use of users, the user's behavior pattern will continue to increase, and the primary and secondary mode classification modes are dynamically added in the smart home system [7].

After receiving the data, the cloud queries the data warehouse for the mode set of the user, and performs pattern matching on the data from the mode set. Finally, after competition, a pattern with the highest matching rate is obtained. The following figure shows a flow chart for classifying user behavior patterns using a classification algorithm (Fig. 3).

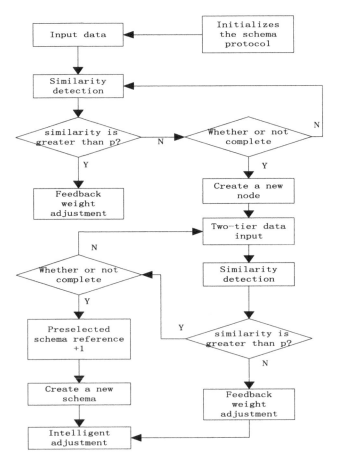

Fig. 3. User behavior pattern classification flow chart

First, initialize the weight vector: Since the system has not been trained yet, there can be only one neuron at the output, and there is no input from the outside world at this time, so the input weight vector is set as follows:

$$b_{ij}(0) = \frac{1}{1+n} \tag{3}$$

In formula (3), $b_{ij}(0)$ is the input weight vector, and the value is 90. Calculate data similarity and match the data [8]. Taking the similarity threshold of 0.8, the similarity between the data is calculated according to the similarity calculation formula shown in the following equation.

$$sim(u, v) = \frac{u \cdot v}{\sqrt{u^2}\sqrt{v^2}} \tag{4}$$

In formula (4), u is the matching template data in the database, v is the input data of the neural network, and $sim(u, v)$ is the degree of similarity. $sim(u, v)$ The smaller the value, the more similar the two data are [9]. In order to make the similarity ratio closer to 1 in the subsequent similar matching, the parameters are adjusted so that the output node can be better fused with the data. If the two data are not similar, that is, no suitable pattern matching is found in the data warehouse, then another level node is added to the neural network to make the large class match successfully.

The second layer of neural network pattern matching will be performed after matching to the large class. The overall process is similar to the first layer, except that after a matching pattern is not matched, a pre-selected mode is set. After the number of occurrences of this mode exceeds the threshold, the system will officially set it to the matching mode. After classifying user behavior, calculate the degree of association between user behaviors so that smart home adjustment control services.

2.3 User Behavior Correlation Calculation

What smart homes need is to discover user habits and provide the right services at the right time. Association rule mining is to discover the relationship between attributes in the database, and measure the relevance with support and credibility to meet the requirements.

The data set of the association rule mining is recorded as D, $D = \{t_1, t_2, \cdots, t_k, \ldots, t_n\}$, in the data set $t_k = \{i_1, i_2, \cdots, i_m, \ldots, i_p\}$. $t_k(k = 1, 2, \cdots, n)$ is called transaction, and $i_m(i = 1, 2, \ldots, p)$ is called item. Let $I = \{i_1, i_2, \cdots, i_m\}$ be the set of all the items in D and any subset W of I be called the set of items of D. The number of transactions in the data set D containing the item set W is referred to as the support number of the item set W, and is denoted as σ_w. The support of item set X is denoted as s(W), and the calculation formula is as follows.

$$s(W) = \frac{\sigma_w}{|D|} \times 100\% \tag{5}$$

In formula (5), $|D|$ is the number of transactions of transaction set D [10]. If $s(W)$ is not less than the minimum support specified by the user, then $s(W)$ is called a frequent item set. If W and V are item sets, and $W \cap V = \Phi$, implied formula $W \Rightarrow V$ is called an association rule, and W and V are respectively referred to as premise and conclusion of association rule $W \Rightarrow V$. The support level of item set $W \cap V = \Phi$ is called the support degree of association rule $W \Rightarrow V$, and is recorded as $s(W \Rightarrow V)$, namely:

$$s(W \Rightarrow V) = s(W \cup V) \tag{6}$$

The confidence level of association rule $W \Rightarrow V$ is recorded as $c(W \Rightarrow V)$, that is,

$$c(W \Rightarrow V) = \frac{s(W \cup V)}{s(W)} \times 100\% \tag{7}$$

After calculating the relevance degree of the smart home user behavior according to the above formula, the classified smart home user behavior data is subdivided again in the same category according to the degree of association.

According to the association rule, the threshold is set to 0.6. In the same user behavior pattern data category, all user behavior pattern data whose association value is greater than the threshold is grouped into one set. User behavior pattern data with a degree of association below the threshold is split into another collection. Until the smart home user behavior data in all categories is subdivided. Use algorithms to analyze smart home user behavior data.

2.4   Analyze User Behavior Pattern Data

Use the Apriori algorithm to analyze smart home users using home device activity associations. First, find all the frequency sets. These frequency sets appear at least at the same frequency as the predefined minimum support. Secondly, strong correlation rules are generated by the frequency set. These rules must meet the minimum support and minimum confidence. Third Use the frequency set found in the first step to generate the desired rule, and generate all the rules that only contain the set items, where each rule has only one right part, and the definition of the middle rule is used here. Once these rules are generated, only those rules that are greater than the minimum confidence given by the user are retained.

Before the Apriori algorithm starts running, input two parameters of minimum support $s(w)$ and minimum confidence $c(w \Rightarrow v)$, and initialize the array data and the vertical array two data structures. Scan the original transaction set to fill the corresponding array vector, and then generate the corresponding vertical array from the array vector. The transaction number of each item is supported by the vertical array statistics (that is, all the transaction numbers in the columns below each item), and the support count of each item needs to be calculated in combination with the number of occurrences of the corresponding transaction in the array vector, and then the support transaction is deleted. The number is less than the minimum support level of $s(w)$, which in turn leads to a frequent 1-item set. Count the number of frequent 1-item centralized transactions. If it is greater than 2, continue to execute downwards. If less than 2, the current 1-frequent item set is the result of the final frequent item set. Except for the transaction code whose transaction length is less than 2 in the vertical array, the candidate 2-item set is obtained by the two-two connection of the items in the frequent 1-item set. The transaction set supporting the candidate 2-item set can be generated by supporting the connection in the vertical array. The support transaction of the two transactions of the item is obtained by intersection, and the frequent 2-item set can be obtained by deleting the candidate 2-item with the support less than the minimum support. And so on, until all user behavior correlations are analyzed.

In order to enable the smart home system to provide services to users accurately and efficiently, a decision tree is established to analyze the user behavior patterns after analyzing the relevance. The data analyzed by the Apriori algorithm generates a data set containing many attributes according to the degree of association. To create a data set containing many attributes into a tree, you need to split the attributes of the data set. This paper chooses the splitting attribute with the maximum gain rate indicator.

The information gain rate is the ratio of the information gain to the amount of information divided. Assuming that the sample data set for training is H and the data set contains H_s tuples, $s = \{1, 2, \cdots, n\}$, the expectation is:

$$i(H) = -\sum_{s=1}^{n} \frac{H_s}{H} \log_2 \frac{H_s}{H} \tag{8}$$

Assume that attribute A has m values of $a_1, a_2, \cdots, a_m$ and divides sample data set H into $\{H_1, H_2, \cdots, H_m\}$. After dividing data set H according to A attribute, it continues to calculate the information entropy required for the next split:

$$i_A(H) = \sum_{j=1}^{n} \frac{|H_j|}{|H|} \times i(H_j) \tag{9}$$

The information gain is the difference between the original information demand and the new demand. The information gain rate normalizes the information gain using the "column information" value. Get the following

$$l_A(H) = -\sum_{j=1}^{n} \frac{|H_j|}{|H|} \times \log_2 \frac{|H_s|}{|H|} \tag{10}$$

This value represents information generated by dividing the training data set D into m partitions corresponding to the m outputs of the attribute A test. A preliminary user behavior decision tree model can be obtained as shown (Fig. 4):

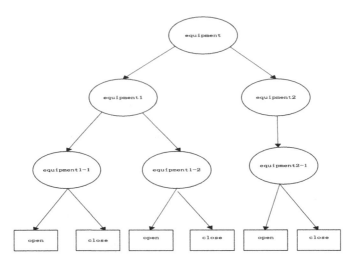

Fig. 4. User behavior decision tree

The smart home system provides users with corresponding services according to the user behavior decision tree, thereby improving the service efficiency of the smart home and reducing energy consumption. So far, the design of cloud computing-based intelligent home user behavior pattern mining analysis method has been completed.

3 Test Experiment

This paper designs a smart home user behavior pattern mining analysis method based on cloud computing. In order to verify the performance of the method, the comparison experiment between the design and the traditional method is carried out, and the relevant verification is completed through experiments.

3.1 Experimental Data Processing

The data used in this experiment is the power consumption data of 2 households for 2 weeks, and is collected by 3 electric meters. The first electric meter collection kitchen mainly includes a microwave oven, an oven, etc.; the second electric meter collects the laundry room, mainly including a washing machine and a drum type dry cleaning machine; and the third electric meter collects a water heater and an air conditioner. Because the data is inevitably erroneous, the missing data points are filled with the average of the last two numbers. The experimental data is processed on a computer configured as shown in the following table (Table 1).

Table 1. Data processing computer configuration.

Project	Configuration	Function
CPU	Intel Core i7-3596 3.25 GHz	Operating platform system
Hard disk	500 G	Storage of experimental data
Graphics chips	AMD RX57960	Drive display
Memory capacity	16 GB	–
Ethernet card	Intel PWLA8391GT	Connect to the internet
Operating system	Windows 8.1	Realize experimental operation

The processed experimental data was used as the experimental object of the experiment, and the relevant experimental verification was completed according to the experimental content.

3.2 Experimental Content

The experiment adopts the form of comparative experiment. The experiment group is the cloud computing-based smart home user behavior pattern mining analysis method designed in this paper. The experimental reference group is the traditional user behavior pattern mining analysis method. The experimental comparison index is the daily power consumption of the smart home system using the experimental group and the reference group. The robustness of the experimental group method and the reference group method is verified by comparing the experimental indexes. In the experimental environment shown in the figure below, the experimental verification is completed (Fig. 5).

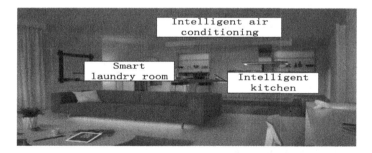

Fig. 5. Lab environment

3.3 Experimental Result

The experimental results are shown in the following table. The data in the table are analyzed and the corresponding experimental conclusions are obtained (Table 2).

Table 2. Power consumption (kW/h)

Experimental days	Experimental group	Control group
1	2.74	5.32
2	2.69	5.06
3	2.55	5.28
4	2.43	5.21
5	2.22	5.54
6	2.28	5.66
7	2.06	5.44
8	2.16	5.05
9	2.16	5.05
10	2.26	5.76
11	2.09	5.49
12	2.15	5.69
13	2.12	5.26
14	2.04	5.60

Analysis of the above table, in the two-week experiment process, the overall power consumption of the smart home system using the experimental group method has a downward trend, and the overall power consumption of the smart home system using the reference group method is constantly fluctuating. Analysis of the data in the table, the power consumption of the smart home system using the experimental group method is significantly lower than the power consumption of the application reference group method. The average power consumption of the smart home system using the experimental group method is 2.28 kW/h, and the average power consumption of the smart home system using the reference group method is 5.34 kW/h, and the reference group is about 2.35 times of the experimental group. In summary, the cloud computing-based smart home user behavior pattern mining analysis method designed in this paper has better robustness and can reduce the energy loss of smart home systems.

4   Conclusion

This paper designs a cloud computing-based smart home user behavior pattern mining analysis method, and compares it with the traditional method to verify that it has better robustness and good application space.

Fund Project: 2019 "climbing plan" Guangdong University Student Science and technology innovation and cultivation special fund project, project name: Based on big data intelligent home Internet of things user behavior pattern mining, project number: pdjh2019b0617.

References

1. Xiao, D., Wang, Q., Cai, M., et al.: Research on implicit interference detection based on knowledge graph in smart home automation. Chin. J. Comput. **42**(06), 1190–1204 (2019)
2. Gao, Y., Bao, F.: Research on mobile user behavior mining integrated with location scenarios. Math. Pract. Theory **48**(16), 72–84 (2018)
3. Wang, Y.: Research on smart home security access control technology based on internet of things and cloud computing. Video Eng. **42**(08), 147–150 (2018)
4. Zhai, P., Fang, X., Liu, X., et al.: Decomposed mining method for process model based on behavior feature net. Comput. Integr. Manuf. Syst. **24**(07), 1690–1697 (2018)
5. Luo, H., Yang, Y., Wang, J., et al.: A cloud computing based mobile user behavior analysis system. Control Eng. China **25**(02), 218–223 (2018)
6. Zhang, Z., Zhang, S., Zeng, J.: Method of attacking temporal pattern privacy of users' behavior in social media. Comput. Eng. Appl. **53**(17), 14–19 (2017). +142
7. Chen, X., Xiao, B.: Emerging sequences pattern mining based on location information. Comput. Sci. **44**(07), 175–179 (2017)
8. Ge, X., Ren, C., Duan, J.: Analysis and research on user behavior patterns in the perspective of socialized electronic commerce. J. Anhui Electr. Eng. Prof. Tech. Coll. **22**(02), 91–95 (2017)
9. Li, S., Liu, J., Shao, F.: Analysis of user's browsing interest data mining combining Web log with user's browsing behavior. Mod. Electron. Tech. **40**(05), 22–25 (2017)
10. Shi, D., Li, H., Yang, R., et al.: Mining user frequent behavior patterns in daily life. J. Natl. Univ. Defense Technol. **39**(01), 74–80 (2017). Author, F.: Article title. Journal 2(5), 99–110 (2016)

Research on Behavior Recognition Method Based on Machine Learning and Fisher Vector Coding

Xing-hua Lu$^{(\boxtimes)}$, Zi-yue Yuan, Xiao-hong Lin, and Zi-qi Qiu

Huali College Guangdong University of Technology, Guangzhou 511325, China
luxinghua5454565@163.com

Abstract. Aiming at the problem that the existing behavior recognition method can not extract the human body interaction area, resulting in low recognition rate, a behavior recognition method based on machine learning and Fisher vector coding is proposed. Constructing artificial neural network based on machine learning, designing the main steps of backward propagation neural network, making the cost function minimum; using the depth continuity of the image to extract the foreground part of the video motion, multiplying with the corresponding 2D video frame to detect the time domain motion Behavior; Solving the dual quadratic programming problem of Fisher support vector machine, obtaining its optimal solution and completing behavior learning; segmenting the current frame image, solving the normal vector to extract the moving target, and completing the behavior recognition method based on machine learning and Fisher vector coding the study. In order to verify the effectiveness of the design method, a comparative experiment was designed. The experimental results show that the average recognition accuracy of the design method is 7.6% higher than the traditional method.

Keywords: Machine learning · Fisher vector coding · Behavior recognition

1 Introduction

Behavior recognition is a technique that uses computer vision techniques to determine whether a particular behavior exists in an image or video sequence. Machine learning has a wide range of applications, especially in the fields of intelligent video surveillance, traffic, and criminal investigation. Therefore, the behavior recognition of machine learning appearance image matching has received more and more attention. Since the two-dimensional image itself is a projection of a three-dimensional object and cannot reflect the space of the real world, an error may occur when extracting the human interaction area. Machine learning and Fisher vector coding have the characteristics of clustering, and the depth values of the same object or objects in contact with each other are continuous. The method in [1] was used to construct a risk prediction model of acute kidney injury (AKI) in severe burn patients, and the prediction performance of machine learning and logistic regression models were compared. Methods The clinical data of 157 patients who met the inclusion criteria for severe burns during the aluminum dust explosion in the "82" Kunshan plant were collected. Univariate

Y.-D. Zhang et al. (Eds.): ICMTEL 2020, LNICST 326, pp. 136–147, 2020.
https://doi.org/10.1007/978-3-030-51100-5_12

analysis was used to screen for factors that may be related to the occurrence of AKI, including patient gender, age, admission time, basic injury, initial admission score, treatment status, and mortality at 30, 60, and 90 days after injury. Mann-Whitney U test, $\chi 2$ test, and Fisher's exact probability test were performed on the data. The P value of 0.1 in univariate analysis and variables that may have clinical significance were included in the construction of the prediction model, and the logistic regression analysis and XGBoost machine learning algorithm were used to construct the AKI prediction model. Calculate the area under the receiver's working characteristic curve (AUC), and the sensitivity and specificity under the optimal threshold. This method, though, identifies clinical symptoms in patients with statistical significance. However, the sample data analyzed by it has screening indicators, so it negates the significance of individual cases and has inaccurate problems. At present, there are many designs for the first and second floors in the smart home field, but in order to realize the true sense of intelligence, in addition to obtaining information and transmitting information, it is necessary to analyze the living data. The development of smart homes can not only rely on the improvement of technology level, but also from the perspective of simple and environmental protection. Therefore, designing smart homes with harmonious interaction has more development prospects.

The existing behavior recognition method can not extract human body interaction area, resulting in low recognition rate. Based on this, this paper proposes a behavior recognition method based on machine learning and Fisher vector coding [2]. Constructing artificial neural network based on machine learning, designing the main steps of backward propagation neural network, making the cost function minimum; using the depth continuity of the image to extract the foreground part of the video motion, multiplying with the corresponding 2D video frame to detect the time domain motion Behavior; Solving the dual quadratic programming problem of Fisher support vector machine, obtaining its optimal solution, completing behavior learning; segmenting the current frame image, solving the normal vector to extract the moving target, and completing the behavior recognition method based on machine learning and Fisher vector coding the study.

2 Research on Behavior Recognition Method Based on Machine Learning and Fisher Vector Coding

The machine learning-based behavior recognition mainly includes the construction of artificial neural network, detecting the time domain motion behavior, using the coding vector to complete the learning, and finally implementing the behavior recognition based on machine learning and Fisher vector coding. The specific process of behavior recognition is shown in Fig. 1:

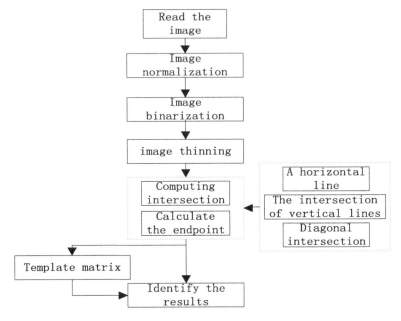

Fig. 1. Behavior recognition process

According to the above process of behavior recognition, the behavior recognition method based on machine learning and Fisher vector coding is studied.

2.1 Building Artificial Neural Network Based on Machine Learning

Machine learning is a scientific rule that uses computers to learn data and to obtain new knowledge and technology by turning data into useful information. This paper uses backward propagation, and the neural network structure is shown in Fig. 2:

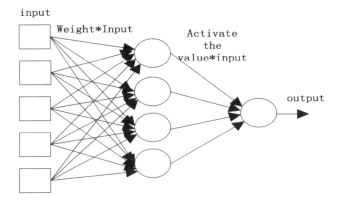

Fig. 2. Back propagation neural network structure

The artificial neural network based on machine learning is a statistical learning algorithm inspired by the biological field. A backward propagation neural network consists of the forward and backward propagation of the input layer, hidden layer and output layer [3]. In detail, backward propagation means that the input signal comes from the input layer, passes through the hidden layer, and is passed to the output layer. If the output layer achieves the expected result, the algorithm ends. Otherwise, the wrong result will propagate back to the output layer through the original connection path and loop continuously to get the error that minimizes the cost function. Before these steps, in order to calculate the activation value, an activation function is set between the input layer and the hidden layer, the hidden layer, and the output layer, as shown in Eq. (1):

$$f(x) = \frac{1}{1 + e^{-\theta x}} \tag{1}$$

In the above formula, $e^{-\theta x}$ represents the training precision during the activation process. The activation function is monotonically increasing and continuous smooth. By setting the parameters, the function can balance the linear and nonlinear relationship, and the function is biased. The calculation of the wrong backpropagation is very important. The number of hidden layers is determined by the number of input and output layers. The gradient descent algorithm is used to mediate the sum of the minimum error squares, which is a common method for training backward propagation neural networks. The training steps for the entire machine learning are shown in Fig. 3:

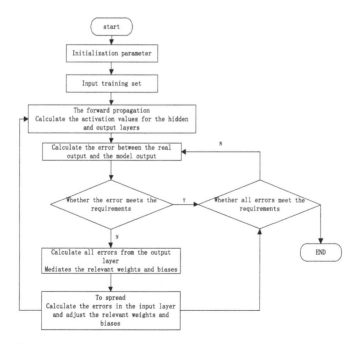

Fig. 3. The main steps of the backward propagation neural network

It is critical to choose a reasonable number of hidden layers. Generally speaking, empirical formulas that are generally accepted by the academic community can be used to obtain parameters. Weight values can be connected to two adjacent layers. The bias term is the mediation input in each layer. Useful items. So far, the construction of the structure and algorithm steps of the artificial neural network based on machine learning is completed.

2.2 Detecting Time Domain Motion Behavior

In order to effectively extract the motion template of the characters in the video stream, this paper uses the weighted cumulative frame difference method to extract the motion time domain. Since the RGB image itself is a two-dimensional projection of a three-dimensional object, in which the depth information of the object is lost, it is inevitable that the segmentation of the RGB video frame will result in over-segmentation or under-segmentation [4]. According to the depth continuity of the depth image, the foreground portion of the video motion can be roughly extracted, and then multiplied by the corresponding two-dimensional video frame to remove the background. On this basis, the weighted cumulative frame difference calculation is performed, and the interference of background noise is effectively removed by this method, and the calculation efficiency is improved. The motion area is then detected in the 2D video frame from which the background is removed. Calculate the time domain difference using the weighted cumulative frame difference method:

$$
\begin{aligned}
A(t) = {} & \omega_{t-n}|f_{t-n}(x,y) - |f_t(x,y)| + \\
& \omega_{t-n+1}|f_{t-n+1}(x,y) - |f_t(x,y)| + \cdots + \\
& \omega_{t-1}|f_{t-1}(x,y) - |f_t(x,y)| + \\
& \omega_{t+1}|f_{t+1}(x,y) - |f_t(x,y)| + \cdots + \\
& \omega_{t+n-1}|f_{t+n-1}(x,y) - |f_t(x,y)| + \\
& \omega_{t+n}|f_{t+n}(x,y) - |f_t(x,y)|
\end{aligned}
\tag{2}
$$

In formula (2), $f(x,y,t)$ represents the video sequence [5] in the GRB image, and the t time frame is $f_t(x,y)$, ω_i is used to indicate the influence of the n frames before and after the tth time [9]. The value of ω_i is expressed as:

$$
\omega_i = \frac{|i|^{-1}}{2\sum_{i=1}^{n} i^{-1}}
\tag{3}
$$

The moving target time_motion region of the time domain portion of the video can be obtained by the above formula. Although multiplication of RGB images with depth images can eliminate some of the interference of complex backgrounds, the depth maps are also affected by noise and other factors in the acquisition. At the same time, there are also parts of the background and the moving human body that have continuous depth, so this part is extracted. The boundary of the human motion area is not clear, and there is also a hollow phenomenon in some motion areas, so it is necessary to extract the human boundary image of the video static frame.

2.3   Using Fisher Vector Coding to Complete Behavior Learning

The Fisher vector uses the GMM model to model the feature points, and calculates the likelihood function gradient to represent the vector of each image according to the parameters of the model. GMM refers to the estimation of the probability density distribution of the image samples [6], usually using two Gaussian distributions are fitted simultaneously. The GMM data is composed of K Gaussian model, and the image is divided into T descriptors. It is assumed that each feature x_i of the image is independently and identically distributed. Both sides take the logarithm at the same time, and the linear combination of Gaussian distribution is used to approximate the description. p_i refers to the Gaussian distribution of feature x_i:

$$\lambda = \{\omega_i, \mu_i, \sigma_i, i = 1, \ldots, K\} \tag{4}$$

In the above formula, ω_i is the weighting coefficient of the i model, μ_i is its first-order mean, and σ_i is the second-order standard deviation. In the process of behavior recognition using Fisher vector coding, the field of pattern recognition technology is involved. The main step of adopting this method is to introduce Fisher's regularity into the support vector machine method and use it for behavior recognition to obtain high-dimensional data for small samples. A better recognition rate, and thus a better recognition of behavior. First, the behavior training video is processed to obtain the sample set:

$$\{(x_i, y_i) | x_i \in R_n, y_i \in \{-1, +1\}\} \\ i = 1, \ldots, l \tag{5}$$

In the above formula, x_i indicates the behavior characteristic in a video, that is, one training sample in the n dimensional real space, and y_i is its identification, indicating that the category is not +1 or −1, and l is the number of samples. The process of obtaining samples is to stack the behaviors directly into an n-dimensional feature [7], or use a feature extraction method to extract n features for training learning. Select the regular factors λ_1 and λ_2, select the positive definite kernel function and its parameters, and calculate the kernel matrix. The role of λ_1 is to control the complexity of the hypothesis space, and the role of λ_2 is to control Fisher's regular influence. The positive definite kernel function is a kernel function that satisfies the positive definite condition and is expressed as:

$$k(x, x^{'}) = (\phi(x))^T \phi(x^{'}) \tag{6}$$

In the above formula, $x, x^{'}$ represents two learning samples, ϕ represents an implicit nonlinear mapping function, and superscript T represents the transposition of a matrix or vector, which can determine a reproducing kernel space in which space, there is a representation theorem that the hypothetical function can be expressed as:

$$f(x) = w^T \phi(x) + b$$
$$= \sum_{i=1}^{l} \alpha_i k(x, x_i) + b \qquad (7)$$
$$= K\alpha + b$$

In the above formula, α and b are the spheroidal coefficients in the hypothesis function, and w is the weight vector, which can be calculated by the following expression:

$$w = \sum_{i=1}^{l} \alpha_i \phi(x_i) = \Psi \alpha \qquad (8)$$

The dual quadratic programming problem of Fisher support vector machine can be solved [8], and the optimal solution is obtained to complete the behavior learning.

2.4 Behavior Recognition

In order to realize behavior recognition, it is necessary to segment the current frame image by spatial domain target detection, thereby extracting a moving target. At the same time, the depth image is a new data source, which embodies the depth information of objects in the image, and the depth information belonging to the same object has continuity characteristics [9]. Therefore, the depth information can be combined to effectively segment the moving target. In the depth map, the normal vector of the surface of the object can effectively represent the geometric information of the object, and the normal vector of the same object surface has only a gradual change from far and near, and a strong mutation information is generated for different objects. Using the normal vector information can effectively extract the edge features of the object. The schematic diagram of the normal vector is shown in the following figure:

Fig. 4. Schematic diagram of surface normal vector

In Fig. 4, the right image is a depth map, and the position of any point in the figure is $P = (x, y)$, and the depth value of the coordinate value is $d(x, y)$, so each pixel in the depth map can be represented by $P = [x, y, d(x, y)]$, which is The method describes an object by combining spatial information in a three-dimensional coordinate system, which is essentially different from the intensity value and spatial information of the RGB image. The normal vector of point $P = (x, y)$ in the depth map can be expressed in the form of a vector cross product:

$$N = S_x \times S_y \tag{9}$$

In the above formula, S_x is the horizontal vector cross of the point, S_y is the longitudinal vector cross of the point, and the two vector forks are calculated in detail to obtain the formula:

$$S_x = \frac{\upsilon}{\upsilon x} \begin{bmatrix} x \\ y \\ d(x, y) \end{bmatrix} \tag{10}$$

$$S_y = \frac{\upsilon}{\upsilon y} \begin{bmatrix} x \\ y \\ d(x, y) \end{bmatrix} \tag{11}$$

Equation (9) can be transformed to get the normal vector of the point:

$$N = S_x \times S_y = \begin{bmatrix} \frac{-\upsilon d(x,y)}{\upsilon x} \\ \frac{-\upsilon d(x,y)}{\upsilon y} \\ 1 \end{bmatrix} \tag{12}$$

After obtaining the normal vector of depth, it is also necessary to fuse the extracted edge features. In this paper, the principle of blending edges is: when a point has only θ or φ detected edges, the feature is accepted, and when there are two corner edges, the simultaneous acceptance and weighted average is adopted [10]. By detecting the edge of the object in the depth map, the resulting human contour is space_motion region. Through the obtained outline, the recognition of the behavior is completed. So far, the research on behavior recognition method based on machine learning and Fisher vector coding has been completed.

3   Experimental Study

In order to verify the effectiveness of the identification method designed in this paper, it is necessary to carry out experiments together with the traditional identification methods, and analyze and compare the experimental results.

3.1   Experimental Preparation

In this paper, the CAD-120 data set was selected experimentally. Setting up the data set consists of 4 experimenters demonstrating 10 different actions, each performed by a different experimenter 3 times. Actions include taking medicine, picking up things, eating, cleaning things, etc. The experimenter performs the same activities with different objects, and the same action of different experimenters also has a background change. The specific parameters of the experiments that need to be used are shown in Table 1:

Table 1. Experimental parameters

The serial number	Project	Parameter
1	Operating system	Windows 7.0
2	Processor	Intel core i5
3	System environment	8 G Lenovo V310
4	Software platform	Matlab2015(a)

Under the above experimental preparation, the experiment was carried out by the conventional method and the method designed in the present paper.

3.2 Experimental Method

In order to improve the credibility of the experiment, the experiment is divided into three parts: In test 1, for each action, one of each experimenter's demonstration is selected as the training set, and the rest is used as the test set. In Test 2, for each action, select two of each experimenter's presentation as the training set, and the rest as the test set. In Test 3, for each action, the actions demonstrated by two experimenters are selected as the training set, and the actions of the remaining two experimenters are used as the test set. For each of the above tests, each test was repeated 100 times, and the confusion level table was obtained, and the recognition rate was analyzed according to the confusion level table, and the accuracy of each test was averaged.

3.3 Experimental Results and Analysis

Under the above experimental environment and experimental method, the experimental results of the two methods in the three tests are obtained. In order to more accurately and intuitively reflect the accuracy of the identification of the two methods, it is necessary to pass the Matlab2015(a) software to the test. Identify the situation for analysis. Due to the similar situation in the test, it is necessary to analyze the degree of confusion between the two methods, and the results of the confusion of the results are shown in Figs. 5 and 6:

	1	2	3	4	5	6	7	8	9	10
1	0.95					0.05				
2		0.91								
3			0.93							
4				0.97						
5					0.99					
6	0.03					0.93				
7							0.91		0.04	
8				0.02				0.96		
9									0.92	
10								0.05		0.94

Fig. 5. Action confusion map of the method

	1	2	3	4	5	6	7	8	9	10
1	0.88			0.10						
2		0.91								0.01
3			0.89				0.08			
4	0.13		0.01	0.85						
5					0.93				0.01	
6			0.08		0.13	0.84				
7							0.86			0.04
8								0.90		
9			0.09			0.11		0.09	0.93	
10										0.84

Fig. 6. Traditional method of action confusion map

In the above two figures, the 1–10 actions are: 1 for planting cereals, 2 for taking medicine, 3 for stacking items, 4 for split piles, 5 for microwave food, 6 for picking things, 7 for cleaning items, 8 For eating, 9 is for items, and 10 for eating. By analyzing the two confusion degree maps, the average recognition rate of the two methods is obtained, as shown in Table 2:

Table 2. Average recognition rate of the two methods

The serial number	Methods of this paper	The traditional method
Test 1	91.3%	90.3%
Test 2	95.1%	86.4%
Test 3	82.6%	69.7%
Average recognition rate	89.7%	82.1%

In this test, action 1 (planting grain) and action 6 (squatting things) are similar, action 2 (medication) and action 8 (eat) are similar. Table 1 shows that the method is identified in test 2. The highest accuracy rate is the lowest in the test three. In Test 2, there are more data sets for training, so the accuracy rate is higher than that of the test. In Test 3, the data sets for training and testing are respectively demonstrated by different experimenters, so there are intra-class changes of the same action. Larger, resulting in lower accuracy. The average recognition accuracy of this paper is 89.7%, and the average recognition accuracy of traditional methods is 82.1%, which verifies the effectiveness of the proposed method.

4 Conclusion

The existing behavior recognition method can not extract the human body interaction area, resulting in low recognition rate. Therefore, the behavior recognition method based on machine learning and Fisher vector coding is proposed. Constructing artificial neural network based on machine learning, designing the main steps of backward propagation neural network, making the cost function minimum; using the depth continuity of the image to extract the foreground part of the video motion, multiplying with the corresponding 2D video frame to detect the time domain motion Behavior; Solving the dual quadratic programming problem of Fisher support vector machine, obtaining its optimal solution and completing behavior learning; segmenting the current frame image, solving the normal vector to extract the moving target, and completing the behavior recognition method based on machine learning and Fisher vector coding the study. In order to verify the effectiveness of the design method, a comparative experiment was designed. The experimental results show that the average recognition accuracy of the design method is 7.6% higher than the traditional method.

5 Fund Project

2019 "climbing plan" Guangdong University Student Science and technology innovation and cultivation special fund project, project name: Research on behavior recognition method based on dense trajectory and Fisher vector coding, project number: pdjh2019b0615.

References

1. Tang, C., Li, J., Xu, D., et al.: Comparison of machine learning method and logistic regression model in prediction of acute kidney injury in severely burned patients. Chin. J. Burns **34**(6), 343–348 (2018)
2. Li, L., Luo, H.-q.: Human action recognition with weighted feature fusion based on STIP and dense trajectory feature. Microelectron. Comput. **34**(04), 110–114 (2017)
3. Qian, M., Zhang, D., Jiang, H.: Recognizing construction worker activities based on accelerometers. J. Tsinghua Univ. (Sci. Technol.) **57**(12), 1338–1344 (2017)
4. Li, Z., Wan, Q., Liu, Y., et al.: Non rigid 3D model retrieval method based on fisher vector encoding and distance learning. J. Comput. Aided Des. Comput. Graph. **30**(7), 1297 (2018)
5. Nguyen, X.S., Nguyen, T.P., Charpillet, F., Vu, N.-S.: Local derivative pattern for action recognition in depth images. Multimedia Tools Appl. **77**(7), 8531–8549 (2017). https://doi.org/10.1007/s11042-017-4749-z

6. Perota, A., Lagutina, I., Quadalti, C., et al.: 203 Single-step gene editing of 3 xenoantigens in porcine fibroblasts using programmable nucleases. Reprod. Fertil. Dev. **29**(1), 210 (2017)
7. He, J., Xue, Y., Li, S., et al.: Head re-identification by local Fisher vector encoded and cross-view quadratic discriminant analysis. J. Tianjin Univ. Technol. **35**(01), 9–15
8. Chen, Z., Wu, S., Fan, B.: Fisher discriminant analysis based on stacked autoencoders. J. S. China Normal Univ. (Nat. Sci. Edn.) **49**(03), 117–122 (2017)
9. Wu, Q., Zhao, X.: Incremental learning algorithm of support vector machine based on vector projection of Fisher discriminant. J. Xi'an Univ. Posts Telecommun. **23**(01), 79–84 (2018)
10. Li, K., Zhang, X., Zhang, M., et al.: n/γ Pulse shape discrimination in Cs2 LiYCl6:Ce3 + crystal using fisher linear discriminant. At. Energy Sci. Technol. **51**(11), 2069–2074 (2017). Author, F.: Article title. Journal 2(5), 99–110 (2016)

Data Scheduling Method of Social Network Resources Based on Multi-Agent Technology

Xing-hua Lu$^{(\boxtimes)}$, Ling-feng Zeng, Hao-han Huang, and Wei-hao Yan

Huali College Guangdong University of Technology, Guangzhou 511325, China
luxinghua5454565@163.com

Abstract. Aiming at the problem that the traditional scheduling method can't deal with a large number of data quickly when dealing with social network resource data, a new scheduling method of social network resource data based on multi-Agent technology is proposed. Firstly, the social network scheduling framework is designed, using the two-level structure of Agent and three CDN management domains to hide the distribution and heterogeneity of different resources, setting the upper limit trigger conditions of data in each management domain of the framework, using reasoning tools to infer and calculate the SLA comprehensive level of each network operation node, calculating the proportion difference between various resources, selecting the appropriate bias a two-stage resource scheduling method is used to realize resource data scheduling. The experimental results show that: compared with the traditional scheduling method, the social network resource data scheduling method based on multi-Agent technology can maintain the processing time in about 10 s with the increase of data volume, and the processing time is shorter, which is more suitable for practical use.

Index Terms: Multi Agent technology · Social network resources · Data scheduling · Processing time

1 Introduction

Agent technology has become a hot topic in the 1990s, even referred to as the next far-reaching breakthrough in the field of software by some literatures. One of the important reasons is that Agent technology is the mainstream technology in the field of computer technology in the network distributed computing, which is also playing an increasingly important role. On the one hand, Agent technology provides an effective way to solve new distributed application problems. On the other hand, it provides a reasonable conceptual model for the comprehensive and accurate study of the characteristics of distributed computing system. The concept and technology of Agent appear in the development of distributed application system, which shows obvious effectiveness [1].

Agent has its own computing resources and its own behavior control mechanism. It can decide and control its own behavior according to its internal state and perceived environmental information without direct external manipulation. Agent can interact with other Agent and implement flexible and diverse interaction with Agent communication language, and can work effectively with other Agent. For example, a user on

Y.-D. Zhang et al. (Eds.): ICMTEL 2020, LNICST 326, pp. 148–158, 2020.
https://doi.org/10.1007/978-3-030-51100-5_13

the Internet needs to use the Agent communication language to present information requirements to the active service Agent. The Agent can sense the environment and respond to related events [2].

Scheduling method refers to the method used by the dispatchers of automobile transportation enterprises when they perform vehicle scheduling. The main scheduling method is empirical scheduling. Experiential scheduling is carried out by means of simple and visualized tools, such as using marks on the scheduling board or transportation network diagram to display the vehicle running dynamics and arrange the vehicle running routes. Using the method of mathematics or artificial intelligence combined with electronic computer to make the plan, at the same time using modern communication technology to transmit and feedback scheduling information, commanding and supervising the vehicle operation, the research on the social network resource data scheduling method based on multi-Agent technology can schedule the social resources in the way of data, and more reasonable allocation of social resources.

2   Data Scheduling Method of Social Network Resources Based on Multi-Agent Technology

2.1   Design the Social Network Scheduling Framework

When designing the social network scheduling framework, virtualization technology is used to hide the distribution and heterogeneity between different resources, so that the network resource data is no longer an independent entity, but all resources are integrated together, so that many virtual machines form a virtual resource pool, which is managed by the management system, the preliminary design of the management framework is shown in the Fig. 1 below:

When there are application request resources, the above management framework will allocate corresponding amount of resources from the resource pool to provide the service in the form of virtual machine. When the application request is completed, the service will release the resources, the system will recycle the virtual machine and put the released resources back to the resource pool. Users do not need to care about the structure and specific implementation methods of the system, but only about the quality of their own services. Because there are different users in the social network and different users have different needs, there will be a great demand fluctuation in the network access end, which requires that the management and scheduling of resources in the network management system can dynamically meet the needs of users and solve the resource utilization rate and application availability, to achieve on-demand allocation [3].

According to the nature of the Agent itself, integrate the framework of Fig. 1, use the interaction between each Agent, combine the learning and adaptability of the Agent, and make automatic adjustment for the current environment. When scheduling, multiple Agent are used. Through coordination and cooperation, the system can make reasonable arrangements for different goals, and finally form an overall scheme. Therefore, when integrating the design framework of Fig. 1, the first level Agent can effectively manage and schedule network resources by controlling multiple second

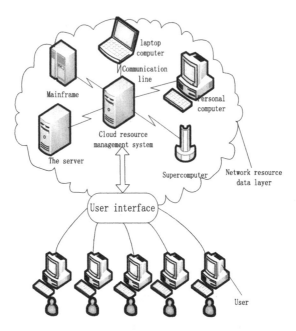

Fig. 1. Management framework designed

level Agent. Then use the hierarchical architecture, two-level structure and three CDN management domains, and appropriately increase the number of Agents and the number of Agent management domains in each layer, the overall framework structure is shown in Fig. 2 below:

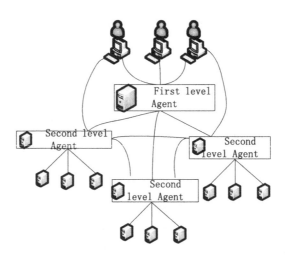

Fig. 2. Architecture diagram for integrating Agent technology

Using the architecture diagram designed in the above figure, the number of monitoring items includes memory utilization and network utilization. In actual monitoring, we only need to ensure that the user determines the upper limit of the amount of usage in the process of establishing the virtual machine instance, that is, the upper limit of the memory size and the bandwidth of the virtual machine can be satisfied without affecting the operation of the scheduling task in the virtual machine. In this way, only the sum of the upper limit of memory and the upper limit of bandwidth of all virtual machine instances on the host needs to be guaranteed within the range of memory and bandwidth resources owned by the physical server. However, in terms of cost, users usually want to use the actual amount of resources used by the virtual machine to count the use of the virtual machine, so a relatively complex scheduling method is needed to schedule effectively, and then set an upper limit trigger condition [4].

2.2   Set the Upper Limit Trigger Condition

The factors that need to be considered for the upper limit trigger conditions mainly include utilization, memory utilization and network utilization. These three monitoring factors represent two different monitoring standards and cannot be monitored by a unified measurement method. Therefore, the three monitoring factors are divided into two groups. The first group is quality monitoring item, which only includes utilization. The main reason why it is called quality monitoring item is that its performance, that is, the computing power provided by the computing center, cannot be measured by the utilization of virtual machine instances alone, because even though the utilization of a specific virtual machine is very low, other virtual machine loads on the same host are the same all of them are very high, resulting in a very high utilization rate of the host, resulting in less time slice allocated by the host to each virtual machine instance, so its computing power is still very low, so it is unscientific to use the utilization rate of the virtual machine as the measurement standard of the virtual machine performance [5].

Another measure is to represent the performance of all virtual machines on the host through the utilization of the host of each virtual machine. This measurement standard is more scientific than the former one, because the higher the utilization rate of the host computer is, the busier the host computer is, the less time can be allocated to each virtual machine, and its computing power will be lower for each virtual machine. This measurement method will perform well in the data center of the same structure, that is, the configuration of the running nodes in the data center is the same. However, due to the different computing power requirements of virtual machine instances running on the work nodes, and the servers in the data center are often heterogeneous, that is, the configuration of servers is often different. Because each running node is different, there are some differences in the computing power between CPUs. Therefore, there must be a big deviation in using the CPU utilization rate to measure the CPU performance of each running node. Therefore, when inferring the upper limit, use the inference tool to synthesize the data value processed by CPU to get the upper limit trigger condition. Use the inference tool as shown in the following Fig. 3 to infer the upper limit trigger condition:

After using reasoning tools, SLA is used to enhance the data quality of conditions. Before evaluation, a group of representative computing tasks will be generated, which

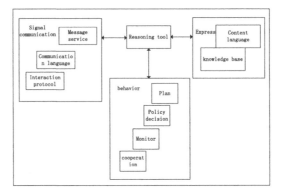

Fig. 3. Reasoning tools used

represent different aspects of CPU computing power, and specify the ideal completion time of each task. After that, the completion time of each task is calculated by executing this group of tasks in all running nodes. Through the combination of these two data and SLA level strategy, the SLA level of each node for each task is calculated. And sum up all SLA levels of each node, and then calculate the SLA comprehensive level of each running node. This is a measure of the CPU's computing power based on the quality of work. It allows the CPU to perform real tasks, and then evaluate its computing power according to its performance. In this way, there is no problem of heterogeneous servers to affect the evaluation of CPU performance of running nodes. And through the selection of SLA level strategy, it can effectively highlight the sensitivity of each virtual machine to the change of CPU computing power and effectively guarantee the work quality of virtual machines with high demand for CPU [6].

One of the problems that should be considered is the virtual machine migration triggered by the instantaneous peak value of all monitoring items on the work node. In the process of virtual machine running, the instantaneous utilization of a monitoring item may increase for some reason, but it will return to the normal level only for a short time. When the monitoring items exceed the preset threshold, the virtual machine will be migrated. When the instantaneous peak value is encountered, many unnecessary migrations will be carried out to reduce the overall performance of the data center, and this instantaneous peak value often occurs. So when calculating the upper limit, follow the flow chart below (Fig. 4):

Run the device at the running node, execute the pre-defined test tasks on all the running nodes every t, record the execution time of each task, calculate the integration $L = (l_1, l_2, l_3, \ldots, l_n)$ of SLA level L of each node for each task combined with the expected execution time of each task, finally calculate the SLA comprehensive level Lr of each node r, and complete the upper limit setting [7].

2.3 Determine Scheduling Parameters

When determining the scheduling parameters, first deploy the tasks that users apply for various types of resources to the cloud to complete their application deployment or

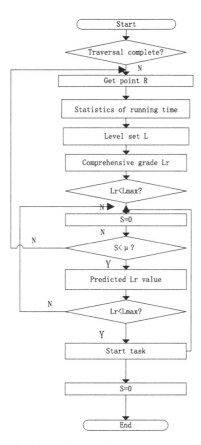

Fig. 4. Execution process

calculation work. Different types of users work with different resource requirements, in addition, the physical devices in the cloud environment data center have different specifications, to design an effective method to get the optimal creation scheme of the virtual machine, make efficient use of resources, reduce resource waste, and at the same time, make the available resources in the cloud be allocated to many users fairly, this is the question that needs to be considered in the resource scheduling algorithm of the virtual machine layer question. Using a game theory based fairness effectiveness trade-off resource scheduling algorithm to solve the resource scheduling problem considering the fairness of resource utilization and resource allocation [8].

In the process of scheduling, we should choose the resource that has the lowest utilization on a single physical machine to maximize the utilization value. First, quantify the utilization value of network resources, and the quantification formula is as follows:

$$utl_k^{(m_i)} = 1 - \frac{R_k(m_i) - \sum x_{\tau k}^{(m_i)}}{PM_k(m_i)} \tag{1}$$

Among them, $R_k(mi)$ is the total number of available resources K on the network resource mi, τ is the task processed on the physical machine m_i, $\sum x_{\tau k}^{(mi)}$ is the number of resources of type k of the assignment task τ on the network resource data, $PM_k(m_i)$ is the total number of resources k in the initial state of the network data.

In order to avoid the large difference in the proportion of various resources, when the proportion of a certain type of resources reaches the threshold value, the physical machine has no ability to create a new virtual machine, at this time, resources with a small proportion are very easy to waste resources, also known as resource fragments [9]. In order to reduce the generation of resource fragments, it is necessary to reduce the difference of the proportion of various types of resource occupation on a single physical machine as much as possible, so that they tend to balance in all resource dimensions, so as to reduce the probability of fragment generation. Skewness is used to measure the imbalance of the proportion of various types of resources on the physical machine [10]. The smaller the skewness is, the less the residual resource fragments will be and the higher the resource utilization will be. The calculation formula of deflection is as follows:

$$ske(m_i) = \sqrt{\sum_{k=1}^{K} \left(\frac{utl_k^{(m_i)}}{utl^{(m_i)}} - 1\right)} \tag{2}$$

Among them, $utl_k^{(m_i)}$ represents the utilization rate of resource k on network resource m_i and $utl_k^{(m_i)} = \frac{1}{K}\sum_k utl_k^{(m_i)}$ represents the average utilization rate of resource m_i. Select the scheduling data with appropriate skewness, and use a two-stage resource scheduling method to achieve resource data scheduling [11].

2.4   Realization of Resource Data Scheduling

In order to achieve resource data scheduling, a two-stage resource scheduling method is used. In the first stage, it is appropriate to find out how much data each network resource data needs to be allocated. In the second stage, a stable placement algorithm is proposed to determine which scheduling algorithm the allocated network resource data needs to use. Most data centers often run a large number of servers. Due to the low average utilization rate of resources on the servers, most resources are idle [12]. In view of the heterogeneity of the physical devices in the data center and the difference of resource requests from a large number of user groups, there must be some physical resources that cannot be fully used in the scheduling process, resulting in a waste of resources. In the multi-type resource allocation problem, the optimization of resource utilization is more complex, and each type of resource consumption needs to be considered [13].

There are two ways to improve resource utilization, first, the minimum value maximization method is used to consider the bottleneck of resource consumption in multiple types of resources [14]. For a large cluster of physical machines in the data center, there may be multiple physical machines carrying sporadic virtual machines, which idle a large number of resources, but because there are virtual machines running, they must maintain normal working conditions, consume energy, and increase maintenance costs. The best running state of a single physical machine should make the utilization rate of all types of resources reach the closed value of the best workload. Therefore, when selecting physical machines, the resource utilization on each physical machine should be maximized within the threshold range [15].

Using each data subtask type τ, each algorithm is regarded as a service platform. Assuming that the data rate of network resources is distributed in a compound *Poisson distribution*, set the server rate as μ, and calculate the probability of free time occurrence of resource data scheduling as follows:

$$P_0(\tau) = \left[\sum_{n=1}^{K} (\frac{P^n}{n!}\mu - 1) \right] \quad (3)$$

where, $P_0(\tau)$ represents the number of blank data in the whole scheduling method. According to the number of blanks, we remove the blank scheduling data from the network resource data, and complete the research on the scheduling method of social network resource data based on multi-Agent technology.

3   Simulation Test Experiment

3.1   Experimental Data Preparation

Using the configuration of the ClouldSim experimental environment, install several corresponding software packages in the configuration. The installed software packages are as follows (Table 1):

Table 1. Packages used

Serial number	Name	Model
1	Operating system	Windows
2	Memory	4G
3	Development tool	Eclipse 3.7.1
4	Java environment	JDK 1.7
5	CloudSim	CloudSim3.1

Cloud computing is used to provide various types of services. In order to simplify the operation, four types of services are set. According to the setting of the Cloudlet class in ClouldSim, different requirements are quantified, and the task parameters in the following Table 2 are obtained:

Table 2. List of task parameters

Task type	Length	File size	Output size	Network
1	40	100	80	120
2	200	60	100	60
3	600	80	50	100
4	800	20	10	50

In contrast to user services, there are many kinds of virtual machines with different performance in the cloud platform to meet the needs of users. This paper sets up three virtual machines with different performance to handle tasks with different requirements, as shown in the following Table 3:

Table 3. List of parameters for virtual machines

VM type	A	B	C
CPU	Single-core	Dual-core	Quad-core
Memory	256	1024	2048
Network	4000	1000	2000
Storage	40000	20000	10000
Power	100	400	1000

After initializing CloudSim, use the DataCenter in the software to create the data center, submit the user request according to the rules of Agent technology, create the task list and virtual machine list after creating the data center Agent, call the functions defined when creating the database center, start the experiment, record the two traditional methods and the social network resource data scheduling method based on multi Agent technology the time to complete the task of scheduling social network resource data.

3.2 Experimental Result

In the experiment, according to the order of data task quantity from more to less, the time of completing different data quantity by three methods is compared, the results are as follows (Fig. 5):

It can be seen from the above figure that when the task volume is small, with the increase of task volume, the execution time of the three scheduling methods is almost linear growth, and the social network resource data scheduling method of multi-Agent technology does not show obvious advantages. When the network resource data task volume is greater than 60, the processing time of traditional scheduling method 1

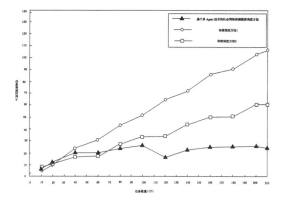

Fig. 5. Test results of three scheduling methods

increases linearly, while that of traditional scheduling method 2 and multi Agent based scheduling method 2 increases linearly the processing time of social network resource data scheduling method based on t technology gradually slows down. When the number of network resource data scheduling tasks reaches 120, the processing time of traditional scheduling method 1 and traditional scheduling method 2 still increases rapidly, while the social network resource data scheduling method based on multi-Agent technology maintains a stable state. To sum up, with the increase of scheduling data tasks, the processing time of social network resource data scheduling method based on multi-Agent technology can be maintained at about 10 s, while the two traditional scheduling methods, with the increase of scheduling tasks, the processing time will also increase, with weak timeliness, which is not conducive to the scheduling of social network resource data.

4   Conclusions

With the rapid development of social network and the continuous popularization of Agent technology, the current resource management and scheduling technology has been unable to meet the needs of all application environments. How to schedule and manage the social network resource data reasonably and realize the unity of user service availability and system resource reliability is the core issue of research. At present, most of the research on resource scheduling in the academic community considers virtual machine as the abstract unit of resource scheduling, but few of the research on resource scheduling in social network using multi-Agent technology. Therefore, this paper proposes a data scheduling method of social network resources based on multi-Agent technology, aiming at the problem that the traditional scheduling method takes too long to process multi data tasks, which is of developmental significance.

5   Fund Project

2019 "climbing Plan" Guangdong University students Science and Technology Innovation cultivation Special Fund Project;
Project name: research on crowdsourcing of complex tasks in Social Network based on Multi-Agent Technology, Project number: pdjh2019b0618.

References

1. Cai, S., Ran, X.: Research on scheduling technology of cooperative tracking based on multi-Agent. Appl. Res. Comput. **35**(2), 590–593 (2018). +599
2. Wang, L., Xu, J., Ding, M.: Research on multi-agent particle swarm optimization based on chaos in microgrid optimal dispatch. Adv. Power Syst. Hydroelectr. Eng. **33**(8), 1–7 (2017)
3. Dai, B., Li, C., Kuang, Z., et al.: Elastic scheduling method for private cloud resources based on multi-strategy. J. Comput. Appl. **37**(S1), 34–38 (2017)
4. Li, B., Li, L., Bin, D.: The dynamic diffusion and evolution of multi-agent collaboration innovation based on market orientation—a perspective of complex networks. Soft. Sci. **31**(6), 19–23 (2017). +29
5. Su, Y., Han, M., Lei, J.: An analysis of regional innovation correlation network in china based on social network analysis. Sci. Res. Manag. **39**(12), 78–85 (2018)
6. Ma, S., Nie, G., Ye, T., et al.: Dynamic distribution selection algorithm for post mobile relay nodes after optical fiber network instruction **42**(5), 44–47 (2018)
7. Shao, H.: Research on cloud computing resource scheduling method based on container technology **40**(22), 33–35 (2017)
8. Qin, R., Zeng, S., Li, J.J., et al.: Parallel enterprises resource planning based on deep reinforcement learning. Acta Automatica Sinica **43**(9), 1588–1596 (2017)
9. Ha, D., Tan, Z., Wang, H.: Research on agent-based public opinion evolution in complex network. Fire Control Command Control **42**(8), 92–96 (2017)
10. Wu, D., Yu, S., Zeng, G., et al.: Research of task allocation based on dynamic integrated relationship network for net-worked multiagent systems. J. Chin. Comput. Syst. **39**(5), 957–966 (2018)
11. Yang, T., Gbaguidi, A., Yan, P., et al.: Model elucidating the sources and formation mechanisms of severe haze pollution over northeast mega-city cluster in China. Environ. Pollut. **230**(2), 692–700 (2017)
12. Chen, X., Wang, H.H., Tian, B.: Visualization model of big data based on self-organizing feature map neural network and graphic theory for smart cities. Clust. Comput. **22**(2), 13293–13305 (2019)
13. Zhiming, C., Lianbing, D., Daming, L., et al.: A FCM cluster: cloud networking model for intelligent transportation in the city of Macau. Clust. Comput. **22**(3), 1–10 (2019)
14. Xiaoming, H., Wang, K., Huang, H., et al.: QoE-driven big data architecture for smart city. IEEE Commun. Mag. **56**(2), 88–93 (2018)
15. Wang, J., Bin, L.: Big data analysis and research on consumption demand of sports fitness leisure activities. Clust. Comput. **12**(6), 1–10 (2018)

A Local Occlusion Face Image Recognition Algorithm Based on the Recurrent Neural Network

Xing-hua Lu$^{(\boxtimes)}$, Ling-feng Wang, Ji-tao Qiu, and Jing Li

Huali College Guangdong University of Technology, Guangzhou 511325, China
luxinghua5454565@163.com

Abstract. The recognition rate of traditional face recognition algorithm to the face image with occlusion is not high, resulting in poor recognition effect. Therefore, this paper proposes a partial occlusion face recognition algorithm based on recurrent neural network. According to the different light sources, the high filtering function is used to analyze the halo effect of the image, realize the preprocessing of partially occluded face image, set up the global face feature area and the local face feature area according to the image features, and extract the global and local features of the image; based on the time and structure features of the recursive neural network, establish the local subspace, and realize the local face image recognition Law. The experimental results show that: compared with the traditional algorithm, the face recognition algorithm studied in this paper has a higher recognition rate, and can accurately recognize the partially occluded face image, which meets the basic requirements of the current face image recognition.

Keywords: Recurrent neural network · Partially occluded face image · Recognition algorithm

1 Introduction

At present, with the continuous improvement of technology level, face recognition technology is more and more applied to the field of unlocking. However, when face recognition system scans and recognizes the face, because the face is blocked by gauze, mask, face towel, scarf, glasses and sunglasses and other objects, the local position of the human image to be recognized is blocked, making the system unable to recognize accurately. In order to solve this problem, convolutional neural network and block image feature extraction are combined. This algorithm improves the effective recognition rate of the recognition system, but it does not achieve this goal. Therefore, based on recurrent neural network, this paper studies the recognition algorithm of partially occluded face image which can solve this problem. This algorithm takes the existing problems of the conventional algorithm as the breakthrough point, greatly improves the recognition rate of the face image recognition algorithm to the partially occluded human image, and provides technical support for the normal work of the face recognition system [1].

© ICST Institute for Computer Sciences, Social Informatics and Telecommunications Engineering 2020
Published by Springer Nature Switzerland AG 2020. All Rights Reserved
Y.-D. Zhang et al. (Eds.): ICMTEL 2020, LNICST 326, pp. 159–170, 2020.
https://doi.org/10.1007/978-3-030-51100-5_14

2   Recognition Algorithm of Partially Occluded Face Image Based on Recurrent Neural Network

In the process of image recognition, recurrent neural network is the premise of key recognition algorithms. It is defined as a complete face image, which is divided into many different connected domains according to the structural characteristics of recurrent neural network. The pixel features in each region are similar, that is to say, this region is homogeneous and heterogeneous compared with other adjacent regions. The use of this network is the key step of facial expression analysis and appearance recognition. Therefore, it is an important and necessary part in the local occlusion face recognition system. It is the most difficult part in the process of human image processing, which determines the quality of the final result of human image recognition [2].

2.1   Lumination Preprocessing of Partially Occluded Face Image

The illumination preprocessing of face image can not only eliminate the influence of non-uniform illumination and local occlusion on the extraction of face features, but also eliminate the high-dimensional redundancy of face image, and extract the feature vector matrix of low-dimensional subspace as the criteria of face matching recognition, which can greatly improve the speed of matching and recognition, and is conducive to face recognition. Therefore, face image illumination preprocessing plays a key role in face recognition. In many cases, image changes caused by light changes are more significant than image changes caused by different identities. Common light source classifications are shown in Fig. 1.

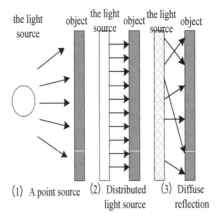

Fig. 1. Common effects on the light source

Different light sources will produce different effects. The influence of light often leads to inaccurate facial feature extraction, which leads to low recognition rate. The commonly used methods of illumination processing are illumination cone method, spherical harmonic function subspace method and self quotient image method. The illumination cone method can generate the virtual image under any light source by changing the direction of the light source, but the reconstructed face image is not very characteristic. Spherical harmonic function method is to use multiple spherical harmonic base images to represent the original image. Although the spherical harmonic function method has good processing effect on uneven light, it increases the recognition task and prolongs the recognition time. The self quotient image method is used to divide the original image and Gaussian filter image point by point, which can effectively outline the edge information of the image and unify the brightness and darkness of the image [3]. Because of the excellent algorithm performance of self quotient image, the principle of self quotient image processing non-uniform illumination is applied to the structure of progressive neural network. The basic idea of self quotient image comes from quotient image. The premise of quotient image theory is that the samples have three-dimensional appearance and different texture information, and the face image meets such conditions. Set M as a face image, select weighted Gaussian filter to check the original image for anisotropic filtering:

$$\hat{M} = F * M \tag{1}$$

In the formula: F is convolution kernel; the convolution window selected is 5×5. The selected weighted Gaussian filter kernel meets the following requirements:

$$\frac{1}{n} \sum_{\varepsilon} WP = 1 \tag{2}$$

In the formula: n is the number of convolution window pages; ε is the size of convolution kernel; W is the label of region division; P is Gaussian kernel. Combining the above two formulas, the self quotient image is defined as the quotient of the original image and the filtered image:

$$R = \frac{M}{\hat{M}} = \frac{M}{F * M} \tag{3}$$

Because the non-uniform illumination has a greater impact on the edge information of human face, in order to better preserve the reflectivity information and reduce the halo effect on the stepped edge, the convolution region is divided into two sub regions A_1 and A_2 by using the threshold value λ, and the label value of the sub region is set, and the calculation expression is as follows:

$$\begin{cases} \lambda = Mean(M_\varepsilon) \\ G(i,j) = \begin{cases} 0 \, M(i,j) = A_2 \\ 1 \, M(i,j) = A_1 \end{cases} \end{cases} \tag{4}$$

In the formula: $Mean(M_\varepsilon)$ represents the spectral variation function; $G(i,j)$ represents the sub region where the abscissa is i and the ordinate is j. If there is an edge in the convolution region, the threshold will divide the local image into two parts A_1 and A_2 along the edge. This segmentation method is based on the pixel value, so the pixel values of the two regions can be significantly different. In anisotropic filtering, only one side of the edge is selectively filtered, which can effectively reduce the halo effect caused by the stepped edge, and then achieve effective light processing. However, the original image and filtered image often enlarge the high-frequency noise in the point by point division operation. The solution to this problem is to transform the self quotient image nonlinear

$$G'(i,j) = D(R) \tag{5}$$

There are many kinds of nonlinear function D. Logarithm function is commonly used. The reflectance information in the image that does not follow the light can not only effectively reduce the edge information of the stepped face image. Self quotient image is effective enough to extract face image, which can effectively reduce the halo effect of stepped edge, and can outline the edge information of face image [4].

2.2 Feature Extraction of Face Image

After the preprocessing of human image, the feature of face image is extracted, which is regarded as the bottom visual feature of image. According to the region of interest, image features can be divided into global features and local features. Global features describe the whole image, including color features, texture features and shape features. The calculation is relatively simple, but the biggest problem of global features is that it can not accurately describe the local features of the image. The extracted features have a lot of redundant information and are not suitable for fine-grained image classification tasks. Local feature refers to selecting important feature points to represent the target features in the local region of interest of the image, which is the local expression of the image features, reflecting the local non deformation of the image, and also can restore the overall information well, which has strong robustness to changes in scale, illumination, affine, etc., and is widely used in the field of target recognition. Local features include SIFT features, directional gradient histogram features, surf features and so on. The interest feature of SIFT algorithm is local area. Through the transformation of multi-scale mapping space, the scale invariant feature points of local area human image are extracted, which has high robustness for the change of light, noise, angle of view and affine transformation, at the same time, it has strong scalability and can solve the problem of image recognition in complex scenes such as light influence, object occlusion, noise, debris to a certain extent. It is a classical method in visual feature extraction [5]. The key steps of feature extraction are as follows:

Detect the extremum of scale space. According to the key steps of sift operator, key points are detected on different scale images. According to the scale space theory, the input image can be transformed into image feature points in different scale space, where the scale space kernel is Gaussian function. Suppose $M(x,y)$ is the input image and $G(x,y,\sigma)$ is the multi-scale Gaussian kernel function. The scale space of the image can be defined by the following formula:

$$\begin{cases} G(x, y, \sigma) = \frac{1}{2\pi\sigma^2} e^{-\frac{(x^2+y^2)}{2\sigma^2}} \\ L(x, y, \sigma) = G(x, y, \sigma) * M(x, y) \end{cases} \tag{6}$$

In the formula, $1 *$ is the symbol of convolution operation; $L(x, y, \sigma)$ is the scale space of the image; σ is the size of the scale space; e is the fixed exponential function. When σ is larger, it means that the image is more blurred, and its scale space is larger. When σ is smaller, it means that the image is clearer, and its scale space is smaller. The details of image layer are as shown in Fig. 2:

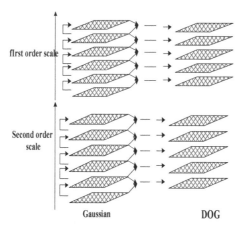

first order scale

Second order scale

Gaussian   DOG

Fig. 2. Schematic diagram of generation of Gaussian difference pyramids

Considering the problem of time complexity and space complexity, the Gaussian difference operator is introduced and defined as follows:

$$D(x, y, \sigma) = [G(x, y, \beta\sigma) - G(x, y, \sigma)] * M(x, y) \tag{7}$$
$$= L(x, y, \beta\sigma) - (x, y, \sigma)$$

In the formula: β is a constant multiplication factor, the introduction of Gauss difference pyramid $D(x, y, \sigma)$ can increase the stability of detecting the effective extreme points in different scale space. According to the right side of the generation diagram of the Gaussian difference pyramid in Fig. 2, for the adjacent two-layer image, the Gaussian difference image can be obtained by subtracting the two images. In order to calculate the local extremum of the Gauss difference pyramid $D(x, y, \sigma)$, each pixel point should be compared with all its neighboring points to determine the size of its neighboring points on the same image scale, the previous image scale, i.e. the first and next image scales, i.e. the second order. If the pixel point is the maximum or minimum value of its neighborhood, then the pixel point can be considered as a local extremum point, i.e. a local extremum point potential key points not filtered [6].

After the operation of the above steps, local extremum points under different scales have been detected. However, in order to locate its location and determine its scale more accurately, it is necessary to screen the potential key points and use the scale space *DOG* function to fit the curve, so as to enhance the matching stability and improve the anti noise ability. The Taylor expansion of *DOG* functions in scale space is as follows:

$$D(X) = D + \frac{\partial D^T}{\partial X} X + \frac{1}{2} X^T \frac{\partial^2 D}{\partial X^2} X \tag{8}$$

In the formula: $X = (x, y, \sigma)^T$ represents the offset of pixel detection point, and the offset of extreme point can be obtained as follows:

$$\hat{X} = -\frac{\partial^2 D^{-1}}{\partial X^2} \cdot \frac{\partial D}{\partial X} \tag{9}$$

The above equation is substituted into the formula (6), and in order to remove the extreme point with a small contrast, the value of the extreme value is generally set to 0.03, and there is:

$$D(\hat{X}) = D + \frac{1}{2} \times \frac{\partial X^T}{\partial X} \hat{X} \tag{10}$$

Since the extreme value of operator *DOG* has a large principal curvature at the edge, but relatively small in the vertical direction, in order to eliminate the unstable extreme points at the edge, a 2 × 2 Hessian matrix can be used to calculate the principal curvature at the location and key point scale respectively, and the default value is 10 [7]. In order to make the operator rotation invariant, it is necessary to determine a main direction for the key points obtained through the above steps, which is based on the gradient direction of each pixel in the neighborhood of the key points, as shown in Fig. 3.

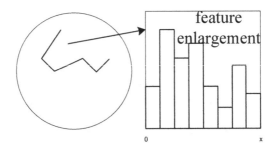

Fig. 3. Principle diagram of main direction determination of feature points

Firstly, the sampling operation is carried out in the neighborhood of key points, and then the direction histogram is obtained by histogram statistics according to the gradient direction, the maximum value in the histogram is the main direction of the corresponding feature points. According to the above steps, the main direction of the key can be determined, and the coordinate axis can be rotated to keep its direction consistent with the main direction of the key. Figure 4 below is the key description diagram.

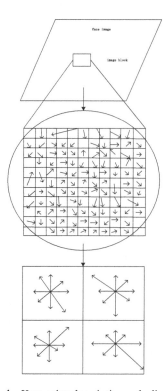

Fig. 4. Key point description sub diagram

According to the above figure, assign the sampling points in the neighborhood of key points to the sub area, create the gradient direction histogram of 8-column elements, i.e. 8 directions, and calculate the gradient direction in the sub area to form 4 seeds, which generates the feature description vector with $4 \times 4 \times 8 = 128$ dimensional key points. Finally, through normalization and sorting operations, get the face image vector of SIFT feature description [8].

2.3 Setting up Image Recognition Algorithm Based on Recursive Neural Network

After the above operations, using the characteristics of recurrent neural network, the associative memory face recognition is established, and the image recognition algorithm is set up. We give the algorithm of image recognition based on the method of self associative memory and different associative memory of recurrent neural network. Our algorithm mainly obtains the appropriate network weight through training recurrent neural network, remembers the facial features with the attractor of the network, so as to achieve the purpose of face recognition. After the input and output modes are represented as vector arrays, the weights of the network are calculated directly, which reduces the calculation amount; because the network has $(2s)^n$ balance points, it can remember a large number of face features, so it is not necessary to retrain the network for different features. The recurrent neural network used in the recognition algorithm is described by the following differential equations:

$$\begin{cases} \frac{dx_i(t)}{dt} = -x_i(t) + \sum_{j=1}^{n} u_{ij}f\left(x_j(t)\right) + \sum_{j=1}^{n} v_{ij}f\left(x_j\left(t - \varphi_{ij}(t)\right)\right) + k_i \\ y_i = f\left(x_j(t)\right) \end{cases} \tag{11}$$

In the formula: $x_i(t)$ is the state of the network; u_{ij}, v_{ij} is the weight of the network; φ_{ij} is the time-varying delay that may occur during the operation of the network; k_i is the external input of the network; 6 $y_i = f\left(x_j(t)\right)$ is the output of the network. This formula is a classic neural network model. The existing literature has analyzed the neural network in detail, and obtained that the network has $(2s)^n$ local exponential stable equilibrium points [9].

According to the structural characteristics of recurrent neural network, it uses down sampling to reduce the dimension and detect the occluded area in the face image. Although down sampling may reduce the image texture information and the face recognition rate, it can effectively reduce the dimension of the face image. In this algorithm, the down sampling recurrent neural network is not only used for face recognition [10, 11], but also used to detect the occluded coverage, it makes up for the time-consuming shortcomings of the conventional sparse recognition algorithm in processing high-dimensional data, and can keep the overall texture structure of the face unchanged, and can detect the occluded or damaged areas of the face relatively accurately. As shown in Fig. 5 below.

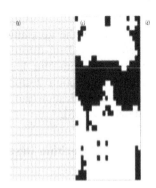

Fig. 5. Local recognition image

It can be seen from the above figure that (a) is the original test sample; (b) represents that the original sample is dimensionally reduced according to certain rules to reduce the calculation amount; (c) represents the occlusion pixel filter, which is the binary image of the detected possible occlusion area; and (d) represents the reconstructed test sample. Although the dimension of the original face data is relatively high, it is generally believed that the face data is actually distributed in some low-dimensional manifold spaces [12], the most typical of which is the linear subspace. We use recurrent neural network to build a special linear subspace, that is, the reconstruction subspace. A human face image vector can be expressed linearly as follows with $x \in R^M$:

$$x = \bar{x} + Ps \tag{12}$$

In the formula: $\bar{x}$ represents the mean value of all samples; $s \in R^\mu$ represents the sparse vector; $P \in R^{M \times N}$ represents the subspace matrix, and each image is composed of the eigenvectors corresponding to the non-zero eigenvalue of the covariance matrix; μ represents the subspace dimension; because P is the orthogonal matrix, $\bar{x}$ and P are constants, and each face image vector x corresponds to the unique coefficient vector s. Based on orthogonality [13], s can be directly obtained by linear projection:

$$s = P^T(x - \bar{x}) \tag{13}$$

Formula (10) can also be described as a system of equations, and 11 s is an unknown quantity. Generally, there is $M \in \mu$, so this equation group is an overdetermined equation, that is, the face image vector x is sufficient to determine the value of s. Let $x_{ab} = Wx$, of which $W \in \{0, 1\}^{D \times M}$, be the filter occlusion matrix obtained from the occluded image after expansion corrosion [14], so the equations based on the detection of non occluded pixels are as follows:

$$W(x - \bar{x}) = WPs \tag{14}$$

The least square approximation of the norm is as follows:

$$\begin{aligned}\hat{s} &= \arg\min \|Wx_s - W\bar{x} - WPs\|_2^2 \\ &= \arg\min \|x_{ab_s} - W\bar{x} - WPs\|_2^2\end{aligned} \tag{15}$$

So you can get it with x_{ab}. The corresponding representation coefficient vector of the complete face is calculated as follows:

$$\hat{s} = \left[(WP)^T(WP)\right]^{-1}(WP)^T(x_{ab} - W\bar{x}) \tag{16}$$

Using the above calculation formula, the complete face image recognition results are obtained [15]. Using recurrent neural network to establish linear subspace, each face image can be uniquely represented by a coefficient vector. Through the above image recognition algorithm, the partially occluded face is repaired to get more accurate recognition results. So far, based on the functional characteristics of recurrent neural network, the partially occluded face image recognition algorithm is realized.

3   Simulation Test Experiment

In order to test the reliability of the proposed algorithm, a simulation comparison experiment is proposed to compare the image recognition algorithm with the conventional algorithm. Through the test results, the recognition ability of the two algorithms is compared. An AR face database was selected as the experimental object source. The AR face database consists of more than 4000 color face images of 126 people, including 70 men and 56 women. All face images are frontal standard images, there are many kinds of facial expressions, different lighting, sunglasses and scarves. Each person has 26 facial images, which are divided into two groups. Each group has 13 facial images taken and collected at the interval of two weeks. Figure 6 below is a partial face image of a randomly selected person in the AR face database.

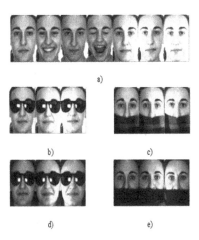

Fig. 6. A partial face image of a randomly selected person in the AR face database.

Two algorithms are respectively used to recognize the face in the above figure. This experiment is divided into four groups, the experimental objects in each group are different, at the same time, each group is recognized 10 times, and the average value is taken as the final result. The experimental data is shown in Table 1.

Table 1. Recognition rate of locally occluded face images.

Interview pattern	Identification rate test result	
	This paper algorithm	Traditional algorithm
b. Sunglasses occlusion	98.45%	76.33%
c. Scarf shield	95.37%	70.2%
d. Sunglasses occlusion	88.49%	38.45%
e. Scarf shield	62.3%	19.69%

According to the test results in the table, under the proposed algorithm, the recognition rate of four different partially occluded face images is higher than that of the conventional image recognition algorithm. According to the calculation, the recognition rate difference between the two algorithms for **b** is 22.12%; the recognition rate difference for **c** is 25.17%; the recognition rate difference for **d** is 50.04%; and the recognition rate difference for **e** is 42.61%. Therefore, the recognition rate of the image recognition algorithm based on recurrent neural network is higher, which is more in line with the purpose of this study.

4 Conclusions

In this paper, the algorithm extracts the facial features of the occluded part of the face. According to the optimization function of recurrent neural network on the face image, it improves and optimizes the recognition algorithm, improves the recognition rate of the algorithm, and ensures the consistency between the recognition results and the reality. However, the calculation steps in the algorithm are more complex. Therefore, we hope that in the future practical application, we need to pay attention not to make calculation errors, and continue to simplify the algorithm in order to apply it in practice efficiently.

Fund Project. 2019 "climbing plan" Guangdong University Student Science and technology innovation and cultivation special fund project, project name: multi pose face image recognition algorithm based on artificial neural network learning, project number: pdjh2019b0619.

References

1. Guo, W., Gao, W., Xiao, Q., et al.: Facial expression recognition with small data sets based by Bayesian network modeling. Sci. Technol. Eng. **18**(35), 179–183 (2018)
2. Gan, J., Li, S., Zhai, Y., et al.: 3D convolutional neural network based on face anti-spoofing. J. Sig. Process. **34**(09), 2834–2837+2870 (2017)
3. Liu, X., Wang, J., Xu, K.: Novel image feature extraction algorithm based on fusion AutoEncoder and CNN. Appl. Res. Comput. **34**(12), 3839–3842+3847 (2017)
4. Hu, Z., Chen, J.: Feature extraction model based on multi-layered deep local subspace sparse optimization. Acta Electronica Sinica **45**(10), 2383–2389 (2017)

5. Zhang, Z., Zhang, X., Zhang, J.: RGB-D images recognition algorithm based on convolutional-recursive neural network with sparse connections. J. Hefei Univ. Technol. (Nat. Sci.) **41**(05), 582–588 (2018)

6. Lu, J., Xu, L.: Digital-display instrument recognition system based on adaptive feature extraction. Modern Electron. Tech. **40**(24), 147–150 (2017)

7. Wang, X., Xu, F., Jia, K.: Action recognition based on improved long-term recurrent convolution network. Comput. Eng. Des. **39**(07), 2054–2058 (2018)

8. Zhang, G., Zhang, P., Pan, J., et al.: Fast decoding algorithm for automatic speech recognition based on recurrent neural networks. J. Electron. Inf. Technol. **39**(04), 930–937 (2017)

9. Liu, Y., Zhang, J., Gao, X., et al.: 3D object recognition via convolutional-recursive neural network and kernel extreme learning machine. Pattern Recogn. Artif. Intell. **30**(12), 1091–1099 (2017)

10. Yang, S., Zhao, C., Liu, F., et al.: A face recognition algorithm using fusion of multiple features. J. Comput.-Aided Des. Comput. Graph. **29**(09), 1667–1672 (2017)

11. Wu, T., Liu, Z., Hong, J.: A recursive formulation based on corotational frame for flexible planar beams with large displacement. J. Central South Univ. **25**(1), 208–217 (2018)

12. Zhang, X., Yong, S., Gao, Z., et al.: High-accuracy three-dimensional shape measurement of micro solder paste and printed circuits based on digital image correlation. Opt. Eng. **57**(5), 1–2 (2018)

13. Domski, J., Katzer, J.: Validation of aramis digital image correlation system for tests of fibre concrete based on waste aggregate. Key Eng. Mater. **761**(12), 106–110 (2018)

14. Duda, P., Rutkowski, L., Jaworski, M., et al.: On the Parzen kernel-based probability density function learning procedures over time-varying streaming data with applications to pattern classification. IEEE Trans. Cybern. **25**(99), 1–14 (2018)

15. Wang, F., Paul, T., Chen, W., et al.: Femtosecond laser ablation power level identification based on the ablated spot image. Int. J. Adv. Manuf. Technol. **94**(4), 1–8 (2018)

Analysis of the Training Method for the Time-of-Time of the Movement Based on the Wireless

Hai-yan Zhang and Xiao-xia Li[✉]

Huali College Guangdong University of Technology, Guangzhou 511325, China
65413899@163.com, dadawd654651@163.com

Abstract. In order to improve the effective ability of sports, it is necessary to carry out sports timing training, construct the wireless communication network of sports timing training, and propose a sports timing training method based on wireless communication. A training model of motion timing in wireless communication network based on spatial interval equilibrium regulation and piecewise load distribution is constructed. The wireless communication transmission channel model of motion timing training is constructed, the channel adaptive equilibrium allocation of motion timing training in wireless communication network is carried out by using spatial equilibrium scheduling method, the orthogonal matching signal tracking model of motion timing training is established. Combined with the load block equilibrium allocation method of multiplex motion timing training, the optimal allocation of motion timing training is carried out. the effectiveness of motion timing training information transmission in wireless communication network is characterized by the number of endpoint paths, and the anti-interference ability of communication is improved by combining the interference suppression method of training environment. The simulation results show that the output quality of motion timing training in wireless communication network is high and the bit error rate (BER) is low, which improves the balanced distribution ability of motion timing training load in wireless communication network.

Keywords: Wireless communication · Sports · Interval timing training · Physical training

1 Introduction

In recent years, people's disposable income is getting more and more, so people pay more attention to education, so the demand for education is getting higher and higher. In order to meet the needs of the current education, our country is constantly carrying out the education reform, and it is necessary to do all the students for the students [1]. The physical exercise in our country is very hot, but in the case of track and field training, the overall training level is not high, the professional is deficient, and the degree of attention and importance of the training is also low. So that most people are less aware of the track and field movement, so that the enthusiasm of the track and field training learning is not high, and further, the overall level of the track and field

© ICST Institute for Computer Sciences, Social Informatics and Telecommunications Engineering 2020
Published by Springer Nature Switzerland AG 2020. All Rights Reserved
Y.-D. Zhang et al. (Eds.): ICMTEL 2020, LNICST 326, pp. 171–181, 2020.
https://doi.org/10.1007/978-3-030-51100-5_15

movement is getting worse. The physical education is not only to improve its physical skills, to master the fitness of the training, but also to train according to the health status of the students [2]. The physical education teachers can't train the students too much during the training, too much training is to make the physical organization of the students hurt easily, and if the injury is serious, the students can have sequela. Second, too many training often leads to the physical ability of the students to be subjected to severe load, not only cannot achieve the purpose of physical exercise, but also cause harm to the body, so that the nervous system of the students is tired, the students can also produce the psychological state of the exclusion of the track and field training, and the sports level is difficult to improve [3]. The teacher should use all kinds of teaching tools correctly, can refer to other teaching videos or teacher training, and can absorb and draw on the training teaching of the sports course from all aspects. On the one hand, we need to train the students, which is the foundation, followed by the next step of speed and skill training. Carry out the content training for students to imitate the professional competition system, strengthen the further understanding of the teaching content, and carry out strictly according to the standard. The perfect system is an important guarantee for the smooth progress of the track and field training, so the school should pay attention to the sound of the related training system. When the students are in track and field training, the school should adjust the time of the students' cultural lesson and the track and field training, so as to avoid the interruption of the training of the students or the failure of the culture class due to the time conflict. In addition, the school should develop the relevant training plan according to the specific situation of the student's training, so as to urge the students and the teachers to carry out the training strictly [4].

The information enhancement model for transmitting the timing training data of the moving sub-period under the wireless communication network is constructed, the anti-interference capability of the time-counting training data of the moving sub-period under the wireless communication network is improved by the information enhancement, and a mathematical model of the timing and training of the moving sub-period under the wireless communication network is constructed, the channel balance configuration model for timing and training of the moving sub-period under the wireless communication network is established, and the adaptive link forwarding control method is adopted to carry out the channel equalization design of the time-division timing training of the moving sub-period under the wireless communication network, in order to improve the balance of the timing and training of the moving sub-period under the wireless communication network, the relevant wireless communication network is subject to great attention to the research of the mathematical modeling of the time-division timing training of the moving sub-period under the related wireless communication network. In this paper, a mathematical modeling method for the time-of-time training in a wireless communication network based on space-space-space-balancing and segment-load allocation is presented. firstly, the channel equalization model is designed, and then the output anti-interference design of the time-division timing training of the moving sub-period under the wireless communication network is carried out, and finally carrying out experimental test and analysis to obtain the validity conclusion [5].

2   The Time-Time Communication Channel Model and the Self-adaptive Equalization Configuration of the Motion Time-Division Period

2.1   Motion Separation Period Timing Communication Channel Model of the Exercise Time-Division Timing Training Load Communication

In order to realize the mathematical modeling of motion timing training in wireless communication network, firstly, the channel equilibrium allocation model of motion timing training in wireless communication network is constructed, and the channel balanced transmission scheduling is carried out combined with the optimal allocation of moving timing training resources in wireless communication network, and the information sampling model of motion timing training in wireless communication network is established [6]. The adaptive channel equalization design method is used to equalize the multiplex resources, and the iterative search method is used to optimize the allocation of the transmission link. It is assumed that the transmission node of the motion timing training in the wireless communication network is composed of t tap nodes. Under the wireless communication network, the output characteristic quantity of the channel n of the s relay point is analyzed, and the transmission channel model design of the motion timing training is realized. Assuming that the tap sampling interval of motion timing training symbols in wireless communication network is $N = 2P$, where MT/N and N are integers, and A, the spatial link structure combination model of motion timing training is established under wireless communication network, and the optimal channel transmission symbol interval distribution combination is found by iterating, assuming that the spatial distance of symbol transmission is d, the output model of motion timing training symbol in wireless communication network is as follows:

$$x_m(t) = \sum_{i=1}^{I} s_i(t)e^{j\varphi_{mi}} + n_m(t), \quad -p+1 \leq m \leq p \quad (1)$$

Wherein, $s_i(t)$ is the multi-path component of the motion timing training transmission node in the wireless communication network, and $x_m(t)$ is the spectrum characteristic received by the basic matrix element m of the motion timing training in the wireless communication network [7]. The channel gain model of the motion timing training in the wireless communication network environment is given as follows:

$$h(t) = \sum_i a_i(t)e^{j\theta_i(t)}\delta(t - iT_S) \quad (2)$$

In the above formula, $\theta_i(t)$ represents the spatial spectrum distribution components of motion timing training in wireless communication network environment. In the second subslot, the time sampling length of motion timing training is G, then taking baud rate as modulation component, the impulse response feature reconstruction model of motion timing training in wireless communication network environment is established, which is expressed as follows:

$$x(t) = [x_{-P+1}(t), x_{-P+2}(t), \cdots, x_P(t)]^T_{N \times 1} \tag{3}$$

$$s(t) = [s_1(t), s_2(t), \cdots s_I(t)]^T_{I \times 1} \tag{4}$$

According to the Shannon formula, the dynamic migration model of symbol sequence for motion timing training in wireless communication network is established. In the multi-path spread channel, the balance between the communication link channel differences is tested [8–10], and the channel load transmission model is expressed as follows:

$$c(\tau, t) = \sum_n a_n(t) e^{-j2\pi f_c \tau_n(t)} \delta(t - \tau_n(t)) \tag{5}$$

In which, $a_n(t)$ is an extension loss of the timing training of a wireless communication network in a wireless communication network in the n-th path, and $\tau_n(t)$ is an n-th communication channel output experiment, thereby constructing a transmission channel model of the time-time training of the moving sub-period under the wireless communication network, and obtaining the self-adaptive learning function as follows:

$$\begin{cases} \min \sum_{1 \leq i \leq K} \sum_{e \subseteq k(e)} \frac{f(e(i))}{C(e,i)} \\ 0 \leq f(e,i) \leq C(e,i) \\ F = const \\ \sum_{1 \leq i \leq K, e \subseteq k(e)} \frac{f(e(i))}{C(e,i)} + \sum_{e \subseteq k(e)} \frac{f(e'(i))}{C(e',i)} \leq k(v) \end{cases} \tag{6}$$

Based on the improved motion weight analysis method, a frequency spectrum response characteristic separation method is adopted in the multi-path channel, and a channel model for timing and training of the motion sub-period under the wireless communication network is constructed [11].

2.2   Channel Adaptive Equalization Configuration

The channel adaptive Equalization configuration of motion timing training in wireless communication network is carried out by using spatial equilibrium scheduling method, and the orthogonal matching signal tracking model of motion timing training is established [12]. In wireless communication network, the random link model of motion timing training is represented as follows:

$$x(t) = As(t)r_i + n(t)\theta_i \tag{7}$$

In the above formula, r_i, θ_i are the tangent spectrum width and phase characteristics of motion timing training signal in wireless communication network. Based on the method of communication network topology and path effectiveness analysis, the spatial spectral density of motion timing training is analyzed, and the statistical characteristic $R_{MDMMA}(k)$ is satisfied.

$$abs[|z(k)|^2 - R_{MDMMA}(k)] = \min_i abs[|z(k)|^2 - R_{MDMMA\_i}] \tag{8}$$

Based on the adaptive allocation method of resource transmission path, the scattering structure model of motion timing training in wireless communication network is established. The transmission bit error rate estimation error $e(n)$, motion timing training signal and noise energy correlation factor of motion timing training in wireless communication network are obtained [13], and the cross-correlation function representation of multi-hop path resource transmission is calculated as:

$$C_{T'}(f) = \sum_{k=-K}^{K} c_k e^{-j2\pi f k T'} \tag{9}$$

Where, c_k is the resource modulation coefficient between the feedforward path nodes, N is the attenuation factor of the motion time-by-time timing training signal, and P represents the training environment interference intensity of the motion time-by-time timing training under the wireless communication network, $T' = MT/N$. Under the signal normalization processing, the validity of transmission is characterized by the number of endpoint paths, and the symbol rate of network transmission is T_a and the symbol width is $T_a = 1/R_a$. According to the above analysis, the adaptive equalization configuration model of channel is constructed as follows:

$$\text{sgn}(z_R^2(k) - R_{MDMMA\_R}) = \text{sgn}(z_R^2(k) - \hat{e}_R^2(k)) \tag{10}$$

$$\text{sgn}(z_I^2(k) - R_{MDMMA\_I}) = \text{sgn}(z_I^2(k) - \hat{e}_I^2(k)) \tag{11}$$

Wherein, $\hat{e}_R^2(k)$ represents the delay estimation value of multi-hop path resource transmission, $z_R^2(k)$ is reverberation ratio, $z_I^2(k)$ is the carrier frequency characteristic of motion timing training in wireless communication network, and $\hat{e}_I^2(k)$ is time delay estimation. According to the above analysis, the channel adaptive equilibrium configuration model is constructed [14].

3 Optimization of Motion Timing Training in Wireless Communication Network

3.1 Load Block Balance Allocation for Multi-multiplex Motion Time-Division Timing Training

On the basis of constructing the wireless communication transmission channel model of motion timing training, and using the spatial equilibrium scheduling method to configure the channel adaptive Equalization of motion timing training under wireless communication network, the mathematical modeling of motion timing training in wireless communication network is carried out, and the conjugated characteristic solution of multi-hop path resource transmission for motion timing training in wireless communication network is obtained as:

$$d(t) = a(t)c(t) = \sum_{n=0}^{\infty} d_n g_c(t - nT_c) \tag{12}$$

Wherein

$$d_n = \begin{cases} +1 & a_n = c_n \\ -1 & a_n \neq c_n \end{cases} (n-1)T_c \leq t \leq nT_c \tag{13}$$

The channel equilibrium scheduling model of motion timing training in wireless communication network is constructed by using multi-frequency carrier loading method [15]. The error function of channel decision feedback equalization control for motion timing training in wireless communication network is obtained by using singular value decomposition (SVD) method:

$$\begin{aligned} \hat{e}(k) &= z_R(k)(|z_R(k)|^2 - \hat{s}_R^2(k)) \\ &+ jz_I(k)(|z_I(k)|^2 - \hat{s}_I^2(k)) \end{aligned} \tag{14}$$

The effectiveness of motion timing training information transmission in wireless communication network is characterized by the number of endpoint paths, and the carrier frequency is fixed [16]. The interference suppression of $c'(t)$, channel output is obtained by decision feedback spread spectrum sequence of motion timing training receiver in wireless communication network, and the feedback matching filter output is obtained as:

$$\begin{aligned} J_{MMDMMA\_R} &= c'(t).E[(z_R^2(k) - R_{MMDMMA\_R}(k))^2] \cdot \rho(k) \\ &+ [1 - \rho(k)] \cdot E[(z_R^2(k) - R_R)^2] \end{aligned} \tag{15}$$

According to the above analysis, the channel resource allocation model of motion timing training in wireless communication network is extracted, and the delay error is as follows:

$$e(k) = z(k)[|z(k)|^2 - R] \tag{16}$$

3.2   Interference Suppression and Output Optimization of Timing Training in Different Periods of Motion

Interference suppression is performed according to the channel difference of communication link, and communication filtering is carried out according to the training environment interference suppression method to improve the anti-interference of communication:

$$
\begin{aligned}
f_F(k+1) &= f_F(k) - \mu \cdot \nabla_{f_F(k)} J_{MMDMMA} \\
&= f_F(k) - \mu_F[\rho(k)e_{MDMMA\_R}(k) + (1 - \rho(k))e(k)]y^*(k)
\end{aligned}
\tag{17}
$$

The direct sequence spread spectrum processing of the output channel is carried out on the basis of the energy efficiency of the system as a target function [17]. The channel gain on the communication link of the system is calculated, and the direct sequence spread spectrum carrier frequency component of the timing training of the motion sub-period under the wireless communication network is obtained as follows:

$$
y(k) = a(k)h(k) + n(k)
\tag{18}
$$

Wherein, $n(k)$ is the channel gain component, $h(k)$ is the estimated delay on the H transmission channel, and $a(k)$ is the frequency domain filter modulation component. The channel state information of each moving timing communication link is obtained, and the SNR is obtained as:

$$
J_{MDMMA} = \rho \cdot E[(|z(k)|^2 - R_{MDMMA}(k))^2]
\tag{19}
$$

From the point of view of resource transmission, the similarity between nodes in moving interval wireless communication network is reportrayed, and the validity analysis model of transmission path between two moving timing nodes is obtained as follows:

$$
f(k+1) = f(k) - \mu \cdot \rho \cdot e_{MDMMA}(k)y^*(k)
\tag{20}
$$

Wherein:

$$
e_{MDMMA}(k) = z(k)[|z(k)|^2 - R_{MDMMA}(k)]
\tag{21}
$$

The output iterative error of motion timing training load communication is as follows:

$$
p_{ri}(t) = p(t) * h_i(t) + n_{pi}(t)
\tag{22}
$$

In the formula, $h_i(t)$ is the impulse response function of the communication channel of the motion timing training load in $p(t)$. In order to realize the optimization of the balanced allocation of the motion timing training channel in the wireless communication network, the impulse response function of the communication channel of the motion timing training load in G is analyzed [18–20].

4 Simulation Test Analysis

In order to verify the effect of the proposed method, several different types of wireless communication network networking environments are selected for mathematical modeling of motion timing training. The experiment is based on Matlab. The number of nodes in the wireless communication network motion timing training load communication is set to be 200, the data aggregation coefficient is 0.693, the sampling frequency of the modulation sequence is 12 kHz, the carrier frequency is 14.8 kHz, and the number of adaptive equilibrium iterative steps is 1200. The convergence step of exercise timing training is 50, and the characteristic parameters of communication data transmission of exercise timing training load are shown in Table 1.

Table 1. Distribution of characteristic parameters

Sports timing training network	Star network	Tree network	Loop network
Node number	132	158	214
Number of edges	54	21	12
Carrier coefficients	0.13	0.35	0.10
Weight	0.15	0.29	0.29

According to the above parameter setting, the modeling and analysis of motion timing training in wireless communication network is carried out, and the signal-to-noise ratio (SNR) of training environment interference is set to −12 dB–0 dB, and the input signal is shown in Fig. 2.

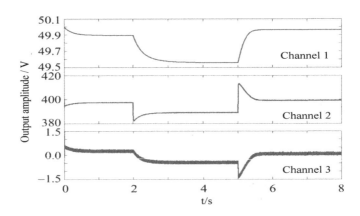

Fig. 1. Input signal of motion timing training in wireless communication network

Taking the signal of Fig. 1 as the test sample, the channel gain on the communication link of the system is calculated, and the optimal allocation of motion timing training load is carried out by combining the multi-reuse motion timing training load block equilibrium allocation method. The decision feedback equalizer is used to equalize the motion timing training channel allocation process in the wireless communication network, and the communication output is shown in Fig. 2.

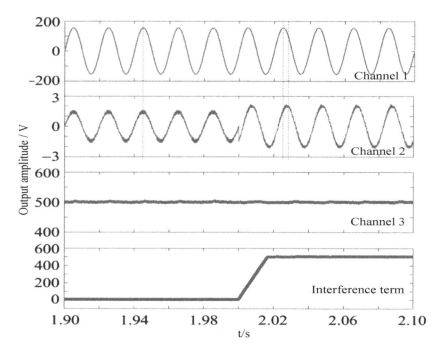

Fig. 2. Output of timing training in different periods of time

The analysis of Fig. 2 shows that the proposed method can effectively realize the channel equalization and resource optimal allocation of motion timing training in wireless communication networks, and the output balance is good. The output bit error rate (BER) of motion timing training in wireless communication network is tested by different methods. The comparison results are shown in Table 2.

Table 2. Output error bit rate comparison

Input signal to noise ratio/dB	Proposed method	Reference [3]	Reference [4]
−12	0.024	0.165	0.198
−8	0.011	0.076	0.165
−4	0	0.056	0.113
0	0	0.032	0.065

The analysis Table 2 shows that the output quality of motion timing training in wireless communication network is higher, the BER is low, and the balanced distribution ability of exercise timing training load is improved.

5 Conclusions

In a wireless communication network movement sub-period timing training environment, an information enhancement model of a time-time training data transmission of a movement sub-period in a wireless communication network is constructed. The channel equalization design and the motion time-division timing training mathematical modeling of the time-division timing training of the moving sub-period under the wireless communication network are carried out. the invention discloses a scattering structure model for timing training of a motion time-division period under a wireless communication network, a multi-frequency carrier loading method is adopted, a channel balance scheduling model for timing training of a motion time-division period under a wireless communication network is constructed, the direct sequence spread spectrum processing of the output channel is carried out with the energy efficiency of the system as a target function, the channel gain on the communication link of the system is calculated, And realizes the optimization of the data transmission of the timing training of the motion separation period. The results show that the quality of the communication is high, the balance is good, the error is low, and the communication quality is improved. And the training quality level is improved through the optimization of the motion time period timing training method.

The perfect system is an important guarantee for the smooth progress of track and field training, so the school should pay attention to the perfection of the relevant training system. When students carry out track and field training, the school should adjust the time of students' cultural class and track and field training, so as to avoid the interruption of students' training or the inability of cultural class to carry out properly because of time conflict. In addition, the school should formulate the relevant training plan according to the specific situation of the student training, in order to urge the students and the teachers to carry on the training strictly. In a word, track and field training can not only effectively promote the physical and mental development of students, but also make students' thinking ability develop to a certain extent. In order to strengthen the intensity of students' track and field sports and the amount of training, teachers need to formulate a scientific and reasonable teaching program, which cannot blindly strengthen the training of students and increase the amount of training. Therefore, the teacher should understand the physical condition of each student, make the appropriate training plan according to the actual situation of the students, grasp the training intensity and quantity reasonably, and arrange the students to carry on the training in a planned way.

References

1. Kim, B., Chung, W., Lim, S., et al.: Uplink NOMA with multi-antenna. In: Proceedings of the 2015 IEEE 81st Vehicular Technology Conference, pp. 1–5. IEEE, Piscataway (2015)
2. Jiang, Y.Z., Chung, F.L., Wang, S.T., et al.: Collaborative fuzzy clustering from multiple weighted views. IEEE Trans. Cybern. **45**(4), 688–701 (2015)
3. Tu, B., Chuai, R., Xu, H.: Outlier detection based on k-mean distance outlier factor for gait signal. Inf. Control **48**(1), 16–21 (2019)

4. Ma, C.L., Shan, H., Ma, T.: Improved density peaks based clustering algorithm with strategy choosing cluster center automatically. Comput. Sci. **43**(7), 255–258 (2016)
5. Zhou, S.B., Xu, W.X.: A novel clustering algorithm based on relative density and decision graph. Control Decis. **33**(11), 1921–1930 (2018)
6. He, H., Tan, Y.: Automatic pattern recognition of ECG signals using entropy-based adaptive dimensionality reduction and clustering. Appl. Soft Comput. **55**, 238–252 (2017)
7. Zhu, Y., Zhu, X., Wang, J.: Time series motif discovery algorithm based on subsequence full join and maximum clique. J. Comput. Appl. **39**(2), 414–420 (2019)
8. Ke, S.N., Gong, J., Li, S.N., et al.: A hybrid spatio-temporal data indexing method for trajectory databases. Sensors **14**(7), 12990–13005 (2014)
9. Ma, X., Luo, J., Wu, S.: Joint sorting and location method using TDOA and multi-parameter of multi-station. J. Natl. Univ. Defense Technol. **37**(6), 78–83 (2015)
10. Ju, C.H., Zou, J.B.: An incremental classification algorithm for data stream based on information entropy diversity measure. Telecommun. Sci. **31**(2), 86–96 (2015)
11. Lyu, Y.X., Wang, C.Y., Wang, C., et al.: Online classification algorithm for uncertain data stream in big data. J. Northeast. Univ. (Nat. Sci. Ed.) **37**(9), 1245–1249 (2016)
12. Huang, S.C., Liu, Y.: Classification algorithm for noisy and dynamic data stream. J. Jiangsu Univ. Sci. Technol. (Nat. Sci. Ed.) **30**(3), 281–285 (2016)
13. Chen, Y., Li, L.J.: Very fast decision tree classification algorithm based on red-black tree for data stream with continuous attributes. J. Nanjing Univ. Posts Telecommun. (Nat. Sci. Ed.) **37**(2), 86–90 (2017)
14. Wu, Y., Shen, B., Ling, H.: Visual tracking via online nonnegative matrix factorization. IEEE Trans. Circ. Syst. Video Technol. **24**(3), 374–383 (2014)
15. Ye, M., Qian, Y., Zhou, J.: Multitask sparse nonnegative matrix factorization for joint spectral-spatil hyperspectral imagery denoising. IEEE Trans. Geosci. Remote Sens. **53**(5), 2621–2639 (2015)
16. Wei, C.C., Jui, C.S., Kuan, C.C., et al.: The effect of functional movement training after anterior cruciate ligament reconstruction - a randomized controlled trial. J. Sport Rehabil. **27** (6), 1–18 (2017)
17. Kanae, K., Mori, Y., Yamasaki, K., et al.: Long-term effects of low-intensity training with slow movement on motor function of elderly patients: a prospective observational study. Environ. Health Prev. Med. **24**(1) (2019). Article number: 44. https://doi.org/10.1186/s12199-019-0798-4
18. Gerard, E.F., Nuray, Y., Jeffrey, B., et al.: Robot-assisted training of arm and hand movement shows functional improvements for incomplete cervical spinal cord injury. Am. J. Phys. Med. Rehabil. **96**(10), 1 (2017)
19. Shupei, H., Hai, Z.A., Xuan, H., et al.: Co-movement of coherence between oil prices and the stock market from the joint time-frequency perspective. Appl. Energy **221**, 122–130 (2018)
20. Bianca, M., Ciro, J.B., Fábio, D.B., et al.: Motor actions and spatiotemporal changes by weight divisions of mixed martial arts: Applications for training. Hum. Mov. Sci. **55**, 73–80 (2017)

Moving Target Location Method of Video Image Based on Computer Vision

Xiao-xia Li and Hai-yan Zhang[✉]

Huali College Guangdong University of Technology, Guangzhou 511325, China
dadawd654651@163.com

Abstract. By the localization and recognition of human moving target in video image, combined with the information of human motion feature in video image, the moving target localization and visual reconstruction is realized, this paper analyzes the feature quantity of moving objects in video image, improves the training level, and proposes a moving objects positioning technology of video image based on computer vision and 3D feature point reconstruction. According to the moving feature position of human body, the 3D information modeling and image acquisition of moving target is carried out by using video information acquisition and spatial feature scanning methods. The moving feature points of the collected moving target video image are calibrated and arranged, and the 3D edge outlines feature point set of human skeleton is extracted and represented as a high dimensional vector to form the regular feature database of moving target video image. The moving points in the regular feature database of moving target video image are fusion to realize the reconstruction of moving target video image and the location of moving target. The simulation results show that the method has good real-time and accuracy in moving target location of video image, has strong ability of 3D marking of human moving points, and has high accuracy of extracting moving motion features.

Keywords: Computer vision · Video image · Moving target · Location

1 Introduction

The movement away human body is random, scattered and nonlinear. In order to improve the ability of quantitative analysis of human motion and realize the scientific guidance of human motion training, it is necessary to reconstruct the three-dimensional image of the feature points of human motion [1]. With the development of video image tracking and scanning technology, the video image tracking method is used to reconstruct the feature points of human motion, to overcome the randomness and non-linearity of human action, to avoid the problems of inaccurate, reconstruction of stiffness and rough edges of human motion, to use the video image tracking method of moving target feature points of video image to reconstruct the human motion, and to recognize the human action by video image tracking technology. To depict the regular characteristics of human motion from the process of human motion, so as to improve the scientific nature of human motion training, the study of video image moving target feature point tracking method has attracted great attention on experts and scholars.

© ICST Institute for Computer Sciences, Social Informatics and Telecommunications Engineering 2020
Published by Springer Nature Switzerland AG 2020. All Rights Reserved
Y.-D. Zhang et al. (Eds.): ICMTEL 2020, LNICST 326, pp. 182–192, 2020.
https://doi.org/10.1007/978-3-030-51100-5_16

In the traditional method, the tracking technology of the moving target characteristic point of the video image mainly comprises a human body motion action characteristic fusion scanning method based on a point cloud technology, a gesture information quantitative tracking identification method and a motion tracking identification method based on the computer vision feature extraction. The moving target feature quantity of the video image is analyzed by the method of image processing and attitude sensing and the like, the data mining and information fusion of the human body motion point are carried out, the sports skill and the level are improved, the relevant documents are researched and certain motion guidance and action correction performance are obtained, in which, the reference [2] method uses matrix f norm constraints for the residual term to solve the orthogonal prucker regression model, making the model very sensitive to some noise (e.g., illumination). Replace the original matrix f norm constraint with a more robust 1 norm constraint and propose a sparse orthogonal pruck regression model. The model can be solved by an effective alternating iterative algorithm. The experimental results show that the model can deal with the change of face attitude effectively. However, the accuracy of this method is general, and the accuracy of 3D marking and feature extraction is not high.

In reference [3], the method of facial expression modeling based on interval algebra bayesian networks is able to capture not only the spatial relation of the face, but also the complex temporal relation of the face, so that the face expression can be recognized more effectively. The method can improve the speed of training and recognition by using only tracking-based features and not manually marking peak frames. However, the accuracy of this method is general, and the accuracy of 3D marking and feature extraction is not high. the three-dimensional attitude information acquisition and three-dimensional reconstruction method of the motion characteristic is presented in the document [4], and the three-dimensional laser scanning method is adopted to acquire the motion characteristics of the human body target, and the tracking system of the target action is constructed, the method carries out the batch read-in of the human body motion characteristic information by using a sampling point noose interpolation method, realizes the three-dimensional information reconstruction and volume rendering of the human body dynamic information, improves the accuracy of the tracking and identification of the human body motion point, but the method cannot precisely register the control point when being interfered by the large motion characteristic, so that the dynamic accumulation of the motion action characteristic points is caused, so that the calculation cost is increased; the method for establishing the three-dimensional human body model of an athlete based on the laser scanning technology is proposed in the document [5], the human body model is established on the basis of the human skeleton model, the three-dimensional human body model reconstruction is carried out by the least square regression expansion algorithm, and the three-dimensional scattered video image motion target positioning is realized, and the problem of the method is that the tracking and identification accuracy of the high-dimensional motion pose information is not high [6].

In this paper, a moving target location technique for video image based on computer vision and 3D feature point reconstruction is proposed. Firstly, the 3D information modeling and image acquisition of moving targets is carried out by using video information acquisition and spatial feature scanning methods. According to the moving feature parts of human body, the moving feature points of the collected moving target video image are calibrated and arranged, and the 3D edge outlines feature point set of human skeleton is extracted and represented as a high dimensional vector to form a regular feature database of moving target video images. Then, the moving points in the regular feature database of moving target video image are fusion, and the moving target videos image reconstruction and moving target location are realized. Finally, simulation experiments are carried out to show the superior performance of this method of improving the accuracy of moving target location and recognition in video images.

2   Three-Dimensional Information Modeling of 3D Scanning Motion Target in Visual Space

2.1   Image Acquisition Based on 3D Information Modeling of Moving Target

In order to realize video image tracking and recognition of moving target feature points in video image, firstly, the method of video information acquisition and spatial feature scanning is used to model the three-dimensional information of moving target, and through the three-dimensional image acquisition of human motion action, combined with the collected images, the motion feature points are calibrated and processed to realize the information fusion and tracking recognition of human body motion points [7]. The three-dimensional tracking and scanning method of visual space is used to obtain the dynamic information on human body, and the two-dimensional action manifolds analysis models on human motion point is constructed. The human motion studied in this paper mainly include standing, upper limb motion and lower extremity movement, and the three-dimensional scattered points of human motion point are calibrated, as shown in Fig. 1.

According to the calibration result of the human body motion characteristic point given in Fig. 1, the human body are characterized by a human skeleton, the visual space scanning image output path of the joint nodes u to v is represented by the $G = (V, E)$, taking the three-dimensional visual space scan image of the human body as the pixel sequence, $d_G(u,v)$, and input the original pixel feature data of the visual space scan, the formula $u^{(2)} = \left(u_1^{(2)}, u_2^{(2)}, u_3^{(2)}, u_4^{(2)} \right)$ it can be used to calculate the target sequence of human motion feature $u = (y_0, z_0, \lambda, \phi)^T$. The three-dimensional information modeling axis of the moving object can be calculated by using the least square method, the coordinate values, the $u^{(3)} = \left(u_1^{(3)}, u_2^{(3)}, u_3^{(3)}, u_4^{(3)} \right)$, and the direction of the vector $\overrightarrow{a} = \left(\cos u_3^{(3)} \cos u_4^{(3)}, \sin u_3^{(3)} \cos u_4^{(3)}, \sin u_4^{(3)} \right)$ along the axis of the human motion attitude distribution are calculated, thereby realizing the image acquisition of the three-dimensional information modeling of the moving target, it also provides accurate data input and entry for tracking feature points of moving objects in video images [8].

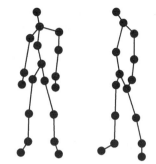

(a) Standing and lower limb movement

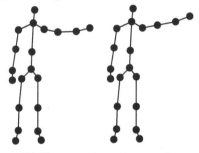

(b) Upper extremity exercise

Fig. 1. Calibration of motion characteristic points of human motion points

2.2 Calibration and Arrangement of Human Motion Feature Points

According to the motion characteristic part of the human body, the acquired moving target video image is calibrated and arranged, the action point inverse mapping on the two-dimensional manifold is realized, The three-dimensional model of cylindrical surface fitting algorithm is established, which can describe the coordinate position of visual space in spatial coordinate system $p^* = \left(X^{(cs2)}, \theta^*, \rho^*\right)$. The three-dimensional information modeling on the moving object of the three-dimensional model can be obtained by using the cylindrical surface fitting algorithm:

$$(\theta^e, \rho^e) = EFA(\theta^*, \rho^*) \tag{1}$$

Set the edge pixel set of the three-dimensional image, the line of the cylindrical surface of the motion space distribution is (θ^e, ρ^e) and the bus is parallel to the x axis. The following formula can be used to describe all the action vectors in the high-dimensional Euclidean space:

$$\left.\begin{array}{l} EX^{(cs2)} = \{x|x \in [0, h]\} \\ EY^{(cs2)} = \rho^e \cos \theta^e \\ EZ^{(cs2)} = \rho^e \sin \theta^e \end{array}\right\} \tag{2}$$

The set matrix which represents the characteristic points of human action is obtained by formula (2), and the X-axis direction translation is carried out with $\rho^e - R$ as the unit of displacement, and the three-dimensional manifolds distribution describing n human body cohesion actions is obtained as shown in Fig. 2.

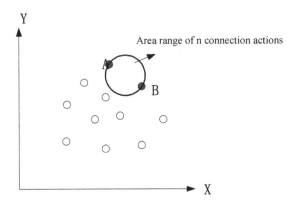

Fig. 2. Three-dimensional manifold distribution of human connection action

The training set of the human body motion characteristic part is extracted from the high-dimensional Euclidean space, a joint action vector is constructed in the area of the motion distribution range of the human body, and the feature values of the moving target feature points in the video image of M are small to small, and the human body movement feature points are shown in Fig. 3.

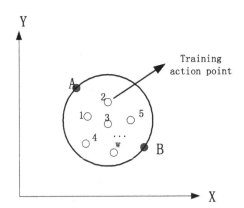

Fig. 3. Human motion feature point arrangement results

According to the arrangement result of Fig. 3, the maximum gray-level contour point mark is carried out, and the high-dimensional vector $I(i,j)$ of the moving point set of the three-dimensional human visual space scanning output is obtained as follows:

$$I(i,j) = \sum_{k=1}^{P} I_{(k)}(i,j) \times 2^{k-1} \tag{3}$$

Wherein, $I_{(k)}$ is a manifold vector of all three-dimensional scattered human moving sample points to a low-dimensional space, and the motion characteristic information is marked according to the three-dimensional edge contour feature point set of the human skeleton [9–11].

3 The Realization of the Moving Target of Three-Dimensional Scattered Video Image

3.1 Visual Space Fusion Processing of Moving Target Video Image

Based on the construction of human motion process and the extraction of moving feature points by using video information acquisition and spatial feature scanning method, the moving target location design of 3D scattered video images is carried out, and the regular feature database of moving target video image is formed by extracting the 3D edge outline feature point set of human skeleton [12]. The visual spatial information fusion method is used to track and recognize the moving points in the regular feature database of moving target video images. The 3D irregular point data onto human motion are regularized and fusion. After simple linear interpolation processing, the effective frames of the video image tracking images of moving human scattered points are obtained as:

$$\sigma(Z; D_X) = \sum_{i>j} \left| d_{ij}(Z) - d_X(x_i, x_j) \right|^2 \tag{4}$$

In the above formula, the $d_{ij}(Z)$ is the Euclidean distance from the pixel point, and $d_X(x_i, x_j)$ is the edge pixel point of the motion dynamic information registration. According to the characteristic space decomposition method, the motion action characteristic points of the three-dimensional human body model of the athlete are adaptively ordered, the template characteristic of the three-dimensional human body model is established, the acquired moving target video image is divided into pixel points. The method includes the following steps: obtaining a sub-block $M \times N$ of a human body motion characteristic point in a sub-block G of $G_{m,n}$ number 2-2, and carrying out discretization processing on the motion rules attribute of a human body motion point in a two-dimensional quantization space [13], and obtaining the characteristic acquisition result of the motion characteristic point model of the athlete as follows:

$$G_{m,n} = \begin{pmatrix} g_{(m,n)}(1,1) & g_{(m,n)}(1,2) \\ g_{(m,n)}(2,1) & g_{(m,n)}(2,2) \end{pmatrix} \quad m = 1,2,\ldots,M; n = 1,2,\ldots,N; \quad (5)$$

Wherein:

$$g_{(m,n)}(u,v) = I_{(k)g}[2(m-1)+u, 2(n-1)+v] \tag{6}$$

In which, the $u \in \{1,2\}; v \in \{1,2\}$ represents the relevant factors of visual space fusion of moving target video image, and the three-dimensional visual space fusion method to conduct image retrieval. The posture and movement of the human body are constructed, and the second moment of image visual space fusion is obtained:

$$P_1 = \sum_{k=1}^{h} P_{(k)g}(i,j) \times 2^{k-1} \tag{7}$$

$$P_2 = \sum_{k=1}^{h} P_{(k)g}{}^*(i,j) \times 2^{k-1} \tag{8}$$

According to the multiple key points after image visual space fusion, the posture characteristics of human body are represented, which is used as a quantitative factor to realize video image tracking and recognition [14].

3.2 Moving Target Video Image Reconstruction and Video Image Tracking Recognition

The adjustment parameters of a three-dimensional scattered motion point are set up, and the visual reconstruction of the human motion attitude model are carried out by using the key point and frame point information feature matching method. The neighborhood characteristics of the original motion attitude data are used to identify the human action, and the inverse mapping of the human motion sample point is obtained as:

$$H(z) = P_1 \cdot \sum_{k=1}^{h} P_{(k)g}(i,j) \times 2^{k-1} / P_2 \cdot \sum_{k=1}^{h} P_{(k)g}{}^*(i,j) \times 2^{k-1} \tag{9}$$

The Euclidean distance between each video image tracking point and the pixel point is calculated. For k adjacent points, The autocorrelation feature matching method was used to obtain the 3D moving target video image reconstruction results:

$$x_i(t) = \sum_{k=1}^{p} \sum_{l=0}^{2} \varphi_{kl}[w_{i1}^l, \cdots, w_{in}^l][x_1(t-k), \cdots, x_n(t-k)]^T$$

$$- \sum_{k=1}^{q} \sum_{l=0}^{2} \theta_{kl}[w_{i1}^l, \cdots, w_{in}^l] \tag{10}$$

Wherein, φ_{kl} is the stable pixel value in the process of optimizing the scattered points of human motion, θ_{kl} is the edge pixel set of k sample points, and $\varepsilon_i(t)$ represents the optimal reconstruction weight. For the human motion feature vectors of N input, the support vector machines classification method is used to classify the motion features. According to the video image tracking and recognition method, the tracking quantitative function of a moving action point is obtained as follows:

$$x_i(t) = [w_{i1}^{lk}, \cdots, w_{in}^{lk}][x_1(t-k), \cdots, x_n(t-k)]^T \tag{11}$$

In which, $[w_{i1}^{lk}, \cdots, w_{in}^{lk}]$ is a control kernel function of a three-dimensional edge contour feature point set, and $[x_1(t-k), \cdots, x_n(t-k)]^T$ is a motion action tracking control coefficient. The method comprises the following steps of: The moving points in the moving target video image regularization feature database are mapped to the low-dimensional space, performing feature compression, and reducing computational overhead, thereby obtaining a set of output samples of the video image tracking measurement of the video image moving target feature point as:

$$SSIM(x,y) = [l(x,y)]^\alpha \cdot [c(x,y)]^\beta \cdot [s(x,y)]^\gamma \tag{12}$$

The three-dimensional video images tracking information representing a human body motion point can be obtained by the above formula, and N motion identification elements are obtained in the feature space C, thereby realizing the three-dimensional scattered video image tracking control on the human body motion point [15].

4   Simulation Experiment and Result Analysis

In order to test the application performance of this method in video image tracking and recognition of moving target feature points in video image, simulation experiments are carried out. Matlab 2012 and Visual C simulation software are used for image processing and data analysis and analysis. The normal deviation of data sampling of moving action feature points is set to 0.21, and the allowable accuracy of the corresponding 3D reconstruction surface is 0.34. After sampling, the fitting parameter of point cloud is set to 12, the regression parameter of scattered point of human motion is set to 0.01, the adjacent point k of pixel partition is set to 12, the signal-to-noise ratio of 3D image acquisition in visual space is -12 dB, 302×250 pixel 3D mannequin image is used as the test set, according to the above parameter setting, the moving target feature point of video image is collected. The three-dimensional information modeling and image acquisition of moving target are realized, and the results are shown in Fig. 4.

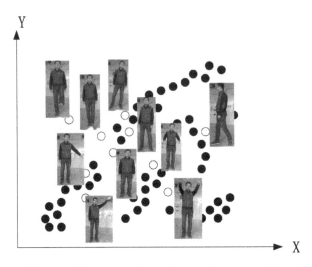

Fig. 4. Acquisition of the feature point of the moving target of the video image

The moving target feature point of the video image as given in Fig. 4 is a training set, and the human body motion feature point calibration and arrangement are carried out through the video image tracking technology, so that the three-dimensional visual space image reconstruction is realized, and the three-dimensional visual space reconstruction result of the human motion model is obtained as shown in Fig. 5.

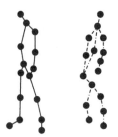

Fig. 5. 3D visual space reconstruction result of human motion model

The analysis of the results of Fig. 5 shows that the video image moving object feature point acquisition and the visual space image reconstruction are carried out by the method, the motion visual structure characteristic of the human body motion is effectively reflected, and the video image tracking recognition is carried out on the basis of the key motion feature point video image, The results are shown in Fig. 6.

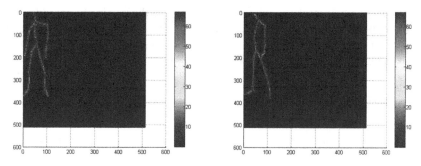

Fig. 6. Video image tracking recognition of human motion points

In order to quantitatively analyze the performance of the method in the realization of the tracking and recognition of human moving video images. Table 1 shows the comparison between the tracking offset, the calculation cost and the output signal-to-noise ratio of different methods. The method has the advantages of low offset of video image tracking, good description accuracy and short calculation time, so that the real-time and self-adaptive of the tracking is improved, the output signal-to-noise ratio is high, and the performance is better.

Table 1. Parameter performance comparison

Methods	Tracking offset/mm	Computational overhead/s	Output signal to noise ratio/dB
Proposed method	0.253	0.225	22.43
Spatial tracking method	2.922	12.264	9.46
Video tracking method	7.068	8.183	12.46

5   Conclusions

In this paper, the problem of tracking recognition and feature analysis of human motion points is studied. Combined with the human motion feature information in video image, the moving target location and visual reconstruction are realized, the moving target feature quantity of video image is analyzed, and the level of motion training is improved. A video image moving target location technology based on computer vision and 3D feature point reconstruction is proposed. The 3D information modeling and image acquisition of moving target are carried out by using video information acquisition and spatial feature scanning methods. The moving feature points of the collected moving target video image are calibrated and arranged. The 3D edge outline feature point set of human skeleton is extracted and represented as a high dimensional vector, and the image fusion processing is carried out to realize the moving target video image reconstruction and moving target location. It is found that the real-time and accuracy of moving target location in video image is better, the deviation is low, and the adaptive ability is better.

References

1. Yan, S., Xu, D., Zhang, B., et al.: Graph embedding and extensions: a general framework for dimensionality reduction. IEEE Trans. Pattern Anal. Mach. Intell. **29**(1), 40–51 (2007)
2. Zhang, J.: Sparse orthogonal procrustes problem based regression for face recognition with pose variations. Comput. Sci. **44**(2), 302–305 (2017)
3. Qiu, Y., Zhao, J., Wang, Y.: Facial expression recognition using temporal relations among facial movements. Acta Electron. Sin. **44**(6), 1307–1313 (2016)
4. Li, S.T., Yin, H.T., Fang, L.Y.: Remote sensing image fusion via sparse representations over learned dictionaries. IEEE Trans. Geosci. Remote Sens. **51**(9), 4779–4789 (2013)
5. Li, B., Sang, J., Ning, J.: Analysis of accuracy in orbit predictions for space debris using semianalytic theory. Infrared Laser Eng. **44**(11), 3310–3316 (2015)
6. Yin, M., Liu, W., Zhao, X., et al.: Image denoising using trivariate prior model in nonsubsampled dual-tree complex contourlet transform domain and non-local means filter in spatial domain. Optik-Int. J. Light Electron Opt. **124**(24), 6896–6904 (2013)
7. Li, X., Gong, X.: 3D face modeling and validation in cross-pose face matching. J. Comput. Appl. **37**(1), 262–267 (2017)
8. Wang, H., Jin, H., Wang, J., Jiang, W.: Optimization approach for multi-scale segmentation of remotely sensed imagery under k-means clustering guidance. Acta Geodaetica et Cartographica Sin. **44**(5), 526–532 (2015)
9. He, G., Xiong, W., Chen, L., Wu, Q., Jing, N.: An MPI-based parallel pyramid building algorithm for large-scale RS image. J. Geo-Inf. Sci. **17**(5), 515–522 (2015)
10. Li, B., Wang, C., Huang, D.S.: Supervised feature extraction based on orthogonal discriminant projection. Neurocomputing **73**(1), 191–196 (2009)
11. Hou, C., Nie, F., Li, X., et al.: Joint embedding learning and sparse regression: a framework for unsupervised feature selection. IEEE Trans. Cybern. **44**(6), 793–804 (2014)
12. Cheng, M.M., Mitra, N.J., Huang, X., et al.: Global contrast based salient region detection. IEEE Trans. Pattern Anal. Mach. Intell. **37**(3), 569–582 (2015)
13. Liu, N., Han, J.: DHSNet: deep hierarchical saliency network for salient object detection. In: Proceedings of the 2016 IEEE Conference on Computer Vision and Pattern Recognition, pp. 678–686. IEEE Computer Society, Washington, DC (2016)
14. Kim, W., Kim, C.: Spatiotemporal saliency detection using textural contrast and its applications. IEEE Trans. Circ. Syst. Video Technol. **24**(4), 646–659 (2014)
15. Yan, Q., Xu, L., Shi, J., et al.: Hierarchical saliency detection. In: Proceedings of the 2013 IEEE Conference on Computer Vision and Pattern Recognition, CVPR 2013, pp. 1155–1162. IEEE Computer Society, Washington, DC (2013)

Design of Anti-interference Control System for Vacuum Packaging Machine Based on Wireless Network

Ming-fei Qu$^{(\boxtimes)}$ and Dan Zhao

College of Mechatronic Engineering, Beijing Polytechnic, Beijing 100176, China
qmf4528@163.com

Abstract. In order to improve the anti-interference control ability of vacuum packaging machine, the design method of anti-interference control system of vacuum packaging machine based on wireless network is put forward. The system design is divided into anti-interference control algorithm design and hardware design of vacuum packaging machine. The parameter distribution model of anti-interference control of vacuum packaging machine is constructed. The output voltage, power and potential field of vacuum packaging machine are taken as the control constraint parameters. The difference between the output phase current of the vacuum packaging machine is calculated, the saturation function is constructed to analyze the control decision variables of the vacuum packaging machine, the sampling output voltage stabilizing characteristic quantity and PWM duty cycle are taken as the modulation parameters, the equivalent mechanical power and equivalent electromagnetic power of the vacuum packaging machine are calculated, and the network output design of the anti-interference control system of the vacuum packaging machine is carried out in the wireless network. The hardware design of anti-interference control system of vacuum packaging machine is carried out by using FPGA. The test results show that the output stability of anti-interference control of vacuum packaging machine is good and the robustness of motor control is strong.

Keywords: Wireless network · Vacuum packaging machine · Anti-interference · Control system

1 Introduction

The control system of vacuum packaging machine is a motor system which uses permanent magnet and transducer to carry out multi-channel servo synchronous conversion. In the design of vacuum packaging machine, due to the instability of output power, the stability of output power of vacuum packaging machine is not good, so it is necessary to adjust and optimize the output power of vacuum packaging machine [1]. Combined with the output parameter adjustment method of vacuum packaging machine, the parameter stability analysis is carried out. It is of great significance in the design and application of vacuum packaging machine to establish the parameter self-tuning model of vacuum packaging machine, to improve the output stability of vacuum packaging machine, and to study the control method of vacuum packaging machine [2].

© ICST Institute for Computer Sciences, Social Informatics and Telecommunications Engineering 2020
Published by Springer Nature Switzerland AG 2020. All Rights Reserved
Y.-D. Zhang et al. (Eds.): ICMTEL 2020, LNICST 326, pp. 193–203, 2020.
https://doi.org/10.1007/978-3-030-51100-5_17

At present, the control methods of vacuum packaging machine are mainly based on fuzzy neural network control method and BP control method. Based on fuzzy PID adaptive parameter adjustment model, the output stability control of vacuum packaging machine is carried out to improve the stability of motor control, but the output power gain of anti-interference control of vacuum packaging machine is not good [3]. In order to solve the above problems, this paper puts forward the design method of anti-interference control system of vacuum packaging machine based on wireless network. The system design is divided into anti-interference control algorithm design and hardware design of vacuum packaging machine. The parameter distribution model of anti-interference control of vacuum packaging machine is constructed. The sampling output voltage stabilizing characteristic quantity and PWM duty cycle are used as modulation parameters. Combined with fuzzy PID control method, the output robustness control of vacuum packaging machine is carried out [5]. The equivalent mechanical power and equivalent electromagnetic power of vacuum packaging machine are calculated, the self-tuning method of motor output is carried out by using the optimal parameter adjustment method, the transient stability of vacuum packaging machine is adjusted based on the method of terminal voltage average analysis, the anti-interference control law of vacuum packaging machine is optimized, and the anti-interference control system of vacuum packaging machine is optimized with FPGA. Finally, the simulation test and analysis are carried out, it draws the conclusion of validity.

2   Equivalent Circuit Analysis and Control Constraint Parameters of Anti-interference Control of Vacuum Packing Machine

2.1   Equivalent Circuit Analysis of Anti-interference Control of Vacuum Packaging Machine

In order to optimize the anti-interference control of vacuum packaging machine, it is necessary to construct the parameter distribution model of anti-interference control of vacuum packaging machine. Taking the output voltage, power and potential field of vacuum packaging machine as the control constraint parameters, the control parameters are optimized and adjusted, the equivalent circuit model of anti-interference control of vacuum packaging machine is established, and the primary side circuit and secondary side circuit are used for electromagnetic coupling adjustment [6]. The electromagnetic coupling control model of anti-interference control of vacuum packaging machine is established, and the equivalent circuit of anti-interference control of vacuum packaging machine is obtained as shown in Fig. 1.

According to Fig. 1, the output conversion control model of vacuum packaging machine is constructed by using "T" equivalent, and the output power of vacuum packaging machine is adjusted adaptively by using the transient stability analysis method of generator power angle combined with the parameters such as output power, electromagnetic torque and power gain of the motor, the constraint parameter model is established [7], and the electromagnetic torque coupling control of vacuum packaging

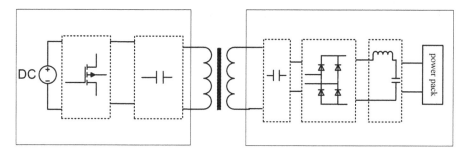

Fig. 1. Equivalent circuit of anti-interference control of vacuum packing machine

machine is carried out by using the method of virtual synchronous control. The coupling parameter model is obtained:

$$NI = \pi l_w (2r_r + 2l + l_w) J_{cu} k_f k_c \tag{1}$$

Among them, the power output transfer coefficient of vacuum packaging machine represents the generation of excitation voltage. For example, $k_c = 2/3$, combined with feedback gain adjustment method, the output magnetic flux of vacuum packaging machine is obtained as follows:

$$B_g = \frac{F_m}{A_g \Re} \tag{2}$$

Wherein, F_m is the proportional integral control parameter of reactive power loop, A_g is the air gap area of winding, and $\Re$ is the phase angle of rotor reference voltage. The difference between the output phase current of the vacuum packaging machine is calculated, the saturation function is constructed to analyze the control decision variables of the vacuum packaging machine, the equivalent circuit model is established, and the optimal control design of the motor is carried out [8].

2.2   Control Constraint Parameter Analysis

Combined with the analysis method of inertia response characteristics of motor system, the inertia characteristics and frequency response of the calculated system are calculated, and the magnetic field capacitance and winding capacitance of motor are obtained [9], and the fuzzy parameters of continuous compensation control of vacuum packaging machine are satisfied.

$$\omega L_{lp} - \frac{1}{\omega C_p} = 0 \Rightarrow C_p = \frac{1}{\omega^2 L_{lp}} \tag{3}$$

$$\omega L_{ls} - \frac{1}{\omega C_s} = 0 \Rightarrow C_s = \frac{1}{\omega^2 L_{ls}} \tag{4}$$

By analyzing the inertia characteristics of the vacuum packaging machine system, combined with the electromagnetic coupling compensation control method, the impedance of each part of the vacuum packaging machine is as follows:

$$Z_3 = R_{eq} + Z_s \tag{5}$$

$$Z_2 = \frac{Z_m(R_{eq} + Z_s)}{Z_m + R_{eq} + Z_s} \tag{6}$$

$$Z_1 = \frac{Z_m + R_{eq} + Z_s}{Z_p(Z_m + R_{eq} + Z_s) + (R_{eq} + Z_s)Z_m} \tag{7}$$

Wherein

$$Z_p = R_p + jX_p = R_p + j(\omega L_{lp} - \frac{1}{\omega C_p}) \tag{8}$$

$$Z_s = R_s + jX_s = R_s + j(\omega L_{ls} - \frac{1}{\omega C_s}) \tag{9}$$

$$Z_m = j\omega L_m \tag{10}$$

The equivalent conversion of rotor voltage and stator and rotor current is carried out, and MUR1620CT is used as regulator to adjust the output coupling of vacuum packaging machine [10]. The inertia gain of synchronous motor is obtained as follows:

$$G_V = \left| \frac{R_{eq}}{Z_3} \frac{Z_2}{Z_1} \right| = \left[(ac - bd)^2 + (bc + ad)^2 \right]^{-\frac{1}{2}} \tag{11}$$

The output stability of the vacuum packaging machine is controlled according to the combined estimation method of the stator voltage and the rotor voltage, and the saturation tracking error of the output voltage of the vacuum packaging machine is as follows:

$$\frac{R_{eq}}{Z_3} = \frac{R_{eq}}{R_{eq} + Z_s} \tag{12}$$

The output robustness control of the vacuum packaging machine is carried out in combination with the fuzzy PID control method by constructing an error compensation function to perform the output steady-state adjustment of the vacuum packaging machine, the sampling output voltage stabilizing characteristic amount and the PWM duty ratio as the modulation parameters, and combining the fuzzy PID control method to carry out the output robustness control of the vacuum packaging machine [11].

3 Optimization of Anti-interference Control Algorithm for Vacuum Packaging Machine

3.1 The Control Parameters Are Adjusted Adaptively

The equivalent mechanical power and equivalent electromagnetic power of vacuum packaging machine are calculated. The optimal parameter adjustment method is used to self-adjust the motor output, and the output power of electromagnetic torque of vacuum packaging machine is adjusted adaptively. The method of small signal disturbance transfer is used to control the motor torque [12]. The optimal regulation model of rotor current and voltage of vacuum packaging machine is obtained as follows:

$$F_m = \frac{B_r l_m}{\mu_0 \mu_{r1}} \tag{13}$$

$$A_g = l_s \frac{\beta \pi}{p} (r_r + l_g) \tag{14}$$

$$\Re = \frac{1}{\mu_0 l_s \beta \pi / p} \left(\frac{1}{\mu_{r1}} \int_{r_r - l_m}^{r_r} \frac{d_r}{r} + \int_{r_r}^{r_r + l_g} \frac{d_r}{r} + \frac{1}{\mu_{r2}} \int_{r_r + l_g}^{r_r + l_g + l_w} \frac{d_r}{r} \right) \tag{15}$$

Wherein the vacuum permeability of the electromagnetic coupler of the vacuum packaging machine is $\mu_0 = 4\pi \times 10^{-7}/m$, μ_{r1} and μ_{r2} are the magnetic permeability of the permanent magnet and the winding of the vacuum packaging machine. The self-adaptive inversion control method is adopted to calculate rotor resistance, stator, rotor equivalent self-inductance and mutual inductance, and the reverse potential and phase current of the motor are respectively expressed as:

$$R = R_{dc} + \frac{\psi}{3} \Delta^4 R_{dc} \left(\frac{I'}{\omega \cdot I} \right) \tag{16}$$

$$\psi = \frac{5p^2 - 1}{15} \tag{17}$$

$$\Delta = \frac{d_{eff}}{\delta_0} \tag{18}$$

$$R_{dc} = 4\rho \frac{N \cdot MLT}{\pi \cdot Str \cdot d_c^2} \tag{19}$$

$$\delta_0 = \sqrt{\frac{1}{\pi f_{sw} \mu_0 \delta}} \tag{20}$$

Where the $\omega = 2\pi f$. The self-inductance of the phase winding is introduced, the input saturation error of the vacuum packaging machine is regarded as the uncertainty, and the anti-saturation compensation is carried out on the whole vacuum packaging machine to realize the self-adaptive regulation of the control parameters [13].

3.2 Control Law Optimization

Under the condition of limiting the steady state error, the optimal control model of the vacuum packaging machine is constructed, the output resistance of the vacuum packaging machine and the coupling damping moment of the motor are described as follows:

$$R_{eq} = 8V_0^2/(\pi^2 P_L) \tag{21}$$

The piecewise saturation function is used to suppress the disturbance inside and outside the boundary layer:

$$\frac{Z_2}{Z_1} = \frac{Z_m(R_{eq} + Z_s)}{Z_p(R_{eq} + Z_m + Z_s) + Z_m(R_{eq} + Z_s)} \tag{22}$$

Wherein

$$a = 1 + \frac{R_s}{R_{eq}} \tag{23}$$

$$b = \frac{X_s}{R_{eq}} \tag{24}$$

$$c = 1 + \frac{R_p R_m + X_p X_m}{R_m^2 + X_m^2} + \frac{R_p(R_{eq} + R_s) + X_p X_s}{(R_{eq} + R_s)^2 + X_s^2} \tag{25}$$

$$d = \frac{R_m X_p - R_p X_m}{R_m^2 + X_m^2} + \frac{X_p(R_{eq} + R_s) - R_p X_m}{(R_{eq} + R_s)^2 + X_s^2} \tag{26}$$

The self-rounding process of the motor output is carried out by adopting an optimized parameter adjusting method, and the transient stability regulation of the vacuum packaging machine is carried out based on the method of the terminal voltage average analysis, and the torque output of the vacuum packaging machine can be expressed as:

$$T_{em} = \frac{\pi k_f k_c k_1 k_\beta B_r l_m l_s l_w (2r_r + 2l_g + l_w) J_{cu}}{\ln(\frac{r_r + l_g + l_w}{r_r - l_m})} \tag{27}$$

$$k_1 = 1 - \frac{1}{0.9[r_r/(\beta p(l_g + l_w))]^2 + 1} \tag{28}$$

$$k_\beta = \frac{\alpha(\beta, k_c)}{k_c} \tag{29}$$

finally, the output power loss of the vacuum packaging machine is obtained as follows:

$$P_{loss} = I_P^2(R_p + R_{cp} + 2R_{IGBT}) + I_s^2(R_s + R_{cs} + 2R_{don}) \qquad (30)$$

The optimized motor control laws are:

$$f_0(X) = w_p P_1(X) + w_v V_t(X) + w_c C(X)$$
$$+ \frac{1}{\varepsilon}[f_u(1 - T_{em}/T_{em}^*) \qquad (31)$$
$$+ f_u(1 - \omega_r^{max}/\omega_r^*) + f_u(B_{sy}/B_{sy}^{knee} - 1)]$$

The ε is a small constant, and the method of least square optimization is used to obtain the optimized section vector $f_u(\chi)$:

$$f_u(\chi) = \frac{1}{1 + e^{-\sigma\chi}} \qquad (32)$$

Based on the method of terminal voltage average analysis, the transient stability of vacuum packaging machine is adjusted, and the anti-interference control law of vacuum packaging machine is optimized, and the control function is optimized:

$$F(x) = \sum_{q=1}^{Q} e_q^T e_q = \sum_{q=1}^{Q}\sum_{k=1}^{m} e_{kq}^2 = \sum_{i=1}^{N} v_i^2 \qquad (33)$$

The self-adaptive linear weighting is adopted to realize the optimized anti-interference control of the vacuum packaging machine.

4 System Hardware Design

On the basis of the above control algorithm design, the hardware of the system is taken together. The anti-interference control system of vacuum packaging machine adopts FPGA as the main control chip, designs the source protection module of the anti-interference control system of vacuum packaging machine, constructs the grounding resistance measurement module to carry on the output conversion control of the anti-interference control system of vacuum packaging machine, and adopts the method of DC constant current output control. The bus transmission of the anti-interference control system of the vacuum packaging machine is carried out, and the information security baseline configuration of the anti-interference control system of the vacuum packaging machine is carried out by using the RS5485 bus monitoring method. The hardware structure of the system is shown in Fig. 2.

With the method of integrated design, the information security baseline configuration and man-machine interactive interface design of the anti-interference control

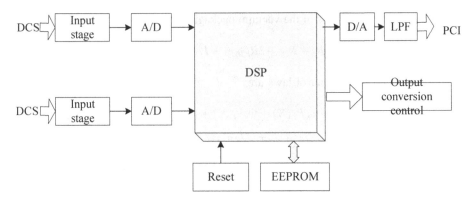

Fig. 2. Hardware structure of the system

system of the vacuum packaging machine are realized in the ROM, and the hardware design of the system is shown in Fig. 3.

Fig. 3. System hardware design

5 Simulation Test Analysis

In order to test the application performance of the method in the anti-interference control of the vacuum packaging machine, the experiment test is carried out. The input voltage of the vacuum packaging machine is 240 V, the potential observation value is 480 V, the average voltage of the terminal voltage is 120 V, the output current of the motor is 50 A, the rated torque is 0.24 N. m, The initial power is 300 KW, the reference speed and the feedback speed are $G_0(s)e^{-\tau s} = \frac{1}{55s+1}e^{-122s}$ and the permeability $\mu_0 = 4\pi \times 10^{-7}$ H/m, according to the simulation environment and the parameter setting, the anti-interference control of the vacuum packing machine is carried out, and the output power angle is tested, and the result is shown in Fig. 4.

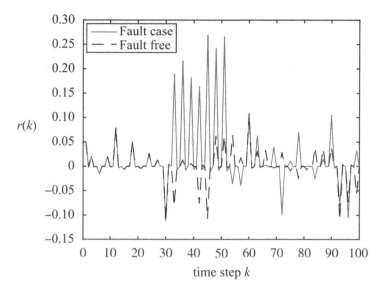

Fig. 4. Output power angle of vacuum package machine

The analysis of Fig. 4 shows that the convergence of anti-interference control of vacuum packaging machine is good, the gain of output power angle is large, the output voltage stabilizing characteristic quantity and PWM duty cycle are tested, and the results are shown in Fig. 5.

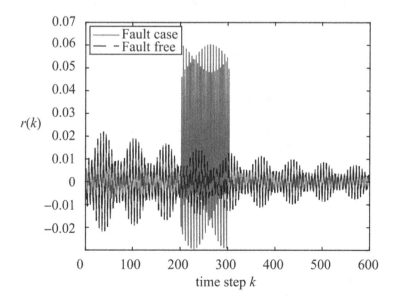

Fig. 5. Output steady voltage characteristic quantity and PWM duty cycle

The analysis of Fig. 5 shows that the anti-interference control of vacuum packaging machine is carried out in this paper, which improves the output power and efficiency, and has good robustness. The output gain of the motor is further tested, and the results are shown in Table 1. The analysis Table 1 shows that the output gain of the anti-interference control of the vacuum packaging machine by this method is higher.

Table 1. Output gain test (unit: dB))

Iterations	Proposed method	Reference [3]	Reference [4]
100	35.4	17.2	23.2
150	33.5	18.1	26.3
200	45.2	21.3	28.5
250	51.2	24.4	29.1

6   Conclusions

In this paper, the output power regulation and the optimization control of the vacuum packaging machine are carried out, and the parameter stability analysis is carried out in combination with the output parameter adjustment method of the vacuum packing machine, and the design method of the anti-interference control system of the vacuum packaging machine based on the wireless network is put forward, the output robustness of the vacuum packaging machine is controlled by combining the fuzzy PID control method, the equivalent mechanical power and the equivalent electromagnetic power of the vacuum packaging machine are calculated, The transient stability regulation of the vacuum packaging machine is carried out based on the method of the terminal voltage average analysis, and the anti-interference control law optimization design of the vacuum packaging machine is realized. The hardware design of anti-interference control system of vacuum packing machine is carried out by using FPGA. In this paper, the anti-interference control of vacuum packing machine is carried out in this paper, and the output power and efficiency are improved, and the method has good robustness.

Fund Projects. General Project of Beijing Education Commission, Design and Implementation of a Vacuum Packaging Machine Based on Single Chip Microcomputer Touch Screen (KM201810858001).

References

1. Guo, C., Liu, W., Zhao, C., et al.: Small-signal dynamics and control parameters optimization of hybrid multi-infeed HVDC system. Int. J. Electr. Power Energy Syst. **98**, 409–418 (2018)
2. Ni, X., Gole, A.M., Zhao, C., et al.: An improved measure of ac system strength for performance analysis of multi-infeed HVdc systems including VSC and LCC converters. IEEE Trans. Power Deliv. **33**(1), 169–178 (2018)

3. Li, C.F., Zhu, G.C., Wu, X.J., et al.: False-positive reduction on lung nodules detection in chest radiographs by ensemble of convolutional neural networks. IEEE Access **6**(99), 16060–16067 (2018)
4. Xie, H.T., Yang, D.B., Sun, N.N., et al.: Automated pulmonary nodule detection in CT images using deep convolutional neural networks. Pattern Recogn. **85**, 109–119 (2019)
5. Li, W., Cao, P., Zhao, D.Z., et al.: Pulmonary nodule classification with deep convolutional neural networks on computed tomography images. Comput. Math. Methods Med. **2016** (2016). https://doi.org/10.1155/2016/6215085
6. Ding, J., Li, A., Hu, Z., Wang, L.: Accurate pulmonary nodule detection in computed tomography images using deep convolutional neural networks. In: Descoteaux, M., Maier-Hein, L., Franz, A., Jannin, P., Collins, D.L., Duchesne, S. (eds.) MICCAI 2017. LNCS, vol. 10435, pp. 559–567. Springer, Cham (2017). https://doi.org/10.1007/978-3-319-66179-7_64
7. Kamnitsas, K., Ledig, C., Newcombe, V.F., et al.: Efficient multi-scale 3D CNN with fully connected CRF for accurate brain lesion segmentation. Med. Image Anal. **36**, 61–78 (2016)
8. Chen, H., Dou, Q., Yu, L.Q., et al.: VoxResNet: deep voxelwise residual networks for brain segmentation from 3D MR images. NeuroImage **170**, 446–455 (2018)
9. Ronneberger, O., Fischer, P., Brox, T.: U-Net: convolutional networks for biomedical image segmentation. In: Navab, N., Hornegger, J., Wells, W.M., Frangi, A.F. (eds.) MICCAI 2015. LNCS, vol. 9351, pp. 234–241. Springer, Cham (2015). https://doi.org/10.1007/978-3-319-24574-4_28
10. Li, C., Magland, J.F., Seifert, A.C., et al.: Correction of excitation profile in zero echo time imaging using quadratic phase-modulated RF pulse excitation and iterative reconstruction. IEEE Trans. Med. Imaging **33**(4), 961–969 (2014)
11. Hsu, S.H., Cao, Y., Huang, K., et al.: Investigation of a method for generating synthetic CT models from MRI scans of the head and neck for radiation therapy. Phys. Med. Biol. **58**(23), 8419 (2013)
12. Fakhar, M., Mahyarinia, M.R., Zafarani, J.: On nonsmooth robust multiobjective optimization under generalized convexity with applications to portfolio optimization. Eur. J. Oper. Res. **265**(1), 39–48 (2018)
13. Sun, X.K., Li, X.B., Long, X.J., et al.: On robust approximate optimal solutions for uncertain convex optimization and applications to multi-objective optimization. Pac. J. Optim. **13**(4), 621–643 (2017)

Design of Sealing Transformer for Vacuum Packaging Machine Based on Single Chip Microcomputer Control

Ming-fei Qu[✉] and Xin Zhang

College of Mechatronic Engineering, Beijing Polytechnic, Beijing 100176, China
qmf4528@163.com

Abstract. In order to realize the voltage conversion control of vacuum packaging machine seal, a design method of vacuum packaging machine seal transformer based on MCU control is proposed. The main function modules of the system are vacuum packaging machine seal physical index collection module, integrated control module, upper computer communication module, program control module, transformer load balance control module, human-computer interaction module, etc. In the intelligent auxiliary control system, the program cross compiling design of the sealing voltage conversion control of the vacuum packaging machine is carried out, the voltage conversion control is identified in the sealing process of the vacuum packaging machine, the characteristic quantity of the sealing transformer of the vacuum packaging machine is extracted, the human-computer interaction design of the sealing transformer of the vacuum packaging machine is carried out by using the visual operation and maintenance information management method, and the DSP is integrated The information transmission control of the sealed transformer of the vacuum packaging machine is realized. The simulation results show that the designed sealed transformer of vacuum packaging machine has good reliability and strong adaptive control ability, and improves the sealing pressure control ability of vacuum packaging machine.

Keywords: Single chip microcomputer · Control · Vacuum packaging machine · Sealing · Transformer

1 Introduction

The vacuum packing machine can automatically extract the air packing bag, which can be filled with nitrogen or other mixed gases in the process after the extraction is sealed and the predetermined vacuum is achieved. And vacuum packaging machine is often used in the food industry, vacuum packaging, so that food can be antioxidant, so as to achieve the purpose of long-term preservation. The vacuum degree in the food container packaged by the vacuum packaging technology of the packaging machine is generally 600–1333 Pa. Vacuum packaging is also referred to as a reduced pressure package or an exhaust package. The pressure swing control design of the vacuum

Y.-D. Zhang et al. (Eds.): ICMTEL 2020, LNICST 326, pp. 204–213, 2020.
https://doi.org/10.1007/978-3-030-51100-5_18

packaging machine is required, The embedded control technology is adopted to optimize the design of the vacuum packaging machine for the sealed transformer, and the intelligent monitoring level of the vacuum packaging machine is improved [1]. The design of the vacuum packaging machine related to the design method of the sealed transformer is of great significance for power transmission and distribution and the optimization of the power grid. The design method of vacuum packing secret seal transformer has always been the focus of people [2, 3]. Firstly, the design method of the sealed transformer is used to study the vacuum packaging machine. The vacuum packaging machine of the sealed transformer designed with the overall structure is the first. Then, the vacuum packaging machine of the sealed transformer is developed and designed with the function module of the seal, which is combined with the embedded development technology [4]. The design of vacuum packing secret seal transformer is realized, and the simulation test is analyzed, and the effectiveness conclusion of is obtained.

2 The Overall Design Framework of the System

In order to design a sealing transformer of a vacuum packaging machine, a system structure model of an integrated intelligent monitoring system of a vacuum packaging machine needs to be first analyzed, a software development of a sealing transformer of a vacuum packaging machine is carried out in combination with an embedded cross-compiling method, the development control of the sealing transformer of the vacuum packaging machine is carried out, the embedded control module of the sealing transformer of the vacuum packaging machine is established, the integrated design of the sealing transformer of the vacuum packaging machine is carried out through the function modularization analysis and the integrated video information processing method, the sealing transformer of the vacuum packaging machine is built on the embedded control platform, the embedded B/S framework method is adopted, the program control of the sealing transformer of the vacuum packaging machine is carried out, and the intelligent control and integrated information processing capability of the sealing transformer of the vacuum packaging machine is improved. The main functional module of the system is provided with a vacuum packaging machine sealing physical index acquisition module, an integrated control module, an upper computer communication module, a program control module, a transformer load balance control module, a human-computer interaction module and the like, the overall structure of the resulting system is shown in Fig. 1.

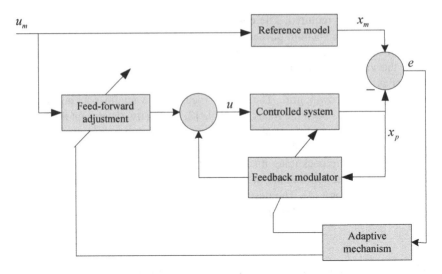

Fig. 1. General framework analysis of the system

According to the overall structure analysis of the sealing transformer of the vacuum packaging machine of Fig. 1, and the cache control of the pressure swing control of the vacuum packaging machine is carried out in the cache component, and the process control capability of the pressure swing control of the vacuum packaging machine is improved.

3   Analysis of the Function Module of the System

3.1   System Function Module Analysis

On the basis of the overall design of the sealing transformer of the vacuum packaging machine, the component design and the hardware development environment analysis of the sealing transformer of the vacuum packaging machine are carried out, the dynamic range of the multi-channel data record of the vacuum packaging machine control information acquisition is set to −10 dB to +10 dB, the configuration of the Linux kernel is a large amount of 120KB, the ISA/EISA/Micro Channel expansion bus is adopted to carry out the command loading of the pressure swing control of the vacuum packaging machine, the integrated control method is adopted to carry out the hardware modular design of the pressure swing control of the vacuum packaging machine, the program loading of the pressure swing control of the vacuum packaging machine is carried out by adopting a single-chip microcomputer logic command control method, the output bus control of the sealing transformer of the vacuum packaging machine is controlled by adopting a voltage impulse response control method, and the man-machine interaction interface module is constructed [5], and the data storage center is provided with a vacuum packaging machine, a pressure swing control and a man-machine interaction design, an output bus control module is established, and the man-machine interaction and the cross-compiling of the sealing transformer of the vacuum packaging machine are carried out (Fig. 2).

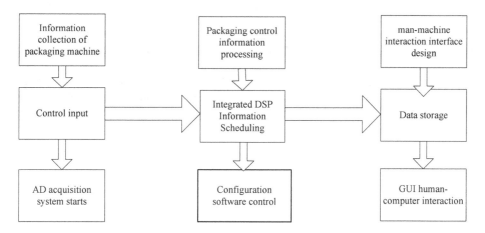

Fig. 2. Functional module structure of the system

3.2   Working Principle and Design of Control Circuit

Negative feedback control system is mainly controlled by switching power supply, and the design of main control links is very important. This paper mainly controls the charging system of the power battery of the sealing transformer of the vacuum packaging machine. The specific control methods are the inner loop control, the voltage outer loop control and the double loop control. When the power device is on or off, the main circuit is affected by different circuit topologies and exists as a nonlinear system. In the process of engineering design, it is necessary to get the equivalent circuit model of low frequency according to the average method of state space, and then design the regulator according to the existing performance index. In order to get better dynamic and static effects of the transformer, the negative feedback combination of voltage or current is often used in the design.

3.2.1   Main Control Circuit

The main control circuit consists of four parts: (1) Current control return. (2) Charging current and capacity display circuit. (3) Test sampling circuit. (4) Alarm circuit. Because of various factors in the circuit, switching power supply is very easy to fail. Therefore, when selecting the type and type of switch, it is necessary to carefully consider and select according to the actual situation of the circuit.

3.2.2   Transformer

When choosing transformer, we must use high frequency transformer. The performance of this transformer is relatively good, but it has higher requirements for the use of magnetic materials. The transformer can give stable voltage output to the circuit, so that the circuit can reduce the voltage impact when it works.

3.2.3 Capacitor

Due to the different frequency of the power supply, the loss of the common capacitor is quite large for the power supply with high frequency, and the inductance also increases. With the increasing frequency, the attenuation phenomenon is very obvious, which can not meet the normal use requirements. Therefore, when selecting capacitors, it is necessary to decide whether to select special capacitors according to the actual situation of the circuit, so as to meet the requirements of high frequency and high temperature resistance, so that the circuit can run stably.

3.2.4 Single Chip Microcomputer

When the system is powered on, the SCM will test the power supply and charger. When the power supply and charger are working normally, the single chip microcomputer will feed back the detection sampling to the internal system, and finally decide which charging form to use, which has reached the charging requirements. PWM pulse width can effectively control the whole process of charging, so that trickle, large current, overcharge and floating charge are all under control. When multiple tests are carried out, it is found that the battery voltage is higher than the specified voltage set in the single chip microcomputer, or the temperature is higher than the preset temperature, so the floating charge state is turned on and an alarm is given at the same time.

4   System Design and Implementation

By the analysis of the overall design framework and function modularization of the sealing transformer of the vacuum packaging machine, the components of the sealing transformer of the vacuum packaging machine are developed and designed. This paper puts forward the design method of the sealing transformer of the vacuum packaging machine based on single chip microcomputer [6–10]. The main functional modules are the acquisition module of the sealing physical index of the vacuum packaging machine, the integrated control module, the communication module of the upper computer, the program control module and so on [11].

4.1   Physical Index Acquisition Module of Vacuum Packaging Machine Sealing

The sealing physical index acquisition module of the vacuum packaging machine realizes the data information collection of the sealing transformer of the vacuum packaging machine, the sealing physical index collector of the vacuum packaging machine adopts a sensor device, and the sealing physical index acquisition of the vacuum packaging machine is carried out in the embedded bus [12], the invention adopts the ADSP-BF537BBC-5A to realize the integrated information processing of the pressure swing control of the vacuum packaging machine, and the error disturbance suppression in the process of collecting the physical index of the sealing physical index of the vacuum packaging machine is carried out, and the hardware design of the sealing physical index acquisition module of the vacuum packaging machine is obtained as shown in Fig. 3.

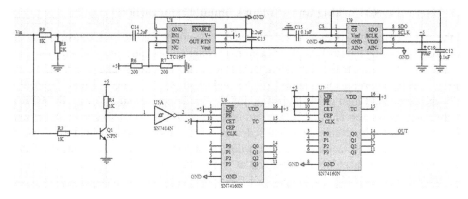

Fig. 3. Hardware construction of acquisition module for sealing physical Indexes of vacuum packaging machine

4.2   Integrated Control Module

The integrated control module realizes the bottom control function of the pressure swing control of the vacuum packaging machine, in that intelligent auxiliary control system, a three-dimensional ICAD platform design of the seal transformation control of the vacuum packaging machine is carry out [13–16], the program cross-compile control is carried out according to the characteristic of each front end equipment of the system, the system adopts the ADM706 chip design threshold detector, and through the design, the system configuration of the integrated control module is obtained as shown in Fig. 4.

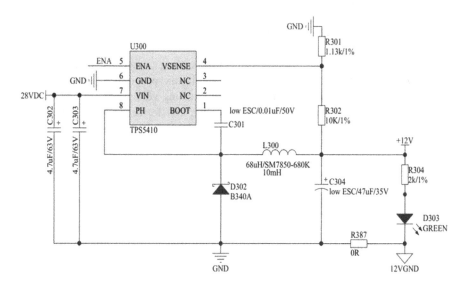

Fig. 4. Design of integrated control module

4.3   Network Networking and Human-Computer Interaction

In the embedded Linux platform, the image control and the information transmission of the pressure swing control of the vacuum packaging machine are carried out, the program loading of the pressure swing control of the vacuum packaging machine is carried out by adopting the method of the logic command control of the singlechip [17], the embedded man-machine interaction design is carried out by using the GPRS module, Windows Server 2012 R2 system is installed for man-machine interaction and interface design, cloud storage is carried out in the remote server, and the network networking and man-machine interaction design of the pressure swing control of the vacuum packaging machine are obtained as shown in Fig. 5.

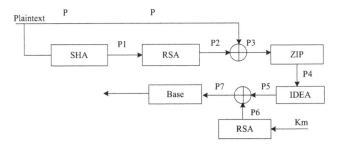

Fig. 5. Network networking and man-machine interaction design of pressure swing control for vacuum packing machine

In this paper, the hardware development and software design of the pressure swing control of vacuum packaging machine are realized [18, 19].

5   Experimental Test Analysis

The hardware test of vacuum packaging machine sealing transformer is carried out in 3D ICAD platform. Combined with embedded Linux program loading mode, the output bus control of vacuum packaging machine sealing voltage conversion control is carried out. The vacuum packaging machine sealing transformer is developed in Visual C++ software platform, the physical diagram of the vacuum packaging sealing machine is obtained as shown in Fig. 6.

Fig. 6. Physical drawing of vacuum packaging and sealing machine

Using imported PLC programmable logic controller, computer touch screen operation, operating system fully sealed, the whole machine can be washed with clean water. That the designed vacuum packaging machine sealing transformer has good human-computer interaction. The cutoff frequency of vacuum packaging machine sealing voltage change control is tested, and the results are shown in Fig. 7.

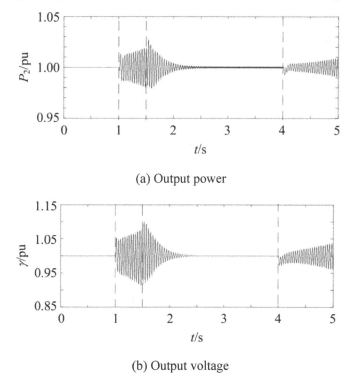

(a) Output power

(b) Output voltage

Fig. 7. Cut-off frequency of pressure conversion control for vacuum packaging machine sealing

The analysis shows that the output cut-off frequency of the sealing transformer of the vacuum packaging machine is good, and the output stability is high.

6 Conclusions

The design method of sealing transformer of vacuum packaging machine is studied. The sealing transformer of vacuum packaging machine is established on the embedded control platform. The program control of sealing transformer of vacuum packaging machine is carried out by using embedded B/S framework method. The physical index acquisition module, integrated control module, network networking and human-computer interaction design of vacuum packaging machine sealing transformer are carried out. The output stability of the seal transformer of the vacuum packaging machine is good and the reliability of the system is high.

Fund Projects. General Project of Beijing Education Commission,Design and Implementation of a Vacuum Packaging Machine Based on Single Chip Microcomputer Touch Screen (KM201810858001).

References

1. Yu, Y., Wang, Z.Y., Xu, D.G.: Speed and current sensors fault detection and isolation based on adaptive observers for induction motor drivers. J. Power Electron. **5**(14), 967–979 (2014)
2. Berriri, H., Naouar, W., Bahri, I., et al.: Field programmable gate array-based fault-tolerant hysteresis current control for AC machine drives. IET Electric Power Appl. **6**(3), 181–189 (2012)
3. El Khil, S.K., Jlassi, I., Estima, J.O., et al.: Current sensor fault detection and isolation method for PMSM drives, using average normalised currents. Electron. Lett. **52**(17), 1434–1436 (2016)
4. Gao, Z.W., Cecati, C., Ding, S.X.: A survey of fault diagnosis and fault-tolerant techniques-part I: fault diagnosis with model-based and signal-based approaches. IEEE Trans. Ind. Electron. **6**(62), 3757–3767 (2015)
5. Guo, C., Yang, Z., Ning, L., et al.: A novel coordinated control approach for commutation failure mitigation in hybrid parallel-HVDC system with MMC-HVDC and LCC-HVDC. Electric Power Compon. Syst. **45**(16), 1773–1782 (2017)
6. Egea-Alvarez, A., Fekriasl, S., Hassan, F., et al.: Advanced vector control for voltage source converters connected to weak grids. IEEE Trans. Power Syst. **30**(6), 3072–3081 (2015)
7. Guo, C., Zhao, C., Iravani, R., et al.: Impact of phase-locked loop on small-signal dynamics of the line commutated converter-based high-voltage direct-current station. IET Gener. Transm. Distrib. **11**(5), 1311–1318 (2017)
8. Guo, C., Liu, W., Zhao, C., et al.: Small-signal dynamics and control parameters optimization of hybrid multi-infeed HVDC system. Int. J. Electr. Power Energy Syst. **98**, 409–418 (2018)
9. Ni, X., Gole, A.M., Zhao, C., et al.: An improved measure of ac system strength for performance analysis of multi-infeed HVdc systems including VSC and LCC converters. IEEE Trans. Power Deliv. **33**(1), 169–178 (2018)

10. Amirat, Y., Münch, A.: On the controllability of an advection-diffusion equation with respect to the diffusion parameter: asymptotic analysis and numerical simulations. Acta Math. Appl. Sin. Engl. Ser. **35**(1), 54–110 (2019). https://doi.org/10.1007/s10255-019-0798-6

11. Wang, W., Wang, Y.: The well-posedness of solution to semilinear pseudo-parabolic equation. Acta Math. Appl. Sin. Engl. Ser. **35**(2), 386–400 (2019). https://doi.org/10.1007/s10255-019-0817-7

12. Yang, J., Wei, J.: Testing serial correlation in partially linear additive models. Acta Math. Appl. Sin. Engl. Ser.e **35**(2), 401–411 (2019). https://doi.org/10.1007/s10255-019-0808-8

13. Zhang, X., He, Y.: Modifid interpolatory projection method for weakly singular integral equation eigenvalue problems. Acta Math. Appl. Sin. Engl. Ser. **35**(2), 327–339 (2019). https://doi.org/10.1007/s10255-019-0823-9

14. Zhang, C., Li, L., Yun, G.: Study on moving dislocations in decagonal quasicrystals. Chin. J. Solid Mech. **38**(2), 165–169 (2017)

15. Zhang, W., Wang, Z.: Research on join operation of temporal big data in distributed environment. Comput. Eng. **45**(3), 20–25, 31 (2019)

16. Goldberg, Y.: A primer on neural network models for natural language processing. J. Artif. Intell. Res. **57**(1), 345–420 (2016)

17. Zhang, H., Li, C., Ke, Y., Zhang, S.: A distributed user browse click model algorithm. Comput. Eng. **45**(3), 1–6 (2019)

18. Gao, J., Huang, X.: Design and implementation of correlation weight algorithm based on hadoop platform. Comput. Eng. **45**(3), 26–31 (2019)

19. Zhou, Q., Chai, X., Ma, K., Yu, Z.: Design and implementation of tucker decomposition module based on CUDA and CUBLAS. Comput. Eng. **45**(3), 41–46 (2019)

Image Segmentation Technology of Marathon Motion Video Based on Machine Learning

Huang Qiang and Liao Yi-de[✉]

Huali College Guangdong University of Technology, Guangzhou 511325, China
pql3@sina.com, liaoyide893@l63.com

Abstract. In order to improve that segmentation quality of the video image of the marathon, a video image segmentation algorithm based on machine learning is proposed. Constructing the edge contour feature detection and the pixel feature point fusion reconstruction model of the marathon moving video image, carrying out multi-level feature decomposition and gray pixel feature separation of the marathon moving video image, and establishing a visual feature reconstruction model of the marathon moving video image, the feature segmentation and the edge contour feature detection of the marathon moving video image are carried out in combination with the block area template matching method, the similarity information fusion model is used for carrying out the video information fusion awareness and the block area template matching in the process of the marathon moving video image segmentation, the fuzzy feature quantity of the moving video image of the marathon is extracted, and the machine learning method is adopted to realize the fusion awareness and the segmentation quality evaluation of the marathon moving video information. The simulation results show that the method is good in image segmentation quality and high in image recognition, and the output signal-to-noise ratio of the motion feature reconstruction of the marathons moving video is high.

Keywords: Machine learning · Marathons · Sports · Video images · Segmentation

1 Introduction

With the development of the computer vision information processing technology, the visual image processing method is adopted to analyze and extract the motion video of the human body, and the segmentation model of the marathon moving video image is established, and the motion characteristic identification and the reconstruction capability of the human body motion are improved. the feature reconstruction of the motion of the human body is established on the basis of the segmentation of the moving video image of the marathon, the non-marked point tracking recognition method is adopted for carrying out the marathon moving video image segmentation processing, and the geometric characteristic analysis model of the marathon moving video image is extracted, through the three-dimensional reconstruction method of the computer vision feature, the method realizes the segmentation and the geometric recognition of the marathon moving video image, extracts the key feature quantity of the marathon

Y.-D. Zhang et al. (Eds.): ICMTEL 2020, LNICST 326, pp. 214–224, 2020.
https://doi.org/10.1007/978-3-030-51100-5_19

moving video image, adopts the pixel tracking and fusion technology, and realizes the image recognition of the marathon moving video [1]. The research on the method of video image segmentation and evaluation of the related marathons is greatly concerned by people [2].

In that traditional method, The method for segmenting the video image of the marathon moving video mainly comprises a HU moment segmentation method, a geometric invariant moment segmentation method, an adaptive edge contour feature segmentation method and the like, a three-dimensional reconstruction model of a marathon moving video image is constructed, a key feature point three-dimensional reconstruction method is adopted [3], the method comprises the following steps of: realizing the segmentation and identification of a marathon moving video image, and acquiring a good marathon moving video image segmentation effect; and a real-time extraction method of a marathon moving video image based on a monocular video is presented in the document [4], In that method, the human motion video follow-up recognition is carried out by adopting a monocular video acquisition method, and the human motion video segmentation is carried out in combination with the correlation fusion method, but the calculation cost of the method is large and the real-time per-formance is not good [5]. A motion image segmentation method based on a sharpening template enhancement technology is presented in the document, and the segmentation detection and the information fusion processing of the two-dimensional marathon moving video image are carried out in combination with the partial region feature matching method, and the image segmentation is realized by extracting the block feature quantity of the marathon moving video image. However, the method has poor self-adaptability and strong anti-interference ability [6].

Aiming at the above problems, this paper proposes a marathon motion video image segmentation algorithm based on machine learning. Firstly, the edge contour feature detection and pixel feature point fusion reconstruction model of marathon motion video image are constructed, the multi-level feature decomposition and gray pixel feature separation of marathon motion video image are carried out, then the visual feature reconstruction model of marathon motion video image is established. Finally, simu-lation experiments are carried out to demonstrate the superior performance of this method in the evaluation of marathon motion video segmentation.

2 Feature Detection of Marathon Motion Video Image and Reconstruction Model of Pixel Feature Point Fusion

2.1 Edge Contour Feature Detection of a Marathon Moving Video Image

In order to realize the image segmentation quality evaluation design of a marathon moving video image based on machine learning, a pixel space fusion model of a marathon moving video image is constructed, and a feature matching method is adopted for carrying out a marathon moving video image characteristic detection, First, the spatial sparsity feature reconstruction of the marathons moving video image is carried out, and the feature point matching of the marathon moving video image is carried out by using the Atanasov extension method, and the template matching model for constructing the marathon moving video image segmentation is shown in Fig. 1.

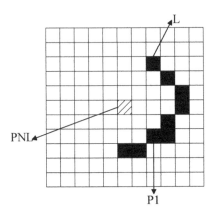

Fig. 1. Template matching model for image segmentation

Assuming that the gray-scale pixel set of the marathon moving video image is (i,j) as a pixel center, a characteristic segmentation model of the marathon moving video image is constructed by adopting a sharpening template block combination method, and the gray value I_{swk} of the marathon moving video image acquired in the k sub-band is determined, in the gray pixel characteristic distribution space [7], the corresponding marathon moving video image gradient characteristic component is obtained as follows:

$$P_{rk} = \left(\frac{\sum_{j=1}^{c} I_{swk}(1,j)}{c}, \frac{\sum_{j=1}^{c} I_{swk}(2,j)}{c}, \dots, \frac{\sum_{j=1}^{c} I_{swk}(i,j)}{c}, \dots, \frac{\sum_{j=1}^{c} I_{swk}(r,j)}{c} \right) \quad (1)$$

$$P_{ck} = \left(\frac{\sum_{i=1}^{r} I_{swk}(i,1)}{r}, \frac{\sum_{i=1}^{r} I_{swk}(i,2)}{r}, \dots, \frac{\sum_{i=1}^{r} I_{swk}(i,j)}{r}, \dots, \frac{\sum_{j=1}^{c} I_{swk}(i,c)}{r} \right) \quad (2)$$

Wherein, c is the number of columns of the LGB vector quantization matrix of the marathon moving video image, and r is the motion blur feature quantity. in combination with a pixel feature point fusion reconstruction method, a human body motion video feature distribution pixel set distribution is obtained, and a video information fusion awareness and a three-dimensional reconstruction are carried out on a marathon moving video image, the feature segmentation and the edge contour feature detection of the marathon moving video image are carried out in combination with the block area template matching method, the gray-scale pixel feature reconstruction of the human motion video is carried out [8], a monocular visual tracking method is adopted, the low-resolution human motion video image is subjected to noise reduction processing, and a sparse characteristic segmentation model of the marathon moving video is constructed, and the output characteristic amount is obtained as follows:

$$G_j(\vec{x}) = \begin{cases} \max\{0, g_j(\vec{x})\}, & 1 \leq j \leq l \\ \max\{0, |h_j(\vec{x})| - \delta\}, & l+1 \leq j \leq p \end{cases} \tag{3}$$

The video information fusion perception and information fusion tracking of human motion are carried out, and the edge outline features of marathon motion video image are detected [9].

2.2 Pixel Feature Point Fusion Reconstruction Model

The edge outline feature detection and pixel feature point fusion reconstruction model of marathon motion video image is constructed, the multi-level feature decomposition and grey pixel feature separation of marathon motion video image are carried out, and the visual feature reconstruction model of marathon motion video image is established. The visual feature distribution of marathon motion video image is as follows:

$$G(\vec{x}) = \sum_{j=1}^{p} G_j(\vec{x}) \tag{4}$$

The adaptive fusion tracking and recognition method is used to mark the key action feature points, and the image segmentation is carried out. The edge segmentation model of marathon motion video image is constructed, and the fuzzy closeness function of human motion video image is obtained as follows:

$$fitness(\vec{x}) = f(\vec{x}) + (Ct)^{\alpha} \sum_{j=1}^{p} G_j^{\beta}(\vec{x}) \tag{5}$$

The bilateral filtering method is used to reduce the noise of marathon motion video image, and the perceptual fusion model of video information fusion is constructed, and the fitness function is obtained as follows:

$$ftiness(\vec{x}) = \begin{cases} f(\vec{x}), & if\ feasible \\ 1 + rG(\vec{x}), & otherwise \end{cases} \tag{6}$$

Considering the gray level pixel level of the marathon moving video image, the multi-dimensional histogram distribution model of the marathon moving video is constructed by adopting a gray-scale invariant moment characteristic decomposition method [10], and the image segmentation model obtained by the fusion of the marathon moving video information is as follows:

$$W_u u(a, b) = e^{j2\pi K \ln a} \times \frac{K}{\sqrt{a}}$$

$$\left\{ \left[\frac{ae^{\frac{j2\pi f_{min}}{a}(b-b_a)}}{f_{min}} - \frac{e^{j2\pi f_{max}(b-b_a)}}{f_{max}} \right] \right.$$

$$+ j2\pi(b - b_a)[Ei(j2\pi f_{max}(b - b_a))$$

$$\left. - Ei\left(\frac{j2\pi f_{min}}{a}(b - b_a) \right) \right] \right\}$$

(7)

Wherein, $b_a = (1 - a)\left(\frac{1}{af_{max}} - \frac{T}{2}\right)$, $Ei(\bullet)$ represents the optimal minimum solution of the visual feature distribution of marathon motion video. Under the action of pixel mean, marathon motion video image segmentation is carried out.

3 Evaluation and Optimization of the Segmentation Quality of the Video Image of the Marathons

3.1 Fuzzy Feature Extraction of a Marathoner's Moving Video Image

The edge contour feature detection and the pixel feature point fusion reconstruction model of the marathon moving video image are constructed, and the multi-level feature decomposition of the marathon moving video image and the basis of the gray pixel feature separation are carried out, In this paper, the segmentation quality assessment and optimization of the video images of the marathons are carried out, and the image segmentation algorithm based on the machine learning is presented in this paper. the feature segmentation and the edge contour feature detection of the marathon moving video image are carried out in combination with the block area template matching method, and the information fusion model of the marathon moving video is constructed based on the local feature adaptive feature matching method [11], the video information fusion sensing model of the image of the marathon moving video is constructed, and the expression of the video information fusion awareness function is obtained as follows:

$$g = k \otimes f + n$$

(8)

Wherein, $\otimes$ represents convolution operator, merges the captured marathon motion video image with vector set, and constructs the edge outline feature decomposition model of marathon motion video [17]. The best resolution eigenvalues of marathon motion video are obtained as:

$$s_{PPM}(t) = \sum_{i=-\infty}^{\infty} \sum_{j=0}^{N_p-1} p\left(t - iT_s - jT_p - c_j T_c - a_i \varepsilon\right)$$

(9)

$$s_{PAM}(t) = \sum_{j=-\infty}^{\infty} d_j p(t - jT_s) \tag{10}$$

The T_s is the spatial pixel gain of volume video motion. The feature reconstruction and reconstruction of marathon motion video is carried out by using similarity reconstruction method. The image pixel decomposition model of marathon motion video is established as follows:

$$x(t) = \sum_{m=1}^{M} \sum_{k=1}^{K(m)} w_{nk} s(t - T_m - \tau_{mk}) + v(t) \tag{11}$$

In the formula, w_{mk} is the fuzzy characteristic component of the marathon moving video, and the image enhancement method is adopted to realize the reconstruction of the gray histogram of the marathon moving video image, and the output is as follows:

$$\begin{cases} x = R \sin \eta \cos \phi & 0 \le \phi \le 2\pi \\ y = R \sin \eta \sin \phi & 0 \le \eta \le \pi \\ z = R \cos \eta & R = D/2 \end{cases} \tag{12}$$

In which, η represents an edge division function, ϕ represents an angle function of a human motion video image segmentation, R represents a template matching coefficient, a gray-scale pixel feature decomposition method is adopted [12], and the feature segmentation and high-resolution reconstruction of the marathon moving video image are carried out, and the output is as follows:

$$\begin{aligned}
\mathbf{D}_{(i+1)} &= \mathbf{B}_{(i+1)} \mathbf{C}_{(i+1)} \\
&= \mathbf{B}_{(i)} \mathbf{C}_{(i)} - \beta_{i+1}^{-1} \left(\mathbf{B}_{(i)} \mathbf{C}_{(i)} \mathbf{w}_{i+1} \right) \frac{\mathbf{w}_{i+1}^T \lambda_i^{-1} \mathbf{C}_{(i)}}{\lambda_i^{-1} \beta_{(i+1)}^{-1} \mathbf{w}_{i+1}^T \mathbf{C}_{(i)} \mathbf{w}_{i+1} + 1} \\
&\quad + \beta_{i+1}^{-1} \mathbf{x}_{i+1} \left(\lambda_i^{-1} \mathbf{w}_{i+1}^T \mathbf{C}_{(i)} \right) - \beta_{i+1}^{-1} \mathbf{x}_{i+1} \frac{\beta_{i+1}^{-1} \lambda_i^{-1} \mathbf{w}_{i+1}^T \mathbf{C}_{(i)} \mathbf{w}_{i+1}}{\beta_{i+1}^{-1} \lambda_i^{-1} \mathbf{w}_{i+1}^T \mathbf{C}_{(i)} \mathbf{w}_{i+1} + 1} \mathbf{w}_{i+1}^T \lambda_i^{-1}
\end{aligned} \tag{13}$$

Based on sparse representation, the fuzzy feature extraction of marathon motion video image is realized. According to the result of feature extraction, the optimal segmentation template matching function of sub-block $G_{m,n}$, with $M \times N$ 2×2 in gradient direction is obtained as follows:

$$G_{m,n} = \begin{pmatrix} g_{(m,n)}(1,1) & g_{(m,n)}(1,2) \\ g_{(m,n)}(2,1) & g_{(m,n)}(2,2) \end{pmatrix} \quad m = 1, 2, \ldots, M; n = 1, 2, \ldots, N; \tag{14}$$

Wherein, the u is the edge pixel point of the marathon moving video image, the $p(i,j)$ represents the gray pixel value of the marathon moving video in the sharpening area, the (i,j) is the image gray scale deviation, and the fuzzy feature extraction of the marathon moving video image is realized through the algorithm design, and performing image segmentation according to the feature extraction result [13].

3.2 Image Segmentation Video Information Fusion Awareness

Setting δ_l^2 as the local variance of the moving video image of the marathon, δ_η^2 is the optimization coefficient of the marathon moving video image, the $\beta = \max\left[\frac{\delta_l^2 - \delta_\eta^2}{\delta_l^2}, 0\right]$, the region block division of the marathon moving video is carried out by using the gradient descent method, so that the sparse characteristic value of the marathon moving video image meets the $C \in S$, According to the sparse prior representation result, the optimal segmentation threshold value at the $F_m(x,y)$ frame m of the marathon moving video image (x,y) is obtained. the template matching of the marathon moving video image is carried out based on the approximate sparse representation method, and the matching coefficient is obtained as follows:

$$g_i^* = \begin{cases} Rs_j, & z \le i \le x - y \\ g_i, & otherwise \end{cases} \tag{15}$$

Wherein, the feature segmentation and edge outline feature detection of marathon motion video image are carried out by combining block region template matching method, and the video information fusion perception is carried out in the process of marathon motion video image segmentation by using similarity information fusion model [14], and the grey edge eigenvalues of local area of marathon motion video image are calculated, in which the maximum gray value of marathon motion video image is as follows:

$$n_{pq} = \frac{\mu_{pq}}{(\mu_{00})^\gamma} \tag{16}$$

By adopting the sparse representation and the super-resolution reconstruction method to carry out the segmentation processing of the marathon moving video image, the machine learning method is adopted to realize the fusion awareness and the segmentation quality assessment of the marathon moving video information, and the sparse segmentation model of the marathon moving video image is expressed as:

$$g(x,y) = f(x,y) + \varepsilon(x,y) \tag{17}$$

Among them, $f(x,y)$, $g(x,y)$, $\varepsilon(x,y)$ represents the original human motion video image, reconstructed image and gray image respectively. Based on the analysis, machine learning method is used to realize the fusion perception and segmentation quality evaluation of marathon motion video information [15].

4 Simulation Experiment and Result Analysis

In order to test the performance of this method in realizing marathon motion video image segmentation, the experimental simulation tool is matlab 7. the sampling data of marathon motion video image is taken from usc-sipi image database. the training sample set of marathon motion video image is 600. the edge contour pixel distribution set of marathon motion video image is 400 * 400. the feature resolution of video information fusion perception is 2000, the edge contour feature decomposition coefficient is 0.34,0.75, and the pixel step size value is 20. According to the simulation parameters, the marathon motion image segmentation is set.

Fig. 2. Marathons moving video images to be segmented

Taking the marathon motion video image of Fig. 2 as the test sample, the information fusion is carried out, the edge outline feature detection and pixel feature point fusion reconstruction model of the marathon motion video image is constructed, the multi-level feature decomposition and gray pixel feature separation of the marathon motion video image are carried out, the automatic segmentation of the marathon motion video image is realized, and the marathon motion video image segmentation is carried out by different methods. The segmentation results are shown in Fig. 3.

(a) PCA method

(b) Proposed method

Fig. 3. Matching result of image pixel spatial fusion characteristics

The analysis of Fig. 3 shows that the quality of the video image segmentation by the method is good, and the error of image segmentation is tested by different methods, and the result of the comparison is shown in Fig. 4.

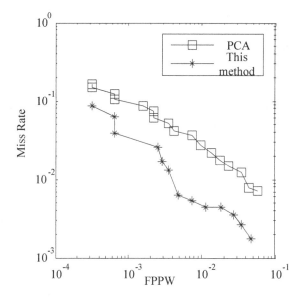

Fig. 4. Error comparison of image segmentation

The test results of Fig. 4 show that the error of memorizing image segmentation is low, and the output peak signal-to-noise ratio (PSNR) of marathon motion video image segmentation is tested by different methods. The results are shown in Table 1. The analysis shows that the output peak signal-to-noise ratio of marathon motion video image segmentation by this method is high.

Table 1. Comparison of psnr for video image segmentation of the line of line marathon(db)

Iterations	Proposed method	Wavelet analysis method	Principal component analysis method
100	43.67	22.89	32.46
200	48.65	25.65	35.56
300	51.52	26.76	37.94
400	54.67	35.43	39.43

5   Conclusions

In this paper, a video image segmentation algorithm based on machine learning is proposed. Constructing the edge contour feature detection and the pixel feature point fusion reconstruction model of the marathon moving video image, carrying out multi-level feature decomposition and gray pixel feature separation of the marathon moving video image, and establishing a visual feature reconstruction model of the marathon moving video image, the feature segmentation and the edge contour feature detection of the marathon moving video image are carried out in combination with the block area template matching method, the similarity information fusion model is used for carrying out the video information fusion awareness and the block area template matching in the process of the marathon moving video image segmentation, the fuzzy feature quantity of the moving video image of the marathon is extracted, and the machine learning method is adopted to realize the fusion awareness and the segmentation quality evaluation of the marathon moving video information. The simulation results show that the method is good in image segmentation quality and high in image recognition, and the output signal-to-noise ratio of the motion feature reconstruction of the marathons moving video is high. This method has good application value in the video analysis of Marathon Sport.

References

1. Mukaino, M., Ono, T., Shindo, K., et al.: Efficacy of brain-computer interface-driven neuromuscular electrical stimulation for chronic paresis after stroke. J. Rehab. Med. **46**(4), 378–382 (2014)
2. Moghaddam, Z., Piccardi, M.: Training initialization of hidden Markov models in human action recognition. IEEE Trans. Autom. Sci. Eng. **11**(2), 394–408 (2014)
3. Amor, B.B., Su, J., Srivastava, A.: Action recognition using rate-invariant analysis, of skeletal shape trajectories. IEEE Trans. Pattern Anal. Mach. Intell. **38**(1), 1–13 (2016)
4. Songlin, L., Yong, J., Yong, G., Xiaoling, Z., Guolong, C.: Moving target tracking algorithm based on improved Camshift for through-wall-radar imaging. J. Comput. Appl. **38**(2), 528–532 (2018)
5. Jie-yu, Z., Hong-ping, Z., Shu, C.: Face recognition based on weighted local binary pattern with adaptive threshold. J. Electron. Inform. Technol. **36**(6), 1327–1333 (2014)
6. Naseem, I., Togneri, R., Bennamoun, M.: Linear regression for face recognition. IEEE Trans. Pattern Anal. Mach. Intell. **32**(11), 2106–2112 (2010)
7. Wagner, A., Wright, J., Ganesh, A., Zhou, Z., Mobahi, H., Ma, Y.: Toward a practical face recognition system: robust alignment and illumination by sparse representation. IEEE Trans. Pattern Anal. Mach. Intell. **34**(2), 372–386 (2012)
8. Wu, J.G., Shao, T., Liu, Z.Y.: RGB-D saliency detection based on integration feature of color and depth saliency map. J. Electron. Inform. Technol. **39**(9), 2148–2154 (2017)
9. Carlson, N.A., Porter, J.R.: On the cardinality of Hausdorff spaces and H-closed spaces. Topology Appl. **160**(1), 137–142 (2017)
10. Yue, X., Mengru, F., Jiatian, P., Yong, C.: Remote sensing image segmentation method based on deep learning model. J. Compu. Appl. **39**(10), 2905–2914 (2019)
11. Gao, H.Y., Wu, B.: Object-oriented classification of high spatial resolution remote sensing imagery based on image segmentation with pixel shape feature. Remote Sens. Inf. **6**, 67–72 (2010)
12. Yuan, J., Wang, D., Li, R.: Remote sensing image segmentation by combining spectral and texture features. IEEE Trans. Geosci. Remote Sens. **52**(1), 16–24 (2014)
13. Krähenbvhl, P., Koltun, V.: Efficient inference in fully connected CRFs with Gaussian edge potentials. In: Proceedings of the 2011 International Conference on Neural Information Processing Systems, pp. 109–117. Curran Associates Inc., New York (2011)
14. Lan, G., Zihan, G., Yao, W.: Gastric tumor cell image recognition method based on radial transformation and improved AlexNet. J. Comput. Appl. **39**(10), 2923–2929 (2019)
15. Huang, B., Zhao, B., Song, Y.: Urban land-use mapping using a deep convolutional neural network with high spatial resolution multispectral remote sensing imagery. Remote Sens. Environ. **214**, 73–86 (2018)

Research on the Adaptive Tracking Method for the Tracking of the Track of the Long-Jump Athletes

Yi-de Liao[✉] and Qiang Huang

Huali College Guangdong University of Technology, Guangzhou 511325, China
liaoyide893@163.com

Abstract. In order to improve the accuracy of long jump in long jump, combined with computer vision image processing method to correct the long jump trajectory in long jump, an adaptive tracking method of long jump trajectory tracking image based on machine vision tracking detection is proposed, and the video point frame scanning method is used to collect the long jump trajectory tracking image. The image of long jump athletes is segmented by adaptive pixel fusion method, and the automatic tracking and recognition of long jumpers' motion trajectory tracking image is carried out based on dynamic feature segmentation. The grey feature quantity of long jump trajectory tracking image is extracted, and the neighborhood distribution model of long jump in long jump is constructed. According to the dynamic evolution characteristic distribution of the long jump trajectory, the dynamic characteristics of the long jump trajectory are analyzed, and the image segmentation of the long jump track tracking is realized by combining the spatial neighborhood enhancement technology, and the adaptive tracking of the long jump trajectory in the long jump is realized according to the image segmentation results. The simulation results show that this method has high accuracy in adaptive tracking image of long jump athletes, and improves the accuracy of long jump in long jump.

Keywords: Long jump · Corner ball · Long jump · Image · Adaptive tracking

1 Introduction

With the development of the intelligent vision image information processing technology, the computer image information processing technology is adopted to carry out the track analysis of the long jump motion in the long jump motion, the motion track tracking image information fusion model of the long jump athlete is constructed, the automatic follow recognition of the track is carried out in combination with the visual evolution characteristic distribution of the moving track tracking image of the long jump athlete, and the identification capability of the long jump athlete motion track tracking image is improved [1], the method of self-adaptive tracking of moving track tracking images of long jump athletes is of great significance in the correction and attitude adjustment of the track of long jump. The method for tracking the track of the moving track of the long jump athlete is based on the automatic segmentation and characteristic information extraction of the image [2], the gray feature quantity of the

Y.-D. Zhang et al. (Eds.): ICMTEL 2020, LNICST 326, pp. 225–235, 2020.
https://doi.org/10.1007/978-3-030-51100-5_20

moving track of the long jump athlete is extracted, the image segmentation and the information fusion are carried out according to the edge contour distribution of the image, in the traditional method, the tracking method for tracking the moving track of the long jump athlete mainly adopts the pixel point tracking method, and the segmentation performance of the image is not good as the gray scale of the pixel distribution is changed [3]. Aiming at the above problems, a method for tracking the moving track of the long jump athlete based on the machine vision tracking detection is proposed, the video point frame scanning method is adopted to carry out the motion track tracking image acquisition of the long jump athlete, and the acquired long jump athlete moving image is divided and processed, Finally, the self-adaptive tracking simulation of the image is carried out, and the validity conclusion is obtained.

2 Imaging and Preprocessing of Track Tracking Image of Long Jump Athletes

2.1 Imaging of Track Tracking Image of Long Jump Athletes

In order to realize the information fusion and feature detection of track tracking images of long jump athletes, the long jump track tracking detection is carried out by combining the image segmentation method, and the feature separation processing of track tracking images of long jump athletes is carried out by using adaptive feature separation and information fusion technology.

The visual image multi-layer grid area distribution model of long jump trajectory planning is constructed. The multi-dimensional video tracking sampling method is used to collect the visual features of the long jump trajectory space [4]. Combined with the video frame point scanning and tracking technology, the spatial visual features of the long jump trajectory are collected distributed. The three-dimensional visual sampling image of the long jump trajectory space is $s(X, Y)$, using the beam scanning method of related frames. The pose distribution mode of multi-frame image with long jump trajectory is obtained as follows:

$$Ncut(A, B) = \frac{cut(A, B)}{assoc(A, V)} + \frac{cut(A, B)}{assoc(B, V)} \qquad (1)$$

Wherein, $assoc(A, V)$ is the amplitude of pixel intersection in the pixel subset G of the spatial vision image of long jump trajectory under machine vision. $assoc(B, V)$ is the 3D edge outline feature quantity of the visual image of long jump trajectory space, and the correlation feature solution of spatial visual feature matching of long jump trajectory is expressed as follows:

$$W_u u(a, b_m) = \frac{1}{\sqrt{a}} \int_{-aT/2+b_m}^{T/2} \left|\frac{1}{\sqrt{T}}\right|^2 dt = \frac{1}{\sqrt{aT}}\left(\frac{T}{2} + \frac{aT}{2} - b_m\right) \qquad (2)$$

The histogram of the moving track space visual image of the long jump and the reference feature point are visually tracked and matched, and a multi-layer segmentation model of the long jump motion track space visual image is established in the local area of the 4×4 sub-block, and the description is as follows:

$$d_{i+1} = 2F(x_{i+1} + \frac{1}{2}, y_i + 2)$$

$$= \begin{cases} 2[\Delta x(y_i + 2) - \Delta y(x_{i,r} + \frac{1}{2} - \Delta xB)] & d_i \leq 0 \\ 2[\Delta x(y_i + 2) - \Delta y(x_{i,r} + 1 + \frac{1}{2} - \Delta xB)] & d_i > 0 \end{cases} \quad (3)$$

In the fuzzy region, the spatial visual information acquisition of the long jump motion track is carry out, and the acquired output is as follows:

$$P(y_{w_3}|x_{w_3}, \theta, \beta) \propto P(y_{w_3}|x_{w_3}, \theta)(y_{w_3}|\beta_i)$$

$$\propto \prod_{k=1}^{K} \alpha_k \frac{1}{\sqrt{2\pi\sigma_k^2}} \exp\left\{-\frac{(x_i - \mu_k)^2}{2\sigma_k^2}\right\} \cdot \frac{1}{Z(\beta_i)} \exp\left(-\sum_{c \subset C} V_c(Y, \beta_i)\right)$$

$$\propto \prod_{k=1}^{K} \frac{\alpha_k}{Z(\beta_i)\sqrt{2\pi\sigma_k^2}} \cdot \exp\left\{-\left[\sum_{k=1}^{K} \frac{(x_i - \mu_k)^2}{2\sigma_k^2} + \sum_{c \subset C} V_c(Y, \beta_i)\right]\right\}$$

$$(4)$$

In summary, the video point frame scanning method is used to collect the motion trajectory tracking image of long jumpers, and the adaptive pixel fusion method is used to segment the image trajectory of long jumpers, so as to improve the adaptive tracking and recognition ability of long jumpers' motion trajectory tracking image [5].

2.2 Image Trajectory Segmentation and Information Enhancement Processing

The grid segmentation of each template in the visual space of the long jump trajectory is carried out, and the binary reconstruction of the correlation frame of the long jump trajectory is carried out in the $m*n$ region. The fuzzy region high resolution feature extraction model of the visual image of the long jump trajectory space is constructed [6–9]. The regional feature distribution points of the spatial visual image of the long jump trajectory are obtained as follows:

$$J(x) = \frac{I(x) - A}{\max(t(x), t_0)} + A \quad (5)$$

Wherein, t_0 represents the structural similarity of the spatial visual image of the long jump trajectory, carries on the template matching in the neighborhood structure of the image 3*3, carries on the spatial segmentation through the acquisition result of the visual image of the long jump trajectory space, considers the common view degree of the new feature point to carry on the spatial visual planning of the long jump trajectory

[10], and the rotation and translation output of the long jump trajectory space are as follows:

$$\overrightarrow{W_iP} = \left\|\overrightarrow{W_iS_k}\right\| \times \cos\partial \times \frac{\overrightarrow{W_iW_j}}{\left\|\overrightarrow{W_iW_j}\right\|} \tag{6}$$

The output of the pixel subset of the spatial distribution of the long jump trajectory is expressed as follows:

$$I(x) = J(x)t(x) + A(1 - t(x)) \tag{7}$$

Wherein, the A is the three-dimensional scale information of the long jump motion track space vision, and $t(x)$ is the edge contour value of the long jump motion track space vision, and the quantitative characteristic distribution set of the long jump motion track space visual image area segmentation is as follows:

$$w(i,j) = \frac{1}{Z(i)} \exp\left(-\frac{d(i,j)}{h^2}\right) \tag{8}$$

Wherein, $Z(i) = \sum_{j \in \Omega} \exp\left(-\frac{d(i,j)}{h^2}\right)$ is the spatial visual gradient feature of long jump trajectory. The adaptive pixel fusion method is used to segment the trajectory of the collected long jumpers' motion image, and the automatic tracking and recognition of the long jumpers' motion trajectory tracking image is carried out based on the dynamic feature segmentation [11], and the fuzzy regional gradient mode features of the input spatial visual image of the long jump trajectory are obtained.

$$\min_c(\min_{y \in \Omega(x)} \left(\frac{I^c(y)}{A^c}\right)) = \tilde{t}(x) \min_c(\min_{y \in \Omega(x)} \left(\frac{J^c(y)}{A^c}\right)) + (1 - \tilde{t}(x)) \tag{9}$$

Wherein, $\tilde{t}(x)$ is the matching set of image frame feature points, A^c is the statistical feature quantity of spatial visual distribution of long jump trajectory, and the image trajectory segmentation and information enhancement processing are realized by comprehensive analysis [12].

3 Adaptive Tracking and Optimization of the Track of the Long-Jump

3.1 Long Jump Track Feature Extraction

On the basis of the above adaptive tracking image design of long jumpers based on the video point frame scanning method, the adaptive tracking image of long jumpers is designed. In this paper, an adaptive tracking method of long jumpers' trajectory tracking images based on machine vision tracking detection is proposed, and the spatial vision planning model of long jumpers is constructed [13]. Combined with visual conduction technology, the position and pose adjustment and attitude correction of long jump motion are carried out, and the quantitative conduction tracking recognition of spatial vision of long jump trajectory is carried out by using modular feature matching technology. The pixel eigenvalues of spatial visual distribution of long jump trajectory are obtained as:

$$w(d_{ij}) = f(|x_i - x_j|) = \frac{1}{\sqrt{2\pi}} \exp\left\{ \frac{(x_i - x_j)^2}{2} \right\} \tag{10}$$

The scene coordinates in the spatial visual distribution area of the long jump trajectory are $M \times N$, according to the spatial rotation and attitude adjustment of the long jump trajectory, the piecewise area planning is carried out, and the feature points of the long jump dynamic trajectory distribution are added to the reconstruction scene [14]. The visual feature quantity extraction and 3D reconstruction of the long jump trajectory are realized, and the reconstruction output is obtained as follows:

$$\beta_i = \exp\left\{ -\frac{|x_i - x_j|^2}{2\sigma^2} \right\} \frac{1}{\text{dist}(x_i, x_j)} \tag{11}$$

The visual image multi-layer mesh distribution model of the long jump motion track planning is constructed, and according to the difference of the acquisition environment of the long jump motion track space visual image, the spatial visual pose offset of the long jump motion track space is obtained as follows:

$$u(x, y; t) = G(x, y; t) \tag{12}$$

$$p(x, t) = \lim_{\Delta x \to 0} [\sigma \frac{u - (u + \Delta u)}{\Delta x}] = -\sigma \frac{\partial u(x, t)}{\partial x} \tag{13}$$

Wherein, Δu is the frame of long jump track tracking image with local correlation pixel point, and F is the spatial visual difference distribution characteristic quantity of long jump track. The grey feature quantity of track tracking image of long jump athletes is extracted [15], and the automatic spatial planning neighborhood distribution model of long jump motion is constructed. The similarity characteristic value of long jump track space is obtained as follows:

$$s(k) = \phi \cdot s(k - 1) + w(k) \tag{14}$$

Wherein

$$\phi = \begin{pmatrix} 1 & 0 & 0 & 0 & 0 \\ 0 & 1 & 1 & 0 & 0 \\ 0 & 0 & 1 & 0 & 0 \\ 0 & 0 & 0 & 1 & 1 \\ 0 & 0 & 0 & 0 & 1 \end{pmatrix}, w(k) = \begin{pmatrix} N(0, \sigma_{\theta(k)}) \\ 0 \\ N(0, \sigma_{x(k)}) \\ 0 \\ N(0, \sigma_{y(k)}) \end{pmatrix} \tag{15}$$

The diffraction R, G, B components of the spatial visual feature distribution of the long jump trajectory are extracted, and the adaptive tracking image of the long jump track is carried out according to the results of feature extraction [16].

3.2   Trajectory Segmentation and Adaptive Tracking of Long Jump

The fuzzy constraint optimization function for strengthening the tracking image information of long jumpers is as follows:

$$
\begin{aligned}
minimize \quad & f(\vec{x}) \quad \vec{x} = (x_1, x_2, \ldots, x_n) \in \Re^n \\
subject\ to \quad & g_j(\vec{x}) \le 0, j = 1, \ldots, l \\
& h_j(\vec{x}) = 0, j = l+1, \ldots, p
\end{aligned}
\tag{16}
$$

The statistical feature distribution model of the track tracking image of long jumpers is obtained as:

$$
L_0(r) = \frac{L(r/2)}{2}, \ H_0(r) = H\left(\frac{r}{2}\right)
\tag{17}
$$

Wherein, r and θ are the coordinates of the frequency domain feature distribution of the long jump trajectory tracking image, and the dynamic characteristics of the long jump trajectory are analyzed in combination with the dynamic evolution feature distribution of the long jump trajectory [17]. The feature high resolution detection of the long jump track tracking image is carried out, and the detection function is obtained as follows:

$$
\Omega = \left\{
\begin{array}{l}
\vec{x} \in s | g_j(\vec{x}) \le 0, j = 1, \ldots, l; \\
h_j(\vec{x}) = 0, j = l+1, \ldots, p
\end{array}
\right\}
\tag{18}
$$

It is assumed that the fuzzy correlation constraint characteristic component of the tracking image of the moving track of the long jump athlete is expressed as follows:

$$
c_1 = \{i | i \in S\}, \quad c_2 = \{\{i, i'\} | i' \in N_i, i \in S\}, \quad C = c_1 \cup c_2
\tag{19}
$$

In the above formula, $i = 1, 2, \ldots, T$, it represents the length of pixel sequence, divides each template in the visual space of long jump motion, merges and filters the visual image of long jump motion space output by frame scanning, and obtains the image enhancement output as follows:

$$
G_j(\vec{x}) = \left\{
\begin{array}{ll}
\max\{0, g_j(\vec{x})\}, & 1 \le j \le l \\
\max\{0, |h_j(\vec{x})| - \delta\}, & l+1 \le j \le p
\end{array}
\right.
\tag{20}
$$

It can be simplified as:

$$
G(\vec{x}) = \sum_{j=1}^{p} G_j(\vec{x})
\tag{21}
$$

By adopting the Harris corner point detection technology to carry out the track tracking and the information marking of the long jump, the motion track tracking image segmentation of the long jump athlete is realized, the self-adaptive tracking of the long jump motion track is realized according to the image segmentation result [18], and the implementation process of the algorithm is shown in Fig. 1.

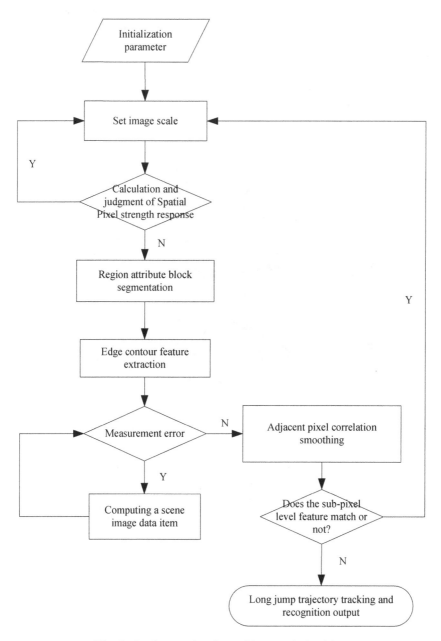

Fig. 1. Implementation flow of improved algorithm

4 Simulation Experiment and Result Analysis

In order to test the application performance of this method in the adaptive tracking and recognition of long jumpers' motion trajectory tracking image, the experimental test and analysis are carried out. Combined with Visual C++ and Matlab, the simulation algorithm of long jumper trajectory tracking image tracking image is designed. The pixel set intensity of adaptive tracking image of long jumpers' motion trajectory tracking image is 200, and the distribution of edge outline features is $400 \leq 400$. The number of iterations of image adaptive tracking learning is 1600 times, and the segmentation coefficient is 0.21. According to the above simulation environment and parameter setting, the adaptive tracking image of long jumpers is carried out, and the original tracking image of long jumpers is obtained as shown in Fig. 2.

Fig. 2. Original long jump athlete's motion track tracking image

Taking the trajectory tracking image of long jumpers as the research sample, the neighborhood distribution model of automatic spatial planning for long jump motion is constructed. Combined with the dynamic evolution feature distribution of long jump trajectory, the dynamic characteristics of long jump trajectory are analyzed, and the segmentation and adaptive tracking of long jump trajectory tracking image are realized, and the tracking results are shown in Fig. 3.

Fig. 3. Tracking adaptive tracking results

The method can effectively realize the self-adaptive tracking of the track-tracking images of the long-jump athletes by adopting the method, and the long-jump precision after the self-adaptive tracking of the moving track of the long-jump athletes is analyzed by adopting different methods, and the comparison result is shown in Fig. 4.

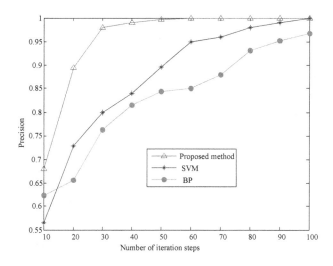

Fig. 4. Precision comparison

The analysis of Fig. 4 results show that the SVM and BP methods are compared with the proposed method, and the adaptive tracking accuracy and adaptive performance of the proposed long jump athlete's tracking image are high. The proposed method has better performance of adaptive tracking image for the long jump athlete.

5 Conclusions

The information fusion model of long jumper trajectory tracking image is constructed, and the visual evolution feature distribution of long jumper trajectory tracking image is automatically followed and recognized, so as to improve the identification ability of long jumper trajectory tracking image. In this paper, an adaptive tracking method of long jumper motion trajectory tracking image based on machine vision tracking and detection is proposed. The video point frame scanning method is used to collect the long jumper motion trajectory tracking image. The collected long jumper motion image is segmented by adaptive pixel fusion method, and the grey feature quantity of the long jumper motion trajectory tracking image is extracted. The automatic spatial planning neighborhood distribution model of long jump motion is constructed. according to the dynamic evolution feature distribution of long jump trajectory, the dynamic characteristics of long jump trajectory are analyzed, and the image segmentation of long jump track tracking is realized by combining spatial neighborhood enhancement technology, and the adaptive tracking of long jump trajectory is realized according to the image segmentation results. It is found that the proposed method has good adaptability to track the long jump trajectory and improves the accuracy of the long jump.

References

1. Ding, Y., Li, N.: Image quality assessment based on non-local high dimensional feature analysis. J. Electron. Inf. **38**(9), 2365–2370 (2016)
2. Wang, H., Jin, H., Wang, J., Jiang, W.: Optimization approach for multi-scale segmentation of remotely sensed imagery under k-means clustering guidance. Acta Geodaet. Cartograph. Sinica **44**(5), 526–532 (2015)
3. Liu, D., ZHou, D., Nie, R., Hou, R.: Multi-focus image fusion based on phase congruency motivate pulse coupled neural network-based in NSCT domain. J. Comput. Appl. **38**(10), 3006–3012 (2018)
4. Hu, L.-J., Yang, J.-Z., Feng, D.-B., et al.: Research on the key design parameters of sleeper for 40 t axle-load heavy haul railway. J. Railway Eng. Soc. **34**(4) 25–29, 74 (2017)
5. Lei, Y.: Multi-focus image fusion method based on NSST and IICM. In: Barolli, L., Zhang, M., Wang, X.A. (eds.) EIDWT 2017. LNDECT, vol. 6, pp. 679–689. Springer, Cham (2018). https://doi.org/10.1007/978-3-319-59463-7_68
6. Yang, L.: Technique for image de-noising based on non-subsampled shearlet transform and improved intuitionistic fuzzy entropy. Optik-Int. J. Light Electron Opt. **126**(4), 446–453 (2015)
7. Wei, X.S., Luo, J.H., Wu, J.: Selective convolutional descriptor aggregation for fine-grained image retrieval. IEEE Trans. Image Process. **26**(6), 2868–2881 (2017)
8. Radenović, F., Tolias, G., Chum, O.: CNN image retrieval learns from BoW: unsupervised fine-tuning with hard examples. In: Leibe, B., Matas, J., Sebe, N., Welling, M. (eds.) ECCV 2016. LNCS, vol. 9905, pp. 3–20. Springer, Cham (2016). https://doi.org/10.1007/978-3-319-46448-0_1
9. Sun, Y., Song, H., Zhang, K., Yan, F.: Face super-resolution via very deep convolutional neural network. J. Comput. Appl. **38**(4), 1141–1145 (2018)
10. Liu, H.M., Bi, X.H., Ye, Z.F., Wang, W.L.: Arc promoting inpainting using exemplar searching and priority filling. J. Image Grapgics **21**(8), 993–1003 (2016)

11. Bharadi, V.A., Padole, L.: Performance comparison of hybrid wavelet transform-I variants and contrast limited adaptive histogram equalization combination for image enhancement. In: Proceedings of the 2017 14th International Conference on Wireless and Optical Communications Networks, pp. 1–8. IEEE, Piscataway (2017)

12. Vishwakarma, A., Bhuyan, M.K.: Image fusion using adjustable non-subsampled shearlet transform. IEEE Trans. Instr. Measur. **PP**(99), 1–12 (2018)

13. Zhang, J.-y., Zhao, H.-p., Chen, S.: Face recognition based on weighted local binary pattern with adaptive threshold. J. Electron. Inf. Technol. **36**(6), 1327–1333 (2014)

14. Naseem, I., Togneri, R., Bennamoun, M.: Linear regression for face recognition. IEEE Trans. Pattern Anal. Mach. Intell. **32**(11), 2106–2112 (2010)

15. Wagner, A., Wright, J., Ganesh, A., Zhou, Z., Mobahi, H., Ma, Y.: Toward a practical face recognition system: robust alignment and illumination by sparse representation. IEEE Trans. Pattern Anal. Mach. Intell. **34**(2), 372–386 (2012)

16. Wu, J.G., Shao, T., Liu, Z.Y.: RGB-D saliency detection based on integration feature of color and depth saliency map. J. Electron. Inf. Technol. **39**(9), 2148–2154 (2017)

17. Carlson, N.A., Porter, J.R.: On the cardinality of Hausdorff spaces and H-closed spaces. Topol. Appl. **160**(1), 137–142 (2017)

18. Ang, L., Cheng, X., Qin, P., Gao, Y.: Non-rigid multi-modal medical image registration based on multi-channel sparse coding. J. Comput. Appl. **38**(4), 1127–1133 (2018)

Application of Big Data's Association Rules in the Analysis of Sports Competition Tactics

Jia Ren[✉] and Chong-gao Chen

Huali College Guangdong University of Technology, Guangzhou, China
renjia123@126.com

Abstract. The problem of low accuracy and poor ability of tactical analysis of current tournament analysis strategy, to improve the statistical intelligent analysis ability of the tactical analysis of sports games, it is necessary to carry out the tactical analysis and statistics of the sports games, and put forward a game strategy analysis and statistical model based on a large data association rule mining. firstly, a data acquisition and diagnosis analysis model of a sports game strategy analysis is constructed, and a sports game tactical analysis data information flow model is constructed, and the statistic characteristic quantity in the sports game tactical analysis is extracted, the method of fuzzy correlation fusion is used to analyze the interference of the statistical data in the tactical analysis of the sports game, and a plurality of known interference frequency components are removed. in that method, a large-data association rule mining algorithm is adopted to carry out statistical data identification and characteristic analysis in a sports game and tactical analysis, an optimization characteristic solution of the game and tactical statistical information analysis is established, and a self-adaptive optimization of the game and tactical statistical information analysis is carried out by adopting a simplified gradient algorithm, the feature analysis and data optimization recognition of the game tactics analysis are realized by combining the self-correlation feature matching method. The simulation results show that the method is used to carry out the tactical analysis of sports games and the accuracy of the statistics, so as to improve the ability of the tactical analysis of the sports games, so as to improve the effect of the competition.

Keywords: Big data · Association rules · Sports games · Tactical analysis · Statistical analysis

1 Introduction

In a large-scale sports event, that tactics of sports match is very important to win, it is necessary to construct the tactical analysis model of the sports game, carry out the tactical analysis of the sports game, extract the statistic feature quantity in the tactical analysis of the sports game, adopt the statistical analysis method, carrying out the tactical analysis and statistics of the sports games, constructing a distributed detection model of the statistical data in the sports game tactical analysis [1], carrying out the characteristic analysis of the tactical characteristics of the sports game according to the statistical data distribution state in the sports game tactical analysis, the research of the statistical data monitoring method in the related sports game tactics analysis is of great

© ICST Institute for Computer Sciences, Social Informatics and Telecommunications Engineering 2020
Published by Springer Nature Switzerland AG 2020. All Rights Reserved
Y.-D. Zhang et al. (Eds.): ICMTEL 2020, LNICST 326, pp. 236–246, 2020.
https://doi.org/10.1007/978-3-030-51100-5_21

concern to the people, the identification of the statistical data in the tactical analysis of the sports game is based on the statistical analysis of the tactical analysis data of the sports game, and a large data analysis method is adopted, Feature extraction and identification of statistical data in the tactical analysis of sports games [2].

Traditionally, the method of statistical analysis, fuzzy feature detection and particle swarm optimization for the tactical analysis and statistical methods of sports games is presented, and the statistical analysis model of statistical data in the tactical analysis of sports games is established, and the method of fuzzy-constrained clustering analysis is combined. And carrying out statistical data detection and identification in the sports game tactical analysis [3]. In reference [4], a statistical data detection method is proposed in the tactical analysis of the sports game based on the feature extraction of the spectrum, according to the spectrum analysis of the statistical data in the sports game tactics analysis by the self-adaptive spectrum detection method, the spectral characteristic quantity of the statistical data in the sports game tactical analysis is extracted, the method of the analysis and analysis is carried out by using the fuzzy correlation fusion analysis, the tactical analysis and the statistics of the sports game are realized, But the computational complexity of the method is high and the real-time performance is not good. In view of the above problems, this paper proposes a game strategy analysis and statistical model based on a large data association rule mining. Firstly, a data acquisition and diagnosis analysis model of a sports game strategy analysis is constructed, and a sports game tactical analysis data information flow model is constructed, and the statistic characteristic quantity in the sports game tactical analysis is extracted, the method of fuzzy correlation fusion is used to analyze the interference of the statistical data in the tactical analysis of the sports game, and a plurality of known interference frequency components are removed [5]. In that method, a large-data association rule mining algorithm is adopted to carry out statistical data identification and characteristic analysis in a sports game and tactical analysis, an optimization characteristic solution of the game and tactical statistical information analysis is established, and a self-adaptive optimization of the game and tactical statistical information analysis is carried out by adopting a simplified gradient algorithm, the feature analysis and data optimization recognition of the game tactics analysis are realized by combining the self-correlation feature matching method. Finally, the simulation experiment is carried out to show the superiority of the method in improving the tactical analysis and statistical ability of the sports game [6].

2 Collection of Statistical Data and Analysis of Characteristics in Tactical Analysis of Sports Competition

2.1 Sampling of Statistical Data in Tactical Analysis of Sports Competition

In order to improve the statistical intelligence analysis ability of sports competition tactical analysis, it is necessary to carry out sports competition tactical analysis and statistics. In this paper, the nonlinear feature sequence analysis method is used to sample the statistical data of sports competition tactical analysis in real time [7]. The collected data are ECG information, real-time brain wave information, cardiac load information, lung flux information and so on. According to the data acquisition results, the intelligent feature analysis and recognition of statistical data in sports competition tactical analysis are carried out, the statistical data collection and information storage model in sports competition tactical analysis is constructed, a statistical analysis model containing physique physiological characteristic information is established, and the statistical data spectrum feature extraction in sports competition tactical analysis is carried out by using feature analysis method [8]. With the preliminary statistics and sampling of statistical data in sports competition tactical analysis, the univariable time series of statistical data in sports competition tactical analysis is constructed as follows: the information flow model of statistical data collection in $\{x_n\}$, sports competition tactical analysis is expressed as follows:

$$x_n = x(t_0 + n\Delta t) = h[z(t_0 + n\Delta t)] + \omega_n \tag{1}$$

Wherein, $h(.)$ is the multivariate quantitative value function of statistical data stream in sports competition tactical analysis, ω_n is the adaptive weighting coefficient, and the real-time collected sports competition tactical analysis data is selected as the original data sample sequence, and the finite data set expression of statistical data in sports competition tactical analysis is obtained as follows:

$$U = \{U_1, U_2, \cdots, U_N\} \tag{2}$$

Wherein U_i is a data transfer model with dimension d dimension, and the high-dimensional mapping vector for transmitting the tactical analysis data of the sports game is $z_n \rightarrow z_{n+1}$ or $z(t) \rightarrow z(t+1)$, so that the transmission time series $\{x(t_0 + i\Delta t)\}$, $i = 0, 1, \cdots, N - 1$ of the transmission sports game tactical analysis data are obtained, and the peak parameter model thereof is expressed as follows:

$$X = [s_1, s_2, \cdots s_K]_\mathbf{n} = (x_n, x_{n-\tau}, \cdots, x_{n-(m-1)\tau}) \tag{3}$$

Wherein, $K = N - (m - 1)\tau$, represents the statistical characteristic quantity of statistical data in sports competition tactical analysis, and gives the statistical data $s_i = (x_i, x_{i+\tau}, \cdots, x_{i+(m-1)\tau})^T$ as a set of scalar sampling sequences in sports competition tactical analysis. Taking lung flux as original data, the characteristic analysis of statistical data in sports competition tactical analysis is carried out, and the statistical information flow is represented as $\{x_i\}_{i=1}^N$, assuming that the input initial information flow of sports competition tactical analysis data is $C_0 = C_{N/2} = 0$, $C_{N-n} = C_n^*$, $n = 0, 1, 2 \cdots N/2 - 1$. The capacity of tactical analysis data for sports competitions is as follows:

$$P_r = \frac{P_t}{(4\pi)^2 \left(\frac{d}{\lambda}\right)^\gamma} \left[1 + \alpha^2 + 2\alpha \cos\left(\frac{4\pi h^2}{d\lambda}\right)\right] \tag{4}$$

The data collection and diagnosis analysis model of sports game tactical analysis is constructed, and the data information flow model of sports game tactical analysis is constructed. The data compression performance of sports game tactical analysis is analyzed by Hession matrix, which is as follows:

$$P_S = p_{2D}^k (1 - p_{2D})^{N-1-k} \sum_{i=1}^{\infty} \lambda_S^i = \frac{\lambda_S}{1 - \lambda_S} \tag{5}$$

In the above formula, the λ_S is the information gain of the sports game tactical analysis data under the non-limited bandwidth and p_{2D} is the information gain of the sports game tactical analysis data under the non-limited bandwidth, According to the characteristic sampling analysis result, the sports game tactics analysis and the statistics are carried out [9].

2.2 Image Trajectory Segmentation and Information Enhancement Processing

In that method, the statistic characteristic quantity in the tactical analysis of the sports game is extracted, and a fuzzy correlation fusion analysis and analysis method is adopted to carry out the filter detection of the statistical data in the sports game tactical analysis [10], by using the matching projection method, the optimized characteristic solution for the analysis of the tactical statistical information of the game and the tactical analysis of the sports game is obtained, and the gradient information component of the output sports game tactical analysis statistical data X can be expressed as:

$$y(k) = s_1(k) + n_1(k); \ \varphi(k) = s_2(k) + n_2(k) \tag{6}$$

$$s_1(k) = AA_H e^{j(\Omega k + \theta_H)}; \ s_2(k) = AA_{H_B} e^{j(\Omega k + \theta_{H_B})} \tag{7}$$

Wherein, A_H, A_{H_B} and θ_H, θ_{H_B} are adaptive feature recognition functions for the statistical data of sports game tactical analysis, and $H(z)$ and $H_B(z)$ represent amplitude response and state feature response, respectively. The simplified gradient algorithm is used to decompose the statistical data in the tactical analysis of sports matches [11]. The boundary conditions of the distribution of statistical data in the tactical analysis of sports competitions are obtained as follows:

$$R_\beta X = U\{E \in U/R|c(E, X) \leq \beta\} \tag{8}$$

$$R_\beta X = U\{E \in U/R|c(E, X) \leq 1 - \beta\} \tag{9}$$

For any two sports competition tactical analysis statistical data blocks m_i and m_j, the basic block characteristic quantity of the sports competition tactical analysis statistical data is the $m_{i,j}(1 \leq i \leq n, 1 \leq j \leq k)$, sports competition tactical analysis statistical data information chain distribution is the $\{\lambda_i : 1 \leq i \leq S\}$, criterion $\{R_j : 1 \leq j \leq L\}$, sports competition tactical analysis statistical data reference frequency f and the key characteristic d_{γ_0} match degree is:

$$\lambda^n(d_{\gamma_0}) = \int_{-\infty}^{+\infty} f(t)d_{\gamma_0}^*(t)dt \tag{10}$$

According to the self-correlation feature matching method, the feature extraction of the statistical data in the sports game tactical analysis is realized [12], and the optimized iterative formula of the feature extraction of the statistical data of the sports game tactical analysis is described as follows:

$$\theta_1(k + 1) = \theta_1(k) - \mu\mathrm{Re}[y(k)\varphi^*(k)] \tag{11}$$

Where μ is the parameter to control the convergence speed and accuracy, which is called the step size of the sports game tactical analysis data recognition; $\varphi(k)$ is the fuzzy parameter of the sports game tactical analysis and statistics, according to the feature extraction results, the sports game tactical analysis and statistical algorithm design [13].

3   Tactical Analysis and Statistical Optimization of Sports Competition

3.1   Mining Algorithm for Large Data Association Rules

On the basis of the above-mentioned data acquisition and diagnosis analysis model for building the tactical analysis of the sports game, and carrying out the tactics analysis and statistics of the sports games on the basis of the construction of the information flow model of the sports game and the tactical analysis, In this paper, a game strategy analysis and statistical model based on large data association rule mining is presented [14]. The analytical model of the statistical data for building the tactical analysis of sports games is expressed as follows:

$$z(t) = x(t) + iy(t) = a(t)e^{i\theta(t)} \tag{12}$$

In the formula, $z(t)$ represents the real component of the statistical data of sports competition tactical analysis, $x(t)$ represents the analytical characteristic quantity of the statistical data, $y(t)$ represents the inherent modal function of the statistical data signal, and decomposes the information component of the statistical data of sports competition tactics analysis into multiple sets of feature sets, and obtains the envelope feature item:

$$a(t) = \sqrt{x^2(t) + y^2(t)}, \ \theta(t) = \arctan\frac{y(t)}{x(t)} \tag{13}$$

Wherein, $\theta(t)$ indicates the high frequency component of sports competition tactical analysis statistical data, $a(t)$ and $\theta(t)$ are the dynamic evolution feature sets of sports competition tactical analysis statistical data, respectively. Using big data association rule mining algorithm, the similarity distribution of statistical data detection is obtained as follows:

$$f(t) = \frac{1}{2\pi} \times \frac{d\theta(t)}{dt} \tag{14}$$

Carrying out the game strategy analysis and the statistical process control to obtain the correlation rule mining characteristic distribution weight as follows:

$$w_{ij} = \beta \times w(e_p k_q) \quad (\beta > 1) \tag{15}$$

On the basis of comprehensive analysis, a large-data association rule mining algorithm is used to analyze and analyze the statistical data in the tactical analysis of sports games [15], and the optimization feature of the analysis of the statistical information of the game is established as follows:

$$r_1 = x(t) - c_1 \tag{16}$$

Based on the above-mentioned processing, a large-data association rule mining algorithm is adopted, and the optimization design of the game and tactical statistical information analysis model is carried out [16].

3.2   Analysis and Output of Competition Tactical Statistical Information

The simplified gradient algorithm is used for adaptive optimization of game tactical statistical information analysis, and the feature analysis and data optimization recognition of statistical data in sports competition tactical analysis are realized by combining autocorrelation feature matching method [17]. The feature transfer function of statistical data in sports competition tactical analysis is expressed as follows:

$$h(\tau_i, t) = \sum_{i=1}^{N_m} a_i(t) e^{j\theta_i(t)} \delta(t - \tau_i(t)) \tag{17}$$

By decomposing the tactical analysis information component into the positive phase sequence and negative phase sequence, the impulse response of statistical data in the game tactical analysis is obtained:

$$h(\tau_i, t) = \sum_{i=1}^{N_m} a_i(t) \delta(t - \tau_i(t)) \tag{18}$$

In the above formula, $a_i(t)$ is the normalization feature solution of the statistical data of sports competition tactical analysis, $\tau_i(t)$ is the time delay, and N_m is the feature reconstruction sequence of the statistical data in the sports competition tactical analysis.

The high-order statistical characteristics of the sports competition tactical analysis are obtained as follows:

$$x_k = \sum_{n=0}^{N-1} C_n \cdot e^{j2\pi kn/N} \quad k = 0, 1, \cdots, N-1 \tag{19}$$

Based on this, the data detection and recognition model in sports competition tactical analysis is constructed, and the time series state equation of data distribution in sports competition tactical analysis is described by using big data association rule mining algorithm:

$$A(x) = AJ(x)a(x) + B(1 - b(x)) \tag{20}$$

So that $A = \{a_1, a_2, \ldots, a_n\}$ is the feature attribute set of describing the statistical data of sports competition tactical analysis, and $G = (V, E, W)$ represents the feature attribute set of describing the statistical data of sports competition tactical analysis. The attribute value of $V = \{v_1, v_2, \cdots, v_N\}$ is the adaptive learning weight of $(u, v) \in E$, the statistical information analysis of sports competition tactics is described as:

$$w_{ij} = \beta \times w(e_p k_q) \quad (\beta > 1) \tag{21}$$

Wherein, β is the close weight coefficient of the statistical data of sports game tactical analysis, and $w(e_p k_q)$ represents the characteristic quantity of tactical state. Combined with big data mining technology, the fuzzy discriminant function of the statistical data of sports game tactical analysis is obtained as follows:

$$\hat{W} = \begin{cases} \text{sgn}(W)(|W| - \alpha Ts) & |W| \geq Ts \\ 0 & |W| < Ts \end{cases} \tag{22}$$

>At $k + 1$ time, the integration state characteristic equation of the statistical data of sports competition tactics analysis is expressed as follows:

$$\begin{cases} w = w(t) * w_{start} & k \geq \alpha \\ w = w(t) * \frac{1}{w_{end}} & k < \beta \end{cases} \tag{23}$$

In which, $\{\alpha, \beta\}$ is the fuzzy clustering center of the statistical data of the tactical analysis of the sports game, the method of the fuzzy C-means clustering analysis is adopted, the statistical characteristic of the statistical data of the sports game is analyzed, and the statistical function is established as follows:

$$J_m(U, V) = \sum_{k=1}^{n}\sum_{i=1}^{c} \mu_{ik}^m (d_{ik})^2 x_i = x_{imin} + cx_i \cdot (x_{imax} - x_{imin}) \tag{24}$$

Wherein, x_i is the sampling scalar time series of sports competition tactical analysis statistical data, x_{imin} is the minimum clustering center weight coefficient, c is the nearest neighbor sample number of sports competition tactical analysis statistical data, the fitness coefficient is adjusted, the data length is assumed to be N, the simplified gradient algorithm is used for the adaptive optimization of game tactical statistical information analysis, and the statistical function $G(Y_j, \omega_i)$ is obtained as:

$$G(Y_j, \omega_i) = \left[p_1 * \sum_{j=1}^{k} l(x) \frac{\sum_{i=1}^{r} N(V_i)}{k} \right] + p_2 * N + p_3 * \frac{\sum_{i=1}^{n} (V_i)}{N_j} \qquad (25)$$

Wherein, $\{p_1, p_2, p_3\}$ is the adaptive weighted parameter of sports game tactical analysis and statistics, $p_1 + p_2 + p_3 = 1$. Based on big data association rules mining algorithm, sports competition tactics analysis and statistics are carried out [18].

4   Simulation Experiment and Result Analysis

In order to verify the application performance of this method in the statistical information analysis of competition tactics to realize the tactical analysis of sports competitions, Matlab and Visual C are used for simulation analysis. The initial sampling interval of physique data is 2 Ms, the collected data have maximum oxygen uptake (VO2max), heart rate and so on, and the discrete sampling frequency of the data is set to 1200 for the length of $f_s = 10 * f_0 \text{Hz} = 10\,\text{KHz}$, sports game tactical analysis data. The interference signal-to-noise ratio of the test sample is-10 dB, and the time-domain waveform of sports game tactical analysis data is shown in Fig. 2.

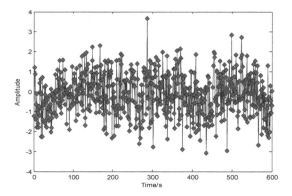

Fig. 1. Tactical analysis of time domain waveforms

Taking the data of Fig. 1 as input, the big data association rule mining algorithm is used to analyze the statistical data and feature analysis in the game tactical analysis, and establish the game tactical statistical information analysis model, and the result of the game tactical statistical information analysis is shown in Fig. 2.

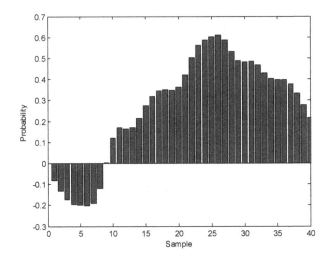

Fig. 2. Tactical information statistical analysis results

Analysis Fig. 2 shows that the method can effectively realize the tactical analysis and statistics of sports games and the exact probability of the test recognition. The results are shown in Table 1. The analysis Table 1 shows that the method is used to carry out the tactical analysis of sports games and the accuracy of the statistics.

Table 1. Comparison of tactical analysis and statistical accuracy of sports competition

Number of experiments	Proposed method	Reference [4]	Reference [5]
50	0.926	0.865	0.878
100	0.965	0.885	0.894
150	0.997	0.943	0.917
200	0.999	0.965	0.938

5   Conclusions

The distributed detection model of statistical data in sports competition tactical analysis is constructed. According to the distribution state of statistical data in sports competition tactical analysis, the characteristics of sports competition tactics are analyzed. In this paper, a sports competition tactical analysis and statistical model based on big data association rules mining is proposed. Firstly, the data acquisition and diagnosis analysis model of sports competition tactics analysis is constructed, and the data information flow model of sports competition tactics analysis is constructed, the characteristic quantity of statistical data in sports competition tactics analysis is extracted, and the interference filtering of statistical data in sports competition tactics analysis is carried out by using fuzzy correlation fusion analysis method. Big data association rule mining algorithm is used to analyze the statistical data and features in the tactical analysis of sports competitions, and the optimal feature solution of statistical information analysis of competition tactics is established. Combined with the autocorrelation feature matching method, the feature analysis and data optimization recognition of statistical data in the tactical analysis of sports competitions are realized. It is found that this method has good accuracy and strong anti-interference ability in the analysis and statistics of sports competition tactics, which improves the adaptability and accuracy of sports competition tactics analysis.

References

1. Wang, X., Zhou, Y., Ning, C., Shi, A.: Image saliency detection via adaptive fusion of local and global sparse representation. J. Comput. Appl. **38**(3), 866–872 (2018)
2. Cheng, M.M., Mitra, N.J., Huang, X., Torr, P.H., Hu, S.M.: Global contrast based salient region detection. IEEE Trans. Pattern Anal. Mach. Intell. **37**(3), 569–582 (2015)
3. Liu, N., Han, J.: DHSNet: deep hierarchical saliency network for salient object detection. In: Proceedings of the 2016 IEEE Conference on Computer Vision and Pattern Recognition, pp. 678–686. IEEE Computer Society, Washington (2016)
4. Kim, W., Kim, C.: Spatiotemporal saliency detection using textural contrast and its applications. IEEE Trans. Circ. Syst. Video Technol. **24**(4), 646–659 (2014)
5. Shan, Y., Wang, J.: Robust object tracking method of adaptive scale and direction. Comput. Eng. Appl. **54**(21), 208–216 (2018)
6. Lei, Y.: Multi-focus image fusion method based on NSST and IICM. In: Barolli, L., Zhang, M., Wang, X.A. (eds.) EIDWT 2017. LNDECT, vol. 6, pp. 679–689. Springer, Cham (2018). https://doi.org/10.1007/978-3-319-59463-7_68
7. Yang, L.: Technique for image de-noising based on non-subsampled shearlet transform and improved intuitionistic fuzzy entropy. Optik-Int. J. Light Electron Opt. **126**(4), 446–453 (2015)
8. Shen, X.X., Zhang, H., Gao, Z.: Behavior recognition algorithm based on Kinect and pyramid feature. J. Optoelectron. Laser **2**, 357–363 (2014)
9. Yan, S., Xu, D., Zhang, B., Zhang, H.-J.: Graph embedding and extensions: a general framework for dimensionality reduction. IEEE Trans. Pattern Anal. Mach. Intell. **29**(1), 40–51 (2007)
10. Wang, X., Zhang, Y., Chen, D.: Face detection based on MB-LBP and eye tracking. Chin. J. Sci. Instr. **35**(12), 2739–2745 (2014)
11. Wei, X.S., Luo, J.H., Wu, J.: Selective convolutional descriptor aggregation for fine-grained image retrieval. IEEE Trans. Image Process. **26**(6), 2868–2881 (2017)
12. Radenović, F., Tolias, G., Chum, O.: CNN image retrieval learns from BoW: unsupervised fine-tuning with hard examples. In: Leibe, B., Matas, J., Sebe, N., Welling, M. (eds.) ECCV 2016. LNCS, vol. 9905, pp. 3–20. Springer, Cham (2016). https://doi.org/10.1007/978-3-319-46448-0_1
13. Azizpour, H., Razavian, A.S., Sullivan, J.: From generic to specific deep representations for visual recognition. In: Proceedings of the 2015 International Conference on Computer Vision and Pattern Recognition Workshops, pp. 36–45. IEEE Computer Society, Washington (2015)

14. Razavian, A.S., Sullivan, J., Carlsson, S.: Visual instance retrieval with deep convolutional networks. ITE Trans. Media Technol. Appl. **4**(3), 251–258 (2016)
15. Tian, B., Yang, H., Fang, J.: Recommendation algorithm based on probability matrix factorization and fusing trust. J. Comput. Appl. **39**(10), 2834–2840 (2019)
16. Hassner, T., Harel, S., Paz, E.: Effective face frontalization in unconstrained images. In: Proceedings of the 2015 IEEE Computer Vision and Pattern Recognition, pp. 4295–4304. IEEE, Piscataway (2015)
17. Huang, B., Zhao, B., Song, Y.: Urban land-use mapping using a deep convolutional neural network with high spatial resolution multispectral remote sensing imagery. Remote Sens. Environ. **214**, 73–86 (2018)
18. Xu, H., Sun, Z.: Fast feature selection method based on mutual information in multi-label learning. J. Comput. Appl. **39**(10), 2815–2821 (2019)

Identification and Analysis of Limb Swing Image in Short Run Training Based on Visual Signal Processing

Chong-gao Chen[✉] and Jia Ren

Huali College Guangdong University of Technology, Guangzhou, China
chenchonggao74@163.com

Abstract. In order to improve the ability of the accurate detection and recognition of the swing of the training limb of the sprinter, a method of image recognition based on the visual signal processing for the motion of the limb is proposed. The method comprises the following steps of: analyzing the motion characteristic quantity of the swing of a sprinting training limb, carrying out a sprinting training limb swinging image acquisition by adopting an infrared characteristic scanning technology, carrying out edge contour detection on the collected sprinting training limb swinging image. Carrying out contour segmentation and characteristic identification of the swinging of the limb of the sprinting training limb in combination with the image segmentation technology, constructing a gray histogram distribution structure model of a sprinting training limb swing image, and carrying out effective extraction of the motion characteristics of the limb swing and the motion characteristic of the sprinting training limb by adopting a regional block matching method, The method of multi-dimensional space reconstruction is adopted to simulate the motion of the limb, and the visual signal processing and the key feature point calibration method are adopted to calibrate and detect the characteristic points of the limb swing of the sprinting training, so as to realize the optimal recognition of the swing of the training limb of the sprinter. The simulation results show that the method of the invention has the advantages of high accuracy, good characteristic identification ability and the capability of improving the swing image recognition ability of the sprinter training limb.

Keywords: Visual signal processing · Sprinting · Training · Limb swing · Image recognition

1 Introduction

In that field of human body kinematics, it is necessary to carry out the optimization recognition of the limb swing of the sprinting training, combine the image recognition and the laser scan tracking technology, carry out the image analysis of the motion of the limb of the sprinting training, establish a laser scanning and image analysis model of the swing of the sprinting training limb [1], the method comprises the following steps of: carrying out the feature extraction and identification of the swing of the limbs of the sprinting training by adopting a laser imaging method, and improving the characteristic

Y.-D. Zhang et al. (Eds.): ICMTEL 2020, LNICST 326, pp. 247–256, 2020.
https://doi.org/10.1007/978-3-030-51100-5_22

identification ability of the sprinting training limb swing; The related sprinting training limb swinging image recognition method has an important significance in promoting the kinematics optimization of the human body, Through the characteristic recognition of the swing of the training limb of the sprinter, the human motion training is guided, and the related sprinting training limb swing image recognition method has been greatly concerned by the people [2].

The image recognition of limb swing in sprint training is based on the analysis of human kinematic image, adopts infrared feature scanning technology of human motion, carries on the image fractal processing, adopts the laser image recognition method of sprint training limb swing, realizes the image recognition of limb swing in sprint training [3]. In the traditional method, the image recognition method of limb swing in sprint training mainly includes Harris corner detection method. Moment analysis method and fuzzy information enhancement method, the dynamic fractal recognition model of limb swing information in sprint training is established, and the laser scanning and feature recognition of human motion are realized by combining scale decomposition method and multi-mode feature reconstruction method. A real-time extraction method of limb swing in sprint training based on monocular video is proposed in reference [4]. Monocular video acquisition method is used to sample and recognize the laser scanning image of limb swing in sprint training, but the calculation cost of limb swing image recognition in sprint training is large and the real-time performance is not good. In reference [5], a method of limb swing image recognition in sprint training based on video tracking is proposed. According to the law of trajectory distribution, the optimal feature extraction of human motion video is realized and the accuracy of recognition is improved. However, the ambiguity of this method is large in the recognition of limb swing image in sprint training. In order to solve the above problems, a method of limb swing image recognition for sprint training based on visual signal processing is proposed in this paper. Firstly, the laser sampling of limb swing information in sprint training is carried out, and then the gray histogram distribution structure model of limb swing image in sprint training is constructed. Combined with the feature point calibration method with large interval and nearest neighbor, the limb swing image recognition in sprint training is realized. Finally, the simulation test and analysis are carried out, and the validity conclusion is obtained [6].

2   Image Sampling and Edge Contour Detection of Limb Swing in Sprint Training

2.1   Image Acquisition of the Motion of the Limbs in the Sprint Training

In order to realize the recognition of limb swinging image in sprint training, firstly, infrared feature scanning technology is used to collect the wobble image of sprint training limb, and the edge outline of the collected sprint training limb wobble image is detected [7]. Assuming that the gray pixel set of sprint training limb swinging laser scanning image is (i, j), as the pixel center, the method of profile compensation is used to combine the sharpening template into blocks. At any level of the 3D surface model of laser imaging, the matching set of pixel imaging template for sprint training limb swinging laser scanning image is as follows:

$$W_u = \frac{1}{\sqrt{aT}}(\frac{T}{2} + \frac{a}{2} - b_m) \tag{1}$$

Where, T represents the ratio of flexion to extension acceleration, a represents the maximum acceleration of oscillation, and b_m represents the oscillation frequency. The level set function reconstruction method is used to reconstruct the laser scanning image of limb wobble in sprint training. The error matching function of swinging laser scanning image of sprint training limb is established by using single frame scanning technology. Combined with pixel reconstruction method, the action feature distribution pixel set of laser scanning tracking of sprint training limb wobble is obtained.

$$s(k) = \phi \cdot s(k-1) + w(k) \tag{2}$$

Where

$$\phi = \begin{pmatrix} 1 & 0 & 0 & 0 & 0 \\ 0 & 1 & 1 & 0 & 0 \\ 0 & 0 & 1 & 0 & 0 \\ 0 & 0 & 0 & 1 & 1 \\ 0 & 0 & 0 & 0 & 1 \end{pmatrix}, w(k) = \begin{pmatrix} N(0, \sigma_{\theta(k)}) \\ 0 \\ N(0, \sigma_{x(k)}) \\ 0 \\ N(0, \sigma_{y(k)}) \end{pmatrix} \tag{3}$$

s stands for high frequency persistence. The R, G, B components of sprint training limb swing laser scanning image W are extracted, and the 3D template matching values A_R, A_G, A_B and W_R, W_G, W_B, of the corresponding sprint training limb swing laser scanning image are extracted during the evolution of the outline curve. According to the above analysis, the laser scanning image acquisition model of sprint training limb swing is constructed, and the feature extraction of sprint training limb swing is carried out taking into account the regional information of the image [8].

2.2 Image Edge Contour Detection

The method comprises the following steps of: carrying out edge contour detection on the collected dash training limb swinging image, carrying out contour segmentation and characteristic identification of the motion of the limb swing by combining the image segmentation technology, calculating the visual characteristic distribution of the swinging laser scanning image of the sprinting training limb to the quantification set [9], the segmentation threshold of the swing laser scanning image of the sprinting training limb is as follows:

$$w(i, j) = \frac{1}{Z(i)} \exp(-\frac{d(i, j)}{h^2}) \tag{4}$$

Where, $Z(i)$ is the template matching value of the sub-region feature matching region, defines the Gibbs prior energy function of the sprint training limb swing laser scanning image, through the edge ambiguity identification method, carries on the edge and the region information combination processing, in the feature mark area, obtains the image gradient information dynamic fusion result, obtains the sprint training limb swing laser scanning image template characteristic distribution:

$$w(d_{ij}) = f(|x_i - x_j|) = \frac{1}{\sqrt{2\pi}} \exp\left\{ \frac{(x_i - x_j)^2}{2} \right\} \tag{5}$$

Using the edge gradient information of the image to carry on the sprint training limb swing laser scanning and the image vision tracking, obtains the image block area size is $M \times N$, according to the sprint training limb swing laser scanning image vision RGB value carries on the pixel characteristic separation, the output is:

$$\beta_i = \exp\left\{ -\frac{|x_i - x_j|^2}{2\sigma^2} \right\} \frac{1}{\text{dist}(x_i, x_j)} \tag{6}$$

The method comprises the following steps of: constructing an active contour model of a sprinting training limb swing, carrying out correlation characteristic matching on the extracted sprinting training limb swinging infrared scanning image, carrying out information fusion and feature extraction at the edge of the sprinting training limb swinging target, The edge contour detection model of the swing image of the training limb of the sprinter is constructed, and the motion attitude recognition is carried out according to the edge contour detection result [10–12].

3   Image Recognition and Optimization of Swing Training Limb Swing

3.1   Visual Signal Processing and Calibration of Key Feature Points

In that method, an infrared characteristic scanning technique is adopted to carry out the image acquisition of the swing training limb, and on the basis of the edge contour detection of the collected dash training limb swing image, the motion of the limb swing image recognition is carried out, In this paper, a method of image recognition based on visual signal processing is presented. a gray histogram distribution structure model of a sprinting training limb swing image is constructed [13], and a regional block matching method is adopted to perform effective extraction of the swing and motion characteristics of the limb swing and motion of the sprinting training limb, and the template matching function $f(g_i)$ of the sprinting training limb swing image is as follows:

$$f(g_i) = c_1 \tilde{\lambda}_i \sum_{j=0}^{N_{np}} \frac{\rho_j \vec{v}_{ij}}{|\vec{v}_{ij}|^{\sigma_1} + \varepsilon} \bigg/ \sum_{j=0}^{N_{np}} \frac{\rho_j}{|\vec{v}_{ij}|^{\sigma_1} + \varepsilon} \tag{7}$$

The background difference component of limb swing image in sprint training is obtained [14]. The reconstruction model of three-dimensional feature distribution region is established by using difference information fusion method. Combined with Gaussian process and deformation model, the dynamic fusion of human motion is carried out. The gray pixel fusion model of infrared information of limb swing in sprint training is established, and the fusion results are satisfied.

$$\partial = arccos\left\{ max\left[\frac{\overline{W_i S_k} \times \overline{W_i W_j}}{\left\| \overline{W_i S_k} \right\| \times \left\| \overline{W_i W_j} \right\|} \right] \right\}$$

(8)

Where, $k = 1, \ldots, M$, $i, j \in \{1, , N\}$, $i < j$, calculates the quantitative set of regional feature distribution of the swinging infrared scanning image of the sprint training limb. $S_i(i = 1, 2, \ldots, M)$, uses the sub-regional feature matching method to fuse the pose information of the two-dimensional outline feature distribution point M $(x_i + \frac{1}{2}, y_{i+1})$, pixel PE1, and constructs the gray edge feature quantity of the swinging infrared scanning image of the sprint training limb.

$$\min_c (\min_{y \in \Omega(x)} (\frac{I^c(y)}{A^c})) = \tilde{t}(x) \min_c (\min_{y \in \Omega(x)} (\frac{J^c(y)}{A^c})) + (1 - \tilde{t}(x))$$

(9)

Where, $\tilde{t}(x)$ is the spatial region pixel of the infrared scanning image of sprint training limb swing, A^c is the gray information component of infrared scanning image, $I^c(y)$ is the transmission intensity of sprint training limb swing under infrared scanning, and the adaptive fusion output of the image is obtained by using the method of region block matching:

$$bnr_\beta(X) = R_\beta X - R_\beta X_1$$

(10)

The image adaptive fusion model of unmarked human motion video is constructed. Multi-dimensional phase space reconstruction method is used to simulate the limb swing of sprint training, and dynamic block matching technology is combined to segment the texture of infrared scanning image of human motion. The super-resolution fusion model of the image is obtained as follows:

$$J(x, y, \sigma) = \begin{pmatrix} \frac{\partial P}{\partial x} \\ \frac{\partial P}{\partial y} \end{pmatrix} = \begin{pmatrix} 1 & 0 & L_x(x, y, \sigma) \\ 0 & 1 & L_y(x, y, \sigma) \end{pmatrix}$$

(11)

Different threshold t is used to segment the infrared scanning image $L_x(x, y, \sigma)$ of human motion, and the fractal estimation and information fusion of the image are realized.

3.2   Feature Extraction and Recognition of Limb Swing in Sprint Training

The 3D reconstruction image of the original human motion infrared scanning image is set as F, the outline of the object in the infrared scanning image of human motion is G, and the block matching is carried out in the affine invariant region. The volume motion attitude transformation analysis is carried out by Kalman filtering method [15]. The attitude transformation matrix is obtained as follows:

$$K_{ab} = \begin{bmatrix} sx & 0 & 0 \\ 0 & sy & 0 \\ 0 & 0 & 1 \end{bmatrix} \tag{12}$$

By adopting the characteristic matching method of the deformation model, the attitude analysis and the deformation characteristic analysis of the human body motion are carried out, and the self-adaptive blocking of the human motion infrared scanning image is carried out on the basis of the combined morphological segmentation method, so that the edge pixel value of the human body motion infrared scanning image is obtained:

$$E_{ext}(V(i)) = \gamma(i)E_{image}(V(i)) + \delta(i)E_{con}(V(i)) \tag{13}$$

Where, E_{image} represents the information component of human motion infrared scanning, combined with wavelet transform method, the fusion filtering of human motion infrared scanning image is carried out, the fractal dimension statistical analysis model of human motion infrared scanning image is established, and the visual signal processing and key feature point calibration methods are used to calibrate the feature points of limb swing in sprint training. The results of super-pixel region reconstruction of human motion infrared scanning image are obtained:

$$P(x_{w_3}, y_{w_3}|\Theta) = \prod_{x_i \in w_3} \prod_{k=1}^{K} \alpha_k g(x_{ij}, y_{ij} \mid \mu_k, \sigma_k^2) \tag{14}$$

The method comprises the following steps of: converting a feature matching method into a one-dimensional sequence $NF_c = \{n : c - k \leq n \leq c + k\}$ with a size of $1 * WN$, combining a two-dimensional spatial feature distribution fusion method, performing visual signal processing and a key feature point calibration of an image, and realizing saliency area feature extraction of the human moving infrared scanning image, The result of the optimized identification of the output of the sprinting training limb is as follows:

$$\begin{aligned} R(x, y) &= \frac{\det(M)}{\det(H)} \\ &= \frac{L_{xx}(x, y, \sigma)L_{yy}(x, y, \sigma) - L_{xy}(x, y, \sigma)L_{xy}(x, y, \sigma)}{1 + L_x^2(x, y, \sigma) + L_y^2(x, y, \sigma)} \\ &= \sigma^2 \frac{L_{xx}(x, y, \sigma)L_{yy}(x, y, \sigma) - L_{xy}(x, y, \sigma)L_{xy}(x, y, \sigma)}{1 + L_x^2(x, y, \sigma) + L_y^2(x, y, \sigma)} \end{aligned} \tag{15}$$

As above, a multi-dimensional space reconstruction method is used to simulate the motion of the limb, and the visual signal processing and the key feature point calibration method are used for the calibration and detection of the characteristic points of the limb swing of the sprinting training, and the optimal recognition of the swing of the training limb of the sprinter is realized.

4   Simulation Test Analysis

In order to verify the application performance of this method in the recognition of limb swing image in sprint training, the simulation experiment is carried out. In the experiment, the fractal dimension of infrared scanning image of human motion is

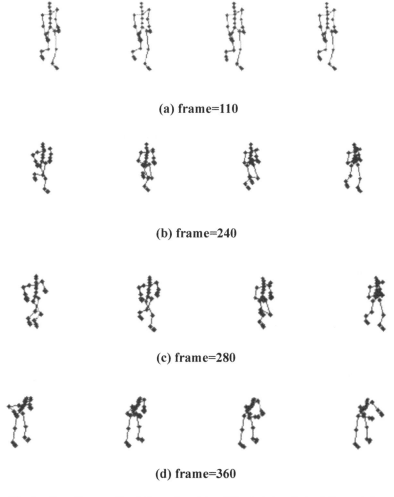

Fig. 1. Sampling results of the swing data of the training limb of the sprinter

estimated to be 5, the hidden variable data X = [2, 5, 6, 8], the sample training scale is 20, and the edge information adjustment parameter of 3DStudio MAX, infrared scanning image of human motion is 1.45. The feature segmentation coefficient is 0.65, and the sampling results of sprint training limb swing data under different sampling frames are shown in Fig. 1.

Taking the sampling result of Fig. 1 as an input, combining the image segmentation technique to carry out the contour segmentation and the characteristic identification of the swing of the limb of the sprinting training, and the characteristic point of the swing of the sprinting training limb is extracted, and the result is shown in Fig. 2.

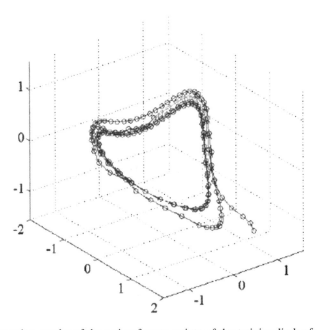

Fig. 2. Extraction results of the swing feature points of the training limb of the sprinter

According to the extraction results of feature points, the motion shape is 43 frames. According to the calibration results of large interval nearest neighbors, the body swing images of sprint training are recognized from different sides, and the recognition results are shown in Fig. 3.

The analysis of Fig. 3 shows that the method can effectively realize the image recognition of limb swing in sprint training, and the feature recognition ability is good. The recognition error is tested and the comparison results are shown in Table 1. The analysis Table 1 shows that the error of human motion feature recognition by this method is low.

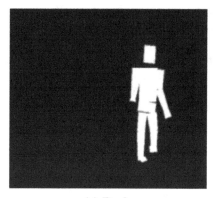

(a) Back

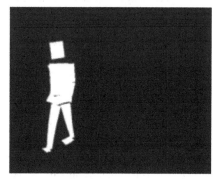

(b) Left side

Fig. 3. Results of image recognition of the swing training limb

Table 1. Error comparison

Iterations	Proposed method	Reference [3]	Reference [4]
100	0.025	0.075	0.176
200	0.012	0.057	0.164
300	0.004	0.045	0.123
400	0.001	0.043	0.087

5   Conclusions

The invention relates to an infrared scanning and image analysis model for establishing sprinting training limb swing, and an image recognition method based on visual signal processing is proposed in this paper. Build a sprint training body active contour model, relevant feature matching body swinging infrared scanning image, extraction of sprint training building block body swinging infrared scanning image fusion model of sprint training, adopt the method of visual signal processing, calibration and the key feature points, the motion of the body for sprint training for the calibration and testing feature points, realized the optimization of sprint training body swinging identification. The results show that this method has the advantages of small error, good recognition effect, high accuracy, strong feature recognition ability, and can improve the image recognition ability of sprinter training body swing, and improve the accurate detection and recognition ability of sprinter training body swing.

References

1. Dan, F., Tobias, S.N., Karl, O., et al.: Skeletal muscle and performance adaptations to high-intensity training in elite male soccer players: speed endurance runs versus small-sided game training. Eur. J. Appl. Physiol. **118**(2), 111–121 (2017)
2. Kim, W., Kim, C.: Spatiotemporal saliency detection using textural contrast and its applications. IEEE Trans. Circ. Syst. Video Technol. **24**(4), 646–659 (2014)
3. Alice, M., Oliver, F., Henner, H., et al.: Sprint interval training (SIT) substantially reduces depressive symptoms in major depressive disorder (MDD): a randomized controlled trial. Psychiatry Res. **1**(12), 265–268 (2018)
4. Li, S., Jia, Y., Guo, Y., et al.: Moving target tracking algorithm based on improved Camshift for through-wall-radar imaging. J. Comput. Appl. **38**(2), 528–532 (2018)
5. Tan, Q.Y., Leung, H., Song, Y., et al.: Multipath ghost suppression for through-the-wall-radar. IEEE Trans. Aerosp. Electron. Syst. **50**(3), 2284–2292 (2014)
6. Gennarelli, G., Soldovieri, F.: Multipath ghosts in radar imaging: physical insight and mitigation strategies. IEEE J. Sel. Top. Appl. Earth Obs. Remote Sens. **8**(3), 1078–1086 (2014)
7. Xiu, C., Ba, F.: Target tracking based on the improved Camshift method. In: CCDC 2016: Proceedings of the 2016 Chinese Control and Decision Conference, pp. 3600–3604. IEEE, Piscataway (2016)
8. Fang, H., Zhou, Y., Lin, M.: Speckle suppression algorithm for ultrasound image based on Bayesian nonlocal means filtering. J. Comput. Appl. **38**(3), 848–853 (2018)
9. Ramos-Llorden, G., Vegas-Sanchez-ferrero, G., Martin-Fernandez, M., et al.: Anisotropic diffusion filter with memory based on speckle statistics for ultrasound images. IEEE Trans. Image Process. **24**(1), 345–358 (2015)
10. Zhou, Y.Y., Zang, H.B., Zhao, J.K., et al.: Image recovering algorithm for impulse noise based on nonlocal means filter. Appl. Res. Comput. **33**(11), 3489–3494 (2016)
11. Peng, X., Gong, G., Liao, X., et al.: Modeling and model identification of micro-position-control hydraulic system. J. Mech. Eng. **53**(22), 206–211 (2017)
12. MA, Z., Chen, W.: Friction torque calculation method of ball bearings based on rolling creepage theory. J. Mech. Eng. **53**(22), 219–224 (2017)
13. Tian, G.H., Yin, J.Q., Han, X., et al.: A new method of human behavior recognition based on joint information. Robot **36**(3), 285–292 (2014)
14. Emmet, C., Andrew, J.H., Mark, L.: The Impact of resistance training on swimming performance: a systematic review. Sports Med. **47**(11), 2285–2307 (2017)
15. Amor, B.B., Su, J., Srivastava, A.: Action recognition using rate-invariant analysis, of skeletal shape trajectories. IEEE Trans. Pattern Anal. Mach. Intell. **38**(1), 1–13 (2016)

Intelligent Agricultural Information Remote Data Storage Method Based on Block Chain

Kun Wang[(⊠)]

Jiangsu Agriculture and Animal Husbandry Vocational College,
Taizhou 225300, China
wangkun010@tom.com

Abstract. In order to improve the secure storage and fault-tolerant ability of intelligent agricultural information remote data storage system, a fault-tolerant method of intelligent agricultural information remote data storage system based on block chain is proposed. Combined with the statistical feature analysis method, the fault-tolerant characteristics of the intelligent agricultural information remote data storage system are analyzed, the correlation characteristics of the intelligent agricultural information remote data are extracted, the block chain control model of the intelligent agricultural information remote data is established, and the block storage and feature matching design of the intelligent agricultural information remote data is carried out by using the autocorrelation feature detection method. The block chain storage structure of intelligent agricultural information remote data security storage is established, combined with the optimized block chain control scheme, the optimal storage structure of intelligent agricultural information remote data is reorganized, the structure reorganization and feature reconstruction of intelligent agricultural information remote data are realized by using fuzzy clustering and vector quantification coding scheme, and the fault tolerant strategy optimization of intelligent agricultural information remote data storage system is realized. The simulation results show that the design of intelligent agricultural information remote data storage system based on this method has good fault tolerance and strong coding and decoding ability, which improves the security of intelligent agricultural information remote data storage and management.

Keywords: Block chain control · Intelligence · Agricultural information · Remote data · Storage

1 Introduction

With the development of the intelligent agricultural information system, the information management of the intelligent agricultural information remote data is greatly concerned, and it is necessary to construct the optimized storage and secure transmission system of the intelligent agricultural information remote data, the intelligent agricultural information remote data encryption and coding design is carried out in combination with the data coding method [1], the safety management capability of the intelligent agricultural information remote data is improved, and the network information encryption and coding design method of the intelligent agricultural information

Y.-D. Zhang et al. (Eds.): ICMTEL 2020, LNICST 326, pp. 257–268, 2020.
https://doi.org/10.1007/978-3-030-51100-5_23

remote data are researched, it has great significance to store and optimize the remote data of intelligent agricultural information. the information management of the remote data of the intelligent agricultural information is based on the fault-tolerant strategy optimization design of the storage system for the remote data of the intelligent agricultural information, and the fault-tolerant strategy of the intelligent agricultural information remote data storage system is constructed, promote the security management and storage of intelligent agricultural information remote data [2].

Based on the detection and feature extraction of intelligent agricultural information remote data, the fault tolerance design of intelligent agricultural information remote data is carried out, and the discrete big data analysis model of intelligent agricultural information remote data is constructed [3], the fault-tolerant design of the intelligent agricultural information remote data storage system is carried out by using a large data mining method. In the traditional method, the intelligent agricultural information remote data fault-tolerance storage design mainly comprises a vector quantization coding method, a fuzzy correlation scheduling method and a hybrid encryption method and the like, the intelligent agricultural information remote data storage design is carried out by adopting a block chain control method, and the safe transmission and storage performance of the intelligent agricultural information remote data are improved. The fault-tolerant design method of the intelligent agricultural information remote data storage system based on the feature space reconstruction is proposed in the paper [4], and the distributed characteristic sequence recombination of the intelligent agricultural information remote data is carried out, The statistic characteristic component of the remote data of the intelligent agricultural information is extracted to carry out the encrypted transmission scheduling, but the calculation cost of the method is large and the real-time property is not good. In the paper [5], the fault-tolerant strategy of the intelligent agricultural information remote data storage system based on the C-means clustering analysis is proposed, and the coding design of the intelligent agricultural information remote data is carried out by adopting the method of the self-adaptive fuzzy clustering analysis, but the self-adaptability of the method is not good, in view of the above problems, this paper proposes a fault-tolerant method of intelligent agricultural information remote data storage system based on block chain. Firstly, the fault-tolerant characteristic analysis of the intelligent agricultural information remote data storage system is carried out in combination with the statistical analysis method, and the correlation characteristic quantity of the intelligent agricultural information remote data is extracted, the optimized storage structure of the intelligent agricultural information remote data is reorganized in combination with the optimized block chain control scheme, and then the structure recombination and the characteristic reconstruction of the intelligent agricultural information remote data are realized by adopting a fuzzy clustering and vector quantization coding scheme. And the fault-tolerant strategy optimization of the intelligent agricultural information remote data storage system is realized. Finally, the simulation experiment is carried out to show the advantages of the method in improving the fault-tolerance performance of the intelligent agricultural information remote data storage system [6].

2   Intelligent Agricultural Information Remote Data Distributed Storage Structure Model and Feature Analysis

2.1   Intelligent Agricultural Information Remote Data Distributed Storage Structure Model

In order to optimize the fault-tolerant design strategy of intelligent agricultural information remote data storage system, firstly, the distributed storage structure of intelligent agricultural information remote data is analyzed, the TinySBSec coding system is embedded into multi-Hoffman table to optimize the coding design of intelligent agricultural information remote data, and the multi-distributed quantitative coding scheme is adopted [7]. The information coding model and statistical information detection model of intelligent agricultural information remote data are established, and the public key is embedded into the master key to carry out the design of intelligent agricultural information remote data distributed coding and block chain control. The intelligent agricultural information remote data distributed collection is constructed by wireless ZigBee networking protocol, and the information fusion of intelligent agricultural information remote data is carried out under the structure system of the Internet of things [8]. The fault-tolerant design model of intelligent agricultural information remote data storage system is constructed, and the quantitative coding of intelligent agricultural information remote data is carried out by using pseudorandom sequence. The collected remote data of intelligent agricultural information is stored optimally through local database and cloud database. The intelligent agricultural information remote data storage system model is shown in Fig. 1.

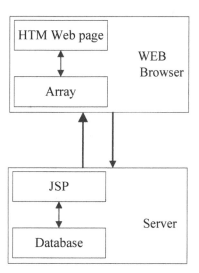

Fig. 1. Model of intelligent remote data storage system for agricultural information

A connected undirected graph $G = V, E, W$ is used to represent the coding center of the intelligent agricultural information remote data storage model, in which $V = \{v_1, v_2, \ldots v_N\}$ is the geometric feature distribution term of the intelligent agricultural information remote data, in which a_j, constructs the coding key agreement protocol of the intelligent agricultural information remote data in the finite field, inputs the key parameters, and obtains the association rule set of the intelligent agricultural information remote data represented by a_j. The simplified geometric model of fault-tolerant storage in intelligent agricultural information remote data storage system can be described by the following formula:

$$\begin{cases} G_1 = b_{11}a_1 + b_{12}a_2 + \ldots + b_{1n}a_n \\ G_2 = b_{21}a_1 + b_{22}a_2 + \ldots + b_{2n}a_n \\ \ldots \qquad \ldots \qquad \ldots \\ G_n = b_{n1}a_1 + b_{n2}a_2 + \ldots + b_{nn}a_n \end{cases} \tag{1}$$

Wherein, G_1 and G_2 indicate that fault-tolerant storage of intelligent agricultural information remote data storage system is related. G_n is the principal component characteristic quantity of intelligent agricultural information remote data coding. a represents the available capacity of the storage node; b represents the load threshold of the storage node. According to the above analysis, the distributed collection and storage structure model of intelligent agricultural information remote data is constructed [9].

2.2 Analysis of Correlation Characteristics of Intelligent Agricultural Information Remote Data

the intelligent agricultural information remote data storage system fault-tolerant characteristic analysis is carried out in combination with the statistical analysis method, the correlation characteristic quantity of the intelligent agricultural information remote data is extracted [10], the block chain control model of the intelligent agricultural information remote data is established, the probability density of the characteristic distribution of the intelligent agricultural information remote data state is obtained by adopting a sample fusion cluster analysis method:

$$w_{ij} = \beta \times w(e_p k_q) \quad (\beta > 1) \tag{2}$$

In which, β is the master key of intelligent agricultural information remote data coding sequence, and $w(e_p k_q)$ represents the length of cyclic shift, and the difference discriminant function of fault tolerance control of intelligent agricultural information remote data storage system is as follows:

$$\hat{W} = \begin{cases} \text{sgn}(W)(|W| - \alpha Ts) \, |W| \geq Ts \\ \qquad 0 \qquad\qquad |W| < Ts \end{cases} \tag{3}$$

Wherein, α is an adaptive adjustment coefficient of the fault-tolerant design of the intelligent agricultural information remote data storage system, W is the fuzzy state characteristic component of the intelligent agricultural information remote data, the value range is $0 \leq \alpha \leq 1$ extracting the correlation feature quantity of the intelligent agricultural information remote data, establishing a block chain control model of the intelligent agricultural information remote data, extracting the intelligent agricultural information remote data characteristic, combining the characteristic classification technology, the intelligent agricultural information remote data storage system fault-tolerant coding control is realized, and a fuzzy information coding model of the intelligent agricultural information remote data is established, and the intelligent agricultural information remote data erasure coding model is obtained as follows:

$$\min_{w,b,\xi} \frac{1}{2}\|W\|^2 + k(x_i, x_j)((W \cdot a) + b) + w(e_p k_q) \geq 1 \tag{4}$$

According to the coupling relationship of intelligent agricultural information remote data, the high dimensional phase space reconstruction is introduced, and the kernel function $k(x_i, x_j)$, which is fault tolerant design of intelligent agricultural information remote data storage system, is obtained. The multi-resolution function of intelligent agricultural information remote data monitoring is as follows:

$$\left.\begin{aligned} \min_{\alpha} \frac{1}{2}\sum_{i=1}^{l}\sum_{j=1}^{l} y_i y_j \alpha_i \alpha_j K(x_i, x_j) - \sum_{j=1}^{l}\alpha_j \\ s.t. \quad \sum_{j=1}^{l} y_j \alpha_j = 0 \\ 0 \leq \alpha_j \leq u(x_j)C, \qquad j = 1, 2, \ldots, l \end{aligned}\right\} \tag{5}$$

The intelligent agricultural information remote data storage system fault-tolerance transfer function is obtained by adopting a bit sequence modulation method to realize the public key output control of the intelligent agricultural information remote data:

$$h(t) = H \sum_{m=1}^{M}\sum_{k=1}^{K(m)} \alpha_{mk}\delta(t - T_m - \tau_{mk}) \tag{6}$$

Combined with the above feature extraction results, the fuzzy cyclic shift method is used to cluster the information of intelligent agricultural information remote data, and the correlation features of intelligent agricultural information remote data are detected [11].

3 Intelligent Agricultural Information Remote Data Storage System Fault Tolerance Strategy

3.1 Block Chain Control Algorithm

On the basis of analyzing the fault-tolerant characteristics of intelligent agricultural information remote data storage system and extracting the correlation characteristics of intelligent agricultural information remote data storage system, the fault-tolerant strategy of intelligent agricultural information remote data storage system is optimized. As a distributed architecture, blockchain provides a new solution for privacy protection and data sharing, which is an extremely hot research direction. Using the block chain technology in the intelligent agricultural information remote data collection base station, the intelligent agricultural information remote data storage alliance chain (DSCB) system is formed. Data sharing among nodes in DSCB is completed by smart contract. Data owners set constraints on data storage, and use computer language instead of legal provisions to regulate the behavior of data visitors, so as to achieve decentralized collective maintenance of a safe and reliable data storage database. In this paper, a fault-tolerant method of intelligent agricultural information remote data storage system based on block chain is proposed. The metadata structure characteristics of intelligent agricultural information remote data are extracted, and the fault-tolerant control of intelligent agricultural information remote data storage system is carried out by using the method of source coding design. The statistical analysis model of fault-tolerance of intelligent agricultural information remote data storage system is obtained.

$$\frac{\partial u_i}{\partial p_i} = \frac{Gh_i}{\sum\limits_{j \neq i} h_j p_j + \sigma^2} \left(\frac{1}{1 + \gamma_i} - \beta_{c_1} \right) \tag{7}$$

The block chain storage structure of intelligent agricultural information remote data security storage is established. Combined with the optimized block chain control scheme, the optimal storage structure of intelligent agricultural information remote data is reorganized, and the non-orthogonal multiple access control of intelligent agricultural information remote data is carried out. The block chain control components of intelligent agricultural information remote data are obtained as:

$$\eta_{comm} = \frac{k_1 \cdot l}{E_{comm}} \cdot \left(1 - p_{drop} \right) \tag{8}$$

Among them, p_{drop} is the symbol output bit sequence of intelligent agricultural information remote data, the output shift symbol $CH_i(i \in C_1)$, which is used to extract the metadata structure characteristics of intelligent agricultural information remote data, and the dynamic load balancing scheduling method is used to carry out the adaptive coding of intelligent agricultural information remote data. The output is as follows:

$$f(x) = \text{sgn}\{\sum_{j=1}^{l} P_{drop}\alpha K k(x_i, x_j) + b\}, \, x \in R^n \tag{9}$$

Wherein, $b^* = y_i - \sum_{j=1}^{l} y_j \alpha_j K(x_j, x_i), \, i \in \{i | 0 < \alpha_i^* < u(x_i)C\}$.

The nearest neighbor query in the process of intelligent agricultural information remote data protection is carried out by using the method of phase space reconstruction. The privacy block chain control output of intelligent agricultural information remote data can be defined as follows:

$$V(u_i) = \left\|\frac{dP(u)}{dt}\right\|_{u=u_i} = \left\|\frac{dP(u)}{dt}\right\|_{u=u_i} \frac{du}{dt}\Big|_{t=t_i} \tag{10}$$

Then

$$\frac{du}{dt}\Big|_{t=t_i} = \frac{V(u_i)}{\left\|\frac{dP(u)}{du}\right\|_{u=u_i}} \tag{11}$$

Ignoring the high order trace H.O.T in the coding process, using the method of fuzzy correlation scheduling, we can get the block chain storage structure increment Δu_{i+1} of intelligent agricultural information remote data security storage:

$$\Delta u_{i+1} = u_{i+1} - u_i = \frac{V(u_i) \times T_s}{\left\|\frac{dP(u)}{u}\right\|_{u=u_i}} = \frac{F \times T_s}{\sqrt{x'^2 + y'^2 + z'^2}} \tag{12}$$

T_s is the curve interpolation period. Based on the analysis, fuzzy clustering and vector quantification coding scheme are used to realize the structure reorganization and feature reconstruction of intelligent agricultural information remote data, and the block chain control of fault-tolerant design of intelligent agricultural information remote data storage system is realized [12].

3.2 Intelligent Agricultural Information Remote Data Storage Security Optimization

In combination with the optimized block chain control scheme, the optimized storage structure of the intelligent agricultural information remote data is reorganized, the intelligent agricultural information remote data is reorganized by the fuzzy clustering method, the data encryption design is carried out, and the N_{ik} is a k-times standard B-spline basis function, according to the fault tolerance control, the intelligent agricultural information remote data optimized and encrypted output is as follows:

$$N_{i,k} = \frac{(u - u_i)N_{i,k-1}(u)}{u_{i+k} - u_i} + \frac{(u_{i+k+1} - u)N_{i+1,k-1}(u)}{u_{i+k+1} - u_{k+1}} \tag{13}$$

The $U = \{u_0, u_1, \ldots, u_{n+k+1}\}$ in the above formula is a feature quantitative set of intelligent agricultural information remote data blockchain control symbol combination feature set, and u is a quantitative coding information distribution independent variable of intelligent agricultural information remote data.

Based on the method of spatial confusion and reorganization, the state characteristics of fault-tolerant encryption of intelligent agricultural information remote data are obtained as follows:

$$
\begin{aligned}
\beta_i^c &= -\sum_{k \in S_s} R_{ik} Q_{kc} - R_{i1} y_c \\
&= -\frac{1}{\det(Q')} \left(\sum_{k \in S_s} (-1)^{i+k} \det\left(Q'_{\setminus ki}\right) Q_{kc} + y_c (-1)^{i+1} \det\left(Q'_{i1}\right) \right)
\end{aligned} \tag{14}
$$

In summary, the vector quantification coding scheme realizes the structure reorganization and feature reconstruction of intelligent agricultural information remote data, improves the security of data storage, and the implementation flow is shown in Fig. 2.

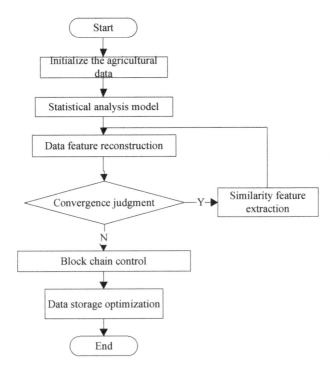

Fig. 2. Fault-tolerant optimization of intelligent agricultural information remote data storage system

4   Simulation Experiment and Result Analysis

In order to verify the performance of this method in the implementation of fault-tolerant control and erasure coding of intelligent agricultural information remote data storage system, combined with MATLAB, simulation experiments are carried out under the environment of VS2010 + opencv2.4.13, windows 10 operating system Intel (R) Xeon (R) CPU e5-2603v4 @ 2.20 GHz, and memory of 32 GB. Set the sampling length of remote data information of intelligent agricultural information as 1024, the test symbol sequence length of data coding as 100, the test symbol sequence length of data coding as 100, the number of training symbols as 500, and the number of iterations as 1000. In the remote data correction and deletion coding of intelligent agricultural information, the length of each group of plaintext blocks is 10000. According to the above simulation parameters, the intelligent agricultural information remote data storage coding is carried out, and the original intelligent agricultural information remote data is obtained as shown in Fig. 3.

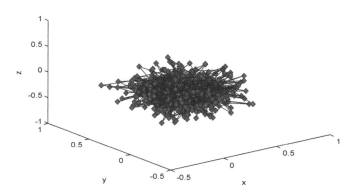

Fig. 3.   Remote data of original intelligent agricultural information

Taking the data of Fig. 3 as the study sample, the block storage and feature matching design of the intelligent agricultural information remote data is carried out by adopting the self-correlation characteristic detection method, and the optimized coding output is shown in Fig. 4.

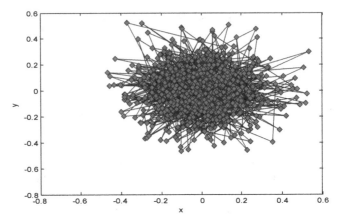

Fig. 4. Optimized code output for medical data

The analysis Fig. 4 shows that the output performance of the intelligent agricultural information remote data block chain control is better by adopting the method, the safe storage capacity of the data is improved, the fault tolerance of the data coding is improved, the comparison result is shown in Table 1.

Table 1. Intelligent agricultural information remote data storage optimization result

Data/Kbit	Proposed method	Chaotic coding	PSO	GP
1000	0.954	0.834	0.823	0.812
2000	0.987	0.858	0.845	0.834
3000	0.991	0.899	0.869	0.868
4000	0.998	0.921	0.884	0.887

According to Table 1, this paper has a good fault tolerance for intelligent agricultural information remote data storage.

In order to further verify the effectiveness of the method in this paper, the computational complexity of the method in this paper and the traditional method are compared and analyzed, and the comparison results are shown in Fig. 5.

According to Fig. 5, the calculation complexity of the method in this paper is up to 28%, which is lower than that of the traditional method, saving calculation time and improving storage efficiency.

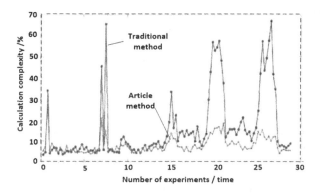

Fig. 5. Comparison results of computational complexity between the two methods

5   Conclusions

Combined with the data coding method, the encryption and coding design of intelligent agricultural information remote data is carried out, and the security management ability of intelligent agricultural information remote data is improved. In this paper, a fault-tolerant method of intelligent agricultural information remote data storage system based on block chain is proposed. The fault-tolerant characteristics of intelligent agricultural information remote data storage system are analyzed by statistical feature analysis method. Fuzzy clustering and vector quantification coding scheme are used to realize the structural reorganization and feature reconstruction of intelligent agricultural information remote data. Based on the method of spatial confusion recombination, the state feature distribution of intelligent agricultural information remote data fault-tolerant encryption is obtained. The fault-tolerant strategy optimization of intelligent agricultural information remote data storage system is realized. It is found that this method can improve the coding ability of intelligent agricultural information remote data and improve the fault-tolerant performance of secure storage.

References

1. Wang, X., Zhang, Y., Xu, M., et al.: Development of integrated network platform for heterogeneous agricultural information remote monitoring terminal. Nongye Gongcheng Xuebao/Trans. Chin. Soc. Agric. Eng. **33**(23), 211–218 (2017)
2. Cai, J., Bai, L., Xu, D., et al.: Remote sensing inversion of land surface temperature based on validation by observed infrared temperature in situ. Trans. Chin. Soc. Agric. Eng. **33**(5), 108–114 (2017)
3. Hai, T., Zhang, L., Liu, X., Zhang, X.: Image enlargement based on improved complex diffusion adaptively coupled nonlocal transform domain model. J. Comput. Appl. **38**(4), 1151–1156 (2018)
4. Grimm, F., Naros, G., Gharabaghi, A.: Closed-loop task difficulty adaptation during virtual reality reach-to-grasp training assisted with an exoskeleton for stroke rehabilitation. Front. Neurosci. **10**, 518 (2016)

5. Huang, J., Huang, H., Ma, H., et al.: Review on data assimilation of remote sensing and crop growth models. Nongye Gongcheng Xuebao/Trans. Chin. Soc. Agric. Eng. **34**(21), 144–156 (2018)
6. Mohammed, E.A., Hani, Z.Y., Kadhim, G.Q.: Assessing land cover/use changes in Karbala city (Iraq) using GIS techniques and remote sensing data. J. Phys: Conf. Ser. **1032**(1), 012047 (2018)
7. Amor, B.B., Su, J., Srivastava, A.: Action recognition using rate-invariant analysis, of skeletal shape trajectories. IEEE Trans. Pattern Anal. Mach. Intell. **38**(1), 1–13 (2016)
8. Liu, S., Zhang, Z., Qi, L., et al.: A fractal image encoding method based on statistical loss used in agricultural image compression. Multimedia Tools Appl. **75**(23), 15525–15536 (2016)
9. Xiu, C., Ba, F.: Target tracking based on the improved Camshift method. In: CCDC 2016: Proceedings of the 2016 Chinese Control and Decision Conference, pp. 3600–3604. IEEE, Piscataway (2017)
10. Li, Z., Yu, J., Bian, C., Wang, Y., Lu, L.: Dynamic data stream load balancing strategy based on load awareness. J. Comput. Appl. **37**(10), 2760–2766 (2017)
11. Zhao, Y., Yuan, Q., Meng, X.: Multi-pose face recognition algorithm based on sparse coding and machine learning. J. Jilin Univ. (Sci. Ed.) **56**(02), 340–346 (2018)
12. Yin, W., Li, J.: Inverse problem of heat source identification based on bayesian differential evolution algorithm. J. Jilin Univ. Sci. Ed. **57**(3), 517–522 (2019)

Design of Multi-parameter Monitoring System for Intelligent Agriculture Greenhouse Based on Artificial Intelligence

Wang Kun[⊠]

Jiangsu Agriculture and Animal Husbandry Vocational College,
Taizhou 225300, China
wangkun010@tom.com

Abstract. In order to improve the multi-parameter monitoring capability of the intelligent agricultural greenhouse, a multi-parameter monitoring system design scheme of the intelligent agricultural greenhouse is proposed based on the artificial intelligence control, the monitoring system mainly comprises a greenhouse multi-parameter information acquisition module, a smart agriculture greenhouse bus control module, a greenhouse temperature information fusion model, a program loading module, a remote communication module, an embedded scheduling module and a human-computer interaction module, the design interface program realizes the man-machine interaction design of the multi-parameter monitoring system of the intelligent agricultural greenhouse, and the main control module of the multi-parameter monitoring system of the intelligent agricultural greenhouse is constructed, and the embedded development of the intelligent agricultural greenhouse integrated intelligent monitoring system is carried out based on the bus under the IEEE488.2 standard, Combined with the application environment of the multi-parameter monitoring system of the intelligent agricultural greenhouse, the self-adaptive output conversion control of the intelligent agricultural greenhouse is carried out, and the optimization design of the multi-parameter monitoring system of the intelligent agricultural greenhouse is realized under the DSP environment. The test results show that the method can be used to monitor the multi-parameter of the intelligent agricultural greenhouse, and the stability of the system is strong.

Keywords: Smart agriculture greenhouse · Intelligent monitoring system · Control · DSP

1 Introduction

Intelligent agricultural greenhouse is an important equipment to realize the monitoring of intelligent agricultural greenhouse. Intelligent agricultural greenhouse is interfered by disturbance harmonics and other factors in realizing the monitoring of intelligent agricultural greenhouse, which leads to the poor output stability of intelligent agricultural greenhouse. The optimal monitoring model of intelligent agricultural greenhouse is constructed, and the integrated control method is used to realize the automatic monitoring and control of intelligent agricultural greenhouse [1]. To improve the output

© ICST Institute for Computer Sciences, Social Informatics and Telecommunications Engineering 2020
Published by Springer Nature Switzerland AG 2020. All Rights Reserved
Y.-D. Zhang et al. (Eds.): ICMTEL 2020, LNICST 326, pp. 269–280, 2020.
https://doi.org/10.1007/978-3-030-51100-5_24

stability and reliability of intelligent agricultural greenhouse, the design method of monitoring system for intelligent agricultural greenhouse is of great value in the design and application of power supply [2]. Based on the analysis of the output parameters of the power supply system of the intelligent agricultural greenhouse, the monitoring system of the intelligent agricultural greenhouse is designed. By the design of information sensing equipment in intelligent agricultural greenhouse, the working condition information of intelligent agricultural greenhouse is collected in real time to realize the control and monitoring of intelligent agricultural greenhouse.

At present, the monitoring methods of intelligent agricultural greenhouse are mainly based on embedded scheduling. Combined with fuzzy adaptive control method, the optimal monitoring and output control of intelligent agricultural greenhouse are carried out [3]. In reference [4], a wireless greenhouse environment intelligent monitoring system based on wireless low-power local area network is proposed. The system consists of sensor sub nodes and sink nodes. The sensor node is powered by two 18650 lithium batteries. The control unit stm32f107 is used as the main control chip, and the sx1278 is used as the Lora RF module to connect the sink node through the star network. The sink node is connected to the sensor node through Lora RF module in the downstream and the server through 4G network in the upstream. At the same time, SD card is designed to store the backup data. However, the intelligent monitoring output error of the agricultural intelligent greenhouse of the system is large, which reduces the monitoring accuracy.

In view of the above problems, this paper designs a multi parameter monitoring system of intelligent agricultural greenhouse based on artificial intelligence. The hardware module of intelligent agricultural greenhouse multi-parameter monitoring system is developed and designed, and the optimal monitoring technology of intelligent agricultural greenhouse based on embedded DSP is put forward. Firstly, the overall framework model of intelligent agricultural greenhouse monitoring system is established. The monitoring system is mainly composed of shed multi-parameter information collection module, intelligent agricultural greenhouse bus control module, greenhouse temperature information fusion model, program loading module. The remote communication module, embedded scheduling module and human-computer interaction module are composed of APP control in MCU control unit, the intelligent control platform of intelligent agricultural greenhouse is constructed, the hardware development of multi-parameter monitoring system of intelligent agricultural greenhouse is carried out with intelligent control chip, and the intelligent control of intelligent agricultural greenhouse is improved. Finally, the experimental test and analysis are carried out. The superior performance of this method in improving the multi-parameter monitoring ability of intelligent agricultural greenhouse is shown.

2   Analysis of the Overall Framework and Function Module of the System

2.1   Design of the Overall Framework of the System

Firstly, the overall design of intelligent agricultural greenhouse integrated intelligent monitoring system is analyzed and introduced. The multi-parameter monitoring system of intelligent agricultural greenhouse is established on the general computer platform, and the modular structure design of intelligent agricultural greenhouse integrated intelligent monitoring system is carried out by using embedded B/S architecture design method. VIX bus control technology is used to realize bus integrated control and information scheduling of intelligent agricultural greenhouse multi-parameter monitoring system, the integrated information processor of intelligent agricultural greenhouse multi-parameter monitoring system is constructed, the instruction design of monitoring system is carried out by using program loading process control method [5], and the hardware development and design of intelligent agricultural greenhouse multi-parameter monitoring system is realized in DSP and FPGA integrated processing environment. Combined with the DC power amplifier intelligent monitoring and power sampling, the dynamic information of the intelligent agricultural greenhouse multi parameter monitoring is extracted, and the dynamic information fusion technology is used to realize the process optimization control of the intelligent agricultural greenhouse multi parameter monitoring. According to the above analysis, the overall structure of multi-parameter monitoring system in intelligent agricultural greenhouse is shown in Fig. 1.

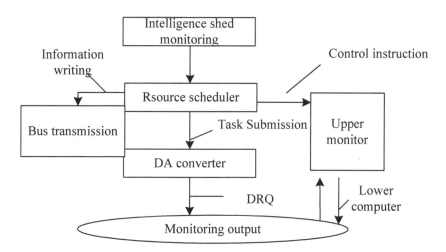

Fig. 1. The overall framework of multi-parameter monitoring system in intelligent agricultural greenhouse

According to the overall design model of multi-parameter monitoring system of intelligent agricultural greenhouse shown in Fig. 1, the component design and hardware development environment analysis of multi-parameter monitoring system of intelligent agricultural greenhouse are carried out [6]. The instruction loading of multi-parameter monitoring of intelligent agricultural greenhouse is carried out by using ISA/EISA/Micro Channel extension bus, and the hardware modularization design of multi-parameter monitoring of intelligent agricultural greenhouse is carried out combined with discrete distributed control method. The monitoring system is mainly composed of greenhouse multi-parameter information acquisition module, intelligent agricultural greenhouse bus control module, greenhouse temperature information fusion model, program loading module, remote communication module, embedded scheduling module and human-computer interaction module. According to the output power and voltage characteristic information of intelligent agricultural greenhouse, the output power consumption of intelligent agricultural greenhouse is tested. The output pulse of the multi parameter monitoring system of the intelligent agricultural greenhouse is tested by the voltage pulse response control method, and the multi parameter monitoring system of the intelligent agricultural greenhouse is logically judged and fuzzy identified [7].

2.2   Description of System Development Environment and Function Module Analysis

On the basis of the overall framework design of the multi-parameter monitoring system of the intelligent agricultural greenhouse, the hardware design of the system is carried out, the control instruction input control of the multi-parameter monitoring of the intelligent agricultural greenhouse is carried out in the executing mechanism, a fuzzy control method is adopted, the output bus design and the automatic monitoring test of the multi-parameter monitoring system of the intelligent agricultural greenhouse are carried out, and the information acquisition module for multi-parameter monitoring of the intelligent agricultural greenhouse is established, by adopting the ITU-656 PPI pattern recognition method, the bus integrated transmission control of the multi-parameter monitoring system of the intelligent agricultural greenhouse is carried out, and the output magnetic induction intensity of the power supply is obtained as follows:

$$B_{tx} = \frac{\mu \times n \times I_{tx} \times a \times b}{4\pi \sqrt{\left(\frac{a}{2}\right)^2 + \left(\frac{b}{2}\right)^2 + x^2}} \times \left(\frac{1}{\left(\frac{a}{2}\right)^2 + x^2} + \frac{1}{\left(\frac{b}{2}\right)^2 + x^2} \right) \tag{(1)}$$

Wherein, n, a and b respectively represent the parameters of the impedance coefficient and the power consumption coefficient of the intelligent agricultural greenhouse, the invention relates to a development and design of a multi-parameter monitoring system of a smart agriculture greenhouse in a combination of network technology and an embedded technology, The man-machine interaction module and the output control module adopt the ADSP21160 as the core processor and use the ISA/EISA/Micro Channel expansion bus to carry out the bus transceiving control of the multi-parameter monitoring system of the intelligent agricultural greenhouse, and the functional module structure of the system is shown in Fig. 2.

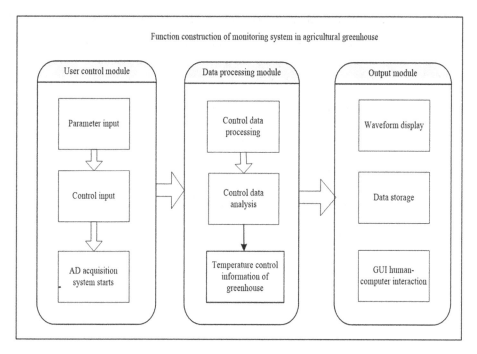

Fig. 2. Functional Module composition of Multi-parameter Monitoring system in Intelligent agricultural greenhouse

In combination with the application environment of the multi-parameter monitoring system of the intelligent agricultural greenhouse, the function modular analysis of the multi-parameter monitoring system of the intelligent agricultural greenhouse is carried out, and the peripheral actuator control of the multi-parameter monitoring system of the intelligent agricultural greenhouse is carried out under the control of the PLC logic programmable chip. The multi-channel data record dynamic range of the intelligent agricultural greenhouse control information acquisition is set to −10 dB to +10 dB, and a large amount of the Linux kernel configuration is 12 KB, and the hardware modular design of the multi-parameter monitoring system of the intelligent agricultural greenhouse is carried out according to the design index [8].

3   The Hardware Design and Implementation of the System

Based on Bus under IEEE488.2 standard, the embedded development of intelligent agricultural greenhouse integrated intelligent monitoring system is carried out. the monitoring system is mainly composed of greenhouse multi-parameter information collection module, intelligent agricultural greenhouse bus control module, greenhouse temperature information fusion model, program loading module, remote communication module, embedded scheduling module and human-computer interaction module [9].

3.1   Multi-parameter Information Acquisition Module for Greenhouse

The multi-parameter information acquisition module of the greenhouse is an original data acquisition function for realizing the intelligent agricultural greenhouse integrated intelligent monitoring system, the data acquisition of the intelligent agricultural greenhouse multi-parameter monitoring system is carried out by adopting the ISA/EISA framework mode, the collected AD information has the output current of the power supply system, information such as voltage, voltage-stabilizing characteristic and power consumption is adopted, the method for adjusting the power factor is adopted [10], the AD information conversion of the intelligent agricultural greenhouse integrated intelligent monitoring system is carried out, a bus development design method is adopted, and the output instruction control of the power supply monitoring is carried out. Using the ADSP-BF537BBC-5A to realize the design and analysis of the intelligent agricultural greenhouse control bus, the multi-parameter information acquisition module of the greenhouse is obtained as shown in Fig. 3.

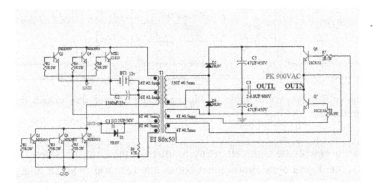

Fig. 3. Multi-parameter information acquisition module for greenhouse

3.2   Bus Control Module

The bus control module realizes the information integration processing of the intelligent agricultural greenhouse multi-parameter monitoring system, designs the automatic control transmission protocol of the intelligent agricultural greenhouse control, and realizes the instruction loading and output conversion control of the intelligent agricultural greenhouse multi-parameter monitoring system in the program loading module [11]. The design circuit of the bus control module is shown in Fig. 4.

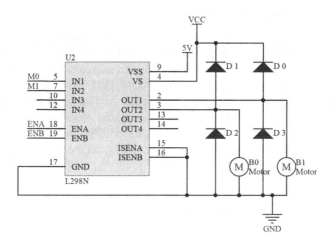

Fig. 4. Bus control module

3.3 Program Loading Module of Greenhouse Temperature Information Fusion Model

The program loading module of the greenhouse temperature information fusion model adopts the PCI bus for embedded development and integrated information processing of the multi-parameter monitoring system of the intelligent agricultural greenhouse. The clock bus circuit and the reset circuit are constructed, the program cross-compiling design of the multi-parameter monitoring system of the intelligent agricultural greenhouse is carried out, and the automatic energy-saving adjustment of the intelligent agricultural greenhouse is realized by adopting the ADSP21160 processor system [12], the design program loading module realizes the program loading of the intelligent agricultural greenhouse integrated intelligent monitoring system, and the obtained program loading module is shown in Fig. 5.

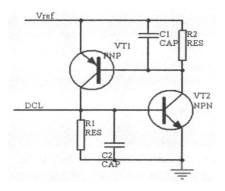

Fig. 5. Programming module design

3.4   Remote Communication Module

The remote communication module adopts the 16-bit 196.608KSa/ Sec/ Chan digitizer HP E1433A for remote communication of the multi-parameter monitoring system of the intelligent agricultural greenhouse, the remote communication module configures the asynchronous memory through the boot ROM [13], uses the PF10 as the SPI interface in the SPI interface, using the high-speed A/ D chip AD9225 as the information transmission center of the intelligent agricultural greenhouse control. And the pulse control and the remote communication of the multi-parameter monitoring system of the intelligent agricultural greenhouse are realized, and the remote communication module is obtained as shown in Fig. 6.

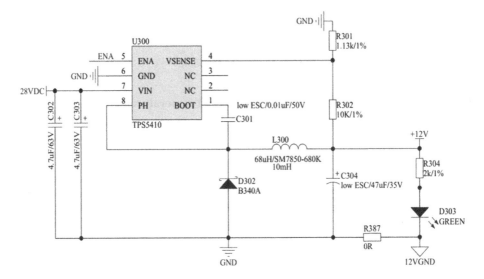

Fig. 6. Upper computer communication module

Comprehensive analysis, combined with the application environment of intelligent agricultural greenhouse multi-parameter monitoring system, the adaptive output conversion control of intelligent agricultural greenhouse is carried out, and the optimal design of intelligent agricultural greenhouse multi-parameter monitoring system is realized under DSP environment [14, 17].

4   System Test Analysis

In order to test the application performance of the intelligent agricultural greenhouse multi-parameter monitoring system designed in this paper, the experimental test analysis is carried out. Figure 7 is an environmental greenhouse intelligent monitoring system of an agricultural greenhouse.

Fig. 7. Intelligent monitoring system of greenhouse environment in agricultural greenhouse

The dynamic coupling parameter of the intelligent agricultural greenhouse is set to be 1.23, the amplification factor of each frequency component of the current is 2.5, the amplitude is 12.4 V, the phase angle is 24 rad/s. The output power loss of the power supply is 15.6 dB and the maximum power value is 34 kW. According to the above simulation parameter setting, the multi-parameter monitoring simulation of the intelligent agricultural greenhouse is carried out, and the output real-time value and the imaginary part value of the monitoring data of the intelligent agricultural greenhouse are shown in Fig. 8.

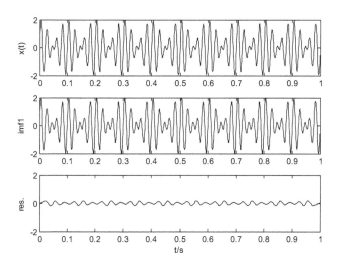

Fig. 8. Output real part value and imaginary part value of monitoring data in intelligent agricultural greenhouse

The analysis of Fig. 8 shows that the method can effectively realize the intelligent monitoring of the intelligent agricultural greenhouse, the anti-interference of the harmonic impedance is good, the voltage amplitude and the current amplitude of the output are tested, and the result is shown in Fig. 9.

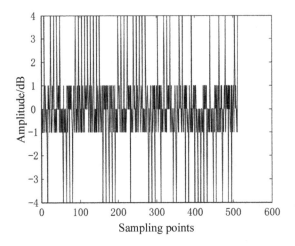

Fig. 9. Output temperature amplitude and humidity amplitude

The analysis Fig. 9 shows that the stability of the output temperature and humidity of the power supply can be improved by using this method, and the output error is measured. The comparison results are shown in Table 1.

Table 1. Comparison of output error of intelligent agricultural greenhouse monitoring

Number of experiments	Proposed method	Reference [4]
100	0.113	0.154
200	0.056	0.134
300	0.012	0.116

Analysis Table 1 shows that the output error of this method to the intelligent agricultural greenhouse monitoring is low.

In order to further verify the effectiveness of this system, the accuracy rate of multi parameter monitoring of intelligent agricultural greenhouse based on this method and traditional method is compared and analyzed.

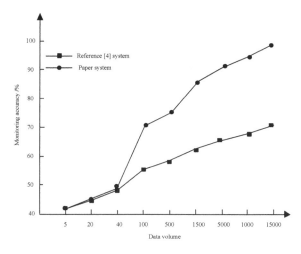

Fig. 10. Comparison of multi parameter monitoring accuracy of intelligent agricultural greenhouse

According to Fig. 10, the multi parameter monitoring accuracy of intelligent agricultural greenhouse in this system can reach up to 100%, which is higher than that of traditional system.

5   Conclusions

In this paper, the design scheme of intelligent agricultural greenhouse multi-parameter monitoring system based on artificial intelligence control is put forward. The monitoring system is mainly composed of greenhouse multi-parameter information collection module, intelligent agricultural greenhouse bus control module, greenhouse temperature information fusion model, program loading module, remote communication module, embedded scheduling module and human-computer interaction module. The integrated information processor of multi-parameter monitoring system in intelligent agricultural greenhouse is constructed, the instruction design of monitoring system is carried out by using program loading process control method, the intelligent monitoring AD sampling of current power supply is carried out with DC power amplifier, the dynamic information of multi-parameter monitoring in intelligent agricultural greenhouse is extracted, and the process optimization control of multi-parameter monitoring in intelligent agricultural greenhouse is realized by using dynamic information fusion technology. The embedded development of intelligent agricultural greenhouse integrated intelligent monitoring system is carried out, and the adaptive output conversion control of intelligent agricultural greenhouse is carried out. The optimal design of multi-parameter monitoring system of intelligent agricultural greenhouse is realized in DSP environment. The analysis shows that the output stability of intelligent agricultural greenhouse monitoring is high, and it can accurately monitor the multi parameters of intelligent agricultural greenhouse.

References

1. Rui, M., Yigeng, H.F., Dongdong, Z., et al.: Modeling simulation and experimental test of proton exchange membrane fuel cells in multiphysical domain. J. Power Supply **17**(2), 3–11 (2019)
2. Quan, L., Chenglin, L.I., Feng, Z., et al.: Algorithm of works' decision for three arms robot in greenhouse based on control with motion sensing technology. Trans. Chin. Soc. Agri. Mach. **48**(3), 14–23 (2017)
3. Drabo, A.: Climate change mitigation and agricultural development models: primary commodity exports or local consumption production? Ecol. Econ. **137**, 110–125 (2017)
4. Zheng, G.L., Wang, T.C.: Design of greenhouse environment intelligent monitoring system based on Lora. Jiangsu Agri. Sci. **47**(10), 216–219 (2019)
5. Ntalli, N., Monokrousos, N., Rumbos, C., et al.: Greenhouse biofumigation with Melia azedarach controls Meloidogyne spp. and enhances soil biological activity. J. Pest. Sci. **91**, 29–40 (2017)
6. Zhang, S., Zhang, C., Ding, J.: Disease and insect pest forecasting model of greenhouse winter jujube based on modified deep belief network. Trans. Chin. Soc. Agric. Eng. **33**(19), 202–208 (2017)
7. Li, Y., Zhou, W., Song, S., et al.: Design of experimental prototype of flexible chassis used in greenhouse. Trans. Chin. Soc. Agric. Eng. **33**(19), 41–50 (2017)
8. Guo-rong, H.A.O., Xu, H.A.N., Wen-jie, D.U., Cheng, L.U.: Fusion estimator with stochastic sensor gain degradation for uncertain systems. Control Decis. **31**(08), 1413–1418 (2016)
9. Liu, Y.: Joint resource allocation in SWIPT-based multi-antenna decode-and-forward relay networks. IEEE Trans. Veh. Technol. **66**(10), 9192–9200 (2017)
10. Du, C., Chen, X., Lei, L.: Energy-efficient optimization for secrecy wireless information and power transfer in massive MIMO relaying systems. IET Commun. **11**(1), 10–16 (2017)
11. Wang, W., Wang, R., Mehrpouyan, H., et al.: Beamforming for simultaneous wireless information and power transfer in two-way relay channels. IEEE Access **5**, 9235–9250 (2017)
12. Hu, S., Ding, Z., Ni, Q.: Beamforming optimisation in energy harvesting cooperative full-duplex networks with self-energy recycling protocol. IET Commun. **10**(7), 848–853 (2016)
13. Wen, Z., Liu, X., Beaulieu, N.C., et al.: Joint source and relay beamforming design for full-duplex MIMO AF relay SWIPT systems. IEEE Commun. Lett. **20**(2), 320–323 (2016)
14. Park, J.J., Moon, J.H., Kim, D.I.: Time-switching based in-band full duplex wireless powered two-way relay. In: URSI Asia-Pacific Radio Science Conference (URSI AP-RASC), pp. 438–441 (2016)
15. Liu, S., Zhang, Z., Qi, L., et al.: A fractal image encoding method based on statistical loss used in agricultural image compression. Multimedia Tools Appl. **75**(23), 15525–15536 (2016)
16. Peter, C., Helming, K., Nendel, C.: Do greenhouse gas emission calculations from energy crop cultivation reflect actual agricultural management practices? – a review of carbon footprint calculators. Renew. Sustain. Energ. Rev. **67**, 461–476 (2017)
17. Green, A., Tzilivakis, J., Warner, D.J., et al.: Problems of benchmarking greenhouse gas emissions in dairy agriculture. Benchmarking Int. J. **24**(3), 12–24 (2017)

Design of Agricultural Network Information Resource Sharing System Based on Internet of Things

Kun Wang[(✉)]

Jiangsu Agriculture and Animal Husbandry Vocational College,
Taizhou 225300, China
wangkun010@tom.com

Abstract. Under the environment of Internet of things, agricultural network information service is open and resource sharing. In order to improve the intelligence of agricultural network information service under the environment of Internet of things, an agricultural network information resource sharing system based on Internet of things is constructed. The overall design description and function modularization analysis of agricultural network information resource sharing system are carried out. The system design includes agricultural network information service resource retrieval module, agricultural network information resource integration processing module, bus control module, resource information fusion module, program loading and compilation module and human-computer interaction module. The bottom module of agricultural network information resource sharing system is designed by using B/S architecture protocol and bus server system, the retrieval of massive agricultural network information service resources is designed based on Internet of things technology, the information dispatching network center of agricultural network information service resources is established under the environment of Internet of things technology, and the Internet of things networking design of agricultural network information resource sharing system is carried out by using network networking methods such as ZigBee and GPRS. The process management and file configuration are carried out under MVB bus control protocol, and the software development and design of agricultural network information resource sharing system are realized under embedded ARM environment. The test results show that the information resource sharing system of agricultural network based on Internet of things technology has good human-computer interaction and resource scheduling, and the execution time cost is small and the reliability is high.

Keywords: Internet of things · Agricultural network · Information resources · Sharing system

1 Introduction

With the continuous progress of science and technology, Internet of things technology is widely used in the sharing of modern agricultural network information resources, especially in the field of agricultural network information service, complex network

Y.-D. Zhang et al. (Eds.): ICMTEL 2020, LNICST 326, pp. 281–293, 2020.
https://doi.org/10.1007/978-3-030-51100-5_25

technology and wireless sensor network technology, the construction of agricultural network information resource sharing system, the use of network control method to realize the agricultural network information service under the Internet of things technology, and the use of new media to promote the improvement of agricultural network information service. So as to provide a better platform for the development of agricultural network information service in China [1]. Under the condition of Internet of things technology, the agricultural network information service platform is constructed, the agricultural network information service resource information is integrated, the agricultural network information agricultural network information resource information sharing level is improved, the communication among various regions is promoted, the agricultural network information service is upgraded in the process of globalization, and the design method of agricultural network information platform under the new media is studied. It is of great significance to improve the intelligent level and automatic control level of agricultural network information service [2].

The design of intelligent independent agricultural network information resource sharing system is based on the network design and software design of the platform, and the transmission and sharing of agricultural network information resources through network and modern media. By using wireless communication technology, Internet technology and Internet of things technology, the network control and resource optimization transmission of agricultural network information service can be realized. The design model of agricultural network information resource sharing system mainly adopts ITU-T H.323 and IETF SIP network signaling control scheme and (Real Time Control Protocol, RTCP), a real-time transmission control protocol for service quality monitoring, to realize the design of agricultural network information service [3], and obtains better platform automatic control efficiency.

In reference [4], an application program development model of agricultural network information resource sharing system based on Linux kernel control is proposed. The platform is developed and designed by using signaling technology, media coding technology and media real-time transmission technology. The information fusion transmission is carried out through ZigBee and wireless communication technology in the network layer, and the output control of agricultural network information service information data is carried out by using VXI bus technology. However, the real-time output performance of media information in this system is not good. In reference [5], a design model of agricultural network information resource sharing system based on VME bus architecture is proposed. The output control of agricultural network information service resource is realized by using the communication bus between special modules, and the original agricultural network information service information is sampled by sensor equipment, RFID label equipment and video equipment, so as to improve the intelligent control ability of agricultural network information service. However, the feedback output error of the system designed by this method is large. In reference [6], an agricultural network information resource sharing system based on TCP/IP is proposed. The non-contact RFID technology is used to activate the electronic label, which realizes the feedback control of the agricultural network information resource sharing system and improves the stability of the platform. The system is prone to errors in process management and file configuration. In reference [7], a design model of agricultural network information resource sharing system based on Internet technology is proposed. The network transmission protocol under the mode of Internet of things is constructed by TCP/IP server or UPD server, and the agricultural network information resource sharing system is designed by using wireless sensor design. The independent control performance of the platform is not good [7].

In view of the above problems, this paper proposes an agricultural network information resource sharing system based on Internet of things. Firstly, the overall framework design and function modular analysis of the platform are carried out, the information processing core control module is then constructed, and the information fusion and integrated dispatching design of the agricultural network information service resources is carried out, the network networking design of the mass agricultural network information service resource retrieval design and the platform is carried out under the Internet of things environment, the software development design of the agricultural network information resource sharing system is realized under the MVB (multivibrator) bus control protocol and the embedded environment, and finally, the simulation experiment analysis is carried out. The advantages of the method in improving the control performance and information transmission capability of the platform are shown.

2 Overall Design and Development Environment Description of the Platform

2.1 General Design Framework of Internet of Things System and Agricultural Network Information Resource Sharing System

In order to realize the design of agricultural network information resource sharing system and the optimal scheduling of agricultural network information service resource information, the overall design framework of the platform is analyzed at first. VXI bus technology is used to collect the information resources of agricultural network information service, and the software of agricultural network information resource sharing system is developed and designed under the embedded kernel. The platform uses LabWindows/CVI to open up the code resources. The agricultural network information resource sharing system is mainly divided into agricultural network information service resource retrieval module, agricultural network information resource integration processing module, bus control module, resource information fusion module, program loading and compilation module and human-computer interaction module [8]. The information perception module is constructed to realize the information collection of agricultural network information service resources, the collected agricultural network information service resource information is processed adaptively, and the underlying database is constructed to realize the storage of agricultural network information service resources. in the local memory module, the program loading and compiling software is used to compile and read and write the control instructions of the new media agricultural network information resource sharing system. The embedded controller PXI-8155 is used to construct the network communication protocol, and the online automatic monitoring and network transmission design of the agricultural network information resource sharing system is carried out under the condition of Internet of things technology [9]. Build ZigBee terminal node, build the Internet of things architecture of agricultural network information resource sharing system. The video equipment is used to monitor the teacher and the indoor environment of the agricultural network information in real time. The user can access the server through the PC machine or mobile phone, and the data fusion and data processing analysis of the collected agricultural network information service platform can be carried out in the central information processing unit. The remote transmission protocol is constructed in the local database to realize the output control and storage of the information sharing system of the new media agricultural network information resources. ZigBee data collection node is designed as the bottom node of the Internet of things, which is uploaded to the remote data center server through GRPS [10], and the sensor node is constructed to realize the original data collection, local information processing and remote data transmission and control of the agricultural network information service. The network structure model of the designed agricultural network information resource sharing system is shown in Fig. 1.

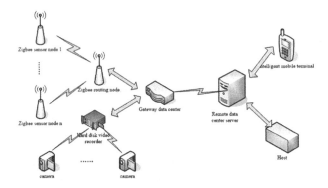

Fig. 1. Internet of things architecture of agricultural network information resource sharing system

According to the architecture of Internet of things shown in Fig. 1, the information dispatching network center of agricultural network information service resources is established under the environment of Internet of things technology, and the network design and system development of agricultural network information service platform are carried out by using network networking technologies such as ZigBee and GPRS. The ZigBee sensor node and hard disk video data are uploaded to the network data center and to the intelligent mobile terminal through the remote data center server. The overall structure of agricultural network information resource sharing system designed in this paper is shown in Fig. 2.

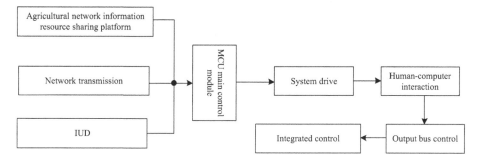

Fig. 2. Overall structural framework of the system

According to the overall architecture shown in Fig. 2, the bus control of agricultural network information resource sharing system is automatically monitored by VIX bus. The sensor group used in the platform adopts ZigBee protocol for ad hoc network and wireless data transmission, and makes full use of open source Linux operating platform to design the internal cache control and human-computer interaction of agricultural network information resource sharing system [11].

2.2   Function Module Analysis and Development Environment Description of the System

On the basis of the overall framework design of the system, the function modular design of the system is carried out, a MySQL construction agricultural network information service management database is constructed, the network design of the agricultural network information resource sharing system is carried out under the B/S structure system, the agricultural network information resource sharing system is divided into an agricultural network information service resource agricultural network information resource integration processing module [12], a control module, an interface module, a program loading and compiling module, a bus module and the like, the program loading and compiling control of the agricultural network information resource sharing system is carried out by using the Native app local application program and the Web app web page application program, the MySQL is used as a database, and the collected agricultural network information service resource information is analyzed and the resource scheduling processing under the embedded system bus. In this paper, an information management system of agricultural network information is constructed, and an open network system model is adopted, and the network networking design and database design of the agricultural network information resource sharing system are carried out. The overall structure design of the agricultural network information resource sharing system designed in this paper is the B/S architecture design, that is the client/server structure [14]. The control protocol of the agricultural network information resource sharing system is constructed by using the GPRS protocol model shown in Fig. 3.

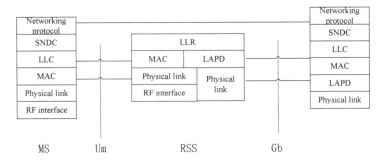

Fig. 3. GPRS protocol model

According to the Internet of Things GPRS protocol model shown in Fig. 3, the GPRS protocol model is divided into a radio frequency interface part, a GPRS air interface layer, a medium access control layer, a program loading and compiling layer, an MCU layer and a physical link layer:

(1) The radio frequency interface part adopts the Um interface to realize the man-machine interaction design of the physical layer access and the radio frequency interface of the agricultural network information resource sharing system, and the physical link layer realizes the physical access and sensor information acquisition of various AD sampling interfaces. A distributed networking architecture is adopted to construct various logical channels of the air interface of the agricultural network information service system under the internet of things.

(2) The MAC bit medium access control layer. The MAC layer adopts a bus control design, carries out process management and bus scheduling under the MVB bus control protocol, Such that the channels can be shared by different mobile stations.

(3) The LLC layer is a logical link control layer, adopts a wireless link protocol of HDLC, and when the running NextTask () enters an infinite loop task, a multi-thread agricultural network information resource sharing system task scheduling method is adopted, and the LLC address and the frame field are designed, and the on-line interface design and program loading and compiling of the agricultural network information service system are completed.

(4) SNDC is called a subnet-dependent binding layer. SNDC adopts an on-line response channel mode to carry out the bus scheduling and the base database design of the agricultural network information service system, and the main function of the invention is to complete the grouping and packing of the data, and to determine the TCP/IP address and the encryption mode.

(5) The protocol SIP of the network layer has a distributed multicast function. SIP also provides good quality of service support, and the network layer protocol uses TCP/IP and X.25 protocols that are transparent to traditional GSM network devices such as BSS and NSS.

According to the analysis, the three-tier architecture of agricultural network information resource sharing system is shown in Fig. 4.

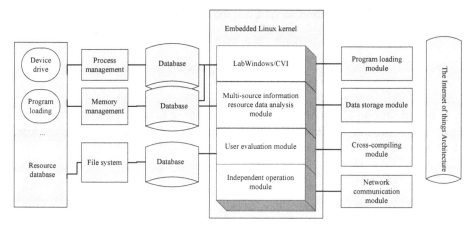

Fig. 4. Three-tier architecture of agricultural network information resource sharing system

3   Development and Design of System Software

3.1   Algorithm Design of Agricultural Network Information Service Resource Retrieval

The bottom module of agricultural network information resource sharing system is designed by using B/S architecture protocol and bus server system, and the retrieval design of massive agricultural network information service resources is carried out based on Internet of things technology. In the above, the overall architecture design and functional index analysis of large-scale agricultural network information resource sharing system are carried out, and the fusion algorithm of agricultural network information service resources is designed. To realize the information resource sharing resource scheduling of new media agricultural network, this paper adopts a fuzzy linear fusion model of agricultural network information resource scheduling. Under the constraint of extreme learning, the fuzzy membership function of agricultural network information service resource fusion is constructed as follows:

$$P_F = \sum_{j=k}^{N} \sum_{\sum u_i = j} \prod_{i=1}^{N} (P_{fi})^{u_i} (1 - P_{fi})^{1-u_i} \tag{1}$$

$$P_D = \sum_{j=k}^{N} \sum_{\sum u_i = j} \prod_{i=1}^{N} (P_{di})^{u_i} (1 - P_{di})^{1-u_i} \tag{2}$$

Wherein, P_{fi} represents the fusion clustering center of big data distribution of agricultural network information service resources. P_{di} is the sampling frequency of agricultural network information service, and the example set of data flow is described as follows:

$$\bar{x} = \frac{1}{N} \sum_{i=1}^{N} |x_i| \tag{3}$$

In the data fusion center of information management system, the data attribute set of agricultural network information service resources is constructed, and the root mean square error of data classification is obtained as follows:

$$\sigma^2 = \frac{1}{N} \sum_{i=1}^{N} |x_i - \bar{x}|^2 \tag{4}$$

In the attribute set distribution space of agricultural network information service resource data, linear regression analysis and correlation analysis are used to obtain the mining results of segmented fusion of agricultural network information service resources:

$$x_i' = \frac{x_i}{\|x_i\|} = (\frac{x_{i1}}{\|x_i\|}, \frac{x_{i2}}{\|x_i\|}, \cdots, \frac{x_{iN}}{\|x_i\|}) \tag{5}$$

Wherein, the dynamic replica value x_N, of agricultural network information service resource data is used in the data clustering space, and the fuzzy C-means and support vector machine algorithm are used to cluster the agricultural network information service resource, and the output characteristic quantity after data clustering is obtained as:

$$X_p(u) = s_c(t)e^{j2\pi f_0 t} = \frac{1}{\sqrt{T}} rect(\frac{t}{T})e^{j2\pi(f_0 t + Kt^2)/2} \tag{6}$$

Wherein, $s_c(t)$ represents the scalar time series in the data set of agricultural network information resource sharing system, $e^{j2\pi f_0 t}$ represents the feature matching set of information fusion, and f_0 represents the reference frequency component, thus realizing the information fusion and integrated scheduling of agricultural network information service resources [15].

3.2   Modularization Design of Software Function

The above designed agricultural network information resource scheduling algorithm realizes the resource information fusion of the algorithm through the resource information fusion module. The SQLServer2012 database is designed in embedded Linux to store the agricultural network information service resource information, and the agricultural network information service resource collection and data loading subroutine is established by using TCP/IP (Transmission Control Protocol/Internet Protocol) transmission control protocol, and the PWM related buffer is set up. The data source is written into the DataSet of agricultural network information resource sharing system, and the data source is bound according to the data in DataSet. The request_irq () function is called to apply for character device driver, and the program loading and compiling and multi-mode control of agricultural network information service resources are realized in cloud computing and Internet of things environment. The trigger bus of agricultural network information resource sharing system is composed of 8 TTL trigger lines and 6 ECL trigger lines, and the minimum communication is carried out by VXI special string protocol. The external controller of agricultural network information resource sharing system is constructed. in the SCSI bus driver design of agricultural network information resource sharing system, the ability of real-time data recording is improved by connecting external PC and VXI bus through MXI-2 bus. The resource information fusion module is the key module to realize the core program processing of the agricultural network information service resource management system. The resource information fusion module adopts the embedded Web service design method, which can realize the collection and adaptive processing of the agricultural network information service resources, construct the ROMFS file system in the physical storage medium, and use ADO. NET to complete the query of the large-scale agricultural network information resource sharing system in the Web programming design. Update and database management, the physical layer and MAC layer of agricultural network information service system adopt IEEE802.15.4 protocol standard. The working rate of distribution node in the middle layer of network is between 20–250kbps. According to the data output from GPRS network, the data bit is sent and received to the RF byte component in the upper layer, which makes the GPRS system meet the required memory, energy consumption and speed. Under the B/S architecture protocol and the bus server system, the software development and design of the independent agricultural network information resource sharing system are carried out. The underlying module of agricultural network information resource sharing system is designed by embedded Boot loader driver module, the process management program is called, and the information collection is carried out through VME bus or local bus transmission technology, thus the software system of agricultural network information resource sharing system is constructed.

4   System Test and Performance Analysis

In order to test the application performance of the agricultural network information resource sharing system designed in this paper, carry on the software debugging and simulation experiment, the agricultural network information resource sharing system provides the user with a simple and unified system calling interface, realizes the information processing and the system integration design, uses the embedded Linux as the kernel to carry on the agricultural network information resource sharing system software development and design. Under X86 architecture, GNU development tool set is used to test the software of agricultural network information resource sharing system, ast_sip_realtime class is used to read data directly from database, Sip protocol stack is used to establish session protocol of agricultural network information service system, sip_call interface is called to create INVITE message outgoing, and channel_bridge function is called to connect two channels, thus the test environment of agricultural network information resource sharing system is constructed. The data block size of data sampling for agricultural network information service resources is 200 m. The task set of agricultural network information service resources scheduling is divided into 10 queue. The parameters of agricultural network information service operation are set in Table 1.

Table 1. Job parameter settings

Number of jobs	Number of tasks	Proportion of agricultural network information service operations
20	1–5	55.7%
13	5–20	25%
10	21–40	10%
8	41–50	6%
6	51–100	2%

According to the above software test environment and parameter setting, the performance of the agricultural network information resource sharing system is tested, and the big data sampling sequence of the information transmission of the agricultural network information service system is obtained as shown in Fig. 5.

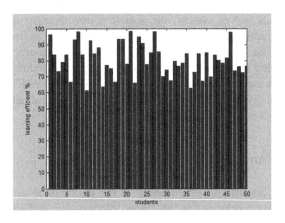

Fig. 5. Big data sampling sequence of information transmission in agricultural network information service system

The agricultural network information service system information shown in Fig. 5 is used as the sample to send the big data sampling sequence, and the network transmission performance of the agricultural network information resource sharing system is tested. Figure 6 shows the time cost of scheduling the agricultural network information service resources under different scale data sets.

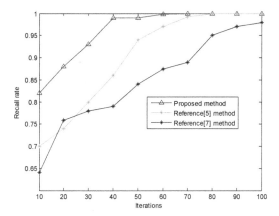

Fig. 6. Comparison of resource recall performance

The analysis of Fig. 6 shows that the recall performance of the new media agricultural network information resource scheduling designed by this method is better, which is 24.5% and 19.8% higher than that of the traditional method. In order to further verify the effectiveness of this system, the execution time cost of this system, document [5] system and document [7] system are compared, and the comparison results are shown in Fig. 7.

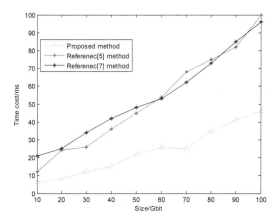

Fig. 7. Comparison of execution time overhead

The analysis of Fig. 7 shows that the execution time cost increases with the increase of the scale of agricultural network information resources sharing resource data. The overall time cost of this method is obviously lower than that of the traditional method, and the execution cost is shortened by 46.7% and 40.4%.

5 Conclusions

In this paper, the agricultural network information service system is constructed to integrate the agricultural network information service resource information and improve the sharing level of the agricultural network information network information resource information, and this paper proposes to construct the agricultural network information resource sharing system based on the Internet of things. The VXI bus technology is used to collect the information resources of agricultural network information service, and the software development and design of agricultural network information resource sharing system are carried out under the embedded kernel, and the network design and system development of agricultural network information service system are carried out by using ZigBee and GPRS and other network networking technologies. B/S framework protocol and bus server system are used to design the underlying module of agricultural network information resource sharing system, and the retrieval design of massive agricultural network information service resources based on Internet of things technology is carried out to realize the core algorithm design and software development of the system. It is found that the agricultural network information resource sharing system under the Internet of things technology designed in this paper has good resource recall performance, low execution time cost and good overall stability. However, this system does not consider the cost when sharing the agricultural network information resources. In the next study, we will take the cost as the research index to further study the agricultural network information resources sharing.

References

1. Huang, H., Xiaotian, G.E., Chen, X.: Density clustering method based on complex learning classification system. J. Comput. Appl. **37**(11), 3207–3211 (2017)
2. Ji, Y., Li, Y., Shi, C.: Aspect rating prediction based on heterogeneous network and topic model. J. Comput. Appl. **37**(11), 3201–3206 (2017)
3. Xiao, K., Du, Z., Yang, L.: An embedded wireless sensor system for multi-service agricultural information acquisition. Sens. Lett. **15**(11), 907–914 (2017)
4. Blanco, A.C., Tamondong, A., Perez, A.M., et al.: Nationwide natural resource inventory of the Philippines using LiDAR: strategies, progress, and challenges. ISPRS J. Photogram. Remote Sens. XL **I**(B6), 105–109 (2018)
5. Slimeni, F., Scheers, B., Nir, V.L., et al.: Learning multi-channel power allocation against smart jammer in cognitive radio networks. In: Proceedings of the 2016 International Conference on Military Communications and Information Systems, Piscataway, NJ, pp. 1–7. IEEE (2016)
6. Eski, İ., Kuş, Z.A.: Control of unmanned agricultural vehicles using neural network-based control system. Neural Comput. Appl. **31**, 583–595 (2019). https://doi.org/10.1007/s00521-017-3026-4
7. Han, B., Li, Y.: Optimization method for reducing network loss of dc distribution system with distributed resource. Photon. Netw. Commun. **37**(2), 233–242 (2018). https://doi.org/10.1007/s11107-018-0805-5

8. Mougin, C., et al.: BRC4Env, a network of Biological Resource Centres for research in environmental and agricultural sciences. Environ. Sci. Pollut. Res. **25**(34), 33849–33857 (2018). https://doi.org/10.1007/s11356-018-1973-7

9. Shi, J., Feng, Z., Liu, J.: Design and experiment of high precision forest resource investigation system based on UAV remote sensing images. Nongye Gongcheng Xuebao/Trans. Chin. Soc. Agric. Eng. **33**(11), 82–90 (2017)

10. Xing, X., Shang, Y., Zhao, R., Li, Z.: Pheromone updating strategy of ant colony algorithm for multi-objective test case prioritization. J. Comput. Appl. **36**(9), 2497–2502 (2016)

11. Zhang, H., Shao, Z., Zhang, Z., et al.: Regulation system of CO_2 in facilities based on wireless sensor network. Nongye Jixie Xuebao/Trans. Chin. Soc. Agric. Mach. **48**(3), 325–331, 360 (2017)

12. Parsley, S.: Accessing good health information and resources. Commun. Eye Health **30**(97), 15–17 (2017)

13. Zhang, X.-B., Li, M., Wang, H., et al.: Location information acquisition and sharing application design in national census of Chinese medicine resources. Zhongguo Zhong yao za zhi = Zhongguo zhongyao zazhi = China J. Chin. Materia Medica, **42**(22), 4271–4276 (2017)

14. Wang, L.: Optimization process of compiling and researching archives in universities under the background of information sharing. Int. Technol. Manag. **6**, 36–38 (2017)

15. Wang, Y., Li, C., Cui, Y., et al.: Construction of PaaS platform based on Docker. Comput. Syst. Appl. **5**(3), 72–77 (2016)

An Evaluation Model of the Efficiency of Agricultural Information Resources Allocation in the Big Data Environment

Kun Wang[(✉)]

Jiangsu Agriculture and Animal Husbandry Vocational College,
Taizhou 225300, China
wangkun010@tom.com

Abstract. In order to improve the ability of optimal allocation of agricultural information resources, analysis of agricultural information resources allocation efficiency, optimize the allocation of agricultural information resources, has become an important issue. An evaluation method of allocation efficiency of agricultural information resources based on huge data is raised, and the software development and design of configuration efficiency evaluation model are carried out in combination with embedded LINUX system. The big data distributed storage structure model of agricultural information resources is constructed. Quantitative regression analysis and adaptive game method are used for quantitative evaluation of agricultural information resources, big data information of agricultural information resources is excavated, regional grid clustering method is used for classification and recognition of agricultural information resources, and information fusion and adaptive scheduling of agricultural information resources are carried out under the optimized information fusion model. Embedded Linux technology is used to develop the evaluation model of agricultural information resource allocation efficiency in C/S client. The system includes data processing module, agricultural information resource allocation module, program loading module, bus scheduling module and human-computer interaction module. The integrated design technology is used to realize the software design of agricultural information resource allocation efficiency evaluation model. The test results show that the designed evaluation model of agricultural information resource allocation efficiency has good reliability and strong human-computer interaction ability, which improves the quantitative evaluation and optimal allocation ability of agricultural information resources.

Keywords: Big data environment · Agricultural information resources · Allocation · Efficiency evaluation

1 Introduction

With the development of the national agriculture and the rural construction, the management and dispatching level of the agricultural information is continuously improved, the information management of the agricultural information resources is continuously promoted, the resource allocation of the agricultural information is

© ICST Institute for Computer Sciences, Social Informatics and Telecommunications Engineering 2020
Published by Springer Nature Switzerland AG 2020. All Rights Reserved
Y.-D. Zhang et al. (Eds.): ICMTEL 2020, LNICST 326, pp. 294–304, 2020.
https://doi.org/10.1007/978-3-030-51100-5_26

becoming more and more popular, and in the development process of the agricultural information resource allocation project, in that invention, the agricultural information resource allocation efficiency evaluation and analysis are needed, a quantitative evaluation model of the agricultural information resource is established [1]. The optimization configuration of the agricultural information resource is carried out in combination with the large data information analysis of the agricultural information resource, the agricultural information resource management and the distribution capability are improved. The evaluation model of the efficiency of agricultural information resource allocation is of crucial importance in raising the use and distribution ability of agricultural information resources [2–4].

The efficiency evaluation of agricultural information resource allocation is based on the resource information and big data information processing technology of cloud computing. Big data mining method is used to explore the relevant characteristics of agricultural information resources. Combined with feature extraction and information fusion methods, the evaluation of agricultural information resource allocation efficiency is realized. The current evaluation model of agricultural information resource allocation efficiency has a long evaluation time, which leads to a slow evaluation efficiency. Therefore, this paper puts forward the evaluation method of agricultural information resource allocation efficiency based on big data, and develops and designs the software of the evaluation model under the embedded Linux system. Firstly, we need to analyze the big data of agricultural information resources, and then design the evaluation algorithm. Finally, the evaluation model of agricultural information resource allocation efficiency is established, and the simulation results are given. The calculation time of this evaluation model is short, which shortens the evaluation time of agricultural information resource allocation efficiency and improves the evaluation efficiency.

2   Big Data Analysis of Agricultural Information Resources

2.1   Big Data Distributed Storage Structure Model

In order to realize the evaluation model of agricultural information resource allocation efficiency in the cloud computing environment, the need for building big data mining and data information storage structure model of agricultural information resources, and use directed graph analysis method to evaluate the allocation efficiency of agricultural information resources [5]. It is assumed that the information storage structure of agricultural information resources is a binary directed graph structure, and the feature distribution attribute set of agricultural information resources is $X = \{x_1, x_2, \cdots, x_n\}$. The big data distributed storage structure model for evaluating the allocation efficiency of agricultural information resources is shown in Fig. 1.

Assuming that the agricultural information resource database dataset $X = \{x_1, x_2, \cdots, x_n\}$, X is the quality of agricultural information resource data mining object set X, H is the selected feature point in the agricultural information resource database, and the key feature point matching method is used for quantitative evaluation of agricultural information resources [6]. The distribution incremental structure of agricultural

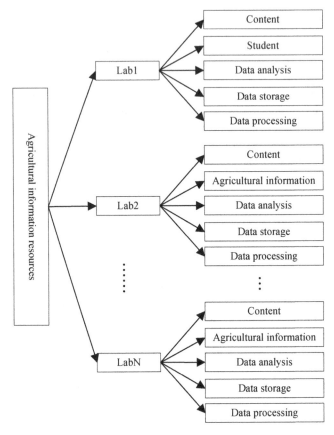

Fig. 1. Big data distributed storage structure model for evaluating the allocation efficiency of agricultural information resources

information resources is represented as an N-dimensional vector, and the information distributed migration model of agricultural information resources is obtained.

The directed graph model is used to building the quantitative evaluation node distribution structure of agricultural information resources, and the fuzzy association feature extraction and information matching are carried out in database. The linear constrained programming model for evaluating the allocation efficiency of agricultural information resources is constructed as follows:

$$\min(f) \; = \; \sum_{i=1}^{m} \sum_{j=1}^{n} H_{ij} X_{ij} \tag{1}$$

Where i is the distribution node and j is the information resource. On this basis, the optimal allocation model of Internet of things nodes is obtained to evaluate the efficiency of agricultural information resource allocation, which is recorded as $L_1, \cdots, L_n$

and $P_1^{\min}, \cdots, P_n^{\min}$. According to the distribution of storage nodes, evaluate and analyze the configuration efficiency [7].

2.2 Big Data Mining of Agricultural Information Resources

Basing on building the Big data distributed storage structure model of the agricultural information resource, the quantitative regression analysis and adaptive game method are used for quantitative evaluation and big data mining [8], and the self-adaptive scheduling parameter $\nabla^2 F(x)$ is constructed, The constraint parameters of agricultural information resource allocation efficiency evaluation are:

$$[\nabla^2 F(x)]_{kj} = \frac{\partial^2 F(x)}{\partial x_k \partial x_j} \tag{2}$$

In combination with that optimal time delay balance control method, the balance control in the evaluation process of the resource allocation efficiency of the agricultural information is carry out, a resource optimization configuration model is established, and in the cloud computing environment, the efficiency evaluation set structure of the agricultural information resource allocation is carried out [9]. The spatial planning model for obtaining the efficiency evaluation of the resource allocation efficiency of the agricultural information is expressed as follows:

$$\begin{cases} C_1(s) = \frac{\lambda_2 \min(f) + 1}{\lambda_1 + 1} \\ C_2(s) = \frac{\prod\limits_{i=1}^{i=n} (T_{mi} \min(f) + 1)}{K_m (\lambda_2 + [\nabla^2 F(x)]_{kj}) s} \end{cases} \tag{3}$$

It is assumed that the dynamic constraint parameter model of agricultural information resource allocation efficiency evaluation is described as follows: $x_j = \{x_{1j}, x_{2j}, \ldots, x_{mj}\}^T$, shares and dispatches according to the attribute distribution of agricultural information resources, and obtains the criteria of agricultural information resource information evaluation factors as follows:

$$S(i,j) = \frac{\sum_{u \in U_{ij}} (V_{u,i} - 3)(V_{u,j} - 3)}{\sqrt{\sum_{u \in U_{ij}} (V_{u,i} - \overline{V}_{.i})^2} \sqrt{\sum_{u \in U_{ij}} (V_{u,j} - \overline{V}_{.j})^2}} \tag{4}$$

Wherein, the evaluation matrix of agricultural information resources is the optimal characteristic solution of the distribution set of $R = (r_{ij}, a_{ij})_{m \times n}$, agricultural information resources:

$$\Phi = diag[e^{j\phi_1}, \cdots, e^{j\phi_P}] \tag{5}$$

The mutual information entropy of agricultural information resources is introduced into high dimensional phase space, namely:

$$\begin{bmatrix} \mathbf{x}(t) \\ \mathbf{y}(t) \end{bmatrix} = \begin{bmatrix} \mathbf{A}(\boldsymbol{\theta}) \\ \mathbf{A}(\boldsymbol{\theta})\Phi \end{bmatrix} \mathbf{s} + \mathbf{n} = \overline{\mathbf{A}}(\boldsymbol{\theta})\mathbf{s} + \mathbf{n} \tag{6}$$

Taking P as the probability density of resource distribution, it is obvious that $\hat{\mathbf{T}} = \left(\mathbf{A}^{\mathbf{H}}\mathbf{A}\right)^{-1}\mathbf{A}^{\mathbf{H}}\mathbf{U}_{\mathbf{s}} = \mathbf{A}^{+}\mathbf{U}_{\mathbf{s}}$, excavates agricultural information resources by big data according to the above analysis [10–12].

3 Evaluation of Allocation Efficiency of Agricultural Information Resources

3.1 Classification and Recognition of Agricultural Information Resources

On the basis of mining big data information of agricultural information resources, the regional grid clustering method is used to classify and identify the agricultural information resources, and the scheduling fusion model [13] is self-adaptive and resource information fusion under the optimized information, and the big data fusion technology is used to manage the information of the relevant resources, and the optimized evaluation set is obtained as follows:

$$F = \mathrm{min}tr\{\mathbf{P}_{\mathbf{A}}^{\perp}\mathbf{U}_{\mathbf{s}}\mathbf{W}\mathbf{U}_{\mathbf{s}}^{\mathbf{H}}\} = \mathrm{max}tr\{\mathbf{P}_{\mathbf{A}}\mathbf{U}_{\mathbf{s}}\mathbf{W}\mathbf{U}_{\mathbf{s}}^{\mathbf{H}}\} \tag{7}$$

The information database of the agricultural information resource is established, and a sample set distribution model of the agricultural information resource pool is obtained to meet the requirements of:

$$T_{i,j}(t) = \frac{\left|p_{i,j}(t) - \Delta p(t)\right|}{p_{i,j}(t)} \tag{8}$$

By using the fuzzy degree function of the evaluation of the efficiency of the agricultural information resource allocation represented by the $U_{i,j}(t)$. The database of resources is reconstructed by using cloud computing method, and the resources of related rule feature set that can extract relevant information are as follows:

$$TF(t, c_i) = \frac{P(t|c_i)}{\sum_{j \to n} P(t_j|c_i)} \tag{9}$$

The distributed storage structure of agricultural information resources is analyzed, and the optimal solution vector of agricultural information resource scheduling is obtained as follows:

$$\mu_{ik} = 1/\sum_{j=1}^{c} (d_{ik}/d_{jk})^{\frac{2}{m-1}} \tag{10}$$

$$V_i = \sum_{k=1}^{m} (\mu_{ik})^m x_k / \sum_{k=1}^{n} (\mu_{ik})^m \tag{11}$$

The regional grid clustering method is used to classify and identify agricultural information resources, and the fuzzy C-means clustering method is used to construct the sub-regional grid clustering center $C(Y)$ of agricultural information resources. The distribution structure of agricultural information resources is reorganized by using similarity evaluation method to realize the autocorrelation feature matching of resources. The optimal clustering model of resources is obtained:

$$l_{d_{ij} \to c_x} = \left(\frac{\sum\limits_{v=0}^{|c_x|} \cosin_{ij \to x}(d_{ij}, d_{xv})}{|c_x|} \right)^{-1} \tag{12}$$

In which, the $\cosin_{ij \to x}(d_{ij}, d_{xv})$ is a fusion clustering feature set of the agricultural information resource, and according to the analysis, the classification identification of the resource is realized, then the resource allocation efficiency evaluation is carried out according to the recognition result [14].

3.2 Information Fusion and Allocation Efficiency Evaluation of Agricultural Information Resources

Using decision similarity (correlation) analysis method, the fuzzy set v_i of the evaluation of agricultural information resource allocation efficiency is obtained as follows:

$$V = \{v_{ij} | i = 1, 2, \cdots, c, j = 1, 2, \cdots, s\} \tag{13}$$

Wherein, V_i is the correlation analysis measure of agricultural information resources [15], and the formula for evaluating the allocation efficiency of resources is obtained by using multiple regression analysis method:

$$U_{i,j}(t) = \exp\left[-b\left[z_i(t) - z_j(t)\right]^2\right] \tag{14}$$

The quantitative regression analysis and the self-adaptive game method of the correlation are used, the sharing degree of the agricultural information is obtained:

$$S_{i,j}(t) = \frac{p_{i,j}(t) - sp_{i,j}(t)}{p_{i,j}(t)} \tag{15}$$

In which: $p_{i,j}(t)$ is the fuzzy correlation feature distribution set of the agricultural information resource sharing, and $\Delta p(t)$ is the fuzzy decision increment value of the agricultural information resource sharing. 4-tuple (E_i, E_j, d, t) is used to represent the main feature quantity of the agricultural information resource sharing schedule, and according to the above analysis, the correlation function of establishing the agricultural information resource information fusion and the configuration efficiency evaluation is as follows:

$$CON(t, c_i) = \log \frac{P(d|t, c_i)}{P(d|t)} = \log \frac{P(d|t, c_i)}{\sum_{i \to m} P(d|t, c_i)} \tag{16}$$

Wherein, $P(d|t, c_i)$ is the distribution probability of c_i agricultural information resource sharing scheduling. Regional grid clustering method is used to classify and identify agricultural information resources. Under the optimized fusion model, information resource fusion and adaptive scheduling are carried out [11].

4   System Software Development and Testing

on the basis of the above-mentioned algorithm design of the agricultural information resource allocation efficiency evaluation model, the software development design of the system is carried out, the embedded Linux technology is adopted to carry out the agricultural information resource allocation efficiency evaluation model software development on the C/S client side [16], the system comprises a data processing module, the resource allocation module, the program loading module, the bus scheduling module and the man-machine interaction module and the like. The device attribute table is configured to configure the DMA0_START_ADDR register, and the bus scheduling method is used for the DMAx_Y_MODIFY, DMAx_PERIPHER-AL_MAP and other register configurations, and the program loading module is used for realizing the load of the evaluation algorithm of the resource allocation efficiency of the agricultural information, and the software implementation diagram of the system is shown in Fig. 2.

According to the software design described above, the software test of the agricultural information resource allocation efficiency evaluation model is carried out, the data length of the buffer data is set to 16 bits, the length of the agricultural information resource data sample is 1024, and the DMM_X_MODIFY of the test set is 2, and the large data analysis part of the agricultural information resource is obtained as shown in Fig. 3.

Big data fusion and resource allocation are carried out by using this method, and the time cost of evaluating the efficiency of agricultural information resource allocation is shown in Fig. 4.

As can be seen from the analysis in Fig. 4, the time cost of the evaluation of agricultural information resources by this method is short, and the response capability of the system is better. the stability of the test system is obtained. According to Fig. 5, the convergence of the system is better, the model designed in this paper is reliable and strong in man-machine interaction capability. And the quantitative evaluation and the optimization configuration capability of the agricultural information resource are improved.

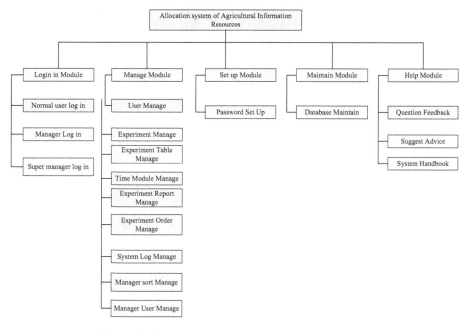

Fig. 2. Software implementation diagram of the system

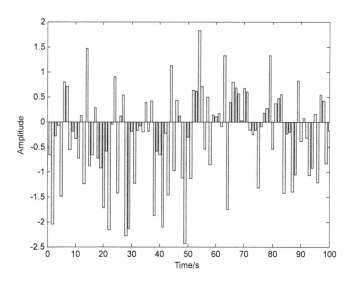

Fig. 3. Large data analysis part of the agricultural information resource

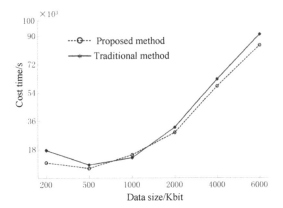

Fig. 4. Time cost of evaluating the allocation efficiency of agricultural information resources

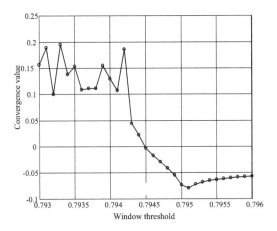

Fig. 5. Convergence test of system

Table 1. Comparison of allocation efficiency of agricultural information resources

Number of iteration steps	Proposed method	Reference [3]	Reference [4]
100	0.973	0.893	0.873
200	0.982	0.901	0.884
300	0.991	0.912	0.911
400	0.994	0.935	0.924

The efficiency of the resource allocation is tested. The results of the comparison are shown in Table 1.

It shows that the efficiency of this method is higher than that of the agricultural information resource allocation.

In order to further verify the effectiveness of the model in this paper, the calculation time of the model in this paper and the traditional model is compared and analyzed, and the comparison results are shown in Fig. 6.

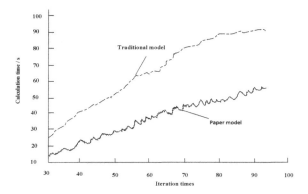

Fig. 6. Comparison results of computational time between the two models

According to Fig. 6, the calculation time of the model in this paper is shorter than that of the traditional model, which shows that the algorithm of the traditional model is more complex, while the calculation complexity of the model in this paper is lower, which shortens the calculation time, thus improving the evaluation efficiency.

5 Conclusions

In this paper, the efficiency evaluation and analysis of agricultural information resources allocation are carried out, the quantitative evaluation model of agricultural information resources is established, the ability of optimal allocation of agricultural information resources is improved, and the evaluation model of agricultural information resources allocation efficiency based on big data is put forward. The big data distributed storage structure model of resources is constructed, and the information fusion and adaptive scheduling of resources are carried out under the optimized information fusion model. The software of agricultural information resource allocation efficiency evaluation model is developed by using embedded Linux technology in C/S client. The test results show that the designed evaluation model of resource allocation efficiency has good reliability, good convergence and strong response ability.

References

1. Wang, S., Tu, H., Zhang, Y.: Cloud service composition method based on uncertain QoS-awareness. J. Comput. Appl. **38**(10), 2753–2758 (2018)
2. Zhao, Y., Hua, Y., Yu, Z.: Improved particle swarm optimization algorithm based on twice search. J. Comput. Appl. **37**(9), 2541–2546 (2017)

3. Wang, Y., Shi, L., Zhang, H., et al.: A data envelopment analysis of agricultural technical efficiency of Northwest Arid Areas in China. Front. Agric. Sci. Eng. **4**(2), 195–207 (2017)

4. Ding, Y., Peng, Z., Zhou, Y., et al.: Design and experiment of motion controller for information collection platform in field with Beidou positioning **33**(12), 178–185 (2017)

5. Kang, N., Shen, J., Xu, M.: The study about intelligent manufacturing resource allocation efficiency based on mutual information criterion. Comput. Integr. Manuf. Syst. **23**(9), 1842–1852 (2017)

6. Adamie, B.A., Balezentis, T., Asmild, M.: Environmental production factors and efficiency of smallholder agricultural households: using non-parametric conditional frontier methods. J. Agric. Econ. **70**(1), 471–487 (2018)

7. Liu, Y.: Joint resource allocation in SWIPT-based multi-antenna decode-and-forward relay networks. IEEE Trans. Veh. Technol. **66**(10), 9192–9200 (2017)

8. Du, C., Chen, X., Lei, L.: Energy-efficient optimization for secrecy wireless information and power transfer in massive MIMO relaying systems. IET Commun. **11**(1), 10–16 (2017)

9. Wang, W., Wang, R., Mehrpouyan, H., et al.: Beamforming for simultaneous wireless information and power transfer in two-way relay channels. IEEE Access **5**, 9235–9250 (2017)

10. Mamut, J., Xiong, Y.-Z., Tan, D.-Y., et al.: Flexibility of resource allocation in a hermaphroditic-gynomonoecious herb through deployment of female and male resources in perfect flowers. Am. J. Botany **104**, 461–467 (2017)

11. Li, X., Rong, Z., Ruan, X.: Attribute reduction of relative indiscernibility relation and discernibility relation in relation decision system. J. Comput. Appl. **39**(10), 2852–2858 (2019)

12. Kompas, T., Chu, L., Van Ha, P., et al.: Budgeting and portfolio allocation for biosecurity measures. Aust. J. Agric. Resour. Econ. **63**(3), 412–438 (2019)

13. Ma, Y., Zhang, Z., Lin, C.: Research progress in similarity join query of big data. J. Comput. Appl. **38**(4), 978–986 (2018)

14. Yuan, Q., Guo, J.: New ensemble classification algorithm for data stream with noise. J. Comput. Appl. **38**(6), 1591–1595 (2018)

15. Liu, H., Yang, H., Zheng, K., et al.: Resource allocation schemes in multi-vehicle cooperation systems. J. Commun. Inf. Netw. **2**(2), 113–125 (2017)

16. Liu, S., Zhang, Z., Qi, L., et al.: A fractal image encoding method based on statistical loss used in agricultural image compression. Multimed. Tools Appl. **75**(23), 15525–15536 (2016)

Seamless and Fast Panoramic Image Generation System Based on VR Technology

Dan Chen[1] and Ding Ren[2,3(✉)]

[1] Dalian University of Science and Technology, Panjin, China
chendan1252@163.com
[2] South China Business College, Guangdong University of Foreign Studies,
Guangzhou, China
yxzcgy@163.com
[3] School of Economics, Jinan University, Guangzhou, China

Abstract. In view of the design of seamless and fast panoramic image generation system, the traditional panoramic image generation system has the problems of poor image generation effect and long calculation time. The design of seamless and fast panoramic image generation system based on VR technology is proposed. According to the image edge processing mechanism, the hardware structure of the system is designed, and the software function of the image processor in the hardware is designed. The process of image edge recognition is described in detail, and the edge is tracked and refined to accurately track the direction and offset of the pixel. The boundary pixel information is recorded by VR technology, and the seamless system of panoramic image is realized by combining the corresponding image data. The experimental results show that the highest generation effect of the system is 90%, which shortens the calculation time and provides effective support for the research of automatic image generation system.

Keywords: VR Technology · Panoramic image · Seamless · Generate

1 Introduction

VR technology has been involved in video conference, network technology and distributed computing technology, and developed to distributed virtual reality. Virtual reality technology has become an important means of new product design and development. In the VR environment for collaborative design, team members can synchronously or asynchronously construct and operate virtual objects in the virtual environment, and evaluate, discuss and redesign virtual objects [1]. The general image reflects the local scene, while the panoramic image reflects the global scene. It has a wide range of application prospects in security monitoring, virtual tourism, education and entertainment, and military fields. There are two kinds of panoramic images: spherical panoramic image and cylindrical panoramic image. Among them, the spherical panorama can reflect the scene in any direction in the space, but it is difficult to deal with it; the cylindrical panorama does not have two parts of the scene: the top cover and the bottom cover, which limits the viewing angle of the user in the vertical

Y.-D. Zhang et al. (Eds.): ICMTEL 2020, LNICST 326, pp. 305–314, 2020.
https://doi.org/10.1007/978-3-030-51100-5_27

direction, but the water square is 360°, which can meet the needs of most applications. Cylindrical panorama is much simpler than spherical panorama, so it is more widely used [2]. Traditional panoramic image generation system has some problems, such as slow speed, low efficiency, and poor image automatic generation effect. For example, in the financial field, the profit drawing is often inaccurate, and the dynamic digital image cannot be edge recognized, resulting in poor image display effect, and algorithm takes a long time [3].

In order to overcome these shortcomings, a seamless and fast panoramic image generation system based on VR technology is proposed. Using the system, the shortcomings of the traditional system image generation method can be overcome without splicing, and the rapid generation of panoramic images can be realized by taking one image.

2   Design of Seamless and Fast Generation System of Panoramic Image

2.1   System Hardware Design

The hardware design of panoramic image automatic generation system is to provide a dynamic expansion mode for the digital under the relevant network service program. According to the requirements of the demander, the large-scale panoramic image is distributed. The hardware design diagram of the system is shown in Fig. 1.

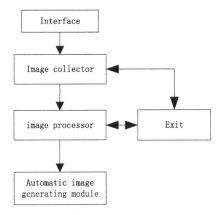

Fig. 1. System hardware design block diagram

It can be seen from Fig. 1 that the design of the image collector is mainly to transmit the collected data from the network interface to the large-scale panoramic image processor, and then transmit it to the top of the single-chip microcomputer for adjustment through the pin of the single-chip microcomputer. When the information and pin transmission of MCU are finished, it is necessary to communicate with other MCU to provide the foundation for image processor. The image processor mainly processes the collected image, and processes the collected image data with the image thread with high sharing efficiency, which can also be realized by programming [4–6]. The automatic image generation module uses a single-chip microcomputer to complete the automatic storage of data, and converts the data into images through the built-in structure, and automatically generates a panoramic image through software program operation [7].

2.2 Function Design of System Software

Aiming at the image processor in the system hardware, the software function is designed. After computer processing, the pattern can be automatically recognized, then we use virtual reality technology to track and refine the image edge [8].

2.2.1 Edge Recognition

In the panoramic image based on VR technology, edge refers to the set of pixels whose gray values $I(x, y, t)$ of surrounding pixels have periodical changes, and the edge recognition method is to recognize the pattern edge obtained by the pattern corrosion and expansion operation. The specific steps are as follows:

(1) Treat structural element (x, y) as a template which is designed to examine the image structure, and its size is generally smaller than the normal image, the calculation formula is:

$$\Delta I(x, y) = \{I(x, y, t+1) - I(x, y, t)\} \tag{1}$$

Where, $\Delta I(x, y)$ represents the pixel gray difference between time $t+1$ and time t of the pixel gray value of the frame video image.

(2) Corrosion is to shrink the edge of the image to the interior, and its function is to clear the boundary action points T, so that the external expansion becomes more expansive, whose expression is:

$$I(x, y) = \begin{cases} 1 & \Delta I(x, y) > T \\ 0 & \Delta I(x, y) \leq T \end{cases} \tag{2}$$

In order to be able to identify the image contour clearly, it is necessary to define an image as a structural element, select a binary image according to the defined structural element, and use the most accurate positioning method for edge positioning [9].

2.2.2 Image Edge Tracking and Thinning

Image edge tracking and thinning is to process and extract the recognized image edge, so as to obtain the edge with a width greater than 1 pixel. In order to track the image edge accurately, the width needs to be set as 1 pixel. In order to solve the tracking problem, it is necessary to find out the boundary pixels of the target image strictly in order to record the corresponding coordinates. According to the edge width of 1 pixel standard, analyze the pixel positions in 8 different fields, and accurately track the direction and offset of the pixel [10–13].

The specific tracking process is as follows:

(1) Scan the top left part of the panoramic image from left to right [14–16], from top to bottom to obtain the first edge point j of the target image, whose expression is:

$$j = \min\{j/d(I_i, I(x, y))\} \leq \theta_1 \tag{3}$$

Where, θ_1 represents the maximum distance threshold between two pixel points in the video image of the subsequent frame; I_i represents the non-zero pixel in the video image, and d represents the spatial dimension.

(2) Assuming that the initial search direction is the lower left corner, this point is taken as the pixel boundary point I_{mean}, and then the coordinates of the boundary point are recorded, set as the background color, and marked as the current coordinates, whose expression is:

$$VR = \sum_{i=1}^{m}(I_i - I_{mean})^2 j \tag{4}$$

(3) Turn the lower left corner of the search direction 90° clockwise to find the subsequent edge points; if the search fails, turn the original search direction 45° counterclockwise to find the subsequent edge points; if no new edge points appear, then there is no new edge point in the range [17].

(4) Repeat until the background color of the entire panoramic image is set.

2.2.3   Automatic Generation

The image information used in the seamless and fast generation system of panoramic image based on VR technology must be real-time. Its structure is that the boundary pixel information recorded is:

```
typedef struct TEdgePoint{
short int X;        //Row of image pixels;
    short int Y;        //Column of image pixels;
    short int Type;      //Boundary point species;
    };
```

For the boundary sampling point, the image edge samples are collected mainly according to the set working time. A seamless and fast panoramic image generation system is designed by processing image information according to schematic diagram.

3 Experiment

In order to verify the rationality of the design of the seamless and rapid panoramic image generation system based on VR technology, the dynamic data of a city's financial trading company is taken as an example.

3.1 Experimental Environment and Parameter Setting

The specific parameter settings are shown in Table 1.

Table 1. Parameter settings

Parameter	Numerical value
Data acquisition floating range	−20–35 dB
Maximum number of overlaps	100 dB
Data collection channel	10 species
Computer data processing power	140 Hz
Image resolution ratio	18 bits
Computer image display resolution	15 bits

3.2 Experimental Condition Setting

Set up several employees of financial trading company to upload data at the same time and record the speed change in time, as shown in Table 2.

Table 2. Changes in the rate of generation

Number of uploads	Generation speed (KB/s)
1	656.22
5	655.13
10	705.12
20	712.16
50	732.13

From Table 2, it can be seen that the automatic generation speed of the system when one company's employees upload data is not much different from that when five, 10, 20 and 50 employees upload data.

3.3 Experimental Results and Analysis

Based on the parameter setting in Table 1 and the change of generation speed in Table 2, the system designed based on VR technology is compared with the seamless and fast generation speed of panoramic image of traditional system, and the specific comparison is as follows.

3.3.1   Co Channel Interference

The same frequency interference refers to the overlapping part of different monitors, and its field strength is the sum of the signal field strength from each monitor. Because of the different signal propagation path, propagation medium and transmission equipment, the signal sent by each monitor is not consistent with the theoretical signal time. It shows that there is delay error between each signal, and then the relative phase difference of each signal is produced. Because of the phase difference, the signals in each overlapping area are interfered by the same frequency, which directly affects the normal monitoring of the system. The system designed with VR technology will not be affected by the same frequency interference, while the traditional system will be affected by the same frequency interference, resulting in poor generation effect. In order to verify this point, the two systems are compared, and the results are shown in Fig. 2.

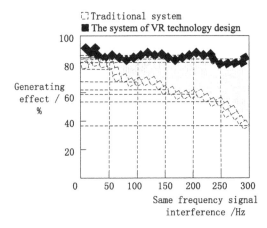

Fig. 2. Comparison of the generation effects of the two systems under the same frequency interference

It can be seen from Fig. 2 that when the intensity of the same frequency interference signal is 50 Hz, the generation effect of the traditional system is 78%, and the generation effect of the system designed based on VR technology is 82%; When the same frequency interference signal strength is 100 Hz, the traditional system generation effect is 70%, and the system generation effect based on VR technology is 81%; When the same frequency interference signal strength is 150 Hz, the traditional system generation effect is 59%, and the system generation effect based on VR technology is 80%; When the same frequency interference signal strength is 200 Hz, the traditional system generation effect is 59%, and the system generation effect based on VR technology is 90%; When the same frequency interference signal strength is 250 Hz, the traditional system generation effect is 54%, and the system generation effect based on VR technology is 79%; When the same frequency interference signal strength is

300 Hz, the traditional system generation effect is 39%, and the system generation effect based on VR technology is 81%. According to the comparison results, under the same frequency interference, the generation effect of the system designed based on VR technology is better than that of the traditional system.

3.3.2   The Influence of Human Factors

In order to illustrate that the system designed based on VR technology has better effect on panoramic image generation than the traditional system, the two systems need to be compared and analyzed, and the results are shown in Fig. 3.

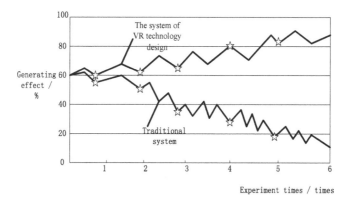

Fig. 3. Path identification of different methods

It can be seen from Fig. 3 that the initial generation effect of the two systems is 60%, when the number of experiments is 1, the generation effect of the traditional system is 58%, and the generation effect of the seamless generation system designed based on VR technology is 63%; When the number of experiments is 2, the generation effect of traditional system is 50%, and the generation effect of seamless generation system based on VR technology is 70%; When the number of experiments is 3, the generation effect of traditional system is 38%, and the generation effect of seamless generation system based on VR technology is 72%; When the number of experiments is 4, the generation effect of traditional system is 30%, and the generation effect of seamless generation system based on VR technology is 80%; When the number of experiments is 5, the generation effect of traditional system is 21%, and the generation effect of seamless generation system based on VR technology is 82%; When the number of experiments is 6, the generation effect of traditional system is 10%, and the generation effect of seamless generation system based on VR technology is 89%. The results show that under the influence of human factors, the system generation effect based on virtual reality technology is better than the traditional system generation effect.

3.3.3   Calculation Complexity

In order to further verify the effectiveness of the system in this paper, take the calculation time of the algorithm as the experimental index, and compare the calculation complexity of the system in this paper and the traditional system. The comparison results are shown in Fig. 4.

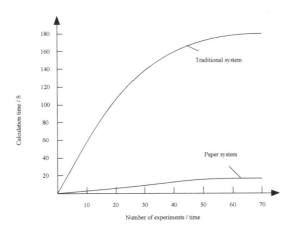

Fig. 4. Calculation time comparison of two systems

According to Fig. 4, when the number of experiments is 50, the algorithm calculation time of this system presents a stable state, when the number of experiments is 70, the calculation time is 16S; while the algorithm calculation time of the traditional method shows an upward trend, when the number of experiments is 70, the calculation time is 180 s. The algorithm calculation time of this system is shorter than that of the traditional system, which shows the calculation time of this system The computational complexity is low.

3.4   Experimental Conclusion

According to the above experimental contents, the experimental conclusion can be drawn:

① Same frequency interference: when the same frequency interference signal strength is 50 Hz, the system generation effect designed based on VR technology is 4% higher than that of traditional system; when the same frequency interference signal strength is 100 Hz, the system generation effect designed based on VR technology is 11% higher than that of traditional system; when the same frequency interference signal strength is 150 Hz, the system generation effect designed based on VR technology is higher than that of traditional system When the same frequency interference signal strength is 200 Hz, the generation effect of the system designed based on VR technology is 31% higher than that of the traditional system; when the same frequency interference signal strength is 250 Hz, the generation effect of the system designed based on VR technology is 25% higher than that of the traditional system; when the same frequency interference signal strength is 300 Hz, the generation effect of the system designed based on VR technology is 25% higher than that of the traditional system The formation effect is 42% higher. Therefore, under the same frequency interference, the system based on VR technology has a better generation effect.

② Influence of human factors: when the number of experiments is 1, 2, 3, 4, 5 and 6 respectively, the generation effect of VR based system is 5%, 20%, 34%, 50%, 61%, 79% and 79% higher than that of traditional system. Therefore, under the influence of human factors, the system based on VR technology is better.

③ Calculation complexity: when the number of experiments is 70, the calculation time of the algorithm of system application designed based on VR technology is 16S, while that of traditional system application is 180 s. Therefore, the calculation complexity of the system in this paper is low and the calculation time is short.

To sum up: Based on VR technology panoramic image seamless fast generation system is reasonable.

4   Concluding Remarks

The seamless and fast generation system of panoramic image based on VR technology is designed, but there is no deep research on other problems. Without a comprehensive analysis on the image interface problem, the probability of interference cannot be determined. Many methods are needed to solve the unknown parameters.

In the more complex network environment, in order to meet the flexibility and reliability requirements of panoramic image automatic generation, it is necessary to use more advanced control equipment to collect image data to ensure the research reliability of the rapid generation system, so as to realize the seamless rapid generation system of panoramic image widely used.

References

1. Wu, L., Hu, Y.: Virtual reality technology of image smoothing in clinic panorama image mosaic. Sci. Technol. Eng. **20**(31), 271–276 (2017)
2. Hu, Y., Wu, L.: Panoramic image generation algorithm in virtual reality based on feature extraction. Sci. Technol. Eng. **17**(32), 285–289 (2017)
3. Wang, G.: Indoor landscape reconstruction technology based on virtual reality. Mod. Electron. Technol. **18**(4), 147–149 (2018)
4. Du, C., Yuan, J., Chen, M., et al.: Real-time splicing of panoramic video based on GPU acceleration and L-ORB feature extraction. Comput. Res. Dev. **54**(6), 1316–1325 (2017)
5. Jiang, X.: Research on automatic splicing algorithm of Railway Environment Video based on vanishing Point Detection. Comput. Eng. Appl. **53**(7), 206–211 (2017)
6. Zhao, S., Xie, M., Chen, Y.: The design and implementation of the panoramic parking system based on the reverse projection. Comput. Eng. Appl. **53**(23), 267–270 (2017)

7. Luo, C., Kong, D., Liu, X., et al.: Implementation of VR panorama video service for smart family. Telecommun. Sci. **16**(10), 185–193 (2017)

8. Yan, Y., Liu, L.: Analysis of VR Film and Television language reform based on Imaging and watching experiment. Film Rev. **14**(12), 59–64 (2017)

9. Qu, Z., Li, X.: Panoramic image splicing seam elimination algorithm based on improved IGG model. Comput. Sci. **44**(12), 274–278 (2017)

10. Jing, Q.: Simulation of image information security protection in multimedia technology. Comput. Simul. **35**(02), 131–134 (2018)

11. Liu, S., Pan, Z., Cheng, X.: A novel fast fractal image compression method based on distance clustering in high dimensional sphere surface. Fractals **25**(4), 1740004 (2017)

12. He, Y., Wang, L., Cai, Y., et al.: Research progress and prospect of catadioptric panoramic system. Chin. Opt. **10**(5), 681–698 (2017)

13. Chen, Y.-C., Tseng, Y.-H.: Advancement of close range photogrammetry with a portable panoramic image mapping system (PPIMS). Photogram. Rec. **33**(13), 196–216 (2018)

14. Hejazifar, H., Khotanlou, H.: Fast and robust seam estimation to seamless image stitching. SIViP **12**, 885–893 (2018). https://doi.org/10.1007/s11760-017-1231-3

15. Yamamoto, K., Watanabe, K., Takeda, S., et al.: Image generation device. Lab. Autom. Inf. Manag. **32**(1), 2105–2109 (2017)

16. Kniaz, V.V., Gorbatsevich, V.S., Mizginov, V.A.: ThermalNet: a deep convolutional network for synthetic thermal image generation. ISPRS – Int. Arch. Photogram. Remote Sens. Spatial Inf. Sci. **42**, 41–45 (2017)

17. Huo, Y., Zhang, X.: Single image-based HDR image generation with camera response function estimation. IET Image Proc. **11**(12), 1317–1324 (2017)

Analysis on Behavior Characteristics of Enterprise Financing Investment Risk Data

Ding Ren[1,2] and Jin-min Du[2(✉)]

[1] South China Business College, Guangdong University of Foreign Studies,
Guangzhou 510545, China
[2] School of Economics, Jinan University, Guangzhou 510632, China
yxzcgy@163.com

Abstract. The existing technical means cannot effectively determine the negative impact of horizontal and vertical data behavioral risk on the return of enterprise financing investment. In order to solve this problem, the behavior characteristics of enterprise financing investment risk data were analyzed. Through determining the subset of risk factors and selecting the redundancy degree of SMT (Securities Margin Trading) index, the risk coefficient evaluation of financing investment was completed. On this basis, through the calculation of investment risk data time expenditure behavior and space expenditure behavior, determine the constraints between various data behavior characteristics, complete the enterprise financing investment risk data behavior characteristics analysis. The results show that the negative influence of horizontal and vertical data behavioral risk on enterprise financing investment is effectively restrained after applying the new investment risk behavior analysis method.

Keywords: Enterprise financing · Investment risk · Data behavior characteristics · Due to the subsets · Redundancy

1 Introduction

Enterprise financing refers to the process of financing with enterprises as the main body to make the capital supply and demand between enterprises and their internal links from unbalanced to balanced [1]. When the capital shortage, with the minimum cost to raise the appropriate period, the appropriate amount of funds; When the capital surplus, with the lowest risk, the appropriate period to put out, in order to obtain the maximum return, so as to achieve the balance of capital supply and demand. Investment risk refers to the loss or bankruptcy risk borne by the investment subject in future business and financial activities, which is the main content of the prediction and analysis conducted by the investment subject before the investment [2]. There are many major factors that cause investment risks, such as changes in government policies, errors in management measures, significant price increases or price drops of important materials that form product costs, and sharp rise in borrowing rates. Investment risk is inevitable in the process of investment, but it can be controlled by relevant means [3]. Specifically, investment risk refers to the deviation between actual investment return and expected return due to uncontrollable or random factors from the beginning of investment

Y.-D. Zhang et al. (Eds.): ICMTEL 2020, LNICST 326, pp. 315–325, 2020.
https://doi.org/10.1007/978-3-030-51100-5_28

decision to the end of the investment period. The deviation between actual investment return and expected return is both higher than the latter and lower than the latter. In other words, both the possibility of suffering economic losses and the possibility of gaining additional gains are the manifestation of the form of investment risk [4].

Existing technical means measure the risk coefficients in the financing investment of enterprises by establishing a decision tree, and then introduce rigid financial indicators to carry out in-depth planning on these risk coefficients, so as to achieve the purpose of analyzing the behavioral characteristics of investment risk data [5]. However, with the progress of scientific and technological means, this method cannot effectively determine the negative impact of horizontal and vertical data behavioral risk on enterprise financing investment, which brings great limitations to the long-term development of enterprises. To avoid the occurrence of the above situation, while keeping the existing research methods on the basis of the application advantages, through the selection of investment risk evaluation index redundancy, conditionality, behavior characteristics on corporate financing and investment risks, analyzing data behavior characteristics and, by means of comparative experiments show that the new methods for analysis of practical value.

2 Evaluation of Risk Factor of Financing Investment

The risk coefficient evaluation of financing investment includes two key links: determining the subset of risk factors and selecting the redundancy of SMT index. The specific operation method can be carried out as follows.

2.1 The Determination of the Subset of Enterprise Financing Investment Risk

The subset of traditional investment risk assessment is excessively dependent on financial indicator factors, and quantitative factors account for too much. For the new enterprise financing investment risk subset, we need to optimize and perfect the traditional subset [6]. The selection of risk factors for financing investment of enterprises should be more dynamic and complicated, and should also be integrated into the characteristics of enterprises themselves [7]. If the selected indicators are not appropriate, the investment loss of enterprises will be caused, so each factor must be carefully screened. The subset of risk factors meeting the standard should meet the requirements of representativeness, feasibility and comprehensiveness [8]. Therefore, selecting investment risk factors with strong theoretical support can not only improve the financing level of enterprises to a certain extent, but also promote the qualitative development of enterprise credit factors [9]. The specific determination method of risk factors subset of enterprise financing investment is shown in formula (1).

$$Q = \sum_{i=1}^{u} (x_{1,2,3,\ldots,n} - \frac{Ew}{P}) \tag{1}$$

Among them, Q represents the subset of enterprise financing investment risk factors, i represents the lower limit of enterprise financing quality, u represents the upper limit of enterprise financing quality, x represents the financial index factor, n represents the position of quantitative factor, E represents the enterprise credit factor, w represents the factor analysis accuracy, and P represents the theoretical constant term coefficient of the index.

2.2   Selection of Redundancy of SMT Evaluation Index

The redundancy of SMT evaluation index refers to the extra spare parameter to ensure the successful completion of the financing investment task [10]. SMT evaluation index redundancy factor refers to the factor that can express the index redundancy. When the redundancy factor increases with the total amount of risk data, the redundancy of SMT evaluation index can be expressed as follows:

$$R_1 = \frac{1}{|Q|} \sum_{d=1}^{U} I_d t \tag{2}$$

Among them, d represents the lower limit of information, U represents the natural number set, I_d represents the upper limit of enterprise financing investment task, and t represents the implementation time of investment. The lower limit of information determines the upper limit of financing and investment tasks, and it will affect the implementation time of investment. When the redundancy factor decreases with the increase of total risk data, the redundancy of SMT evaluation index can be expressed as follows:

$$R_2 = \frac{|Q|}{\sqrt{\displaystyle\sum_{d=1}^{U} I_d t}} \tag{3}$$

3   Analysis of Data Behavior Characteristics Based on Risk Factor Assessment

On the basis of enterprise financing investment risk coefficient evaluation, data time expense behavior, data space expense behavior and other steps are determined to complete the analysis of enterprise financing investment risk data behavior characteristics based on risk coefficient evaluation [11].

3.1   Time Cost

Time cost refers to the measurement of enterprise financing investment risk factor in unit time. The time cost can be analyzed from the perspectives of underlying communication and investment result invocation, among which the most basic is the transmission cost of investment data [12, 13]. For enterprises with the most basic financing investment ability, the risk data delay is constant, and in terms of time structure, one data transmission can only realize one pair of minimum data transmission. The specific transmission mode is shown in Fig. 1.

Fig. 1. Detailed diagram of transmission mode of time consuming behavior

According to Fig. 1, during the transmission of enterprise financing investment risk data [14], the transmission delay is not only constant but also equal to the access time of Shared data. If α represents the transmission delay, the time consumption behavior of enterprise financing investment risk data can be expressed as:

$$K = \frac{(R_1 + R_2)}{\alpha \prod^{a=1} \lambda f} \tag{4}$$

Where, K represents the time expense behavior of enterprise financing investment risk data, a represents investment result call constant, λ represents data transmission expense, and f represents the limit of enterprise basic financing investment ability.

3.2 Data Space Overhead Behavior

The cost of data space mainly comes from the risk factor of financing investment and investment consistency agreement [15, 16]. In addition, there is the risk of data transfer communication buffer overhead, maintenance of consistent investment results, and so on. According to the above knowable, in corporate finance investment risk under the condition of constant coefficient evaluation result, the data of time overhead transmission result and there is a proportional relationship between transmission delay, and in most cases, the specific value can be Shared by calculation time delay of the data access time way, this is also the result data timing is always the main reason for stable [17]. On this basis, let ζ represent the communication buffer of venture capital data transmission, and formula (4) can express the space expenditure behavior of enterprise financing investment risk data as follows:

$$G = \left| \frac{\log_{(R_1 + R_2)} \zeta \cdot l^2}{Mc} \right| \tag{5}$$

Among them, G represents the spatial expenditure behavior of enterprise financing investment risk data, l represents the consistent financing investment result, M represents the buffer coefficient of investment risk data [18], and c represents the constant communication buffer time.

3.3   Determination of Constraints Between Behavioral Characteristics

On the premise of the existence of investment risk coefficient, behavior characteristics of enterprise financing investment risk data are the main indicators to describe whether the investment results are feasible [19]. When the data time consumption behavior shows a gradually rising trend under the influence of risk delay, the data transmission communication buffer of venture capital will also increase, and the increase of data space expenditure behavior becomes an inevitable trend [20]. This is the result of the change of all indexes caused by the change of one physical quantity, which is called the restriction between the behavior characteristics of enterprise financing investment risk data. Let χ represent the synchronization index between time expenditure behavior and space expenditure behavior. With the support of formula (4) and formula (5), the restriction relationship between behavior characteristics of enterprise financing investment risk data can be expressed as:

$$C = \int_{G=1}^{K \to \infty} \chi \cdot (z+s)^2 \tag{6}$$

Where, C represents the restriction relationship between the behavior characteristics of enterprise financing investment risk data, z represents the specific value of the initial investment risk data behavior, and s represents the specific value of the last investment risk data behavior.

On the basis of determining the constraints among various data behavior characteristics, the behavior characteristics of enterprise financing investment risk data are analyzed.

4   Experimental Results and Analysis

In order to verify the practical value of the behavior characteristic analysis method of enterprise financing investment risk data designed in this paper, the following comparative experiment is designed. Taking a financing investment behavior of a certain enterprise as the experimental object, the change of the negative impact of the data behavior before and after the application of this method on the return of financing investment of an enterprise was recorded during the 5-month experimental period.

4.1 Horizontal Data Behavior on the Negative Impact of Enterprise Investment Returns

The figure below shows the change in the degree of negative impact of horizontal data behavior on enterprise investment returns during the 5 months of the experiment.

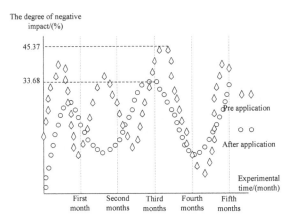

Fig. 2. Contrast chart of negative impact of horizontal data behavior on enterprise investment returns

Analysis Fig. 2 shows that with the increase of experimental time, application of new type of enterprise financing risk investment behavior characteristics data analysis method, the horizontal data behavior the negative effect on the enterprise investment income presents the tendency of rising and falling appear alternately, test time between 3 months to 4 months, the transverse data behavior of negative impact of enterprise investment income reached a maximum of 45.37%; Application of the new corporate finance investment risk behavior data analysis method, the horizontal data behavior the negative effect on the enterprise investment income also shows the tendency of rising and falling appear alternately, test time to three months when lateral data behavior on negative impact of enterprise investment income reached a maximum of 33.68%, far lower than that before using this method.

4.2 Comparison of Negative Impact of Longitudinal Data Behavior on Enterprise Investment Returns

The figure below shows the change in the degree of negative impact of longitudinal data behavior on the investment returns of enterprises during the 5-month experiment period.

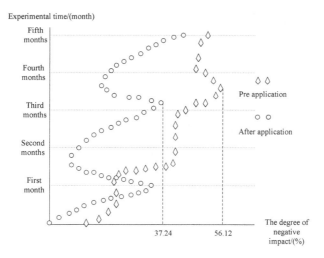

Fig. 3. Comparison chart of negative impact of longitudinal data behavior on enterprise investment returns

Analysis Fig. 3 shows that with the increase of experimental time, application of new type of enterprise financing risk investment behavior characteristics data analysis method, the longitudinal data behavior the negative effect on the enterprise investment income is gradually rising trend, the experiment time between 3 months to 4 months, the longitudinal data behavior of negative impact of enterprise investment income reached a maximum of 56.12%; Application of the new corporate finance investment risk behavior data analysis method, the longitudinal data behavior the negative effect on the enterprise investment income appear alternately trend of rise and fall, the time between 3 months to 4 months, the longitudinal data behavior of negative impact of enterprise investment income reached a maximum of 37.24%, far lower than that before using this method.

4.3 Comparison of Analysis Accuracy of Different Methods

In order to further verify the advantages of this method, this method and traditional methods are used to analyze the behavioral characteristics of enterprise financing investment risk data and compare the accuracy of different methods. The experimental results are shown in Fig. 4.

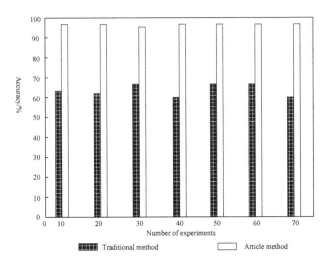

Fig. 4. Comparison of analysis accuracy of different methods

It can be seen from the analysis above that the analysis accuracy of the traditional method is between 61% and 70%, while the analysis accuracy of this method is always higher than 96%, far higher than the traditional method, so this method can realize the accurate analysis of enterprise financing risk. The main reason is that the method of this paper selects the redundancy of the index of securities margin trading and completes the evaluation of the risk coefficient of financing and investment by determining the subset of risk factors. On this basis, by calculating the time expenditure behavior and space expenditure behavior of investment risk data, the constraint relationship between various data behavior characteristics is determined. Through horizontal and vertical data behavior risk, the behavior characteristics of enterprise financing investment risk data are analyzed. Therefore, this method has high analysis accuracy.

4.4 Time Cost Comparison of Different Methods

On the basis of the above experiments, this paper uses the methods in this paper and traditional methods to analyze the behavioral characteristics of enterprise financing investment risk data, and compares the time cost of different methods. The experimental results are shown in Fig. 5.

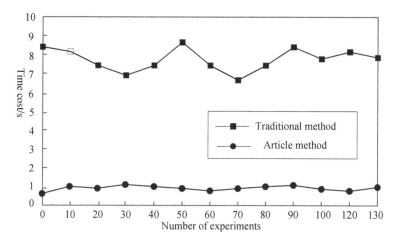

Fig. 5. Comparison of time cost

According to the analysis of Fig. 5, the time cost by traditional methods in analyzing the behavioral characteristics of enterprise financing investment risk data varies from 6.5 s to 8.8 s. The time cost by this method in analyzing the behavioral characteristics of enterprise financing investment risk data is always less than 1.5 s, which is far lower than that of traditional methods. It shows that this method can complete the behavioral analysis of enterprise financing investment risk data in a short time Feature analysis.

5   Conclusion

Although there are many studies on the risk of enterprise financing investment, the conclusions are often different and even contradictory. Due to the complexity of the problem, it is difficult to extract the behavior characteristics of enterprise financing investment risk data. Driven by interest and risk management, group companies and multinational companies often operate multiple projects at the same time. On the one hand, operators need to carry out effective investment and financing management of these projects; on the other hand, investors also need to understand the management level and moral hazard status of operators. Therefore, this paper analyzes and studies the behavioral characteristics of enterprise financing investment risk data. Under the influence of behavioral risks of horizontal and vertical data, the return of financing investment of enterprises will show a trend of gradual decline. In order to fully enhance the economic value of enterprises and reduce the risk of financing investment, this paper analyzes the behavior characteristics of enterprise financing investment risk data by determining the subset of risk factors. The comparison of experimental data shows that the influence of horizontal and vertical data behavioral risk on the return of enterprise financing investment is effectively controlled after the application of the new method for analyzing the behavioral characteristics of enterprise financing investment risk.

Fund Project. Social Science Youth Project of Educational department of Guangdong Province: 2018WQNCX304; Guangzhou Social Science Co-construction Project: 2018-JD-04; and Guangdong Regional Financial Policy Research Center Project:2018-JDZD-01.

References

1. Yang, J., Shi, Z., Liu, Z.: Simulation of terminal user information acquisition under big data analysis. Comput. Simul. **35**(02), 441–445 (2018)
2. Cao, K., Yan, M.: Analysis of bidding behavior characteristics of online auction bidders in China – an empirical study based on functional sparse data clustering method. Mod. Econ. Sci. **39**(6), 115–121 (2017)
3. Wu, C., Sun, C., Chu, D., et al.: Clustering of several typical behavioral characteristics of commercial vehicle drivers based on GPS data mining. Transp. Res. Rec. J. Transp. Res. Board **2581**(2581), 154–163 (2016)
4. Tsuji, K., Fukuda, M., Yamato, E.: An analysis of the eating behavior and the psychological characteristics affecting clinical indicators in diabetes patients: the behavioral economics approach. J. Jpn. Diab. Soc. **59**(2), 114–120 (2016)
5. Bazhayev, N.A., Lebedev, I.S., Krivtsova, I.E.: Analysis of statistical data from network infrastructure monitoring to detect abnormal behavior of system local segments **17**(1), 92–99 (2017)
6. Jin, H., Li, G., Park, S.T., et al.: The effects of consumer characteristics on information searching behavior in wireless mobile SNS: using SEM analysis. Wirel. Pers. Commun. **93**(1), 1–16 (2016). https://doi.org/10.1007/s11277-016-3523-2
7. Basurto-Hurtado, J.A., Morales-Hernández, L.A., Osornio-Rios, R.A., et al.: An approach based on the exploratory data analysis to relate the wear behavior with the microstructure of ductile cast irons. Adv. Mater. Sci. Eng. **2016**(2), 1–11 (2016)
8. Annink, A., Dulk, L.D., Amorós, J.: Different strokes for different folks? The impact of heterogeneity in work characteristics and country contexts on work-life balance among the self-employed. Int. J. Entrep. Behav. Res. **22**(6), 880–902 (2016)
9. Zhou, Q., Yang, J., Han, J.: Research on electricity consumption behaviors of the capacity expansion users based on big data analysis. Electr. Power **50**(10), 176–180 (2017)
10. Han, Z., Wu, M., et al.: Growth and developmental parameters and behavioral characteristics of infant rhesus monkeys. Chin. J. Comp. Med. **26**(4), 24–34 (2016)
11. Vakulchyk, O., Protasova, Y.: Unsystematic risk and enterprise investment attractiveness. Adv. Eng. Forum **22**(1), 107–111 (2017)
12. Salomon, T., Gomes, I., Ozahata, M.C., et al.: Social and behavioral characteristics of male blood donors and their sexual partners: an analysis to define risk subsets. Transfusion **59**(8), 134–141 (2019)
13. Hoffman, L., Delahanty, J., Johnson, S.E., et al.: Sexual and gender minority cigarette smoking disparities: an analysis of 2016 Behavioral Risk Factor Surveillance System data. Prev. Med. **113**(8), 1–12 (2018)
14. Chippendale, T., Raveis, V.: Knowledge, behavioral practices, and experiences of outdoor fallers: implications for prevention programs. Arch. Gerontol. Geriatr. **72**(9), 19–24 (2017)
15. Zhang, Y., Liu, Z., Zhang, B., et al.: Empirical research on the effect of decision-makers' psychological factors on the behavior alienation in company intellectual capital investment. Manag. Rev. **56**(7), 143–155 (2017)

16. Li, C., Wang, R., Ning, H., et al.: Characteristics of meteorological drought pattern and risk analysis for maize production in Xinjiang, Northwest China. Theor. Appl. Climatol. **133**(1), 1–10 (2017). https://doi.org/10.1007/s00704-017-2259-6

17. Shao, Y.-H., Zhan, S.: Group management and enterprise overinvestment: an analysis based on the perspective of internal capital market and external governance environment. Financ. Theory Pract. **33**(6), 15–22 (2017)

18. Lei, G., Liu, M., Wang, W.: Management quality and state-owned enterprise investment efficiency. Frontiers **75**(6), 34–46 (2017)

19. Zhao, Y., Hong, Y., Huang, Y.J., et al.: Relationship between R&D investment and business performance from the perspective of environmental regulation: takeing the heavy-polluting industries from 2011 to 2016 as an example. Ecol. Econ. **75**(3), 213–226 (2017)

20. Chen, L.-W., Wang, S.-T., Wang, L.-W., et al.: Behavioral characteristics of autism spectrum disorder in very preterm birth children. Mol. Autism **10**(1), 1–10 (2019)

Web Database Sharing Platform Design Based on Large Data Visualization of Learning Behavior

Fang Meng[1(⊠)] and Guo-gen Fan[2]

[1] Huali College Guangdong University of Technology,
Guangzhou 511325, China
mengfang845@163.com
[2] Guangzhou Huali Science and Technology Vocational College,
Guangzhou 511325, China

Abstract. In order to improve the sharing ability of network database in the visual environment of learning behavior big data, a design method of network database sharing platform based on big data visual analysis of learning behavior is proposed. The piecewise linear coding method is used to collect the characteristics of the network database in the visual environment of learning behavior. The characteristics of association rules of network database shared resources in big data visual environment are extracted, the optimal structure of network database shared resources is reorganized by adaptive spatial resource reorganization method, the optimal storage spatial distribution model of network database shared resources is established, and the statistical analysis method is used to search the association of network database shared resources in big data visual environment. The feature quantity of association rules of network database sharing resources is extracted, and security sharing of network database sharing resources is carried out according to the clustering of feature quantity. The network database sharing platform is designed in embedding ARM environment. The simulation results show that this method has good adaptability and security, and improves the level of resource sharing.

Keywords: Learning behavior · Big data · Visualization · Network database · Shared platform

1 Introduction

With the development of information security construction, under the visual environment of learning behavior big data, it is necessary to construct the security sharing model of network database shared resources, combined with the distributed storage structure and characteristic distribution of network database shared resources, to optimize the scheduling and sharing of network database shared resources under big data visual environment. To improve the ability of optimal storage and distributed scheduling of shared resources in network database [1]. Under the condition of information construction, through the establishment of network database sharing in big data visual environment of learning behavior, the optimal management and retrieval

© ICST Institute for Computer Sciences, Social Informatics and Telecommunications Engineering 2020
Published by Springer Nature Switzerland AG 2020. All Rights Reserved
Y.-D. Zhang et al. (Eds.): ICMTEL 2020, LNICST 326, pp. 326–337, 2020.
https://doi.org/10.1007/978-3-030-51100-5_29

ability of shared resources in a network database can be improved. With the integration technology of mobile terminal and big data, the information sharing design of network database sharing resources under big data visualization environment of learning behavior is carried out, and the retrieval and information management level of network database sharing resources under big data visualization environment of learning behavior is improved. Optimal storage design of resources is carried out, and the statistical analysis method and adaptive information retrieval method are used to improve the optimal scheduling ability of shared resources in network databases. It is of great significance to study the related resource sharing scheduling methods in the optimal management of shared resources in network databases [2].

Traditionally, sharing scheduling methods of network database under the visual environment of learning behavior big data mainly include fuzzy information clustering method, statistical analysis method, association rule scheduling method and so on [3]. Shared resource management and allocation model of network database under the visual environment of learning behavior big data is established, and the adaptive allocation and optimal scheduling of resource information are carried out in combination with association rule mining violation. To improve the ability of big data feature collection and optimal allocation of network database under big data visual environment of learning behavior. In reference [4], a sharing scheduling method of network database under big data visualization environment of learning behavior based on fuzzy statistical analysis is proposed. Combined with quantitative evaluation model, it is possible to mine the information of shared resources of network database under the visual environment of learning behavior. The fuzzy clustering method is used to classify and identify the shared resources of network database in big data visual environment, but the computational overhead of this method is large and the adaptability of this method is not good. In reference [5], a resource security sharing method based on directed graph analysis is proposed, and the spatial information sampling technology is combined to optimize the collection and scheduling of resources, but the anti-interference of this method is not good [6].

In view of the above problems, the present invention provides a method for sharing a network database in a big data visualization environment based on big data visualization analysis of learning behavior. The method includes the following steps:

1. Extracting the feature quantity of the association rule of the shared resource. Using fuzzy comprehensive clustering method, combined with learning behavior, the information clustering processing of network database shared resources are performed. Establish a big data feature acquisition model based on the statistical feature distribution set of shared resources to obtain feature quantity.
2. Optimize the storage structure of the database. Through the related statistical analysis method, the similarity of network database sharing is determined, and the semantic ontology feature set of shared resources is obtained. The fuzzy C-means clustering method is used to construct the user perception model, and the database distribution structure method is used to realize the network database sharing.
3. Optimized structural reorganization of the network database shared resources.
4. Using the auto-correlation feature matching method, based on the distribution of storage nodes, under the big data visualization environment of learning behaviors,

quantitative assessment of the network database shared resources is performed to realize the reorganization of network database shared resources.

5. Feature extraction and secure sharing. Combining oriented clustering is performed for database resource retrieval. By statistical analysis, the feature quantity is searched by correlation. According to the clustering of feature quantity, secure sharing of network database shared resources.

By building a network database sharing platform, it not only effectively integrates decentralized and different standards of network data information, but also systematizes network data, improves the management level of network data information, and optimizes the management model of data information. Development to create a healthy environment for sustainable development

2   Feature Acquisition and Optimization of Storage Structure of Big Data in Network Database

2.1   Feature Collections of Big Data in Network Database

In order to realize the network database sharing under the visual environment of learning behavior big data, it is necessary to construct the optimal storage model of network database sharing resources under the visual environment of learning behavior big data. Combined with the spatial information sampling method, the network database sharing design under the visual environment of learning behavior big data is carried out, and the resource access is realized from the user interface. The replica manager is used to process the network database sharing, resource scheduling and replica correlation fusion in big data visual environment, and the collection and information scheduling model of network database sharing resources in big data visual environment is obtained [7].

According to the semantic feature distribution set of the shared resource of the network database under the large data visualization environment of the learning behavior, the judgment criteria for determining the intelligent sharing and scheduling of the shared resource of the network database under the large data visualization environment of the learning behavior [8] are as follows:

$$S(i,j) = \frac{\sum_{u \in U_{ij}} (V_{u,i} - 3)(V_{u,j} - 3)}{\sqrt{\sum_{u \in U_{ij}} (V_{u,i} - \overline{V_{.i}})^2} \sqrt{\sum_{u \in U_{ij}} (V_{u,j} - \overline{V_{.j}})^2}} \tag{1}$$

The network database sharing resource pool fusion processing is carried out in combination with the characteristic distribution perceived by the user, and the information clustering processing of the shared resource of the network database under the large data visualization environment of the learning behavior is carried out in combination with the fuzzy comprehensive clustering method [9], the method comprises the following steps of: performing a user-aware network database large-data feature association rule feature quantity in a clustering center as follows:

$$V_{u,i} = \frac{D_i^-}{D_i^+ + D_i^-}, \quad \overline{V}_j = \frac{R_i^+}{R_i^+ + R_i^-} \tag{2}$$

Constructing a self-adaptive fusion cluster analysis model of a network database shared resource in a large data visualization environment of a learning behavior [10], the invention realizes the reconstruction of the fuzzy index set of the shared resource of the network database under the large data visualization environment of the learning behavior, and obtains the fuzzy output set of the network database shared resource fusion scheduling as the $E_k \in E(k = 1, 2, \ldots, t)$, The integration model of the intelligent sharing of the large data features of the user-aware network database under the large data visualization environment of the learning behavior is $P_i \in P(i = 1, 2, \ldots, m)$, and the statistical analysis and the quantitative regression analysis method [11] are adopted, the method comprises the following steps of: calculating a text feature vector vi and a $v_i = ((w_1, t_1), (w_2, t_2), \ldots (w_j, t_j))$ of a large-data feature library of a user-aware network database in a large-data visualization environment of a learning behavior, and adopting a decision similarity (correlation) analysis [12] method to obtain a fuzzy set of the network database shared resource acquisition:

$$V = \{v_{ij} | i = 1, 2, \cdots, c, j = 1, 2, \cdots, s\} \tag{3}$$

In which, V_i is a statistical characteristic distribution set of a network database shared resource in a large-data visualization environment of learning behavior, and based on the analysis, a large-data characteristic acquisition model of a network database is established, and a fusion cluster analysis is carried out according to the information acquisition result so as to improve the resource sharing level [13].

2.2   Database-Optimized Storage Structure

Combined with feature mining method, the database distribution structure of user-aware network is reorganized. Assuming that user-aware network dataset $X = \{x_1, x_2, \ldots, x_n\}$, n is the number of dataset X in big data visual environment. The formula for intelligent sharing of shared resources in a network database under big data visualization environment is obtained.

$$U_{i,j}(t) = \exp\left[-b\left[z_i(t) - z_j(t)\right]^2\right] \tag{4}$$

By using the correlation statistical analysis method, the similarity of network database sharing under the big data visualization environment of learning behavior is obtained as follows:

$$S_{i,j}(t) = \frac{p_{i,j}(t) - sp_{i,j}(t)}{p_{i,j}(t)} \tag{5}$$

In which: $p_{i,j}(t)$ is the fuzzy correlation feature distribution set shared by the network database, and $\Delta p(t)$ is the fuzzy decision increment value [14] shared by the network database. The invention relates to a fuzzy degree characteristic distribution set of a network database shared resource in a large data visualization environment of a learning behavior by using a 4-tuple (E_i, E_j, d, t), wherein the E_i, E_j are the statistic feature quantity and the correlation rule feature quantity, and a distributed sensing and fusion method is adopted, the feature reconstruction of the shared resource of the network database is carried out [15], and the semantic ontology feature set of the shared resource of the network database under the large data visualization environment of the learning behavior is extracted to be as follows:

$$TF(t, c_i) = \frac{P(t|c_i)}{\sum_{j \to n} P(t_j|c_i)} \tag{6}$$

Wherein, t is the statistical characteristic quantity of the shared resources of the network database, and the multiple regression distribution model of the fusion and sharing of the shared resources of the network database under the visual environment of the learning behavior of big data is expressed as follows:

$$\mu_{ik} = 1 / \sum_{j=1}^{c} (d_{ik}/d_{jk})^{\frac{2}{m-1}} \tag{7}$$

$$V_i = \sum_{k=1}^{m} (\mu_{ik})^m x_k / \sum_{k=1}^{n} (\mu_{ik})^m \tag{8}$$

The fuzzy C-means clustering method is used to construct a user-aware model in a large-data visualization environment of learning behavior, and a resource structure recombination method is combined to realize the sharing of the network database, and the characteristic cluster analysis is realized in the fuzzy center $C(Y)$, and the resource security sharing level is improved [16].

3   Network Database Sharing and Optimization

3.1   Optimized Structural Reorganizations of the Network Database Sharing Resource

on the basis of the analysis of the large data characteristic acquisition and the information storage structure of the network database under the large data visualization environment of the learning behavior by adopting the segmented linear coding method, the optimization design of the network database sharing is carried out, In this paper, a method of network database sharing based on learning behavior and large data visualization analysis is presented in this paper [17]. The difference fusion feature quantity of the network database sharing under the large-data visualization environment of learning behavior is expressed as follows:

$$J_m(U, V) = \sum_{k=1}^{n} \sum_{i=1}^{c} \mu_{ik}^{m} (d_{ik})^2 \tag{9}$$

The method of autocorrelation feature matching is used to quantitatively evaluate the shared resources of network database in big data visual environment of learning behavior. The distribution incremental structure of shared resources of network database in big data visual environment of learning behavior is expressed as a dimension vector [18], and the optimal migration model of shared resources of network database is described as follows:

$$p(e_k|v_k) \sim t_{(v_k + d_e)}(u_{e|v,k}, \Sigma_{e|vk}) \tag{10}$$

The quantitative evaluation node distribution structure of shared resources in learning behavior big data visualization environment is constructed by using directed graph model, and the optimal storage space distribution model of network database shared resources is established as:

$$\min(f) = \sum_{i=1}^{m} \sum_{j=1}^{n} C_{ij} X_{ij} \tag{11}$$

$$\text{s.t} \begin{cases} \sum_{j=1}^{m} X_{ij} = a_i, \, i = 1, 2 \ldots m \\ \sum_{i=1}^{m} X_{ij} = b_i, \, j = 1, 2 \ldots n \\ X_{ij} \geq 0, \, i = 1, 2 \ldots m, \, j = 1, 2 \ldots n \end{cases} \tag{12}$$

According to the distribution of the storage nodes, carrying out a quantitative evaluation on the shared resources of the network database under the large data visualization environment of the learning behavior, and realizing the structure recombination of the shared resource of the network database [19].

3.2 Implementation of Feature Extraction and Security Sharing

The statistical analysis method is used to search the shared resources of the network database under the visual environment of big data. The interference signal-to-noise ratio (SNR) of the distributed environment of the shared resources of the network database under the visual environment of big data is defined as follows:

$$SNKR_i = (3/2)|\sigma^4/\gamma|\lambda SNR_i^2 \tag{13}$$

The distributed link fusion set of database resource retrieval is constructed, combined with association rule mining and fuzzy C-means clustering method, the feature directional clustering of database resource retrieval is carried out, and the clustering function is obtained as follows:

$$J_m(U, V) = \sum_{k=1}^{n} \sum_{i=1}^{c} \mu_{ik}^m (d_{ik})^2 x_i = x_{imin} + cx_i \cdot (x_{imax} - x_{imin}) \qquad (14)$$

The self-adaptive optimization method is adopted to realize the user-aware network under the large-data visualization environment of learning behavior, and the optimized solution is obtained:

$$\sum_{i=1}^{c} \mu_{ik} = 1, k = 1, 2, \ldots, n \qquad (15)$$

Under the visual environment of learning behavior big data, the output of network database sharing is as follows:

$$x_{n,G} = x_{n,G} + \Delta x_i \qquad (16)$$

in a comprehensive analysis, an association search of a shared resource of a network database in a large data visualization environment of a learning behavior is carried out by adopting a statistical analysis method, an association rule feature quantity of a shared resource of a network database is extracted [20]. According to the clustering of the feature quantity, security sharing of the shared resources of the network database is carried out, the overall implementation process is shown in Fig. 1.

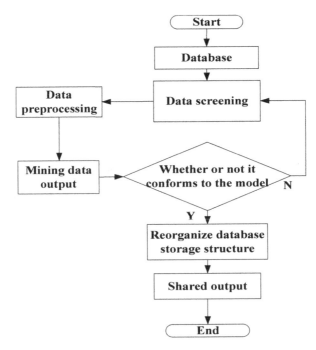

Fig. 1. Implementation flow of network database sharing in big data visual environment of learning behavior

4 Simulation Experiment and Result Analysis

In order to verify the application performance of this method in realizing the visual environment of learning behavior big data, the simulation experiment is carried out with Matlab. The length of information retrieval of network database shared resources using MySQL, is set to 2000, the distribution coefficient of information entropy is 0.46, the coefficient of association rules is 0.89, and the fuzzy membership parameter is set to 1.5, the length of information retrieval of shared resources of network database is set to 2000, the distribution coefficient of information entropy is 0.46, the coefficient of association rules is 0.89, and the fuzzy membership parameter is 1.5. According to the above parameters, the APP login interface of the network database sharing platform is shown in Fig. 2.

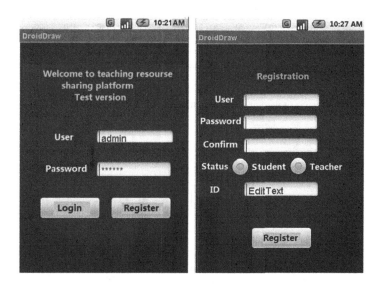

Fig. 2. APP login interface of network database sharing platform

Combining association rule mining and fuzzy C-means clustering method, directional clustering of retrieval features and big data analysis was performed, and the results of big data visualization analysis were obtained, as showed in Fig. 3.

In Fig. 3, the network sharing information nodes is densely distributed and show a good sharing effect, which proves the effectiveness of the method in this paper. The sampling interval of shared resources in the network database is 16 ms, and the carrier frequency of network link transmission perceived by users in big data visual environment is 50 kHz. Taking the above resource data set as the research object, the resource sharing level is obtained as showed in Fig. 4.

The analysis in Fig. 4 shows that the level of resource sharing of the traditional method is low, and the level of resource sharing of this method is higher than that of the traditional method. Reduce the interference signal-to-noise of the distributed link

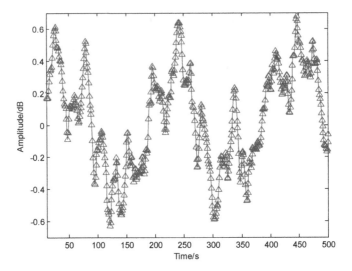

Fig. 3. Large data visualization analysis results

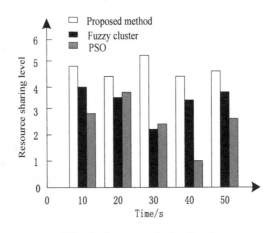

Fig. 4. Resource sharing level

fusion set of resource retrieval and improve the order of the set. Database resource retrieval feature-oriented clustering combining association rule mining and fuzzy C-means clustering method improves the convergence of sets and increases the level of resource sharing. Based on the above research, the sharing rate is tested and analyzed. The results are shown in Fig. 5.

It can be seen from Fig. 5 that the information sharing rate of the method in this paper is much higher than that of traditional methods, and the rate of change does not increase with the number of iterations, while the ratio of the traditional method changes with the number of iterations The amplitude is large, and the stability of the method is poor. Because when extracting the feature quantity of the association rule of the shared

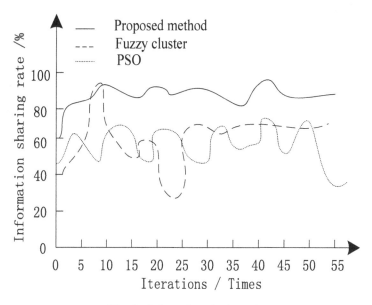

Fig. 5. Information sharing rate

resource, the comprehensive fuzzy clustering method is used to perform the clustering process, so that the similar and detailed information is gathered, and the information sharing ratio is improved. Under the analysis of the analysis rate, the accuracy of the information is compared to determine the superiority of the method in this paper. It has an improved level of information sharing.

It can be seen from Table 1 that the accuracy of the two traditional methods is low, and the accuracy changes greatly as the number of iterations increases. However, the accuracy of the methods in this paper is higher than that of traditional methods, and the increase of the number of iterations, the accuracy changes less, and it shows stability. Because the method in this paper uses the auto-correlation feature matching method, based on the distribution of storage nodes, the network database shared resources are quantitatively evaluated to obtain the optimal migration model of shared resources. The model optimizes the distribution of storage nodes and improves the accuracy of resource sharing.

Table 1. Precision comparison

Iterations	Proposed method	Fuzzy cluster	PSO
100	0.943	0.864	0.917
300	0.995	0.912	0.929
500	0.999	0.932	0.934

5   Conclusions

In this paper, a design method of network database sharing platform based on big data visual analysis of learning behavior is proposed. The piecewise linear coding method is used to collect the characteristics of the network database in the visual environment of learning behavior. The characteristics of association rules of network database shared resources in big data visual environment are extracted, the optimal structure of network database shared resources is reorganized by adaptive spatial resource reorganization method, the optimal storage spatial distribution model of network database shared resources is established, and the statistical analysis method is used to search the association of network database shared resources in big data visual environment. The feature quantity of association rules of network database sharing resources is extracted, and security sharing of network database sharing resources is carried out according to the clustering of feature quantity. The network database sharing platform is designed in embedding ARM environment. The simulation results show that this method has good adaptability and security, and the level of resource sharing is improved.

Fund Project. 2019 Guangdong Higher Education Teaching Reform Project "Research on Network Database Learning Based on Learning Behavior Big Data Visualization"; 2019 Huali College Guangdong University of Technology Project "Research on Network Database Learning Based on Learning Behavior Big Data Visualization" (GGDHLYJZ[2019]No.32).

References

1. Wang, Y., Fang, G., Zhang, F., et al.: RC-loaded planar half-ellipse antenna for impulse radar application. Electron. Lett. **51**(23), 1841–1842 (2015)
2. Ma, Y., Zhang, Z., Lin, C.: Research progress in similarity join query of big data. J. Comput. Appl. **38**(4), 978–986 (2018)
3. Yuan, Q., Guo, J.: New ensemble classification algorithm for data stream with noise. J. Comput. Appl. **38**(6), 1591–1595 (2018)
4. Evangelio, R.H., Patzold, M., Keller, I.: Adaptively splitted GMM with feedback improvement for the task of background subtraction. IEEE Trans. Inf. Forensics Secur. **9**(5), 863–874 (2014)
5. Wang, S., Tu, H., Zhang, Y.: Cloud service composition method based on uncertain QoS-awareness. J. Comput. Appl. **38**(10), 2753–2758 (2018)
6. Zhao, Y., Hua, N., Yu, Z.: Improved particle swarm optimization algorithm based on twice search. J. Comput. Appl. **37**(9), 2541–2546 (2017)
7. Zhang, R., Ho, C.K.: MIMO broadcasting for simultaneous wireless information and power transfer. IEEE Trans. Wirel. Commun. **12**(5), 1989–2001 (2013)
8. Wu, Z.H., Hu, P.: Analysis on VANET routing protocols. J. Commun. **36**(Z1), 75–84 (2015)
9. Chen, Y., Fang, M., Shi, S., et al.: Distributed multi-hop clustering algorithm for VANETs based on neighborhood follow. EURASIP J. Wirel. Commun. Netw. **2015**(1), 98 (2015). https://doi.org/10.1186/s13638-015-0327-0
10. Matilainen, M., Nordhausen, K., Oja, H.: New independent component analysis tools for time series. Stat. Probab. Lett. **105**, 80–87 (2015)
11. Liu, Y.: Joint resource allocation in SWIPT-based multi-antenna decode-and-forward relay networks. IEEE Trans. Veh. Technol. **66**(10), 9192–9200 (2017)

12. Du, C., Chen, X., Lei, L.: Energy-efficient optimization for secrecy wireless information and power transfer in massive MIMO relaying systems. IET Commun. **11**(1), 10–16 (2017)

13. Wang, W., Wang, R., Mehrpouyan, H., et al.: Beamforming for simultaneous wireless information and power transfer in two-way relay channels. IEEE Access **5**, 9235–9250 (2017)

14. Zeng, Y., Zhang, R.: Full-duplex wireless-powered relay with self-energy recycling. IEEE Wirel. Commun. Lett. **4**(2), 201–204 (2015)

15. Li, X., Rong, Z., Ruan, X.: Attribute reduction of relative indiscernibility relation and discernibility relation in relation decision system. J. Comput. Appl. **39**(10), 2852–2858 (2019)

16. Bhuvaneshwar, K., Belouali, A., Rao, S., et al.: Abstract 2604: the Georgetown Database of Cancer (G-DOC): a web-based data sharing platform for precision medicine. Cancer Res. **77** (13), 2604 (2017)

17. Teresa, S.: Sharing data in the platform economy: a public interest argument for access to platform data. Soc. Sci. Electron. Publ. **54**(4), 1017–1071 (2017)

18. Wei, J.H., Huang, X.Y., Liu, W.F., et al.: Cost-effective and scalable data sharing in cloud storage using hierarchical attribute-based encryption with forward security. Int. J. Found. Comput. Sci. **28**(7), 843–868 (2017)

19. Bai, T., Dou, H.J., Zhao, W.X., et al.: An experimental study of text representation methods for cross-site purchase preference prediction using the social text data. J. Comput. Sci. Technol. **32**(4), 828–842 (2017). https://doi.org/10.1007/s11390-017-1763-6

20. Witold, D., Rafał, W., Wojciech, C.: Ivga: a fast force-directed method for interactive visualization of complex networks. J. Comput. Sci. **21**(1), 448–459 (2017)

Network APT Attack Detection Based on Big Data Analysis

Guo-gen Fan[1(✉)] and Jian-li Zhai[2]

[1] Guangzhou Huali Science and Technology Vocational College, Guangzhou
511325, Guangdong, China
fanguogen@foxmail.com
[2] Huali College Guangdong University of Technology, Guangzhou 511325,
Guangdong, China

Abstract. In order to improve the security of the distributed optical fiber
sensing network, the self-adaptive detection of the fiber sensing network needs
to be carried out, and an overlap detection algorithm under the APT attack of the
distributed optical fiber sensing network based on the spectral characteristic
component and the big data analysis is proposed. the large data sampling model
of the network APT attack is constructed, the attack characteristics and the
related properties of the distributed optical fiber sensing network virus are
simulated by adopting the spectrum correlation characteristic detection and the
large-data quantization characteristic coding, and the large-data fusion and
feature extraction of the APT attack information are realized, the output
abnormal characteristic detection of the distributed optical fiber sensing network
is carried out through the feature extraction result, a distributed optical fiber
sensing network intrusion large data statistical analysis model is constructed,
and a narrow-band signal spectrum offset correction method is adopted, And
calculating the connection probability density and the individual infection
probability of the APT attack node, and improving the detection capability of
the network APT attack. The simulation results show that the algorithm can
effectively implement the network APT attack detection, improve the security
detection capability of the network APT attack, and has a good network security
protection capability.

Keywords: Big data analysis · Network · APT · Attack detection · Sensing
network

1 Introduction

With the development and popularization of the network technology, the network
security is becoming more and more concerned. The Internet has the characteristics of
openness, no competence and non-security, and the network attack network virus is on
the rise of the number and the degree of harm [1]. The present situation of network
security is worrying due to the direction and non-regularity of the virus and the
invisibility. according to the results of the American VIRUS official statistics, the
average global average of 30 million computers has been attacked by various viruses,
and the detection of network attack is an important means to protect the security of the

Y.-D. Zhang et al. (Eds.): ICMTEL 2020, LNICST 326, pp. 338–348, 2020.
https://doi.org/10.1007/978-3-030-51100-5_30

computer system, and how to establish a high-efficiency network APT attack detection method, It is a focus of many experts in this field [2]. At present, the new type of network virus's invasion and propagation is carried out in a normal way for continuous attack. It is difficult to detect, and it is necessary to effectively detect the APT attack. It is of great significance to study the detection algorithm of distributed optical fiber sensing network virus under continuous attack [3].

The aggressive behavior of the network virus is a distributed optical fiber sensing network APT attack signal in the data of the computer network, and the intrusion attack is carried out on the network user in the form of data information. The traditional method is difficult to realize the effective detection, and the main detection method is based on the detection method of the ant colony algorithm, the detection method based on the immune genetic algorithm and the detection method based on the neural network algorithm. Among them, the most common is the overlapping detection method of APT attack based on the neural network algorithm [4]. Distributed optical fiber sensing network APT attack detection algorithm with any large frequency, Which is suitable for realizing large-frequency signal detection, but has limited detection performance for multi-frequency network intrusion signals, high calculation complexity and difficulty in implementation [5]. Interference attack location method is proposed to optimize the state transition feature of the intrusion tolerant system, and the intrusion path of the virus is analyzed and analyzed. The structure level characteristic decomposition of the potential intrusion signal is realized, and a certain effect is obtained. However, the algorithm cannot effectively realize the overlapping detection of the continuous attack virus, and proposes an overlap detection algorithm under the APT attack of the distributed optical fiber sensing network based on the spectral characteristic component and the big data analysis [6]. By the improved design of the algorithm, the test performance of the network APT attack is improved, and the performance verification of the simulation experiment shows its effectiveness.

2 APT Attack Model of Distributed Optical Fiber Sensing Network

In order to extract the continuous attack signal model of virus, it is necessary to construct the continuous attack model of distributed optical fiber sensor network virus, design the virus state transition model of distributed optical fiber sensor network, describe the virus system of distributed optical fiber sensor network as five states of Markov chain HMM, and analyze the security attributes of intrusion tolerance system [7]. Spectrum correlation feature detection and big data quantitative feature coding are used to simulate the attack characteristics and related properties of distributed optical fiber sensor network virus, and big data fusion and feature extraction of APT attack information are realized. described by Langevin equation, the APT attack of distributed optical fiber sensor network is a bistable nonlinear driving multi-frequency resonance model, and the expression of Langevin equation is as follows:

$$\frac{dx}{dt} = ax - bx^2 + s(t) + \Gamma(t) \tag{1}$$

In the formula, a, b is the system parameter. By adjusting the system parameters, the interference noise can be described by mathematical model as follows:

$$f(x) = sgn\left\{ z \sum_{i=1}^{l_1} \alpha_i^+ y_i K(x_i, x) + \sum_{i=1}^{l_2} \alpha_i^- y_i K(x_i, x) + b \right\} \tag{2}$$

In the process of APT attack in distributed optical fiber sensor network, assuming that the amplitude of APT attack signal is A, the amplitude adjustment coefficient of input signal is as follows:

$$x(t) = \sum_{i=0}^{p} a(\theta_i) s_i(t) + n(t) \tag{3}$$

Firstly, the local extreme point of the signal in the stochastic resonance system is determined. In order to improve the detection performance of the continuous attack, the APT attack behavior is transformed into a convex combinatorial optimization problem. Using the wrapper feature selection model and the method of marking the average value of the upper and lower envelope lines, the EMD difference component of the APT attack signal is obtained by the nonlinear mapping function $\{(x_1, y_1), (x_2, y_2), \cdots (x_i, y_i), \ldots (x_n, y_n)\}$ of the sample set $\varphi(x)$:

$$\bar{\tilde{u}}_{e|v,k}^* = \tilde{u}_{e|v,k} + h(x_k) \tag{4}$$

The optimal classification hyperplane structure is carried out in the high dimensional feature space:

$$f(x) = w \cdot \varphi(x) + b = 0 \tag{5}$$

In the formula, w represents a weight vector, and b represents a threshold value. In order to minimize structural risk, the optimal classification plane should meet the following constraints:

$$y_i \cdot (w \cdot \varphi(x_i) + b) \geq 1 \tag{6}$$

The label information of the APT attack file block and the file block is correlated to the S-Table, a normal resonance function is introduced, the non-negative relaxation variable ξ_i is adopted to improve the classification SVM generalization ability of the learning method, and each grid point can only be occupied by one virus intrusion adsorption chain node, then the attack detection and optimization problem of the virus under the continuous attack is changed to:

$$\min \tfrac{1}{2} w \cdot w + c \sum_{i=1}^{n} \xi_i$$
$$s.t. y_i(w \cdot x_i + b) \geq 1 - \xi_i, \ \xi_i \geq 0, \ i = 1, 2, \ldots, n \tag{7}$$

In the formula, the artificial immune method is used to carry out the transmission impedance and immunity of the virus [8], and the Lagrange multiplier is introduced to transform the above optimization problem into dual form.

$$\min \frac{1}{2} \sum_{i,j=1}^{n} \alpha_i \alpha_j y_i y_j \left(\varphi(x_i) \cdot \varphi(x_j) \right) + \sum_{i=1}^{n} \alpha_i \tag{8}$$

At the same time, the following conditions need to be met:

$$\sum_{i,j=1}^{n} \alpha_i y_i = 0, c \geq \alpha_i \geq 0 \tag{9}$$

The algorithm calculation process is realized by MPI interface based on chain growth. The APT attack model of distributed fiber sensing network is constructed. The block diagram of model design is shown in Fig. 1.

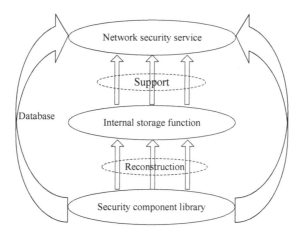

Fig. 1. APT attack detection model of distributed optical fiber sensing network

3 Propagation Probability of APT Attack in Distributed Optical Fiber Sensor Networks

The probability model of APT attack propagation in distributed optical fiber sensor network is analyzed to realize the overlapping detection of continuous attack signals. The APT attack of distributed optical fiber sensor network is connected to mobile devices through a single connected virus. The success of transmission is related to the time of connection establishment and the propagation time of virus. The classification attribute based on information entropy is used to describe the population size of virus transmission [9]. The time-frequency analysis Viterbi algorithm is used to estimate the instantaneous frequency under APT attack, which can expand the frequency of APT attack on distributed optical fiber sensor network and reduce the attack efficiency. The single frequency signal of continuous attack signal of distributed optical fiber sensor network is described as follows:

$$s(t) = a(t) \cos \phi(t) \tag{10}$$

Since the instantaneous frequency of the distributed optical fiber sensing network is time-varying, the instantaneous spectrum corresponding to the instantaneous frequency should be present, the time-frequency analysis Viterbi algorithm is adopted, the average frequency of the continuous attack signal spectrum of the distributed optical fiber sensing network virus is equal to the time average of the instantaneous frequency, then:

$$f(t) = \frac{1}{2\pi} \frac{d}{dt} [\arg z(t)] \tag{11}$$

Thus, the average frequency of the instantaneous spectrum is the instantaneous frequency, and the instantaneous frequency is the derivative of the phase of the analytical signal. Assuming that the time required for virus transmission is t_{virus}, the probability of successful transmission of the virus is the probability that the connection is established at t_{virus} or longer:

$$P_{t_{virus}} = 1 - F_{link}^{v1}(t_{virus}) = \frac{1}{\pi(b-a)} \int_0^\pi \int_0^{\frac{2R}{t_{virus}}} v\sqrt{1 - \left(\frac{vt_{virus}}{2R}\right)^2} g(v, \phi, v1) dv d\phi \tag{12}$$

Many viruses are targeted only for specific vulnerabilities, such as for a particular bluetooth version, a particular operating system's vulnerable point, or even a particular vendor's device. Therefore, under the invasion of APT, the normal resonance of the network is suppressed, the time-frequency characteristic of the non-stationary continuous attack signal is extracted by using the time-frequency analysis method, the instantaneous frequency is estimated, and the frequency expansion is realized [10, 11]. As shown in Fig. 2, a continuous attack model from A to B in the coverage of the virus is obtained, as shown in Fig. 2, and is defined as a signal model and a propagation probability model in the distributed fiber-sensing network APT attack by the time from the node A to the node B through all the distances, And provides a signal basis for realizing the APT attack detection.

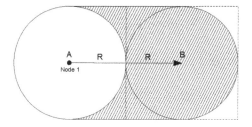

Fig. 2. Attack node distribution range of distributed optical fiber sensor networks

3.1 Improved Implementation of Detection Algorithm

The traditional detection method realizes the detection of the APT attack by using the hierarchical detection algorithm of the interference attack positioning state transfer feature extraction, and the algorithm does not adapt to the feature selection parameters under the continuous attack, and the detection performance is not good. In this paper, an overlapping detection algorithm based on a distributed optical fiber sensing network (APT) attack based on spectral characteristic component and big data analysis is presented [12, 13]. On the basis of the above-mentioned APT attack signal design, it is assumed that the amplitude of the continuous attack signal is A, and if the c_k is a fraction, the phase $\phi(t)$ is a non-uniform sample. the effect of the phase difference of the sampling interval is different, where S is the time sampling step (corresponding to Δt), and the spectrum characteristic of the narrow-band signal is as follows:

$$g(v, \phi, v1) = \frac{u(h(v,\phi,v1)-a)-u(h(v,\phi,v1)-b)}{h(v,\phi,v1)}$$
$$h(v, \phi, v1) = \sqrt{v^2 + v1^2 + 2vv1 \cos \phi} \tag{13}$$

Where the F_{link}^{v1} represents the accumulated time of the connection, $v1$ represents the mobile speed of the node, the sg represents the relative movement speed of the node, and the selection of the class 1 in the model may be a "Smartphone X 'using the' Bluetooth V2". It is assumed that the virus is moving at a constant speed under a continuous attack, then:

$$v_{average} = \frac{a+b}{2} \tag{14}$$

As a kind of narrowband signal, APT attack signal produces spectrum offset through normal resonance. In this paper, the narrowband signal spectrum offset correction method is used to improve the detection performance, and the connection probability of APT attack node and the infection rate of individual can be expressed as a matrix [14–17]. Thus, the connection probability of the same class is allowed to be different, and the maximum propagation probability is defined as:

$$trans_{rate\,Max} = \frac{1}{t_{virus}} \tag{15}$$

Therefore, the connection probability can be defined as:

$$Contact_{rate} = \min\{node_{rate}, trans_{rate\,Max}\} \tag{16}$$

Finally, the dynamic system equation of the overlapping detection under the APT attack of the distributed optical fiber sensing network based on the spectral characteristic component and the big data analysis can be generalized as follows:

$$\begin{aligned}
\frac{dS_k(t)}{dt} =& O_k(t)(P_{os1_k} + P_{os2_k}) + T_k(t)P_{tsk} - S_k(t)P_{spk} \\
& - S_k(t)\beta_{ak} - S_k(t)\left(\beta_{u_k(t)} + \beta_{l_k(t)}\right) - S_k(t)(P_{so1_k} + P_{so2_k})
\end{aligned} \tag{17}$$

$$\begin{aligned}
\frac{dE_k(t)}{dt} =& S_k(t)\left(\beta_{u_k(t)} + \beta_{l_k(t)}\right) + X_k(t)P_{xe_k} - E_k(t)P_{ex_k} - E_k(t)P_{et_k} \\
& - E_k(t)(P_{ei1_k} + P_{ei2_k})
\end{aligned} \tag{18}$$

$$\frac{dP_k(t)}{dt} = T_k(t)P_{tp_k} + S_k(t)P_{sp_k} \tag{19}$$

$$\frac{dT_k(t)}{dt} = I_k(t)P_{it_k} + E_k(t)P_{et_k} - T_k(t)P_{tp_k} - T_k(t)P_{ts_k} - T_k(t)(P_{to1_k} + P_{to2_k}) \tag{20}$$

Through the improved design of the above algorithm, the overlapping detection algorithm under the APT attack of the distributed optical fiber sensing network based on the frequency spectrum characteristic component and the big data analysis is realized, and the next step is to perform the performance verification through the simulation experiment [18–20].

4 Simulation Experiment and Result Analysis

In order to test the detection performance of this algorithm under APT attack on distributed optical fiber sensor network, the virus database is DARPA database, which is the real simulation and reproduction of distributed optical fiber sensing network data, and contains a wealth of continuous attack signal types. The decision threshold $G_T = 20\sigma^2$, adopts constant false alarm probability $p_f = 0.1$. With the collected network continuous signal, the signal is preprocessed by noise reduction filter, and the narrowband signal spectrum offset correction is used to detect and optimize the signal. The distribution of big data of the network attack is shown in Fig. 3.

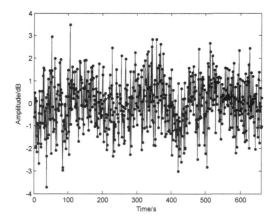

Fig. 3. Big data distribution of network attacks

The gain node tree with self-interference channel is set as $L = 2$, $N = 4$. For the convenience of calculation, the influence of APT attack probability of distributed optical fiber sensor network under different propagation time is shown in Fig. 4 through the design of the above simulation environment, the influence of APT attack infection probability of distributed optical fiber sensor network under the condition of fixed average node speed is obtained through the design of the above simulation environment.

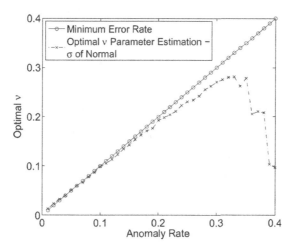

Fig. 4. Infection probability of APT attack in distributed optical fiber sensor networks

As you can see from Fig. 4, the time required for all users to infect is 50 days; when the action distance is 100 m, the time required for all people to infect is only 5 min. In order to further compare the detection performance of the algorithm under APT attack, the overlap detection algorithm designed in this paper is compared with the traditional method, and the detection performance curve is shown in Fig. 5. It can be seen from the diagram that the proposed algorithm effectively improves the detection performance of network APT attacks and improves the overlapping detection ability of APT attacks.

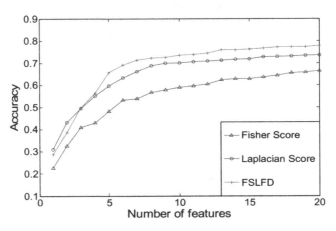

Fig. 5. Detection performance

5   Conclusions

The traditional network attack detection methods have the problems of weak security and poor detection results. An APT detection algorithm of the distributed optical fiber sensing network is proposed based on the spectral characteristic component and the big data analysis. The large data sampling model of the network APT attack is constructed, the attack characteristics and the related properties of the distributed optical fiber sensing network virus are simulated by adopting the spectrum correlation characteristic detection and the large-data quantization characteristic coding, and the large-data fusion and feature extraction of the APT attack information are realized, the output abnormal characteristic detection of the distributed optical fiber sensing network is carried out through the feature extraction result, a distributed optical fiber sensing network intrusion large data statistical analysis model is constructed, and a narrow-band signal spectrum offset correction method is adopted, And calculating the connection probability density and the individual infection probability of the APT attack node, and improving the detection capability of the network APT attack. The simulation results show that the algorithm can effectively implement the network APT attack detection, improve the security detection capability of the network APT attack, and has a good network security protection capability. This method has good application value in network security protection and virus intrusion detection.

Fund Project. 2019 Guangdong Higher Education Teaching Reform Project "Research on Network Database Learning Based on Learning Behavior Big Data Visualization"; 2019 Huali College Guangdong University of Technology Project "Research on Network Database Learning Based on Learning Behavior Big Data Visualization" (GGDHLYJZ[2019]No.32).

References

1. Huang, H., Lu, D., T., H.: Chover type law of iterated logarithm of NSD sequences. J. Jilin Univ. **56**(05), 1113–1118 (2018). Science Edition
2. Li, X., Kang, Z.: Ultra low Power and High Linear LNA based on double Cross Coupling Capacitance feedback. Autom. Instrum. **7**, 326–330 (2018)
3. Houg, X.F., Wang, H., Li, Y.: Research on efficient processing method of large amount of data based on HIVE and distributed Cluster. J. China Acad. Electron. Inform. Technol. **13**(3), 315–320 (2018)
4. Zhao, L.X.: Research and implementation of vehicle-mounted Charger based on DSP. J. Power Supply **15**(3), 158–162 (2017)
5. Guo, H.P., Dong, Y.D., Mao, H.T., et al.: Logistic discrimination based rare-class classification method. J. Chin. Comput. Syst. **37**(1), 140–145 (2016)
6. Gao, N., He, Y.Y., Gao, L.: Deep learning method for intrusion detection in massive data. Appl. Res. Comput. **35**(4), 1197–1200 (2018)
7. Zhang, Y.Z., You, R.: Wavelet variance analysis of EEG based on window function. Chin. J. Biomed. Eng. **23**(2), 54–59 (2014)
8. Yang, L., Kong, Z., Shi, H.: Multi-controller dynamic deployment strategy of software defined spatial information network. Comput. Eng. **44**(10), 58–63 (2018)
9. Liu, Y., Du, Z., Zhao, Q.: Bifurcation analysis of the ENSO recharge oscillator with time-delayed feedback. Appl. Math. Mech. **39**(10), 1128–1136 (2018)
10. Niu, W., Zhang, X., Yang, G., et al.: Modeling attack process of advanced persistent threat using network evolution. IEICE Trans. Inf. Syst. **100**(10), 2275–2286 (2017)
11. Shen, X., Qin, S.: Anomaly detection based on synthetic minority oversampling technique and deep belief network. J. Comput. Appl. **38**(7), 1941–1945 (2018)
12. Yang, Y.H., Huang, H.Z., Shen, Q.N., et al.: Research on intrusion detection based on incremental GHSOM. Chin. J. Comput. **37**(5), 1216–1224 (2014)
13. Liu, L., Liu, S.: Dynamic fuzzy clustering algorithm based on weight difference. J. Jilin Univ. **57**(03), 574–582 (2019). (Scientific version)
14. Ma, Y., Zhang, Z., Lin, C.: Research progress in similarity join query of big data. J. Comput. Appl. **38**(4), 978–986 (2018)
15. Du, Z., Zhao, Q.: Bifurcation analysis of the ENSO recharge oscillator with time-delayed feedback. Appl. Math. Mech. **39**(10), 1128–1136 (2018)
16. Xu, X., Wang, S., Li, Y.: Identification and predication of network attack patterns in software-defined networking. Peer-to-Peer Netw. Appl. **12**(1), 1–11 (2018)
17. Bang, J., Cho, Y.-J., Kang, K.: Anomaly detection of network-initiated LTE signaling traffic in wireless sensor and actuator networks based on a Hidden semi-Markov Model. Comput. Secur. **65**(6), 108–120 (2017)

18. Yin, C., Xia, L., Zhang, S., et al.: Improved clustering algorithm based on high-speed network data stream. Soft. Comput. **22**(4), 1–11 (2017)
19. Park, Y.H., Yun, I.D.: Arrhythmia detection in electrocardiogram based on recurrent neural network encoder–decoder with Lyapunov exponent. IEEJ Trans. Elect. Electron. Eng. **14**(2), 1273–1274 (2019)
20. Brito, C.J., Miarka, B., de Durana, A.L.D., et al.: Home advantage in Judo: analysis by the combat phase, penalties and the type of attack. J. Hum. Kinet. **57**(1), 213–220 (2017)

Two Particle Filter-Based INS/LiDAR-Integrated Mobile Robot Localization

Wanfeng Ma, Yong Zhang, Qinjun Zhao$^{(\boxtimes)}$, and Tongqian Liu

School of Electrical Engineering, University of Jinan, Jinan 250022, Shandong, China
elephantfff@163.com, {cse_zhangy,cse_zhaoqj}@ujn.edu.cn

Abstract. In order to achieve high precision localization, this paper presents an integrated localization scheme employs two particle filters (PFs) for fusing the inertial navigation systems (INS)-based and the light detection and ranging (LiDAR)-based data. A novel data fusion model is designed, which considers the robot position error, velocity error, and the orientation error. Meanwhile, two-PFs based data fusion filer is designed. The position errors measured by the two-PFs in real tests is 0.059 m. The experimental results verify the effectiveness of two-PFs method proposed in reducing the mobile robot's position error compared with the two-EKF method.

Keywords: Mobile robot localization · INS · LiDAR · Particle filter

1 Introduction

At present day, the mobile robots play a vital role in various fields, such as medical treatment, automatic driving, transportation, warehousing, indoor rescue and so on. These works usually need to be completed in complex indoor environment, and robots have to complete the precise movement, which depends on accurate location information. Consequently, the localization of the mobile robots in indoor environment has gradually become a key research (Wang 2017, Sherwin 2018, Xu 2018).

At present, mobile robot localization is usually achieved by a single method, Global Positioning System (GPS) is a famous example. But for indoor localization, it is difficult to achieve high accuracy positioning, because receiving signal become difficult in indoor environment. Nowdays, indoor navigation method based on local positioning system (LPS) has been proposed (Xu 2017, Zhang 2015, Cui 2016, Cao 2019). For example, a probabilistic UHF RFID tag localization (Cao 2018) algorithm has been proposed for the robot localization (Jian 2018). At the same time, the ultra wide band (UWB) system is also used for mobile robot localization.

However, using a single method is difficult to get rid of the inherent disadvantages. For example, to overcome the disadvantage of UWB dependence on

Y.-D. Zhang et al. (Eds.): ICMTEL 2020, LNICST 326, pp. 349–358, 2020.
https://doi.org/10.1007/978-3-030-51100-5_31

additional devices, the no beacon-based approaches have been proposed. The inertial navigation systems (INS) is one famous example (Monica 2018). However, noted that the INS navigation is poor in long-term navigation. In this case, the light detection and ranging (LiDAR) is used to improve the localization accuracy in long-term navigation. For example, a LiDAR-based localization is proposed (Huang 2016). Figure 1 shows the automatic driving car using the LiDAR to complete localization. It should be pointed out that although the LiDAR-based localization is accuracy, its processing speed is low.

Fig. 1. Automatic car.

In order to achieve high precision robot localization in indoor environment, and overcome disadvantages of localization using single method. Many researchers began to study the integrated localization scheme. Therefore, the integrated navigation method develop rapidly.

An integrated localization scheme fusing the inertial navigation systems (INS)-based and the light detection and ranging (LiDAR)-based data is proposed in this work. In this model, the INS and the LiDAR measure the robot position in parallel. A novel data fusion model is designed, which considers the robot position error, velocity error, and the orientation error. Meanwhile, two particle filters (PFs) are used as the data fusion filter, one PF estimates the LiDAR-derived robot position, the other PF fuses the INS-based and the LiDAR-based data. The experimental results have been done to verify that the two-PF method proposed in this work is effective.

The rest of the paper is organized as follows: the INS/LiDAR integrated model for two particle filter is designed in Sect. 2, the proposed two particle filters' performance is investigated in Sect. 3, Sect. 4 give the conclusions.

2   The INS/LiDAR Integrated Model for Two Particle Filter

Figure 2 displays the INS/UWB integrated navigation scheme using two particle filter. In this work, the LiDAR and the INS are fixed on the mobile robot. The LiDAR measures the LiDAR-based robot position $\mathbf{Po}^L$ by fusing the distances between the corner points (CPs) and the mobile robot via the PF. Meanwhile, the INS provide the INS position $\mathbf{Po}^I$, and the PF uses the difference between $\mathbf{Po}^L$ and $\mathbf{Po}^I$ to obtain error estimation of the INS position, which is used to compensate the $\mathbf{Po}^I$.

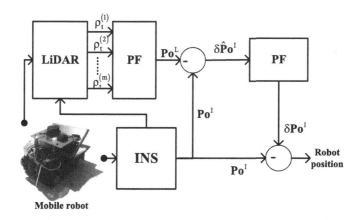

Fig. 2. The two particle filter-based INS/LiDAR integrated navigation scheme.

2.1   The LiDAR-Based Localization Model

The LiDAR-based localization model will be studied in this subsection. To the robot localization, the 2D position (x, y) in east and north directions, velocity V, and the orientation ϕ are considered in LiDAR-based localization model. The state equation of the PF for the LiDAR-based localization is listed as Eq. 1.

$$\underbrace{\begin{bmatrix} x_k \\ y_k \\ V_k \\ \varphi_k \end{bmatrix}}_{\mathbf{X}^1_{k|k-1}} = \underbrace{\begin{bmatrix} x_{k-1} + T \cdot V_{k-1} \sin\left(\varphi_{k-1}\right) \\ y_{k-1} + T \cdot V_{k-1} \cos\left(\varphi_{k-1}\right) \\ V_{k-1} \\ \varphi_{k-1} \end{bmatrix}}_{f\left(\mathbf{X}^1_{k-1}\right)} + \omega^1_k, \tag{1}$$

where T is the sample time, k represents the time index, $\omega^1_k \sim N\left(0, \mathbf{Q}_1\right)$ is the system noise. Using the CPs position, the observation equation is listed as Eq. 2.

$$
\underbrace{\begin{bmatrix} d_{1,k} \\ d_{2,k} \\ \vdots \\ d_{m,k} \end{bmatrix}}_{\mathbf{y}_k^1} = \underbrace{\begin{bmatrix} \sqrt{\left(x_k - x^{(1)}\right)^2 + \left(y_k - y^{(1)}\right)^2} \\ \sqrt{\left(x_k - x^{(2)}\right)^2 + \left(y_k - y^{(2)}\right)^2} \\ \vdots \\ \sqrt{\left(x_k - x^{(m)}\right)^2 + \left(y_k - y^{(m)}\right)^2} \end{bmatrix}}_{h\left(\mathbf{X}_{k|k-1}^1\right)} + \nu_k^1, \tag{2}
$$

where $\left(x^{(i)}, y^{(i)}\right), i = 1, 2, \ldots, m$ is the CP's position, here, the m is the number of the CP, $d_{i,k}, i = 1, 2, \ldots, m$ is the distance between the CP and the mobile robot, $\nu_k^1 \sim N\left(0, \mathbf{R}_1\right)$ is the measurement noise.

2.2   The INS/LiDAR Localization Model

Based on the LiDAR-based localization model, the INS/LiDAR localization model will be investigated in this subsection.

The position error $(\delta x_k, \delta y_k)$ can be computed by the follows

$$
\delta x_k = \delta x_{k-1} + T \cdot \delta V x_{k-1}, \tag{3}
$$

$$
\delta y_k = \delta y_{k-1} + T \cdot \delta V y_{k-1}, \tag{4}
$$

where $(\delta x_k, \delta y_k)$ is the 2D position error, and $(\delta V x_k, \delta V y_k)$ is the 2D velocity error. It should be emphasized that the mobile robot's velocity in east and north directions is not easy to be measured.

The most common method is to calculate the robot's velocity by using the encoder-derived velocity and the orientation. Thus, we can get the following conclusion.

$$
\begin{aligned}
\delta V x_k &= \tilde{V}_k \sin \tilde{\varphi}_k - V_k \sin \varphi_k \\
&= \tilde{V}_k \sin \tilde{\varphi}_k - \left(\tilde{V}_k - \delta V_k\right) \sin \left(\tilde{\varphi}_k - \delta \varphi_k\right),
\end{aligned} \tag{5}
$$

$$
\begin{aligned}
\delta V y_k &= \tilde{V}_k \cos \tilde{\varphi}_k - V_k \cos \varphi_k \\
&= \tilde{V}_k \cos \tilde{\varphi}_k - \left(\tilde{V}_k - \delta V_k\right) \cos \left(\tilde{\varphi}_k - \delta \varphi_k\right),
\end{aligned} \tag{6}
$$

where $\tilde{V}_k$ is the velocity measured by the encoder at the time index k, δV_k is the velocity error at the time index k, $\tilde{\varphi}_k$ is the orientation measured by the INS at the time index k, $\delta \varphi_k$ is the error of the orientation at the time index k.

Thus, Eqs. 3 and 4 can be rewritten as the follows.

$$
\delta x_k = \delta x_{k-1} + T \cdot \left(\tilde{V}_k \sin \tilde{\varphi}_k - \left(\tilde{V}_k - \delta V_k\right) \sin \left(\tilde{\varphi}_k - \delta \varphi_k\right)\right), \tag{7}
$$

$$
\delta y_k = \delta y_{k-1} + T \cdot \left(\tilde{V}_k \cos \tilde{\varphi}_k - \left(\tilde{V}_k - \delta V_k\right) \cos \left(\tilde{\varphi}_k - \delta \varphi_k\right)\right), \tag{8}
$$

For the INS/LiDAR localization, the state equation of the PF can be written as the following.

$$
\underbrace{\begin{bmatrix} \delta x_k \\ \delta y_k \\ \delta V_k \\ \delta \phi_k \end{bmatrix}}_{\mathbf{X}^2_{k|k-1}} =
$$

$$
\underbrace{\begin{bmatrix} \delta x_{k-1} + T \cdot \left(\tilde{V}_k \sin \tilde{\phi}_k - \left(\tilde{V}_k - \delta V_k \right) \sin \left(\tilde{\phi}_k - \delta \phi_k \right) \right) \\ \delta y_{k-1} + T \cdot \left(\tilde{V}_k \cos \tilde{\phi}_k - \left(\tilde{V}_k - \delta V_k \right) \cos \left(\tilde{\phi}_k - \delta \phi_k \right) \right) \\ \delta V_{k-1} \\ \delta \phi_{k-1} \end{bmatrix}}_{f\left(\mathbf{X}^2_{k-1}\right)} + w_k^2, \tag{9}
$$

where $w_k^2 \sim N\left(0, \mathbf{Q}_2\right)$ is the system noise. The observation equation can be written as the follows.

$$
\underbrace{\begin{bmatrix} \delta \tilde{x}_k \\ \delta \tilde{y}_k \end{bmatrix}}_{\mathbf{y}_k^2} = \begin{bmatrix} x_k^I - x_k^L \\ y_k^I - y_k^L \end{bmatrix} = \underbrace{\begin{bmatrix} \delta x_k \\ \delta y_k \end{bmatrix}}_{h\left(\mathbf{X}^2_{k|k-1}\right)} + \nu_k^2, \tag{10}
$$

where $\left(x_k^I, y_k^I\right)$ is the INS position, and $\left(x_k^L, y_k^L\right)$ is the LiDAR position in east and north directions, $\nu_k^2 \sim N\left(0, \mathbf{R}_2\right)$ is the measurement noise.

3   Tests and Discussion

3.1   Environment

In this paper, in order to verify the proposed algorithm's effectiveness, the real test is done. Figure 3 shows the real test environment. The real test was done in the University of Jinan. The test employs one LiDAR, one IMU, and one robot with the encoder. Here, the LiDAR and IMU are fixed on the mobile robot, which are capable of providing the distances between the CPs and the robot, LiDAR-derived position, and INS-based position. 0.02 s is selected as the sample time in this work. It should be emphasized that the test area is small due to the limited detection range of the LiDAR used in the test. Figure 4 shows the mobile robot used in the real test.

The position of the corner point, the reference path, and the paths provided by the LiDAR and DR are shown in Fig. 5. In this figure, we can find that the path estimated by the LiDAR with the corner points' positions is stable. Compared with the LiDAR, the path estimated by the DR is not suitable.

Fig. 3. Test environment.

Fig. 4. Mobile robot.

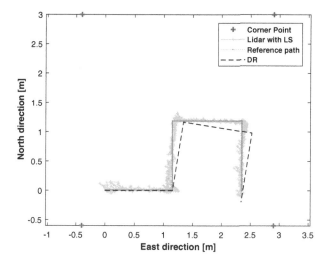

Fig. 5. The reference path, the paths provided by the LiDAR and DR, and corner point.

3.2 Performance of the Two PF

The two PF's and the two EKF's performances will be investigated in this subsection. The trajectories estimated by the TKF and TPF are showed in Fig. 6. From the figure, we can see obviously that the TKF has divergence. Compared with the TKF, the TPF is closer to the reference path.

The position errors measured by the TKF and TPF are shown in Fig. 7 and Fig. 8. At the same time, Table 1 shows the difference of the TKF and TPF in the aspect of position error. It is easy to see from the figure that the error of PF is less than that of KF. The position root-mean-square error (RMSE) of two-PF proposed in this work in east direction is 0.073 m, and in north direction is 0.044 m.

Table 1. Position error of two methods.

Method	RMSE (m)		
	East	North	Mean
Two EKF	0.209	0.243	0.226
Two PF	**0.073**	**0.044**	**0.059**

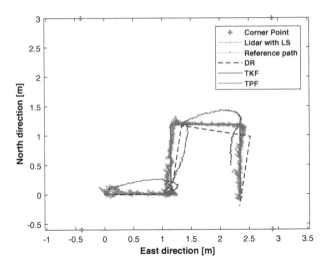

Fig. 6. The trajectories estimated by the TKF and TPF.

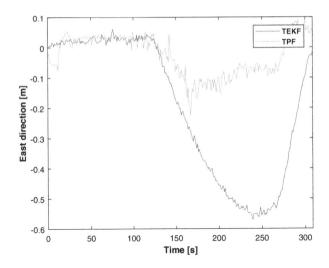

Fig. 7. Position error in east direction.

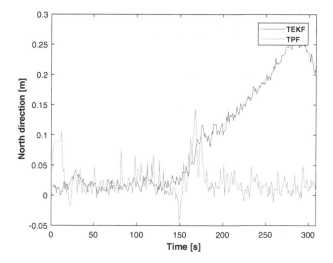

Fig. 8. Position error in north direction.

4   Conclusions

A localization method for INS/LiDAR-integrated mobile robot based on two particle filter is proposed in this work. In this scheme, two PFs are used, one is used for the LiDAR localization, the other one is used for fusing the INS-based and the LiDAR-based data. The experimental results verify the effectiveness of two-PF method proposed in the aspect of reducing the position error compared with the two-EKF method.

Acknowledgment. This article was partially funded by Shandong Key research and Development Program 2019GGXI04026 and 2019GNC106093, was partially supported by Shandong Provincial Natural Science Foundation project ZR2018LF010, was partially supported by the Shandong High school science and technology project under Grant J18KA333.

References

Wang, L., Cheng, X., Li, S.: IMM-RKF algorithm and its application in integrated navigation system for agricultural robot. J. Chin. Inert. Technol. **25**(3), 328–333 (2017)

Sherwin, T., Easte, M., Chen, A.T., et al.: A single RF emitter-based indoor navigation method for autonomous service robots. Sensors **18**(2), 585 (2018)

Xu, Y., Ahn, C.K., Shmaliy, Y.S., et al.: Adaptive robust INS/UWB-integrated human tracking using UFIR filter bank. Measurement **123**, 1–7 (2018)

Xu, Y., Shmaliy, Y.S., Li, Y., Chen, X.: Uwb-based indoor human localization with time-delayed data using EFIR filtering. IEEE Access **5**, 16676–16683 (2017)

Zhang, X., Zhang, R., Guo, M., et al.: Yaw error self-observation algorithm for pedestrian navigation via foot-mounted inertial navigation system. J. Chin. Inert. Technol. **23**(4), 457–466 (2015)

Cui, B., Chen, X., Xu, Y., et al.: Performance analysis of improved iterated cubature Kalman filter and its application to GNSS/INS. ISA Trans. **66**, 460–468 (2016)

Cao, H., Zhang, Y., Han, Z., et al.: Pole-zero-temperature compensation circuit design and experiment for dual-mass MEMS gyroscope bandwidth expansion. IEEE/ASME Trans. Mechatron. **24**(2), 677–688 (2019)

Cao, H., Zhang, Y., Shen, C., et al.: Temperature energy influence compensation for mems vibration gyroscope based on RBF NN-GA-KF method. Shock Vibr. 1–10 (2018)

Jian, Z., Lyu, Y., Patton, J., Senthil, C.G.P., Roppel, T.: BFVP: a probabilistic UHF RFID tag localization algorithm using Bayesian filter and a variable power RFID model. IEEE Trans. Ind. Electron. **PP**(99), 1 (2018)

Monica, S., Ferrari, G.: Improving UWB-based localization in IoT scenarios with statistical models of distance error. Sensors **18**(5), 1592 (2018)

Huang, H., Chen, X., Zhang, B., Wang, J.: High accuracy navigation information estimation for inertial system using the multi-model EKF fusing Adams explicit formula applied to underwater gliders. ISA Trans. **66**(1), 414–424 (2016)

Design of Parametric CAD System for Ceramic Products Based on Virtual Reality Technology

Jia-bei Ye[1(✉)] and Guo-qiang Cui[2]

[1] Department of Design, Hubei Institute of Fine Arts, Wuhan, Hubei, China
yejiabei252@tom.com
[2] PetroChina Xinjiang Oilfield Company Research Institute of Exploration
and Development, Karamay, Xinjiang, China

Abstract. Aiming at the problem that the drawing of ceramic products designed and produced by the original system is low in definition, which leads to poor picture effect, this paper proposes the design of parametric CAD system of ceramic products based on virtual reality technology. Through sensor-mcu control system, complete data collection, build a computer control system platform, select the appropriate data transmission port, complete data transmission; Application of virtual reality technology, and through the data query, modify, and 3 d parametric regeneration to complete its structure system design work process, improve the search efficiency of menu file, according to user requirements, remove or add a menu item, calculating weights of the Bezier curve, design the user interface and high efficiency, adjust the memory image file, complete the system design. The comparison experiment is designed in CAD software, and the image effect of the system in this paper is compared with that of the traditional system. The ceramic products produced by the design system have higher clarity and better effect.

Keywords: Virtual reality technology · Ceramics · CAD

1 Introduction

There are many types of ceramic products, and the shape and structure are complicated. At present, the development of new products for ceramic products still follows the traditional manual method, which is mainly based on imitation. This method has a long development cycle and high cost. Therefore, the application of advanced manufacturing technologies such as CAD to the development and production of ceramic products is an inevitable trend in the development of the ceramic industry, and an important aspect of transforming traditional industries with information technology [1]. Ceramic products are indispensable for modern families. The design, manufacture and use of ceramic products has a long history in China. Since the beginning of the year, the total output of China's ceramic products has ranked first in the world and has become a major producer and consumer of ceramics. However, in terms of product quality, China's ceramic products belong to the middle and low grades. The products produced by foreign-funded enterprises and joint ventures together with imported products occupy the main market of domestic high-end products. For the current hand-

© ICST Institute for Computer Sciences, Social Informatics and Telecommunications Engineering 2020
Published by Springer Nature Switzerland AG 2020. All Rights Reserved
Y.-D. Zhang et al. (Eds.): ICMTEL 2020, LNICST 326, pp. 359–369, 2020.
https://doi.org/10.1007/978-3-030-51100-5_32

workshop-based product development model of ceramics manufacturing, the application of technology to the design and development of ceramic products can improve product quality, shorten product development cycle, reduce development costs, and improve the company's ability to respond to the market and adaptability [2]. This is of great significance in promoting the standardization and informationization development of China's ceramic enterprises. How to make ceramic products meet the needs of modern society in terms of quality, variety, function and shape is the key to the development of China's ceramic industry. The traditional ceramic products and mold design and manufacturing process is long and complicated, and it has not been able to adapt to the increasingly fierce market competition. Therefore, the parametric CAD system design of ceramic products based on virtual reality technology is proposed. At present, advanced manufacturing technology represented by high-tech such as CAD/CAE/CAM/RP has developed to a new stage [3]. The use of high technology to transform the traditional ceramic industry is an inevitable trend of China's ceramic enterprises to adapt to the world's development trend. The development of CAD software for ceramic products is one of the important contents. Parametric design not only enables CAD system to have interactive drawing function, but also has automatic drawing function. The special product design system developed by parametric design means that designers can free themselves from a lot of tedious drawing work and greatly improve design efficiency. And reduce the amount of information stored.

2 Hardware Design of Parametric CAD System for Ceramic Products

2.1 Overall Structural Design

The system selects sense-mcu as the core console, selects the appropriate data transmission port, complete data transmission, applies virtual reality technology, and completes its structure design through data query and modification of 3-d parameter regeneration. The data acquisition of the simulation training system is completed by the sensor-single-chip microcomputer control system, and the collected signals are transmitted to the virtual reality platform, and the final operation result is displayed in the display. The specific design scheme is as follows (Fig. 1):

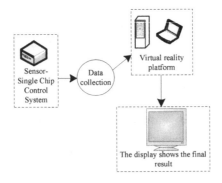

Fig. 1. Hardware system design

According to the overall structure, the structure of each part is designed separately. Firstly, the computer control system platform is built and the appropriate data transmission port is selected.

2.2   Data Transmission Port Selection

With the rapid development of computer hardware technology, the original system has been on the verge of being eliminated. This is an extremely fatal problem of the original system and urgently needs to be solved. The parallel port and serial port of the computer are common ports for transmitting data. Among them, parallel port programming is relatively simple, and it is more economical for building a computer control system platform, which makes the parallel port widely used in electronic control fields, such as robots. The field of single-chip programmers and home automation, and the serial port transmission speed is slower than the parallel port. Therefore, considering the actual requirements of the system for reading and writing the transmission port, the system control software module selects the parallel port of the computer as the data transmission port [4]. The parallel port is also the printer interface of the computer. Its main purpose is to connect the printer to the computer, and the mouth is also born. Therefore, the parallel port is often called the printer port, which is the female end of a needle. The 25 pins of the 25-pin parallel port are as follows (Fig. 2):

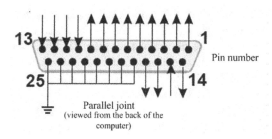

Fig. 2. 25-pin parallel pin map

The 25-pin parallel port is divided into a data area, a control area, and a status area. The data area transmits data, the control area controls the peripheral device, and the status signal returned by the peripheral device is transmitted to the computer through the status area. Data registers, control registers, and status registers are connected internally to these three areas. The specific information of each pin of the parallel port is shown in the Table 1.

Table 1. Parallel port 25 pin specific function list

Stitch	Function	Transmission direction	Register	Logic
1	gate	output	control channel0	Yes
2	data channel0	Input/output	data channel0	No
3	data channel1	Input/output	data channel1	No
4	data channel2	Input/output	data channel2	No
5	data channel3	Input/output	data channel3	No
6	data channel4	Input/output	data channel4	No
7	data channel5	Input/output	data channel5	No
8	data channel6	Input/output	data channel6	No
9	data channel7	Input/output	data channel7	No
10	data channel8	Input/output	data channel8	No
11	data channel9	Input/output	data channel9	No
12	affirm	Input	status channel6	No
13	busy	Input	status channel7	Yes
14	select	Input	status channel5	No
15	error	Input	status channel4	No
16	initialization	output	control channel1	No
17	select	Input	control channel2	No
18–25	–	–	–	–

As described above, the data area, the control area, and the status area of the parallel port are respectively connected to corresponding registers in the computer, so these registers are operated in the program. These registers, which can be found in the standard parallel port, include data registers, control registers, and status registers. The data register is connected to the data area, the control register is connected to the control area, and the status register is connected to the status area [5]. So writing different contents to these registers will cause the corresponding voltage in the corresponding area of the parallel port, and the specific voltage can be measured with a multimeter. Similarly, the voltage applied to the parallel port can also be read by the register.

3 System Software Design Based on Virtual Reality Technology

The three-dimensional parametric CAD system is based on the actual needs of ceramic product design work, using computer software technology, designed and developed a set of engineering and technical personnel for ceramic production enterprises, based on computer systems, CAD system that is easy to operate and use [6]. Including the human-computer interaction interface design, three-dimensional parametric design, etc., above the system base layer and support layer is the application layer of the product parametric CAD system. The human-computer interaction interface design refers to the application development tool to design the system menu, dialog box and toolbar, etc., requiring the human-computer interaction interface to be clear and intuitive, and the design result and the command appear in the same window.

3.1 Overall Structure Optimization

The data on ceramic products is deep and wide, and the mold mechanism is flexible. Not all data and design processes can be parameterized, and some must be determined by the experience of mold designers. In order to provide convenience for the designer and to make the system standardized and orderly, the system establishes a three-dimensional system with the following data types for query, modification and regeneration. The workflow of its structural 3D parameterization system is usually as shown in the following figure (Fig. 3):

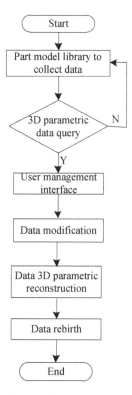

Fig. 3. Work flow chart

The parameterized system soil consists of three parts: a three-dimensional parameterized part model library, a user-managed interface, and a main program of the system. Establish a design subsystem that optimizes the calculation of the local shape. Here, it is mainly for the flow channel of ceramic products, to establish a reasonable mathematical model of fluid dynamics, to use the computational fluid dynamics method for flow channel analysis, to optimize the design, and to perform a simple overall analysis and verification of the established three-dimensional solid model. Model geometry and physical properties [7].

3.2 Menu Efficient Design

Careful menu design can significantly improve the efficiency of CAD operations. Through detailed analysis of the menu file structure, we can re-edit it according to certain grammar rules, not only can customize our own system interface, mainly including drop-down menus, toolbars, prompt information and other parts.

It is also possible to normalize most of the interfaces. Each menu section includes several menu items. Users can delete or add menu sections or menu items as needed. When deleting a menu section or menu item, you only need to delete all the corresponding menu section files; when adding, you should add the corresponding menu file to the source menu file according to certain grammar rules, but note that the total number of menus after adding must not exceed the system. Desired point. The menu items in the menu file are defined in the order of arrangement. If you want to change the position of a menu item, just adjust the position defined in the menu file [8]. Similarly, the user can redefine the access key and hotkey as needed, as long as the access key or hotkey letter in the corresponding file line in the menu file is modified, or the definition access key is added thereto, but in the process, Avoid duplication. When the drop-down menu is finished, the corresponding menu item in the menu file and the menu name or menu command of each sub-menu item are changed to Chinese, and the letter and hotkey command of the access key are reserved [9]. For ease of use, the toolbar can be modified in the menu file, or some of the command buttons can be deleted. Similarly, users can add menu files to create new toolbars or command buttons based on certain grammar rules. To normalize the toolbar, just change the names of all toolbars and command buttons in the toolbar menu file to Chinese. The user adds a new menu command or command button, and can add corresponding prompt information in the menu-specific help menu section file. It must be noted that the identifier of the prompt information should be the same as the identifier of the corresponding menu command or command button, and the Chinese prompt Information, customizing a more efficient system 3D solid modeling user interface.

3.3 Bezier Curve Weight Calculation

The shape of the curve is uniquely determined by the two endpoints of the curve and a number of points that are not on the curve. These two endpoints and several points are called the vertices of the Bezier feature polygon or the control points of the Bezier curve. Let n + 1 vertices of a given spatial feature polygon, $P_i(i = 0, 1, \ldots, n)$, define the vector function of the n-time Bezier curve as:

$$P(t) = \sum_{i=0}^{n} B_{n,i}(t)P_i \tag{1}$$

$B_{n,i}(t)$ of them are Bernstein's functions. Some properties of the Bezier curve can be obtained from the properties of Bezier curve equation and Bernstein root function. The end and end points of the curve pass through the starting point of the feature polygon respectively, and the derivative property of the $B_{n,i}(t)$ function can be derived:

$$P(t) = n \sum_{i=0}^{n} \left(B_{n-1,i-1}(t) - B_{n-1,i}(t-1) \right) \tag{2}$$

According to the nature of the Bernstein function, the shape of the curve is unchanged after the control point is reversed, but the direction is reversed. The Bezier curve is located in the convex hull formed by its control vertices. If the plane control polygon is convex, the Bezier curve is also convex. The shape of the curve does not change with changes in the coordinate system. For a planar Bezier curve, the number of intersections between any line in the plane and the Bezier curve is not more than the number of intersections between the line and the control polygon. Normally, only three Bezier curves are used in the graphics package, which brings design convenience on the one hand, and avoids a large increase in computation due to high-order polynomials. The cubic Bezier curve is generated by four control points, and n = 3 is substituted:

$$P(t) = (1-t)^3 \times P_0 + 3t(1-t)^2 \times P_1 + 3t^2(1-t) \times P_2 + t^3 P_3$$
$$0 \leq t \leq 1 \tag{3}$$

Write it as a matrix:

$$P(t) = \begin{bmatrix} t^3 & t^2 & t & 1 \end{bmatrix} \times M_{Bez} \times \begin{bmatrix} P_0 \\ P_1 \\ P_2 \\ P_3 \end{bmatrix} \tag{4}$$

$$0 \leq t \leq 1$$

Among them, the Bezier matrix is:

$$P(t) = \begin{bmatrix} t^3 & t^2 & t & 1 \end{bmatrix} \times M_{Bez} \times \begin{bmatrix} P_0 \\ P_1 \\ P_2 \\ P_3 \end{bmatrix} \tag{5}$$

$$0 \leq t \leq 1$$

It can be seen from the above calculation that only the control points of each curve are adjusted, and each control point is drawn as a hollow circle, and the shape of the curve changes when the mouse clicks on the movement control point.

3.4   Memory Image File

A memory image file allows a disk file to be mapped to a specific range of memory addresses. The application obtains the file on disk by using a pointer in memory instead of executing a traditional file read function. More importantly, applications can use this mechanism to share memory. Normally, in Windows, each application runs in its own address space, and all memory allocations are made in this space. This space is private to the process and cannot be used by other processes. Using a memory image file allows multiple processes to access the same data file at the same time. Memory image file data is not actually read from disk except when it is accessed in memory. Therefore, it requires less physical memory and disk operations, and is more efficient; only the file segments that are actually changed are Write back to disk, reducing the number of disk operations and improving execution performance; accessing only one linear address space, the code is simple and clear; you can share a file between processes. When programming a memory image file, creating a memory image file can be done either in the editor process or in the master process. The implementation method should be decided by the programmer according to the requirements of the system integration [10]. If the size of the file exceeds the mapped image, then only the mapped range is valid and the rest of the file cannot be updated: if the file mapping object is larger than the file, the file end flag on the disk will be expanded to fit the file object Size; if you plan to extend the length of a file, it is necessary to estimate the maximum size of the file, create a file map large enough, and a large enough file image; finally, because the image is only in-memory data, if the length of the file When changes occur, it is necessary to call SetFilepointer and SetEndofFile before closing the file to adjust the end of file flag.

4   Simulation Test

In order to verify the effectiveness of the above-mentioned parametric CAD system of ceramic products based on virtual reality technology, a simulation experiment was designed. The ceramic model rendering effect of the designed system is compared with the original effect, and the experiment is completed.

4.1   Experimental Preparation

The CAD software used in this experiment has higher requirements on the operating system. To ensure the smooth progress of the experiment, the following conditions must be met: (Table 2)

Table 2. Experimental platform requirements

Name	Parameter
CPU	Intel core dual core or above
Internal storage	More than 8 GB DDR4
GPU	NVIDIA GT 740 M, 830 M, 930 M The above and similar products
Network	Minimum 512 Kb, recommended 2 Mb and above network configuration
Hard disk	18 GB (including temporary swap space) Recommendation: Intel 540(480 GB) SSD

Under the premise of meeting the above requirements, the semi-finished products of ceramic products that have not been rendered are randomly selected as follows:

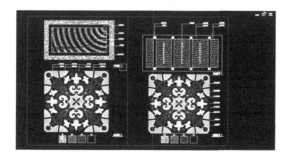

Fig. 4. Ceramic product not rendered

Figure 4 shows an unrendered semi-finished product of a ceramic tile product. Comparative experiments were performed under otherwise identical conditions.

4.2 Experimental Result

After the above preparations are completed, the designed system and the original system are used, and the ceramic product renderings are modified and designed, and the results are simultaneously magnified by the same multiples. The comparison results are as follows (Figs. 5 and 6):

According to the comparison results in the above figure, it can be clearly seen that the product map obtained by the original system has lower definition and the image is more blurred, and the obtained product map has poor effect, which has an impact on subsequent operations and requires the designer's later stage. Repair, resulting in a waste of human resources. The effect diagram obtained by the designed system is clear and clear, and the obtained product map has a good effect and can meet the user's needs.

Fig. 5. Original system result

Fig. 6. Designed system results

Making product images in a fixed time. the generation time period of the traditional system and the system in this paper is intercepted in the simulation environment, and the same pixel quality of the graph is compared separately, and the results are shown in Fig. 7.

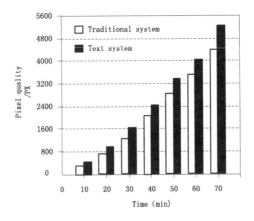

Fig. 7. Image quality testing

According to the data of Fig. 7, it can be clearly seen that the image generation quality of this system is higher than that of the traditional system in a fixed period of time. After the actual calculation can be affirmed, the specific efficiency increase ratio of more than 15%.

5   Conclusion

The development and application of the system solves the problems of automatic parameter design and product realism display of ceramic products, avoiding the repeated labor of designers, and the designer can quickly and easily obtain the required design results, which will greatly shorten the product development cycle. Reduce development costs and improve the market competitiveness and economic benefits of enterprises.

6   Fund Project

Research results of Wuhan Business School "Engineering Animation Design and Application Research team", subject number 2018TD016.

Wuhan Business School <Digital Creative and Design Research Center> Research Results, Project No. 2018 YJZX.

References

1. Zhang, Z.: Parameterized design of fabricated structural shear wall under virtual reality technology. Shanxi Archit. **44**(36), 42–43 (2018)
2. Hu, M., Wang, D.: Virtual reality technology based CAD three-dimensional modeling system of mechanical industry product. Mod. Electron. Tech. **42**(09), 142–144 (2019)
3. Jin, F., Xie, L.: The research ergonomics on MTM and NIOSH method based on virtual reality. J. Jiangxi Norm. Univ. (Nat. Sci. Edn.) **41**(04), 338–343 (2017)
4. Zhao, W., Guo, W.: Design and implementation of virtual simulation system for TBM and its working process. Comput. Technol. Dev. **28**(04), 169–173 (2018)
5. Li, T., Fang, X., Lin, R., et al.: 3D virtual human rapid modeling method based on top-down modeling mechanism. Chin. J. Ship Res. **12**(01), 38–44 (2017)
6. Xing, J., Gan, Y., Dai, X.: Auto-programming system based on the workpiece model for industrial robot. Robot **39**(01), 111–118 (2017)
7. Li, Y., Wang, Y., Yang, Z.: The development of parameterization finite element analysis system based on Nx Nastran. Min. Res. Dev. **38**(05), 84–87 (2018)
8. Zhuang, S., Zhao, W., Yang, X., et al.: CAD software development for sealing ring on AutoCAD platform. J. Rocket Propul. **43**(03), 47–52 (2017)
9. Xue, B., Deng, J.: A modified CST representation method and CAD oriented wing parameterization of civil aircrafts. Aeronaut. Comput. Tech. **48**(04), 11–15 (2018)
10. Xie, L., Huang, C., Tan, M., et al.: CAD parametric design and application on extrusion die with porthole for aluminium alloy pipes based on UG software. Forg. Stamp. Technol. **42**(04), 188–193 (2017)

Numerical Simulation of Remaining Oil Distribution Based on Oil Field Data Analysis

Guo-qiang Cui[1][(✉)], Chang-jun Diao[1], Qiang Zhang[2], Ji-gang Zhang[1], and Jia-bei Ye[3]

[1] PetroChina Xinjiang Oilfield Company Research Institute of Exploration and Development, Karamay 834000, Xinjiang, China
cuiguoqiang1465@tom.com
[2] PetroChina Xinjiang Oilfield Company Development Company, Karamay 834000, Xinjiang, China
[3] Department of Design, Hubei Institute of Fine Arts, Wuhan, Hubei, China

Abstract. In view of the narrow data source range of traditional residual oil distribution numerical simulation, a numerical simulation method of residual oil distribution based on oilfield data analysis is studied. Firstly, the principle of big data was put forward to complete the collection and analysis of oilfield information. Then, the three-dimensional simulation model of oilfield was designed by haiyan software. Then, the grid structure of oilfield saturation setting model was divided. By comparing the range of data sources, it is verified that the proposed numerical simulation method can effectively extend the range of data sources and improve the accuracy of numerical simulation.

Keywords: Data analysis · Residual oil distribution · Numerical simulation · Data fitting

1 Introduction

With the deepening of oilfield development, most of China's oilfields, especially the eastern onshore oilfields, have gradually stepped into the late stage of high water cut development [1, 2]. In the face of the shortage of reserves and national energy in the new area of the old oilfield, how to improve oil recovery and reverse the passive situation of oilfield development in the high water cut period has become a serious issue for oilfield development workers. A large number of studies have shown that the average recovery rate of secondary oil recovery is about 35%, and it is estimated that about 20% of movable oil is still not injected into water wave due to the heterogeneity of the reservoir, and this part of movable oil can be exploited by deepening reservoir understanding, changing oil production technology and other ways [3]. Therefore, in the stage of high water cut development, it is of great significance to carry out fine reservoir description and remaining oil distribution research, so as to provide technical support for the potential tapping adjustment of old oilfields. In order to solve the problems existing in the actual development of some oilfields, such as many oil-bearing

Y.-D. Zhang et al. (Eds.): ICMTEL 2020, LNICST 326, pp. 370–381, 2020.
https://doi.org/10.1007/978-3-030-51100-5_33

series, small thickness of single oil layer, poor physical properties, low reserve abundance and different oil well productivity, further tap the potential of remaining oil, improve the level of reservoir development, deepen the understanding of reservoir geology, and design the numerical simulation method of remaining oil distribution based on the analysis of oilfield data.

In the study of oil field distribution, numerical simulation combined with oil data analysis can effectively improve the accuracy of distribution research results, improve the effect of oil field development, and further improve the recovery factor. The so-called oilfield data analysis refers to the process of using appropriate statistical analysis methods to analyze a large amount of collected oilfield data, extract useful information, form conclusions, and conduct detailed research and summary on the data [4]. This technique provides a basis for numerical simulation and ensures the validity of distribution results. It improves the precision of numerical simulation and provides technical support for the future development of petroleum industry.

2 Numerical Simulation Method of Remaining Oil Distribution Based on Oil Field Data Analysis

According to the past research on the distribution data of the remaining oil, in order to ensure that the simulation method of the remaining oil distribution can get more accurate simulation results, the oilfield data analysis technology is introduced into the method design.

2.1 Oil Field Data Collection and Analysis

Big data technology is used to obtain oilfield data. Oilfield data is the original data collected by oilfield enterprises for geological research and scientific management. It is a form of independent data storage and management for the original data collected from the source [6]. These data are one of the most important embodiment of oil field. Through digital transformation, data is transformed into the most important information, which is essentially the basic oil and gas materials. In order to ensure the accuracy and universality of the data source, the oil field data source is set as shown in Fig. 1 below:

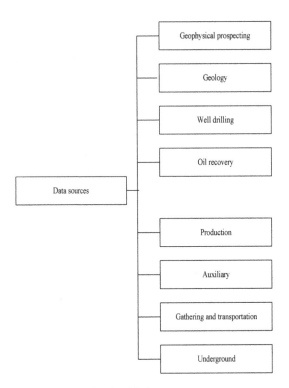

Fig. 1. Oil data sources

Through the above process to complete the acquisition of oilfield data. The data results are stored in the database and analyzed. In the process of analysis, using big data technology, in different types of data, cross analysis to obtain data value, promote the design of numerical simulation method. In the construction of numerical simulation method, flexible data analysis ability from multiple angles is needed. Taking the numerical model as an example, not only the development situation changes of different oil fields and different development units, but also the development situation changes of different types of reservoirs, different displacement modes, different recovery degrees and other angles, as well as the impact analysis of social factors and natural factors, etc. The results are applied to the numerical simulation. To ensure the design sequence, the design process is shown in Fig. 2 below:

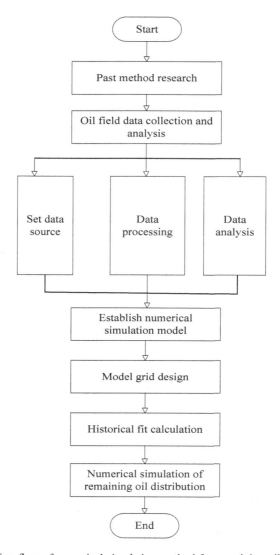

Fig. 2. Design flow of numerical simulation method for remaining oil distribution

Use the above process to complete the design process of numerical simulation method, introduce big data technology in the field data analysis [5], expand the data source, improve the accuracy of data simulation analysis results, and ensure the effectiveness of the method design.

2.2 Establish Numerical Simulation Model

Based on the above data collection and analysis results, a numerical simulation model is built. According to the interface provided by petrel software, the 3D fine geological model is transformed into the geological model required by VIP numerical simulation software. The specific model image is as follows (Figs 3 and 4).

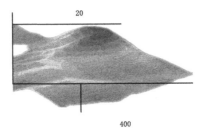

Fig. 3. 3D model of oil field

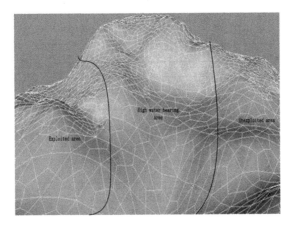

Fig. 4. Oilfield geological model

In this data simulation, it mainly includes: reservoir geological parameters [7], including reservoir depth, sand thickness, effective thickness, permeability, porosity, etc.; physical property constant of balance area, including original reservoir pressure, original saturation pressure, oil-water interface and capillary pressure corresponding to the interface, etc. special core analysis data [8], including oil-water and gas-water relative permeability curve, rock compression coefficient; PVT data of high pressure physical properties of crude oil, including curves of oil phase volume coefficient, oil phase compression coefficient, oil porosity and other changes with pressure; physical properties constant of formation water, including water porosity, density, compression coefficient, etc.; dynamic data, including well location, well type, completion data, production and injection volume, pressure, etc.

The parameters involved in the numerical simulation include matrix porosity, matrix permeability, matrix initial oil saturation, effective thickness, fracture porosity, fracture permeability and so on. By using the geological parameters of the corresponding intervals of each well point in the study area and using petrel software [9], the data field of the actual reservoir geological parameters is established. Based on the data field, the model grid is divided and data simulation is realized.

2.3   Model Grid Design

Using the model set above, the mesh generation is completed. It is assumed that there is a residual oil accumulation area in the reservoir, which is square in shape and relatively high in oil saturation. If the square area is taken as the plane size of the numerical simulation grid, the following situation may occur after grid division, that is, no complete grid falls on the remaining oil area. As the saturation displayed in the grid is the average value of the grid, the saturation on the remaining oil area is allocated to four or two adjacent grids, the simulated remaining oil will be dispersed, and the oil saturation will drop. Even in the simulation results, it is difficult to see that the oil saturation is relatively high for the enriched remaining oil, and the shape and center position of the simulated remaining oil will also change. Obviously, this kind of grid division is not consistent with the actual situation. If a production well is designed to exploit the remaining oil on this basis, it may lead to class failure (Fig. 5).

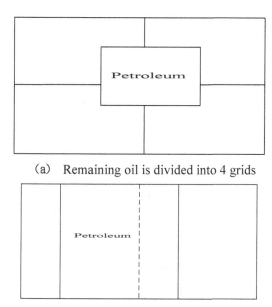

（a） Remaining oil is divided into 4 grids

（b）Remaining oil is divided into 2 grids

Fig. 5. Schematic diagram of remaining oil being meshed

The above method has poor control power. In order to improve the control power of the grid on the model, at least one grid is set at the center of the enriched remaining oil, then the area and center position of the enriched remaining oil can be determined, and the area and oil saturation of the remaining oil can also be controlled. The larger the area of remaining oil enrichment is, the more grid control will be obtained under this grid size, and the better the control result will be; however, if the grid size is too large, the remaining oil enrichment will not get more grid control, and the remaining oil in numerical simulation will be dispersed, and the oil saturation will decline, so that it is difficult to find the existence of the remaining oil enrichment. Conventional numerical simulation of remaining oil area requires that the grid size should meet the requirements of no less than three grid nodes between two well points. If the number of grid junctions between two well points is less than three, the accuracy of calculation and the characterization of oil saturation will be affected. Therefore, the total number of grid nodes in the model is 800000, including 400 in the east-west direction (X direction), single grid step of 30 m, 100 in the north-south direction (Y direction), and single grid step of 30 m. There are 20 layers vertically. The total number of nodes is 400 * 100 * 20 = 800000. According to the operation speed of the existing computer and the effective area of the actual simulation, the fault is selected as the closed boundary, and the invalid area is cut as the simulation area. The number of effective grids in the simulation area is 400000 to ensure the normal operation of the model.

2.4   Historical Fit Calculation

As the geological model changes with the development stage, the differences of geological models in different stages need to be considered, so the stage fitting method is used in the fitting. Due to the limitation of data, the change of infiltration curve is not considered in this simulation. The fitting of the comprehensive indicators of the unit in each stage is as follows. On this basis, a better dynamic fitting is carried out. Historical fitting is to use the actual dynamic data to verify the geological model [10], so that the simulated dynamic production data is basically consistent with the actual data. When fitting the production data of the model, it takes one month as a time point, and adopts the fixed oil production mode, which is fitted from four aspects: fault block index, well group index and single well index. The difference equations of the model are solved by the full implicit method. The maximum time step of the iteration is 10, and the maximum number of iterations is 100. In this way, the convergence of the iterative calculation and the stability of the model are guaranteed. The specific fitting results are as follows (Tables 1 and 2).

Table 1. Reserve matching data of numerical model reservoir (excluding fuzzy layer)

The layer number		XI	XII	XIII	XIV	Total
Modified reserves (10^4t)		170.50	259.70	225.0	58.0	713.2
Fitting	Matrix reserves (10^4t)	141.50	228.25	201.50	52.0	623.25
	Fractured reserves (10^4t)	27.0	28.0	20.20	3.60	78.8
	Total (10^4t)	339	515.95	446.7	113.6	1415.25
	Percentage of fractured reserves (%)	16.0	11.0	9.0	6.5	10.625
Error (%)		−1.0	−1.5	−1.2	−5.0	2.175

Table 2. Reserve matching data of numerical model reservoir (including fuzzy layer)

The layer number		XI	XII	XIII	XIV	Total
Modified reserves (10^4t)		170.50	259.70	225.0	58.0	713.2
Fitting	Matrix reserves (10^4t)	150.50	235.25	201.50	52.0	639.25
	Fractured reserves (10^4t)	28.0	28.0	20.20	3.60	9.8
	Total (10^4t)	349	522.95	446.7	113.6	1432.25
	Percentage of fractured reserves (%)	16.0	11.0	9.0	6.5	10.625
Error (%)		5.0	2.0	−1	−2	1

The actual reserves of this area after the reserves are changed are 14 million tons. The calculated reserves of the model are compared by stratified reserves. As the actual calculated reserves do not include fuzzy layers, 30 stratified reserves are deducted, and the error is controlled between 5%, the overall reserves are relatively small, with a total error of 2%, in which the fracture reserves account for 10.0% of the total reserves, the stratification ratio is between 6.0% and 12.0%, and the vertical distribution of fractures from top to bottom becomes poor. According to the fitting results of the overall reserves, the geological model has high accuracy and can meet the needs of numerical simulation.

2.5   Numerical Simulation of Remaining Oil Distribution

Through the above fitting data combined with the remaining oil distribution standard to complete the design of data simulation. According to the current classification standards of remaining oil in domestic major oil fields, the remaining oil in the model is divided into the following five types: structural factor control type, interlayer interference type, incomplete injection production type, single well drilling type and water flooded type. Among them, water flooded type is the most, accounting for 38.0%, followed by structural factor control type, accounting for 27.5%. This is because of the development of underwater distributary channels in this area, and the distribution of oil fields is mostly positive rhythm and compound rhythm. The general trend is that the bottom is thick and the top is fine, and the physical properties are good and bad. The coarse-grained sandstone in the lower part has good physical properties, and it can see water quickly after waterflooding development, which is the main part that causes the injection water to rush rapidly and forms the short-circuit cycle of injection production. But the physical properties of the upper and middle parts are poor, forming more remaining oil. The specific distribution of remaining reserves is shown below (Table 3).

Table 3. Distribution of remaining recoverable reserves

Type of remaining oil	Remaining recoverable amount/10^4t	Proportion/%
Structural factor control type	8.60	27.5
Interlayer interference type	3.65	11.5
Incomplete injection production	4.25	14.0
Single well drilling type	2.90	9.0
Watered out type	12.50	38.0
Total	31.9	100

According to the category distribution in the above table, combined with the data simulation model, the data model is displayed in the form of formula, and the specific formula is as follows.

$$A_{t-o} = A_i, B_{t-o} = B_i \tag{1}$$

$$\frac{\partial A}{\partial n} = 0 \tag{2}$$

$$\frac{\partial}{\partial x}\left(\frac{A * A_i}{\partial} * \frac{\partial A}{\partial x}\right) + \frac{\partial}{\partial y}\left(\frac{A * A_i}{\partial} * \frac{\partial A}{\partial y}\right) + \partial = \frac{\partial B_i}{\partial i} \tag{3}$$

In the above formula, formula (1) and formula (2) represent the boundary conditions of the numerical simulation model, A is the result of grid transformation, B is the final result of grid division, i is the set grid number, n is the cell boundary, x, y are the coordinates of cells, and ∂ is the distribution coefficient of remaining oil. Through the above formula to complete the research on the distribution of remaining oil, the actual oil field data is brought into the formula, and the design method of this paper is used to complete the research on the distribution of remaining oil in the oil field. According to the prediction results of data simulation, the actual oil volume is exploited to improve the exploitation and utilization efficiency of the remaining oil volume. In order to verify the effectiveness of the numerical simulation method of remaining oil distribution based on the analysis of oil field data, the experimental links are set up to obtain the research results.

3   Experimental Results and Analysis

In order to verify the validity of the numerical simulation method of remaining oil distribution based on the analysis of oil field data designed in this paper, a comparative test is set up to complete the research on the difference between the original numerical simulation method and it. In this experiment, the comparative amount is set as the range of data source of numerical simulation.

3.1   Experiment Preparation Process

In order to ensure the effectiveness of the experiment, the oil field in the same area is selected to complete the data simulation research, and the numerical simulation method designed in this paper and the original numerical simulation method are used to carry out the simulation. In order to ensure the order and consistency of the experimental process, the experimental equipment and samples are set as follows (Table 4).

Table 4. Setting of experimental equipment

Direction of use	Equipment	Parameter
Model processing software	Petrel	
Data storage	Data base	SQL2013
Image processing software	Remote sensing image processing system	
Analog computation	CPU	Intel
Comprehensive treatment	Operating platform	Microsoft

Using this equipment to complete the numerical simulation process, and set its range sample, compare the original method and the data source of this method numerical simulation to complete the experiment process, the data sample is as follows (Table 5).

Table 5. Experimental samples

Number	Sample
Y1	Geophysical prospecting
Y2	Geology
Y3	Well drilling
Y4	Oil recovery
Y5	Production

The above samples are used to complete the experiment, and the experimental results are represented by images, based on which the experimental results are analyzed.

3.2   Simulation Experiment Results and Analysis

Set the experimental results of this method as the experimental group, the results of the original method as the control group. The specific experimental results are as follows:

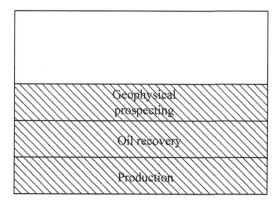

Fig. 6. Original method data source

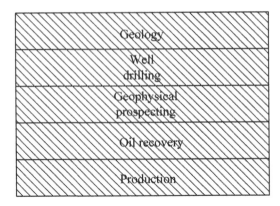

Fig. 7. Data sources of this method

In the above experimental results, the overlapped part between the original method and the data source range of the method in this paper and the experimental sample is shown in shadow. From Figs. 6 and 7, we can see that the data source and sample of the design method in this paper have always been, and the data source of the original method is different from the experimental sample. It can be seen from the above that in the case of the same experimental target, the richer the data source, the higher the accuracy of the numerical simulation results, and the more persuasive. Therefore, the accuracy of the numerical simulation method designed in this paper is higher than that of the original method.

The experiment shows that the accuracy of remaining oil numerical simulation can be effectively improved by using oil field data analysis in remaining oil distribution. The application of this design method in life can effectively improve the research effect of oil industry on oil field reserves, and deal with the rapid development of oil enterprises.

4 Conclusion

For the simulation of remaining oil distribution in the oil field, the total grid number is used to control the accuracy of the simulation results. The computer with appropriate row energy and speed is selected to support the calculation process, so that the numerical simulation can not only describe the distribution of remaining oil, but also meet the requirements of calculation speed. It can be seen from the distribution simulation of remaining oil in most oilfields at present that the remaining oil mainly exists in the edge of the oilfields, the layers with low permeability and the areas with imperfect well pattern. Because the remaining oil in these areas has a large accumulation, a reasonable grid number is set to control the remaining oil characterization results of its distribution, so as to complete the numerical simulation research of remaining oil distribution. In the research, the data processing part is added to improve the accuracy of numerical simulation and provide technical support for the future development of petroleum industry.

References

1. Li, W., Yin, T., Zhao, L., et al.: Architecture characteristics of low sinuosity distributary channel reservoir and its controlling factors on residual oil distribution: a case study of Xingbei Oilfield China. Geoscience **32**(01), 173–182 (2018)
2. Tan, H., Fu, Q., Li, L., et al.: Application of streamline numerical simulation method to study of remaining oil distribution in high water-cut stage oilfield. J. Chengdu Univ. Technol. (Sci. Technol. Edn.) **44**(1), 30–35 (2017)
3. Zhang, J., Lin, C., Zhang, X., et al.: Remaining oil distribution of point bar reservoir based on reservoir architecture and reservoir numerical simulation. Lithol. Reserv. **29**(4), 146–153 (2017)
4. Zhou, Y., Zhang, L., Luo, J., et al.: The numerical simulation study of remaining oil distribution in M reservoir. Unconv. Oil Gas **4**(2), 95–98, 90 (2017)
5. Tian, F., Shi, P., Bai, Y.: Study on numerical simulation and remaining oil distribution law of Yan 912 in Zhangyaoxian Area of Dingbian Oilfield. **4**(3), 70–74 (2017)
6. Zhu, W., Zhang, X., Han, H., et al.: Effect of coordination number on distribution of remaining oil and oil recovery. Contemp. Chem. Ind. **46**(1), 64–67 (2017)
7. Li, H., Zheng, B., Liu, Y., et al.: Fine characterization of the remaining oil after chemical flooding in the thick-layer reservoir—Taking X oilfield as an example. J. Chongqing Univ. Sci. Technol. (Nat. Sci. Edn.) **20**(01), 26–30 (2018)
8. Zhang, W., Guo, L., Chen, D., et al.: Study on current situation and production optimization of L block in Jiyuan Oilfield. Liaoning Chem. Ind. **47**(11), 1175–1177 (2018)
9. Liu, C., Li, Y., Zhang, W., et al.: Remaining oil distribution pattern controlled by interlayer in a oilfield in Bohai Sea. Lithol. Reserv. **29**(05), 148–154 (2017)
10. Fu, X., Yu, G., Ge, J.: Analysis on influence of sandwich on remaining off in Tahe bottom water sandstone reservoir. China Energy Environ. Protect. **39**(10), 199–203 (2017)

Multiple Frame CT Image Sequencing Big Data Batch Clustering Method

Xiao-yan Wang, Guo-hui Wei, Zheng-wei Gu,
Ming Li[(⊠)], and Jin-gang Ma

Shandong University of Traditional Chinese Medicine, Jinan, China
lmzhj@126.com

Abstract. CT image diagnosis technology had developed rapidly in China. In clinical testing, large-scale data gradually existed in the form of sequences. Data clustering was the integration of different substances in an image according to certain properties, but there were still many problems in the use of commonly used data clustering methods in medicine. The current sequencing big data clustering method analysis was still in the research stage and had very important significance. This paper proposed a large-scale batch clustering method based on multi-frame CT images, which was compared with the traditional clustering method, and hoped to provide assistance for clinical applications.

Keywords: Multi-frame CT · Sequencing data · Clustering method

1 Introduction

With the development of CT image technology, the application in clinical detection has been extensive in recent years. However, under actual circumstances, CT technology is affected by many objective conditions, and the needs of clinical testing must also be considered. Data imaging is somewhat defective. How to collect large quantities of data and reconstruct CT images completely and accurately is of great significance for clinical testing, both theoretical and practical [1, 2]. In recent years, although many relatively mature data clustering methods have been studied, the application is also very extensive. For example, filtered back projection data clustering method and iterative image sequencing data clustering method, but the calculation amount is very large, the clustering integrity of the data is low, and the imaging effect is not ideal [3, 4]. Therefore, neither of these methods can be applied to image sequencing big data batch clustering.

In recent years, the technical requirements for medical imaging are very high. In clinical testing, large quantities of data exist in the form of sequences [5]. Because the human body's organizational structure is quite complex, it is difficult to deal with some large-structure images with large data volume. Therefore, many methods of data clustering are not suitable for clinical imaging detection [6]. At present, many medical sequence imaging data clustering methods are in the exploration and research stage. In recent years, many medical scholars have studied data clustering [6], proposed a fuzzy clustering method (CFN), and tested it in medical sequence imaging, but the results

Y.-D. Zhang et al. (Eds.): ICMTEL 2020, LNICST 326, pp. 382–393, 2020.
https://doi.org/10.1007/978-3-030-51100-5_34

show that this method is very sensitive to the initial value of the data. In order to improve this deficiency, the researchers have proposed many ways to improve [8]. For example, based on the genetic algorithm of CFN, although this method can satisfy the shortcomings of the CFN method, the speed of clustering data is very slow [9]. In addition, researchers have proposed a density-based data clustering method, through the density distribution model as a prerequisite for data clustering. If the initial values set are small, the adjacent density is combined, but the accuracy of this method is relatively low. In order to improve the accuracy of the image, a data clustering method based on texture features has been proposed. This method is to generate a matrix according to the texture of the collected data [10]. The accuracy of this method is very high, but the matrix after data generation is sparse, so that there is an influence between each data, affecting the speed of clustering and imaging quality [11]. In general, the above several methods have their own problems, the difference in imaging will directly affect the judgment of certain conditions, not to be underestimated. By analyzing and summarizing the previous research results and experience, this paper proposes a DD-TV clustering method based on multi-frame CT image sequencing data, and achieves a good clustering effect.

In this paper, through the analysis of multi-frame CT image imaging principle, the multi-frame CT image clustering method is studied, and a new method of clustering data with incomplete projection data (DD-TV method) is proposed, which has a high value.

2 Application Analysis of Multi-frame CT Image in Data Batch Clustering

2.1 Principle Analysis of Multi-frame CT Imaging

Medical imaging technology has developed rapidly in clinical testing and is widely used, thus further enhancing the importance of image analysis and research [12]. To some extent, the accuracy of the image is an important basis for clinicians to judge the condition. Medical data clustering plays an important role in the analysis of images. It is also an imaging method under computer simulation technology. With the aid of computer simulation technology, the data is collected, analyzed and studied, and finally imaged [13].

Especially in recent years, with the increasing demand for imaging diagnostic applications, medical image data is more in clinical form in the form of large-scale sequence images [14]. At the same time, the anatomical structure of the human body is very complicated, which makes some traditional clustering methods have some inapplicability in processing such medical sequence images with very complicated structure and very large data volume [15, 16].

In the process of CT image reconstruction based on computer simulation technology, many researchers tend to explore the image reconstruction technology, and have formed a better reconstruction method [17]. For example, image reconstruction based on data analysis, simple operation, small amount of calculation, and fast image reconstruction speed are widely used in clinical detection [18]. However, this method requires very high data integrity. If the projected data is incomplete, it will cause artifacts, and if it is serious, it may cause partial image distortion [19, 20].

The principle of multi-frame CT imaging is shown in Fig. 1 below.

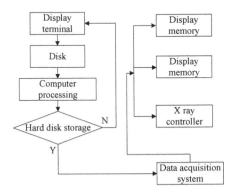

Fig. 1. Principle of multi-frame CT imaging

The basic principle of CT image is to scan a layer of a certain thickness of the inspection part of the human body with an X-ray beam. After the X-ray is received by the detector and transformed into visible light, it is transformed from an photoelectric converter into an electrical signal, which is then converted into a digital signal by an analog/digital converter and fed into a computer for processing. The processing of image formation is like dividing the selected plane into several cuboids with the same volume, which are called voxels. The X-ray attenuation coefficient or absorption coefficient of each voxel is calculated and arranged into a matrix, that is, a digital matrix. The digital matrix can be stored on disk or cd-rom. A CT image is made by converting each digit in the digital matrix into a small square of gray varying from black to white through a digital/analog converter.

2.2 Multi-frame CT Image Sequencing Big Data Bulk Clustering Method Analysis

The traditional multi-frame CT image sequencing big data batch clustering method directly processes the original data. However, the differences between the data samples are particularly small, the speed of clustering is very slow, and the phenomenon of repeated clustering is prone to occur, which increases the difficulty of clinical detection to some extent. Therefore, this paper proposes the DD-TV clustering method by spatially correlating the data of medical image sequencing. This method can convert the data of the original space into the feature space, which not only greatly reduces the amount of data, but also improves the speed of clustering. More importantly, the transformed data can display its own attributes in the feature space, greatly improving the accuracy of clustering.

The flow chart of multi-frame CT image reconstruction is shown in the following Fig. 2:

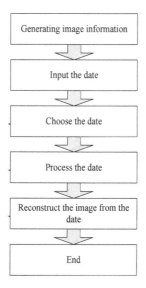

Fig. 2. Multi-frame CT image reconstruction flowchart

Multi-frame CT image program:

```
Begin
clear all;
clc
load matlab;
%reconstruct
Figure(1)
title('original image')
imshow(P);

%the size of image
N = 258;
%coordinate of image
center= floor((N + 1)/2);
xleft = -center + 1;
x = (1:N) - 1 + xleft;
x=repmat(x,N,1);

ytop = center - 1;
y= (N:-1:1).' - N + ytop;
y = repmat(y, 1, N);

%angle change

theta1 = theta1*pi/180;
costheta = cos(theta1);
sintheta = sin(theta1);

len = size(R1,1);
ctrIdx = ceil(len/2);
img = zeros(N,class(R1));
for i = 1:length(theta1)
 proj = R1(:,i);
 t = x.*costheta(i) + y.*sintheta(i);
 a = floor(t);
 img=img+(t-a).*proj(a+1+ctrId+(a+1-t).*proj(a+ctrIdx);
 img = img*pi/(2*length(theta1));

%show reconstruction image
    Figure(2);
     imshow(img,[]);
  end
```

A flowchart of a DD-TV data clustering method based on a multi-frame CT image is shown in Fig. 3:

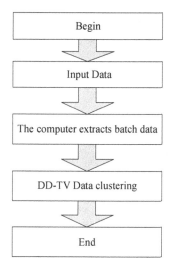

Fig. 3. DD-TV data clustering method flow chart

DDTV data clustering procedure:

```
price = [1.1,1.2,1.3,1.4,10,11,20,21,33,34]

increase = [1 for i in range(10)]

data = np.array([price,increase],dtype='float32')

class Myhcluster( ):

def __init__(self):

print('start system clustering')

'''The start function of the system clustering method, there are two input
parameters of the input variable and the distance calculation method'''

def prepare(self,data,method='zx'):

if method == 'zx'

self.zx(data)

'''Center of gravity method for system clustering'''

def zx(self,data):
token = len(data[0,:])

flu_data = data.copy()

classfier =[[] for i in range(len(data[1,]))]

LSdist     =     np.array([0 for i  in range(token ** 2)],
dtype='float32').reshape([len(data[0, :]), token])

index = 0

while token > 1:

'''Calculating the distance matrix'''

for i in range(len(data[0,:])):

for j in range(len(data[0,:])):

LSdist[i,j]=round(((flu_data[0,i]-flu_data[0,j])**2+(flu_data[1,i]- flu_data[1,j])*
*2)**0.5,4)

end

#Implementation of System Clustering
> rm(list=ls())
> a <- Sys.time()
> price <- c(1.1,1.2,1.3,1.4,10,11,20,21,33,34)
> increase <- rep(1,10)
> data <- data.frame(price,increase)#generate sample data frame
> d<- dist(data)#create sample distance array
> hc <- hclust(d,'centroid')#systematic clustering with center of gravity>
cbind(hcmerge,hcmerge,hcheight)# demonstrate the classification process
```

First, we first detect the distance-driven operation of the image orthographic projection. We select the circular plate with uniform size as the pseudo-true image. The distribution of the projection values obtained by the distance-driven operation of the image orthographic projection is shown in Fig. 4 The horizontal axis represents the detector, and the number of detectors is 120; the vertical axis represents the projection value detected by the corresponding detector. From the Fig. 4, we can find that the projection value calculated by the distance projection of the image is almost stable, and there is no fluctuation.

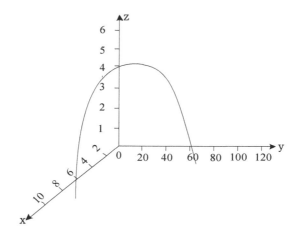

Fig. 4. Distance-driven orthographic projection

Let the image be initialized to W, and set the number of times of the DD-TV method to i, $i = 1$, $W[i] = 0$.

Constrain the multi-frame CT image, and set the constrained image to $p[n]$, that is: if $p[n] \geq 0$, $p[n] = W[i]$, otherwise, $p[n] = 0$.

The speed algorithm finds the minimum value of the objective function, and the number of times is t, $t = 1, 2, \ldots, N_t$. When t = 1,

$$P[n, t] = P[n] \tag{1}$$

When the number of DD-TV method is $i = i + 1$,

$$W[i + 1] = W[i] \tag{2}$$

$$N = i_1 g_1 + i_2 g_2 \tag{3}$$

The DD-TV algorithm flow chart is shown in Fig. 5.

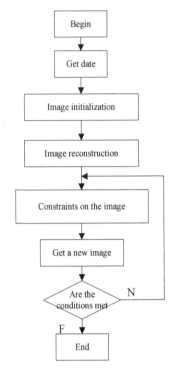

Fig. 5. DD-TV algorithm flow chart

3 Experimental Design and Result Analysis

In order to verify the application effect of the method of multi-frame CT image sequencing big data clustering, a simulation experiment was carried out. The experimental operating system is Windows 10, and the simulation software is matlab 7.0. The traditional method is selected as the experimental comparison method to comprehensively compare the performance of different methods. The experimental data are shown in Fig. 6.

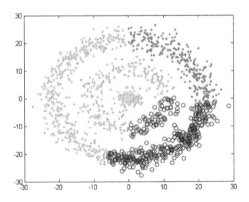

Fig. 6. Experimental data

The results are shown in Table 1, Fig. 7 and Fig. 8.

Table 1. Performance comparison

Method	Precision	Speed
Traditional method	91.86%	321.71 s
DD-TV method	95%	168.3 s

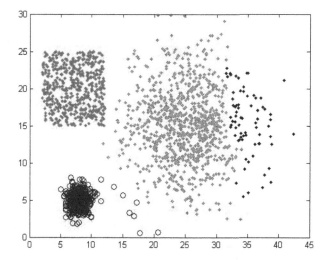

Fig. 7. Clustering effect of traditional method

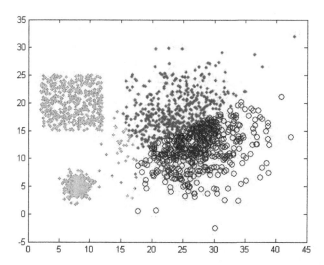

Fig. 8. Clustering effect of DD-TV method

The study found that the DD-TV method not only has high clustering accuracy, but also greatly improves the speed of image data processing.

The DD-TV method does not need to store a large number of data matrix systems, but calculates the individual data in the matrix sequence at all times, saving a lot of time and space. At the same time, this method does not need to go through the entire detector and image, just cyclically calculate the data on the projection line. Compared with the traditional iterative data clustering method, the overall speed is improved, and combined with the principle of data standardization optimization, it has an important impact on the quality of reconstructed images.

With the development of technology, the way of CT scanning is very different from the past, and multi-frame images can be obtained in a short time. Because the scanning time is very short, a movie image can be obtained, which can prevent image artifacts after motion. For the research and analysis of DD-TV data clustering based on multi-frame CT images, there are also many shortcomings in the experiment. In this paper, the image is reconstructed only under 2D conditions, and image reconstruction under 3D conditions can be achieved in later studies. Moreover, other optimization methods can be used in subsequent studies when optimizing the objective function, making the calculation more accurate. It is hoped that the research in this paper can provide some help for clinical testing.

4   Conclusion

Along with the development of image processing technology, image feature analysis method is used for medical diagnosis has become one of the important tool of case analysis, common medical images with CT image, ultrasound image and X-ray image, etc., for case analysis and diagnosis of CT image which provides a powerful data support and intuitive image, in the CT image acquisition, the need for more frame scan and gathering, finally realizes the sequencing batch clustering large data, analysis of CT image can improve the efficiency and capacity, is of great significance in the aspect of doctors for patients. On the basis of studying the characteristics of traditional clustering methods, a multi-frame CT image sequencing method is proposed. The simulation results show that this method has high clustering accuracy and low clustering time. The method proposed in this paper provides a new idea for the further development of multi-frame CT image sequencing big data clustering technology, which improves the efficiency and ability of CT image analysis and plays an important role in the accurate acquisition of patients' conditions by doctors.

References

1. Bricq, S., Collet, C.H., Armspach, J.P.: Unifying framework for multimodal brain MRI segmentation based on hidden markov chains. Med. Image **23**(12), 22–25 (2017)
2. Gilbert: Ultrasonic detection based on computer simulation technology, **36**(4), 94–95 (2017)
3. Liew, A.W.C., Yan, H.: An adaptive spatial fuzzy clustering algorithm for 3-D MR image segmentation. IEEE Trans. Med. Imaging **11**(2), 60–62 (2017)

4. Zhang, D.-Q., Chen, S.-C.: A novel kemelized fuzzy c-means algorithm with application in medical image sementation. Artif. Intell. Med. **19**(2), 37–38 (2017)
5. Chuang, K.S., Tzang, H.L., Chen, T.-J.: Fuzzy c-means clustering with spatial information for image segmentation. Comput. Med. Imaging Graph. **3**(10), 123–124 (2017)
6. Liu, S., Pan, Z., Cheng, X.: A novel fast fractal image compression method based on distance clustering in high dimensional sphere surface. Fractals **25**(4), 1740004 (2017)
7. Tang, H., Dillenseger, J.L., Bao, X.D., Luo, L.M.: A vectorial image soft segmentation method based on neighborhood weighted gaussian mixture model. Comput. Med. Imaging Graph. **42**(12), 34–36 (2017)
8. Raghuvira Pratap, A., Vani, K.S., Rama Devi, J., KnageeswaraRao, V.A.: An efficient density based improved K-medoids clustering algorithm. Int. J. Adv. Comput. Sci. Appl. **3**(9), 25–27 (2017)
9. Chabat, F., Yang, G.-Z., Hansell, D.-M.: Obstructive lung diseases: texture classification for differentiation at CT. Radiology **5**(34), 57–58 (2017)
10. Kuo, W.-F., Lin, C.-Y., Sun, Y.-N.: MR images segmentation. In: Computer Society Conference on Computer Vision and Pattern Recognition, vol. 27, no. 5, pp. 67–69 (2017)
11. Yang, J., Xie, Y., Guo, Y.: Panel data clustering analysis based on composite PCC: a parametric approach. Cluster Comput. **34**(5), 1–11 (2018)
12. Huang, S., Ren, Y., Xu, Z.: Robust multi-view data clustering with multi-view capped-norm K-means. Neurocomputing **311**, 197–208 (2018)
13. Bo, Y.: The data clustering based dynamic risk identification of biological immune system: mechanism, method and simulation. Cluster Comput. **7330**, 1–14 (2018). https://doi.org/10.1007/s10586-018-1960-2
14. Payne, W.V., Heo, J., Domanski, P.A.: A data-clustering technique for fault detection and diagnostics in field-assembled air conditioners. Int. J. Air-Cond. Refrig. **26**, 1850015 (2018)
15. Das, P., Das, D.K., Dey, S.: A new class topper optimization algorithm with an application to data clustering. IEEE Trans. Emerg. Top. Comput. **PP**(99), 1 (2018)
16. Ma, R., Angryk, R.A., Riley, P., et al.: Coronal mass ejection data clustering and visualization of decision trees. Astrophys. J. Suppl. **236**(1), 14 (2018)
17. Karpinski, P., Patai, A., Hap, W., et al.: Multilevel omic data clustering reveals variable contribution of methylator phenotype to integrative cancer subtypes. Epigenomics **10**(3), 1289–1299 (2018). epi-2018-0057
18. Fan, W., Bouguila, N., Du, J.X., et al.: Axially symmetric data clustering through Dirichlet process mixture models of Watson distributions. IEEE Trans. Neural Netw. Learn. Syst. **PP**(99), 1–12 (2018)
19. Popova, O., Kuznetsova, E., Sazonova, T.: Algorithms of data clustering in assessing the transport infrastructure of the region. In: MATEC Web of Conferences, vol. 170, no. 3, pp. 123–130 (2018)
20. Sriadhi, S., Gultom, S., Martiano, M., et al.: K-means method with linear search algorithm to reduce Means Square Error (MSE) within data clustering. In: IOP Conference Series Materials Science and Engineering, vol. 434, no. 3, p. 012032 (2018)

Research on Scale Space Fusion Method of Medical Big Data Video Image

Xiao-yan Wang, Guo-hui Wei, Zheng-wei Gu, Jin-gang Ma, Ming Li,
and Hui Cao[✉]

Shandong University of Traditional Chinese Medicine, Jinan, China
sdnuwxy@163.com

Abstract. In the research of scale space fusion of medical big data video image, due to the different spatial management methods of multi-source video image, the efficiency of multi-dimensional scale space fusion is low, so a new image scale space fusion method is designed according to the characteristics of medical big data video image. From the aspect of video image visualization and multi-dimensional space fusion, the space fusion method is designed respectively, and the sampling survey method is adopted for experimental analysis to obtain experimental data. The experimental results show that the proposed method is feasible and reliable.

Keywords: Medical treatment big data · Video image · Scale space fusion

1 Introduction

Image fusion is the integration of two or more complementary bands and useful information of a sensor into a unified image or integrated image feature for observation or further processing through a fusion system to achieve more accurate and comprehensive recognition of the target or scene. Analyzed image processing method [1]. With the development of society and the advancement of technology, the application of digital medical equipment in hospitals has become more widespread [2], so medical video data is growing at an unimaginable speed. However, until now, medical video image storage and management methods have lagged behind, which has led to great challenges in medical image video storage and processing [3].

The images of different imaging technologies, imaging directions and anatomical parts are mixed together, which need to be fused and managed for further analysis and utilization [4]. Therefore, the problem of video image fusion and processing under medical big data has become a social hot issue. Medical big data video image contains a lot of information [5]. There are usually many images for the same scene, so it is necessary to integrate them to realize information visualization, which can obtain more accurate and reliable description for the same scene, and improve the accuracy of medical diagnosis [6]. There are many research achievements on the scale-space fusion method of medical big data video images, such as the multi-feature based scale-space fusion method of medical big data video images. Firstly, edge features and average gradient features of the low-frequency coefficients after multi-scale decomposition

Y.-D. Zhang et al. (Eds.): ICMTEL 2020, LNICST 326, pp. 394–402, 2020.
https://doi.org/10.1007/978-3-030-51100-5_35

were extracted, and the correlation signal intensity ratio features of the high-frequency coefficients were extracted. Then, the edge feature level fusion is used to guide the pixel level image fusion to obtain the high frequency coefficient. In order to solve the problem that the simple weighting method in the synthesis module can easily cause local blurring of edges or textures, the multi-scale decomposition coefficients of the same position are synthesized in two cases. Finally, the low frequency coefficients of fusion images are obtained by means of adaptive weighting of average gradient features, and the low frequency and high frequency coefficients are inverted by multi-scale transformation to obtain the fusion images. However, this method has the problem of poor fusion image quality, and the practical application effect is not good.

It is very important for the hospital information system that the video image scale space under the medical big data can achieve complete fusion. Instead of simply overlaying the video images together, they form a composite image with more information, reducing the uncertainty of the information. The systematic improvement of medical image can make the hospital staff master the patient's medical record information more accurately, simplify the work flow, greatly improve the efficiency of the hospital [7, 8], and make the hospital no longer be unable to distinguish each person's electronic information because of the number of patients, thus leading to the decline of the efficiency of the people's medical treatment. Therefore, in the hospital big data environment, the processing and management of video image is very important [9–11]. Then, from the different attributes of video image to explore, we can design the scale space fusion scheme of medical big data video image.

2 Design of Scale Space Fusion Method for Medical Big Data Video Image

In terms of the design of video image scale space fusion method under medical big data, the visualization and multi-dimensional animation in image video should be considered first, because the data form of these modes is complex [12, 13], and the attribute problem should be considered to fuse them, as shown in Fig. 1, which is the image scale space fusion method designed under medical big data.

It can be seen from Fig. 1 that in the process of video image scale space fusion under medical big data [14], the steps of data processing, visual fusion and multi-dimensional scale space fusion are carried out at the same time, then the image format of the same attribute is screened, and the image of the same attribute is fused, and finally the fusion result is output.

2.1 Visual Fusion Design of Medical Big Data Video Image

Medical data information system is a system that integrates large-scale data, so it is necessary to fuse the scale space of image and video image retained in the medical process [15], so as to facilitate the management of staff. Video image visualization is a process that can not be ignored for video image processing, and it is also a key part for medical big data video image to realize scale space fusion [16]. The computer technology is applied to the construction of video image informatization under the medical

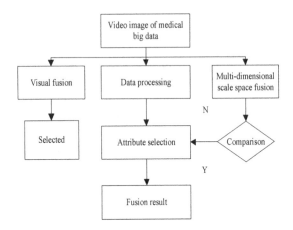

Fig. 1. Image spatial fusion method

big data. Through the processing of the computer in the video image visualization level and multi-dimensional animation level, the same attribute data fusion is carried out, so as to organize the medical big data more conveniently. Therefore, the computer technology is very important in the video image processing and data attribute screening fusion [17].

In the process of video image processing, computer visual fusion method can sort out the same format of visual image. The problem of medical security is very important. Like the financial information system of the hospital, the video image of the hospital should also ensure that the patient's data cannot be leaked, because once the medical data is leaked, the consequences will be unimaginable. Then the video image visualization data processing also needs to have the function of medical data protection, so as to realize the orderly and efficient work of the hospital. The visual fusion method of video image under the medical big data can guarantee the data screening of the hospital video image without changing the format, attribute and size, so as to lay the foundation for the realization of the scale space fusion of video image under the medical big data [18].

2.2   Multi Dimension Scale Space Fusion Design of Medical Big Data Video Image

In the scale space of video image, multi-dimensional data is very common, and it is also common in medical information system, so it is a highly feasible method to use multi-dimensional scale space fusion method to carry out spatial fusion of medical big data image, this method is to recombine and fuse the data packets with different information content. It is the result of upgrading and fusing the video image by using the key technology of information technology. It uses the relevant functions of data recognition by computer to fuse the medical video image data in scale space, and uses the public to filter the data attributes, so as to better manage the video image data [19]. The multi-dimensional scale space fusion method of computer data can also be called the production tool of video image informatization under medical big data. The multi-dimensional scale space fusion method of computer data can recognize the size, attributes, format of image and whether the image can be fused, and filter the data through the following formula to achieve the goal of data fusion.

$$S_x = \frac{1}{n} \sum_{i=1}^{n} (x_j - X_j)(x_j - X_j)^T \qquad (1)$$

Formula: T represents the magnitude of multi-source video image data. Since the feature matrix S_x does not satisfy the diagonal matrix in the geometric matrix, it is necessary to find the orthogonal matrix W of multi-source data, and meet the relationship of $W^T S_x W$ related diagonal matrix. Unilateralization is carried out for matrix S_x, and the geometric features of the matrix are decomposed in the process of unilateralization. The feature polynomial of feature matrix S_x should meet the following conditions,

$$|S_x - \lambda I| = 0 \qquad (2)$$

In the formula: I represents the sequence characteristics of the correlation matrix; λ represents the data satisfying the characteristic values of all multi-source video image data. The absolute value is the single direction of the support vector. Because the multi-source video image scale space features need to express all the multi-source data, the size of the guarantee value is enough [20]. Take λ into the correlation diagonal matrix, and set the corresponding feature vector as V, and establish the relationship as follows:

$$X_j S_x W = \mathrm{diag}(\lambda) V \qquad (3)$$

The orthogonal matrix W of multi-source video image data features is obtained by formula (3), and W contains $[V, V_1, \cdots, V_X]$; V, which represents the intersection features of multi-source data.

3 Experimental Demonstration and Analysis

In order to verify the effectiveness of the proposed scale space fusion method for medical big data video image, a simulation experiment is designed. During the experiment, the video image archiving of a hospital is taken as the experimental object, and the computer fusion experiment is carried out for the different attribute video images in this system. The traditional method is compared with the scale space fusion method of video image proposed in this paper, so as to effectively analyze the applicability of the two methods and the practicability in the scale space fusion of video image. Firstly, the speed and stability of video image data fusion management after the application of the two methods are compared. The better the index is, the better the comprehensive performance of the method is. Then the image resolution of different fusion methods is compared. The higher the image resolution is, the better the fusion image quality is. Finally, the lower the error rate is, indicating that the higher the fusion accuracy is, the better the image is the clearer the image. The design of simulation experiment parameters is shown in Table 1.

Table 1. Simulation experiment parameter design

Project	Parameter
CPU	Intel Xeon
CPU hard disk capacity	1.5T
CPU frequency	1.2 GHz
Random access memory	128 GB
Operating system	Windows 10
Monitor resolution	1280*1024
Simulation software	MALTAB 7.11

The experimental data are shown in Table 2.

Table 2 Experimental data

	Parameter	Remarks parameter
Multiple video image management coefficient	6.75	Ensure it is within the controllable range of the experiment
Number of multiple video image data sources	7–8	Random collocation
Number of multiple video image data sources	6G	Standard limit unchanged
Data integration accuracy	1.65TH	±0.5TH

An example of data sample is shown in the figure below (Fig. 2).

After the above experimental preparation process is ready, the data will be sampled and compared with the scale space fusion method proposed in this paper by using the traditional method. The experimental results are shown in Fig. 3.

As shown in Fig. 3, the number of video images of the traditional method is between 0–63, and the number of video images of the method in this paper is between 0–91, which shows that the video image scale space fusion method proposed in this paper has higher management speed than the traditional method, and the data fusion management is relatively stable, which shows that the method in this paper is effective and reliable.

Figure 4 are the image separation rates after the scale space fusion of medical video image using the traditional method and the method in this paper, which are the main reflection of the fusion image quality.

It can be seen from the analysis of Fig. 4 that the resolution of the output image is always lower than 80 dpi after using the traditional method for medical video image spatial fusion. After using the method in this paper for medical video image spatial

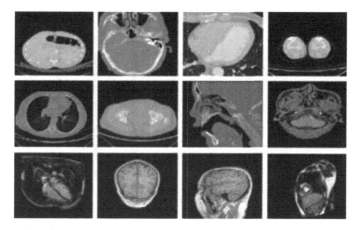

Fig. 2. Example of medical big data video data

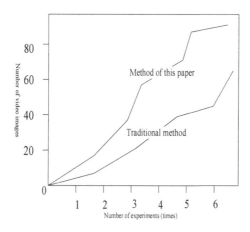

Fig. 3. Comparison diagram of video image data fusion

fusion, the resolution of the output image is about 300 dpi, the imaging quality is high, more clear, and the actual application effect is good.

Image fusion error rate comparison test is shown in Fig. 5.

From the analysis of Fig. 5, it can be seen that the fusion error rate of the traditional method is between 19% and 23%, while the error rate of the method in this paper is always lower than 5%, which shows that the image scale space fusion error of the method in this paper is far lower than that of the traditional method, with high fusion accuracy and feasibility.

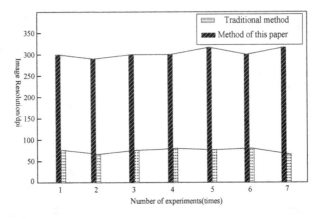

Fig. 4. Different methods of fusion image resolution comparison

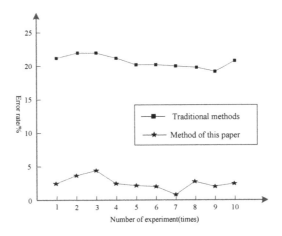

Fig. 5. The error rate of different methods is compared

4   Conclusions

In the aspect of video image information fusion, it is necessary to classify the database generation and images with different attribute formats, and to achieve a large number of fusion of image scale space efficiently to a certain extent, so as to promote the continuous progress of medical information management technology. So according to the characteristics of medical big data video image, this paper designs a new image scale space fusion method. From the aspect of video image visualization and multi-dimensional space fusion, the space fusion method is designed respectively, and the sampling survey method is adopted for experimental analysis to obtain experimental data. The experiment verifies the feasibility and reliability of the design method. This method is very important for the improvement of medical system, the effective arrangement of medical data, the convenience of staff operation, and the promotion of medical development. It is also of clinical application value for the people's life and the development of the country. In the future research, we should further describe the local features of medical images, and build a fusion classification model combining local and global features to further improve the classification performance.

References

1. Shao, J., Chang, H., Zheng, Z., et al.: Image informatization construction analysis. China Tissue Eng. Res. **21**(23), 3767–3772 (2017)
2. Zhang, W., Guo, W., Yang Society.: Based on the medical big data. Comput. Simul. (8), 142–145 (2006)
3. Xie, X., Jiang, B., Liu, J.: Visual tunnel fire simulation system development. Comput. Simul. (06), 221–231+159 (2008)
4. Tao, H., Zou, W., Yang, H.: Robust dissipative iterative learning fault-tolerant control for Medical big data. Control Theor. Appl. **33**(3), 329–335 (2016)
5. Liu, S., Pan, Z., Cheng, X.: A novel fast fractal image compression method based on distance clustering in high dimensional sphere surface. Fractals **25**(4), 17–22 (2017)
6. Gao, Z.: Space target image fusion method based on image clarity criterion. Opt. Eng. **56**(5), 53–60 (2017)
7. Liu, S., Zhang, Z., Qi, L., et al.: A fractal image encoding method based on statistical loss used in agricultural image compression. Multimed. Tools Appl. **75**(23), 15525–15536 (2016). https://doi.org/10.1007/s11042-014-2446-8
8. Yu, L., Xun, C., Wang, Z., et al.: Deep learning for pixel-level image fusion: recent advances and future prospects. Inf. Fus. **42**(6), 158–173 (2018)
9. Yu, L., Xun, C., Ward, R.K., et al.: Image fusion with convolutional sparse representation. IEEE Sig. Process. Lett. **23**(12), 1882–1886 (2016)
10. Li, S., Kang, X., Fang, L., et al.: Pixel-level image fusion: a survey of the state of the art. Inf. Fus. **33**(6), 100–112 (2017)
11. Wang, Z., Shuai, W., Ying, Z., et al.: Review of image fusion based on pulse-coupled neural network. Arch. Comput. Methods Eng. **23**(4), 659–671 (2016). https://doi.org/10.1007/s11831-015-9154-z
12. Ghassemian, H.: A review of remote sensing image fusion methods. Inf. Fus. **32**(PA), 75–89 (2016)
13. Fakhari, F., Mosavi, M.R., Lajvardi, M.M.: Image fusion based on multi-scale transform and sparse representation: image energy approach. IET Image Proc. **11**(11), 1041–1049 (2017)
14. Ayhan, B., Dao, M., Kwan, C., et al.: A novel utilization of image registration techniques to process mastcam images in Mars Rover with applications to image fusion, pixel clustering, and anomaly detection. IEEE J. Sel. Top. Appl. Earth Obs. Remote Sens. **99**(99), 1–12 (2017)
15. Hansen, N.L., Kesch, C., Barrett, T., et al.: Multicentre evaluation of targeted and systematic biopsies using magnetic resonance and ultrasound image-fusion guided transperineal prostate biopsy in patients with a previous negative biopsy. BJU Int. **120**(5), 631 (2016)
16. Stecco, A., Buemi, F., Cassarà, A., et al.: Comparison of retrospective PET and MRI-DWI (PET/MRI-DWI) image fusion with PET/CT and MRI-DWI in detection of cervical and endometrial cancer lymph node metastases. Radiologia Medica **121**(7), 537–545 (2016). https://doi.org/10.1007/s11547-016-0626-5
17. Wang, K., Qi, G., Zhu, Z., et al.: A novel geometric dictionary construction approach for sparse representation based image fusion. Entropy **19**(7), 306 (2017)

18. Wang, H.P., Liu, Z.Q., Fang, X., et al.: Method for image fusion based on adaptive pulse coupled neural network in curvelet domain. J. Optoelectron. Laser **27**(4), 429–436 (2016)
19. Bungert, L., Coomes, D.A., Ehrhardt, M.J., et al.: Blind image fusion for hyperspectral imaging with the directional total variation. Inverse Prob. **34**(4), 1–12 (2018)
20. Du, L., Sun, H., Wang, S., et al.: High dynamic range image fusion algorithm for moving targets. Acta Optica Sinica **37**(4), 45–52 (2017)
21. Shibata, T., Tanaka, M.: Versatile visible and near-infrared image fusion based on high visibility area selection. J. Electron. Imaging **25**(1), 013016 (2016)
22. Hafner, D., Weickert, J.: Variational image fusion with optimal local contrast. Comput. Graph. Forum **35**(1), 100–112 (2016)
23. Yu, L., Xun, C., Hu, P., et al.: Multi-focus image fusion with a deep convolutional neural network. Inf. Fus. **36**, 191–207 (2017)
24. Xu, X., Dong, S., Wang, G., et al.: Multimodal medical image fusion using PCNN optimized by the QPSO algorithm. Appl. Soft Comput. **46**(6), 588–595 (2016)
25. Ma, K., Li, H., Yong, H., et al.: Robust multi-exposure image fusion: a structural patch decomposition approach. IEEE Trans. Image Process. **PP**(99), 1 (2017)

Data Mining Method of Malicious Attack Based on Characteristic Frequency

Jia Luo[(⊠)] and Chan Zhang

School of Information Technology, Guangdong Industry Polytechnic,
Guangzhou, China
luojia314@163.com

Abstract. Aiming at the problem of high false alarm rate and failure rate in traditional data mining methods of malicious attacks, a data mining method of malicious attacks based on characteristic frequency is designed. Preprocess the original data in the data set, select the minimum attribute subset, use the discretization to process the unified data format, take the new subset as the input of feature frequency extraction of malicious attack data, extract the feature frequency according to the different protocols of malicious attack data transmission, integrate it into the value data mining algorithm, and use the spatial mapping principle to realize the malicious attack data excavate. The experimental results show that: compared with the traditional data mining method, the false alarm rate and failure rate of the designed malicious attack data mining method based on the feature frequency are reduced by 0.3 and 0.2 respectively, which shows that the method is more suitable for practical projects.

Keywords: Feature frequency · Malicious attack · Data mining · Spatial mapping principle

1 Introduction

Various attacks against Android are emerging in an endless stream. Malware detection for Android has become a very important link in the field of mobile security in recent years. Among them, web browsing accounts for a very large proportion of these activities. Because of this, many lawbreakers and hackers aim at the vulnerability of people's weak awareness of network security and deliberately carry out malicious activities attacking and intruding into the user's system, launching malicious attacks from different terminals used by the user, no matter web page or software, are extremely vulnerable to serious harm, which is the most serious problem of network security at present, greatly endangering the data security of the user using the Internet, and even causing serious economic losses [1].

Due to the continuous improvement of network speed and database technology, the number of access and operation log data generated in the Internet is increasing [2]. In the early stage, only relying on human power to extract the characteristic data of malicious attacks and normal behaviors from the log data has been unable to cope with the current large and complex network environment, so it is necessary to make corresponding improvement according to the actual needs. Using data mining method is a simple and effective countermeasure.

Data mining refers to the process of extracting effective and potentially useful knowledge and patterns from a large number of uncertain and rough data, which is suitable for extracting behavioral features from a large number of historical data [3]. The technical characteristics of data mining meet the application requirements of building rule base. This can not only improve the accuracy of mining malicious attack data, but also effectively update the rule base intelligently, greatly ensuring the data security [4]. However, the traditional data mining methods can not extract the characteristics of malicious attack data completely, which makes it easy to mine out the normal security data when mining malicious attack data, resulting in data loss. When using the relevant data, there are different failures, and even the property loss of users. Therefore, the data mining method of malicious attack based on the characteristic frequency is designed, and the problems existing in the traditional data mining method are solved by using the characteristic of the characteristic frequency.

2 Design of Data Mining Method for Malicious Attacks Based on Characteristic Frequency

2.1 Data Preprocessing

The main task of data preprocessing stage is to randomly sample N records of normal data and malicious attack data specified in data set D, then filter all attribute $Q = \{Q_1, Q_2, \cdots Q_n\}$ of the selected records, and then filter out the required sub attribute set $q = \{Q_1, Q_2, \cdots Q_n\}$ according to the expression meaning and processing needs of each attribute for the next stage of processing.

Assuming that there are T normal data and I malicious attack data in database D, what we need to do in this stage is to sample N_1 normal data set D_1 from T normal data and N_2 attack connection data set D_2 from T malicious attack data. Take normal data extraction as an example, open the file containing data set D, read a record in the file as *line*, judge *line* as empty, then close the file, otherwise generate a random number between [0, T] *temp*, judge whether *temp* is less than or equal to N_2, if the result is "yes", then add the record to D_1, otherwise, continue to read the data in the file, cycle the above operations until all the numbers according to the completion cycle [5].

According to the above process, the algorithm is executed once for malicious attack data, and the required normal data subset D_1 and malicious attack data subset D_2 are selected. The process flow chart is shown in Fig. 1:

The purpose of the above filtering process is to filter out the relevant attributes with important meanings from the alternate attribute set. At the same time, ensure that the filtered data is the minimum set of attributes that can fully describe the network behavior [6].

After the completion of data filtering, discretization is carried out to deal with the data format. The continuous variables in the data are discretized. According to the defined functions, the functions are divided into specific linear intervals and given membership degree. In the very complex network connection data, the field types are

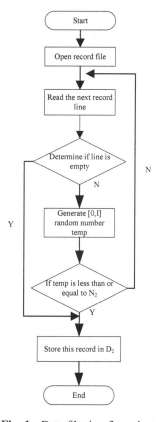

Fig. 1. Data filtering flow chart

binary, discrete and continuous [7]. In many previous studies, the treatment of continuous variables is to divide them into specific intervals according to different interval settings, which is the division of Cartesian sets [8]. The filtered data q in the data set is shown in Table 1:

Table 1. q data example table

Serial number	TID	q
1	001	500
2	002	400
3	003	600
4	004	700
5	005	800

The conversion function of variable q is defined as:

$$f(x) = \begin{cases} low & x \le 400 \\ mid & 400 \le x \le 700 \\ high & x \ge 700 \end{cases} \tag{1}$$

According to the above functions, q of all records is transformed into linear interval q', and the division results are shown in Table 2.

Table 2. q data example discretization table

TID	q	q'
001	500	Mid
002	400	Low
003	600	Mid
004	700	High
005	800	High

In the above contents, mid, low and high represent that the q-transform of data set is divided into three linear intervals. The membership functions of dividing q to these three linear intervals are given as follows:

$$f_{low}(x) = \begin{cases} 1.0 & x \le \alpha \\ \frac{x-\alpha}{\eta-\alpha} & \eta \le x \le \alpha \\ 0 & x \ge \alpha \end{cases} \tag{2}$$

$$f_{mid}(x) = \begin{cases} 0 & x \le \alpha \\ \frac{x-\mu}{\alpha-\eta} & \eta \le x \le \alpha \\ 1.0 & x = \alpha \\ \frac{x-\omega}{\alpha-\omega} & \alpha < x < \omega \\ 0 & x \ge \omega \end{cases} \tag{3}$$

$$f_{high}(x) = \begin{cases} 0 & x \le \alpha \\ \frac{x-\alpha}{\omega-\alpha} & \alpha \le x \le \omega \\ 1.0 & x \ge \omega \end{cases} \tag{4}$$

The membership functions defined by the above three formulas are shown in Fig. 2.

The database information processed by the above membership function is shown in Table 3.

After discretizing the malicious attack data set D_2 and normal training data set D_1 processed in the previous stage with the above membership functions, a new attack training data set D_{2c} and normal training data set D_{1c} are formed as the input of feature frequency extraction in the next stage.

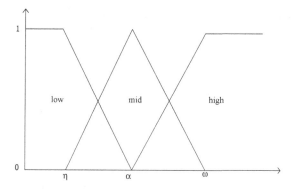

Fig. 2. Membership function

Table 3. Discrete processing data information

TID	q		
	q_{low}	q_{mid}	q_{high}
001	0.5	0.5	0
002	1.0	0	0
003	0	1.0	0
004	0	0.5	0.5
005	0	0	1.0

2.2   Extract Characteristic Frequency of Malicious Attack Data

Although there are many kinds of malicious attacks, they can be roughly divided into three forms (because Internet protocol is TCP/IP protocol, network layer is IP datagram, network layer is mainly two protocols, TCP protocol and UDP protocol, one is connection oriented protocol, the other is datagram service) [9].

The first is network packet data itself. Generally speaking, network data packets of different protocols are generally divided into two parts: Protocol head and data. Protocol head includes relevant management and control information for network packet transmission [10]. The information of data part load is generally divided into two kinds: one is protocol control and management information, the other is data information. The protocol control and management information of the protocol header and the data part load are strictly regulated by different protocols. Data information is produced in various network applications, which can be ordinary binary data sequence or string sequence [11]. At the IP network packet level, IP network packet encapsulation mainly includes Internet control message protocol, IGMP (Internet Group Management Protocol), TCP (transmission layer control protocol) and UDP (User Datagram Protocol). Most of the network malicious attacks are also realized through these four protocols. In the attack process, the network packet from the protocol header data and content may be different from the normal access characteristics [12].

The second form is the relationship between network packet and packet (packet sequence). It can be found that in some malicious attacks, although a single data packet conforms to RFC standard, the sequence of consecutive packets is different from the normal sequence. Because the data packets transmitted on the network are not arbitrary but according to the corresponding protocol, the sequence of packets must have its regularity, showing a specific frequency [13].

The third form is aimed at the statistical characteristics of network connection. In terms of the performance of data packets, some malicious attacks are similar to normal packets on the surface of a single packet, and the short-term packet sequence also conforms to the normal network transmission protocol. However, the statistics of various ways for a certain period of time or a certain length of network connection will form unique statistical characteristics, which can be distinguished from normal network access.

According to the above characteristics of malicious attacks on the transmission data, we use different data mining algorithms to analyze the huge amount of network data stored in the database, extract the appropriate characteristic frequency of malicious attacks data, and ensure that the extracted characteristic frequency does not take any subjective factors.

Malicious attack data is transmitted according to certain rules and protocols, and the characteristic frequency is shown in two aspects: one is reflected in the protocol header of each layer from the data link layer to the application layer, and the other is reflected in the fixed byte string TCP flow of the data part of the data part of the network data packet. Through the above analysis, the feature frequency is extracted.

First of all, historical data is classified: each kind of malicious attack data as a category, normal access data as the background class Z, because the main network protocol on the Internet is TCP/IP protocol, most of the malicious attack data is also carried out by TCP/IP protocol, so the main parsing method of TCP /IP protocol is different. For the common TCP protocol, because the TCP protocol is a connection oriented transport layer protocol, there is no connection between the whole data generated by the application program and the real single TCP packet, so the protocol data part takes all the data transmitted in the complete connection as the analysis object, and the data part of the single TCP packet as the analysis object. UDP protocol is a datagram protocol in the transport layer, which is not connection oriented. The data generated by the application program is completely reflected in each UDP packet, so the UDP protocol takes a single UDP packet as the protocol data analysis object.

For protocol header data, ICMP and IGMP protocols treat each value of each specified field as an item in the item set. All values of all specified fields constitute the item set $z = \{z_1, z_2, \cdots z_n\}$, and all header field values of each network packet constitute a transaction, that is, the item set. The historical database is transformed into a transaction database. The Apriori algorithm is used to find the frequent k-term set which satisfies the minimum support degree for the transaction database of protocol head type of network data transformation in the attack process. For these k-item sets in the transaction database which is the normal access data grouping transformation of the background class Z, the support degree of the background class Z is calculated as $S(x)$, and then the support degree of the background class Z is calculated as $Q(x)$. When $Q(x)$ is greater than or equal to the minimum support degree, it indicates that this frequent k-item set has specific malicious attack data in the process of malicious attack, and the change of the support degree of malicious attack data is the characteristic frequency of malicious attack data, the algorithm of data mining based on feature frequency is used to mine malicious attack data.

2.3   Implementation of Malicious Attack Data Mining

Assuming that the malicious attack data obey the spherical distribution, the kernel function is used to map the data space to the high-dimensional kernel space, find a hypersphere that can contain all the data in the kernel space, find a minimum containing sphere that contains normal data, and solve the minimum containing sphere (sphere center, radius) by the minimum maximization method [14]. When identifying a new data, if the data is inside the sphere, it is considered normal, otherwise it is abnormal.

Firstly, the input space is mapped to a high-dimensional space by kernel function, in which a sphere containing all training data is constructed; the data points on the sphere are the obtained support vectors [15]. Assuming that model $r(x : \alpha)$ represents a kind of closely bounded data set, the goal of optimization is to find a minimum sphere with a center of x and a radius of α, and make all samples of the training set fall in the sphere. Define a minimization problem:

$$R(x, \alpha, \eta) = x^2 + E \sum_i \eta \tag{5}$$

Make this sphere satisfy:

$$\begin{cases} (x^2 - \alpha) \leq \eta_i \\ \eta_i > 0, \forall i \end{cases} \tag{6}$$

In formulas 5 and 6, x represents the center of the sphere, α represents the radius of the sphere, η represents the relaxation variable, and E represents the influence of the adjustment relaxation variable. By using Lagrange function to solve the minimum optimization problem under the above constraints, it can be judged that the data belongs to this class and should meet the following requirements:

$$(z - x) \leq \alpha^2 \tag{7}$$

In the formula, z represents a normal class, otherwise it is an abnormal class, that is, a class with malicious attack data. The criteria for determining whether the data belongs to this class are:

$$(z \cdot z) - 2 \sum_i zx + \sum_i x_i \leq \alpha^2 \tag{8}$$

In the formula, α represents the distance from any support vector to the spherical center x. When the data in the input space does not meet the spherical distribution, the input space can be mapped to the high-dimensional space first through the kernel technique, and then solved in the mapped high-dimensional space. If the above conditions are rewritten as follows:

$$J(z \cdot z) - 2\sum_i Jzx + \sum_i Jx_i \leq \alpha^2 \tag{9}$$

In the formula, J represents a linear kernel function. In normal data, the number of malicious attacks is more, which means that the malicious attack data itself is active and the behavior is complex. Therefore, the feature frequency is integrated into the data mining algorithm to find the most suitable hypersphere for data mining, and the malicious attack data is included in the hypersphere as much as possible, so as to reduce the false alarm rate of data mining.

The characteristic frequency of malicious attack is integrated into the algorithm: the normal data activity frequency matrix $y = [y_1, y_2, \cdots, y_n]$ is defined, and n is the number of training data.

$$y_i = \frac{\sum\limits_{j=1}^{m} b_{ij}}{\max\left(\sum\limits_{j=1}^{m} b_{ij}\right)} \tag{10}$$

In the formula, i and j are variables, n represents the number of data, m represents the characteristic frequency, p represents a matrix of m × n, then the problem of function minimization is as follows:

$$\min R(x, \alpha, \eta) = x^2 + E \sum_i y_i \eta_i \tag{11}$$

Adjust the corresponding constraints through the above formula:

$$\sum_i x_i = 1, 0 \leq x_i \leq y_i \tag{12}$$

By constraining the center of data sphere, the feature frequency is introduced into the algorithm. According to the principle of spatial mapping, the sphere of normal data and malicious attack data are constructed respectively, so as to realize the mining of malicious attack data.

3   Simulation Experiment of Data Mining Method of Malicious Attack

3.1   Data Extraction

Because of the large number of software users in the Android software market, the data is reliable. The data selection method in reference Android malware outlier detection based on feature frequency is used to extract the data. Therefore, use data of Google store, app store, app Bao and other software were collected as normal sample test sets, a total of 1,823. 1619 malware was extracted from the above data sources as a negative sample data test set. In order to ensure the data quality, the missing data processing, repeated data processing and abnormal data processing are carried out. Then decompile these apps with apktool and other tools, run them to obtain manifest and small files, and complete the data extraction. Then we extract the feature frequency of attack data, and get 874 feature frequencies. Then we integrate the feature frequency of each sample into the mining algorithm as a new feature.

3.2   Evaluation Index

In order to accurately describe these two concepts and avoid unnecessary misunderstanding, 4 parameters and 2 evaluation criteria were introduced into the experiment. Four parameters are as follows:

FP: determine the data as normal data, which is actually the number of malicious data.

TN: determine the data as malicious data, which is actually the number of malicious data.

TP: determine the data as normal data, which is actually the number of normal data.

FN: determine the data as malicious data, which is actually the number of normal data.

2 evaluation criteria are as follows:

False positive rate: normal data is mined as malicious attack data. The calculation formula of false positive rate M is:

$$M = \frac{FN}{FN + TP} \times 100\% \qquad (13)$$

Failure rate: malicious attack data is not successfully mined. The calculation formula of failure rate O is:

$$O = \frac{FP}{TN + FP} \times 100\% \qquad (14)$$

3.3   Test Steps

Randomly select 1000 normal data as training set and other normal data and malicious attack data as test set. The frequency is the number of features contained in each data. Normalize it and then use it as data mining feature. Traditional data mining methods based on clustering analysis and data mining methods based on feature frequency are used respectively. For the convenience of description, a group using the traditional data mining method is called the control group, and a group using the feature frequency based data mining method is called the experimental group. Two groups of data mining experiments at the same time, according to the experimental results for comparative analysis.

3.4 Experimental Results and Analysis

Through the above process, the data mining is completed, and the statistical software is used to count the false alarm rate and mining failure rate results. The statistical results are as follows.

As can be seen from Fig. 3, the overall trend of the experimental results of the false alarm rate of the data mining method based on the characteristic frequency is stable at about 0.1, with small fluctuation; the false alarm rate of the traditional data mining method is initially around 0.2, with the increase of the number of experiments, the false alarm rate gradually rises, and finally stabilizes at about 0.4; compared with the two, the data mining method based on the characteristic frequency of malicious attacks the false alarm rate of the method is lower than that of the traditional data mining method, which shows that in the data mining method, the feature frequency is used to effectively reduce the false alarm rate, which proves that the method is better.

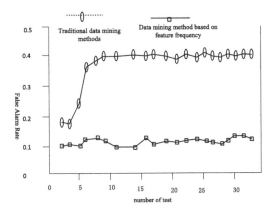

Fig. 3. False alarm rate results of different methods

It can be seen from Fig. 4, the failure rate of data mining method based on the characteristic frequency tends to 0 in many experiments, while in the traditional data mining method, the fluctuation range is large, the lowest is 0.1, the highest is 0.4, and the overall trend is high. Compared with the two methods, the failure rate of malicious attack data mining method based on feature frequency is lower, which shows that this method is better than the traditional data mining method.

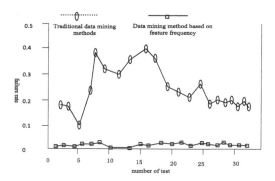

Fig. 4. Failure rate results of different methods

4 Conclusions

At present, with the rapid development of network, all kinds of network channels used by users are vulnerable to malicious attacks, resulting in data loss, even economic loss. Traditional malicious attack data mining methods have high false alarm rate and failure rate. In order to solve this kind of problem, a malicious attack data mining method based on the characteristic frequency is designed, which uses the stability and regularity of the characteristic frequency to reduce the false alarm rate and failure rate of the data mining method. Through many comparative experiments, it is proved that the data mining method of malicious attacks based on feature frequency effectively improves the problems existing in traditional data mining. However, because of the inherent characteristics of data extraction, the data experimental samples often mix with malicious behaviors, resulting in the deviation of experimental results. These problems need more in-depth research and discussion.

References

1. Liu, Y., Yuan, H.H.: Parallel discretization of data preparation optimization in data mining. J. Sichuan Univ. (Nat. Sci. Edn.) **55**(05), 103–109 (2018)
2. Zhang, Y., Yin, C.H.: Android malware outlier detection based on feature frequency. CAAI Trans. Intell. Syst. **13**(02), 168–173 (2018)
3. Wang, J., Zhang, Y.S., Chen, R.Y., et al.: Identification of user's role and discovery method of its malicious access behavior in web logs. Comput. Sci. **45**(10), 172–208 (2018)
4. Cui, Y., Song, W., Peng, Z.Y., et al.: Mining method of association rules based on differential privacy. Comput. Sci. **45**(06), 42–62 (2018)
5. Wang, J.Y., Liu, C., Fu, X.C., et al.: Crucial patterns mining with differential privacy over data streams. J. Softw. **30**(03), 158–176 (2019)
6. Zhang, B., Li, G.: Design of web anomaly data mining software based on improved clustering algorithm. Mod. Electron. Tech. **42**(08), 81–89 (2019)
7. Xiang, Z., Xiang, S.B.: Data mining based on fuzzy genetic algorithm. Control Eng. China **24**(05), 947–951 (2017)

8. Mei, Y., Xiong, T., Luo, S.B.: Research on NoSQL distributed big data mining method in complex attribute environment. Sci. Technol. Eng. **26**(09), 244–248 (2017)

9. Zhang, K.F., Liu, J.H., Zhang, J.F.: Local outlier mining algorithm for large scale high dimensional data set. Microelectron. Comput. **12**(03), 116–119 (2018)

10. Xu, L., Wang, J.X.: Data mining algorithm of abnormal network based on fuzzy neural network. Comput. Sci. **46**(04), 79–82 (2019)

11. Han, X., Du, S., Li, Z., et al.: Diagnosis of electric shock fault based on time-frequency singular value spectrum of leakage current and fuzzy clustering. Nongye Gongcheng Xuebao/Trans. Chin. Soc. Agric. Eng. **34**(04), 217–222 (2018)

12. Zhang, D., Yin, G., Jin, X., et al.: Two-stage and bi-direction feature selection method for EEG channel based on CSP and SFFS-SFBS. Dongnan Daxue Xuebao (Ziran Kexue Ban)/ J. Southeast Univ. (Nat. Sci. Edn.) **49**(01), 125–132 (2019)

13. Janus, T., Skomra, M., Marcin, D.: Individual security and network design with malicious nodes. Information (Switzerland) **9**(09), 214 (2018)

14. Cetinkaya, A., Ishii, H., Hayakawa, T.: A probabilistic characterization of random and malicious communication failures in multi-hop networked control. SIAM J. Control Optim. **56**(05), 3320–3350 (2017)

15. Preeti, P., Fawzia, G.F., Richard, S., et al.: Documenting attacks on health workers and facilities in armed conflicts. Bull. World Health Organ. **95**(01), 79–81 (2017)

Research on Image Recognition Algorithm Based on Depth Level Feature

Chan Zhang[(✉)] and Jia Luo

School of Information Technology, Guangdong Industry Polytechnic,
Guangzhou, Guangdong, China
zhangchan332@163.com

Abstract. In order to solve the problem that the traditional image recognition algorithm can not guarantee a relatively stable recognition accuracy and poor robustness under a variety of interferences, the image recognition algorithm based on depth level features is studied. After preprocessing, such as filtering and enhancing, the image to be recognized is segmented. The segmented image is input into convolution neural network, and the feature of depth level is extracted from the neural network. The feature points of the extracted deep level features are matched to realize image recognition, and the algorithm of image recognition based on the deep level features is designed. Compared with the traditional image recognition algorithm, the designed image recognition algorithm can ensure a more stable recognition accuracy and has better robustness.

Keywords: Depth level features · Image recognition · Algorithm research

1 Introduction

Image recognition technology plays an extremely important role in various fields. Good recognition technology is the key. How to improve the recognition rate and speed is of great significance, which is directly related to the practicability and security of image recognition. Image data, as a common information source, is characterized by huge information content, complex structure and redundancy. Therefore, compared with other types of data, digital image processing is more difficult. Image features are the centralized and simplified expression of image information. Due to different shooting angles, shooting environments or photographers, the same object will present different shapes on different images, however, the features used to express the object should be as stable as possible [1]. Therefore, image features are designed to express the invariable and essential information of the object in the image. No matter what shape the object presents in the image, the features of the object in the image can be used as invariable marks, which can be effectively identified by the computer.

Image recognition is one of the important research topics in the field of computer vision and pattern recognition. It has a wide range of application prospects in practice, and it is also an important tool to realize the intelligent society in the future [2]. Deep level feature is an important theory in deep learning. Based on convolution neural network, the objects of input network are expressed in deep level feature, which is

Y.-D. Zhang et al. (Eds.): ICMTEL 2020, LNICST 326, pp. 415–425, 2020.
https://doi.org/10.1007/978-3-030-51100-5_37

helpful for subsequent processing. Based on the above analysis, this paper designs an image recognition algorithm based on depth level.

2   Research on Image Recognition Algorithm Based on Depth Level Feature

2.1   Image Preprocessing

In practical application, the image to be recognized will contain interference factors that affect the recognition accuracy due to the influence of acquisition equipment, personnel, environment and other factors. Therefore, image preprocessing is needed before image recognition.

Firstly, the image is filtered to remove the noise in the image. When the number of pixels in a region is less than a fixed threshold, it is judged as noise, and the region is filled as background color to be removed. The size of each connected region is calculated by identifying the connected region of the whole picture. That is, all pixels belonging to the same connected domain are marked with the same region. Taking the 4-connected identification method as an example, first apply for a piece of identification space, scan the image from top to bottom, from left to right, for any pixel with a value of 0 in the image, the pixel above is t, and the pixel on the left is r. If r = t = 0, a new identifier will be given to p; if r and t have one of 1, a marker of 1 will be given to p; if r = t = 1, and there is the same marker, the marker will be given to p; if r = t = 1, but there are different markers, a smaller value will be given to P, indicating that the two markers are equivalent. Merge all the equivalent tags, scan again until the tags no longer change, and complete the image filtering. After image filtering, the image details are enhanced to facilitate the subsequent extraction of image features [3].

In this paper, image enhancement is realized by gray level transformation or histogram equalization. The gray level transformation does not depend on the position of the pixel in the image. Using the transformation T, the original brightness P in the range $[p_0, p_k]$ is transformed into a new range $[q_0, q_k]$. The gray level transformation for enhancing image contrast is shown in the following figure (Fig. 1).

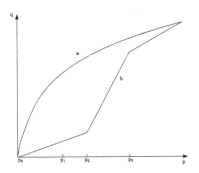

Fig. 1. Gray level transformation

The curves a and b in the image are two different mapping of gray level changes. The $[p_0, p_1]$ and $[p_2, p_3]$ areas in a and b are the areas of image contrast enhancement. The pixel value difference between these two areas is enlarged. For 256 color gray-scale image, only 256 bytes of storage space is needed to save a look-up table. The content of the table is the transformed gray-scale value. The original gray-scale value is used as the look-up index of the table, and the pixel value of each point in the image is searched and replaced, that is, the gray-scale transformation of the image is completed. In order to make the object to be recognized have the same gray value in the whole brightness range, histogram equalization is used.

For an image with G gray levels and size of M × N, create an array H with length of G, and initialize its elements to 0. Establish image histogram: scan each pixel, and increase the corresponding H value. When the pixel p has brightness g_p, there are:

$$H[g_p] = H[g_p] + 1 \tag{1}$$

Thus, a cumulative histogram H_c is formed:

$$\begin{cases} H_c[0] = H[0] \\ H_c[p] = H_c[p-1] + H_c[p] \quad p = 1, 2, \ldots, G-1 \end{cases} \tag{2}$$

Set up $T[p]$, Make $T[p]$ meet the following formula:

$$T[p] = round \frac{G-1}{NM} H_c[p] \tag{3}$$

Rescan the image, for the pixel point with gray value of g_p, make the new gray value of $T[g_p]$, and get the image after histogram equalization [4]. After image pre-processing, the image is segmented.

2.2   Image Segmentation

Because a digital image contains too much information, it will bring great interference to the intelligent recognition of the object in the image. In order to separate some areas of useless information from the areas of interest, we need to use the means of image segmentation. In this paper, the edge based segmentation method is used to segment the preprocessed image.

When detecting the edge of the target, firstly roughly detect its contour points, then connect the detected contour points according to certain principles, test and link the missing contour points, and remove the wrong boundary points at the same time [5]. Use the 3 × 3 operator template as shown in the figure below to segment the image after detecting the edge (Fig. 2).

Z_1	Z_2	Z_3
Z_4	Z_5	Z_6
Z_7	Z_8	Z_9

Fig. 2. 3×3 operator template

Define the gradients in horizontal g_x and vertical g_y directions:

$$\begin{cases} g_x = \dfrac{\partial f}{\partial x} = (Z_7 + Z_8 + Z_9) - (Z_1 + Z_2 + Z_3) \\ g_y = \dfrac{\partial f}{\partial y} = (Z_3 + Z_6 + Z_9) - (Z_1 + Z_4 + Z_7) \end{cases} \tag{4}$$

Define gradients in the direction of g'_x and g'_y diagonals:

$$\begin{cases} g'_x = (Z_2 + Z_3 + Z_6) - (Z_4 + Z_7 + Z_8) \\ g'_y = (Z_6 + Z_8 + Z_9) - (Z_1 + Z_2 + Z_4) \end{cases} \tag{5}$$

According to this definition, the generated operator template is as shown in the following figure (Fig. 3):

Fig. 3. Prewitt operator template

After calculating the gradient, the image is segmented according to the gradient. After image segmentation, deep features of image are extracted.

2.3 Deep Feature Extraction of Image

The image deep feature extraction in this paper is carried out in the convolution neural network. The segmented image is input into the input layer of the convolution neural network. After processing in the neural network, the feature map is generated, and then the deep feature of the image is extracted from the feature map [6].

Each layer of CNN structure contains several feature graphs, each of which is expressed from different scales and layers. Low level feature images can be understood directly through visualization. They capture the edge of the object and the sharp changes of the pixel information in the image. The detail texture structure of the original image is still preserved in the feature image. The visualization results of the feature map on the high level are not easy to understand, and the high level features are abstracted and iterated to express the semantic information of the image.

In CNN hierarchical structure, each layer of feature map expresses image information from different aspects. Making full use of the information of feature map to describe image can make the constructed image features have stronger expression ability. Because the feature images at different levels have different sizes, the higher the level is, the smaller the size of the feature image is. Therefore, in order to facilitate the extraction of hierarchical features, it is necessary to adjust the feature images at different levels to the original image size. In this paper, the bilinear interpolation method is used to sample the feature map at different levels, making it have the same size as the original image, stacking all the feature maps to build a three-dimensional matrix $F \in R^{N \times H \times W}$, where H is the height of the image, W is the width of the image, and N is the number of feature maps. F can be expressed as:

$$F = [up(F_1), up(F_2), \cdots, up(F_L)] \tag{6}$$

Among them, up is the upper sampling operation, and the number of characteristic graphs at the level of $up(F_l) \in R^{N_l \times H \times W}$ and N_l [7]. For any region Q on the image, its descriptor can be represented by N-dimensional vector as $D_Q \in R_N$, and the i-dimensional d_i of the descriptor represents the result of describing the corresponding region pixels on the i-level feature map.

DHF feature extraction process is as follows: the trained CNN model is used in the original image, and the convolution output layer is selected to construct the image hierarchy. Re adjust the size of the feature map to the original image. For the feature extraction unit on the original image, determine its corresponding area on the feature map, and count the pixel information contained in the area on the feature map. The low-level feature image still retains rich texture information, and the method of information entropy is used to count the pixels in the feature area. The maximum and minimum values of pixels in the statistical region are divided into several intervals. Count the number of pixels in each interval $n_i, i = 1, 2, \cdots, bins$, $bins$ is the number of divided intervals, and calculate the probability of pixels falling into each interval p_i is the total number of regional pixels.

$$p_i = \frac{n_i}{total} \tag{7}$$

where *total* is the total number of area pixels. Calculate the information entropy of area pixels:

$$H = -\sum_{i=1}^{bins} p_i \cdot \log_2 p_i \tag{8}$$

Information entropy is a kind of quantity used to measure the degree of information confusion. Specifically, in this paper, the location distribution of significant changes in the region with lower entropy rate is relatively centralized, and the location of significant changes with higher entropy rate is widely distributed in the whole characteristic region [8]. The feature graph at high level has strong abstract semantic information. In this paper, region average method is used to reduce the influence of noise in the region. Finally, the DHF feature descriptor of feature extraction unit is constructed by integrating the high and low level feature map information. Complete the deep feature extraction of the image to be recognized, match the feature points, and realize the image recognition.

2.4 Image Recognition

After the feature points in the image are extracted, they need to be matched and correlated. Image feature matching and association is to find the feature points extracted from one image and find the matching feature points in another image. This step is completed by calculating the feature descriptors of the extracted image feature points, and then calculating the similarity between the feature descriptors. Image feature descriptor is a kind of vector which can describe the local structure features of image quantitatively. It can fully represent the local shape and texture structure features near the feature points. After extracting feature points, the matching and association of feature points are based on the similarity between feature descriptors. The cosine distance of the included angle shown in the following formula is used to calculate the similarity.

$$d = \frac{\sum_{i=1}^{n} x_i y_i}{\sqrt{\sum_{i=1}^{n} x_i^2} \sqrt{\sum_{i=1}^{n} y_i^2}} \tag{9}$$

In the above formula, x_i and y_i are the feature points to be matched. Generally speaking, the smaller the distance between two vectors is, the higher the similarity is. However, in the process of feature matching and association, it is simply considered that the feature points with the smallest distance between feature descriptors are matched points, which may cause some mismatches. If there is a feature point A in the reference image, its feature descriptor is $Desc_a$, there may be two mismatches: one is that the real feature points corresponding to A in the image to be matched are not extracted, at this time, only other wrong feature points can be matched; the other is that in the image to be matched, there may be multiple feature points with the minimum distance between the feature descriptor and $Desc_a$, at this time, there is a one to many matching problem [9].

In order to reduce the problem of mismatching, we use the ratio of the nearest distance to the next nearest distance to associate feature point pairs [10]. Suppose that there are two feature points B_1 and B_2 in the image to be matched, their feature descriptors are $Desc_{b1}$ and $Desc_{b2}$ respectively. Compared with the feature descriptors of all other feature points, the distance between $Desc_a$ and $Desc_{b1}$ is the smallest, while the distance between $Desc_a$ and $Desc_{b2}$ is the second smallest. At this time, it is not directly considered that point A and point B_1 are matched, but the distance between $Desc_a$ and $Desc_{b1}$ divided by the distance between $Desc_a$ and 12 is calculated, when the ratio is less than a certain threshold, point a and point B_1 are considered to match each other.

Through feature matching and association, the next step of image matching is to solve a certain spatial transformation model according to the spatial coordinates of these matching feature points. For two images that need to be matched, one of them can be regarded as the result of some spatial transformation for the other, and the two can be modeled according to some spatial transformation model. In image matching, affine transformation is generally used to model the spatial transformation relationship between the reference image and the image to be matched. The mathematical model is shown in the following formula.

$$
\begin{bmatrix} x' \\ y' \\ 1 \end{bmatrix} = \begin{bmatrix} a_1 & a_2 & t_x \\ a_3 & a_4 & t_y \\ 0 & 0 & 1 \end{bmatrix} \begin{bmatrix} x \\ y \\ 1 \end{bmatrix} \tag{10}
$$

Among them, (x, y) and (x', y') represent the coordinates of the midpoint of the two images respectively, (t_x, t_y) represents the amount of translation, and $a_j, j = 1, 2, 3, 4$ represents the parameters of image rotation, scaling and other transformations. After the parameters t_x, t_y and a_j are calculated by certain methods, the transformation relationship of spatial coordinates between the two images can be obtained.

Assume that there are N pairs of matching feature points found in feature matching and association steps. For affine transformation model, it needs at least 4 pairs of matching feature points to solve its parameters. For the remaining $n - 4$ pairs of matching points, assume that the coordinate of reference image is $A_i(i = 1, 2, \cdots, N - 4)$, and the coordinate of matching point corresponding to $B_i(i = 1, 2, \cdots, N - 4)$ is, take A_i into the result obtained in the previous step, and calculate the transformed coordinate, assuming that it is 4 $A_i'(i = 1, 2, \cdots, N - 4)$. Calculate the distance D_i between A_i' and B_i. If the distance is less than a preset threshold T, the correct matching point of the point is considered as the internal point. If it is not satisfied, the point is considered as the wrong matching point, which is called the external point. Make a note of all the inner points, find 4 new pairs in the matching point pairs, perform the above steps again, and record the inner points every time. After repeating the above process many times, compare the number of interior points obtained each time. The parameter obtained in the most number is the required solution parameter. Using the obtained parameters, the spatial matching of feature points is completed and the matching results are output. At this point, the research of image recognition algorithm based on depth level feature is completed.

3   Algorithm Test Experiment

In order to verify the performance of the algorithm, we choose the image data as the experimental data in YouTube labeled video dataset (https://research.google.com/youtube8m/), exclude the unavailable data, take the remaining data as the experimental sample set, and carry out the comparative experiment with three kinds of commonly used images A cognitive algorithm is designed. The experimental hypothesis was verified by comparison.

3.1   Experimental Content

In this section, we compared the robustness of the two image recognition algorithms to evaluate the advantages and disadvantages of the two algorithms. The experimental method was comparative experiment. The experiment verification process is completed under the control of other variables except the experimental variation.

The object of the experiment is 300 images randomly selected from the library, and each image is then selected 5 images with higher similarity as interference items. The experiment was divided into three groups, the first group added noise to the experimental image; the second group did blur processing, namely the reverse processing of sharpening processing; the third group reduced the brightness of the image. The image recognition algorithm designed in this paper will be compared with the recognition algorithm based on neural network, the recognition algorithm based on information fusion matching and the recognition algorithm based on template matching. Taking the above three algorithms as the reference group of the comparative experiment, the algorithm proposed in this paper is the experimental group, recording the relevant experimental data, and completing the experiment.

Add quantization interference to the experimental image according to the quantization table of external interference degree of the experimental image shown below. 300 images were randomly divided into three groups. After adding different interferences, the experiment was carried out (Table 1).

Using the image recognition algorithm based on the depth level feature designed in this paper and its comparative recognition algorithm to recognize the image with interference, comparing the image recognition accuracy of different algorithms, and judging the robustness of four image recognition algorithms under the external interference.

Table 1. Quantization table of external interference degree of experimental image

Degree of interference	Add noise /pixels	Fuzzy processing /%	Reduce the luminance cd/m^3
1	10	20	0.05
2	20	40	0.10
3	30	60	0.15
4	40	80	0.20

3.2 Experimental Result

Under the noise interference, the recognition accuracy of the proposed recognition algorithm and the recognition algorithm based on neural network for the image of the experimental object is shown in the table below (Table 2).

Table 2. Recognition accuracy under noise interference/%.

Degree of interference	Experimental group algorithm	Reference group algorithm
1	96.42	88.97
2	95.84	84.43
3	95.76	81.69
4	95.43	79.75

It can be seen from the above table that the recognition accuracy of the experimental group algorithm is higher than that of the reference group algorithm after adding different levels of noise to the image. With the increase of the interference degree, the recognition accuracy of the experimental group algorithm has no significant change, and the recognition accuracy of the reference group algorithm has a downward trend, and the decline range is large. It shows that the recognition algorithm proposed in this paper can guarantee higher recognition accuracy when adding noise interference to the image.

After the experimental image is fuzzy processed, the recognition accuracy of the proposed recognition algorithm and the recognition algorithm based on information fusion matching for the experimental object image is shown in the table below (Table 3).

Table 3. Recognition accuracy after fuzzy processing/%.

Degree of interference	Experimental group algorithm	Reference group algorithm
1	91.16	74.28
2	93.27	72.75
3	91.56	71.97
4	92.48	67.31

It can be seen from the above table that the recognition accuracy of the experimental group algorithm is higher than that of the reference group after image fuzzy processing, and does not fluctuate with the increase of the fuzzy degree, but the recognition accuracy of the reference group algorithm will decrease with the increase of the interference degree.

After reducing the gray level of the image, the recognition accuracy of the proposed recognition algorithm and the recognition algorithm based on information fusion matching for the experimental object image is shown in the table below (Table 4).

Table 4. Recognition accuracy after gray level reduction/%.

Degree of interference	Experimental group algorithm	Reference group algorithm
1	85.47	65.64
2	86.05	64.59
3	87.16	61.53
4	86.28	60.44

After analyzing the above table, the accuracy of the two groups of image recognition algorithms is affected after the gray level of the image is reduced. However, with the gray level getting lower and lower, the accuracy of the reference group algorithm is getting lower and lower, but the recognition rate of the experimental group algorithm does not fluctuate greatly. In conclusion, the image recognition algorithm based on the depth level features designed in this paper can guarantee high recognition accuracy and good robustness under various levels of image interference.

4 Conclusions

In this paper, an image recognition algorithm based on depth level features is designed. Firstly, the image is preprocessed. Secondly, the segmented image is input into the input layer of convolution neural network, and the feature mapping is generated in the neural network. Finally, the deep features of the image are extracted from the feature mapping. Finally, the effectiveness of the algorithm is proved by the comparative experiment of three traditional image recognition algorithms The algorithm designed in this paper can ensure high recognition accuracy and good stability under different levels of interference.

References

1. Yang, J., Zhou, T., Guo, L., et al.: Lung tumor image recognition algorithm based on cuckoo search and deep belief network. J. Comput. Appl. **38**(11), 3225–3230 (2018)
2. Gao, Y., Wang, B., Guo, Z., et al.: Clothing image recognition and classification based on HSR-FCN. Comput. Eng. Appl. **55**(16), 144–149 (2019)

3. Liu, Y., Yang, J., Wang, C.: Optimization of behavior recognition algorithm based on low-level feature modeling. Sci. Technol. Eng. **18**(21), 69–75 (2018)
4. Zhang, Q., Guan, S., Xie, H., et al.: Image adaptive target recognition algorithm based on deep feature learning. J. Taiyuan Univ. Technol. **49**(04), 592–598 (2018)
5. Huang, X., Ling, Z., Li, X.: Discriminative deep feature learning method by fusing linear discriminant analysis for image recognition. J. Image Graph. **23**(04), 510–518 (2018)
6. Yi, L., Ya, E.: Based on Gobor feature and deep belief network face recognition methods. Comput. Simul. **34**(11), 417–421 (2017)
7. Sang, S., Feng, H., Wang, L.: Image true-false decision algorithm based on improved SURF coupled hierarchical clustering. Comput. Eng. Des. **38**(06), 1602–1607 (2017)
8. Li, Y., Yang, Q., Lei, H., et al.: Improved Criminisi algorithm based on DIBR. Comput. Eng. Des. **38**(05), 1287–1291 (2017)
9. Li, Q., You, X., Li, K., et al.: Deep hierarchical feature extraction algorithm. Pattern Recognit. Artif. Intell. **30**(02), 127–136 (2017)
10. Ma, X., Sang, Q.: Handwritten signature verification algorithm based on LBP and deep learning. Chin. J. Quantum Electron. **34**(01), 23–31 (2017)

Research on Shadow Detection Method of Infrared Remote Sensing Image Based on Artificial Intelligence

Shuang-cheng Jia[✉] and Tao Wang

Alibaba Network Technology Co., Ltd., Beijing, China
jiashuangcheng1@2980.com

Abstract. In the process of the development of science and technology in China, in order to maximize the use of network and high-tech resources, more and more fields are increasingly being used for artificial intelligence during this period to meet the growing demand for high technology and requirements. Artificial intelligence is necessary to detect the shadow of infrared remote sensing images. Therefore, in the field of image detection, artificial intelligence must be applied appropriately. In this paper, through the research on the characteristics of artificial intelligence and the artificial intelligence infrared shadow image detection method, the importance of artificial intelligence for infrared remote sensing image detection is deeply analyzed. The significance of research on infrared remote sensing image shadow detection based on artificial intelligence is emphasized.

Keywords: Artificial intelligence · Infrared remote sensing image · Shadow image detection · Detection method

1 Introduction

Due to the limitation and influence of imaging technology, imaging conditions and other factors, there are more or less degradation phenomena in the formation of color remote sensing image, and image shadow is a typical representative [1]. The existence of shadow will disturb the image processing of computer vision, affect the accurate interpretation and interpretation of image information, and bring many difficulties to the follow-up remote sensing image processing, such as target classification and recognition, image matching, etc., so it is very necessary to detect image shadow.

At present, there are many research results on shadow detection of infrared remote sensing image. In reference [2], a shadow detection method based on depth information is proposed. In order to solve the problem of automatic shadow detection in complex scenes, an automatic shadow detection algorithm for single image based on depth information is proposed. Firstly, the depth information is used to estimate the normal and point cloud information of the image, and multi-scale texture filtering is applied to the image; secondly, the normal, point cloud and chroma information are used to estimate the shadow confidence and brightness confidence of the filtered image at different scales, and the shadow boundary correlation multi-scale fusion is applied to

© ICST Institute for Computer Sciences, Social Informatics and Telecommunications Engineering 2020
Published by Springer Nature Switzerland AG 2020. All Rights Reserved
Y.-D. Zhang et al. (Eds.): ICMTEL 2020, LNICST 326, pp. 426–436, 2020.
https://doi.org/10.1007/978-3-030-51100-5_38

the two confidence maps, At the same time, the complex shadow boundary information and structure information are preserved. Finally, Laplace operator is used to optimize the shadow confidence and get more accurate shadow detection results. However, this method is too complex and has a long time-consuming problem. In reference [3], a shadow detection method of infrared remote sensing image based on support vector machine is proposed. Firstly, the image is segmented into independent regions; secondly, the high-order energy equation is built by using support vector mechanism to model the shadow layout information; finally, the minimum equation is used to determine whether the region is a shadow, but the detection accuracy of this method is low, and the actual application effect is not ideal.

Artificial intelligence technology has the new characteristics that the previous science and technology systems do not have. The design and application of artificial intelligence technology under the Internet background should also be adapted to the new era and new requirements. The construction of infrared remote sensing image shadow detection method under artificial intelligence technology should also be adapted to the modern situation [4]. In order to combine the innovation of science and technology in the development of image detection methods in the contemporary development, we must design and construct the infrared remote sensing image detection technology under the Internet according to the actual situation, which really plays the role of artificial intelligence technology [5]. There is also a big innovation and reform in the detection method of shadow images, which makes the artificial intelligence technology more and more important and the inevitability and importance of using artificial intelligence technology to carry out technological innovation in various fields [6].

Because most methods of infrared remote sensing image shadow detection rely on manual work and have strong subjectivity, the detection accuracy decreases. Although some researches have put forward methods of infrared remote sensing image shadow detection by computer, there are some defects. In order to solve the problems existing in the traditional methods, this paper puts forward an infrared remote sensing image shadow detection method based on artificial intelligence. This method can solve the problem of complex scene shadow detection, promote the further development of image shadow detection technology, and can be better applied in many fields.

2   Research on the Characteristics of Artificial Intelligence

In recent years, more and more industries have gradually realized the positive significance of artificial intelligence [7]. Especially in the era of the Internet, many companies have increased the design and application of artificial intelligence technology, and gradually pay attention to the new methods of using modern technology and digital technology in the process of infrared remote sensing image shadow detection. However, in the actual application of artificial intelligence, some enterprises or fields are not optimistic after the successful use of artificial intelligence technology. This is because many companies have succeeded in completing the artificial intelligence technology under the Internet background. On the contrary, the requirements for the accuracy and accuracy of technical work have gradually relaxed, which eventually led to the negative effect [8].

When looking at the artificial intelligence technology in the context of the development of the Internet, even if new technologies have been formed, it is necessary to pay attention to the emergence of various other problems. It is necessary to exert the true value of artificial intelligence technology under the Internet, rather than letting it flow, but sometimes it will affect the work [8]. Many large companies' optimism about artificial intelligence makes them want to build and use this technology in the enterprise to improve the efficiency and accuracy of their work. Due to its uniqueness, artificial intelligence often has relatively high technical requirements in the process of application [10]. Especially for developers, artificial intelligence-based infrared remote sensing image shadow detection method is the latest method at this stage [11]. Under such a background, the research on artificial intelligence-based infrared remote sensing image shadow detection method has gradually become an important topic. It is necessary to seize the opportunity, give play to the important role of science and technology, promote scientific and technological progress and innovation, improve the updating and upgrading of shadow image detection methods, and strengthen the innovation and upgrade of image detection methods in the intelligent context [12].

3 Research on Shadow Detection Method of Infrared Remote Sensing Image Based on Artificial Intelligence

China's high-tech has shown a state of rapid development. Infrared remote sensing image shadow detection has also received more and more attention. The solution to the problem of shadow detection is also mentioned on the agenda [13]. Due to the shadow of infrared remote sensing images, the inspectors are often in a state of long-term intense work, which not only exacerbates the psychological pressure of the staff, but also increases the difficulty of image discrimination [14].

According to Table 1, in the context of intelligence, the Internet and artificial intelligence present new features that China has not had before, in terms of technological innovation, application, and implementation [15]. This uniqueness has created the inevitability and particularity of the rapid development of various fields in the Internet age [16]. Artificial intelligence infrared remote sensing image shadow detection method has new features that traditional image detection methods do not have [17]. For the development and innovation of detection systems in the context of artificial intelligence, it is also necessary to adapt to the new era and new requirements, and the improvement of detection methods should also be adapted to the modern situation.

Table 1. Artificial intelligence technology information sheet

Constitute	Availability	Effective rate
Computer technology	87.4%	38.2%
Data base	69.2%	65.8%
Visual technology	76.4%	67.2%

According to Figs. 1 and 2, it can be known that the projection method of infrared remote sensing images plays an important role in the detection of shadows. In the projection of an image, the probability of projection for a region can be expressed by the following formula:

$$P(A/B) = P(B/A) * P(A)/P(B) \tag{1}$$

This formula shows the probability that an A event will also occur under the condition that the B event occurs, which is equal to the conditional probability of the occurrence of the B event under the condition of the A event, and then multiplied by the probability of the A event, and then divided by the probability of the occurrence of the B event [18]. When A and B are replaced by S and T, the total probability values of S and T and the conditions to be satisfied can be expressed by the following formula:

$$Rc(s) = \{s|I(s,t) > 0\} \tag{2}$$

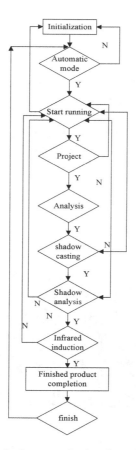

Fig. 1. Image projection flow chart

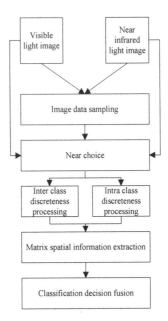

Fig. 2. Image shadow information collection flow chart

According to Fig. 3, with the modernization of China, in recent years, the state's investment in artificial intelligence technology and remote sensing technology is gradually increasing. This has enabled the technical work in various parts of the country to be carried out in an orderly manner, and the demand for shadow image detection and recovery is growing. It has led to the booming image detection industry and artificial intelligence technology [19]. For radiance in remote sensing technology, the following formula can be used to calculate:

$$Le = dLe/d \cos \theta \tag{3}$$

Fig. 3. Infrared remote sensing image map

In the formula for radiance, θ is the angle between the given direction and the normal of the source cell. The research on shadow detection method of artificial infrared infrared remote sensing image is to analyze and research the modern image detection problem on this basis. Also, it discusses and discusses the solutions to the common problems in the current shadow image detection process, improving the quality and efficiency of shadow image detection. At the same time, the technical support for scientific and technological personnel is strengthened and the harmonious development of science and technology is jointly promote in all aspects of China [20].

4 Verification of Shadow Detection Method for Infrared Remote Sensing Image Under Artificial Intelligence

The research on shadow detection method of artificial infrared infrared remote sensing image is based on such a society, in order to alleviate the psychological pressure of staff and enable them to concentrate on their work. If the person inspected does not have artificial intelligence awareness and works blindly without professional training, it may cause mishandling of the monitoring work or even cause an accident. If the staff does not have good physical and psychological qualities, they will not be qualified for the

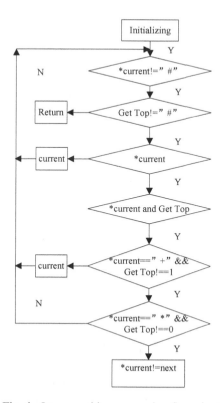

Fig. 4. Image position conversion flow chart

shadow detection of infrared remote sensing images. Therefore, inspectors must conduct job tests and professional training before working, especially to know the characteristics and characteristics of artificial intelligence.

According to Fig. 4, the development of modern social science and technology is very rapid. Work in all industries is linked to technology, the Internet, and artificial intelligence. Artificial intelligence infrared remote sensing image shadow detection method is the product that emerged in such a large environment (Fig. 5).

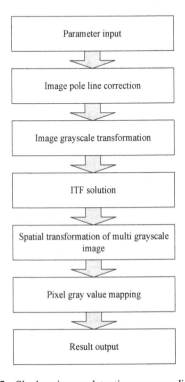

Fig. 5. Shadow image detection process diagram

As you can see from the above figure, when testing, you must first put your own safety first. In the process of testing, all units and enterprises must make every effort to ensure the full use and utilization of artificial intelligence technology, increase the effectiveness of detection, and avoid the occurrence of detection errors. As a new type of high-tech detection method, artificial intelligence infrared remote sensing image shadow detection method can effectively improve the technology and innovation consciousness of the inspectors. It can also reduce the psychological burden and psychological pressure of the workers, ensure the completion of the project on time, quality and quantity, and improve the quality and effectiveness of shadow image detection.

According to Table 2, the application of artificial intelligence technology in the Internet age and the design of image detection methods are in line with modern work requirements. In actual work, it has to play a positive role and truly achieve technological innovation. The development of modern society is very fast, and the work of various industries must be related to technology, the Internet and artificial intelligence technology. The artificial intelligence-based infrared remote sensing image shadow detection method is a product that emerges in such a large environment (Figs. 6 and 7).

Table 2. Infrared remote sensing shadow detection table

Detection project	Definition	Shadow influence
Infrared camera	High	Great
Infrared radiometer	Low	Great
Color infrared photography	High	Small

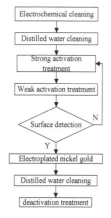

Fig. 6. Planar image stereoscopic structure

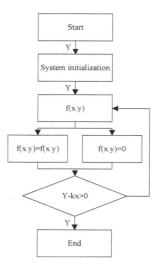

Fig. 7. Infrared remote sensing shadow detection flow chart

According to the above two figures, the image detection system under the background of rapid development of science and technology has a big innovation and reform. This has caused the importance of artificial intelligence technology and infrared remote sensing technology in image detection, and the difficulty and necessity of constructing artificial intelligence in various regions. Therefore, there must be a dedicated technical staff to carry out technological innovation, fundamentally solve the problems of image detection, and ensure the smooth progress of shadow image detection.

In order to further verify the superiority of the artificial intelligence-based infrared remote sensing image shadow detection method proposed in this paper, a comparison experiment of detection accuracy was conducted. The experimental results are shown in Fig. 8.

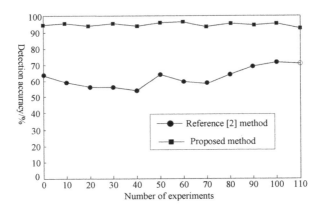

Fig. 8. Comparison of detection accuracy of different methods

The analysis of the figure above shows that the detection accuracy of reference [2] method is 54–73%, and the fluctuation is unstable, indicating that the detection accuracy of traditional methods is low and unstable. The detection accuracy of the proposed method remains above 94% and the fluctuation is relatively stable, indicating that the method in this paper can accurately detect the shadow of infrared remote sensing image with good stability.

Based on the above experiments, the detection time of different research methods is compared, and the results are shown in Table 3.

According to the above table, the detection time of the reference [2] method is between 13.5 s–18.1 s, while the detection time of the proposed method is before 1.2 s–1.6 s, which is much lower than that of the experimental comparison method, indicating that the infrared remote sensing image stealth detection method based on artificial intelligence has a short detection time and high efficiency.

Table 3. Comparison of testing time of different methods

Number of experiment	Reference [2] method	Proposed method
20	13.5 s	1.2 s
40	16.0 s	1.6 s
60	14.8 s	1.4 s
80	13.7 s	1.6 s
100	18.1 s	1.3 s
120	14.7 s	1.5 s
140	17.6 s	1.2 s
160	15.2 s	1.6 s

5 Conclusion

According to the unique characteristics of remote sensing image shadows, artificial intelligence infrared shadow image detection method is proposed to improve the detection accuracy of shadows. It is necessary to combine the innovation of artificial intelligence in the development of image detection methods in contemporary development. Therefore, we should carry out the improvement and update of the infrared remote sensing shadow image detection method under the Internet according to the actual situation, and truly play the role of artificial intelligence. In the era of the development of artificial intelligence, the design method of infrared remote sensing shadow image detection should meet the modern operation requirements. It plays an active role in actual work to truly achieve technological innovation.

References

1. Shen, J., Xuan, J.I.: Cloud and cloud shadow multi-feature collaborative detection from remote sensing image. J. Geo-Inf. Sci. **18**(5), 599–605 (2016)
2. De zheng, X.U., Tang, X.M., Zhu, X.Y., et al.: Shadow detection method of infrared remote sensing image based on depth information. Geomatics Spat. Inf. Technol. **11**(7), 1112–1117 (2017)
3. Yang, M.: Shadow detection method of infrared remote sensing image based on support vector machine. Geospat. Inf. **10**(3), 358–362 (2017)
4. Kang, X., Huang, Y., Li, S., et al.: Extended random walker for shadow detection in very high resolution remote sensing images. IEEE Trans. Geosci. Remote Sens. **56**(2), 867–876 (2017)
5. Li, J., Hu, Q., Ai, M.: Joint model and observation cues for single-image shadow detection. Remote Sens. **8**(6), 484 (2016)
6. Zhen-Yu, L.I., Wang, H.C., Wang, G.L., et al.: Face detection system based on cascade's algorithm of adaboost and principal component analysis. Sci. Technol. Eng. **162**(5), 667–674 (2018)
7. Xuan, L.I., Zhang, H.: Color image edge detection based on fuzzy algorithm. Sci. Technol. Eng. **12**(1), 66–69 (2018)

8. Wang, R.J., Niu, Z.X., Song, C.H., et al.: An improved shot boundary detection algorithm based on mutual information. Sci. Technol. Eng. **26**(1), 44–49 (2018)

9. Liu, S., Pan, Z., Cheng, X.: A novel fast fractal image compression method based on distance clustering in high dimensional sphere surface. Fractals **25**(4), 1740004 (2017)

10. Zhao, Y.L., Tao, Q.C., Qian-Wen, L.U., et al.: The adaptive-canny threshold selection algorithm based on the second derivative of image gradient. Sci. Technol. Eng. **12**(4), 78–82 (2018)

11. Liu, S., Zhang, Z., Qi, L., et al.: A fractal image encoding method based on statistical loss used in agricultural image compression. Multimedia Tools Appl. **75**(23), 15525–15536 (2016)

12. Qi, C., Zhang, G., Yang, X., et al.: Single image shadow detection and removal based on feature fusion and multiple dictionary learning. Multimedia Tools Appl. **77**(14), 18601–18624 (2018)

13. Hosseinzadeh, S., Shakeri, M., Zhang, H.: Fast shadow detection from a single image using a patched convolutional neural network, vol. 78, no 8, pp. 1–12 (2017)

14. Russell, M., Zhou, J.J., Fang, G., et al.: Feature-based image patch classification for moving shadow detection. IEEE Transactions on Circuits & Systems for Video Technology **29**(9), 2652–2666 (2017)

15. Qiao, X., Yuan, D., Li, H.: Urban shadow detection and classification using hyperspectral image. J. Indian Soc. Remote Sens. **45**(6), 945–952 (2017)

16. Wang, J., Li, X., Hui, L., et al.: Stacked conditional generative adversarial networks for jointly learning shadow detection and shadow removal, vol. 12, no 7, pp. 56–62 (2017)

17. Vicente, T.F.Y., Hoai, M., Samaras, D.: Leave-one-out kernel optimization for shadow detection and removal. IEEE Trans. Pattern Anal. Mach. Intell. **99**, 682–695 (2018)

18. Kim, D.S., Arsalan, M., Park, K.R.: Convolutional neural network-based shadow detection in images using visible light camera sensor. Sensors **18**(4), 960–966 (2018)

19. Wang, Q., Yan, L., Yuan, Q., et al.: An automatic shadow detection method for VHR remote sensing orthoimagery. Remote Sens. **9**(5), 469 (2017)

20. Silva, G.F., Carneiro, G.B., Doth, R., et al.: Near real-time shadow detection and removal in aerial motion imagery application. ISPRS J. Photogram. Remote Sens. **140**, 104–121 (2017). S0924271617302253

Research on Fault Intelligent Detection Technology of Dynamic Knowledge Network Learning System

Shuang-cheng Jia[✉] and Tao Wang

Alibaba Network Technology Co., Ltd., Beijing, China
jiashuangcheng1@2980.com

Abstract. The rapid development of computers has improved the scope of dynamic knowledge network learning applications. Online learning has brought convenience to people in time and place. At the same time, people began to pay attention to the efficiency and quality of online learning. At present, the network knowledge storage system is distributed storage system. The distributed storage system has great performance in terms of capacity, scalability, and parallelism. However, its storage node is inexpensive, and the reliability is not high, and it is prone to fault. Based on the designed fault detection model detection path, relying on building the knowledge data node fault detection mode, constructing the knowledge data link fault detection mode, completing the fault detection model detection mode, and finally realizing the dynamic knowledge network learning system fault intelligent detection technology research. The experiment proves that the dynamic knowledge network learning system fault intelligent detection technology designed in this paper reduces the fault rate of the network learning system by 37.5%.

Keywords: Network learning · Fault detection · Intelligent detection · Technology research

1 Introduction

Network learning advocates students as the main body, while intelligent network learning system is characterized by students' personalized learning [1]. The organization of domain knowledge and intelligent navigation are the basic problems to realize personalized learning in intelligent network learning system [2]. In this era of information explosion, learning determines its own competitiveness. However, many people spend a lot of time and money to enrich themselves through various channels. As a result, they find that what they finally master is fragmented information, which can not form a complete knowledge framework [3]. These isolated knowledge can not be used to solve practical problems, so it is particularly important to build a perfect knowledge learning system.

The dynamic knowledge network learning system jointly created by network technology, computer technology and communication technology has become an emerging learning method, providing the masses with convenient conditions for learning anywhere and anytime [4]. The storage system in the network learning system

© ICST Institute for Computer Sciences, Social Informatics and Telecommunications Engineering 2020
Published by Springer Nature Switzerland AG 2020. All Rights Reserved
Y.-D. Zhang et al. (Eds.): ICMTEL 2020, LNICST 326, pp. 437–448, 2020.
https://doi.org/10.1007/978-3-030-51100-5_39

is composed of multiple storage points, but multiple storage points are prone to data synchronization failure and serial effects [5]. When a virus invades one of the storage points, the relevant storage points may be implicated. Based on the above situation, the network learning system should adopt the fault intelligent detection technology to automatically detect the entire learning system before the network knowledge system fails, and find the place where the fault may occur, by backing up, copying, transferring, etc. the knowledge data. Which means to process the network learning system to ensure the integrity of the knowledge data and the security of the network learning system [6]. The experiment proves that the network learning system using the automatic fault monitoring technology can greatly reduce the fault rate of the system itself. In order to reduce the failure rate of dynamic knowledge network learning system, this paper proposes a new fault detection technology for dynamic knowledge network learning system.

2 Fault Detection Path Design of Dynamic Knowledge Network Learning System

The most common faults in dynamic knowledge network learning systems are data loss and data confusion. The system loses a lot of data and the system knowledge cannot be acquired normally.

Set the data loss rate of the dynamic knowledge network learning system as $u_k = Kx_k$, the following formula can be obtained.

$$\begin{cases} x_{k+1} = A_d x_k + (B_0 + DF(\tau_k)E)u_{k-d+1} + (B_1 - DF(\tau_k)E)u_{k-d} \\ y_k = Cx_k \end{cases} \tag{1}$$

Assuming the probability of data confusion is r, then:

$$P(\zeta_k = 0) = r, P(\zeta_k = 1) = 1 - r \tag{2}$$

If the estimated error of the state observation parameters of the dynamic knowledge network learning system is set as $e(k) = x(k) - \widehat{x}(k)$, no data loss or confusion will occur. The state estimation error can be calculated by using the following formula:

$$e_{k+1} = Ae_k + BKe_{k-d+1} + B_1Ke_{k-d} + DFEKe_{k-d+1} - DFEKe_{k-d} \tag{3}$$

In the above formula, the following formula can be obtained by introducing the augmented vector $\theta_k = [x_k, e_k]^T$.

$$\theta_{k+1} = \begin{bmatrix} A & 0 \\ 0 & A \end{bmatrix} \theta_k + \begin{bmatrix} (B_0 + DFE)K & 0 \\ DFEK & B_0K \end{bmatrix} \theta_{k-d+1} \\ \begin{bmatrix} (B_1 - DFE)K & 0 \\ -DFEK & B_1K \end{bmatrix} \theta_{k-d} \tag{4}$$

The following formula is used to represent the estimation error of state observation parameters in the case that data of dynamic knowledge network learning system cannot be obtained.

$$e_{k+1} = (A - LC)e_k + B_0 Ke_{k-d+1} + B_1 Ke_{k-d} + DFEKx_{k-d+1} - DFEKx_{k-d}$$

(5)

The fault detection path model of random switching control can be established by using the following formula:

$$z(k+1) = A(\xi_k)z(k) + A_3 z(k-d+1)$$

(6)

The following state observation parameters can make the fault path detection model approach stable.

$$\xi(k+1) = \begin{bmatrix} \overline{A_{c11}} & \overline{B_{c1}} \\ 0 & I \end{bmatrix} \xi(k) + \begin{bmatrix} \rho(k+1) \\ 0 \end{bmatrix} + K(k)$$
$$[\lambda(k+1) - \begin{bmatrix} \overline{A_{c21}} & \overline{B_{c2}} \end{bmatrix} \xi(k)]$$

(7)

In the above formula, $K(k)$ is used to describe the kalman filter increment.

According to the method described above, the fault detection path of dynamic knowledge network learning system is designed by using the residual of observation parameters. The detection path is shown in Fig. 1.

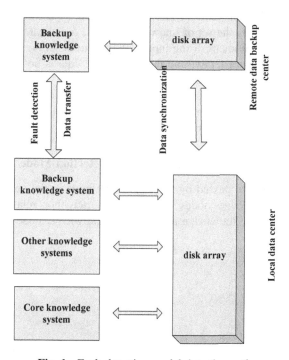

Fig. 1. Fault detection model detection path

The fault detection path ensures the security of the knowledge data in a single disk by copying and transferring [7, 8]. If the knowledge data in the storage system is lost, all knowledge acquisition in the entire network learning system cannot be performed normally [9]. Therefore, ensuring the security of knowledge data in the system is a top priority.

3 The Fault Detection Model of Dynamic Knowledge Network Learning System Is Constructed

In the dynamic knowledge network learning system, each operation execution time and system feedback time delay of acquiring knowledge are negligible [10]. The network learning system applies network technology to transmit knowledge information, and at the same time, the system has the possibility of fault [11].

3.1 Building Knowledge Data Node Fault Detection Mode

Let G = (π, Λ) represent the network in the knowledge learning system, G is a vector, and n = (1,..., n) represents the set of knowledge storage points in the knowledge learning system [12]. Then, $\Lambda \subseteq \pi \times \pi$ represents a collection of knowledge links in the knowledge learning system. Expressed as function [13]:

$$F_Y = F_X \times 2^\pi \tag{8}$$

Where F_Y is the value range of the knowledge system, F_X is the natural number set, and formula (1) represents the set of knowledge nodes. A indicates the set of storage node faults at a certain moment. If the input data produces set A, it indicates that the knowledge data node is not faulty, and the knowledge data is not lost in the storage system [14]. If the input data does not generate the set A, it indicates that the knowledge data node is faulty, and the corresponding knowledge data is lost. The dynamic knowledge network learning system will automatically detect the cause of the loss and synchronize the data in time.

3.2 Building the Knowledge Data Link Fault Detection Mode

The link refers to the path passed by the knowledge node in the network knowledge system. The two knowledge nodes belong to the neighbor relationship, and the network path from the m knowledge node to the n knowledge node is represented by m-n, and the two adjacent relationship knowledge nodes in the knowledge system [15], using neighbor(n) to represent its path set. There are two functions for the link between the node m and the n node, namely: send$_{m,n}$(A) and receive$_{m,n}$(A). The former is to pass the information A in the knowledge node m to the knowledge node n, if the knowledge node n receives the information A in the knowledge node m, then the knowledge node m passes the latter function to the knowledge point n [16]. Expressed by function:

$$y_m = \begin{cases} y_m, y_m \geq T_d \\ y_m - R, y_m \leq T_d \end{cases} \tag{9}$$

Where y_m is the information amount of the m node, T_d is the difference between the information amounts of the m node and the n node, and R is a natural integer. For the knowledge storage nodes m and n, under the premise that the m-n link is complete, the knowledge storage node m transmits information to the n through the link. If the send$_{m,n}$(A) and receive$_{m,n}$(A) functions are displayed in the system, it means that the link is not faulty, and the information won't be lost while transmitted in the link. If both send$_{m,n}$(A) and receive$_{m,n}$(A) functions are not displayed in the system, or only one [17] is displayed, it indicates that there is a problem between the two knowledge nodes, the dynamic knowledge network learning system will automatically monitor the cause of the problem and fix it in time.

3.3   Establishment of Intelligent Fault Detection Model

When a knowledge node or a link in the dynamic knowledge network learning system has problems, it will affect the normal operation of the knowledge learning system [18, 19]. The introduction of fault self-energy monitoring technology is mainly to automatically detect the entire learning system and find out where the fault may occur before the network knowledge system fails [20]. Before the fault occurs, the network learning system is processed by means of backing up, copying, and transferring the knowledge data to ensure the integrity of the knowledge data and the security of the network learning system [21, 22]. The fault detection algorithm is as follows:

Var Dp: //Fault detection module of initial process p;

Rp "π": The initial process p has a corresponding timer for any of the processes in the set π;

Initialization:

Dp=φ;

Forall q do rp "q=δ+υ";

Start sending process,send message with interval δ:

Forall q do send <alive> to q;

Receive process, q reset after receiving <alive> message:

Rp "q=δ+υ";

Detecte faults when rp "q" exceeds interval δ:

Dp=Dp ∪ q

The fault detection technology is based on the delay of knowledge node information [23], δ is the transmission period of information fault detection, and the knowledge data node sends the <alive> message [24, 25] according to the δ period, if the response feedback message has not been received within a certain time, which indicates that the dynamic knowledge network learning system has failed (Fig. 2).

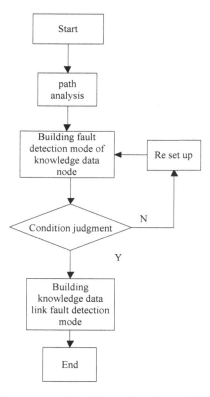

Fig. 2. Implementation process of intelligent detection model for network learning

Based on the fault detection model detection path design, the knowledge data node fault detection mode is built, the knowledge data link fault detection mode is built, and the network learning system fault intelligent detection model is realized.

4 Experimental Design and Result Analysis

In order to verify the effectiveness of the research on the fault intelligent detection technology of the dynamic knowledge network learning system proposed in this paper, the simulation test is carried out. During the test, two different dynamic knowledge network learning systems are used as test objects to test whether the system which gained knowledge per unit time failed. The knowledge data of two learning systems, English, mathematics, and physics are simulated. In order to ensure the accuracy of the simulation test, multiple simulation tests are performed, and the data generated by multiple tests are presented in the same data chart.

4.1   Data Preparation

In order to ensure the accuracy of the simulation test process and results, the test parameters are set. The simulation test uses two different dynamic knowledge network learning systems as the simulation test objects, simulates the number of system faults, and analyzes the simulation test results. Due to the amount of knowledge, the complexity of knowledge information, and the difficulty level of knowledge information contained in different stages and levels of knowledge data are different, the amount of correct knowledge is also different, and it has an impact on the test results. Therefore, it is necessary to ensure that the difficulty, subject and study time are consistent during the test. Set the tester's network learning time to 24 h. The test data setting results in this paper are shown in Table 1.

Table 1. Test parameters setting

Type	Complexity
Junior middle school	English
	Math
	Chemistry
	Physics
High school	English
	Math
	Chemistry
	Physics
University	English
	Chemistry
	Math
	Physics
Graduate student	English
	Math
	Chemistry
	Physics

4.2   Analysis of Test Results

The experimental results are counted as a contract collection schedule, and the test results are shown in Table 2.

Table 2. Number of system faults when acquiring knowledge

System type	Subject	Number of faults
Traditional system	English1	0
	English2	1
	English3	1
	English4	2
	Math1	1
	Math2	0
	Math3	1
	Math4	1
	Physics 1	0
	Physics 2	1
	Physics 3	1
	Physics 4	2
	Chemistry1	0
	Chemistry2	0
	Chemistry3	1
	Chemistry4	2
The system designed in this paper	English1	0
	English2	0
	English3	0
	English4	0
	Math1	0
	Math2	0
	Math3	0
	Math4	1
	Physics 1	0
	Physics 2	0
	Physics 3	0
	Physics 4	0
	Chemistry1	0
	Chemistry2	1
	Chemistry3	0
	Chemistry4	1

The numbers behind the subjects in the table indicate the difficulty of knowledge. The larger the number, the more complicated and difficult the relevant knowledge is. Because 12 different execution parameters are set during the test, it is impossible to obtain the experimental results at a glance, thus affecting the comparative analysis of the two systems. According to Table 2, the comparison of the number of faults of the system when acquiring knowledge is shown in Fig. 3.

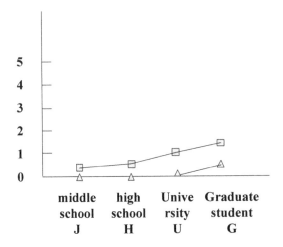

Fig. 3. Number of system faults when acquiring knowledge

In the figure, the abscissa is the degree of difficulty of knowledge, and the ordinate is the number of times the system fails when acquiring knowledge. The horizontal and vertical coordinate data are referred to Table 2. It can be seen from Fig. 3 that the dynamic knowledge network learning system fault intelligent detection technology research is significantly reduced compared with the traditional system.

In order to further verify the superiority of this method, the failure rate of dynamic knowledge network learning system is compared after the application of different methods. The results are shown in Table 3.

Table 3. System failure rates were compared by different methods

Number of experiment	Traditional system	The system designed in this paper
20	39.7%	0.6%
40	40.2%	0.9%
60	38.1%	0.5%
80	35.6%	1.0%
100	38.2%	0.4%
120	37.4%	0.6%
Average	38.2%	0.7%

As can be seen from the above table, the intelligent fault detection technology of dynamic knowledge network learning system designed in this paper reduces the failure rate of network learning system by 37.5%.

5   Conclusion

This paper proposes a research on intelligent detection technology for dynamic knowledge network learning system fault, based on the design of fault detection model detection path, relying on building knowledge data node fault detection mode, constructing knowledge data link fault detection mode, the construction of fault detection model detection mode is completed, and finally the fault intelligent detection technology studied in this paper is realized. The tests in this paper show that the research on fault intelligent detection technology is effective. It is hoped that the research of fault intelligent detection technology in this paper can provide a theoretical basis for the research of fault intelligent detection technology in dynamic knowledge network learning system.

References

1. Ji, J.: Research on extraction and detection of intrusion feature information in mobile network. Computer Simulation **34**(3), 289–292 (2017)
2. Zhou, Q., Yan, P., Xin, Y.: Research on a knowledge modelling methodology for fault diagnosis of machine tools based on formal semantics. Adv. Eng. Inform. **32**(9), 92–112 (2017)
3. Pandey, R.K., Gupta, D.K.: Intelligent multi-area power control: dynamic knowledge domain inference concept. IEEE Trans. Power Syst. **32**(6), 4310–4318 (2017)
4. Koperwas, J., Skonieczny, Ł., Kozłowski, M., Andruszkiewicz, P., Rybiński, H., Struk, W.: Intelligent information processing for building university knowledge base. J. Intel. Inf. Syst. **48**(1), 141–163 (2016). https://doi.org/10.1007/s10844-015-0393-0
5. Saiprasert, C., Pholprasit, T., Thajchayapong, S.: Detection of driving events using sensory data on smartphone. Int. J. Intel. Transp. Syst. Res. **15**(1), 17–28 (2015). https://doi.org/10.1007/s13177-015-0116-5
6. Shi, D., Fang, W., Zhang, F., et al.: A novel method for intelligent EMC management using a "knowledge base". IEEE Trans. Electromagn. Compat. **60**(6), 1621–1626 (2018)
7. Sun, L., Wu, J., Jia, H., et al.: Research on fault detection method for heat pump air conditioning system under cold weather. Chin. J. Chem. Eng. **12**(1), 88–96 (2017)
8. Ji, H., Park, K., Jo, J., Lim, H.: Mining students activities from a computer supported collaborative learning system based on peer to peer network. Peer-to-Peer Netw. Appl. **9**(3), 465–476 (2015). https://doi.org/10.1007/s12083-015-0397-0
9. Idris, N.H., Salim, N.A., Othman, M.M., et al.: Prediction of cascading collapse occurrence due to the effect of hidden failure of a protection system using artificial neural network. J. Elect. Syst. **13**(2), 366–375 (2017)
10. Cui, Q., Li, J., Wang, P., et al.: Cascading failure of command information system bi-layer coupled network model. Harbin Gongye Daxue Xuebao/J. Harbin Inst. Technol. **49**(5), 100–108 (2017)
11. Dan, L., Zhou, Y., Hu, G., et al.: Fault detection and diagnosis for building cooling system with a tree-structured learning method. Energy Build. **127**, 540–551 (2016)
12. Li, Yu., et al.: Image fusion of fault detection in power system based on deep learning. Clust. Comput. **22**(4), 9435–9443 (2018). https://doi.org/10.1007/s10586-018-2264-2

13. Bhattacharya, S., Roy, S., Chowdhury, S.: A neural network-based intelligent cognitive state recognizer for confidence-based e-learning system. Neural Comput. Appl. **29**(1), 205–219 (2016). https://doi.org/10.1007/s00521-016-2430-5

14. Keliris, C., Polycarpou, M.M., Parisini, T.: An integrated learning and filtering approach for fault diagnosis of a class of nonlinear dynamical systems. IEEE Trans. Neural Netw. Learn. Syst. **28**(4), 988–1004 (2017)

15. Boella, G., Caro, L.D., Humphreys, L., Robaldo, L., Rossi, P., van der Torre, L.: Eunomos, a legal document and knowledge management system for the Web to provide relevant, reliable and up-to-date information on the law. Artif. Intel. Law **24**(3), 245–283 (2016). https://doi.org/10.1007/s10506-016-9184-3

16. Tribe, J., Liburd, J.J.: The tourism knowledge system. Ann. Tour. Res. **57**(2), 44–61 (2016)

17. Li, J.: Exploring the logic and landscape of the knowledge system: multilevel structures, each multiscaled with complexity at the mesoscale. Engineering **2**(3), 276–285 (2016)

18. Mccullough, E.B., Matson, P.A.: Evolution of the knowledge system for agricultural development in the Yaqui Valley, Sonora, Mexico. Proc. Nat. Acad. Sci. U.S.A. **113**(17), 4609 (2016)

19. Santoro, G., Vrontis, D., Thrassou, A., et al.: The Internet of Things: building a knowledge management system for open innovation and knowledge management capacity. Technol. Forecast. Soc. Chang. **136**(2), S0040162517302846 (2017)

20. Kaggal, V.C., Elayavilli, R.K., Mehrabi, S., et al.: Toward a learning health-care system – knowledge delivery at the point of care empowered by big data and NLP. Biomed. Inform. Insights **8**(Suppl. 1), 13–22 (2016)

21. Herrick, J.E., Beh, A., Barrios, E., et al.: The Land-Potential Knowledge System (LandPKS): mobile apps and collaboration for optimizing climate change investments. Ecosyst. Health Sustain. **2**(3), e01209 (2016)

22. Dong, T.P., Hung, C.L., Cheng, N.C.: Enhancing knowledge sharing intention through the satisfactory context of continual service of knowledge management system. Inf. Technol. People **29**(4), 807–829 (2016)

23. Taraba, P., Trojan, J., Kavkova, V.: Development of the knowledge system based on formation of holistic competence of project managers in the Czech Republic. In: International Scientific & Technical Conference on Computer Sciences & Information Technologies (2017)

24. Arru, M., Negre, E., Rosenthal-Sabroux, C., et al.: Towards a responsible early-warning system: Knowledge implications in decision support design. In: IEEE 10th International Conference on Research Challenges in Information Science (2016)

25. Golovachyova, V.N., Menlibekova, G.Z., Abayeva, N.F., et al.: Construction of expert knowledge monitoring and assessment system based on integral method of knowledge evaluation. Int. J. Environ. Sci. Educ. **11**(2), 162–170 (2016)

Design of Buoy Positioning System for Ocean Monitoring Based on Visual Feature Recognition

Ye Liu[1,2,3(✉)] and Lei Liu[1,2,3]

[1] Institute of Oceanographic Instrumentation, Qilu University of Technology
(Shandong Academy of Sciences), Qingdao, China
ly0822cn@163.com
[2] Shandong Provincial Key Laboratory of Ocean Environmental Monitoring
Technology, Qingdao, China
[3] National Engineering and Technological Research Center of Marine
Monitoring Equipment, Qingdao, China

Abstract. Because the latitude and longitude feedback of the traditional ocean monitoring buoy is not accurate, a method of ocean monitoring buoy positioning based on visual feature recognition is proposed. By selecting buoy shape and material, the communication module and image acquisition module are designed Complete hardware design. In the software design, according to the angle between the lowest pixel, the highest pixel and the horizontal direction, the positioning analog signal is selected. Through the E-R model and the buoy information table field, the database design is completed. So far, the design of the buoy positioning system based on visual feature recognition is completed. According to the simulation results, the longitude and latitude coordinates of the design system feedback can be accurate to four decimal places, which shows that the designed positioning system is more accurate.

Keywords: Visual feature recognition · Marine monitoring buoy · Positioning system design

1 Introduction

The sea is the origin of life, containing countless treasures and resources. The rational use and development of the oceans have an important impact on our economic development and social progress. At the same time, various natural disasters caused by the oceans also have a huge impact on social development and human life. China's marine disasters are relatively serious, which are affected by marine pollution, red tide, typhoon, storm surge and so on. It is urgent to strengthen the monitoring and research of marine environment [1]. At present, the main methods for locating buoys are GPS, simulated annealing and extended Kalman filter. Among them, GPS technology is to send the buoy signal to the remote monitoring center through the wireless GPRS network, and use the network technology to obtain the buoy positioning information.

© ICST Institute for Computer Sciences, Social Informatics and Telecommunications Engineering 2020
Published by Springer Nature Switzerland AG 2020. All Rights Reserved
Y.-D. Zhang et al. (Eds.): ICMTEL 2020, LNICST 326, pp. 449–460, 2020.
https://doi.org/10.1007/978-3-030-51100-5_40

The simulated annealing algorithm can locate the target effectively by establishing the target function of the buoy system and establishing the reasonable receiving and stopping criterion. The extended Kalman filtering algorithm uses the relative azimuth information of the aerial sonar buoy and the aircraft to determine the position of the buoy. However, the longitude and latitude feedback of the traditional marine monitoring buoy positioning system is not accurate enough, so a visual feature recognition based marine monitoring buoy positioning system is designed. Visual feature recognition is a method of feature recognition based on the main features of the content image (such as color, texture, and shape). Visual feature recognition is not only applied in the field of computer, but also widely used in industrial design, civil architecture and geographic mapping. For example, in the production of industrial equipment parts, through the application of visual feature recognition method, it can be intuitively analyzed whether there are defects in the shape of parts. This paper will carry out buoy positioning through this mechanism. The innovation point of this paper is that when setting the buoy position, the camera is used for pixel calibration, and some sampling points are selected on the spatial physical coordinate plane, the pixel coordinate difference is considered, and the relative uniform part of the difference is selected to set, thus the scientific distribution of the buoy position is raised.

2 Design of Buoy Positioning System for Ocean Monitoring Based on Visual Feature Recognition

Marine monitoring technology is a comprehensive high-tech which integrates computer, information and sensors, database, remote communication and other disciplines. It integrates the development achievements of many disciplines and represents the development frontier of high technology. With the development of related disciplines and technologies, real-time image processing technology has been more and more integrated into various fields of society. As an important part of the three-dimensional monitoring network of marine environment, the marine buoy monitoring system based on real-time monitoring image has the advantages of stable operation, strong resistance to external damage, large bearing capacity and long working time [2]. A positioning system is designed for the marine monitoring buoy, including the buoy system, shore station receiving system and upper computer. The overall structure is shown in the figure below (Fig. 1):

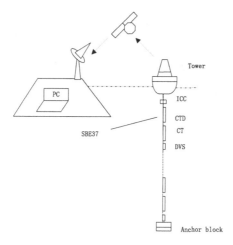

Fig. 1. Marine monitoring buoy positioning system

The hardware design of buoy positioning system mainly includes buoy body, power supply system module, protective equipment, sensor, anchoring system. In the software design, we make full use of DSP/BIOS real-time operating system and scom communication module to manage various tasks, and use TI's class/micro driver model and CSL's API to optimize the algorithm design. This design not only improves the utilization rate of driver code, but also ensures the real-time positioning of the system [3]. Next, the hardware and software of the system are designed respectively.

3 Hardware Design

3.1 Design Buoy

It mainly includes buoy components, batteries, solar panels and various sensors, etc. To prove that the foundation of stable operation of buoy on the sea surface is similar to the cone-shaped buoy, as shown in the following figure (Fig. 2):

Fig. 2. Cone like floating body

Therefore, the design of the buoy is very important. It is necessary to analyze the wave response of the conical buoy in this paper. By analyzing the roll response and heave response, the buoy shape that is most suitable for the design conditions of this paper is selected [4]. According to the size of the conical buoy, the deck diameter is 3 M, the bottom diameter is 1.5 m, the depth and draft are 0.4 m, and the displacement is 3 T. The Rao (floating body response under the action of unit regular wave amplitude) of the target at different wave angles has the following response function with time under simple harmonic $R(\omega, \beta, t)$:

$$R(\omega, \beta, t) = AR_e\left[|H(\omega, \beta)|e^{i(\omega t + \varphi)}\right]* \tag{1}$$

In formula (1), A is the incident amplitude value; R_e is the heave response; $H(\omega, \beta)$ is the transfer function; $e^{i(\omega t + \varphi)}$ is the frequency. As for the selection of the material of the buoy, it is very important for the stable and continuous operation of the buoy. Especially in the sea areas with high temperature, high salinity and frequent sea conditions in South China, the influence of target materials is very obvious. At present, the buoy materials at home and abroad are mainly steel, plastic and chin alloy. Their comparisons are as follows (Table 1):

Table 1. Performance comparison of buoy materials

Floating body material	Anticorrosive	Advantage	Disadvantages
Steel	Poor	Mature, low cost	Easy to corrosion
Stainless steel	Good	Heat and high temperature resistance, a wide range of applications, many categories	The high cost
Engineering plastics	Good corrosion resistance	High rigidity, high mechanical strength	The price is expensive and the output is small

Comparing the anticorrosive properties, merits and demerits and cost of several materials, the standard skeleton of the buoy chooses 316 stainless steel with good corrosion resistance. The buoyancy chamber of the standard body selects EVA material as the foam floating body to provide support for the buoy. So far, the design of the buoy body has been completed.

3.2 Design Image Acquisition Card

Real time image processing technology has been more and more integrated into various fields of society. As an important part of the three-dimensional monitoring network of marine environment, the marine buoy monitoring system based on real-time monitoring image has the advantages of stable operation, strong resistance to external damage, large bearing capacity and long working time [5]. Image acquisition card is the foundation of buoy positioning system based on visual feature recognition. It needs to meet the requirements of miniaturization, lightweight, low power, long life, safety and no pollution. At present, most of the offshore buoys are powered by batteries and solar panels. Due to the constraints of the environment and battery life of the offshore buoys, the batteries need to be replaced every three months or so. Based on the existing power supply equipment, this paper designs the image acquisition card, uses the new marine energy (wind energy, wave energy) to realize the self power supply of the acquisition card, extends the maintenance free period, and ensures the long-term stability of the buoy. First, the circuit connection diagram of the acquisition card is designed as shown in the following figure (Fig. 3):

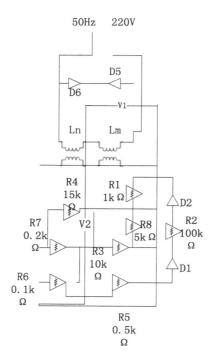

Fig. 3. Circuit connection diagram of acquisition card

Description of the circuit connection diagram of the acquisition card: in the whole circuit board, if the power start button is started, the contactor ln is powered on and self-locking, and the normally open contacts d5 and D6 are closed, the whole acquisition card circuit board is powered on. The control signal is fed back to the lower computer through R1 1 kΩ serial interface, to ensure that the acquisition card drives the horizontal or vertical DC motor to rotate in the positive and negative directions according to the acquired control signal [6]. The control voltage of the circuit board is realized by two switch type step-down regulators D1 and a single channel analog switch. According to the analog switch of control signal management channel, the acquisition card selects a reasonable resistance, and then regulates the output voltage. So far, the hardware design of the system has been completed.

4 Software Design

The working environment of the designed and developed buoy positioning system is long-term, continuous and unattended. Considering that LabVIEW software has powerful functions, flexible programming and friendly human-computer interface, it is specially selected as the foreground development tool, while SQL server has powerful data management functions, as a network database, and the system functions realized by the monitoring system are shown in Fig. 4:

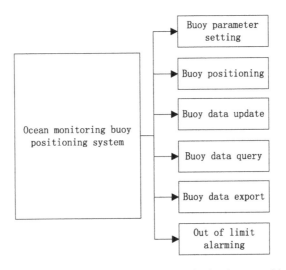

Fig. 4. Functional structure diagram of marine monitoring buoy positioning system

Next, the software of the detection buoy positioning system is designed.

4.1 Select Positioning Analog Signal

Analog signal includes current signal and voltage signal, which are located through serial port. The system obtains the target information through two CCD cameras [7]. Based on the principle of binocular vision (head up binocular vision principle, and some adjustments are made), the triangle relationship between the target point and two cameras is used to locate the target. The system studies the target positioning according to the following steps: first, determine the position and orientation of the two buoy cameras in the work area, the distance between the two cameras (baseline distance); determine the corresponding relationship between the pixel coordinates and the physical angle; use the triangle principle to calculate the physical coordinates of the intersection of the two projection lines. Select a number of sampling points on the existing spatial physical coordinate plane (sampling at equal intervals), find out the pixel coordinates of the camera corresponding to the sampling points, observe the pixel coordinates corresponding to each sampling point, verify the pixel coordinates difference between each sampling point, select the parts with relatively uniform difference, determine the lowest pixel point and the highest pixel point selected, and measure the angle. The calculation formula is:

$$\frac{P\_End - P\_Start}{\theta_Q} = \frac{P\_End - Pixel}{\theta} \tag{2}$$

In formula (2), P_End is the highest pixel, P_Start is the lowest pixel, θ_Q is the camera angle corresponding to the selected lowest pixel and the highest pixel, as the maximum field angle. In the case of a single camera, the angle relationship between them is shown in the following figure (Fig. 5):

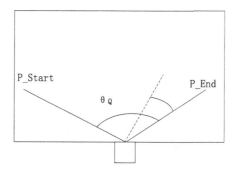

Fig. 5. Relationship between angles

After obtaining the angle relationship, the corresponding relationship between the spatial physical coordinates of the sampling point and the pixel coordinates of the image can be established: The horizontal distance between the two cameras is L, and the width of the delimited area W is used for projector projection. The angle between the highest pixel of the left camera and the horizontal direction is θ_L, and the angle between the lowest pixel of the right camera and the horizontal direction is θ_L. According to these two included angles, the positioning analog signal is finally determined.

4.2   Database Design

Database is a collection of organized and shareable large amount of data stored in computer for a long time. The data in database is described, organized and stored according to a certain data model, which has the characteristics of permanent storage, organization and shareable [8]. In the database design of this paper, the amount of buoy positioning data that users need should be reasonably stored, and the stored data should have the ability of fast feedback, which can effectively and quickly realize the secondary development of users' data. In the conceptual structure design of the database, the E-R model is used to represent the data logic. The E-R diagram of the buoy is shown as follows (Fig. 6):

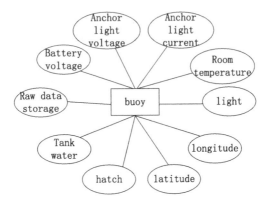

Fig. 6. E-R chart of buoy

In conceptual structure design, E-R model is a logical representation of data, which is not constrained by any DBMS and is widely used as a tool of data modeling in database design. The logical structure design of the database is to convert the basic E-R diagram designed in the conceptual structure design stage into the logical structure consistent with the data model supported by the DBMS, to ensure that the basic table structure is reasonable, to reduce data redundancy, and to improve the utilization rate of storage space [9]. This system adopts the classical relational database architecture to determine the number of tables in the database and the relationship between tables. The buoy body information table records the element values related to buoy body safety, with the whole time as the primary key. The details are as follows (Table 2):

Table 2. Field description of buoy information table

Field meaning	The field name	The data type	Whether the primary key
The hour of time	IntegralTime	Datetime	Not null
Sampling time	SampleTime	Datetime	Null
Battery voltage	BatteryVoltage	Nvarchar [50]	Null
Anchor light voltage	LightVoltage	Nvarchar [50]	Null
Anchor light current	LightCurrent	Nvarchar [50]	Null
Anchor light current	CabinTempt	Nvarchar [50]	Null
light	Light	Nvarchar [50]	Null
longitude	Longitude	Nvarchar [50]	Null
latitude	Latitude	Nvarchar [50]	Null
hatch	DoorAlarm	Int	Null
Tank water	WaterAlarm	Int	Null
Raw data storage	SaveDate	Int	Null

After getting the E-R diagram and field table, the database can be created. SQL Server 2005 provides us with rich graphical management tools, which facilitates the creation and configuration of database. The specific steps are as follows: (1) First, select the appropriate version of SQL Server database according to the existing laboratory conditions, computer hardware resources and operating system environment. Windows XP is selected as the operating system and SQL Server 2005 is selected as the database version; (2) After the completion of database installation, define the database, name the database inmarsatbuoy, and create the database with graphical method or T-SQL statement; (3) Create all kinds of table spaces to be used – InMarsatATPressure, InMarsatBuoyBody, InMarsatHumidity, Watertemper, Wave, Wind, etc. And create tables with graphical methods or T-SQL statements. The workflow of the buoy positioning system based on visual feature recognition is as follows (Fig. 7):

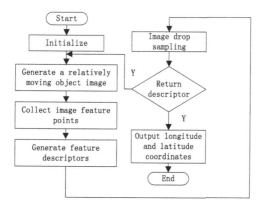

Fig. 7. System work flow chart

So far, the design of buoy positioning system based on visual feature recognition is completed.

5 Simulation Test Experiment

In order to verify the effectiveness of the designed system, we need to design simulation experiments, and use the traditional positioning system as a contrast, and analyze the experimental results.

5.1 Experimental Environment

The hardware emulator xds560 is selected as the bridge between DSP processing platform and PC to ensure that the simulation results of the system are consistent with the actual operation results. Make full use of the fast characteristics of this hardware emulator to realize fast code download and online debugging. The system connection using the hardware emulator is as follows (Fig. 8):

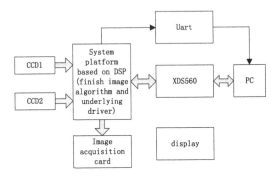

Fig. 8. System experiment environment

According to different functions, the experimental system is divided into the following main parts: (1) Feature acquisition: CCD1 and CCD2 represent two cameras respectively, real-time acquisition of images waiting for DSP platform processing. (2) Signal processing part: the DSP used in the experiment is TMS320DM642 digital signal processor of TI company, and the design of software system is completed on SEED-VPM642 development board provided by hezhongda company, in which video coding and decoding equipment and UART communication module have been integrated. TMS320DM642 is the core device of the scheduling management system. It manages the related equipment and runs the finger recognition and positioning algorithm. The experiment was carried out in this experimental environment and the results were analyzed.

5.2   Experimental Results and Analysis

Because of the limitation of marine environment (such as the influence of sea breeze and wave), some external conditions and factors cannot be determined, so the method of qualitative analysis cannot be carried out. In addition, because of the combination of qualitative and quantitative experimental methods, it has a subjective effect on the experimental results to some extent, so this experiment will be carried out by quantitative analysis. In the above experimental environment, the original system and the system designed in this paper are compared. The experimental results are shown in the following table (Table 3):

Table 3. Experimental result

Location feedback time	The original system latitude and longitude	Latitude and longitude of the system	Latitude and longitude of traditional systems
7:00	120.3 39.1	120.2835 39.0708	122.45 40.64
8:00	120.3 40.9	120.3055 40.8654	121.32 39.72
9:00	120.6 39.0	120.875 39.0282	121.34 40.21
10:00	120.4 39.0	120.3771 39.0146	119.87 30.73
11:00	120.3 39.6	120.3029 39.5894	120.86 40.12
12:00	120.3 39.6	120.3084 39.6027	121.02 39.76
13:00	120.3 39.5	120.3222 39.5259	120.642 40.43

Using the original positioning system and the system designed in this paper, we can receive the longitude and latitude coordinates fed back by the system every hour. When the feedback coordinates are retrieved and analyzed, the longitude and latitude of the original system can only be accurate to one decimal place. The longitude and latitude coordinates of the feedback system designed in this paper can be accurate to four decimal places. It can be seen that the positioning system designed in this paper is more accurate.

6   Conclusion

Because the longitude and latitude feedback of traditional positioning system of ocean monitoring buoy is not accurate enough, a positioning system of ocean monitoring buoy based on visual feature recognition is designed. Through the design of hardware and software, the positioning system of ocean monitoring buoy based on visual feature recognition is designed. According to the simulation results, the designed system feedback longitude and latitude coordinates can be accurate to four decimal places, indicating that the designed positioning system longitude and latitude coordinates positioning is more accurate. Especially in the severe weather, the buoy positioning system can monitor the marine hydrological and meteorological parameters in an all-round way, and provide valuable data support for the meteorological research of the marine sector, which has the particularity that other monitoring methods can not replace. Therefore, the design and analysis of the marine buoy positioning system can better promote the progress of marine positioning technology and make contributions to the marine monitoring industry.

References

1. Zhao, J., Wang, Z., Hui, L., et al.: Design of a marine multi-point water quality monitoring system based on underwater acoustic communication. J. Dalian Fish. Univ. **32**(6), 747–752 (2017)
2. Cao, W., Sun, Z., Li, C., et al.: Design and application of data collecting system and data receiving system for water quality monitoring buoy. J. Trop. Oceanogr. **37**(5), 1–6 (2018)
3. Kong, W., Yang, Z., Ma, S.: Design of ultra-low power consumption ocean drifting buoy collector based on MSP430. Mod. Electron. Tech. **40**(20), 146–149 (2017)
4. Rao, K.-y., Ji, X.-p., Chen, J.-m., et al.: Design and implementation of the low-power management scheme for the Polar Drift-Towing Ocean Profiler. Mar. Sci. **41**(9), 27–33 (2017)
5. Wang, S., Tian, Y., Tian, K.: Application of BeiDou satellite navigation system in wave energy self-powered marine Buoy. GNSS World China **43**(04), 130–134 (2018)
6. Zhao, T., Qi, J., Ruan, D.-s., et al.: Design of an ocean buoy auto-warning system based on geomagnetic-infrared detection. J. Ocean Technol. **36**(5), 19–25 (2017)
7. Zhang, Z., Wu, N., Yu, J.: Design and implementation of underwater acoustic identification system based on feature template matching. Comput. Digital Eng. **46**(11), 2274–2278 (2018)
8. Zhang, K., Wang, H., Chen, X.-d.: Visual dispensing system based on automatic recognition of workpieces. Modular Mach. Tool Autom. Manuf. Tech. **533**(7), 43–47 (2018)
9. Wan, Q., Yu, H., Wu, D., et al.: Survey of multiple objects tracking based on three-dimensional visual systems. Comput. Eng. Appl. **53**(19), 33–39 (2017)

Application of Iridium Data Communication System in Information Transmission of Ocean Monitoring Buoy

Ye Liu[1,2,3(✉)] and Yu-zhe Xu[1,2,3]

[1] Institute of Oceanographic Instrumentation, Qilu University of Technology
(Shandong Academy of Sciences), Qingdao, China
ly0822cn@163.com
[2] Shandong Provincial Key Laboratory of Ocean Environmental Monitoring
Technology, Qingdao, China
[3] National Engineering and Technological Research Center of Marine
Monitoring Equipment, Qingdao, China

Abstract. In view of the problem of poor real-time transmission of the traditional information transmission method of marine monitoring buoy, the transmission speed is slow. Based on this, iridium data communication system is applied to the information transmission of ocean monitoring buoy. Through the establishment of the overall framework of Iridium satellite communication system, determine the buoy information transmission network protocol. On the basis of the network protocol, use Iridium satellite data communication system to obtain the location information of the marine monitoring buoy, and then process the obtained information. Finally, upload the processed buoy information to complete the transmission of the marine monitoring buoy information. Compared with the traditional method of information transmission of ocean monitoring buoy, the experimental results show that the method of information transmission of ocean monitoring buoy using iridium data communication system can complete the transmission of buoy information in a shorter transmission time, with better real-time transmission.

Keywords: Iridium data communication system · Marine monitoring · Buoys · Information transmission

1 Introduction

With the development of operational marine monitoring system, marine monitoring technology is also developing rapidly. China is speeding up the construction and improvement of the marine environment three-dimensional monitoring system covering China's coastal waters. At present, there are many kinds of instruments and sensors used in the marine environment monitoring system, with different working principles and positions. They cover the observation elements from shore to offshore, from air to water, from water to seabed, including dynamic elements, ecological elements and geological parameters [1–3]. The real-time/quasi real-time data acquisition of various automatic monitoring instruments and equipment is the key to ensure the operational

© ICST Institute for Computer Sciences, Social Informatics and Telecommunications Engineering 2020
Published by Springer Nature Switzerland AG 2020. All Rights Reserved
Y.-D. Zhang et al. (Eds.): ICMTEL 2020, LNICST 326, pp. 461–471, 2020.
https://doi.org/10.1007/978-3-030-51100-5_41

operation of the observation system. The offshore marine monitoring system is far away from the ground, and the conventional cable, short wave, GSM/CDMA and other communication modes are difficult to meet the requirements. At present, the widely used communication mode is all kinds of satellite systems with communication ability [4–7].

Large scale ocean data buoy is a kind of fully automatic and advanced ocean hydrological and meteorological telemetry equipment, which can monitor the ocean hydrological and meteorological parameters of a certain anchor point for a long term, continuous, fixed-point and automatic way, and provide real-time data for the disaster marine environment prediction, ocean development and ocean engineering. It is the main source and important component of the data in the ocean disaster early warning and prediction system [8]. Due to the high requirement of real-time marine monitoring data, the real-time data transmission system of marine data buoy is an important part of the buoy. Since the development of ocean data buoy in China, the real-time data transmission system has adopted a variety of data communication methods, including short wave communication, Inmarsat-C satellite communication and GPRS/CDMA communication. All kinds of communication modes have their own advantages and limitations. Short wave communication has poor anti-interference ability, high bit error rate and low data receiving rate. Inmarsat-C satellite communication has high reliability and data receiving rate of more than 95%, but the communication cost is high, which is not suitable for data transmission. GPRS/CDMA communication cost is low, but the communication signal is limited by the distance from buoy to shore [9]. According to the technical requirements of the data transmission of the buoy system, iridium data communication is used to transmit large amount of real-time data, which can improve the stability and reliability of the information transmission of the marine monitoring buoy, with the remarkable characteristics of high speed, low signal delay and small signal loss [10]. Based on the above analysis, the application of iridium data communication system in the information transmission of ocean monitoring buoy is described.

2   Application of Iridium Data Communication System in Information Transmission of Ocean Monitoring Buoy

2.1   General Architecture of Iridium Communication System

Iridium BD terminal module 9602 introduced by iridium company is used in iridium communication system. The SBD service of bidirectional real-time short data transmission in the form of data package is mainly used for the application development of regional automation and remote data tracking. In view of the special sea area of marine monitoring buoy, the data transmission is realized by using iridium BD. The SBD service of iridium SBD terminal module 9602 is realized through RS-232C interface, and the baud rate is 19200 bit/s by default. The module can receive up to 270b data or send 340B data at a time, and does not need to install a SIM card. When there is data receiving, it will ring. The average standby current of the module is 5 mA, while the average current of iridium SBD is 95ma and 45 mA respectively. The user application monitoring center uses iridium SBD terminal module 9602 to transmit and receive data through iridium communication network.

Because the logic level of RS-232C standard is not compatible with the logic level of TTL digital circuit, when the communication interface of iridium SBD terminal module 9602 adopts RS-232C standard, the level conversion of the communication interface should be carried out first when the hardware circuit is connected. In order to realize RS-232C level conversion, the interface device adopts the ax3232e chip of Maxim company, which is a low power consumption level conversion chip with data transmission rate up to 250 kb/s and two transmitters and two receivers. The overall framework of iridium communication system is shown in Fig. 1.

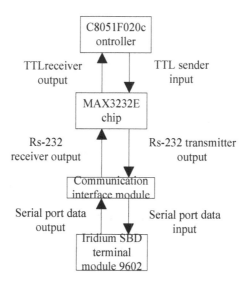

Fig. 1. General framework of iridium communication system

The software core of iridium SBD communication is the development of 9602 driver of iridium SBD terminal module. The software part of its iridium data communication system includes several modules, and its main functions are as follows. The main functions of the data acquisition module include: switching the extended serial port of imp16c554; collecting data according to the communication protocol of each equipment; compiling the collected data. The main function of data transmission module is to dial and transmit data. In the data transmission module, it mainly focuses on three aspects: the first is the processing of the shore station program timeout and unresponsive after dialing successfully; the second is the response timeout retransmission control; the third is the processing of data verification errors in the process of data transmission. The data transmission module packs the transmitted data into frames, each 32 bytes is a frame, and adds CRC16 verification. In the process of data receiving and sending, after the connection between the transmitting module and the receiving shore station is established, the shore station verifies each received frame of data, and responds to the transmitting module according to the verification results.

The iridium data communication system is applied to the information transmission of marine monitoring buoy, as described below.

2.2   Determination of Buoy Information Transmission Network Protocol

Network communication needs network protocol, so it is very important to choose appropriate network protocol to ensure data transmission. TCP/IP protocol is used as the buoy information transmission network protocol. In the TCP/IP protocol, each terminal has an IP address, and different applications on the terminal have a port number. On the same terminal, different applications can be distinguished according to the port number. There are two kinds of TCP/IP protocols: connection oriented reliable transport protocol TCP and connectionless unreliable transport protocol UDP. When using UDP protocol to communicate, you only need to know the IP address and port number of the other party to send the data. You don't need to establish a connection, but you can't guarantee the integrity of the data, which is prone to data loss. When using TCP protocol to communicate, you should first establish a connection between the two sides of the communication, so as to prepare for the subsequent communication. In TCP communication, data can be confirmed and retransmitted in case of transmission error, so as to ensure that the data will be transmitted to the other party. The communication protocol in this software is TCP/IP protocol based on client/server mode. As a client, the offshore buoy host should actively establish a TCP connection with the server-side shore station receiving system with fixed public IP address and fixed monitoring port, Then the receiving system of the shore station sends the corresponding command to the buoy host through the connected socket, waiting for the buoy host to receive and send the data to the shore station.

2.3   Acquisition of Position Information of Marine Monitoring Buoy

The underwater data acquisition module in the iridium data communication system uses the wave energy to descend by itself, rise to the set depth, and start to collect data. When it rises to a certain distance from the sea surface buoy, the NdFeB magnetic block embedded in the glass fiber reinforced plastic at the top of the data acquisition system will trigger the magnetic sensitive switch circuit embedded in the glass fiber reinforced plastic at the bottom of the buoy to generate the interrupt signal and wake up the main control board in the dormant state. Then, the main control board receives and saves the data from the electromagnetic coupling system through the BCB serial port. After receiving the data, the underwater data acquisition system descends again to collect the data. At the same time, the main control board sends the received data to the monitoring center through the iridium communication terminal, and enters the sleep state again, waiting for the next data arrival.

Assuming that the signal frequency of the ocean monitoring buoy (radiation source) is f_D, when the satellite in the iridium data communication system moves towards the direction close to the radiation source, the signal frequency received by the satellite will be greater than the signal frequency sent by the radiation source f_D, When the satellite flies over the radiation source and the connection between them is perpendicular to the movement direction of the satellite, the signal frequency received by the satellite will be equal to the signal frequency f_D emitted by the radiation source. When the satellite moves away from the radiation source, the signal frequency received by the satellite will be less than the signal frequency f_D emitted by the radiation source. The relationship between the sending frequency of the radiation source signal and the receiving frequency of the satellite signal can be expressed as follows:

$$f_R = \left(1 + \frac{|v| \cos \theta}{c} \right) f_D \tag{1}$$

Among them, f_R is the signal receiving frequency, v is the speed vector of the satellite, c is the propagation speed of electromagnetic wave in the medium, θ is the angle between the connection between the satellite and the radiation source and the speed direction of the satellite. Assuming that the receiving frequency of the signal from the radiation source is measured by the satellite at t_N time, the included angle t_N can be calculated according to Formula 1 when the transmitting frequency of the radiation source signal is known. From a geometric point of view, in three-dimensional space, all points with an included angle of θ_N with the direction of satellite movement can form a conical surface with a fixed point of satellite and a conical angle of θ_N. When the radiation source is at any position on the cone surface, the receiving frequency of the satellite for the radiation source signal is equal when the signal transmitting frequency is constant, so the cone surface is also called the equal frequency surface. If the satellite gets two equal frequency surfaces at t_1 and t_2 respectively, If the conic angles of these two equal frequency surfaces are θ_1 and θ_2 respectively, two curves will be formed when the two equal frequency surfaces intersect the earth sphere.

The marine monitoring buoy is considered as a stationary target during the period of satellite visibility. According to the Doppler frequency offset effect, the measurement frequency of the ith received signal can be expressed as:

$$\begin{aligned} f_{ri} &= f_e \left(1 - \frac{V_{si}^T (L_{si} - L_b)}{c|L_{si} - L_b|} \right) + n_i \\ &= f_e \left(1 - \frac{V_{sxi}(x_{si} - x) + V_{syi}(y_{si} - y) + V_{szi}(z_{si} - z)}{c(x_{si} - x)^2 + (y_{si} - y)^2 + (z_{si} - z)^2} \right) + n_i \end{aligned} \tag{2}$$

Among them, f_e is the carrier frequency of the signal, $L_b = [x, y, z]^T$ is the position vector of the marine monitoring buoy in the ECEF coordinate system, $V_{si} = [V_{sxi}, V_{syi}, V_{szi}]^T$, $L_{si} = [x_{si}, y_{si}, z_{si}]^T$ are the speed vector and position vector of the satellite in the i-th positioning respectively, n_i is the signal noise.

According to the signal receiving frequency measured at different times, the position coordinates of the marine monitoring buoy can be located. Because the satellite transmits information on two fixed VHF working channels (161.975 MHz and 162.025 MHz). Therefore, when the carrier frequency of the signal is known and the earth surface equation is combined, two equal frequency surface equations are established, and then the position vector of the ocean monitoring buoy can be obtained by solving the equations composed of three equations. According to the intersection of these two curves, the position of the ocean monitoring buoy can be determined.

2.4   Information Processing of Marine Monitoring Buoy

The information of ocean monitoring buoy is mainly related to the ocean. The specific processing contents are as follows:

Calculation of meteorological and hydrological data: according to the requirements of coastal observation specification, it is necessary to observe the wind speed and corresponding wind direction, maximum wind speed and corresponding wind direction and its occurrence time, maximum wind speed and corresponding wind direction and its occurrence time, daily maximum wind speed and corresponding wind direction and its occurrence time. The wind parameters are sampled once every 3S, and the wind direction is sampled in integral time of every 3S. Instantaneous wind speed: take the average wind speed of 3S before sampling as the instantaneous wind speed of this sampling. Instantaneous wind direction: add the direction obtained by the electro-magnetic compass and the direction of the wind sensor itself, and then put it into the main value range 0–360. At the zero second of every minute, the instantaneous wind data obtained in the previous minute is calculated on a minute average. If 11 valid sampling data are obtained in this minute, the data in this minute will be considered as valid, and one minute average calculation will be carried out, otherwise no processing (no calculation, no storage) will be carried out. The wind speed is calculated by averaging 21 samples from 0 s in the previous minute to 0 s in the current minute. The wind direction is decomposed and added by the vectors of 21 sampling values from 0 s of the previous minute to 0 s of the current minute, and then synthesized. Zero (North) if 0. At the 0 s of every minute, the average wind data of one minute obtained in the last ten minutes is calculated in ten minutes. If there are more than six valid one minute average wind data within the ten minutes, the ten minute data is considered to be valid, and the ten minute average calculation is carried out, otherwise no processing is carried out. The wind speed is the sliding average of the first 11 1 min average wind speeds. The wind direction is the decomposition, addition and synthesis of the first 11 1-minute average wind direction vectors. Zero (North) if 0.

Calculation of air temperature and air pressure parameters: the sampling interval is 3 s, and the air temperature and air pressure values are sampled every 3 s. One minute average value: 21 samples from the first 1 min 0 s to the end of this minute 0 s are obtained by averaging the maximum 3 values and the minimum 3 values.

Calculation of the main wave direction: the wave direction here refers to the external wave direction, which is different from the wave direction that describes the internal structure of the wave. It refers to the direction of each specific wave on the sea surface. The direction of each specific wave on the sea surface is generally different, so the main direction of each specific wave at a certain time is called the main wave direction. The wave in the actual ocean is very complex. When the system calculates the wave direction, the wave on the sea surface is simplified as a two-dimensional single wave. When the buoy is in the direction from the wave peak to the wave trough, the direction of the buoy inclination is the wave direction. It is divided into 16 directions, with the geographic north direction as zero degree, and calculated in a clockwise direction. The relationship between the direction and the angle is shown in Table 1.

Table 1. Orientation and angle

Bearing	Degree/°	Bearing	Degree/°
N	348.76–11.25	S	168.76–191.25
NNE	11.26–33.75	SSW	191.26–213.75
NE	33.76–56.25	SW	213.76–236.25
ENEE	56.26–78.75	WSW	236.26–258.75
E	78.76–101.25	W	258.76–281.25
ESE	101.26–123.75	WNW	281.26–303.75
SE	123.76–146.25	NW	303.76–326.25
SSE	14.25–168.75	NNW	326.26–348.75

As shown in Table 1, the wave sensor finally transmits the wave direction occurrence rate of 16 directions (360° bisection), and the azimuth with the largest occurrence rate is the main wave direction. The main wave direction is usually calculated by drawing direction spectrum. Direction spectrum (two-dimensional spectrum) can show the distribution of component wave energy according to frequency and propagation direction at the same time. After analyzing the direction spectrum, the main wave direction can be obtained. The wave sensor obtains the wave direction occurrence rate of 16 directions. In order to calculate the azimuth with the largest occurrence rate, this paper adopts the sliding average filtering method for the main wave direction. The 16 wave occurrence rates are grouped, and the average of each wave occurrence rate is calculated by adding before and after. The largest set of calculated numbers is the main wave direction.

Calculation of wave height and period: according to GB/t14914-2006 code for coastal observation, wave height and period eigenvalues and their codes are defined as follows:

Maximum wave height (Hmax): the maximum value of wave height in continuous wave records;

Maximum wave period (Tmax): the period corresponding to the maximum wave height;

One tenth of the wave height (H1/10): the average value of the first one tenth of the total wave height in successive wave records, arranged from large to small;

One tenth period of large wave (T1/10): the average value of each period corresponding to each wave height of one tenth of large wave;

Effective wave height (H1/3): the average value of the first third of the total wave height in successive wave records, arranged from large to small;

Effective wave period (T1/3): is the average value of the corresponding period of each wave height of the effective wave height;

Average wave height (hmean): it is the average value of all wave heights in continuous wave records;

Tmean: is the average value of the period corresponding to each wave height of the average wave height; Average wave height hmean is a basic characteristic quantity, which represents the average value of each wave height, and can roughly reflect the average state of sea wave height. The average wave height of some large waves, such as the effective wave height and the one tenth of the wave height, represent the significant part of the waves, which are concerned in general navigation and port design; the maximum wave height Hmax is the maximum value of the observed wave height, which is also the most important in practical application. What kind of wave height is used in practical application depends on the purpose of actual use. The wave sensor of this system can measure all these characteristic wave heights with some representative significance. Daily statistical calculation of meteorological and hydrological data: the system is set to work in a fixed time mode, once every half an hour, and other parts are powered off to achieve the maximum power saving; the buoy system can also receive the control command sent by the processing system according to the shore station data, and switch between the working mode of one hour and half an hour. We make daily statistics according to the received and stored meteorological and hydrological data and display them on the real-time interface. According to the knowledge of ocean observation, the daily statistical value of meteorological parameters is updated at 20:00 every day, and the hydrological parameters are updated at 0:00 every day. The essence of daily statistical calculation of data is to read the database and use SQL statements to calculate the data. Several main SQL math functions are used: AVG: arithmetic average; COUNT: count records; FIRST and LAST: return the last data in the first data field of a field; Max and Min: return the maximum and minimum values of a field; sum: return the SUM of a specific field or operation.

2.5   Upload of Information of Marine Monitoring Buoy

The information needed to be transmitted by the marine monitoring buoy includes marine meteorological and hydrological data, acoustic array, acoustic fingerprint information and video information. By default, the marine meteorological and hydrological data are uploaded once every half an hour, and each packet of data is about 1.2 kb. The sound information is transmitted every 10 min, and there are three kinds of data packets with different contents according to different settings. The specific content form of every 1 min packet is as follows: content 1: it is the basic transmission packet, including packet time, array attitude information (depth, roll, pitch, true direction), detection sign, target direction and reserved part. The size of content 1 packet is about 9.6 kb. Content 2: add processing results (C4 band beamforming results) on the basis of basic transmission packets, and the content 2 packet size is about 350 kb. Content 3: on the basis of content 2 packet, the processing result (beam domain data) is added, and content 3 packet size is about 1.5 MB. Video information is uploaded once an hour, and the amount of data transmitted is about 30 MB. It can be seen that the amount of information transmitted by buoy to shore station data receiving and processing system is very large, and at the same time, it is necessary to ensure that the data is sent to shore station safely, reliably and accurately. After receiving the data, according to the communication protocol between the shore station and the buoy host, first determine whether the command code is 0x01 sent by the buoy host. After the authentication is successful, send the data query command. The shore station becomes the main controller, waiting for the buoy host to send the data. After receiving the data, analyze the logarithmic data, Set different elements into different arrays, and store the parsed data in different arrays for convenient display and storage.

In conclusion, iridium data communication system is applied to the information transmission of marine monitoring buoy, which improves the real-time performance of the information transmission of marine monitoring buoy.

3   Experiment

The iridium data communication system is applied to the information transmission of marine monitoring buoy, and compared with other information transmission methods of marine monitoring buoy to verify whether the iridium data communication system applied to the information transmission of marine monitoring buoy can improve the transmission speed of marine monitoring buoy information.

3.1   Experimental Process

Firstly, the information parameters of the ocean monitoring buoy are set. Some parameter information is shown in Table 2.

Table 2. Partial parameter data transfer format table

Byte symbol	Data values	Byte meaning
1	Way to work	0: Dormancy mode 1: Way to work Others: reserved
2	Buoy attitude information upload mode	0: Instructions to upload 1: Implementation of transmission Others: reserved
3	Data upload mode	0: Automatically upload 1: Real-time transmission Others: reserved
4	Update the logo	0x91: Instruction parameter update 0x92: Instructions to update 0x93: Parameters are updated Others: reserved

After setting the parameters, the iridium data communication system is used to transmit the information of the marine monitoring buoy, and the real-time transmission is tested, which is expressed by the time of information transmission, and compared with the traditional method of information transmission of the marine monitoring buoy. In order to ensure the accuracy of the experiment, five experiments were carried out.

3.2 Analysis of Experimental Results

Using two kinds of information transmission methods of marine monitoring buoy, the comparison results of information transmission time are shown in Fig. 2.

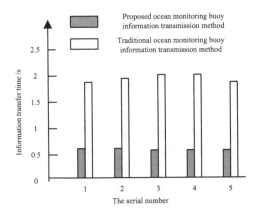

Fig. 2. Information transmission rate comparison results

It can be seen from Fig. 2 that the information transmission time of traditional marine monitoring buoy information transmission method is between 1.8–2 s, while that of iridium data communication system applied to marine monitoring buoy information transmission method is about 0.6–0.7 s. Through comparison, it is found that the iridium satellite data communication system is applied to the information transmission method of marine monitoring buoy, which significantly improves the transmission speed of the information of marine monitoring buoy, indicating that the proposed information transmission method of marine monitoring buoy has higher real-time performance and stability.

4 Conclusion

In view of the poor real-time transmission of the traditional marine monitoring buoy information, the iridium satellite data communication system is applied to the marine monitoring buoy information transmission, which improves the shortcomings of the traditional method. Through the comparative experiment, the information transmission speed is improved by comparing with the traditional marine monitoring buoy information transmission method. It is hoped that it can provide some basis for the study of the information transmission method of the ocean monitoring buoy.

References

1. Duan, S.: Design for STM32-based automatic data transceiver system of HM2000 iridium buoy. Mine Warfare Ship Self-Defence **25**(4), 46–50 (2017)
2. Zhang, S., Wang, D., Shen, R.: Design of a data automatic transceiver for HM2000 iridium profiling float. J. Ocean. Technol. **37**(5), 53–59 (2018)
3. Zhang, H., Dou, Y., Chen, Y., et al.: Design and application of sea-ice-gas unmanned ice station monitoring system for Arctic. Chin. J. Electron. Devices **42**(3), 749–755 (2019)
4. Zheng, Y., Zhao, Y., Liu, W., et al.: Forest microclimate monitoring system based on Beidou satellite. Trans. Chin. Soc. Agricult. Mach. **49**(2), 217–224 (2018)
5. Hu, S., Dou, Y., Ma, C., et al.: Design and application of arctic sea ice comprehensive monitoring system based on iridium 9602. Mod. Electron. Tech. **41**(20), 127–131 (2018)
6. Xu, L., Hou, Z., Yan, S., et al.: Design of a wireless real-time observation data transmission system for deep ocean mooring. Telecommun. Sci. **34**(6), 29–35 (2018)
7. Wang, Y., Yu, H., Yang, J.: Investigation on satellite technology for rapid report data transmission. Seismol. Geomagn. Obs. Res. **38**(4), 203–206 (2017)
8. Chen, X., Liu, B.: Application of real-time monitoring buoy in monitoring red tide. J. Trop. Oceanogr. **37**(5), 20–24 (2018)
9. Zhao, J., Wang, Z., Hui, L., et al.: Design of a marine multi-point water quality monitoring system based on underwater acoustic communication. J. Dalian Fish. Univ. **32**(6), 747–752 (2017)
10. Kong, W., Yang, Z., Ma, S.: Design of ultra-low power consumption ocean drifting buoy collector based on MSP430. Mod. Electron. Tech. **40**(20), 146–149 (2017)

Virtual Force Coverage Control System of Wireless Sensor Network in the Background of Big Data

Jia Xu[1,2(✉)] and Yang Guo[2]

[1] Dalian Jiaotong University, Dalian, China
[2] Dalian Institute of Science and Technology, Dalian, China
yu2018030211@163.com

Abstract. In view of the low virtual force coverage of traditional wireless sensor networks. A virtual force coverage control system based on wireless sensor network is designed. Hardware design mainly includes network interface, processor, control chip and network coordinator. In the software part of the system, firstly, the virtual force coverage control node is selected. On this basis. The optimal control of virtual force and coverage of wireless sensor networks. The virtual force coverage control system of wireless sensor network is designed under the background of big data. The experimental results show that. Under the background of big data, the coverage of virtual force control system of wireless sensor network is higher than that of traditional system. It has a certain practical significance.

Keywords: Big data · Wireless sensor · Network · Virtual force · Cover · Control

1 Introduction

As one of the basic problems of wireless sensor network. The research of network virtual force coverage control has attracted extensive attention of scholars at home and abroad. A series of effective methods for different coverage requirements are developed. Different applications have different interpretations and requirements for coverage. The coverage control problem can be regarded as the case when the sensor node energy, wireless network communication bandwidth, computing capacity and other resources are generally constrained. Through network sensor node deployment and routing and other means. Finally, all kinds of resources of wireless sensor network are allocated optimally. So as to further improve the perception, communication and other service quality.

Due to the intensive deployment of nodes in most sensor networks. If each node communicates with a certain power, it will increase communication interference and cause coverage redundancy. Therefore, a certain sleep mechanism can not only balance the energy consumption of nodes, optimize the network coverage, but also extend the network lifetime. Aiming at the problem of virtual force coverage control system in traditional wireless sensor networks. A virtual force coverage control system for wireless sensor networks in the background of big data is designed. In this design, the energy constraints and coverage requirements of wireless sensor networks are taken into account. Combined with antenna theory, the coverage control problem of wireless sensor networks is reduced to a multi-objective nonlinear programming problem. Thus, a mathematical model of multi-objective nonlinear programming problem is derived and established. The

© ICST Institute for Computer Sciences, Social Informatics and Telecommunications Engineering 2020
Published by Springer Nature Switzerland AG 2020. All Rights Reserved
Y.-D. Zhang et al. (Eds.): ICMTEL 2020, LNICST 326, pp. 472–487, 2020.
https://doi.org/10.1007/978-3-030-51100-5_42

experimental results show that. Under the background of big data, the virtual force coverage control system of wireless sensor network is designed. The coverage of the control system is higher than that of the traditional system. It has a certain practical significance.

2 Overall Architecture

The virtual force coverage control system of wireless sensor network is designed. In order to solve the problem of low coverage of network virtual baggage, the overall framework of the design is shown in Fig. 1:

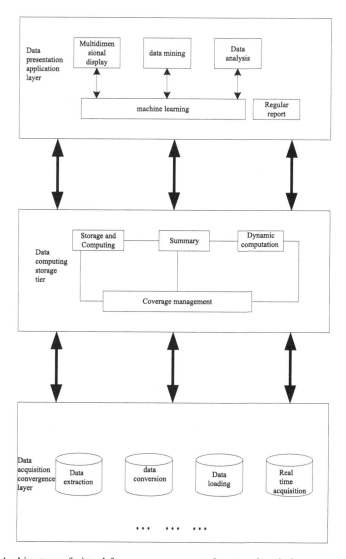

Fig. 1. Architecture of virtual force coverage control system in wireless sensor network

The whole technical architecture is divided into three layers: Data acquisition convergence layer. Wireless sensor network is adopted. As the main collection tool of real world perception data. Gather other big data collection tools [1]. Collect different information of various kinds of sensing devices, and provide data aggregation and storage for the upper layer. Data storage computing layer adopts the current information technology industry. More mature distributed storage and computing framework. To meet the need of virtual force coverage in wireless sensor networks, and to support the increase of hardware nodes, the expansion of data storage space is completed smoothly. All kinds of algorithms required for data presentation application layer and integrated data analysis are encapsulated into analysis modules required for various scenarios. Both terminal app and personalized data analysis application can be built quickly through various components.

3   Hardware Design

The design of system hardware circuit is based on processor. Including network interface design, processor design, interface circuit design, network coordinator design, the following is a specific introduction.

3.1   Network Interface Design

The FPGA processor of Xilinx company is used to control the driving control of the whole network interface. It is connected with network interface chip [2] AX88180 by bus. The internal register of AX88180 is configured by the network driver to realize the transmission and reception of Ethernet data, so as to realize the data communication between the system and the network. The connection between AX88180 chip and 88Ellll chip adopts Gigabit Ethernet media independent interface (GRMII) mode. The function of network interface layer in TCP/IP protocol architecture is realized, including link layer protocol and physical layer protocol. 88E1111 is connected with RJ45 network interface to realize the transmission and reception of bit stream on the network cable. It includes chip selection signal, read enable signal, write enable residence, address bus, data bus, interrupt signal, clock signal, reset signal, read clock signal, write clock signal, etc.

The network interface chip AX88180 reset [3] adopts the combination of power on automatic reset and manual reset, and the frequency of external crystal oscillation circuit is 12 MHz. P1 port line, INT0 and VSE are used for network data acquisition. The P1 port is an 8-bit network data acquisition bus, INT0 is the network data acquisition interrupt control, VSE is the control signal line of the network data acquisition channel. Because the network interface chip AX88180 has only 1 K bytes, it can not meet the requirements of the system. Therefore, 32 byte HM156 is used to expand the system. The P0 port line is address data multiplexing, which is used for low byte address locking. The P2 port line outputs high byte address.

3.2   Processor Design

Control part of virtual force coverage control system in wireless sensor network. With DSP as the core, DSP processor is connected with FPGA. Connection signals include: address bus, data bus [4], chip selection signal, bus hold signal, clock signal, preparation signal, interrupt signal, read signal and write signal. The control signal of SRAM chip is generated by FPGA chip, and its read-write operation is controlled by DSP chip and FPGA chip respectively. When receiving data, FPGA writes human data to SRAM, and DSP reads data from SRAM. When sending data, DSP writes data to SRAM and FPGA reads data from SRAM. The DSP processor uses DFHEF45 as the interface chip, DFHEF45 is an embedded chip launched by CYPRESS. The chip can communicate with wireless sensor as well as wireless sensor. The chip provides 8 bit wide data bus and interrupt support, which makes it easy to connect with micropro-cessor, microcontroller and DSP. Internal 256 byte RAM, two sets of parallel registers support ping-pong operation. By controlling pin AO, address and data can be distin-guished, and address auto increment mode is supported. The working voltage is 3.3 V, and the interface is compatible with 5 V level. The functional module diagram is as follows (Fig. 2):

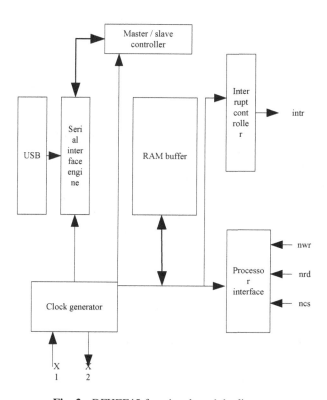

Fig. 2. DFHEF45 functional module diagram

DFHEF45 interface chip is characterized by low cost, low power consumption, high performance, strong reliability, fast instruction execution speed, flexible addressing mode and high efficiency. ARM microprocessor is widely used in embedded system development. Because of its high speed and good compatibility, it is widely used in industrial control, network technology, video acquisition and other fields.

3.3 Control Chip Design

The control chip used in this system is CC2430. It is an on-chip wireless sensor network control product complying with IEEE802.15.4 standard. It integrates ZigBee RF front-end, memory and microcontroller on a single chip [5]. It uses an 8-bit MCU (8051), 128 KB programmable flash memory and 8 KB ram. It also includes an analog-to-digital converter (ADC), four timers, a watchdog timer, a 32 kHz crystal oscillator sleep mode timer, a power on reset circuit, a power down detection circuit, and 21 programmable I/O pins. CC2430 only needs a few peripheral components. Its peripheral circuit includes crystal clock circuit, RF input circuit and output matching circuit. The local oscillator signal of 151 chip can be provided by either external active crystal or internal circuit. RF input and output matching circuit is mainly used to match the input and output impedance of the chip, and provide DC bias for PA and LNA inside the chip. The following figure shows the hardware application circuit of CC2430 chip (Fig. 3).

The control chip uses an unbalanced antenna to connect the unbalanced transformer, which can improve the antenna performance. The unbalanced transformer in the circuit is composed of capacitance C341, inductance L341, L321, L331 and a PCB microwave transmission line. The whole structure meets the requirements of RF input and output matching resistance (50Q). R221 and R261 are bias resistors [6], and R221 mainly provides a suitable working current for the 32 MHz crystal oscillator, A 32 MHz crystal oscillator circuit is composed of a 32 MHz quartz resonator (X1) and two capacitors (C191 and C211). A 32.768 kHz crystal oscillator is composed of a 32.768 kHz quartz resonator (X2) and two capacitors (C441 and C431). The voltage regulator supplies power to all pins and internal power supply which require 1.8 V voltage. C241 and C421 are decoupling capacitors, which are used to realize power filter and improve the stability of the chip. For the design of analog part, in order to reduce the interference of other parts and improve the RF performance, anti-interference measures need to be taken. For example, add magnetic beads or inductors at the input end of the analog power supply; separate the analog ground and the digital ground, and ground them at one point. In order to reduce the influence of the distribution parameters, the ground should be paved as large as possible, and holes should be punched properly. The capacitance used for filtering should be close to the chip as much as possible.

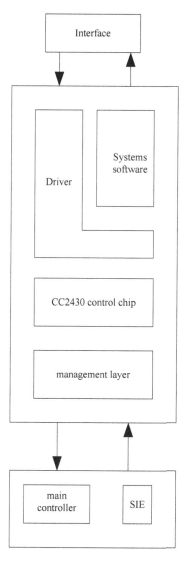

Fig. 3. CC2430 control chip

3.4 Design of Network Coordinator

The network coordinator needs to display the current network status, so the network coordinator is composed of CC2430, serial port, key and LCD. The circuit block diagram is shown in Fig. 4. RFD node and ROUTER node are composed of CC2430, photoresist, serial port expansion interface and street light dimming control circuit.

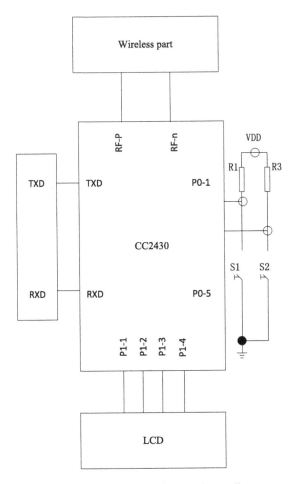

Fig. 4. Circuit diagram of network coordinator

The network coordinator uses the I/0 port of CC2430 to control the LCD directly, and outputs the data and debugs the program through the serial port. S1 and S2 are used to control the switch status of the whole network street lamp. It also monitors the key at any time. If the key is pressed, it will send data to each street lamp control node through the network and display the current power switch status of the whole network. RFD node and ROUTER node can also detect their own current light conditions, and determine whether to turn on the street lights by judging the light conditions, so as to achieve energy-saving control.

The network coordinator first initializes CC2430 and LCD [7], then initializes the protocol stack and opens the interrupt. After that, the program starts to format a network. If the network format is successful, the physical address of the corresponding network coordinator, the network ID number and channel number of the established network will be displayed on the LCD screen.

4   Software Implementation

4.1   Selection of Virtual Force Coverage Control Nodes in Wireless Sensor Networks

Before selecting the virtual force coverage control node in wireless sensor networks, a perception model is established to achieve the goal of path planning. The decision tree algorithm is used to consider whether the node is a candidate work node or not according to the node energy, the number of unselected work nodes and the number of neighbor nodes. When the nodes switch states, the energy information of their neighbors is introduced to make decisions, which makes the energy consumption in the network more balanced.

The virtual potential field method is used to simulate the movement of charged particles from high potential point to low potential point in the electric field. Each sensor node in the network is regarded as a virtual charge, and the target and obstacle are regarded as low potential point and high potential point respectively. By using the force of potential field on the node, the node moves to the target, and at the same time, all kinds of obstacles in the moving process can be avoided. When each node in the wireless sensor network is affected by the virtual force of other nodes, it spreads to other areas in the target area, and finally reaches the equilibrium state, that is, to achieve the full coverage state of the target area. Or the uniformity of network coverage is taken as the goal, and the non-uniformity of node deployment is regarded as the obstacle. Using virtual potential field to realize network redeployment [8], the network coverage area can be maximized.

In the virtual force model defined, the virtual force of a sensor node is represented as follows:

$$D = \sum_c hF_d + df \tag{1}$$

In formula (1), D is the sensor node, $\sum_c h$ needs the resultant force of the virtual gravity of the coverage area, F_d is the sensor node at the obstacle, df the resultant force of virtual repulsion (Fig. 5).

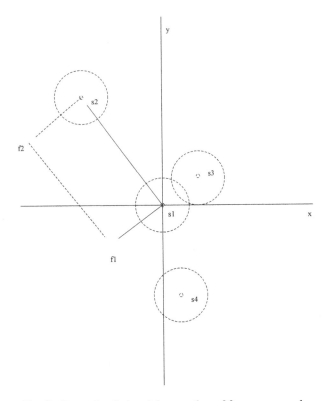

Fig. 5. Example of virtual force action of four sensor nodes

From the above analysis, if the value is set artificially, the monitoring area can be covered according to a certain density, or the coverage intensity of the detection area can be adjusted. However, on the one hand, energy saving is not considered; On the other hand, the density of the final layout depends on the critical distance from the definition. When the distance is too small, the layout of wireless sensor nodes is too close to ensure the coverage requirements; When the distance is too large, the sensor nodes are sparse, which is easy to form a blind area. In order to solve this problem, we will optimize the virtual force coverage control in the next step.

4.2   Optimization of Virtual Force Coverage Control in Wireless Sensor Networks

Based on the selection of virtual force control nodes in wireless sensor networks, the control optimization of virtual force coverage [9] in wireless sensor networks is carried out. At the same time, before optimizing the virtual force coverage control of wireless sensor network, the network model is established. The sensor nodes in the network are randomly and evenly deployed in the two-dimensional square area with side length L, and the node density is large enough, if all nodes are in working state, the whole area a can be completely covered, it is assumed that the network has the following properties:

First, the coverage of each node is far smaller than the whole network area.

Second, all nodes will not be moved after deployment, without human maintenance.

Thirdly, each node has a fixed sensing radius. The nodes in the sensing range can receive the information sent by the node, while the nodes outside the sensing range can not receive the information.

Fourth, all nodes are isomorphic and have the same initial energy.

Fifth, the time synchronization between nodes in the network reaches second level.

Assuming that the minimum power [10] that can detect and decode the signal correctly, i.e. the minimum value of G is J, the minimum transmission power of the transmitting node is:

$$X = \frac{D(VN)^T}{JH * J^2} \tag{2}$$

In formula (2), X represents the relationship between transmission power and distance, JH represents the minimum power consumed by the whole network, J^2 represents the minimum power consumed by the whole network, $X\, D(VN)^T$ represents the balanced power consumed by sensor nodes.

Therefore, the energy saving optimization target model can be expressed as follows: assuming D is the monitoring target area and N sensors are used to cover the nodes, the coverage matrix is as follows:

$$\begin{bmatrix} A_1 \\ A_2 \\ \vdots \\ A_r \end{bmatrix} = G * \begin{bmatrix} z_{11} & z_{12} & \cdots & z_{1f} \\ z_{21} & z_{22} & \cdots & z_{21} \\ \vdots & \vdots & & \vdots \\ z_{r1} & z_{r2} & \cdots & z_{rf} \end{bmatrix} \begin{bmatrix} x_1 \\ x_2 \\ \vdots \\ x_r \end{bmatrix} \tag{3}$$

In matrix 3, A_1, A_2, A_r respectively represent the coverage area of sensor nodes. Constraints x_1, x_2, x_r can ensure that there is no blind area in the coverage area, constraints G can ensure the connectivity of the network, and take wireless interference into account. Based on the above mathematical model, the energy-saving wireless sensor network coverage control problem is reduced to a multi-objective nonlinear programming problem.

On this basis, the method of setting objective optimization function and using artificial fish swarm algorithm to solve the coverage control problem is to simplify the coverage problem into a function, find the solution of the extreme value of the function and the corresponding extreme value, so as to correspond to the node working state of the sensor coverage problem. The problems related to covering optimization are integrated into a function, which is called optimization objective function. The process of target optimization is as follows (Fig. 6):

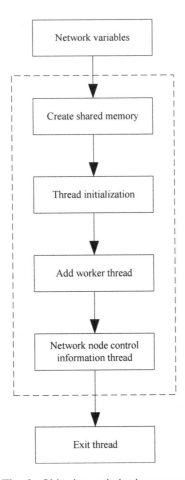

Fig. 6. Objective optimization process

The above is the calculation process of network coverage, and the specific calculation is shown in the following formula:

$$D = RF \frac{df}{\sum_{s} fD * GH} \tag{4}$$

Among them, D is the total number of sensor nodes, RF is the number of working sensor nodes, $\sum_{s} fD$ represents the global energy balance coefficient, GH represents the remaining energy in the network nodes, df represents the coverage of the monitoring area.

When the target area is completely covered by the sensor's sensing range, it is easy to have unnecessary repeated coverage. Adopting the optimal deployment strategy of nodes can save energy consumption, and also provide a good topology structure for information fusion processing, hierarchical routing and other follow-up technologies. In this scheme, virtual force acts between sensor nodes, which can be expressed as:

$$NF = \frac{V}{\sum_a c \Rightarrow v} \tag{5}$$

In formula (5), NF is the distance between the two sensor nodes, $\sum_a c$ is the square of the sensing radius of the two nodes, is the sensor area dimension of the node, v represents the node value of the minimum energy consumption in the point, V represents the weight coefficient of the two sub targets.

5 Experimental Comparison

This design is to prove the effectiveness of the virtual force coverage control system of wireless sensor network under the background of big data designed above, and to ensure the preciseness of the experiment, the traditional virtual force coverage control system of wireless sensor network is designed. Under the background of big data, the virtual force coverage control system of wireless sensor network is compared, and the virtual force coverage of the two systems is compared.

5.1 Experimental Platform

The experimental system is composed of three small mobile agents driven by two wheel differential as the experimental platform, as shown in the figure below (Fig. 7):

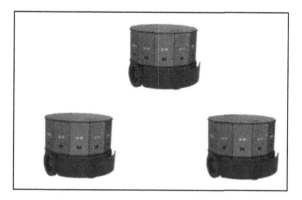

Fig. 7. Small mobile agent

The wireless communication system is based on cc2430zigbee control chip. The communication between the wireless communication system and the control system adopts serial port communication mode. The control system is composed of upper computer and lower computer. The upper computer is developed based on VC. It is mainly used to receive wireless communication information, obstacle distance information, and real-time calculation to get the motion control information of the agent. The main controller of the lower computer is the 2000 series DSP chip of TI company, with the main frequency of 40 MHz, It is mainly used to collect ultrasonic information and encoder information, and control the left and right driving wheels of the agent according to the control instructions issued by the lower computer.

This system is based on IOS 5.1 system to realize the augmented reality client. Therefore, during the test process, an iPhone 4 mobile phone running IOS 5.1 or above system version is needed to watch the experiment. The server is developed in Python, so a web server supporting Python language is also needed. In addition, the iPhone 4 mobile phone should have WiFi or 3G network environment for communication with the server. The experimental platform is designed as follows (Fig. 8):

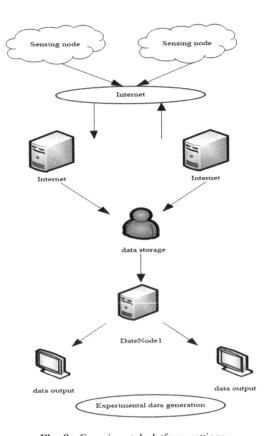

Fig. 8. Experimental platform settings

On the basis of the above experimental environment design, the experimental scheme is designed. In the square monitoring area with side length of 100 m, 100 sensor nodes are randomly and evenly deployed. Supposing that the virtual cell is divided into square areas with side length of 20 m, in order to ensure that the nodes of adjacent cells can communicate with each other, the communication radius and sensing radius of the nodes are respectively 45 m and 13 M. At the same time, it can be assumed that the initial energy of all nodes is 50 J, the energy consumed by each round of nodes elected as cluster heads is 1 J, the working time of each round of cluster heads is certain, there is no energy consumption under the node sleep state, the energy of the center of mass is 50 J, and it will not change with the operation of the network. Because there are 4 nodes in each cell, and each node will die after 50 rounds of cluster heads are selected, the total number of rounds of cluster heads selected in each cell is 200, and the lifetime of the whole cell is the product of the number of rounds of cluster heads selected by all nodes and each continuous working time. In the initial stage, the sensor nodes are randomly and evenly deployed in the whole monitoring area. The above is preparation for the experiment.

5.2   Analysis of Experimental Results

Compared with the coverage of the traditional system and the designed system, the experimental results are generated by the same energy model as LEACH protocol. The specific experimental results are as follows (Fig. 9):

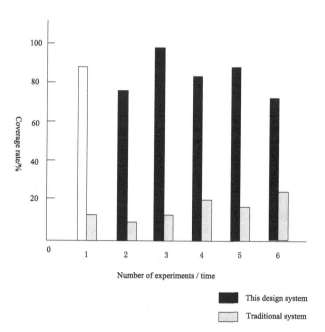

Fig. 9. Comparison of experimental results

Analysis of the above comparison figure shows that in the five experiments, under the background of big data, the virtual force coverage of the wireless sensor network virtual force coverage control system is higher than that of the traditional system. In the second experiment, the difference between the two is the largest.

Therefore, through the above experiments, it can be proved that under the background of big data, the coverage of the virtual force coverage control system of wireless sensor network is higher than that of the traditional system, which proves that under the background of big data, the effectiveness of the virtual force coverage control system of wireless sensor network has a certain practical application significance.

6   Concluding Remarks

In view of the low coverage of the traditional virtual force coverage control system in wireless sensor networks, a virtual force coverage control system in wireless sensor networks is designed under the background of big data. The design of the system is completed from two aspects of hardware design and software design. The experimental results show that under the background of big data, the virtual force coverage control system of wireless sensor network is higher than that of traditional system. The system has good convergence and universality to solve the multi-objective nonlinear programming problem. It can meet the coverage control requirements of wireless sensor network, maximize the life cycle of the network, and improve the performance of the system.

There are still some deficiencies in this design, which need to be improved in the future practical application to meet the virtual force coverage requirements of wireless sensor.

References

1. Yang, H.: Energy-efficient construction of virtual coordinates in WSN. J. Chin. Comput. Syst. **39**(2), 245–248 (2018)
2. Cui, P., Wang, M.: An optimal deployment strategy for wireless sensor networks based on virtual force oriented genetic algorithm. Electron. Des. Eng. **25**(7), 87–91 (2017)
3. Zhang, Y., Qiao, Y., Zhang, H.: Coverage enhancing for underwater acoustic sensor networks based on virtual force and fruit fly optimization algorithm. J. Shanghai Jiaotong Univ. **51**(6), 715–721 (2017)
4. Dang, X., Wang, H., Hao, Z., et al.: Covering algorithm related with area division and virtual forces in three-dimensional. Comput. Eng. Appl. **53**(2), 107–111 (2017)
5. Qi, C., Dai, H., Zhao, X., et al.: Distributed coverage algorithm based on virtual force and Voronoi. Comput. Eng. Des. **39**(3), 606–611 (2018)
6. Liu, L., Pan, M., Tian, S., et al.: A non-cooperative game-theoretic energy allocation for distributed data gathering in wireless sensor networks. Eng. J. Wuhan Univ. **50**(3), 384–389 (2017)
7. Yuan, H.: Wireless sensor network saving access protocol algorithm. Comput. Digit. Eng. **45** (9), 1798–1801 (2017)

8. Qi, F., Sun, Y.: Wireless sensor network coverage efficiency optimization simulation. Comput. Simul. **34**(8), 297–301 (2017)
9. Xu, Z., Tan, L., Yang, C., et al.: Node coverage optimization algorithm in directional heterogeneous wireless sensor network. J. Comput. Appl. **37**(7), 1849–1854 (2017)
10. Mao, K., Xu, H., Fang, K., et al.: Design and realization of WSNs routing protocol based on virtual gravity. Transducer Microsyst. Technol. **36**(12), 98–101 (2017)

Author Index

Printed in the United States
By Bookmasters